Logically Identical P

Abbreviated Name	*Syn*	
DN	ϕ,	$--\phi$
AS	ϕ_1 & $(\phi_2$ & $\phi_3)$,	$(\phi_1$ & $\phi_2)$ & ϕ_3
AS	$\phi_1 \vee (\phi_2 \vee \phi_3)$,	$(\phi_1 \vee \phi_2) \vee \phi_3$
ID	$\phi \vee \phi$,	ϕ
ID	ϕ & ϕ,	ϕ
Dist	ϕ & $(\theta_1 \vee \ldots \vee \theta_n)$,	$(\phi$ & $\theta_1) \vee \ldots \vee (\phi$ & $\theta_n)$
Dist	$\phi \vee (\theta_1$ & $\ldots$ & $\theta_n)$,	$(\phi \vee \theta_1)$ & $\ldots$ & $(\phi \vee \theta_n)$
DeM	$-(\phi_1 \vee \ldots \vee \phi_n)$,	N$[\phi_1]$ & $\ldots$ & N$[\phi_n]$
DeM	$-(\phi_1$ & $\ldots$ & $\phi_n)$,	N$[\phi_1] \vee \ldots \vee$ N$[\phi_n]$
Cont	$\phi \supset \theta$,	N$[\theta] \supset$ N$[\phi]$
E/I	$(\phi$ & $\theta) \supset \psi$,	$\phi \supset (\theta \supset \psi)$
$\supset$ / v	$\phi \supset \theta$,	N$[\phi] \vee \theta$
$-(\supset)$ / &	$-(\phi \supset \theta)$,	ϕ & N$[\theta]$
$-(\&)$ / $\supset$	$-(\phi$ & $\theta)$,	$\phi \supset$ N$[\theta]$
$\equiv$ / $\supset$	$\phi \equiv \theta$,	$(\phi \supset \theta)$ & $(\theta \supset \phi)$
$-(\equiv)$ / $\equiv(-)$	$-(\phi \equiv \theta)$,	$\phi \equiv$ N$[\theta]$
v^e / $\equiv$	$\phi \; v^e \; \theta$,	$\phi \equiv$ N$[\theta]$
v^e / &	$\phi \; v^e \; \theta$,	$(\phi \vee \theta)$ & $-(\phi$ & $\theta)$
Com	$\phi \equiv \theta$,	$\theta \equiv \phi$
Com	ϕ & θ,	θ & ϕ
Com	$\phi \vee \theta$,	$\theta \vee \phi$

CRITICAL THINKING

CRITICAL THINKING

An Introduction to Reasoning

FRANCIS WATANABE DAUER

This edition published by Barnes & Noble, Inc.,
by arrangement with Oxford University Press, Inc.

1996 Barnes & Noble Books

ISBN 0-76070-137-7

Printed and bound in the United States of America

M 9 8 7 6 5 4 3 2 1

FG

To My Father,
Satosi Watanabe,
who taught me the art of reasoning
from my earliest days

Preface

Since ancient times instruction in the art of reasoning has been a central mission of philosophy. Today this mission is entrusted to courses with such titles as "Elementary Logic" and "Critical Thinking," and it is probably fair to say that Irving Copi's *Introduction to Logic* has set the standard for texts in such courses. Despite its seriousness and its comprehensiveness, some have been dissatisfied with Copi's text; the present text is intended as an alternative that overcomes two major sources of dissatisfaction.

Some instructors, having found insufficient intellectual content in Copi's text, have converted introductory instruction in the art of reasoning into abstract and theoretical courses, often involving quantification theory. This is unfortunate because such courses only pay lip service to the art of reasoning and in truth are nothing but simplified courses in mathematics. It is my fundamental belief that virtually all students are in need of a course that will help them to reason about matters they face in daily life. My text is intended to be such an aid, and I hope that its intellectual content will encourage those who have opted for quasi-mathematical courses to return to our ancient mission of instructing the young in the art of reasoning.

A second source of dissatisfaction has been that Copi's text often appears to be irrelevant in much the way academia as a whole appeared irrelevant to many students of the sixties. It is no doubt true that any text that emphasizes the study of logic at the expense of demonstrating its value will be considered irrelevant. The easy way to meet this charge is to drop the serious study of logic altogether; this is indeed the route taken by many watered-down texts that have come out in the last two decades. It seems to me clear that natural deduction at the level of the propositional calculus is the only easily accessible systematization of ordinary thinking that has been achieved in two millennia. To forgo this achievement in favor of a spurious search for relevance strikes me as bordering on sheer madness.

It is not hard to understand why the traditional study of logic strikes students as irrelevant. They are told that logic is only concerned with validity, not soundness; that the truth or falsity of the premises and the conclusions are of no concern to logic. This is surely the easiest way to incur the charge of irrelevance: after all, truth and falsity are what ultimately matter. The value of logic cannot be properly demonstrated unless the issue of soundness, or the acceptability of the premises and conclusions, is faced. This text does precisely that. In this way, while placing appropriate emphasis on the study of logic, the text is intended as an alternative to elementary logic texts that fail to focus on the actual world among all the possible worlds.

Given this overall purpose of the text, something should be said of the several chapters that compose it. Chapter 1 is a short introduction that ties together much of the text. Indeed, one of the principal aims in writing this text has been to give a unified and coherent account of reasoning rather than a patchwork of disparate topics as seen in so many texts. Chapter 1 indicates the kind of unity I envision in this work. Chapter 2 is concerned with the assessment of evidence and the background within which we work. Clearly these epistemological issues must be faced if the acceptability of the premises (and hence the conclusions) is to be discussed. The main test that is developed in Chapter 2 is coherence theoretic in its approach. Because this approach tends to be controversial, I have included a short section (Section 2.1) that can be read in lieu of the bulk of Chapter 2. On the other hand, even foundationalists tend to think of coherence as a test for justification; furthermore, it has been my experience that many students find the material in Chapter 2 to be both interesting and useful.

Chapter 3 is a reasonably standard account of natural deduction in the propositional calculus. Two points may be made about that chapter's approach: First, because Chapter 4 urges analyzing ordinary arguments by supplying missing premises that convert them into deductively valid ones, more than the ordinary amount of emphasis in Chapter 3 is placed on finding missing premises. Second, the emphasis throughout Chapter 3 is on enhancing the ability to reason in ordinary situations, which has three consequences: (a) The truth table method is not the principal method of this text; the value of such a pencil-and-paper method in enhancing our reasoning ability is limited, and it is entirely useless for discovering missing premises. However, the method is presented in the starred, optional Section 2.4 because of the theoretical insights it provides; Section 2.4 may be skipped without any loss in continuity. This method of noting optional text and more difficult exercises is used throughout the book. (b) The method of natural deduction presented is extremely liberal in the number of inference rules allowed. There is no point in insisting on a theoretically elegant system for a course in reasoning, and students should in any event become acquainted with most of the permissible inferential maneuvers that are easy to grasp. (c) Although conditional proofs (as well as *reductio* proofs) are covered in Chapter 3, the method of natural deduction presented does not include conditionalization as an inference rule. Whatever conditionalization allows in normal contexts can be accomplished by an auxiliary conditional derivation, and the derivation of theorems or tautologies (where conditionalization *is* a genuine simplification) does not seem to be a proper task for a course in reasoning. Finally, it should be noted that there is a summary of the inference rules at the end of Chapter 3; students may be well advised to consult this summary as they work through Chapter 3.

Chapters 4 and 5 show how the material in Chapters 2 and 3 can be combined to assess arguments and their conclusions. Roughly, the message of Chapter 4 is that the conclusion of a deductively valid argument is justified at least to the degree to which the conjunction of the (given and missing) premises is justified. Chapter 5 is concerned with nondemonstrative arguments. The text conceives of nondemonstrative legitimacy in terms of the conclusion being the best available explanation of the premises, where A is taken to explain B if A along with justified auxiliary premises constitute deductively valid reasons for B.

Chapter 6 is devoted to language and the various levels or dimensions of meaning: syntax, semantics, illocutionary forces, pragmatics, empirical meaning, and the evaluative charge of certain uses of language. While it is largely meant as a consciousness-raising chapter, some issues of a slightly more theoretical nature are touched on in this chapter. The more theoretical sections (or parts of sections) have been starred and may be safely skipped.

The starred Chapter 7 is meant as a transition chapter to a more advanced course in reasoning. Section 7.1 covers quantificational structures (without going into deductions in quantification theory); the Venn diagram test for syllogisms is included, not because I think it is intrinsically valuable, but because some law school entrance examinations seem to require a passing knowledge of syllogisms. Section 7.2 is a fairly detailed introduction to the rudiments of probability theory.

Discussion of fallacies is integrated with the material in the text and is principally found in Sections 2.6 and 4.7, as well as in the various sections of Chapter 6. In some instances, the fallacies have been given more rigid definitions than the standard ones to avoid vagueness. Fallacies are classified into one of four categories depending on the type of diagrammatic analyses they call for. A separate list of fallacies follows the table of contents, and a summary inside the back cover of the text summarizes all the fallacies according to the four categories.

While every attempt has been made to make the presentation clear, simple, and intuitive, it is possible that the material covered in this text is slightly more difficult than that found in the average critical-thinking text. The reader may want to recall that reasoning in ordinary situations is not really simple, and if a course in reasoning is to have genuine and lasting benefits, students must be encouraged to make serious efforts at mastering the art of reasoning. A whole course can be spent learning truth tables, Venn diagrams, and the names of fallacies; this makes the course easy for students (and instructors). But that would be ignoring the important task of providing useful instruction in the art of reasoning. Another point to consider is that, rather than presenting rules and maxims *ex cathedra,* the text attempts to make them plausible at an intuitive level.

Such an intuitive understanding is the best path to achieving a mastery of the art of reasoning. On the other hand, the exercises are generally designed so that they can be done without understanding the rules and maxims that underlie them. Inevitably, students vary widely in both their interests and their abilities; the text aims at neither depriving the more talented students of a deeper understanding nor penalizing others for not going into material that is beyond them.

Accompanying this text is an instructor's manual that contains answers to all exercises in the text, provides some other exercises (and their answers) that might be used for additional work or examinations, and briefly explains why I chose certain approaches to various topics. Some of the material (especially in Chapters 2 and 4) is controversial, and I have sometimes chosen to oversimplify rather than going into complicated philosophical issues, especially in epistemology. Thus the instructor's manual, with its more professional audience, serves as a means to clarify, defend, or qualify statements in the text with respect to these complications.

Inevitably a text of this kind is indebted to the personal support of many individuals. Among my colleagues, I have particularly benefited from Noel Fleming and Nathan Salmon. Over the years many teaching assistants in my critical-thinking course have provided suggestions and encouragements. Dr. Kwang-su Kim and Mr. Wayne Waxman have been particularly helpful, and I also owe thanks to Dr. Patricia Johnson Forgie, Dr. Elias Savellos, Mr. Mark McLeod, Mr. Christopher Belshaw, and Ms. Karen Lucas, just to mention a few. Particular thanks go to my former student Dr. Jig-chuen Lee, who was instrumental in persuading me to write an instructor's manual. Ms. Kathy McKinney has been most generous in supporting this project and making the capabilities of the department office available; I am also indebted to Ms. June Kelley and Ms. Meredith Sedgwick for typing the earliest versions of the text, and Ms. Paula Ryan for printing some of the later versions. I am as always appreciative of the support my parents have provided over the years, and I thank my children, Hilary and Karen, for their forbearance while I was engaged in this project. My debt to the students of UCSB, who have endured less satisfactory versions of this work, goes without saying.

This text is primarily meant as a practical text in the art of reasoning. In writing it I have tried to cull from philosophy all that is easily accessible and useful to this end. A by-product of this attempt is that the material presented here provides a decent background for a number of courses in philosophy: logic, philosophy of science, philosophy of language, and epistemology. Needless to say, it would be gratifying if this text should transform the practical concerns of at least a few students into an interest in the further pursuit of philosophy.

Santa Barbara, Calif. F. W. D.
February 10, 1987

Contents

* This section may be skipped or be read in lieu of Sections 2.2–2.5.
† This section is optional and may be skipped.

‡ Contains more difficult material and may be skipped.

‡ Contains more difficult material and may be skipped.

List of Fallacies

Fallacy Categories

Inferential Fallacies
Presuppositional Fallacies
Fallacies of Relevance
Fallacies of Substance

Individual Fallacies

Accent
Accident
Affirming the Consequent
Amphibole
Appeal to the Imagination
Argument from Ignorance
Argumentum ad Hominem
Argumentum ad Populum
Begging the Question
Black and White Fallacy
Complex Question
Composition
Confusing the Two 'or's
Denying the Antecedent
Division
Emotional Appeals
Equivocation
False Appeal to Authority
False Cause
*Gambler's Fallacy
Hasty Generalization
Ignorance
*Ignoring Antecedent Probabilities
*Ignoring *De Re* Uses
*Ignoring Intensional Contexts
Illicit Redefinition
Irrelevant Conclusion
*Modal Fallacy with [ ]
*Modal/Deontic Fallacy with < >
Use/Mention Fallacy

* Discussed in the more difficult starred portions of the text.

CRITICAL THINKING

1

Introduction to Critical Thinking

In our daily lives we have occasion to say and think a variety of things. One of the things we desire is that what we say or think should be true. There are of course myriad other things we may desire of what we think or say; for example, one may want his statements to be elegant, another may want her speech to incite others, and yet another may want his thoughts to be exciting. Still, one of the things we aim at in our thought and speech is truth. This text is concerned with that kind of thinking and talking in which at least a primary goal is to think and say what is true.

Given this goal, we should like some canons or guidelines by which we can assess the truth claims we make. Critical thinking may be taken as the art of assessing truth claims according to certain general principles or canons. If we were like God and our knowledge were infallible and complete, there would be little need for developing canons of truth assessment. But such is not our lot: characteristically we know certain things but are ignorant of a lot more. Let us look at a simple example to see what sorts of things may be involved in assessing truth claims. Once we recognize the activity of assessing truth claims, we'll have a better idea of what canons we are looking for.

Suppose that Jane goes to Professor C's office to ask for her term paper. He says that he put it in the box outside along with the other term papers. When Jane doesn't find the paper there and asks C about it, he says he put it there, and adds that he *distinctly* remembers putting it there. So far Jane may have good reasons to think that the paper was put there and somehow got lost. Being told that she got a "B" on it, she doesn't give it much thought until she returns to her room. But then, remembering C having said that he *distinctly* remembers putting her paper in the box, she begins to wonder why he should distinctly remember this. Her last name doesn't begin with an "A" and the chances of her paper being on the top of the pile seem small. Isn't C perhaps protesting too much? Furthermore, since the box was a large one, the paper couldn't have fallen out. Recalling also that his office was a mess with dozens of papers strewn around, Jane begins to think that there is a chance that C simply lost her paper.

Her suspicions having been aroused, she talks to her friends and discovers that her paper isn't the first one to have mysteriously disappeared outside C's office.

To test her suspicions, she goes back to C to see what he may be able to say about the content of her paper. The conversation goes like this:

Jane: What did you think of my paper?
C: Although it may not have been outstanding, I thought that it was a solid piece of work.
Jane: What did you think of my argument about justice for the warrior class?
C: That was quite interesting, but I thought it could use some further development.
Jane: Do you have any further suggestions?
C: Well, just keep up the good work and with a little more effort you might get an "A" the next time.

Being further reinforced by these evasive answers, Jane takes the bold step of asking C about something quite preposterous that wasn't in the paper at all.

Jane: Just one last thing. What did you think about my idea that existentialist themes could be found in Plato's *Republic?*
C: I thought that that was quite provocative but misguided; ultimately it was the weakest part of your paper.

Jane now knew that C had never read her paper.

Perhaps the most important thing to notice is that throughout the example certain things are taken to be unproblematic while others are taken to be problematic. On the unproblematic side are claims or beliefs that are accepted as true and not questioned, and they include the evidence Jane had or collected as well as items of general knowledge. The principal claim that is problematic in the example is C's claim that he had read and graded the paper. This is the claim whose truth or falsity Jane wishes to assess, and to this end she infers conclusions that are relevant to the claim from the things she unproblematically accepts.

Among the things Jane accepts without question are that she did not mishear what C in fact said, that her eyes were not deceiving her when she looked for her paper in the box, that she correctly remembers (in her room) that C used the word "distinctly," that her last name does not begin with an "A," that things tend to get lost in messy rooms, that her friends were telling the truth when they said their papers had mysteriously disappeared outside C's office, that C should be able to say something about a paper if he had read it, and that C wouldn't talk about the paper's wild idea of existentialist themes in the *Republic* if he had read the paper and knew that no such idea was suggested in the paper. Here are a couple of examples of Jane's reasoning or inferences:

[A] The pile C put in the box was alphabetically arranged or not.
If it was alphabetically arranged, her paper wouldn't be at the top.

If it was not alphabetically arranged, there is only a small chance that her paper was on the top of the pile.
If her paper was not at the top of the pile, C will not have distinctly remembered putting her paper outside his office.
Thus, there is at most only a small chance that C distinctly remembers putting her paper outside his office.

[B] If her paper didn't have the wild suggestion that there are existentialist themes in the *Republic* and C read the paper, C knows that there was no such suggestion in the paper.
If C knows that there was no such suggestion in the paper, C wouldn't say that the suggestion was provocative but misguided.
The paper didn't have the wild suggestion.
C did say that the suggestion was provocative but misguided.
Thus, C did not read the paper.

We now see that two basic aspects of the activity of truth assessment are (1) *isolating* and *gathering* a stock of things that may be accepted without question, and (2) *reasoning* from those accepted things to (at least the likely) *truth* or *falsity* of the claims that are taken to be *problematic.* Given that these aspects of the activity of truth assessment, among the maxims or canons we are looking for are (a) maxims for helping us to determine what may be accepted without question, and (b) canons for recognizing what reasons are good reasons. Thus, critical thinking involves isolating a stock of things that may be accepted without question according to (a) and reasoning according to (b) from the accepted things to the truth or falsity of the problematic claims.

There is, however, a third aspect involved in the activity of truth assessment: an appreciation of exactly what is stated by the use of words. Language is the primary instrument for thought and communication, and we are liable to mislead or miss something if we do not pay careful attention to the use of language. Aside from noting C's use of the word "distinctly," Jane was reinforced in her suspicion by the first segment of her conversation with C. Why? If we look at the things C said, they say nothing specific and assert in slightly differing ways that her paper was a "B" but not an "A." Just because C said nothing beyond this, Jane recognized his remarks as evasive and took the bold course of trying to trip up C—a course we may suppose an intelligent woman like Jane would not have taken if she had not found strong reasons for thinking that C hadn't read her paper! Beyond our example, most of us have had the experience of misleading ourselves or others by failing to attach a clear meaning to our words. Thus, for the purpose of critical thinking, in addition to (a) and (b), we need (c) maxims for determining the meanings conveyed by the use of language.

In a broad way, the aim of this text is the practical one of improving one's ability in critical thinking. The hope is that by learning a number of general canons for critical thinking and by applying them in exercises, readers will be in a position to keep improving their thinking on their own after having finished the text. Thus, the bulk of this book will be concerned with presenting general canons or maxims of type (a), (b), and (c). Specifically, Chapters 2–6 cover the following topics. In Chapter 2 we shall be concerned with what may be accepted as unproblematic. While part of what may be so accepted would normally be considered "evidence," the unproblematic will also be seen to include general background claims through which the evidence is assessed. In Chapter 3 we shall shift gears and focus on the "deductive" kind of reasoning. Chapters 2 and 3 will then give us some rules or guidelines for recognizing what is unproblematic and what constitutes a good reason. Chapter 4 will finally allow us to merge this material to develop and enhance our critical thinking skills; that is, we shall be in a position to assess truth claims according to the general principles that were developed in Chapters 2 and 3. The topic of Chapter 5 will be the kind of reasoning that is used in scientific and ordinary contexts that is not amenable to the kind of analysis suggested in Chapter 4; the material developed in Chapters 2 and 3 will again prove useful to this end. Thus, the seemingly disconnected Chapters 2 and 3 are preparatory chapters for Chapters 4 and 5, which are the two "payoff" chapters. In Chapter 6 we shall turn to the long-delayed topic of discerning the meaning of the words we use; here we shall find that our language is possessed of various levels, each level generating a level of meaning.

Beyond the canons of good thinking that the text is primarily concerned with, all of us are prone to fall into certain forms of bad thinking. There are infinitely many bad forms of thinking, but it is a fact of human nature that certain forms of erroneous reasoning are particularly apt to convince us. From the Middle Ages logicians have tried to collect and categorize appealing forms of bad reasoning by presenting long and complicated lists of fallacies. Ultimately, these lists of fallacies represent the human psychology of bad thinking. Without attempting to present a complete psychology of this kind, we shall note standard fallacies at various points in the text as they relate to the main topics under discussion. All the fallacies discussed in this book are summarized by types inside the back cover of the text.

The material in Chapters 2–6 makes fairly minimal demands on one's ability to deal with symbolic or formal techniques. However, some aspects of reasoning call for more advanced formal techniques that are essentially beyond the scope of an introductory text in reasoning. Other than a short discussion of syllogisms that is included because certain graduate entrance exams seem to place some value on them, Chapter 7 is intended to give the interested reader a glimpse of a more advanced study of reasoning. Specifically, it is meant to acquaint the reader with (a) the deeper logical structures that were not covered in the text up to that point, and (b) the elementary basis for probabilistic thinking. In certain situations the material of this chapter can be used to enhance or augment the techniques that were investigated in Chapters 2–6.

One final introductory remark is in order. While this text is primarily concerned with presenting canons or principles of critical thinking, one must not become obsessed by them. Many of the canons are mere rules of thumb; others, while decisive, tend to be limited in scope and application. In the end, critical thinking is an art (in the sense of a craft). This means that a few guidelines, sober common sense, attentiveness to what one is thinking and saying, and a lot of practice will carry one a long way toward becoming a deft practitioner of the art.

2

Accepting the Unproblematic

In our example of Chapter 1 Jane accepted a variety of claims without questioning them, and these claims allowed her to make inferences about claims that were initially more problematic. Rules for legitimate inferences will be covered in Chapter 3, and this chapter is concerned with offering guidelines for accepting certain claims as unproblematic. Chapters 2 and 3 will then form the basis for Chapter 4, which presents a broadly applicable method of assessing truth claims. Given this preview and turning to the topic of this chapter, one may wonder: isn't it dangerously uncritical to accept any claim as unproblematic, especially when such a claim could be mistaken? In response to this worry, two things should be noted:

(1) Some philosophers have indeed claimed that truth assessments must always start with claims that are certain and immune from error. Whether or not such an approach is in principle possible, it is clearly impractical. At best it would take a complex and lengthy reasoning process to arrive at even the most obvious claim. Most of us take it as unproblematic that John F. Kennedy has been dead for some time. Some may remember the assassination, but no one is immune from misremembering. Even if one consults others and historical records, these sources are not infallible. Considerations of this kind may make one wonder whether we can ever know anything of the past. While this is an interesting philosophical question, our more pressing practical needs do not allow us to devote much attention to such a question. We simply have to accept certain claims as unproblematic in our daily lives even if we cannot rule out the possibility of error.

(2) To accept a claim without question does not commit one to never questioning the claim in the future. Aside from perhaps having to defend such a claim if one is questioned or challenged by someone, circumstances could always arise that would force us to reopen the issue. Suppose that someone claims to be John F. Kennedy and that his fingerprints

match those of our former president. He explains that he made a deal with Lyndon Johnson to avoid being exposed in a scandal involving Marilyn Monroe, and produces a diary in the handwriting of Kennedy to substantiate the point. If all of this and more were to happen, we might no longer be able to accept the death of Kennedy as unproblematic. Our earlier acceptance of Kennedy's death as unproblematic does not force us to close our eyes in light of such new evidence. On the other hand, this remote and wild possibility of having to reopen the issue should not prevent us today from accepting as unproblematic the claim that Kennedy is dead. In short, as long as one doesn't dogmatically foreclose the possibility of raising questions in the future, the attitude of accepting some fallible claims as unproblematic is rational because, without it, useful truth assessments cannot get off the ground.

Given that certain claims have to be accepted as unproblematic, which claims should be so accepted? Clearly, some rules for making this choice are desirable. Unfortunately, while there is no doubt that all thinking persons rely on *some* guidelines in choosing the unproblematic, there is no codified set of rules for making this choice. In part this is because the choices are dependent on the combinations of surrounding circumstances, which are too numerous to catalogue in an exhaustive way. Beyond this, the choices often require subtle judgments whose subtlety cannot be reflected in a manageable set of rules. Given these difficulties, we must either remain silent or present a set of rules that is to be taken with a grain of salt. We shall opt for the latter course. In fact, we shall present two sets of rules. In Section 2.1 we shall present an abbreviated set of rules that is somewhat intuitive. Readers wishing to proceed to other topics may skip Sections 2.2–2.5, in which a less abbreviated and more systematic set of rules is developed. Alternatively, readers wishing to pursue the more complex set of rules may skip Section 2.1. In Section 2.6 we discuss fallacies related to accepting claims as unproblematic.

Whether one chooses the set of rules given in Section 2.1 or the one in Sections 2.2–2.5, two things must be kept in mind:

(1) The rules give a rough outline or model for determining the unproblematic. In applying the rules in practical cases, one may want to add additional refinements or even depart from the rules if special reasons for such a departure are present. We call our rules a "model" because they behave a bit like models in the sciences. The Bohr model of the atom takes the atom to have a nucleus of protons and neutrons analogous to the sun and a set of orbiting electrons analogous to the planets. While this model explains many useful relations between subatomic particles, the "solar system model" only approximates the atom, and not everything true of the model is true of the atom. If a set of rules gives us a model for determining the unproblematic that even begins to approximate the usefulness of the Bohr model, we will have gone a long way toward providing canons for accepting the unproblematic.

(2) The rules will determine certain claims to be unproblematic to the

exclusion of others. The purpose of the rules is to determine a sufficient variety of claims to be unproblematic, so that other claims (which may be as justified as those ruled to be unproblematic) can be inferred with relative ease from the stock that is specified as unproblematic. While we shall often refer to the non-unproblematic claims as "problematic," "problematic" should be understood to include claims that are "inferential" or "inferred from the unproblematic." Thus, if a claim the reader is inclined to consider unproblematic becomes labeled as "problematic," this may only mean that the claim can be inferred with relative ease from the claims officially recognized as "unproblematic."

*2.1 A Short Account of the Unproblematic

Our discussion of the questions that might be raised about Kennedy's death suggests that for a claim to be accepted as unproblematic (by a given person at a given time), there should be no doubts about the claim beyond "wild" doubts, that is, doubts of a kind that would undermine virtually any claim. We shall therefore insist that for a claim C to be unproblematic for a person P at a time t, C must pass the "Absence of Practical Doubt" (or APD) test:

(APD) *All the grounds for doubting C that are available to P at t are such that if P were to accept them as legitimate, similar or analogous doubts could be raised with "equal justice" for virtually all other claims.*

Consider my situation now with respect to the claim that Kennedy has been dead for some time. I of course have to grant that evidence for the assassination having been a hoax *could* arise. If this *possibility* were taken as legitimate grounds for doubting that Kennedy has been dead for some time, analogous doubts could be raised with "equal justice" for virtually all other claims. For example, I take myself to be seeing various things now. But isn't it possible that I am dreaming or that some neurophysiologist is tampering with my brain so that it would *seem* to me that I am seeing those things? There seems to be little basis for labeling this doubt as illegitimate while labeling the doubt about the Kennedy assassination as legitimate. Hence, the claim that Kennedy has been dead for some time passes the APD test. Of course if the evidence for the assassination having been a hoax should actually become available to me, *at that time* the claim "Kennedy has been dead for some time" would no longer pass the APD test.

Beyond the APD test, it is desirable to limit the kinds of claims that can be counted as unproblematic so that we minimize the chances of error while still having a sufficiently large stock of unproblematic claims.

*This section may be skipped or be read in lieu of Sections 2.2–2.5.

We shall propose limiting the unproblematic to claims of the following five kinds:

OBSERVATIONAL (OR OB) CLAIMS *or beliefs concern what one does or did more or less directly observe or experience,* for example see, hear, touch, feel. Included in this category are claims about one's psychological states (such as 'I'm in pain'), which are more or less directly available. Among the OB claims we shall also include observational claims of others that are reported to us.

PARTICULAR FACTUAL CLAIMS (OR PF CLAIMS) *are those made by appropriate experts* such as scientists, encyclopedias, textbooks, newspapers, atlases, and TV newscasts. By a particular factual claim we shall understand claims limited to what happened or is the case in a reasonably restricted chunk of space and time; furthermore, it must be independent of the kinds of interpretations and inferences experts can disagree on. Examples of PF claims include 'Caesar was assassinated in 44 B.C.', 'Texas is larger than Rhode Island', and 'Jupiter is farther away from Earth than Mars'.

INTUITIVE (OR INT) CLAIMS *are simple claims of which one can be assured by merely reflecting on the matter a bit* (and without relying on having learned it by observation or in the past or from some other source). Typical of this category are simple claims of logic, mathematics, and meaning relations such as "If 'A' and 'if A, then B' are both true, then 'B' must be true," '2 + 2 = 4', and "If X knows that p, 'p' is true."

GENERAL CLAIMS OF SCIENCE AND MATHEMATICS (OR SM CLAIMS) *are those made by appropriate experts* such as scientists, textbooks, or encyclopedias. Laws of physics, chemistry, and biology, as well as various theorems of mathematics, are examples of SM claims.

GENERAL CLAIMS OF COMMON SENSE (OR CS CLAIMS) *are the final kind.* For our purpose, we shall say that C is a general claim of common sense for P just in case P has confirming evidence for C, no disconfirming evidence against C, and there is general agreement that the generalization C is correct among knowledgeable and intelligent people P has met. 'Things don't vanish into thin air' and 'People don't walk on water' are likely to have been general claims of common sense even for cavemen who were without the benefits of modern science.

The unproblematic claims can now be specified as follows:

> *C is unproblematic for P at t and if and only if C passes the APD test* **and** *C is a OB, PF, INT, SM, or CS claim that is directly available to P at t (by observation, reading, reflection, etc.) or, in the case of an OB, PF, or SM claim, is transmitted to P at t by P's memory and/or testimony of other people (including ordinary nonexperts).*

Thus, for example, that a cure for skin cancer has been discovered would be an unproblematic claim for me if it passes the APD test and my friend (with no record of being unreliable) told me that, according to the *New*

York Times she read yesterday, researchers at Harvard Medical School had announced the discovery of a cure for skin cancer.

The material of this section may be summarized or abbreviated by the following chart:

C is an unproblematic claim =

(1) C passes the APD test, i.e., doubts about C are wild, and analogous doubts would undermine most claims, *and*
(2) C is a claim of one of the following five types:
- OB: Presently observed, remembered, or reported claim about an observed event.
- PF: Expert claim about an uncontroversial particular fact, which is now read (heard), remembered, or reported by a third party.
- INT: Present reflection alone shows C must be true.
- SM: Expert claim of a law of science or math, which is now read (heard), remembered, or reported by a third party.
- CS: C is presently remembered to be a personally confirmed, generally acknowledged, undisconfirmed general claim (of common sense).

While this account suppresses many complications and relies heavily on one's judgment in applying the APD test, it should suffice for readers wishing to go on to other topics. The rules presented in Sections 2.2–2.5 dispense with the APD test and elaborate on the different types of unproblematic claims.

EXERCISES—SECTION 2.1

Given your situation at this moment, which of the following claims are unproblematic? For each claim that is, identify it as OB, PF, INT, SM, or CS claim, *and* briefly justify your answer. Assume yourself to be "I," and choose the words in brackets that make the statement true (of you).

(a) I [do, do not] have a headache now.
(b) I [have, have not] had an affair with a person from Iran.
(c) Obesity causes a strain on one's heart.
(d) If Tom is taller than Mary and Mary is taller than Jim, then Tom is taller than Jim.
(e) Other things being equal, on flat terrain it is slower to walk than to ride a bicycle.
(f) One gets what one pays for; the more one pays, the better the merchandise is.
(g) Current first-mortgage rates [are, are not] at the double-digit level.
(h) Nothing can travel faster than the speed of light.
(i) Venus is smaller than Earth.
(j) The sum of the angles of a triangle is 180°.

2.2 Candidates for Unproblematic Acceptance

In the following four sections we shall present a fairly elaborate set of rules for determining the unproblematic. In this section and the next we shall specify the class of claims that are candidates for unproblematic acceptance. Such candidates should be accepted as unproblematic unless there are reasons against so accepting them. The reasons against unproblematically accepting a candidate fall into two categories: (a) A candidate for unproblematic acceptance C_1 conflicts with another candidate for unproblematic acceptance C_2. In such a case we clearly cannot accept both C_1 and C_2. (b) Even if a candidate for unproblematic acceptance does not conflict (or were not to conflict) with other candidates, there may be some ground for questioning the reliability of the person making the claim. Thus, an eyewitness report should not be accepted as unproblematic if we have reasons to think that the witness was drunk out of his mind at the time of the incident. In Section 2.4 we shall discuss this kind of reason for doubting a claim, and in Section 2.5 we shall suggest ways of dealing with conflicts between candidates for unproblematic acceptance. Such is the general strategy to be pursued in our specification of the unproblematic in Sections 2.2–2.5.

The claims that are candidates for unproblematic acceptance may be divided into five groups: observational (or OB) claims, particular factual (or PF) claims, intuitive (or INT) claims, general claims of science and mathematics (or SM) claims, and general claims of common sense (or CS) claims. What is meant by these categories will become clearer as we consider the kinds of claims that fit into these categories.

Observational (or OB) Claims. Perhaps the most conspicuous class of unproblematic claims involves *claims or beliefs concerning what one more or less directly observes or experiences (i.e., sees, hears, touches, feels, etc.).* We shall call these claims OBSERVATIONAL CLAIMS and consider them to be candidates for unproblematic acceptance for the observer at the time of observation. Candidates of this type include claims like the claim that there is a book in front of me (made while seeing the book) and the claim that he said such and such (made immediately upon hearing him). Also included are claims like 'I feel depressed' made while being aware of one's feeling of depression. Expressions like 'Seeing is believing' and 'I want to see it with my own eyes' suggest that we consider observational claims to be the least problematic. This category of candidates, as well as the others we shall discuss, are demarcated in terms of "content"—that is, what the claim is about—and one's access to the claim. Thus, the candidates we have just isolated may be summarized in the following way:

Claim Type	*Content*	*Access*
OB	What was observed	Observer at the time of observation

A summary like this must of course be understood and applied within the background of a number of clarifications and elaborations, to which we now turn.

(1) In counting a claim as an OB claim, one must take care that the claim doesn't go beyond what can plausibly be claimed to be directly observable. 'The book in front of me is *The Women's Room*' is an observational claim for me when made on the basis of seeing the book. But it is not an observational claim that the book in front of me is a best-seller. That this book is a best-seller is not something anyone can directly observe (although one may observe a claim of testimony on the cover that it is a best-seller). The distinction between what can be directly observed and what involves an inference or an interpretation is crucial when dealing with eyewitnesses in the courtroom. An eyewitness can testify about what he or she directly observed; interpretations or inferences a witness puts on the evidence, as well as what is reported on the basis of hearsay, are disallowed and the jury is instructed to disregard them. Roughly, one should count a claim as an observational claim only if one thinks that it could be accepted as an eyewitness report in a courtroom. This rule of thumb as well as the qualification 'more or less directly observable' are admittedly imprecise. However, there is no substitute for good judgment, and trying to make the distinction too precise is liable to result in curious and impractical philosophical theories.

(2) When I see Snooz sleeping, my observational claim can take either the form 'I see Snooz sleeping' or 'Snooz is sleeping'. We shall not insist that an OB claim explicitly contain a verb of perception like "see" or "hear." Suppose we take the claim in the form, 'Snooz is sleeping'. This claim has the kind of content that, under an appropriate circumstance, allows it to be an observational claim. If the claim is made by me while seeing Snooz sleep, my claim is an OB claim. On the other hand, you might make the same claim 'Snooz is sleeping', on the basis of an inference from his absence at the party and his dormant propensities. Thus, whether a claim is an OB claim depends on whether it is based on an observer observing the claimed event.

(3) Suppose a day passed since my seeing Snooz sleep, and I claim 'Snooz was (seen) sleeping'. Is this an observational claim for me? In a sense it doesn't matter what we call it as long as we are clear on the fact that my claim depends on both my past observation and my present memory of this past observation. We could say that 'Snooz was (seen) sleeping' is not an OB claim, but a claim of memory concerning an OB claim made in the past. Alternatively, we could consider 'Snooz was (seen) sleeping' to be an OB claim and insist that my present position with respect to the claim is not that of an observer at the time of observation. For our purpose it will be convenient to adopt the second terminology.

To sum up, an OB claim must be about what was more or less directly observed. Whether a claim is an OB claim depends neither on the explicit present of a verb of perception in the claim nor only on the form of the claim; whether it is an OB claim for a person P depends on whether P's basis for the claim involves some observer having observed the claimed event. Even when a claim or statement is counted as an OB claim for P, whether or not it is a candidate for unproblematic acceptance for P depends on P's access to the claim. So far we have only allowed that an OB claim is a candidate for unproblematic acceptance for P if it is made by P at the time of observation. Thus, my subsequent claim that Snooz was sleeping is so far not counted as an OB *candidate* for unproblematic acceptance for me. The discussion of reliance on memory will be postponed to Section 2.3.

Particular Factual (or PF) Claims. If we read in an encyclopedia or a history text that the Battle of Actium took place in 31 B.C., we take it as unproblematic that the battle did take place at that time, and similarly we take it as unproblematic that Israeli planes bombed Iraqi nuclear plants when we read this in the newspaper. Upon seeing an atlas we take it as unproblematic that Rhode Island is smaller than Texas. These are examples of what we shall call particular factual claims, and lumped under this category are three different kinds of claims:

(1) Claims that could have been one's own observational claim without too much difficulty if one were at the right place at the right time. 'Caesar was assassinated in 44 B.C.' would be an example of this type.
(2) Claims that involve a compilation of a number of observations. An example would be 'Nebraska is smaller than Texas'. It would be silly to think that a person could walk around Nebraska and Texas and easily perceive that one is smaller than the other. And this certainly was not the way reference sources arrived at the claim. Rather, a great number of surveyors were employed and their observations were compiled to produce a reasonably accurate map of the land; based on such a map, political boundaries were established and superimposed on the map. An atlas in which we can "see" Nebraska to be smaller than Texas is expert testimony based on such a compilation, which reports how the geographic features and the political boundaries were at the time of publishing the map.
(3) Claims about a particular fact involving uncontroversial inferences from observations such as a claim that a certain star is three light-years away from Earth.

For our purposes, we may define a PARTICULAR FACTUAL (or PF) CLAIM as *a claim that is limited to what happened or is the case in a reasonably restricted chunk of space and time and is free of interpretations and inferences, except those over which disagreement among experts is implausible.* The qualification concerning interpretations and inferences is meant to exclude from PF claims a claim like '48 percent of the TV audience watched the Super Bowl', when this is based on an inference from the viewing behavior of several hundred families in a Nielsen poll. Similarly, interpretive statements like 'The real cause of the Civil War was not slavery but the issue of states' rights' are intended to be excluded. On the other hand, a scientist's claim that a certain star is three light-years away from Earth will be counted as a PF claim; although the claim is based on inferences from certain observations, the inferences only require utterly uncontroversial applications of well-established laws of physics. When an inference or interpretation is involved in a claim, in order to accept it as a PF claim one must be satisfied that serious disagreement among experts over such a claim is unlikely or implausible.

Given this understanding of particular factual claims, the basic idea is to count PF claims as candidates for unproblematic acceptance when they are made presently available to us by appropriate experts such as scientists, encyclopedias, textbooks, newspapers, atlases, and TV newcasts. In a broad sense, we can conceive of PF candidates for unproblematic acceptance as expert testimony concerning particular facts. However, something more needs to be said about experts.

By an "expert" we shall understand publicly recognized experts such as recognized scientists and historians, commonly used textbooks, and reference sources that are generally reliable, such as *Encyclopedia Britannica* and the *New York Times*. In some cases the experts are experts in particular fields such as physics or medicine, while in other cases they are accredited as expert transmitters of information—examples being standard reference sources and reliable newspapers. A historian might be seen as falling into both of these categories. The term "expert" will *not* be extended beyond publicly recognized experts; for example, we shall not consider each person to be an "expert" on his or her own name or feelings.

While what is intended by the term "appropriate expert" should be reasonably clear, it may often be difficult to determine beyond a shadow of doubt that someone or some source is in fact an appropriate expert. No doubt we have often heard that the *New York Times* is a reliable newspaper; some of us may also have often read the newspaper and seen very few of its stories controverted by other sources. Still, can we be absolutely sure that the *New York Times* is generally reliable? To avoid impoverishing our stock of PF candidates, we introduce the notion of a presumption. Let us say: X can be PRESUMED if there are some grounds for thinking X to be true and no specific grounds for thinking X to be false. Our account of PF candidates for unproblematic acceptance then becomes this:

> *A particular factual claim C is a candidate for unproblematic acceptance for P if C is made presently available to P by a source P can presume to be an appropriate expert.*

The following chart summarizes PF candidates.

Claim Type	*Content*	*Access*
PF	Uncontroversial particular facts	Made available by a presumed expert source at time of accepting the claim

We conclude our discussion of PF candidates with a few remarks about when we can presume a source to be an expert source. Typically the grounds one has for something or someone being an expert source is the general reputation of the source and the office or position occupied by the person. The *Encyclopedia Britannica,* the *Rand McNally Atlas,* the *New York Times,* and the *Los Angeles Times* are examples of sources having national or local reputations. Somewhat similarly, that a textbook is widely used at leading universities would count toward its being an appropriate source. Being a professor of biology at Harvard or Berkeley, being a special assistant for Middle East Affairs in the State Department, and being the curator of the National Gallery would be examples of grounds for thinking that the person is an expert in his or her field.

Except for the observational claims of reporters (i.e., "expert observers" whom a current-event source tacitly endorses by continuing to use them as reporters or critics), an expert should base his or her particular factual claims on a number of observations that are carefully assessed and/or compiled. A reputable scientist does not announce his or her results until the experiment has been repeated several times and the reliability of the observations and the experimental setup has been carefully assessed. A historian takes great care that there is enough evidence for an event having occurred and no serious evidence against its having occurred; this is especially true when the event is in the remote past where the evidence is both scanty and liable to involve a mistransmission somewhere along the line. Except for what was directly observed by a reliable reporter, a reliable newspaper won't print a story unless it has been independently confirmed by several sources. This is reflected in newspaper statements like "Israeli planes attacked Iraqi nuclear power plants, and the Israeli government announced that there were no Israeli casualties in the raid." That there was such an attack and that the government made such an announcement about the casualties are considered to be sufficiently confirmed and corroborated for the newspaper to put its reputation on the line. However, it is not willing to vouch for the correctness of the announcement, because the paper evidently lacked independent confirmation of there being no Israeli casualties. [If we consider the Israeli government to be an expert source, we may eventually want to consider the casualty claim to be a candidate for unproblematic acceptance. This possibility will have to await our discussion in Section 2.3, because the announcement was not made directly available to us (by our hearing it) but only indirectly through the newspaper article.]

Our discussion of the last paragraph can be put in the following way: Normally, part and parcel of taking a particular factual claim to have been made available by an expert source is taking the claim to have been based on a number of observations that were carefully assessed or compiled; thus, the grounds for presuming the former should normally also be grounds for presuming the latter. The only significant exception involves observation claims by a person whom a current-even source like a newspaper continues to use as a reporter, critic, or columnist. A newspaper continuing to use such a person suggests that it is at least willing to vouch for the person keeping the observational facts straight. Thus, we may presume that such a person is at least an expert observer, so that claims that are entirely limited to what the person directly observed may be counted as PF candidates. These considerations must be kept in mind upon leaving the news section of the newspaper and entering the opinion or review sections, where the paper absolves itself of the responsibility of separating news from opinion. Particular factual claims in those sections may be considered PF candidates only if we have grounds for thinking that the author is an expert in the field who has carefully assessed or compiled a number of observations (by one or more persons), or—barring that—that the claim is limited to what the author directly observed.

Intuitive (or INT) Claims. There is a relatively small class of candidates for unproblematic acceptance that depends neither on observation nor on expert testimony. Examples are claims like 'One can't be in two places at the same time', '13 + 12 = 25', and 'If all men are mortal and Socrates is a man, then Socrates is mortal'. For the lack of a better term, we might call claims of this type "intuitive claims." For our purpose:

> *A claim is an* INTUITIVE CLAIM *for P when by merely reflecting on the matter a bit (and without having learned it in the past or from some other source), P can assure him- or herself (or "see" with the "mind's eye") that the claim is (or has got to be) true.*

We can then say that a claim is a candidate for unproblematic acceptance for P if it is an intuitive claim for P. Where "content" under the Access column refers to what is under the Content column, the INT candidates may be presented in chart form:

Claim Type	*Content*	*Access*
INT	Reflection alone shows it must be true.	The "content" is easily ascertained at the time of accepting the claim.

Three features tacit in our characterization of INT candidates are essential for categorizing a claim as intuitive in type:

(1) Since reflection alone is supposed to be sufficient to assure us of its truth, an INT claim must not depend on collecting or having collected observational evidence for it. Consider for example '12 + 13 = 25'. If we put 12 rabbits together with 13 rabbits in a cage and find the next day that there are 27 rabbits in the cage, we would not say that we have uncovered evidence that 12 + 13 might not be 25. We would say that someone put some other rabbits into the cage or that the rabbits had reproduced as is their wont. In short, we count no observation as falsifying '12 + 13 = 25'. But then we can claim '12 + 13 = 25' without collecting observational evidence, because we are antecedently assured that nothing will count as evidence against it. Somewhat similarly, if prosecution's witness claims that the suspect was seen at the murder site on the night of the murder and the suspect's witness claims that the suspect was playing poker all night, we conclude that one of the two witnesses must be lying or mistaken. We would not consider this as potential evidence that someone might be in two places at the same time. If our conception of the world precludes our accepting anything as observational evidence again 'A person can't be in two places at the same time', we can accept this claim without worrying about observational evidence. The same type of consideration applies to the Socrates example.

(2) Intuitive claims are supposed to be claims we can in some sense "see" to be true without relying on our having learned it in the past. Our examples of INT claims seem to have this feature. For most of us, however, a present reliance on the Pythagorean theorem (the square of the hypotenuse is equal to the sum of the squares of the other two sides) would not involve our "seeing" it to be true; rather, it would be a case of our relying on having learned it in the past. Thus, although observational evidence may be irrelevant to the truth of the Pythagorean theorem, for most of us it would not count as an INT candidate.

(3) INT candidates are supposed to be claims that require little reflection. For someone who has just constructed or gone through a proof for the Pythagorean theorem, his or her reliance on the theorem would perhaps involve "seeing" the theorem to be true. However, a proof for the theorem is reasonably complex and requires more than a bit of reflection. Thus, even for the person who has just gone through the proof, the theorem should not be counted as an INT candidate. In order to minimize the possibility of error among the unproblematic claims, we have limited INT candidates to reasonably obvious claims requiring little reflection.

In this age of computers and calculators, perhaps the following remarks are in order. Complex mathematical and logical relations can indeed be easily ascertained by using such devices. Yet we shall not consider a result thus ascertained to be an intuitive claim, because we are ultimately relying on the machine (and its operator) to function correctly and do not "see" with the "mind's eye" that the result must be correct. While for OB candidates we allow certain mechanical and electronic observational aids such as eyeglasses, telescopes, and automobile odometers, our attitude toward INT candidates is to disallow electronic aids, taking results that depend on their use as inferences based on the generalization that computing machines are normally reliable.

Strongly Supported General Claims. Most of us would consider general claims of the following kind to be unproblematic: 'Things don't vanish into thin air', 'All men are mortal', 'The square of the hypotenuse is equal to the sum of the squares of the other two sides', 'People can't walk on water', 'The period between conception and birth is approximately nine months for human beings', and 'Things tend to get lost in messy rooms'. These are general claims that virtually no intelligent and knowledgeable persons would deny, and except for mathematical claims, they are well corroborated by experience.

Leaving aside mathematical claims, it is true that the generalizations just mentioned are in some sense derived or inferred from observations. However, if someone claimed that a local hero called Bear was (seen) walking on water, we would respond that the speaker must be kidding (or must have been on drugs). This response critically depends on treating 'Men cannot walk on water' as unproblematic and taking it to *override* the contrary claim of a solitary witness. That this is a rational procedure seems to be beyond question. On the other hand, the rationale for this procedure is less clear and is a sourse of philosophical controversy. It may be the result of scientific results having been developed over the ages and having been corroborated by countless witnesses, so that the evidence for the unreliability of the solitary contrary witness is overwhelming. It may be because, without the scientific laws we have developed over time, there is no coherent framework for assessing alleged observations. In any event, we certainly do allow certain generalizations to override some observational claims. Of course if Bear had repeatedly performed his feat in front of numerous witnesses, and investigators could not discover any "gimmick," we would have to rethink our science.

One class of generalizations we should count as candidates for unproblematic acceptance are *general claims of science and mathematics (or SM claims),* made presently available to us by what can be presumed to be an expert source—either a scientist herself (in her writings) or by an accredited transmitter such as a textbook, encyclopedia, teacher, or newspaper. The SM candidates may be presented in chart form.

Claim Type	*Content*	*Access*
SM	General laws of science and math	Made available by a presumed expert source at time of accepting the claim

Beyond SM candidates is another class of generalizations that should be candidates for unproblematic acceptance, and they might be called the *general claims of common sense (or CS claims).* There is little chance of a scientist working on establishing that things tend to get lost in messy rooms; yet the claim should be a candidate for unproblematic acceptance. Again, even cavemen who were without the benefit of science should have been able to accept as unproblematic the claim that men can't walk on water. On the other hand, "common sense" can be a dangerous appeal. Someone might say, "It's just common sense that capital punishment would deter crime." But this claim should not be taken as a candidate for unproblematic acceptance.

To specify the CS claims appropriately, let us use the usual terminology of confirmation and disconfirmation. A generalization like 'All ravens are black' tells us that any observed raven is black; thus, whenever we determine an observed raven to be black, we have a bit of evidence in favor of the generalization because this is what the generalization predicted. But of course the observation of no single black raven, and not even any group of a thousand black ravens, *proves* that *all* ravens are black. Because it is only a bit of evidence in favor of the generalization and not a proof, sightings of black ravens are said to confirm the generalization that all ravens are black. Much in the same way, each time we step into the bathtub and find our feet going to the bottom, we have a confirmation of the claim that no one can walk on water.

Suppose now that someone claims to have observed a white raven. Now if there really was a white raven, this would make the generalization 'All ravens are black' false. But of course a claim to have seen a white raven can be mistaken; thus, given such an alleged observation, we would not immediately say that the generalization has been falsified. Still the generalization is clearly false if there is nothing amiss with the alleged observation of the white raven. To indicate that the generalization is in trouble without being conclusively falsified, the observational claim that a white raven was seen is often said to disconfirm the generalization that all ravens are black. Since 'disconfirm' is sometimes used synonymously with 'falsify', we shall often speak of *apparent* disconfirmation and *apparently* disconfirming instances to emphasize that the available evidence is not decisive. However, it should be clear that if we are to maintain a generalization in face of an (apparent) disconfirmation, we must be confident that it can be explained away in terms of something being amiss with the observation.

Given this much, for our purposes we can say:

> *C is a* GENERAL CLAIM OF COMMON SENSE *(or a CS claim) for P just in case the following three conditions are met: (i) numerous confirming instances of C have been observed by P, (ii) there is general agreement on C's correctness among knowledgeable and intelligent people P has met, and (iii) when there are apparently disconfirming instances, either in P's own observation or in some testified to P, it is plausible to P that these instances can somehow be explained away.*

Conditions (i)–(iii) may be explained as follows: Consider the claim that things don't vanish into thin air. Conditions (i) and (ii) are presumably met for most of us. However, there are some apparently disconfirming instances. Aside from the tricks of magicians, sometimes when we lose something, it is as if it had vanished into thin air. In these cases we usually do not know what the true explanation of the apparent anomaly is. However, we do take it as plausible that the apparent disconfirmation can *somehow* be explained away. That is the intent of condition (iii). On the other hand, that capital punishment deters crime is not a candidate for unproblematic acceptance, because neither condition (i) nor (ii) is satisfied.

When the CS candidate is a claim like 'It *almost* never snows in Santa Barbara', condition (iii) must be construed in a special way. The only snowfall of the last fifty years in 1946 does not constitute a disconfirmation. On the other hand, if someone claimed that it snowed for two solid weeks in Santa Barbara last year, this would constitute an apparent disconfirmation. In face of such an apparent disconfirmation, 'It almost never snows in Santa Barbara' can be maintained as a CS candidate only if it is plausible that the apparent disconfirmation can somehow be explained away. Given my knowledge of the Santa Barbara climate, it is plausible to me that the claim about the two-week snowfall can be explained away in some way or other; perhaps the person was joking or under the influence of some drug.

Given this understanding of condition (iii), let us say that a general claim is a CS candidate for unproblematic acceptance for P if (with the help of memory) P can ascertain that conditions (i)–(iii) are satisfied. Where "content" under the Access column refers to what is under the Content column and 'undisconfirmed' abbreviates feature (iii), the CS candidates may be presented in chart form.

Claim Type	*Content*	*Access*
CS	Personally confirmed, generally acknowledged, undisconfirmed generalization of common sense	With the help of memory, "content" is ascertained at the time of accepting the claim.

SM and CS candidates are sometimes confused with PF and INT candidates. Thus, something should be said about what separates them. The distinction between strongly supported general claims (i.e., SM and CS claims) and PF claims is this: Even when made by an expert source, PF claims are typically about some particular objects, and in general, compiling the behavior of the one or more objects covered by a PF claim is a practical way of trying to determine decisively the truth or falsity of the claim. SM and CS claims, on the other hand, are general claims that explicitly or implicitly involve the word "all" in a way that makes it impractical to determine their truth by compiling the behavior of all the instances involved. 'Socrates is mortal' is a PF claim that applies only to Socrates, and finding out Socrates's fate is a practical way of determining its truth or falsity. 'All men are mortal' is an SM or CS claim because of the use of 'all', which makes the generalization apply to anyone, past, present, or future; as such, there is no practical way of trying to determine it decisively to be true by compiling the dates of all its instances. Sometimes this generalization is expressed in the singular form 'Man is mortal'; yet this counts as an SM or CS claim because the intent of that statement is that all men are mortal, not just that this or that man is mortal. A claim like 'All Japanese rivers are shorter than the Urubamba River of South America' is a PF claim despite the use of 'all', because checking the length of the Urubamba and all the rivers in Japan (in an atlas) is a practical way of decisively determining its truth or falsity.

Two factors may be relied on in separating INT claims from SM and CS claims:

(1) The complexity of the claim or the terms involved in the claim. INT claims are supposed to be simple claims that we can "see" to be true simply by reflecting on the matter. The most general laws of physics are complex or use complex terms (like "kinetic energy," whose definition requires some knowledge of calculus). Complexity is the typical earmark of SM claims.

(2) The conceivability of observations that would have shown the claim to be false. Although we in fact did not have observations of that kind, and a few reports of such an observation would have had no effect, we can at least conceive of the possibility of having had a large number of observations that would have shown 'No one walks on water' to have been false. Such is not the case with INT candidates, because by and large INT candidates determine how we are going to treat or conceptualize any possible observation. The conceivability of falsifying observations is an earmark of CS claims and perhaps low-level SM claims (like Boyle's law), which are fairly closely tied to observations.

This completes our catalogue of the types of candidates for unproblematic acceptance. One feature we have not sufficiently emphasized is that a claim C could be a candidate for a person P at time t and not be such a candidate for P at another time t′. P may now be observing a wart on the neighbor's forehead, but twenty years later it may be the vaguest of recollections that the (previous) neighbor had a wart. P may not have known the Los Angeles News Agency to be unreliable last year but now he does; in that case their "expert testimony" ceases to be expert testimony. What was an intuitive claim for P at one moment may not be intuitively clear to him at another. What is now a general claim of common sense would not be a CS candidate later if disconfirming instances should occur in the interim. Thus, strictly speaking, we should say 'C is a candidate for a person P at time t' rather than 'C is a candidate for P'. Except for the somewhat hybrid CS candidates, the relevant sources of all the candidates discussed in this section are presently given: OB candidates relate to present observations, PF and SM candidates involve presently reading or hearing an expert source, and INT candidates require present reflection. Even with the hybrid CS candidates involving memory, it must be presently ascertained that it is personally confirmed and generally acknowledged. In a slightly stretched sense of "directly given," we can say that all the candidates discussed in this section are candidates at the time they are "directly given." Table 2.1 near the end of Section 2.3 (as well as the summary of Sections 2.2–2.5 at the end of the chapter) summarizes the material covered in this section and the next (where we shall consider transmitted OB, PF, and SM claims).

EXERCISES—SECTION 2.2

Some of the problems in this section do not have unique correct answers. The answers can depend on one's own particular situation, and some cases can involve judgment calls over which reasonable people can disagree. Thus, it is important to justify your answers when the problem asks for it.

1. Consider the following eyewitness report by Mrs. McGillicutty:

   Oh yes, I saw Mr. Crispin stab his wife. He used a kitchen knife, he did. Probably the very one Mrs. Crispin used to prepare his dinner with. He is an evil man, he is. One look at him and you'd know. I was scared out of my mind, I was, and all I wanted to do was run away. As he kept stabbing her over and over, he kept saying, "I finally have my freedom!" He's getting rid of his wife to marry some floozie in London—that's what everyone in the village says. God will punish him, He will!

   Assume that Mrs. McGillicutty is not lying and that she correctly remembers what she saw or experienced on the day of the murder. Which of the following statements were (presently given) OB candidates for Mrs. McGillicutty at the time of the murder? Briefly justify your answers.

   (a) Mr. Crispin is stabbing his wife repeatedly with a kitchen knife.
   (b) Mr. Crispin is stabbing his wife with the knife Mrs. Crispin used to prepare his dinner with.
   (c) Mr. Crispin is an evil man.
   (d) Mr. Crispin is killing his wife to get his freedom.
   (e) Mr. Crispin is killing his wife so that he could marry a floozie in London.
   (f) Mrs. McGillicutty is scared out of her mind.
   (g) Mrs. McGillicutty wants to run away.
   (h) Mr. Crispin keeps saying things as he stabs his wife.
   (i) God will punish Mr. Crispin.

2. Assume that you are reading the following passage from the *Los Angeles Times:*

   WASHINGTON—Interrupting his Falkland Islands shuttle mission, Secretary of State Alexander M. Haig, Jr., returned here Tuesday to report to President

Reagan while Britain and Argentina consider "new ideas" to resolve the crisis.

Haig . . . refused to characterize himself as either optimistic or pessimistic about the prospects of averting war. . . .

Before leaving London . . . Haig sounded a note of anxiety about the possibility of conflict. . . .

The situation "is dangerous, and increasingly so," he said. "Therefore, there is great urgency to find a political solution."

Based on reading this passage, which of the following statements (or paraphrases) are PF candidates for unproblematic acceptance for you? Briefly justify your answer.

(a) Haig interrupted his Falkland Islands shuttle mission and returned to Washington to report to President Reagan.
(b) Britain and Argentina are considering "new ideas" to resolve the crisis.
(c) Haig is neither optimistic nor pessimistic about the prospects of averting war.
(d) Haig is anxious about the possibility of conflict.
(e) The situation is dangerous and increasingly so.

3. Repeat the instructions in exercise 2 for the following column written by a former senior advisor to President Jimmy Carter for Middle Eastern affairs:

Israel's withdrawal from the Sinai has converted the historically complex question of Middle East peace into a relatively simple issue: Do the Arabs, and particularly the Saudis, really want peace? Withdrawal from the Sinai is conclusive evidence of Israel's willingness to make peace with its neighbors. The hollowness of Arab rhetoric has been demonstrated by Israel's relinquishment of more than 90 percent of the territory it has occupied since 1967—territory that constituted a vital defense buffer zone against renewed aggression. It is now irrelevant to talk about Saudi Arabia's sensitivities or to waste time trying to convince the Saudis or the Palestine Liberation Organization of Israel's right to exist.

(a) Israel has withdrawn from more than 90 percent of the Sinai.
(b) Withdrawal from the Sinai is conclusive evidence of Israel's willingness to make peace with its neighbors.
(c) The Sinai constituted a vital defense buffer zone (for Israel) against renewed aggression.
(d) Now that Israel has withdrawn from the Sinai, it is irrelevant to talk about Saudi Arabia's sensitivities.
(e) It is a waste of time trying to convince the Saudis or the Palestine Liberation Organization of Israel's right to exist.

4. Repeat the instructions in exercise 2 for the following article by a music critic in the *Los Angeles Times.*

BERKELEY—Rickie Lee Jones' concert Sunday night at the Berkeley Community Theater was . . . a boozy affair mixing equal parts of celebration and sentimentality.

Typical of the bizarreness of the evening, Jones, in her first California concert in nearly three years, did almost the entire show in sheer lacy lingerie.

It was stylish lingerie, to be sure, a sort of top-of-the-line Frederick's of Hollywood. And, given Jones' instinct for camp theatricality, you might even be tempted to dismiss the attire as part of a vampish stage persona.

But the costume seemed simply one in a series of unsettling signs that here was a performer who might be operating close to an emotional edge: lusty swigs from a Jack Daniels bottle, constant embraces with band members for reassurance, some embarrassingly incoherent chatter between songs, and repeated strip-show bumps and grinds.

For some of the 3600 people who filled the auditorium, the eccentric behavior added up to tedious indulgence. There were numerous walkouts near the end of the two-hour performance. The *San Francisco Examiner* music critic labeled the concert a "disgrace."

To most on hand, however, the concert was an absorbing experience: the chance to see a major pop figure battle the tensions and insecurities of the creative process.

(a) Jones gave her first California concert in almost three years at the Berkeley Community Theater on Sunday night.
(b) The concert was bizarre.
(c) Jones did almost the entire show in sheer lacy lingerie.
(d) The lingerie she wore was a sort of top-of-the-line Frederick's of Hollywood.
(e) Jones has an instinct for camp theatricality.
(f) There was a series of unsettling signs that she was operating close to an emotional edge.
(g) She took swigs from a Jack Daniels bottle and embraced band members a number of times.
(h) She embraced band members for reassurance.
(i) For some of the audience the eccentric behavior added up to tedious indulgence.
(j) There were numerous walkouts near the end of the two-hour performance.
(k) The concert was a disgrace.
(l) In the concert Jones battled the tensions and insecurities of the creative process.

5. On the basis of the material covered in Section 2.2 (and summarized in that part of the chart at the end of Section 2.3 not having to do with transmitted claims), which of the claims (a)–(k) below are candidates for unproblematic acceptance for you? For each claim that is such a candidate, identify it as an OB, PF, INT, SM, or CS candidate, and *justify* your answer. In (a)–(c), assume yourself to be "I" and choose the words in brackets that are true of you. For (i)–(k), assume that you have just read the following article from the *Encyclopedia Britannica:*

   The mass of the earth is found by comparing its gravitational attraction on a small sphere at its surface with that of a large sphere of known mass on the small sphere. The attractive force satisfies the law of gravitation, namely, that the force produced on a given small body is proportional to m/r^2, where m is the mass of the attracting body and r is the distance of its center. If the forces produced and the distances are known, we can find the ratio of the masses. Boys and Braun independently found the mass [of the earth] to be 5.98×10^{21} metric tons.

   (a) I [do, do not] have a headache now.
   (b) I [do, do not] have a father who is alive.
   (c) I [have, have not] had an affair with a person from Iran.
   (d) One gets what one pays for; the more one pays, the better the merchandise is.
   (e) Obesity causes a strain on one's heart.
   (f) $2483 \times 484 = 1,201,772$.
   (g) Other things being equal, on flat terrains it is slower to walk than to ride a bicycle.
   (h) If Tom is taller than Mary and Mary is taller than Jim, then Tom is taller than Jim.

(i) The attractive force produced by a large sphere on a given small body is proportional to m/r^2, where m is the mass of the attracting body and r is the distance of its center [from the center of the small body].
(j) Given the law of gravitation, if the forces produced on the small sphere by Earth and the other large sphere are known as well as the distances between the centers of these bodies, one can determine the ratio of the masses of Earth and the other large sphere.
(k) The mass of the Earth is 5.98×10^{21} metric tons.

2.3 Transmission of Claims

Given the account of Section 2.2, OB, PF, and SM claims are candidates for unproblematic acceptance for me at the moment that I am observing the event in question or reading an "expert source" like an encyclopedia. But once the event is over and once I close the encyclopedia, the involved claims are no longer directly given, and thus, they are no longer candidates according to the account so far given. If John is on a date with Ginny, it is a present-tense observational claim for John that he is dating Ginny. But the next day, the claim 'I had a date with Ginny last night' is no longer a present-tense observational claim for John. But surely, that he had a date with Ginny should be a candidate for unproblematic acceptance for John on the next day. Similarly, if my friend tells me that he read in the newspaper yesterday that the Raiders won the 1984 Super Bowl, that the Raiders won should be a candidate for unproblematic acceptance for me. Clearly, the stock of things we could rely on in our truth assessments would be impoverished if we relied only on directly given claims and did not use claims that are transmitted in one way or another. This section will enlarge the class candidates for unproblematic acceptance by including certain transmitted OB, PF, and SM claims.

One way a claim can be transmitted is by memory. Of course, all of us have had the misfortune of misremembering something. On the other hand, most readers presumably don't have serious doubts as to whether they had breakfast this morning or whether they had a date last night. In the example of Jane's missing term paper in Chapter 1, when she got back to her room, Jane unhesitatingly relied on her memory that Professor C used the word "distinctly." We unhesitatingly rely on the remembered fact that Reagan was elected president and the previously learned fact that water is made up of hydrogen and oxygen. Other than what we are *now* observing or reading, almost everything we know is based on memory in one form or another. Thus, if we did not rely on OB, PF, and SM claims that are transmitted by memory, the activity of truth assessment would be *severely* hampered.

Even granting that the unproblematic cannot be limited to claims that are immune from error, it would be wise to put some limitations on the kind of reliance on memory that can be used in generating candidates for unproblematic acceptance. If the remembered observation was in the recent past or if we recently read the expert testimony of a PF or SM claim, we need not seriously worry about our memory leading us astray. In order to have a short term, let us call these claims *recently acquired claims.*

Problems arise when our initial acquisition of an OB, PF, or SM claim is not in the recent past but somewhat more remote. One kind of memory of even the remote past on which we normally rely involves memory of an event that has some particular significance. Thus, one is likely to remember correctly the first boy or girl one kissed in a quasi-romatic way. Finally seeing the place you always wanted to see, seeing a crucial game in which your favorite team was involved, and a particularly embarrassing experience are all events that are likely to be remembered correctly because of their significance. Similarly, reading or hearing a PF or SM claim in a standard text or a class lecture is likely to be remembered correctly if the claim (or the acquisition of the claim) had a particular significance for us. Reading about a battle in which one's great-grandfather had a role, an amusing or otherwise memorable way in which a professor made a claim, and losing a significant amount of money on a bet over the claim may be ways in which claims can become unforgettable for us. Let us say that a claim is a *memorable claim* for a person if the claim or its acquisition was of particular significance for the person. Remembered type OB, PF, and SM claims that are memorable are normally reliable.

Other kinds of claims involving memory on which we place strong reliance are remembered claims that have been corroborated a number of times since their initial acquisition. Suppose that I (seem to) remember going to Lake Como before going to Venice on my trip to Europe. The kinds of corroboration this memory claim may have had are

(1) I mentioned this order of events in the past to my traveling companion and she agreed with me (or at least didn't contradict me).
(2) The photo album of the trip has pictures of Lake Como before the pictures of Venice, and I looked at this album a number of times.
(3) I (seem to) remember being in St. Moritz on that trip, and from this I infer that the natural route would have been to go to Lake Como first and Venice second rather than the other way around.

Corroboration usually takes the form in which others who know of the event are in agreement (or do not contradict) or other (seeming) memories of one's own cohering with the memory in question. Similar considerations apply to PF and SM claims that we remember. For example, that Lincoln was shot is unproblematic for us, and this is true despite our inability to remember which expert (i.e., book or teacher) first made it available to us. We place strong reliance on this memory because we are likely to have been in a number of situations in which the shooting of Lincoln was corroborated for us. We might have read it again in another context or used the claim as an example (as I am now doing) without incurring the protest or objection of the hearer. My memory that Newton's second law states that force equals mass times acceleration has a similarly strong status because it has been corroborated for me a number of times in books and conversations.

In discussing memory, one feature deserves particular attention: The more specific the claim is, the less confident we tend to be. Thus, that I took a trip to Europe seems beyond doubt, and that I went to Italy is about as indubitable. That I went to Lake Como before Venice is perhaps a little more doubtful; that I ate ravioli (rather than cannelloni) for lunch on the shores of Lake Como seems quite dubitable (in the absence of some specific significance about the ravioli lunch). This can be seen roughly as a matter of the degree of corroboration. I have a number of seeming memories of being in Europe; they corroborate each other, and the supposition that they are all mistaken would create a serious discontinuity in my life as I know it. That I went to Lake Como first is corroborated in the ways we have already discussed. As to whether I had ravioli or cannelloni lunch, either claim fits in with my other memories, and to this extent, my memory of the ravioli lunch receives no corroboration from my seeming memories. Similarly, 'The Japanese attacked Pearl Harbor' seems a bit more reliable for most of us than 'The Japanese sank the battleship *Arizona*'. Even the most casual newscast reminds us annually of Pearl Harbor Day on December 7, and to this extent the broader claim has had repeated corroboration. That the battleship *Arizona* was sunk is not as frequently mentioned, and to this extent it has a slightly lesser corroboration. (It is also true that broader claims are often more significant and memorable to us than particular details, which tend to be less significant.)

OB, PF, and SM claims that seem to be remembered are most reliable when they are recently acquired, memorable, or corroborated claims. However, that a claim C is recently acquired, memorable, or corroborated is often at least as problematic as the claim C itself. The problem is most acute with respect to corroboration. Consider 'Lincoln was shot' or 'Force equals mass times acceleration'. My grounds for thinking that these claims have been corroborated are that the contents of the claims are things that many people know about, that I'm likely to have made these claims in their presence, and that insofar as the memory survives in me, the people I made the claims to did not disagree with me. But the claim that 'Lincoln was shot' has been corroborated for me is more problematic than the claim that Lincoln was shot. In short, an allegedly corroborated claim C may have an unproblematic status even if the claim 'C has been corroborated' is somewhat problematic. Clearly, we cannot say that a remembered claim C is unproblematic for us only if its being recently acquired, memorable, or corroborated is unproblematic for us.

To get around this difficulty, we shall once again rely on the idea of presumption introduced in Section 2.2 and say:

> An allegedly remembered OB, PF, or SM claim is a candidate if one can presume that it is recently acquired, memorable, or corroborated.

The kind of grounds for presuming a claim to have been corroborated has already been mentioned. The grounds for presuming that a remembered claim is a recently acquired claim is typically the content of the claim itself. Suppose I (seem to) remember 'There was a plane crash in London yesterday', perhaps because I seem to remember reading it in the newspaper. My grounds for thinking that this PF claim was recently acquired are my seeming to remember that the plane crash occurred *yesterday*. Content is again significant for being able to presume a claim to be memorable. 'Sally was the first girl whom I kissed' is a memorable claim for me because of the significance that the alleged event had for me. My grounds for thinking that it has a significance for me are people's interest in their first (quasi-)romance, the content of the claim (which makes it clear that what is allegedly remembered is something about the first romance), and perhaps the persistence of this seeming memory in me to this very day.

Memory is one way OB, PF, and SM claims can be transmitted. Another way they can be transmitted is by the testimony either of expert transmitters (like newspapers) or ordinary people. Suppose we read in the newspaper: "The National Center for Communicable Diseases has announced that the Russian flu has reached an epidemic level in the Southwest." That the center made such an announcement is a candidate for unproblematic acceptance by the account of Section 2.2; however, that the flu has reached an epidemic level should also be a candidate for unproblematic acceptance. Nor is our reliance on testimony limited to expert transmitters. We typically rely on what others say when we ask what the time is, whether Wilbur was at the party last night, what the paper says about last night's game, what the physics book our roommate is reading says Newton's third law is, and so on.

If an appropriate expert X (like a scientist) makes a claim C, and this in turn is transmitted to us by an expert transmitter (like a newspaper) in a statement, "(The expert) X claimed C," the danger of error is not significantly increased from the circumstance (covered in Section 2.2) in which the expert X makes C directly available to us. Thus, we may say:

> OB, PF, and SM claims that are transmitted by presumed expert transmitting sources are candidates.

When we turn to ordinary people or "nonexpert" transmitters, there is no doubt that the danger of error is significantly increased. While we do rely on nonexpert testimony, we all have had the misfortune of being lied to or misled by unreliable people. When the need arises, we can question any particular eyewitness report or nonexpert testimony as to what the paper or encyclopedia said. But we cannot seriously question all or most of them at any given time. How, for example, would we check up on the reliability of a particular eyewitness? One relevant factor would be how reliable the person was in the past, and determining this typically involves asking others whether they have been misled by the person; but in doing this we are relying on the testimony of these other people. Our reliance on nonexpert testimony is ubiquitous, and we cannot adopt the policy of accepting nonexpert testimony only after the reliability of the person testifying has been first checked out. Clearly, some OB, PF, and SM claims transmitted by nonexpert testimony should count at least as *candidates* for unproblematic acceptance.

To investigate the matter of nonexpert testimony, let us consider the following reasonably simple case: Suppose that Ted tells me that he saw Jock at the basketball game last night. Later in the day when Wilbur asks me whether I know why Jock wasn't at the party last night, I tell him that Jock was at the basketball game. Even in this simple case, Wilbur's access to the fact depends on the following chain of events: (1) Ted correctly observed that Jock was at the game. (2) Ted correctly remembers what he observed when he told me about it. (3) Ted wasn't misspeaking or lying to me; that is, he told me what he believed. (4) I correctly heard what Ted said. (5) I correctly remembered what Ted told me when I spoke to Wilbur. (6) I wasn't misspeaking or lying when I talked with Wilbur. (7) Wilbur correctly heard what I said. Schematically, the chain of transmission is given in Figure 2.1. The portion that is boxed by solid lines is not directly available to Wilbur; all that is directly available to Wilbur is my nonexpert testimony. A further complication from Wilbur's point of view is that I did not say, "Ted told me that he saw Jock at the game," but only, "Jock was at the game." Wilbur might assume that there is some chain of transmission going back to someone's observation of Jock at the game, but he certainly does not know the details of the chain that is boxed schematically by the dashed lines. On the last column of Figure 2.1 are the various things that might have gone wrong in the actual chain of transmission. Roughly 'Jock was at the game' can be a candidate for unproblematic acceptance for Wilbur at time t_5 only if he can presume that the various things that could have gone wrong did not. PF and SM transmitted claims differ from the present example only in that the alleged initial source is the directly given expert testimony in newspapers, encyclopedias, textbooks, etc., rather than the directly given observation.

How can one presume that the various things that might have gone wrong didn't go wrong? Insofar as we have already counted initially acquired observational claims as candidates for unproblematic accep-

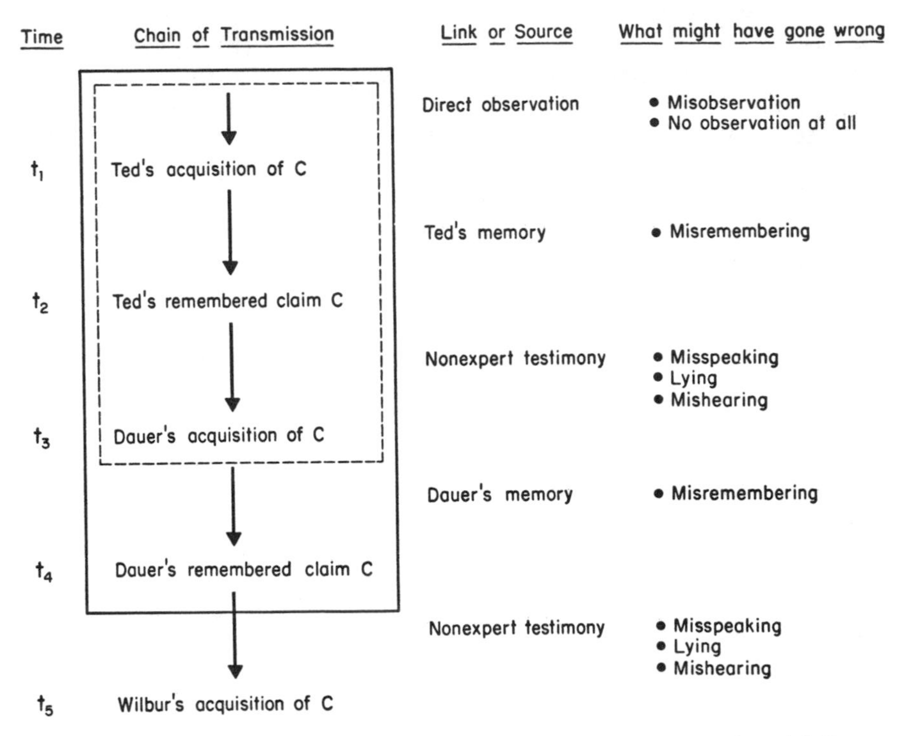

Figure 2.1. Transmission of the claim C ('Jock was at the game last night').

tance, in our example Wilbur can presume that there is no misobservation at the beginning of the chain, and that no one in the chain misheard what was said. We may also presume that people generally manage to say what they intend to say; thus, Wilbur may presume that there was no case of misspeaking. We have already seen that we cannot check on the reliability of each nonexpert testifier before accepting the claim of nonexpert testimony; thus, we must be allowed the general presumption that people aren't lying. Specific grounds for thinking that someone is lying may arise, and these conditions will be discussed in Section 2.4. But as far as being a *candidate* for unproblematic acceptance goes, one may presume that a nonexpert testifier is not lying. What this means for our purpose is that we may generally presume that misobservation, misspeaking, mishearing, and lying did not occur at various points in the chain.

Given our earlier discussion of memory, we may say: if the content of the claim and other general considerations allow one to presume that the claim was recently acquired, memorable, or corroborated for the people involved in the chain of transmission, one may presume that there was no misremembering. In our example, because the claim is about Jock's whereabouts *last night,* Wilbur can presume that it is a recently acquired claim for the people involved in the chain, and hence he may presume that no particular person misremembered.

What remains from Figure 2.1 is the issue of how we may presume that claim actually started with an observation or the reading of some expert source vis-à-vis a PF or SM claim. If part of the nonexpert testimony states the appropriate initial source, we may presume that the claim did get started in the right way. Thus, if I say to Wilbur, "Ted told me that he saw Jock at the game last night," Wilbur may presume that the chain started with an actual observation. Similarly, if you tell me that you read in the paper that Hacksaw Reynolds was traded to the Forty-Niners, I may presume that this transmitted PF claim was initially acquired by you from a directly given expert source (i.e., the newspaper you read). But what should we do when the source isn't given? What is Wilbur's position in our example and mine if you simply tell me that Hacksaw was traded? How can one presume that the chain didn't originate with an inference or in some other inappropriate way? If time and circumstance permit, one could ask for the source. But time or circumstance do not always permit further questioning.

Our attitude will allow us to presume that a claim started with a directly given observation or expert source, if we can presume that the originating source (or an equally good one) is readily available. The rationale for this attitude is that if the source was readily available, a person in the chain is likely to have gotten it from such an available source or else to have gotten it from someone else who got it from such a source. Furthermore, if the source (or an equally good one) is readily available, the claim could have been easily checked; thus the chain is likely to terminate fairly quickly if it started out incorrectly, and a person is least likely to try to deceive others if the deception could be easily uncovered. Thus, if you tell me that Hacksaw Reynolds was traded, I can presume that this could be easily checked in the newspapers: a source that either is, or is as good as, your source. Wilbur's situation is more complicated. If he can presume that a number of people he knows saw Jock at the game, he may presume that my claim got started with an observation; on the other hand, if Wilbur has reason to think that at best only one person he knows saw Jock, he can't presume that the claim started with an observation unless I can provide him with the originating source (who is Ted in our example).

The concern in the last two paragraphs has been about whether a transmitted claim was *appropriately initiated.* Our results may be summarized as follows:

> A claim of nonexpert testimony can be presumed to be appropriately initiated if the originating source is given or an equally good originating source can be presumed to be readily available.

Having completed our survey of various things that may have gone wrong in the transmission in Figure 2.1, we may say:

> An OB, PF, or SM claim of nonexpert testimony is a candidate if one can presume that it was appropriately initiated and recently acquired, memorable, or corroborated for each transmitting link.

Although the various things in Figure 2.1 that could have gone wrong in a chain of transmission have been covered, one additional factor needs to be noted. As the chain of transmission of the kind envisioned has more and more links, the chance of error is correspondingly increased. That is, there is an increased possibility that *at least one* of the links in the chain involves a mistransmission or that a series of minor distortions adds up to a major distortion. Fortunately, we can presume that errors of this kind are absent when we can presume that the chain was appropriately initiated. It is unlikely that the last transmitter can give a satisfactory account of the ultimate source of the information if he or she were at the receiving end of a long chain of transmission with numerous links. Thus, to presume appropriate initiation, we must be able to presume that an equally good originating source is readily available; but in that case, we can also presume that transmission errors would have been caught relatively quickly, so that the length of the chain in itself has no direct impact on the acceptability of the claim.

We may summarize the discussion of Section 2.3 in streamlined form if we note two things: (a) Transmission by memory alone is just a simple instance of the more complicated type of transmission we have been considering more recently. (b) When an expert transmitting source is involved, either the originating source is cited and appropriate initiation is thereby presumable, or else the claim becomes a directly given PF or SM claim for which the transmitting source is vouching. Thus, everything we have said can be summarized as follows:

> A transmitted OB, PF, or SM claim is a candidate if one can presume an appropriate initiation and transmission of direct observation or expert testimony.
>
> Appropriate initiation is presumable: Transmission is entirely by one's own memory from observation or expert source, *or* it is accompanied by such an originating source, *or* one can presume that an equally good originating source is readily available.
>
> Appropriate transmission is presumable: One can presume that the transmission is by an expert transmitting source, *or* that the claim is recently acquired, memorable, or corroborated for each transmitting link.

TABLE 2.1. Candidates for Unproblematic Acceptance

Claim Type	*Content*	*Access*[a,b]
OB	What was observed	Direct: Observer at the time of observation. Transmitted: Appropriate initiation and transmission of a direct observation is presumable.
PF	Uncontroversial particular facts	Direct: Made available by an expert source at the time of accepting the claim. Transmitted: Appropriate initiation and transmission of direct expert testimony is presumable.
INT	Reflection alone shows it must be true	"Content" easily ascertained at the time of accepting the claim.
SM	General laws of science and mathematics	Direct: Made available by an expert source at the time of accepting the claim. Transmitted: Appropriate initiation and transmission of direct expert testimony is presumable.
CS	Personally confirmed, generally acknowledged, undisconfirmed generalization of common sense	With the help of memory, "content" is ascertained at the time of accepting the claim.

[a]Appropriate initiation is presumable: Transmission is entirely by one's own memory from observation or expert source, *or* it is accompanied by such an originating source, *or* one can presume that an equally good originating source is readily available.

[b]Appropriate transmission is presumable: One can presume that the transmission is by an expert transmitting source, *or* that the claim is recently acquired, memorable, or corroborated for each transmitting link.

This completes our account of the candidates for unproblematic acceptance. They are the directly given candidates discussed in Section 2.2 and the transmitted candidates just specified. Table 2.1 (as well as Table 2.6, at the end of Chapter 2) summarizes all the candidates for unproblematic acceptance. It should be noted in Table 2.1 that no transmitted INT or CS claim is a candidate for unproblematic acceptance. INT candidates were supposed to be intuitively obvious at the time of considering them without relying on our memory or the testimony of others. The point of these qualifications would be defeated if we allowed transmitted INT claims to be candidates for unproblematic acceptance. As for a CS claim, one should not rely on it if there is no personal confirmation but only the testimony of others that it is a claim of common sense. Nor should one rely only on one's memory of having taken a claim to be a CS candidate in the past. After all, the situation may have changed since the last time one ascertained a claim to be personally confirmed, generally acknowledged, and undisconfirmed.

EXERCISES—SECTION 2.3

1. In each of the following, assume yourself to be "I" and choose the word in brackets that is true (of you). For each of the examples, determine whether it is a candidate, and if it is, (i) determine whether it is an OB, PF, INT, SM, or CS candidate, and (ii) whether it is a recently acquired, memorable, or corroborated claim for you. Briefly justify your answers.

   (a) I [did, didn't] attend my high school graduation.
   (b) I [did, didn't] attend the last lecture of this class.
   (c) The [Democratic, Republican] candidate won the last presidential election.
   (d) The period between conception and birth is approximately nine months for human beings.
   (e) Israel has had a number of wars with its Arab neighbors since 1947.
   (f) The Earth is not flat.

2. Assume that you have just read the following item in the *Los Angeles Times:*

   DEAR ABBY: I've been stood up on dates more times than I can count. I took a girl out to a nice restaurant, wined her and dined her, then she excused herself to go "powder her nose" and never came back. I tried a dating service and was sent a hooker. I swore off singles bars forever because all the "single" women I've met there were either separated, engaged, or out cheating on their husbands. All I want is a woman who's reasonably attractive, intelligent, and sincere.

   SQUARE & FRUSTRATED

   Determine which of the following claims are candidates for unproblematic acceptance, and for those that are, identify them as OB, PF, INT, SM, or CS candidates. Briefly justify your answers.

   (a) "Square & Frustrated" took a girl out to a restaurant and she never came back after she excused herself to powder her nose.
   (b) "Square & Frustrated" will never go to a singles bar again.
   (c) All women at single bars "Square & Frustrated" attended were separated, engaged, or cheating on their husbands.
   (d) "Square & Frustrated" wants a reasonably attractive, intelligent, and sincere woman.

3. Determine which of the following claims are candidates for unproblematic acceptance, and for those that are, identify them as OB, PF, INT, SM, or CS candidates and state whether they are directly given or transmitted. Briefly justify your answers.

   (a) If Tom loves Jane but Jane doesn't love Tom, Tom and Jane don't love each other.
   (b) The sum of the angles of a triangle is 180°.
   (c) The speed of light is approximately 186,000 miles per second.
   (d) Nothing can travel faster than the speed of light.
   (e) The area of a circle is π times the square of the radius.
   (f) The Pacific Ocean is the largest ocean.
   (g) The robbery rate is lower when people have less economic need to steal.
   (h) Other things being equal, the less one eats, the less weight one gains.
   (i) $E = mc^2$.
   (j) Venus is smaller than Earth.

(k) Current mortgage rates [are, are not] at the double-digit level. (Choose the term that makes the sentence true.)

2.4 Grounds for Doubting a Candidate

We said earlier that a candidate for unproblematic acceptance should be accepted as unproblematic unless there are specific grounds for doubting the reliability of the claim, or the claim conflicts with other candidates for unproblematic acceptance. In this section, we shall concern ourselves with specific grounds for doubting the reliability of a candidate for unproblematic acceptance.

Suppose that I am the observer at the appropriate time for 'I see a woman crossing the street'. Clearly this is an OB candidate for unproblematic acceptance. Given such a claim, barring a conflict with other claims, if I don't have any particular reasons for doubting it (as I normally wouldn't), no further reason is needed to accept it beyond my impression that I am seeing her cross the street. However, now consider the following circumstances:

(1) I saw only the back of the person and I'm taking the person to be a woman because of the shoulder-length hair I espied. Back in the fifties there would be no reason for doubting my claim, but since the late sixties men started having long hair. Thus, in the context of the seventies and the early eighties, there are reasons for thinking that I did not get a good enough look at the person, and this constitutes a specific reason for doubting the reliability of my claim.

(2) Although the person is unknown to me, I saw the person from the front and noticed facial makeup and the apparent physiological features of a woman. Normally there would be no reason for doubting my claim in this kind of a circumstance; however, in this particular circumstance, after crossing the street, the person walked into a transvestite bar. Knowledge of this circumstance (either on my part or on the part of a hearer to whom I made the claim) constitutes specific reasons for doubting the reliability of my claim.

(3) The person crossing the street is my former wife to whom I just said good-bye. In this case, not only are there no reasons for doubting my claim, but there are also exceptionally strong reasons that virtually eliminate all possibilities of error.

These kinds of examples suggest that it may be convenient to assign "reliability grades" to candidates for unproblematic acceptance as follows:

"A"—A candidate for unproblematic acceptance for which we have additional strong reasons that virtually eliminate all possible grounds for doubt.

"B"—A candidate we have no particular reason to doubt and no particular reason to accept beyond the fact that it is a candidate for unproblematic acceptance.
"C"—A candidate for unproblematic acceptance we have some particular reason to doubt.

'I see a woman crossing the street' has the grade "A" for me in circumstance (3) above. Another example of a grade "A" candidate might be an experimental or observational result scientists arrive at in their laboratories after carefully checking and rechecking their experiments. 'I see a woman crossing the street' has a reliability grade "B" in circumstance (1) if the claim was made in the fifties, as well as in circumstance (2) if there were no transvestite bars around the area. 'I see a woman crossing the street' has the grade "C" in circumstance (1) if the claim was made in the seventies or early eighties, as well as in circumstance (2) as actually described.

It would be a mistake to conclude from our examples that a claim can be unproblematically accepted only if it has a reliability grade of "A." If we always adopted a skeptical attitude and worried about remote possibilities like the one that the person may be a transvestite, the activity of truth assessment could hardly get off the ground. Other things being equal, a candidate for unproblematic acceptance should be accepted if it has a reliability grade of "B." What we have to worry about is that a candidate actually has a reliability grade "B" rather than "C." That is, we should examine the available evidence to make sure that there are no particular reasons to doubt the claim.

As a step toward cataloguing the various grounds for doubt, we may note the variety of candidates we have discussed are based on the reliability of one or more of the following faculties or sources: (a) observation, (b) memory, (c) nonexpert testimony, (d) expert testimony, and (e) intuition. OB candidates always depend on (a), typically on (b), and often on (c), and where it does depend on (c), it depends on (a) once again to the extent of having correctly heard what was testified. CS candidates depend on (a), (b), and (c). PF and SM candidates rely on (a) and (d), typically on (b), and often on (c). Finally, INT candidates depend on (e). If there are grounds for doubting any of these faculties or sources, or what must be presumed about them, there are also doubts about the candidates based on those faculties or sources or presumptions. Specific grounds for doubting one or more of (a)–(e), or what a candidate must presume about them. may roughly be divided into six kinds:

(i) If one did not get a good enough look in one's observation, if one's memory is somewhat hazy, or if in making an intuitive claim one has a psychological sense of unclarity or uncertainty, then there is a significant possibility of error and there are grounds for doubting the claim made. Similarly, if one is under the influence of alcohol or hallucinogens, there are grounds for doubting the reliability of claims partially based on observation, memory, or intuition. One class of grounds for doubt may be characterized as shown here:

> The particular circumstances surrounding a claim's use of observation, memory, or intuition involves a significant possibility of error.

Included in this class are particular circumstances like the presence of a transvestite bar in our earlier example. Also included are emotional factors that are liable to have interfered with the proper functioning of observation or memory. Our perceptual or observational judgments are unreliable when we are distraught or overexcited. For example, if we are in a hurry and can't find something, how often do we fail to see what is in front of our noses? Given emotional influences like fear and surprise, one often receives significantly differing eyewitness accounts of a murder or assassination. Emotional interferences are also very common with memory. Wanting to see oneself in a good light, one often forgets, suppresses, or alters untoward things one has done in the past; there is often also the danger of putting the past (such as one's first love affair) in a rosier light than it actually was.

(ii) Suppose Ted tells me: "The person standing there is Eric Lipsowich. I met him yesterday and he told me his name." 'He is Eric Lipsowich' is for me a transmitted observational claim. If I know or find out that Ted is notoriously unreliable in remembering names, because Ted's memory is a link in the transmission, I have grounds for doubting the transmitted claim that the man's name is Eric Lipsowich. Again, although I am not color-blind, there has been a history of my calling blue things green and green things blue. Based on this history, unless I was being very careful, I would have grounds for doubting my own observational claim that the curtain I saw in his room was green. Most of us have had the misfortune of having acquaintances whose sincere nonexpert testimony concerning OB, PF, and SM claims has often proved to be wrong. Whether his difficulty is with observation or memory, given this type of history, we have grounds for doubting things he testifies to us. Even some experts can be unreliable about certain things, and if this is so, their claims about those things should be doubted. Finally, some people frequently make errors concerning even the most obvious logical or geometric relations; such a person has grounds for doubting his own intuitive claims in the area in which he has often been mistaken in the past. Thus, the second kind of grounds for doubt is as shown here:

> An expert or nonexpert source, or a person's use of observation, memory, or intuition, has a record of unreliability in the area of the claim.

(iii) When we rely on what was made available to us or to another by observation or expert testimony, we often do not have direct access to what was observed or to what the expert source testified. But sometimes we do. I might remember El Capitan and Half Dome being on the same side of Yosemite Valley—either on the basis of my having been there or on the basis of my friend's testimony. If I now go to Yosemite (again) and see El Capitan and Half Dome on opposite sides of the valley, I have the strongest possible grounds for doubting my previous claim. Similarly, some PF or SM claim may have been transmitted to me by my memory or some nonexpert testimony. If I now have direct access to the newspaper, text, or reference work that originated the transmitted claim (or a source that is just as good as the particular reference source that happened to be involved in the transmission), and this is at odds with what was transmitted to me, I have strong grounds for doubting the transmitted claim. For example, suppose that I seem to remember the Blue Nile having tributaries in Uganda, and I come upon the atlas that originated this claim for me (or another one that is just as good). If I now discover that the Blue Nile starts in Ethiopia rather than Uganda, I have exceptionally strong grounds for doubting the remembered claim that the Blue Nile starts in Uganda. The third kind of grounds for doubt then is as shown here:

> The reliance on observation, memory, or nonexpert testimony in a transmitted claim is undermined by one's direct access to the ultimate (or an equally good) basis for the claim.

(iv) The fourth kind of grounds for doubt may be characterized as follows:

> The impartiality of expert or nonexpert testimony is made dubious by identifiable motives or grounds that may well have been operative.

The testimony of an accused person concerning his whereabouts at the time of the crime should not be accepted as unproblematic. To the extent that the person is accused of the crime (or is even a suspect), he may well be the criminal, and if he is the criminal, he certainly has a motive for lying about his whereabouts. Thus, the impartiality of his testimony is made dubious by the motive of saving his skin that may well have been operative. Under these circumstances, there are grounds for doubting his claim about his whereabouts. In this kind of case, we need not *establish* that he has the motive (which may involve establishing that he is the criminal). On the other hand, there must be enough grounds for thinking that he may very well have the motive in question; being accused of the crime or being suspected by the police would be grounds enough.

Even when expert testimony is involved, one must be on one's guard against potential motives or grounds that would cast doubt on a person's impartiality. A famous example is a Russian biologist between the two world wars who, in order to satisfy the communist ideology, wanted to prove that environmental needs can bring about genetic changes in animals. He constructed an experiment in which the environment would make it advantageous for nonspotted fish to develop spots for camouflage. When the fish didn't develop those spots, he surreptitiously painted spots on the fish and announced his "discovery" to the world. For someone reading these "discoveries," their convenience for the communist ideology and the totalitarian nature of Stalinist Russia would be grounds for thinking that the biologist may very well have had a motive for achieving such a "discovery." This would be enough for doubting the impartiality of the expert and the expert testimony itself. Similar considerations apply to Russian historians (of the fifties), who were continually "discovering" that American inventions were actually first invented by little known and little appreciated Russians.

Though less extreme, the history text of any country written by a citizen of that country is suspect if the claims involve the "fine deeds" of that country. Grammar school texts, and even some high school texts, in American history describe the War of 1812 as the second war of independence—that is, a war whose aim was to gain American freedom of the seas. In fact, it is more likely that the main aim of the war was to conquer and annex the territory that is now Canada. Claims in newspapers and magazines with a political slant are at least somewhat suspect if the claims enhance and support the political ideology of the paper or magazine. These examples should make it clear that when an expert or nonexpert has an axe to grind, his testimony may be colored by his special desire to make his point. When the lack of impartiality on the part of the testifier is suspect, there are grounds for suspecting the testimony itself.

(v) The next class of grounds for doubt may be characterized as follows:

> The alleged expertise of an "expert" is dubious relative to the claims of the "expert" testimony.

If one discovers that one's doctor has not read any medical journals in the last twenty years, this would constitute grounds for doubting his expertise and his prognosis as well. If we suspect that the news service that is the sole source of a story in a newspaper employs a very high percentage of inexperienced reporters, we would have grounds for doubting the expertise of the news service, and with this there are doubts about the story as well. What is particularly dangerous about expert testimony is that the expert may be overstepping his area of expertise into another (usually related) field in which he has little or no expertise. A particularly interesting example of this idea concerned the psychiatrist Wilhelm Reich, who claimed that a variety of disorders were due to the Russians bombarding us with orgone and who subsequently urged President Eisenhower to start a program of building orgone boxes in order to protect our citizens. Another example of this idea of overstepping the area of expertise concerns the nutritionist Adelle Davis. Her expertise in the field of nutrition is beyond doubt, but occasionally she overstepped her bounds, made medicinal claims that she had no expertise to make, and subsequently had to retract them. Another form of expert testimony that one should doubt involves areas in which it is doubtful that anyone has expertise. Thus, expertise of financial advisers who write books like *How to Become a Millionaire in Your Spare Time* should be doubted because *no one* has expertise in the area of how to become a millionaire in one's spare time. When the expertise of the expert testifier becomes dubious, so does the testimony itself.

(vi) For transmitted OB, PF, and SM candidates, we had to be able to presume appropriate initiation and appropriate transmission. Because circumstances may arise in which these presumptions become dubious, the last class of grounds for doubt may be characterized as follows:

> Revelations or circumstances make the presumption of appropriate initiation or appropriate transmission of transmitted candidates dubious.

For example, the presumption of an OB claim's appropriate initiation becomes dubious when we learn that it was most unlikely for anyone to have been at the right place at the right time; with this doubt, the observational claim itself becomes doubtful. With respect to a claim for which the originating source was not specified, the presumption of appropriate initiation becomes dubious if we fail in our attempt to check up on the claim: other observers of the event cannot be found or standard reference sources in which the claim should be found make no reference to what is claimed. When the presumption of appropriate initiation has become dubious, so does the claim itself.

The presumption of appropriate transmission by nonexpert transmitters becomes dubious if we have grounds for doubting the claim to have been recently acquired, memorable, or corroborated for the persons involved in the chain of transmission. For example, suppose Tom tells me that our friend Jackie has gone through Zadar because she did so on her trip to Europe last summer. Because the reported event appears to be in the recent past, I may presume that all the memories in the chain were recently acquired. But suppose I discover that Tom's source was Gail and Gail tells me that she talked with Tom about Jackie's first trip to Europe ten years ago and not the trip last summer. Doubt has now arisen about whether the memories are reliable, because we can no longer presume that the claim was recently acquired for everyone in the chain; given this doubt, there are grounds now for doubting that Jackie did go through Zadar. To take a different example, suppose that Sherwin tells me what the atomic weight of gold is and adds that he should remember this because he once lost a $50 bet on this matter. Because of the bet, I may presume that the claim about gold's atomic number is a memorable one. But if I should discover that Sherwin is wealthy and has lost many bets like this one, I have reasons then to doubt that gold's atomic number is particularly memorable for him; given this doubt, I also have grounds for doubting Sherwin's claim (unless I have an independent basis for the claim).

In sum, (i)–(vi) represent the kinds of doubt there may be about the faculties or sources involved in claims or what needs to be presumed about them for the claims to be candidates. When specific doubts or suspicions of these kinds arise with respect to a candidate, the candidate must be assigned a reliability grade of "C." These bases for assigning the reliability grade of "C" are again summarized in Table 2.2, near the end of this section. Before concluding our discussion of the grounds for doubting a candidate, one technical point needs to be made. For certain claims to be candidates, we had to be able to *presume* expertise or appropriate initiation or appropriate transmission, and this meant in part that there were no reasons against the source being an expert source or the initiation or transmission being appropriate. If there are doubts of kind (v) or (vi) about the expertise of a source or the appropriate initiation or transmission of a transmitted claim, is the claim still a candidate, albeit one with a reliability grade of "C," or does it cease being a candidate altogether? Because candidates with the grade of "C" will be precluded from becoming unproblematic claims, for all practical purposes, nothing hangs on the distinction. However, to aim for some uniformity in our exercises, we might say: if doubts about the expertise or appropriate initiation or transmission remain at the level of suspicions, the claim is a candidate for the grade of "C"; if these doubts are more thoroughly established and tend to undermine completely the presumption of expertise or appropriate initiation or transmission, the claim is not a candidate at all.

Because the reliability grade of "B" should be assigned to a claim unless it has a grade of "C" or "A," something needs to be said about the reliability grade of "A." Although we initially characterized this grade in terms of having additional reasons that virtually eliminate all possible doubt, for the sake of concreteness and simplicity we shall give it a narrower characterization. As we shall see in Section 2.5, the main reason for having the reliability grade of "A" is the functional role it can play in resolving conflicts between candidates for unproblematic acceptance. Because this role is most easily conceived if we limit the "A" grade to a relatively short list, we do so. In the end, our ultimate interest is not in the reliability grade of "A" but in the class of unproblematic claims it helps to determine.

With one exception to be noted shortly, the narrower characterization of the reliability grade of "A" is this:

(1) No CS claim will have the grade of "A."
(2) Experts will be limited to scientists, although we can be a bit liberal about who counts as a scientist (e.g., mapmakers, coroners, and laboratory analysts may be construed as scientists).
(3) No transmitted claim will have the grade of "A," although we can be a bit liberal about what qualifies as "presently given": a few hours, and perhaps even a day in same cases, might be taken to be covered by "presently given" as long as the transmission only involves one's own memory.
(4) INT claims should be devoid of all uncertainties, and both OB and INT candidates should satisfy a *"centrality requirement": the rejection of the claim would force the rejection of a host of other candidates.* For example, if I just said good-by to my former wife who is now crossing the street, rejecting the claim 'A woman is crossing the street' would force the rejection of a host of other candidates, including those concerning the conversation I just had, not to mention the history of our marriage. Metaphorically, rejecting a central claim would amount to finding oneself in "The Twilight Zone."

The one exception to our characterization involves claims like 'Reagan is the president' (made in 1985) and 'Reagan is not Carter'. *These claims assert or deny the identity of individuals; that is, they assert or deny that A and B are exactly the same person or thing. We shall call these claims* IDENTITY CLAIMS. Identity claims like 'Reagan is the president' must of course be kept separate from ordinary claims like 'Reagan is *a* Republican', which does not assert of any A and B that A and B are exactly the same person or thing. 'Reagan is a Republican' only asserts that Reagan has the feature of being a Republican, a feature Reagan shares with a number of other people.

Identity claims are central to much of our speech and thought: If asked what the president did today, one might answer, "Reagan left for Santa Barbara," thereby taking it for granted that Reagan is the president. Similarly, we think that the claim 'Carter is from Texas' is denied by the claim 'Carter is from Georgia', thereby taking it for granted that Texas is not Georgia. This suggests that certain identity claims should be given an "A" grade even though they are typically transmitted OB or PF candidates. However, many identity claims are problematic, and some, even if unproblematic, shouldn't be given the grade of "A": 'Tomasello is the Masked Murderer' can obviously be problematic, and 'Tom is Billy's father' may deserve no better than a "B" grade (from the perspective of most people). Let us say a transmitted claim of identity is *completely corroborated for a person P if P remembers it to be generally acknowledged and undisputed and P can presume that it was based on a significant number of direct observations.* An identity claim may then be given the reliability grade of "A" even if it is a transmitted OB or PF claim as long as it is completely corroborated.

For our purpose, then, a full characterization of candidates with the reliability grade of "A" becomes the following:

> OB Candidates: Completely corroborated identity claims and directly given central claims.
> PF Candidates: Completely corroborated identity claims and directly given scientific claims.
> INT Candidates: Central claims devoid of all uncertainties.
> SM Candidates: Directly given scientific claims.
> CS Candidates: None.

Readers should adhere to this list carefully and avoid the error of being overly generous with the reliability grade of "A." As we shall see in the next section, once a candidate has the grade of "A," it is very difficult to dislodge it from being an unproblematic claim. A summary of all the reliability grades is given in Table 2.2 (and again in Table 2.6).

EXERCISES—SECTION 2.4

Consider yourself to be Inspector Brown having the following "conversation":

Inspector Brown: Silky! Get into the car and tell me what you saw last night on Rodeo Drive.

Silky: This sure is a nice Chevy you have here, Inspector.

B: It's actually a Plymouth.

S: Well, whatever. What did I see on Rodeo Drive last night? Yeah, I saw Jane Fonda walking out of one of the fancy stores loaded down with packages.

B: See any of your friends?

S: I wouldn't call him my friend, but I did see Mr. Ricardo get out of a 1982 BMW.

B: How did you know him to be Mr. Ricardo?

S: I only saw his back but I knew because he was wearing an expensive German fedora and a pair of Bally shoes made in Switzerland.

B: How did you know that it was an *expensive German* fedora and that the Bally shoes were those made in Switzerland rather than Italy?

TABLE 2.2. Reliability Grades

Claim Type	*"A" Grade*	*"B" Grade*	*"C" Grade*
OB	Completely corroborated identity claim *or* directly given and central	Any type of candidate whose reliability grade isn't "A" or "C"	Any type of claim where specific reasons bring about one or more of the following: (1) Circumstance of using an involved faculty has significant chance of error. (2) An involved faculty or source has a record of unreliability. (3) A transmission is undermined by direct access to (something as good as) the original source. (4) Testifier may well have a motive that would cast doubt on the impartiality of the testimony. (5) Presumed expertise of an expert is dubious for an alleged claim of "expert" testimony. (6) Presumption of appropriate initiation or transmission is dubious.
PF	Completely corroborated identity claim *or* directly given by scientific source		
INT	Devoid of all uncertainty *and* central		
SM	Directly given by scientific source		
CS	*None*		

C is a completely corroborated identity claim = C asserts of some A and B that A and B are exactly the same person or thing, C is remembered to be generally acknowledged and undisputed, and C can be presumed to be based on a significant number of direct observations.

C is central = The rejection of C would force the rejection of a host of other candidates.

Note: If doubts of types 5 and 6 are sufficiently established to undermine the presumption, the claim would cease being a candidate altogether.

S: Look, I own a hat store. If I don't know fedoras, who does? And I looked at his fedora several times, since it's an expensive type that I sell only about twice a week. And I know about his shoes because, having been in the hat business, I know all about men's furnishings.

B: Alright. Go on.

S: As Mr. Ricardo came out of the car, I see my girlfriend come out of the store she works at—at the corner of Rodeo and Wilshire. As I go toward her, she doesn't notice me and gives this Ricardo guy a big hug. They start kissing right on the street and she starts acting as if she hasn't seen a man in years. I was so surprised and jealous I could have killed the SOB on the spot.

B: You sure it wasn't your girlfriend you wanted to kill? After all, she's the one who's dead, not Mr. Ricardo or whoever that man was.

S: I love her, Inspector. How could I kill her? Ricardo is the man who seduced her heart away from me.

Problem 1: For each of the following candidates for unproblematic acceptance, determine whether it has the reliability grade of "A," "B," or "C." For those with the reliability grade of "A," justify this grade; for those with a reliability grade of "C," state the specific reason for doubting the claim.

1. Silky was walking down Rodeo Drive (last night).
2. Jane Fonda walked out of a fancy Rodeo Drive store last night loaded down with packages.
3. The man getting out of the car was Mr. Ricardo.
4. The man who got out of the car wore an expensive German fedora.
5. The man got out of a 1982 BMW.
6. The man who got out of the car wore Bally shoes made in Switzerland.
7. The woman coming out of the store was Silky's girlfriend.
8. Silky's girlfriend works at a store on the corner of Rodeo and Wilshire.
9. Silky's girlfriend was "friendly" with the man claimed to be Mr. Ricardo.
10. Silky's girlfriend was acting as if she hadn't seen a man in years.
11. Silky wanted to kill the man claimed to be Mr. Ricardo.
12. Silky loved his girlfriend.
13. Silky thinks that the man rather than his girlfriend was at fault.
14. I (Inspector Brown) just finished having a talk with someone responding to the name "Silky."

Problem 2: Suppose that you (as Inspector Brown) come across the following items the next day: (a) A gossip column claiming that Jane Fonda hates the Beverly Hills scene and wouldn't be caught dead shopping on Rodeo Drive. (b) A report on Silky stating that he has been in the hat business for only two weeks. (c) A report on Silky's girlfriend stating that she has an identical twin who works in the same store. Furthermore, going to the store where Silky's girlfriend worked, you (as Inspector Brown) discover that the store is on the corner of Rodeo Drive and Santa Monica Boulevard. Given these revelations, and assuming that something given a day ago is too long ago to count as "presently given," would any candidate with the grade of "B" or better in problem A have to be downgraded? If so, specify the specific reasons for lowering the reliability grade.

2.5 Unproblematic Claims

We are now in a position to move from claims that are candidates for unproblematic acceptance to claims that can be treated as unproblematic. The first step is to eliminate all candidates with a reliability grade of "C," because they should not be accepted as unproblematic even if they do not conflict with other candidates. Having done that, we have to worry about how to resolve conflicts among the remaining candidates. If a conflict arises and *other things are equal,* the rational course is to eliminate all parties to the conflict from the class of unproblematic claims.

However, other things are not always equal when a conflict arises. Consider the following three cases:

(a) Tom states, "The person crossing the street is a woman," but Jane, who happens to be there when Tom says this, knows the person crossing the street to be her brother dressed up as a woman. Where (a_1) is based on Tom's testimony of his observation and (a_2) is based on Jane's observation and a host of other things (like, perhaps, having helped him into his costume), the conflicting claims are these:

(a_1) The person crossing the street is a woman.
(a_2) The person crossing the street is not a woman.

At least *for Jane,* because (a_2) has a reliability grade of "A," she should be able to retain (a_2) and reject (a_1). For someone other than Jane, as long as Jane doesn't explain why Tom is mistaken, (a_1) and (a_2) may both have the reliability grade of "B," so that neither is retained as unproblematic.

(b) Allan testifies that he saw Fast Joe at the bar at time t, whereas Burt testifies that he saw Fast Joe at the mansion at t. The following claims conflict:

(b_1) Fast Joe was at the bar at time t.
(b_2) Fast Joe was at the mansion at time t.
(b_3) A person can't be in two places at the same time.

Surely in this case (b_3) should be retained and (b_1) and (b_2) be eliminated from the class of unproblematic claims.

(c) An apparently sober man testifies that he saw the local hero called Bear walking on water, and let us suppose we have no reasons to think that he has a motive to deceive us. We would then have a conflict between (c_1) and (c_2):

(c_1) Bear walked on water.
(c_2) No one can walk on water.

The rational course is to retain (c_2) as unproblematic and reject (c_1).

To formulate appropriate rules that will have these results, let us first state what constitutes a conflicting class of claims. The three conflicting classes displayed in the last paragraph are paradigms of conflicting classes. Paradigmatically, then, *a class of claims is a* CONFLICTING CLASS *if it is impossible for all of its members to be true.* However, there is a complication to be noted. Consider the class {(b_1), (b_2), (b_3)}. Because this is a conflicting class, so is the four-membered class {(b_1), (b_2), (b_3), 'Reagan is the president'}: because it's impossible for the first three members to be all true, clearly it isn't possible for all four members to be true. In this kind of case, we shall use the term '*relevant* conflicting class' to refer to the class made up of just (b_1), (b_2), and (b_3); it would cease being a relevant conflicting class if an irrelevant member like 'Reagan is the president' were added. Our interest is in relevant conflicting classes rather than conflicting classes that contain irrelevant members. Furthermore, we shall understand 'relevant conflicting class' to exclude classes that have two separately conflicting subclasses. Thus, although {(b_1), (b_2), (b_3), (c_1), (c_2)} is a conflicting class, the last two members are irrelevant to the conflict created by the first three members. Thus, we shall not consider this five-membered class to be a relevant conflicting class; rather the relevant conflicting classes are {(b_1), (b_2), (b_3)} and {(c_1), (c_2)}.

Consider now the following two transmitted OB candidates:

(d_1) Kathy and Bob first met in Santa Barbara.
(d_2) It was snowing when Kathy and Bob first met.

The fact is that it almost never snows in Santa Barbara—once every thirty or forty years. Given this background, although it is not impossible for (d_1) and (d_2) to bc both true, it is exceptionally unlikely that they are both true. That is, {(d_1), (d_2), 'It almost never snows in Santa Barbara'} is a *virtually* conflicting class. To characterize this kind of conflict, let (d^*) and (d_3) be given by:

(d^*) It never snows in Santa Barbara.
(d_3) (d^*) is almost exceptionless (i.e., it almost never snows in Santa Barbara, or, it's very unlikely for it to snow in Santa Barbara).

For someone knowledgeable about the Santa Barbara climate, (d_3) is a CS candidate, and we assumed that (d_1) and (d_2) were transmitted OB candidates. The sense in which (d_1), (d_2), and (d_3) are conflicting candidates is this: if (d_3) were replaced by (d^*), we would have the strictly conflicting class {(d_1), (d_2), (d^*)} in which it is impossible for all three members to be true.

Given this background, the kind of conflicting classes we are interested in may be summarized as follows:

S is a relevant conflicting class = S contains no member irrelevant to the conflict, *and*

(1) S is strictly conflicting: it is impossible for all members of S to be true, *or*
(2) S is virtually conflicting: S contains 'X is virtually exceptionless', and replacing this by X would result in a strictly conflicting class.

It should be understood that 'X is virtually exceptionless' may have variant forms of the kind indicated in (d_3) above.

Let us now turn to the idea that all members to a conflict may not be of equal standing. We shall cash this idea in terms of the following four rules of preference:

(P1) An OB or PF claim with the reliability grade of "A" is preferred over OB and PF claims with the reliability grade of "B."

(P2) An INT or SM claim with the reliability grade of "A" is preferred over INT and SM claims with the reliability grade of "B."
(P3) An INT or SM or CS claim with the reliability grade of "B" or better is preferred over OB and PF claims with the reliability grade of "B."
(P4) An INT claim with the reliability grade of "A" is preferred over all other claims (unless in an SM claim with the reliability grade of "A" scientists or mathematicians have determined that the INT claim is to be rejected).

These preference relations are summarized in Figure 2.2, which should be read as follows: A candidate X with a given grade is preferred over another candidate Y with a given grade if and only if a downward line connects X to Y. Thus, P4 is reflected in Figure 2.2 by a downward line connecting "A" grade INT candidates to all other candidates. On the other hand, an "A" grade OB candidate has neither a higher nor a lower preference rank than "A" grade or "B" grade SM candidate, because there is no downward line on Figure 2.2 between an "A" grade OB claim and any SM claim.

The first three rules of our model or approximation for arriving at unproblematic claims can now be stated as follows:

(A) Eliminate all members with the reliability grade of "C" from the total class of candidates for unproblematic acceptance.
(B) Given what remains after (A), if there is a relevant conflicting subclass S, eliminate members of S according to the following rule:
    (B1) If S contains members that are preferred over other members, retain any member that is preferred over some other member,

Figure 2.2. Preference rankings. Asterisk indicates unless explicitly denied by a grade "A" SM candidate.

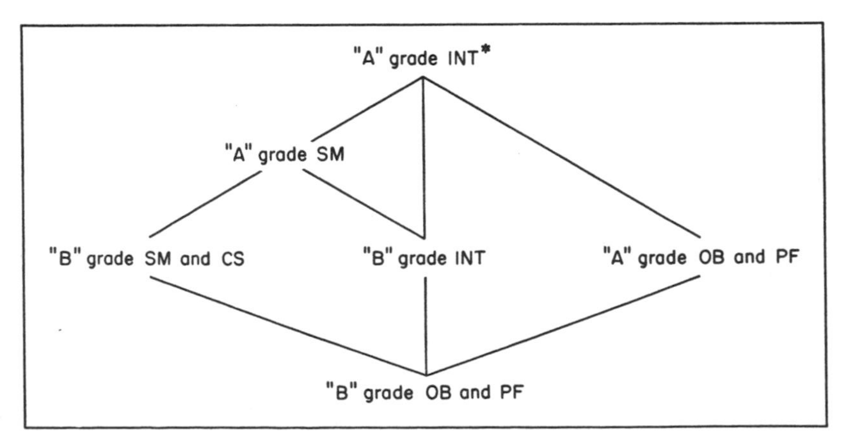

and eliminate the remaining members that are not preferred over any other members.

(B2) If the reduced subclass S continues to conflict, repeat step (B1) if it is applicable.

(C) Given what remains after (A) and (B), if S or the reduced S still conflicts, eliminate all its remaining members.

After performing steps (A)–(C), sometimes certain readjustments are needed. To see this, suppose Mrs. Yakuza testifies that her husband was at home sleeping last night around ten o'clock, and Mr. Yakuza's associate testifies that he was instead at a Las Vegas casino around ten o'clock the same night. Consider the following four claims:

C: Mr. Yakuza was at home around ten o'clock last night.
X: Mr. Yakuza was at a Las Vegas casino around ten o'clock last night.
I: A person can't be at two places at the same time.
C*: Mr. Yakuza was sleeping around ten o'clock last night.

{C, X, I} is a relevant conflicting subclass, and by rule B1 above, both C and X would be eliminated. C* doesn't belong in the relevant conflicting subclass, because it is neither impossible nor *extremely* unlikely that Mr. Yakuza was sleeping in a Las Vegas casino (which typically includes a hotel). But surely we should not count C* as unproblematic. Roughly, C and C* sink or swim together, because they are both based on Mrs. Yakuza's testimony; C* is no more preferred than C, and if the associate's testimony were true, this would cast doubt on both C and C* (C would be outright false and C* would be at least questionable). In general let us say that C* is a *near relative* on an eliminated member C just in case: *C and C* have the same basis, C* is no more preferred than C, C was eliminated due to its conflict with a claim X, and the truth of X would cast doubt on C* as well as C.* Given this much, the readjustment that is needed after rule (C) is this:

(D) Eliminate near relatives of members that were eliminated due to a conflict.

Except for having to repeat steps (B)–(D), if we started with more than one relevant conflicting subclass, the residue is the class of unproblematic claims. Thus, the final two rules are[1]:

(E) Repeat steps (B)–(D) if the original class contained more than one relevant conflicting subclass.

(F) The final residue, which is free of all conflicts, is the class of unproblematic claims.

1. These rules need to be understood in a special way when a member C belongs to two conflicting subclasses S1 and S2. Even if C got eliminated by applying (B)–(D) on S1, in applying (B)–(D) to S2, S2 must be construed still to contain C. In applying (F), C must be eliminated as long as it got eliminated by applying (B)–(D) to at least one of the conflicting subclasses.

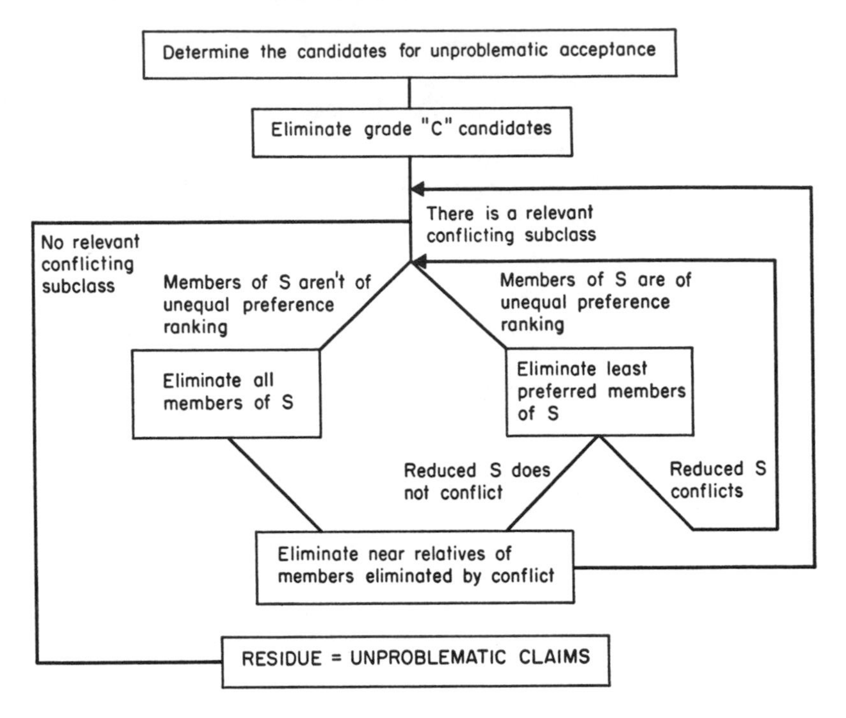

Figure 2.3. Flowchart for selecting the unproblematic.

S conflicts = S strictly conflicts (it's impossible for all members of S to be true) **or** S virtually conflicts (contains 'X is virtually exceptionless' and replacing this by X would make S strictly conflicting).

C* is a near relative of eliminated C = C* and C have the same basis, C* is no more preferred than C, C was eliminated due to a conflict with some X, and X would cast doubt on both C and C* if X were true.

If C belongs to two conflicting subclasses S1 and S2, treat S1 and S2 separately, and eliminate C from the final residue if C was eliminated from either S1 or S2.

Rules (A)–(F) for determining the unproblematic can be summarized by a "flowchart" of the steps to be taken. This flowchart is given in Figure 2.3, which is to be read as follows: The boxed items indicate the steps to be taken, and these steps should be performed sequentially by following the lines in a downward path. An exception to this sequential order is indicated by an "arrow" indicating the need to return upward and repeat an earlier step. Where a downward path divides into several branches, the condition for choosing a given branch is indicated to the side of that branch.

To see how these rules work, let us consider the following example and put ourselves in the position of the narrator:

> This was the worst morning since I joined Softdisk Corporation as a section chief three months ago. First, our ace programmer Ms. Malm

calls in to tell me that she crashed her car yesterday afternoon and couldn't come to work because of the injuries she suffered as a result.

Shortly afterward Dr. Horner, the psychiatrist in the personnel department, came to see me. He told me that as he was leaving last night, he saw my programmer Perry going through wastebaskets in another person's office. This, according to him, was 11 P.M. because he had just checked the clock before leaving. Dr. Horner finished his story by saying: "I have previously diagnosed Perry to be suffering from deep emotional hostility and in need of psychiatric help—I put this in writing to the previous section chief; but I never thought that Perry's hostility would lead him to become a spy against his own company." Very vaguely I seem to remember someone else outside my section saying that Perry was often hostile.

No sooner had Dr. Horner left, but Perry's officemate Jones came into my office. He asked that he be moved to another office away from Perry. According to Jones, Perry came to his apartment last night for a small party with Ms. Malm. Perry got drunk, and in an ensuing argument he punched Jones. Becoming curious (and confused), I asked Jones when all of this occurred. Jones said that Ms. Malm and Perry came over around 8 P.M. and stayed till around 11:15 when the incident occurred and the party broke up.

Construing "presently given" broadly to cover the entire morning and understanding "scientists" liberally to include psychiatrists, let us take our task to be that of determining which among the following claims are unproblematic.

(1) Ms. Malm was sufficiently injured by an accident yesterday afternoon to prevent her from going to work today.
(2) I joined Softdisk three months ago.
(3) Perry is suffering from deep emotional hostility and is in need of psychiatric help.
(4) Perry is spying on his own company.
(5) People other than Horner have reported that Perry is often hostile.
(6) Perry was going through wastebaskets in someone else's office at 11 P.M. last night.
(7) Perry was at Jones's apartment at 11 P.M. last night.
(8) Perry punched Jones around 11:15 P.M. last night.
(9) A person cannot be in two places at the same time.
(10) No one who attends a party shortly after having an accident is sufficiently injured by the accident to prevent her from going to work on the next day.
(11) (10) is virtually exceptionless.
(12) Ms. Malm had an accident yesterday afternoon.
(13) Ms. Malm attended a party around 8 P.M. last night.
(14) If (12) and (13) are true, Ms. Malm attended a party shortly after having an accident.

TABLE 2.3

Claim	Cand.?	Reliability Grade	Member of RCC S1?	Member of RCC S2?	OK or Reason for Elimination
(1)	T-OB	B		Y	Least preferred member of S2
(2)	T-OB	B			OK
(3)	D-PF	A			OK
(4)	No				Inferential at best
(5)	T-OB	C			Significant chance of error because of memory vagueness
(6)	T-OB	B	Y		Least preferred member of S1
(7)	T-OB	B	Y		Least preferred member of S1
(8)	T-OB	B			Near relative of (7)
(9)	INT	A	Y		OK
(10)	No				Disconfirmed
(11)	CS	B		Y	OK
(12)	T-OB	B		Y	Least preferred member of S2
(13)	T-OB	B		Y	Least preferred member of S2
(14)	INT	A		Y	OK

The best way to deal with this kind of case is to form a chart of the sort given in Table 2.3. We list first the involved claims and identify them as not being a candidate or as a candidate of a certain type with a given reliability grade. For (4) and (10), which are not candidates, we put down the reason they are not candidates. When the short statement of the reason isn't entirely obvious, we should add at the bottom a comment like:

(10) is disconfirmed because in a few cases, the extent of the injuries becomes apparent only the next day.

As for those that are candidates, we should identify them first by type: OB, PF, INT, SM, or CS. In the case of OB, PF, and SM candidates, we should indicate whether they are direct (D) or transmitted (T) candidates. The net effect of the "Cand?" column in our example is to eliminate (4) and (10) from being unproblematic claims, and this completes the first step on the flowchart given in Figure 2.3.

Proceeding to the next step of the flowchart in Figure 2.3, the column for reliability grades becomes filled, and in cases in which a "C" grade is assigned, the reason is stated in the "reason" column. If the reason given for a "C" grade is highly abbreviated, a comment should be added at the bottom. The effect of the column for reliability grades in Table 2.3 is to eliminate (5) from being a unproblematic claim.

Having eliminated the "C" grade candidates, to follow Figure 2.3, we need to determine whether there are any relevant conflicting (sub)classes (RCC), and if there are, what these conflicting classes are. Intuition and common sense (in broader senses than the ones involved in INT and CS claims) should at least allow one to suspect conflicts. In our example, the claims about Perry's whereabouts at 11 P.M. certainly seem to conflict. Though less obvious, there seems to be a conflict of some sort between Ms. Malm's claim that she is too badly injured to work and Jones's claim that she was partying last night. However, because (10) was given the grade "C," we can only anticipate a virtually conflicting subclass concerning the extent of Ms. Malm's injuries. In this way intuition and common sense (broadly construed) usually allow one to determine, or at least to suspect, that there are *some* conflicts. But finding the exact composition of a conflicting subclass can be a bit complicated at times. Thus, a few words on this topic seem to be needed.

A strongly conflicting class is one in which it is impossible for all the claims in the class to come out true. The simplest example would be a class like {C, not-C}, in which all the members can't come out true because affirming C forces one to deny not-C. More complex cases are classes like {C, D, E, F} where, for example, affirming C together with D and E forces one to deny F; clearly, if C, D, and E together force one to deny F, the class as whole can't come out true. This suggests a general strategy for finding a conflicting subclass:

> *Starting with some claim C, find other claims E, F, G, . . . so that together their affirmation will force one to deny yet another claim X belonging to the entire class; the subclass {C, D, E, F, . . . , X} is then a strongly conflicting subclass.*

This strategy needs to be filled in two ways: (i) Which claim C do we start with? (ii) How do we know or find out which of the other claims force one to deny an X that also belongs to the entire class?

As for (i), one guideline is

(iA) *Start with a claim C with the lowest preference ranking,* and this will typically involve a grade "B" OB claim. Thus, in the obvious conflict about Perry's whereabouts at 11 P.M., start with either claim (6) or (7): it doesn't matter which one. When the conflict isn't immediately evident, the conflict typically involves a number of background claims that we tend to accept as unproblematic, and these background claims have to be brought into play to determine the composition of the conflicting subclass. Thus, a second guideline is

(iB) *Start with a claim C that "hooks on" directly to one of the background claims.* In our example and exercises, it will typically be a claim C such that there is also the background claim 'If C is [or: if C, D, and E are all] true, then. . . '. In our example, guideline (iA) suggests choosing claim (1), (12), or (13). Claims (12) and (13) both directly hook onto the background claim (14), while (1) doesn't directly hook onto anything. Thus, we start with claim (12) or (13) expecting to rely on the other one very quickly.

Turning to question (ii) above, how do we find out which of the other claims are needed if the denial of an X is to be forced? *To some extent we shall have to rely on our intuitions of these things,* and sometimes, this is entirely sufficient. Thus, consider the conflict concerning Perry's whereabouts at 11 P.M. Let us say that we start with claim (6), namely Perry being in someone's office at 11 P.M. Affirming this along with the background claim (9) that one can't be in two places at the same time forces us to deny (7), namely, that Perry was at Jones's home at 11 P.M. Thus, one of the conflicting subclasses is {(6), (7), (9)}.

In more complex cases, intuitions may need to be augmented by additional guidelines, and one guideline will prove to be particularly useful for our example and the exercises:

> *Affirming the claims D1, . . . , Dn and 'if D1, . . . , Dn are true, then E' will force one to affirm 'E' (and deny 'not-E').*

In a degenerate case, there may of course be only one D; in other words, *n* may equal 1. This guideline may be applied to the conflict concerning the extent of Ms. Malm's injuries. Assuming that we start with claim (12), we immediately rely on (13) as well, because the two together will hook onto (14). Because (12), (13), and (14) fit the pattern of the guideline, their affirmation forces us to affirm that:

(a) Ms. Malm attended a party shortly after having an accident.

We noted already that we can only expect a virtually conflicting class. Given that (11)—that is, '(10) is virtually exceptionless'—is a remaining candidate, we look for a strong conflict by replacing (11) by

(10) No one who attends a party shortly after having an accident is sufficiently injured by the accident to prevent her from going to work on the next day.

Because we have already been forced to affirm (a), affirming (10) as well forces us to affirm that she wasn't sufficiently injured to prevent her from going to work the next day. But this is to deny that:

(1) Ms. Malm was sufficiently injured to prevent her from going to work.

Alternatively, we might think along the following lines: Given (a) and (1), we are forced to affirm that someone who attended a party shortly after an accident is sufficiently injured to prevent her from going to work. But this forces us to deny (10). Either way, {(1), (12), (13), (14), (10)} is a strongly conflicting class and {(1), (12), (13), (14), (11)} is a virtually conflicting subclass. This virtually conflicting subclass is the second conflicting subclass of our example.

Returning to filling in Table 2.3 by following Figure 2.3: because our example has two relevant conflicting subclasses, we form two columns: "Member of RCC S1?" and "Member of RCC S2?". In general, we should form as many such columns as there are relevant conflicting subclasses among the candidates that remain after eliminating "C" grade candidates. For each remaining claim, we insert a "Y" under "Member of RCC

S1?" if it belongs to the relevant conflicting class S1, and then do the same for S2. In the case of strictly conflicting classes like {(6), (7), (9)}, no comment needs to be added. But in the case of virtually conflicting classes like {(1), (11), (12), (13), (14)}, we should add at the bottom a comment like:

{(1), (11), (12), (13), (14)} is a virtually conflicting class because if (11) were replaced by (10), we would have a strictly conflicting class.

Having gotten this far, we follow the central portion of the flowchart given in Figure 2.3. Starting with S1, we note that claims (6) and (7) are least preferred; thus, they are eliminated and the reason is placed on the "reason" column in Table 2.3. The reduced class S1, which now only contains claim (9), does not conflict. The next step is to check whether any near relative needs to be eliminated, and in our case (8) is such an example. Because "near relative of (7)" is too abbreviated a reason, we should add a comment like the following:

> (7) and (8) have the same basis (Jones's testimony), (8) is no more preferred than (7), (7) was eliminated because of a conflict with Dr. Horner's testimony (6), and if (6) were true, this would cast doubt on (8) as well; that is, it would be somewhat doubtful that in fifteen minutes Perry could have finished whatever he was doing in the office, go over to Jones's place, and get involved in something like an argument that resulted in him punching Jones.

It might be noted that (13)—Ms. Malm's attendance at the party around 8 P.M.—is not a near relative of the eliminated (7), because Horner's testimony casts no doubts upon Ms. Malm attending a party at Jones's apartment. In any event, this completes our consideration of S1.

Again, following the flowchart given in Figure 2.3, we are to "loop back" and determine whether there are any relevant conflicting subclasses. Because S2 is such a class, we go through the "main loop" again. This results in (1), (12), and (13) being eliminated as least preferred members. When we loop back a second time to determine whether there are any further relevant conflicting subclasses, we see that there are none in the remaining class {(2), (3), (9), (11), (14)}; this residue, then, is the class of unproblematic claims, and we indicate this by inserting "OK" in the last column of Table 2.3.

Suppose that in the position of the narrator of the story, we learn a few days later that (a) Jones is notorious for playing jokes on his friends, (b) Ms. Malm and Perry are Jones's friends, and (c) Dr. Horner has an intense hatred for Perry. With these additional revelations, Table 2.3 would be altered significantly, resulting in Table 2.4 and its appended comments. With the revelation we have imagined, the minimal conflicting subclasses disappear in that crucial items in the conflicts have been eliminated early because they have a reliability grade of "C." Of course this result, which makes Ms. Malm's testimony unproblem-

TABLE 2.4.

Claim[a]	*Cand.?*	*Reliability Grade*	*OK or Reason for Elimination*
(1)	T-OB	B	OK
(2)	T-OB	B	OK
(3)	T-PF	C	Doubts of impartiality because of hatred of Perry
(4)	No		Inferential at best.
(5)	T-OB	C	Significant chance of error because of memory vagueness
(6)	T-OB	C	Same as (3)
(7)	T-OB	C	Record of unreliability
(8)	T-OB	C	Record of unreliability
(9)	INT	A	OK
(10)	No		Disconfirmed
(11)	CS	B	OK
(12)	T-OB	B	OK
(13)	T-OB	C	Record of unreliability
(14)	INT	A	OK

[a]Comments: (3) is a *transmitted* (T) PF claim because a few days have passed since Dr. Horner's testimony. For (7), (8), and (13), Jones has a record of playing practical jokes on his friends, and Ms. Malm and Perry are friends of Jones; thus, Jones has a record of unreliability in testimony like the one he gave.

atic, depends on us having no reason to attribute any motives of deception to her.[2]

This then is our model for determining what may be accepted as unproblematic. While the model can no doubt use refinements and adjustments, it provides the basic outline of how the unproblematic may be selected and it has a relatively clear application to a significant number of examples. For the sake of concreteness, we present in Table 2.5 a format for use in determining the unproblematic.

For the sake of easy reference, a summary of all the major points covered in Sections 2.2–2.5 is reproduced at the end of this chapter.

One postscript may be in order. Given our preference rankings, which assign a fairly high preference rank to SM and CS claims, one may wonder how such claims can ever be discredited. An examination of the preference rankings shows that an SM claim is not preferred over a PF claim with the reliability grade of "A." Thus, when an accepted scientific theory conflicts with a scientific report of a carefully conducted new experiment,

2. It is arguable that our model of determining the unproblematic is a bit too charitable with Ms. Malm's testimony. A more refined model might add further reliability grades so that Jones's claims remain reliable enough to create a conflict with Ms. Malm's claims. On the other hand, being a notorious practical joker would detract from a person's ability to make other people's apparently sincere claims problematic; if we think of the boy who cried "Wolf!", our model may not seem too far off the mark.

TABLE 2.5. Format for Determining the Unproblematic, Along with Possible Answers for Each Column

Claim	*Cand.?*	*Reliability Grade*	*Member of*[a] RCC S1	*OK or Reason for Elimination*[b]
Claim number	No	A	Y	Reason for noncandidacy
	T- or D-OB	B	Blank	Reason for "C" grade
		C		Least preferred member of S1
	PF	Blank		Member of eliminated class S1
	SM			Close relative of member eliminated by conflict
	INT			OK
	CS			

[a]Form as many columns as there are relevant conflicting classes and for any virtually conflicting class; add comment indicating why it is virtually conflicting.

[b]Unless the reason given on the format is obvious, add comments below to explain the reason.

we have a conflict between an SM claim and a grade "A" PF claim that would result in both claims being eliminated from the class of unproblematic claims. (While a conflicting grade "A" OB claim might in principle have the same effect, to produce a genuine conflict with a scientific theory usually requires an elaborate experimental setup, which only a scientist can devise.) When an SM claim and a conflicting grade "A" PF claim are both rendered problematic, scientists will seek a resolution of the conflict. If these attempts result in the new experiment being (partially) discredited, the PF claim is given the reliability grade of "C" or "B," with the consequence that the new experimental result is eliminated from the class of unproblematic claims and the theory is reintroduced as an unproblematic claim. On the other hand, if the theory is discredited, scientists will revise the theory so that the revised theory will agree with the new (as well as the old) experimental results; in this case, the new experimental result as well as the revised theory will attain the unproblematic status, while the original theory will cease being an SM candidate.

The situation with CS candidates is in principle somewhat simpler. Once it becomes implausible that apparently disconfirming instances can be explained away, the claim ceases being a CS candidate. If most of the plausible gimmicks were checked to be absent, and a number of sober witnesses claimed to have observed the local hero called Bear walking on water, we could no longer claim that 'No one can walk on water' is undisconfirmed. On the other hand, in our scientific age CS claims like 'No one can walk on water' tend to have some SM analogues that are not that easily eliminated. Their elimination will normally require conflicting grade "A" PF claims of the sort discussed in the last paragraph.

EXERCISES—SECTION 2.5

Problem Set A

1. For each of the following classes of claims, determine the relevant conflicting subclass(es), and briefly explain how the subclass(es) (were found to) conflict. [Assume that the same person or times are referred to by the same names or descriptions within each class of claims. d(4) and e(6) are so numbered for easy reference, but they are not part of the class.]

   (a) (1) Tom is dating only one woman.
   (2) Tom is dating Mary.
   (3) Tom thinks that Mary is more intelligent than Veronica.
   (4) Tom is scared of dating very intelligent women.
   (5) Tom is dating Veronica.

   (b) (1) Mary was home by 10 P.M.
   (2) Mary was at the bar only between 9:00 and 9:30 P.M.
   (3) Tom was still working at his office at 9 P.M.
   (4) Tom saw Mary at the bar.
   (5) Tom wasn't at the bar between 9:00 and 9:30 P.M.

   (c) (1) Jill is very sweet to her father.
   (2) Jim's father loves his daughter Jill.
   (3) Jim's father loves only one of his children.
   (4) Jim broke his father's computer.
   (5) If (3) is true, then if Jim's father loves Jill, Jim's father doesn't love Jim.
   (6) Jim's father loves Jim.

   (d) (1) Tom is dating Mary.
   (2) Mary is in Tom's logic class.
   (3) The following claim is nearly exceptionless:
   (4) No man dates a woman he is scared of dating.
   (5) Tom finds Mary to be an intelligent woman.
   (6) Tom is scared of dating women he finds to be intelligent.
   (7) If (5) and (6) are true, Tom is scared of dating Mary.

   (e) (1) Scott likes the owner of the Good Time Bar.
   (2) Scott had a drink at the Good Time Bar at 7 P.M on Friday.
   (3) Scott had dinner at Rififi's at 7:15 P.M. on Friday.
   (4) Scott strongly disapproves of having a drink before dinner.
   (5) The following claim is nearly exceptionless:
   (6) If someone strongly disapproves of something, that person will never do that thing.
   (7) Scott has no way of going from the Good Time Bar to Rififi's except by using the crowded city streets.
   (8) The distance from the Good Time Bar to Rififi's is fifteen miles on city streets.
   (9) No can cover fifteen miles on crowded city streets in fifteen minutes or less.
   (10) If (2), (7), and (8) are true, then if (3) is true, Scott covered fifteen miles on crowded city streets in fifteen minutes or less.

2. For each class of statements given below, let each member's candidate type, reliability grade, and membership in conflicting subclasses be given by the displayed chart. You do not need to know what these numbered statements represent. For each class determine which are the unproblematic claims (assuming that there are no conflicts with any unmentioned statements). Assume

unless otherwise indicated, that there are no near relatives and that each conflicting subclass ceases to conflict once a member is eliminated from it.

	Statement	*Cand. Type*	*Reliability Grade*	*Member of RCC*	
				S1?	*S2?*
(a)	(1)	OB	C		
	(2)	OB	B	Y	
	(3)	INT	B	Y	
	(4)	OB	B	Y	
	(5)	PF	B		
	(6)	CS	B		
(b)	(1)	OB	C		
	(2)	INT	B	Y	
	(3)	SM	B	Y	
	(4)	PF	A	Y	
	(5)	OB	B		
(c)	(1)	PF	B	Y	
	(2)	OB	B	Y	
	(3)	CS	B	Y	
	(4)	SM	C		
	(5)	INT	A		Y
	(6)	PF	A		Y
	(7)	SM	B		Y
	(8)	OB	B		
(d)	(1)	SM	B		
	(2)	PF	A	Y	
	(3)	OB	B	Y	
	(4)	OB	B	Y	
	(5)	PF	A	Y	
	(6)	INT	A	Y	
	(7)	PF	C		
	Assume that {(2), (5), (6)} also conflicts.				
(e)	(1)	OB	B		
	(2)	OB	B	Y	
	(3)	OB	B	Y	
	(4)	SM	B	Y	
	(5)	INT	A		Y
	(6)	SM	B		Y
	Assume that (1) and (2) have the same basis and that (3) would cast doubt on both (1) and (2).				
(f)	(1)	CS	B		
	(2)	SM	B	Y	
	(3)	PF	A	Y	
	(4)	OB	A	Y	
	(5)	OB	B	Y	
	(6)	PF	B	Y	
	(7)	INT	B		
	Assume that {(2), (3), (4)} also conflicts.				

3. In each of a–e below, take the numbered statements to refer to the statements with the same number in exercise 1a–e. Furthermore, take these claims to be the indicated candidate types with the indicated reliability grades. Assuming that there are no near relatives (or conflicts with unmentioned statements), determine the unproblematic claims for each of a–e.

	Statement	*Cand. Type*	*Reliability Grade*		*Statement*	*Cand. Type*	*Reliability Grade*
(a)	(1)	PF	B	(b)	(1)	OB	B
	(2)	OB	B		(2)	OB	B
	(3)	OB	B		(3)	OB	C
	(4)	PF	C		(4)	OB	B
	(5)	OB	B		(5)	OB	B
(c)	(1)	OB	B	(d)	(1)	OB	B
	(2)	OB	B		(2)	OB	B
	(3)	PF	B		(3)	CS	B
	(4)	OB	C		(4)	Not a candidate	
	(5)	INT	A		(5)	PF	B
	(6)	OB	B		(6)	PF	B
					(7)	INT	A
(e)	(1)	OB	B				
	(2)	OB	B				
	(3)	OB	B				
	(4)	OB	C				
	(5)	CS	B				
	(6)	Not a candidate					
	(7)	OB	B				
	(8)	PF	A				
	(9)	CS	B				
	(10)	INT	B				

Problem Set B

Consider the following story and put yourself in the position of the narrator at the end of the story:

> It was summer, so it was still light as I was driving home in the slow-moving traffic on Main Street. As I was passing a liquor store called The Liquor Barrel, I saw Tom going into the store. I guess Tom was preparing to have a drink on the sly. I remembered the time as 7 P.M., because I was listening to the car radio and they announced the time just then. Tom's wife called me the next morning and asked me where Tom was last night, because he didn't come home till five minutes after the seven o'clock news started. Knowing her strong views against drinking, I discreetly said that I didn't know. Her question, however, surprised me, because I seem to remember the distance from The Liquor Barrel to Tom's house on the other side of the town to be over ten miles on congested city streets. To make sure, I checked the distance again on a map and it was indeed a little over ten miles.

Problem 1: Assuming that mapmakers are scientists, determine the unproblematic claims among (1)–(6) below by filling in the chart of the sort indicated in Table 2.5.

(1) Tom went into The Liquor Barrel at 7 P.M. last night.
(2) Tom was preparing to have a drink on the sly.
(3) The distance from The Liquor Barrel to Tom's house is more than ten miles on city streets.
(4) One cannot cover more than ten miles on city streets in five minutes.
(5) Tom was back at his house by 7:05 P.M.
(6) If (3) and (4) are true, then if Tom went into The Liquor Barrel at 7:00 P.M. last night, he wasn't back at his house by 7:05.

• • •

Suppose the story continues again as follows, and put yourself in the narrator's position at the end of this second stage of the story.

My surprise was diminished when Tom's wife added: "I'm mad at Tom since his n'er-do-well twin brother came into town yesterday and was calling from a liquor store to arrange a lunch with Tom for today. I looked like a fool not knowing where Tom was." Given that he's a n'er-do-well, no wonder I hadn't heard about Tom's twin brother before.

Problem 2: Add (7) and (8) below to the list of statements, continue assuming mapmakers to be scientists, and determine the unproblematic claims among (1)–(8) by filling in the chart of the sort indicated by Table 2.5.

(7) Tom's twin brother came into town yesterday.
(8) Tom's twin brother is a n'er-do-well.

• • •

Suppose the story continues again as follows, and put yourself in the narrator's position at the end of this third stage of the story.

When the afternoon paper came out, I was shocked to read: "Armed robbery at the Liquor Barrel, owner injured. Around 7 P.M. last night there was a holdup at the Liquor Barrel. When the owner tried to ring the alarm, he was shot in the leg, and the assailant took off with about $5000." The paper went on to give the owner's description of the suspect, and it certainly did fit Tom (or his twin brother).

Problem 3: Add (9) to the list of statements, continue assuming mapmakers to be scientists, and determine the unproblematic claims among (1)–(9) by filling in a chart of the sort indicated by Table 2.5.

(9) There was an armed robbery at the Liquor Barrel around 7 P.M. last night.

Problem Set C

Consider the following story and put yourself in the position of the narrator:

As I entered the case, the inspector made the police records available to me and the following facts were stated in them: (i) Jane was found dead in her house. (ii) The coroner's report stated that from the laboratory tests it was determined that Jane died between 10:00 and 11:30 P.M. on Friday due to stab wounds by the knife that was found there. (iii) Jane's watch was shattered and had stopped at 11:15 P.M. (iv) Tom acknowledged the knife to be his, but claimed that it had been missing since a month ago. (v) Prior to dying, Jane had managed to scribble on a piece of paper that Tom attacked her, and handwriting experts confirmed it to be Jane's handwriting. (vi) According to neighbors, Tom hosted a party in his house that night, and upon questioning the participants, it was determined to be a swingers' party involving around ten couples, some of whom Tom hardly knew. (vii) All of the participants testified that although Tom was out between 9 and 10 P.M. to get some more liquor, he was at the party from ten o'clock until it broke up around midnight and was seen every half an hour during those two hours.

It struck me as curious that a group of swingers in a state of undress would be able to testify so exactly concerning Tom's presence from ten o'clock to midnight. However, upon talking to them, I learned that it was a rule of these distasteful gatherings that everyone would assemble every half an hour in the living room to change partners, and that for this purpose the host provided a clock in the living room, which chimed on the hour and the half hour. Looking at the map, and checking it with my own car several times, I determined the distance between Tom's house and Jane's house to be twenty-five miles on the Ventura freeway. Returning to the police, I inquired about the traffic on the Ventura freeway; I was told that on Friday nights it is moderately congested until about 11:30 and that it was heavily patrolled because of the number of drunk drivers on Friday nights.

Problem 1: Construe "presently given" sufficiently broadly so that all the items the narrator learned in the above story are taken to be presently learned. Assuming coroners and mapmakers are scientists, and that all time references are to Friday night, put yourself in the position of the narrator and determine which among (1)–(10) below are unproblematic claims by filling in a chart of the sort indicated by Table 2.5.

(1) Jane was killed between 10:00 and 11:30 P.M. on Friday.
(2) The exact time of murder was 11:15 P.M.
(3) The knife that killed Jane belonged to Tom.
(4) Tom had been missing his knife since a month ago.
(5) Tom hosted a swingers' party.
(6) Tom was seen at the swingers' party every half an hour between ten o'clock and midnight.
(7) Jane's house is twenty-five miles from Tom's house on the Ventura freeway.
(8) If (1), (6), and (7) are true, then if Tom killed Jane, Tom covered fifty miles on the Ventura freeway in thirty minutes or less between 10:00 and 11:30 P.M.
(9) If Tom covered fifty miles on the Ventura freeway in thirty minutes or less between 10:00 and 11:30 P.M., then Tom averaged 100 miles or more per hour on the Ventura freeway between 10:00 and 11:30 P.M.
(10) The Ventura freeway was moderately congested and heavily patrolled between 10:00 and 11:30 P.M.
(11) No one can average 100 miles or more per hour on a freeway that was moderately congested and heavily patrolled.
(12) Tom killed Jane.

• • •

Suppose the story continues as follows:

As I was about to leave after further questioning one of the swingers at Tom's party, she asked me what time it was. I told her, but then noticing her watch, I asked her what was wrong with hers. She replied, "Nothing now. On the night of Tom's party, I noticed when I was leaving that it had somehow gained an hour; but I guess it lost it again. I really should buy one of those quartz watches." I did not think much of this until I questioned another one of the swingers. He was visibly annoyed with my questions and he finally said in exasperation, "I really can't remember that much about the party. I was so drunk that I must have slept a while in the car on the way home without later remembering it. It was 1:20 by the time I got home, and I live only five miles from Tom's house. We'd been drinking since four in the afternoon, and I wouldn't even have been able to tell you about Tom except that when he came back from the liquor store he made such a big point of saying, 'ten o'clock, only two more hours left,' '10:30, only an hour and a half left,' and so on."

Problem 2: Maintaining the assumptions in problem 1 and extending the "presently given" to cover the latest revelations, redo problem 1 in light of these new revelations.

Problem Set D

Consider the following narration and put yourself in the position of the author:

> In studying the life of Stephen Douglas, I come across a biography of him written by his father-in-law, James Madison Cutts. In it an incident is reported:
>
> > After returning to Illinois in late August 1854, he attended a meeting on September 1 where he stood before a hostile crowd and attempted to justify his introduction of the Kansas–Nebraska Bill [which reopened the slavery question]. Upon looking at his watch, Douglas left the meeting telling the crowd: "It is now past midnight and it is Sunday morning—I'll go to church and you may go to Hell."
>
> In checking up on this story, I found old newspapers that covered his return to Illinois at the end of August. They do report on the meeting of September 1 where he defended his bill in front of a hostile crowd. Yet, none of the papers I could find report his witty comment. However, two papers, one in Chicago and one in Detroit, state that Douglas left when the meeting came to an end at 10:30 P.M. Furthermore, consulting a perpetual calendar in the library, I discovered that September 1, 1854 was a Friday. Finally, the accounts of the papers make it quite clear that Douglas did not attend any public meeting on that weekend except for the one on September 1.[3]

Problem 1: For the sake of determining direct accessibility, assume that all the documents are presently available to you. Furthermore, assume that Cutts can be presumed to be a reliable historian, that the perpetual calendar is a work of scientists, and that you know of a few (but only of a few) public meetings that lasted over twenty-four hours. On this basis, determine the unproblematic claims among (1)–(10) by filling in a chart of the sort indicated by Table 2.5.

(1) On September 1, 1854, Douglas stood before a hostile crowd and attempted to justify his introduction of the Kansas–Nebraska Bill.
(2) At the end of the September 1 meeting, Douglas said: "It is now Sunday morning—I'll go to church and you may go to Hell."
(3) Douglas left the September 1 meeting past midnight.
(4) When Douglas left the September 1 meeting (i.e., the one that started on September 1), it was Sunday.
(5) Douglas left the September 1 meeting at 10:30 P.M.
(6) If Douglas left the September 1 meeting at 10:30 P.M. of that day, Douglas did not leave the meeting after midnight.
(7) September 1, 1854 was a Friday.
(8) No public meeting lasts over twenty-four hours.
(9) (8) is virtually exceptionless.
(10) If (7) and (8) are true, Douglas did not leave the September 1 (public) meeting on Sunday.

• • •

Problem 2: Redo problem 1 by canceling the assumption that Cutts is an accredited historian and assume that he backs up his account of Douglas's remark by saying: "As is well known from the newspaper accounts of the meeting, Doug-

3. This narration is adapted from Jacques Barzun and Henry Graff, *The Modern Researcher,* New York: Harcourt, Brace and Co., 1957, pp. 94–96.

las said at its conclusion, 'It is now past midnight. . . .'" In fact, Cutts is a discredited historian, although he did not back up his account of the incident in the way imagined.

Problem Set E: The Dreyfus Affair[4]

Phase I: The Court-Martial of 1894

In light of certain information that became available to French Military Intelligence, Captain Alfred Dreyfus of the artillery (and recently attached to the War Office) was arrested on October 15, 1894 and charged with providing foreign governments with secret military documents. The court-martial of Captain Dreyfus lasted from December 19 to 22, 1894. He was found guilty and sentenced to life in prison on Devil's Island.

The evidence presented at the court-martial came in two parts: (i) evidence presented at the closed court but in the presence of the defendant and his lawyer, and (ii) a secret file passed to the presiding officers of the court-martial (i.e., the "judges") and not shown to the defendant or his lawyer—an irregular procedure even by the lax standards of French courts-martial.

Evidence Presented at the Court-Martial in Presence of the Defense

CM1: A document generally referred to as the *bordereau* ("the list") was a letter addressed to Colonel Schwartzkoppen (the German military attaché in Paris) that was surreptitiously obtained from the German embassy in Paris by French counterespionage agents. In this unsigned and undated document, its author promises to provide Schwartzkoppen with five secret French military documents, three of which concern the French artillery. The document closes by saying, "I'm off to maneuvers." This document reached French Intelligence on September 26, 1894.

CM2: Three handwriting experts testified that the *bordereau* was written in Dreyfus's handwriting, and two handwriting experts testified that it was not.

CM3: Government officials testified that some of the documents promised in the *bordereau* did not exist and were not anticipated prior to July 1894.

CM4: French Intelligence testified that they had determined the *bordereau* was written in April 1894.

CM5: Major Henry (one of the three leading men of the French military intelligence) testified that as early as March 1894 he was warned of a traitor in the War Office, and that in June he was specifically warned that Dreyfus was the traitor. Henry refused to disclose his source beyond saying that the informant was a man of honor.

CM6: Dreyfus denied all charges and protested that he was innocent.

The Evidence of the Secret File

SF1: A biographical sketch of Dreyfus, prepared by French Intelligence, stated that Dreyfus began his career as a spy at the School of War in 1890. It listed as evidence: (i) a charred copy of some classified artillery instructions found

4. This set of problems relates to the Dreyfus affair in France, which started in 1894 and lasted a decade. It eventually touched on such issues as the honor of the French army, the integrity of various French governments, and anti-semitism; Emile Zola's famous *J'Accuse* letter was in connection with one government's handling of the Dreyfus affair, and various political parties had much at stake on the outcome of the affair. This set of problems bypasses all the political complications and restricts itself to the evidence surrounding the guilt or innocence of Captain Dreyfus. For the sake of this set of problems the evidence has been somewhat "doctored"; however, most of the material in these problems is quite close to the truth as we know it and was drawn from Guy Chapman, *The Dreyfus Case,* London: Rupert Hart-Davis, 1963.

in Dreyfus's quarters, and (ii) the discovery by French counterespionage agents that the German embassy possessed a copy of a sensitive manual given in a course at the School of War.

SF2: *The canaille* [*scum*] *D letter.* A letter from Schwartzkoppen to Panizzardi (the Italian military attaché in Paris) that was intercepted by French counterespionage agents. While the letter itself had no date, it was dated April 16, 1894 by French Intelligence. It ran in part: "Herewith twelve large-scale [fortification] plans of Nice, which that scum [*canaille*] D. handed to me for you."

SF3: *The Panizzardi telegram.* A telegram in code that was sent from Panizzardi to Rome on November 2, 1894. It was intercepted and partially deciphered by the French Foreign Office. The decoded content was: "Captain Dreyfus arrested. Precautions taken, emissary warned."

Problem 1: Put yourself in the position of the judges of the court-martial. Among other things this means that you have no reason to doubt the integrity of French Intelligence and regard the French Intelligence as an expert source. Consider the following thirteen statements and determine the unproblematic claims among them by filling in the chart of the sort indicated by Table 2.5.

(1) The author of the *bordereau* promises to provide Schwartzkoppen with secret French military documents.
(2) The author of the *bordereau* is Captain Alfred Dreyfus.
(3) Some of the documents identified and promised in the *bordereau* neither existed nor were anticipated until July 1894.
(4) The *bordereau* was written in April 1894.
(5) No one will be able to identify and promise the delivery of material that neither existed nor was anticipated at the time of making the promise.
(6) If (3) and (5) are true, the *bordereau* was not written in April 1894.
(7) Major Henry was warned that there was a traitor in the War Office and that the traitor was Dreyfus.
(8) Dreyfus was the traitor in the War Office.
(9) Dreyfus is innocent of all charges.
(10) Dreyfus started his career as a spy at the School of War in 1890.
(11) Schwartzkoppen received fortification plans of Nice for Panizzardi from an agent he referred to by the initial "D."
(12) Dreyfus handed over to Schwartzkoppen fortification plans for Nice.
(13) The arrest of Dreyfus was attended by Panizzardi taking precautions and warning the emissary.

Phase II: Picquart's Discovery of 1896

In 1895 Lieutenant Colonel Picquart took over French Intelligence, and in March 1896 French Intelligence surreptitiously obtained from the German embassy an unmailed letter addressed to a certain Esterhazy (a major in the French army). The letter (called the *petite bleu* for the type of paper on which it was written) requested clarification on an earlier point Esterhazy made. In August French Intelligence received specimens of Esterhazy's handwriting. Although no handwriting expert was available, careful scrutiny by Picquart and others in Intelligence left no doubt that the handwriting of the Esterhazy specimen and that of the *bordereau* were the same. Picquart now began to worry about the Dreyfus case and examined the secret file, which was supposed to contain decisive evidence against Dreyfus. The only potentially relevant items he found in it were the "finding" of the French Intelligence that Dreyfus authored the *bordereau* (although the basis of the findings were no longer in the file) and the *canaille* D letter (SF2). [The biographical sketch (SF1) and the Panizzardi telegram (SF3) were no longer in the file (although not having known the initial contents of the secret file, Picquart could not know that any items were missing). Nor was the transcript of the trial of 1894 available to Picquart.] (1)–(6) below then were the claims relevant to the Dreyfus case available to Picquart.

Problem 2: Put yourself in Picquart's position, treat statement (1) below to be a candidate for unproblematic acceptance with the reliability grade of "B," and assume "the handwriting looks the same" means that even under careful scrutiny ordinary observers cannot detect the difference between the samples of handwriting. Assume also that many people have seen both Dreyfus and Esterhazy and no one ever suggested that Dreyfus and Esterhazy might be the same person. On this basis and construing "presently given" sufficiently broadly to cover Picquart's inspection of all the documents, determine the unproblematic claims among (1)–(6) by filling in the chart of the sort indicated by Table 2.5.

(1) Dreyfus wrote the *bordereau.*
(2) Esterhazy was in contact with Schwartzkoppen.
(3) The handwriting of the Esterhazy specimen and that of the *bordereau* look the same.
(4) If the handwriting on a number of documents looks the same, the same person wrote those documents.
(5) (4) is virtually exceptionless.
(6) Esterhazy isn't Dreyfus.
(7) If (3), (4), and (6) are all true, then Esterhazy rather than Dreyfus wrote the *bordereau.*
(8) Schwartzkoppen received fortification plans of Nice for Panizzardi from an agent he referred to by the initial "D."

Epilogue to Phase II: Needless to say, Picquart found the case for Dreyfus's guilt virtually nonexistent. Indeed he became convinced that Dreyfus was innocent. When he approached his superiors in the War Office on the matter, he was informed that the Dreyfus case could not be reopened because the honor of the French army depended on the case having been properly conducted. (His resistance to this line of thought resulted in his removal from French Intelligence and transferral to an outpost in southern Tunisia.)

Phase III: Cavaignac's Disclosure of 1898

Between 1896 and 1898, a number of events occurred that once again brought the Dreyfus case to the center of attention. Leaks to the newspaper suggested that there had been a secret file in the 1894 court-martial, Esterhazy was found not guilty of espionage principally because handwriting experts testified that the *bordereau* was not written by Esterhazy, and the *petite bleu* could not be entered as evidence because it was never posted by Schwartzkoppen. In an attempt to put an end to the matter, when Cavaignac became minister of war in June 1898, he went through the secret file and found three documents, which he found particularly useful: the *canaille* D letter [SF2], and the following two:

SF4: A letter dated March 1894 from Panizzardi to Schwartzkoppen that stated: "Since I cannot come to you, will you please come to me tomorrow morning, for D has brought me a number of interesting things and the work must be shared as we have only ten days left."

SF5: A letter dated September 1896 from Panizzardi to Schwartzkoppen that stated: "I have read that a Deputy is going to interpellate [i.e., grill a minister in the lower house of the French Parliament] about Dreyfus. If new explanations are required at Rome, I shall say I have never had relations with this Jew. You understand. If you are asked, say the same thing, for no one must ever know what happened with him."

On July 7, 1898, in a speech to the Chamber of Deputies, Cavaignac conceded that Esterhazy was the likely author of the *bordereau,* but affirmed his absolute certainty that Dreyfus was guilty of passing information. In support of this he read out the SF2, SF4, and SF5, and he was greeted with cheers by the chamber (which was relieved that the Dreyfus affair could be put behind them).

Problem 3: Putting yourself in Cavaignac's position upon examing the files, determine the unproblematic claims among (1)–(5) below by filling in a chart of the sort indicated by Table 2.5.

(1) Schwartzkoppen received fortification plans of Nice for Panizzardi from an agent he referred to by the initial "D."
(2) Dreyfus provided plans of the Nice fortification to Schwartzkoppen.
(3) An agent referred to by the letter "D" provided Panizzardi with "interesting" information.
(4) Dreyfus provided Panizzardi with "interesting" information.
(5) Panizzardi advised Schwartzkoppen to deny knowledge of Dreyfus, adding that no one must know what happened with Dreyfus.

Problem 4: Repeat problem 3 by putting yourself in Picquart's position in 1898, recalling the epilogue to Phase II and assuming that Picquart remembers that in August 1896 the secret file contained nothing remotely significant beyond the *canaille* D letter, and that Picquart had not seen the file since August 1896.

The Final Phase: 1898–1904

During these years, more and more evidence emerged supporting Dreyfus's innocence. This evidence may be divided into those concerning the *bordereau* and those concerning the other (alleged) items. To determine what was unproblematic, put yourself in a position involving total hindsight that may not have been available to anyone even at the conclusion of the Dreyfus affair.

The Evidence Surrounding the Bordereau

(a) The contents of the *bordereau* (CM1), which finished with the statement "I'm off to maneuvers."
(b) The 1894 findings of the French Intelligence that Dreyfus wrote the *bordereau.*
(c) The testimony by government officials that some of the documents identified and promised in the *bordereau* neither existed nor were anticipated until July 1894 (CM3).
(d) Testimony from the War Office that Dreyfus did not go and was not scheduled to go on maneuvers any time after July 1, 1894, and that Esterhazy did attend several maneuvers in August 1894.
(e) Of the three handwriting experts who testified in 1894 that the handwriting of the *bordereau* was that of Dreyfus (cf. CM2), one was no longer available by the time the appeals court met. A second testified to the appeals court that had he seen Esterhazy's handwriting in 1894, he would have identified the handwriting of the *bordereau* as that of Esterhazy. The third handwriting expert, Bertillion, maintained in the appeals court that the handwriting of the *bordereau* was that of Dreyfus. However, Bertillion's system had often been questioned as unintelligible, and a special commission of savants (including the famous French mathematician Henri Poicare) (i) destroyed the basis of Bertillion's system to the satisfaction of all other experts, and (ii) established Esterhazy to have written the *bordereau.*

Consider the following claims that relate to the *bordereau:*

(1) Dreyfus wrote the *bordereau.*
(2) Some of the documents identified and promised in the *bordereau* neither existed nor were anticipated until July 1894.

(3) No one would be able to identify and promise the delivery of material that neither existed nor was anticipated at the time of making the promise.
(4) If (2) and (3) are true, the *bordereau* was not written until July 1894.
(5) The author of the *bordereau* was off to maneuvers.
(6) If (1) and (5) are true and the *bordereau* was not written until July 1894, Dreyfus was off to maneuvers sometime after July 1, 1894.
(7) Dreyfus was not off to maneuvers anytime after July 1, 1894.
(8) Esterhazy did attend maneuvers in August 1894.
(9) The handwriting of the *bordereau* is that of Dreyfus. [Judge this claim entirely on the basis of item (e).]
(10) The handwriting of the *bordereau* is entirely that of Esterhazy.
(11) Dreyfus isn't Esterhazy.
(12) If (10) and (11) are true, Dreyfus did not write the *bordereau.*

Problem 5: Though somewhat unrealistic, assume that claim (1) is a candidate for unproblematic acceptance with the grade of "B," and that evidence (a)–(e) is presently available to you. Furthermore, because handwriting analysis does not seem to be a science in any reasonably strict sense of the term, assume that although handwriting experts are experts in handwriting analysis, there are no scientists in this field. Finally, assume that many people saw Dreyfus and Esterhazy and that no one ever suggested Dreyfus and Esterhazy might be the same person. On this basis, and being mindful of the first footnote of Section 2.5, determine the unproblematic claims among (1)–(12) above by filling in a chart of the sort indicated by Table 2.5.

Problem 6: Assume (as was indeed the case) that the only basis French Intelligence had for (1) was the handwriting experts mentioned in (e). Cancel the assumption that (1) has a reliability grade of "B," and redo problem 5 by maintaining the other assumptions.

The Evidence Surrounding Other Items

(a) Major Henry's testimony of 1894 about being warned in 1894 of a spy in the War Office, and of Dreyfus being that spy (CM5).
(b) A biographical sketch of Dreyfus prepared by French Intelligence in 1894 (SF1). Subsequent investigation of the Intelligence files showed that the claim of Dreyfus having started his career as a spy at the School of War in 1890 rested entirely on the two bits of evidence given there: (i) a charred copy of some classified artillery instructions found in Dreyfus's quarters, from which alone it was inferred that he had copied those instructions and failed in destroying the original; and (ii) the discovery by French counterespionage agents that the German embassy possessed a copy of a sensitive manual given in a course at the School of War. However, later investigations showed that the manual was found by French Intelligence in the German embassy only in 1894, whereas Dreyfus attended the School of War from 1890 to 1892.
(c) The *canaille* D letter (SF2), dated April 16, 1894 by French Intelligence. At the appeals court, French Intelligence officers admitted that the letter was dated only after October 1894 (when Dreyfus became a suspect). One Intelligence officer seemed to recall vaguely getting the letter in 1892, while another seemed to recall vaguely getting it in December 1893.
(d) The Panizzardi telegram (SF3), received by French Intelligence in 1894 from, and deciphered by, the Foreign Office. The version shown at the 1894 court-martial stated: "Captain Dreyfus arrested. Precautions taken, emissary warned." In a thoroughly corroborated testimony, the Foreign Office testified as follows: The first attempt to decipher the telegram (which used a new code) only produced certainty about the word "Dreyfus" and hypotheses all of

which were judged to be dubious by the cryptographers themselves. One hypothesis did approximate the version used in the court-martial. However, the War Office was warned of the dubious nature of these hypotheses. By November 13, 1894 (a full month before the court-martial), the telegram was fully deciphered and forwarded to French Intelligence, and it read: "If Captain Dreyfus has not had relations with you, it would be well to order the Ambassador to publish an official denial, in order to avoid press comment."

(e) SF4 dated March 1894 and read by Cavaignac, in which Panizzardi (allegedly) said: "D has brought me a number of interesting things." Investigation of the Intelligence files established that a copy of the original letter showed a "P" in the place where the "D" had appeared in the letter Cavaignac saw.

(f) SF5 dated September 1896, read by Cavaignac, and (allegedly) from Panizzardi to Schwartzkoppen. It expressed concern about the upcoming interpellation involving Dreyfus, and urged denial of any knowledge of Dreyfus. Close examination by French Intelligence agents disclosed that the body of the letter was on a different paper from the paper on which the signature and letterhead occurred. In a transcript of an interrogation of Major Henry, Henry admitted to having forged the letter, and Henry committed suicide while in prison.

Problem 7: Assume that evidence (a)–(f) is available to you, and determine the unproblematic claims among (1)–(7) below by filling in a chart of the sort indicated by Table 2.5.

(1) Major Henry was warned in 1894 that there was a spy in the War Office.
(2) Dreyfus started his career as a spy at the School of War in 1890.
(3) Schwartzkoppen received fortification plans of Nice for Panizzardi from an agent he referred to by the initial "D."
(4) Schwartzkoppen received the fortification plans of Nice (for Panizzardi from an agent he referred to by the initial "D") before 1894.
(5) With the arrest of Dreyfus, Panizzardi took precautions and warned the emissary.
(6) An agent referred to by the letter "D" provided Panizzardi with "interesting" information around March 1894.
(7) In September 1896, Panizzardi advised Schwartzkoppen to deny knowledge of Dreyfus, adding that no one must know what happened with Dreyfus.

2.6 Related Fallacies

As we noted in Chapter 1, a list of fallacies represents the human psychology of bad thinking. In general we can understand a FALLACY as *an erroneous but frequently persuasive way of being led from a reason or circumstance to a conclusion.* In this chapter, we have been discussing the circumstances under which we may accept a claim as unproblematic. However, if we are not careful, we may be beguiled into accepting a number of problematic claims as unproblematic or at least as less problematic than they are. Thus, we conclude this chapter with a discussion of some fallacies that are likely to result in our acceptance of a problematic claim as (relatively) unproblematic. Some of these fallacies relate to considerations we appealed to in Sections 2.2–2.5, and others have a less direct bearing on what we have discussed.

Two preliminary points need to be made: First, most fallacies can be considered from two points of view. Sometimes one is said to commit a fallacy when one relies on an erroneous form of thinking in attempting to persuade someone—often knowing full well that one is presenting an illegitimate form of reasoning. Seen in this way, the fallacy is a "speaker's fallacy." But a fallacy can also be seen as a "hearer's fallacy," or being persuaded by an erroneous form of thinking presented by others or even by oneself. Because the same form of bad thinking is involved in either case, we can largely ignore this distinction. The second point is that a number of schemes for classifying fallacies into a variety of types have been proposed over the years, and this text classifies fallacies into four types, three of which are presented in this section. While these classifications are ultimately of little practical significance, they do put some order into a motley collection of fallacies. Our scheme divides fallacies according to the kind of analyses they demand, and this should be of some help in approaching the exercises. Using this scheme, a grand summary of all the fallacies covered in this text is given inside the back cover of the text. With this much said, let us discuss the fallacies with which this chapter is concerned.

(1) Fallacy of the Argument from Ignorance. Most of us have probably heard claims of the following kind: "I believe in God's existence; after all, no one has proved that He doesn't exist." Such a claim is often made with sincerity, and it seems to have some force in rebutting the agnostic's doubts. Yet, when we make the form of reasoning explicit, it amounts to:

Because there is no disproof of C ('God exists'), C is true.

This is clearly an erroneous form of reasoning: We may have no disproof or evidence against Cleopatra having eaten figs on the day of her death. Yet this is hardly a reason for thinking that she did eat figs on that fatal day; this is a matter about which we are unlikely to have any evidence one way or the other. The erroneous form of reasoning involved in the theist's claim is an instance of the FALLACY OF THE ARGUMENT FROM IGNORANCE.

This fallacy may be defined as the one we (as hearers) commit when *we are led to accept a claim C* **just** *because there are no reasons against C or because C hasn't been disproved.* The source of this fallacy is easy to diagnose: A claim C is either true or false. However, there are three possible positions one may occupy with respect to a claim: (a) one may have reasons favoring C, (b) one may have neither reasons for C nor reasons against C, and (c) one may have reasons against C. The fact that C is either true or false can lead one to forget about (b), and thus lead one to accept (a) from the elimination of possibility (c).

To abbreviate the definition, and to expedite the work in the exercises, we may represent the Fallacy of the Argument from Ignorance as follows:

> Fallacy of the Argument from Ignorance
>
> No (decisive) reason against C → C is true.

In a diagram of this kind, 'A → B' should be understood as 'A alone is mistakenly taken to be (or is offered as) a good reason or basis for accepting B', and to have a term, we shall say that any fallacy that can be conveniently represented in the form 'A → B' is an INFERENTIAL FALLACY:

> Inferential Fallacies
>
> A → B: A alone is mistakenly taken to be (or offered as) a good reason or basis for accepting B.

The analysis of a fallacy committed by a passage (or a line of thought) should (a) identify the fallacy by name, (b) show that the fallacy's definition applies to the passage (or line of thought) by filling in variables like 'C' in the fallacy's abbreviating diagram, and (c) if it is not obvious from step (b) that the case fits the fallacy's definition, justify the claim that the case does fit the definition. In short,

> Analysis of Fallacies
>
> (1) Name the fallacy.
> (2) Fill in the fallacy's abbreviating diagram.
> (3) Justify what is not obvious.

Given this machinery, we shall analyze our initial example simply as:

Ignorance: No decisive reason against 'God exists' → God exists (or 'God exists' is true).

Step 3 of the analysis may be omitted because it's obvious that the Fallacy of the Argument from Ignorance has been committed. As another example, consider a claim often made by the tobacco industry: "It should be remembered that no one has proved that smoking actually causes cancer." Though not explicitly stated, it is clearly suggested that smoking is (or may be) safe. Understanding 'safe' as 'doesn't cause cancer', the tobacco industry view should be analyzed:

Ignorance: No decisive reason against 'Smoking is (or may be) safe' → Smoking is (or may be) safe.

A comment in accordance with step 3 should be needed if it isn't obvious that 'Smoking is safe' is the conclusion the hearer is invited to draw.

In light of the present discussions, it may appear that we were committing the Fallacy of the Argument from Ignorance in urging that a candidate for unproblematic acceptance is "innocent until proven guilty," that is, a claim that should be accepted as unproblematic in the absence of reasons against doing so. However, it must be remembered that insofar as a claim was a candidate for unproblematic acceptance, there were strong reasons for accepting it, for example, that I (seem to) see a book in front of me is a strong reason for claiming that there is a book in front of me. Thus, if there are no reasons against a candidate, one can accept it without committing the Fallacy of the Argument from Ignorance. Clearly, this attitude cannot be extended to claims we have no reasons for accepting; that is, accepting such a claim *just* because there are no reasons against it is to commit the Fallacy of the Argument from Ignorance.

The consideration of the last paragraph brings out an important point about many of the fallacies we shall be discussing: While a fallacy may be committed in accepting B solely on the basis of A, we often have good reasons for accepting B when *A is supplemented with some other factor.* This suggests that we must not be too hasty in accusing someone of committing a fallacy, because there may be an additional factor that the person thinks is too obvious to mention. On the other hand, this kind of a principle of charity must not be extended to accepting fallacious forms of reasoning. The best approach in an everyday context is to avoid the extremes: In the absence of other factors that are explicitly given or contextually obvious, tentatively accuse the person (or oneself) of having committed a fallacy, and thereby invite the person (or oneself) to make explicit the other factors that are deemed relevant.

(2) Fallacy of False Cause. Suppose that studies by sociologists disclose that there is a significant correlation between being black and performing poorly on academic tasks. It would surely be tempting for a person with racist inclinations to conclude that being black is a cause of poor test performances, in short, that blacks genetically have an inferior intelligence. The high percentage of black players in the National Basketball Association may also lead to the conclusion that blacks are genetically superior basketball players. To convince ourselves that these are erroneous forms of reasoning, consider an old Inca custom: The priests performed certain rituals on June 22 to prevent the sun from going too far to the North, and this ritual was of course always followed by the sun's return to the Southern Hemisphere. The Incas evidently inferred on the basis of this correlation that the rituals were a cause of the sun's return, that the priests *brought back* the sun. The examples of this paragraph commit the Fallacy of False Cause.

The most general characterization of this fallacy is that of mistaking what isn't a cause for a cause. For our purpose, we shall single out one form of it (whose Latin name is *post hoc ergo propter hoc,* or, "after this, therefore, because of this"). We shall say that the FALLACY OF FALSE CAUSE is committed when *one is led to accept a causal relation* **merely** *on the basis of a correlation or the fact that one event (the alleged cause) occurred one or more times prior to the other event (the alleged effect).* Of course a correlation is often a sign of a causal relation, but one must consider the other causal factors that may have been operative: socioeconomic condition is clearly one such a factor in our racial example. Needless to say, one must be on one's guard against the Fallacy of False Cause in accepting a claim as a general claim of common sense. An abbreviated representation of the fallacy is as follows:

Fallacy of False Cause
C (frequently) occurs with E → C causes (or is causally related to) E.

Thus, our initial example would be analyzed.

False Cause: Being black frequently occurs with poor academic performance → being black causes poor academic performance.

Superstitions also involve this fallacy: Ever since his team won a crucial game when he wore a sweater (which could only be described as ugly), the 1986 coach of St. John's basketball team called it his lucky sweater. If he even half-believed this, he committed the Fallacy of False Cause:

False Cause: Wearing the sweater occurred with winning → Wearing the sweater causes winning.

Perhaps a more subtle example is the following: Suppose eight in ten users of Miracle Cure are rid of their common colds within two days. It is tempting to infer that Miracle Cure cures the common cold; in other words, it causes the cold to go away. But this commits the Fallacy of False Cause.

False Cause: Taking Miracle Cure (very) frequently occurs with being rid of the cold → Taking Miracle Cure cures the cold.

Other factors must be considered before making a causal claim. Colds may generally go away in a couple of days; perhaps the directions for taking Miracle Cure urged drinking lots of orange juice along with the drug and it was the juice that was causally relevant.

(3) Fallacy of Hasty Generalization. Perhaps not a few American students have been discouraged by their professors who have told them that

European students are better educated than American students. At least some of these professors are likely to have reached this conclusion on the basis of having observed in their own classes the superior performance of the European foreign students. Should we accept the inference of such professors? It won't do much good to complain that he or she is inferring from "some" to "all"; general claims (including legitimate ones) are often based on such an inference, because no one can examine *all* the instances. But when we make such an inference, we must be able to presume that the instances constitute a fair or representative sample. And this is where our professor goes awry. Typically, a country sends its best students abroad for further study; thus, one cannot presume that the European students studying in America constitute a fair sample of European students in general. The professor who bases his or her conclusion on the performances of European students in the American classroom commits the FALLACY OF HASTY GENERALIZATION.

We define this fallacy as the one we commit when *we accept a generalization on the basis of instances that cannot be presumed to constitute a "fair" sample.* Clearly, in accepting a claim as an unproblematic general claim of common sense, one must be careful that one is not committing the Fallacy of Hasty Generalization. In our scheme for classifying the fallacies we shall call this a PRESUPPOSITIONAL FALLACY. The crux of these fallacies is that although an inference from A to B is often acceptable, a condition for its acceptability is that certain presuppositions can at least be presumed to be satisfied; the fallacy is committed when the presupposition cannot be presumed. Presuppositional Fallacies and their abbreviating diagram may be generally understood as follows:

> Presuppositional Fallacies
>
> A → B; NOT {X}: A is a poor reason for accepting B in the context at hand because the inference from A to B requires that we can presume X, and X cannot be presumed in the context.

Because the inference of a generalization from its instances requires being able to presume the instances to form a fair sample, the Fallacy of Hasty Generalization may be diagrammed as:

> Fallacy of Hasty Generalization
>
> G is true of instances I → G is true in all (most or large number of) cases; NOT {I is a fair sample}.*
>
> *Note that step 3 of the analysis (explaining the unobvious) is needed with respect to fairness of the sample; that is, one should explain why the fairness of the sample cannot be presumed.

Our initial example should then be analyzed as follows:

Hasty Generalization: 'Being better than American students' is true of European students studying in America → 'Being better than American students' is true of all (or most European students; NOT {European students studying in America form a fair sample}.

- Because a country typically sends its best students abroad, it cannot be presumed that the European students studying in America form a fair (i.e., unbiased) sample of European students.

To be able to presume that a sample is fair actually has two dimensions: (a) The sample is not biased in some way, and (b) the sample is sufficiently large. As in our example concerning the professor's inference, the Fallacy of Hasty Generalization is often committed, because the sample cannot be presumed to be an unbiased one. Nisbett and Ross[5] report an interesting and frequent version of the Fallacy of Hasty Generalization that concerns insufficient sample size: A consumer armed with relevant statistics from *Consumer's Guide* on the strong performance of Volvos abandons his plans to buy a Volvo when he hears a horror story about his friend's Volvo. In giving disproportionate weight to the one horror story, he commits the Fallacy of Hasty Generalization:

Hasty Generalization: 'Performing poorly' was true of his friend's Volvo → 'Performing poorly' is true of a large number of Volvos; NOT {his friend's Volvo forms a fair sample}.

- The single instance is not a sufficiently large sample to conclude that a large number of Volvos perform poorly.

More obvious instances of the Fallacy of Hasty Generalization are advertisements for the supermarket chains that are often seen. Week after week we endure seeing happy shoppers with their bags of groceries exclaiming: "I saved $7.48," "I saved $12.67," and so on. We are told that what they saved is based on the prices for the same items at some competing grocery store, and it is concluded that you really do save at such and such a chain, say Fine Food. We would analyze the fallacy as follows:

Hasty Generalization: 'Being cheaper than other stores' is true for items selected by the shoppers in the advertisement → 'Being cheaper than other stores' is true of most or all items at Fine Food; NOT {items selected form a fair sample}.

- Given the context of an advertisement, we cannot presume that the items selected by the people in the ad constitute an unbiased sample of grocery items at Fine Food.

Though less explicit, the advertisement also seems to suggest that Fine Food is cheaper than all or most other grocery stores. If so, the Fallacy of

5. Richard Nisbett and Lee Ross, *Human Inference: Strategies and Shortcomings of Social Judgment,* Englewood Cliffs, N.J.: Prentice-Hall, 1980.

Hasty Generalization is committed a second time, because the sample of competing stores cannot be presumed to be fair.

When a fallacy is as obvious as the ones in grocery chain advertisements, there is a temptation to think that no one is really going to be deceived. But two points should be kept in mind: (a) It's unlikely that companies spend good money on expensive TV advertisements if they have no effect in persuading potential customers. (b) Even if one isn't convinced that a certain chain *is* cheaper, one may be led to think: "Maybe that chain is cheaper; I should perhaps try that store." But on the basis of the advertisement, there is very little reason to single out a particular grocery chain even in this limited way. In a slightly extended sense, one commits the fallacy even if one is persuaded only in such a partial or limited way.

(4) Fallacy of the False Appeal to Authority. The Nobel Prize-winning chemist Linus Pauling has gone to great length in claiming the powers of vitamin C to prevent and cure such things as the common cold, and this has convinced many people of the medicinal virtues of vitamin C. While Pauling is undoubtedly a distinguished chemist, his expertise does not extend to medicine. Thus, while Pauling's claims should be accepted as expert testimony in chemistry, it would be a mistake to accept his claims for vitamin C as expert testimony, and to do so is to commit the FALLACY OF THE FALSE APPEAL TO AUTHORITY.

This fallacy may be defined as the one we commit when *we are led to accept the testimony of an (alleged) authority who has no expertise in the relevant area.* We have in effect already covered this fallacy in Section 2.4, where we discussed grounds for doubting the expertise of an alleged expert; the four examples given there can all be seen as instances of the Fallacy of the False Appeal to Authority. We shall classify this fallacy as a presuppositional fallacy and diagram it as follows:

False Appeal to Authority

Alleged authority P claims C is true → C is true; NOT {P has expertise in the area relevant for C}.*

*Note that one should say why P has no expertise in the relevant field.

If someone is persuaded by Pauling's claims about vitamin C, we would thus analyze the fallacy as follows:

False Appeal to Authority: The Nobel Prize-winning chemist Linus Pauling claims that vitamin C has medicinal powers → Vitamin C has medicinal powers; NOT {Pauling has expertise in medicine}.

- While Pauling has expertise in chemistry, his expertise doesn't extend to medicine.

Suppose your economics professor says: "I think that the Bank of America stocks are going to be a good investment and I'm going to buy some." It is tempting to think that the Bank of America stocks *are* going to be a good investment (and that one should invest in the Bank of America), because after all, an economist said so. But to think so is to commit the Fallacy of the False Appeal to Authority:

False Appeal to Authority: An economics professor claims that the Bank of America stocks are going to be a good investment → Bank of America stocks are going to be a good investment; NOT {An economics professor's expertise extends to the stock market}.

- It cannot be presumed that someone with expertise in economic theory and its applications has expertise on how to invest in the stock market.

Because this instance of the Fallacy of the False Appeal to Authority seems to be so prevalent, it may be worth pointing out that there seems to be no reliable theory for predicting the behavior of Wall Street. Even if there were, it is unlikely to have great predictive power, because there are likely to be too many parameters that are too complex to determine (such as political developments, purchasing behavior of others, and the weather that affects agriculture and related enterprises).

(5) Fallacy of *Argumentum ad Populum.* Many of us have had an experience in which someone makes a claim that seems to be clearly false—for example, a claim that philosophers are helpless when it comes to practical matters. I try to refute this argument by citing the example of Harry, a philosophy professor who is wealthy because he increased his real estate holdings many times over and also played a central role in the statewide Democratic party. My opponent is unimpressed and simply replies, "Well, (as they say) the exception proves the rule." So many people have claimed that the exception proves the rule that it has become a widely accepted piece of conventional wisdom. However, a little reflection should make it plain that, in the form in which it is often accepted,[6] it is a piece of rank nonsense: How can finding an A that isn't a B prove the rule that A's are B's? It certainly *dis*proves the claim that all A's are B's, and it casts doubt on the looser claim that most A's are B's. It would seem that many people accept a plainly false version of 'The exception proves the rule' simply because of the circumstance that so many people believe it, and to do so is commit the Fallacy of *Argumentum ad Populum.*

This fallacy has been variously described as "directing an emotional appeal to the masses," "the attempt to win popular assent by arousing

6. There is a reading of 'The exception proves the rule' that might be a bit more plausible. Because there is something exceptional, unusual, or abnormal about an A that isn't a B, A's are normally B's. Unfortunately, the saying is often used as a means of defending generalizations from counterinstances. Max Black has also pointed out that the saying is a corruption of the sound maxim that the exception probes the rule; that is, a test for the correctness of a rule or general claim is that it exceptionless. (See Max Black, *Critical Thinking,* Englewood Cliffs, N.J.: Prentice-Hall, 1952.)

emotions rather than appealing to the relevant facts," and "an attempt to create a bandwagon effect." We shall consider the appeal to emotions as a separate fallacy and define the FALLACY OF *Argumentum ad Populum* as the one in which:

> *We are led to accept a claim C* just *because so many people accept C, a reason that isn't decisively relevant to the truth or correctness of C.*

We could treat this fallacy as an inferential fallacy and abbreviate it as 'So many people believe C → C is true'. On the other hand, it is somewhat implausible that people accept the inference in such a blatant form. Because so many people accept C is typically not so much a reason for believing C as part of the surrounding circumstance that unwittingly (and perhaps even subconsciously) leads us to accept C; however, the fact that so many people believe C isn't decisively relevant to the truth or falsity of C. We shall therefore abbreviate or diagram the Fallacy of *Argumentum ad Populum* as follows:

> Fallacy of *Argumentum ad Populum*
>
> So many people accept C ⇝ C is true.

Because the circumstance that leads us to accept C isn't (decisively) relevant to the truth of the claim that we finally accept, the Fallacy of the *Argumentum ad Populum* belongs to the category of fallacies we shall call FALLACIES OF RELEVANCE, and their abbreviating diagram can be explained and summarized as follows:

> Fallacies of Relevance
>
> A ⇝ B: While the circumstance A isn't (decisively) relevant to the truth or correctness of B, A surreptitiously leads one to accept B.

Thus, we would analyze our example as:

Argumentum ad Populum: So many people accept 'The exception proves the rule' ⇝ The exception proves the rule.

The Fallacy of *Argumentum ad Populum* has been committed far more often than we might think. For years it was conventional wisdom that heavier objects fall faster to the ground.[7] It took Galileo's famous but

7. It is true that Aristotle was the leading authority for most of the two thousand years preceding Galileo, and it was certainly Aristotle's doctrine that heavier objects fall faster to the ground. However, in those days, it was likely that many people believed the false claim, not because they read Aristotle or because some expert told them of this, but simply because so many of their neighbors claimed it. It was these people who committed the Fallacy of *Argumentum ad Populum.*

simple experiment of dropping objects of unequal weight from the Leaning Tower of Pisa to convince people that differences in weight do not affect how fast an object falls to the ground. At least in many instances the pre-Galilean people can be taken to have committed the following fallacy:

Argumentum ad Populum: So many people accept that heavier things fall faster to the ground ⇝ Heavier things fall faster to the ground.

Iron ships were relatively late innovations, which suggests that many people committed the Fallacy of the *Argumentum ad Populum* in accepting 'A ship can't be built of iron'. The prevalent belief in witchcraft in the old days of Salem, Massachusetts, might again be partially attributable to the people having committed the Fallacy of *Argumentum ad Populum.* Nor should we think that we are immune from this fallacy today. Often winning a string of primaries creates a bandwagon effect for a presidential candidate; evidently, a number of people commit the following fallacy:

Argumentum ad Populum: So many people accept that 'X is the best candidate' ⇝ X is the best candidate (therefore the one for whom one should vote).

A more delicate example is the immediate and massive rejection (not to mention outrage) directed at the published research of some Stanford researchers, who claimed that they had evidence for the inferior intelligence of blacks. Several things ought to be noted immediately: (a) Scrutiny by scientific experts revealed pretty quickly that the alleged research was shoddy and fatally flawed. (b) The alleged results were at odds with the evidence that had been accumulated over the years. (c) It has been argued, not without plausibility, that even if the findings were correct, they should not be published in light of the adverse social effects such a publication was likely to have. If someone rejected the alleged results on the basis of (a), (b), or (c), such a rejection would certainly have justification. But it is also possible that many people immediately rejected the alleged findings because of their conviction that the races are equal in intelligence, a conviction that merely developed as a result of so many people having claimed it in the past. Such a person would have committed the Fallacy of *Argumentum ad Populum.*

The Fallacy of *Argumentum ad Populum* points out the need for great caution in accepting something as an unproblematic general claim of common sense. This is why we have insisted that such a claim must be personally confirmed. We have also required that others agree with the claim; but the others had to be people who can be presumed to be intelligent and knowledgeable. The peculiar marks of the Fallacy of *Argumentum ad Populum* are (i) there is no independent basis for the claim beyond others having claimed it, and (ii) there is no presumption that the others exercised judgment in making the claim. One is not committing this fallacy when the claim has an independent basis and one can presume that those who corroborate the claim are exercising judgment. In such a circumstance, corroboration gives us *a* supporting reason for the claim that has an independent basis. As with many other fallacies, the Fallacy of *Argumentum ad Populum* is committed when the *mere* acceptance of a claim by others leads us to accept it as well.

(6) Fallacy of Emotional Appeals. When Eisenhower was running for president in 1952, his running mate, Richard M. Nixon, was accused of financial improprieties by various people. To answer the charges, he went on national television, listed his various holdings and debts, and then said:

> It isn't very much. But Pat and I have the satisfaction that every dime we have got is honestly ours. I should say this, that Pat doesn't have a mink coat. But she does have a respectable Republican cloth coat, and I always tell her that she would look good in anything. One other thing I probably should tell you, because if I don't, they will probably be saying this about me, too. We did get something, a gift, after the election. A man down in Texas heard Pat on the radio mention that our two youngsters would like to have a dog, and, believe it or not, the day before we left on this campaign trip we got a message from Union Station in Baltimore, saying they had a package for us. We went down to get it. You know what it was? It was a little cocker spaniel dog, in a crate that he had sent all the way from Texas, black and white spotted, and our little girl, the six-year-old, named it Checkers. And, you know the kids, like all kids, loved the dog, and I just want to say this, right now, that regardless of what they say about it, we are going to keep it.

This speech, generally referred to as the "Checkers Speech," is often taken as a classic example of appealing to our sense of pity. After talking about his wife who has only a "respectable Republican cloth coat," he turns his attention to his children's love for Checkers and how his critics will no doubt be asking that the dog be taken away from the kids. The overall effect was to arouse the listener's sense of pity toward the poor Nixon family, and this evidently led many voters to accept the view that Nixon was a poor, honest man who was unfairly charged with improprieties by his critics; in any event, public opinion turned favorable to Nixon after the "Checkers Speech," Eisenhower kept him as a running mate, and in November they were elected. In making the emotional appeal Nixon committed the FALLACY OF (MAKING) EMOTIONAL APPEALS, and to let one's sense of pity lead to the acceptance of Nixon's financial propriety is to commit the FALLACY OF (BEING GUIDED BY) EMOTIONAL APPEALS.

Hearers commit this fallacy when *emotional appeals lead them to accept a claim,* and speakers commit this fallacy *when they attempt to persuade people of a claim by appealing to their emotions.* It should be obvious that this is a fallacy of relevance. Reasons for a claim are relevant to the correctness of the claim, and not the emotions that may have been aroused. Thus, whether it is a speaker's or hearer's fallacy, we shall diagram or abbreviate it as:

> Emotional Appeal
>
> An appeal to an emotion E* ⇝ C is true or correct.
>
> *Note that step 3 (explaining the unobvious) should be performed to the extent of briefly explaining how the emotional appeal is made.

Thus our example would be analyzed as follows:

Emotional Appeal: An appeal to pity ⇝ Nixon didn't commit any financial improprieties.

- Appeal to pity is made by talking about Pat's cloth coat and the children's love for Checkers, a love that Nixon isn't going to deny them regardless of what the critics say.

If we understand 'emotions' in a broad sense, appeals can be made to our sense of pity, hate, indignation, fear, hope, flattery, humor, and desire for sexual or romantic gratification, just to mention a few. An example of appealing to two emotions is represented in the following mailer:

> Dear California Republican:
>
> Are you going to let Rose Bird and a few hand-picked Democrats in Sacramento steal your vote for the next twenty years? Thanks to the help of over 2.7 million Republicans, we forced the Democrats to bring their self-serving, unfair reapportion plan out into the open and put it to the test of a statewide vote on June 8, 1982. As a last resort, the Democrats took our successful Referendum drive to the Supreme Court of California. And—to the surprise of no one—[the Democrat governor] Jerry Brown's hand-picked Chief Justice Rose Bird cast her decision in favor of the Democrat reapportion plan. *In effect, Rose Bird told 3.5 million Republicans to drop dead.* That's why the California Republican party has launched a new campaign. And we need your personal signature.
>
> What happens if this petition drive loses? . . . State spending will skyrocket as liberals introduce more pork-barrel projects. And hard-core criminals will roam the streets, thanks to more liberal laws which will protect murderers and rapists from prosecution and mandatory jail sentences. That's why we desperately need you to sign.

The fallacy committed by this letter may be analyzed as follows:

Emotional Appeal: The appeal to fear as well as hate and indignation ⇝ One should support the reapportionment petition.

- Hate and indignation are aroused by using expressions like 'steal your vote' and 'told 3.5 million Republicans to drop dead'.

- Fear is aroused by talking about higher taxes and more hard-core criminals roaming the streets.

Media advertisements clearly rely on appealing to a variety of emotions in an attempt to get the reader or listener to buy their products. The omnipresent dandruff advertisements appeal to fear; car and airline advertisements almost inevitably have an attractive woman to appeal to the male buyer's hope for romantic or sexual gratification. Hope for some relief from the miseries of oven cleaning can make one susceptible to an advertisement for any product that promises to make life a little easier. Praise or flattery makes one feel good, and thereby receptive to the follow-up suggestion that one should buy something. Thus, depicting the progress women have made since the turn of the century, Virginia Slims advertisements proclaim, "You've come a long way, Baby!" The woman of today is supposed to feel good by this praise and smoke Virginia Slims (so that she can die of lung cancer just like men). For years Alka-Seltzer and Volkswagen advertisements relied on finding something funny that could result in the suspension of one's critical faculties and lead to the acceptance of an insufficiently supported claim. In the context of media advertisements, it is of course unlikely that any hearer fully accepts the claim that one should buy product X. The danger is that one finally accepts a limited and qualified claim like, "Well, (who knows) maybe X is worth a try." As noted in our discussion of the Fallacy of Hasty Generalization, if one is led to accept even such a limited and qualified claim, one has already committed the Fallacy of (Being Guided by) Emotional Appeals.

It would be a mistake to think that such appeals to emotions occur only in contexts of getting people to buy a product. The appeal to fear is made by 'Only an *idiot* would fail to see that C is true', and the appeal to flattery is made by 'The *intelligent* reader can now see that C is true'; both appeals can surreptitiously lead one to accept C. A well-known debating tactic is to ridicule one's opponent, and it is sad but true that this often succeeds where reason fails. It could also be conjectured that an appeal to hope may have led some people to accept certain strange religious doctrines.

Although perhaps it is not strictly an emotional appeal, we should include in this category appeals to vividness or concreteness. One or more vivid or concrete examples often prove to be far more effective in producing conviction than carefully rehearsed reasons. Nisbett and Ross cited the following example[8]:

> In his book on the press coverage of the 1972 presidential campaign, Timothy Crouse reported that, on the eve of the election, the reporters covering Senator George McGovern agreed unanimously that he could not lose the [presidential] election by more than ten points. The reporters all knew that McGovern was trailing by twenty points in all the

8. Nisbett and Ross, *Human Inference*, p. 56.

> polls and that no major poll had been wrong by more than 3 percent in twenty-four years. What information had caused these reporters to disregard both polls and the base-rate information on the accuracy of the polls? Crouse's guess—and ours—is that it was the concrete evidence of their own experience. The reporters had seen wildly enthusiastic crowds acclaiming McGovern all over the country, and they gave this vivid information . . . disproportionate weight.

We would analyze the fallacy committed by the reporters as follows:

Emotional Appeal: Appeal to vividness ⇝ McGovern will not lose by more than ten points.

- Personally seeing the cheering crowds of McGovern supporters made a vivid impression.

Virtually all emotional appeals have an appeal to vividness, and in our exercises we should identify the fallacy in terms of the more obvious emotions involved when we have such appeals to pity, fear, etc. However, there are some cases like the present one where no particular emotion is involved and the sheer vividness or concreteness of an example leads one to accept a claim connected with it.

It is of course neither desirable nor possible for us to eliminate our emotions. However, one has to be on guard so as not to let them interfere with the normal functioning of critical abilities. In particular, we should not be guided by our emotions into accepting claims as unproblematic, or less problematic than they are. If one can at least recognize the claim as problematic and in need of justifications, one has already done much to defuse the illegitimate appeal to emotions.

EXERCISES—SECTION 2.6

Unless the person or group A is specified in a problem, take A to be the speaker or hearer of the following statements. Analyze in the manner indicated in the text the most likely fallacy that is or may be committed by A.

1. You should be pleased that your girlfriend is going away for a while. As they say, absence makes the heart grow fonder.
2. [Advertisement for Mateuse Wines:] Have you ever heard of anyone who doesn't like Mateuse?
3. [Argument in the California Voter's Pamphlet for Proposition 9, which would have allowed private-school students to borrow state textbooks:] *My son is severely handicapped and neurologically impaired.* Since our local school does not have an appropriate education program for him, Sean attends [a private school]. As a concerned parent I urge you to vote "yes" on Proposition 9 so that my son and thousands like him will be able to borrow textbooks.
4. That the Creation theory is as good as the theory of Evolution has finally been established. The Arkansas legislature made it a law that the two theories must be taught as being equally plausible.
5. [KNBC TV editorial against the mandatory bottle deposit initiative in Cali-

fornia:] Every store and supermarket selling beverages will have to buy empties back, sort them all dirty, sticky, and smelly for later collection. . . . The bottle bill, we fear, is a well-intentioned mistake.

6. When the IQs of Japanese children were compared to the IQs of American and British children of similar socioeconomic backgrounds, on the average, the Japanese children scored almost ten points higher than the American and British counterparts. Now we know why Japan is doing so well: the Japanese are genetically just smarter!
7. Virtually every Japanese tourist I have seen in America walks around with a camera. The Japanese must regularly walk around with cameras whereever they are.
8. Because there are no signs of Russia's serious desire to negotiate an arms agreement, it's reasonable to think that they have no such desire.
9. Virtually every divorced couple had sex before getting married. Clearly, premarital sex is a cause of divorce.
10. [Marx and Engels in the *Communist Manifesto*:] Owing to the extensive use of machinery and to division of labor, the work of the proletarian has lost all individual character. He becomes an appendage of the machine. In proportion as the repulsiveness of the work increases, the wage decreases. No sooner is the exploitation of the laborer by the manufacturer at an end than he is set upon by the other portions of the bourgeoisie, the landlord, the shopkeeper, and pawnbroker, etc. . . . The proletarians have nothing to lose but their chains. Working men of all countries, unite [for the Communist revolution]!
11. [Student to a philosophy professor:] I don't see why you gave me a "C" for this term paper. My political science professor looked at it and said that it was an excellent philosophical paper.
12. Don't you believe all those nice tourist brochures about Turkey! Turkey is a terrible place for tourists; my sister went there and had the most awful time.
13. The average income of people with a college education is substantially higher than that of those who did not go to college. Increase your earning power by attending college!
14. [Argument against Proposition 21 from the California Voter's Pamphlet:] A similar measure, Proposition 6, was rejected [two years ago] with 61 percent of the voters against it. This reflected a well-deserved negative response.
15. [From Nisbett and Ross[9]:] The mastectomies performed on the wife of President Ford and Mrs. Rockefeller in the fall of 1974 produced a flood of visits to cancer-detection clinics by women [Group A]. Widely disseminated statistics about the lifetime risk for breast cancer (5 percent) had never produced an impact approaching that of these two highly publicized cases.
16. Fifty Nobel Laureates have come out for nuclear disarmament. Isn't it time we listened to the wise people of our age?
17. [Argument for a mandatory bottle deposit initiative (Proposition 11) in the California Voter Pamphlet:] In the long run, Proposition 11 will save consumers millions of dollars. . . . A price study shows that *average beverage prices for consumers are lower* in four of the five "bottle bill" states surveyed than in neighboring states.
18. [Husband to wife:] We can't let our kids eat just what they like. Ask anyone, and they'll tell you that children can't get a balanced diet by eating only what they like.
19. [An example drawn from Nisbett and Ross[10]:] In a psychology experiment involving a question-and-answer game, the "questioners" were told to ask challenging but not impossible questions, judge the correctness of the answers

9. Ibid.
10. Ibid., pp. 65–83.

provided by the "contestants," and provide the correct answer when the contestant's answers were wrong. A random choice determined who were to be the "questioners" and who were to be the "contestants." A third set of subjects were chosen as "observers" [Group A] and the setup of the game and the procedure for selecting "questioners" and "contestants" was carefully explained to them. Again and again the questioners displayed esoteric knowledge in providing answers to questions the contestants could not answer. When the observers [Group A] were asked to rate the level of general knowledge possessed by the questioners and the contestants, they rated the questioners almost twice as knowledgeable as the contestants.

20. No news is good news. (Do not treat this as an *Argumentum ad Populum.*)

SUMMARY OF SECTIONS 2.2–2.5

TABLE 2.6 Candidates and Reliability Grades

Type	*Content*	*Access* [a,b]	*Reliability Grade "A"* [c,d]
OB	What was observed	Direct: Observer at the time of observation. Transmitted: Appropriate initiation and transmission of a direct observation is presumable.	Completely corroborated identity claim *or* directly given and central
PF	Uncontroversial particular facts	Direct: Made available by an expert source at the time of accepting the claim. Transmitted: Appropriate initiation and transmission of direct expert testimony is presumable.	Completely corroborated identity claim *or* directly given by scientific source
INT	Reflection alone shows it must be true	Content is easily ascertained at the time of accepting the claim.	Devoid of all uncertainty *and* central
SM	General laws of science and mathematics	Direct: Made available by an expert source at the time of accepting the claim. Transmitted: Appropriate initiation and transmission of direct expert testimony is presumable.	Directly given by a scientific source
CS	Personally confirmed, generally acknowledged, undisconfirmed generalization of common sense	With the help of memory, "content" is ascertained at the time of accepting the claim.	*None*

[a]Appropriate initiation is presumable: Transmission is entirely by one's own memory from observation or expert source, *or* it is accompanied by such an originating source, *or* one can presume that an equally good originating source is readily available.

[b]Appropriate transmission is presumable: One can presume that the transmission is by an expert transmitting source, *or* that the claim is recently acquired, memorable, or corroborated for each transmitting link.

[c]C is a completely corroborated identity claim = C asserts of some A and B that A and B are exactly the same person or thing, C is remembered to be generally acknowledged and undisputed, and C can be presumed to be based on a significant number of direct observations.

[d]C is central = The rejection of C would force the rejection of a host of other candidates.

TABLE 2.6 Candidates and Reliability Grades (*continued*)

Reliability Grade "B": A candidate that is neither an "A" nor a "C" grade candidate.

Reliability Grade "C": Specific reasons bring about one or more of the following doubts (and if doubts of types 5 and 6 completely undermine the presumption, the claim ceases being a candidate altogether):

(1) Circumstance of using an involved faculty has a significant chance of error.
(2) An involved faculty or source has a record of unreliability.
(3) A transmission is undermined by direct access to (something as good as) the original source.
(4) Testifier may well have a motive that would cast doubt on the impartiality of the testimony.
(5) Presumed expertise of an expert is dubious for an alleged claim of "expert" testimony.
(6) Presumption of appropriate initiation or transmission is dubious.

TABLE 2.7. Format for Determining the Unproblematic, Along with Possible Answers for Each Column

Claim	*Cand.?*	*Reliability Grade*	*Member of RCC S1* [a]	*OK or Reason for Elimination*[b]
Claim number	No	A	Y	Reason for noncandidacy
	T- or D-	B	Blank	Reason for "C" grade
	OB	C		Least preferred member of S1
	PF	Blank		Member of eliminated class S1
	SM			Close relative of member eliminated by conflict
	INT			
	CS			OK

[a]Form as many columns as there are relevant conflicting classes and for any virtually conflicting class, add comment indicating why it is virtually conflicting.

[b]Unless the reason given on the format is obvious, add comments below to explain the reason.

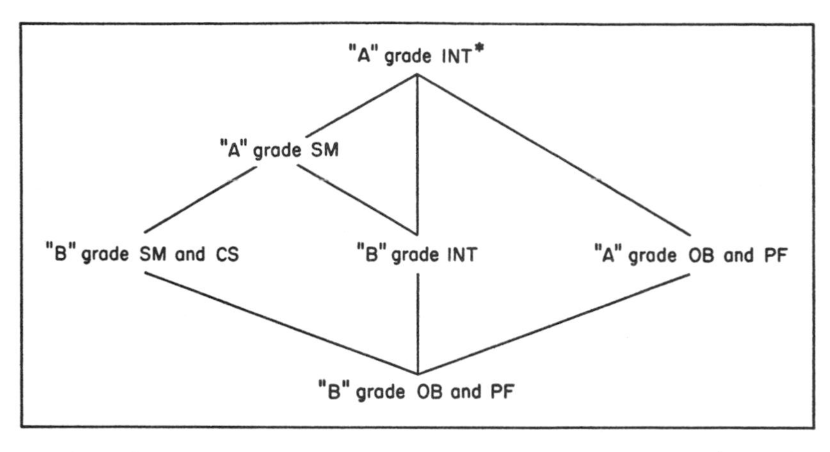

Figure 2.4. Preference rankings. Asterisk indicates unless explicitly denied by a grade "A" SM candidate.

Figure 2.5. Flowchart for selecting the unproblematic.

S conflicts = S strictly conflicts (it's impossible for all members of S to be true) **or** S virtually conflicts (contains 'X is virtually exceptionless' and replacing this by X would make S strictly conflicting).

C* is a near relative of eliminated C = C* and C have the same basis, C* is no more preferred than C, C was eliminated due to a conflict with some X, and X would cast doubt on both C and C* if X were true.

If C belongs to two conflicting subclasses S1 and S2, treat S1 and S2 separately, and eliminate C from the final residue if C was eliminated from either S1 or S2.

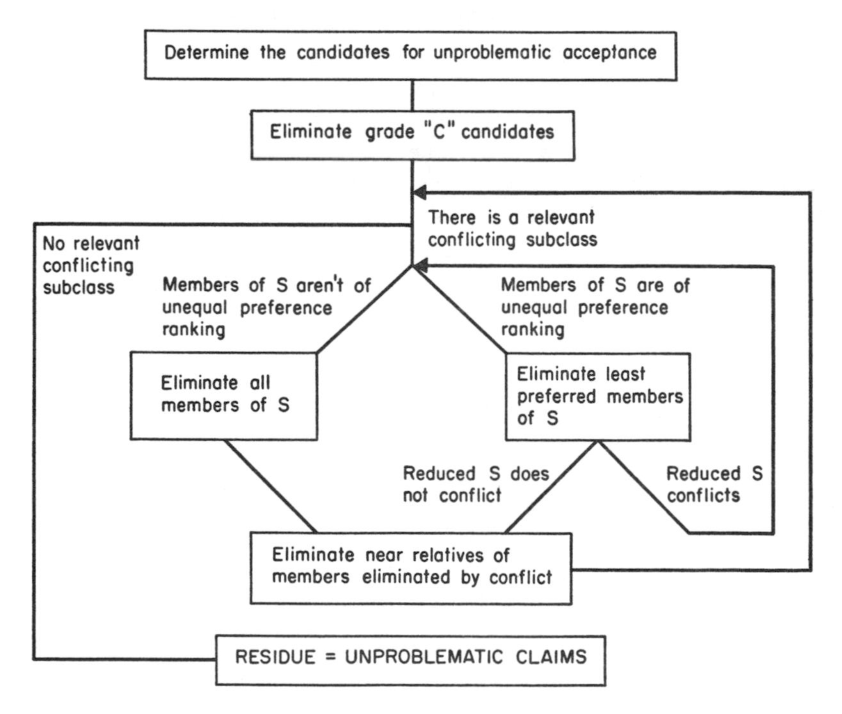

3

Deductive Reasoning

In Chapter 1 we saw that the activity of truth assessments has two major dimensions: (1) isolating and gathering a stock of things that may be accepted as unproblematic, and (2) reasoning from these unproblematic claims to the truth or falsity of the problematic claims that we wish to assess. Insofar as critical thinking was taken as the art of making truth assessments according to general principles or maxims, we seek principles or rules to guide us in (1) and (2). In giving us maxims for isolating the unproblematic, Chapter 2 gave us half of what we wanted. What we now need is a set of rules that will give us a standard of good reasoning, and this is the topic to which we now turn. Because the rules for good reasoning and the maxims for isolating the unproblematic are very different kinds of rules, the reader will rightly sense that there has been a sudden change of topics between Chapters 2 and 3. While the need to shift gears for a while is unavoidable, it should be plausible that if the materials from Chapters 2 and 3 are combined, we shall have a set of rules that can guide us in making truth assessments. Such is indeed the case, and Chapters 4 and 5 will be the "payoff" chapters: in those chapters the discussions from Chapters 2 and 3 will merge to give us methods for assessing truth claims that have a wide range of applications.

The concern of this chapter is actually a bit more limited than that of specifying a standard of good reasoning in general. This chapter is concerned with the standards of reasoning called *deductive* reasoning. We concentrate on deductive reasoning in part because it is the one type of reasoning for which systematic rules have been developed. Beyond this, as we shall see in Chapters 4 and 5, knowledge of deductive relations allows us to develop standards for other types of reasoning. Thus, the material covered in this chapter forms an essential tool for developing general standards of good reasoning, and this in turn will allow us to develop the promised methods for assessing truth claims.

3.1 Preliminaries

While a more complete discussion of reasoning will be postponed to Chapter 4, in order to get into our topic of deductive reasoning, we must say a few preliminary things about reasons in general. When we say that A is a reason for B, or again, when we say that we are reasoning from A to B, we shall require that A and B be things that can be true or false. For our purposes, we shall take statements to be the things that can be true or false. Of course beliefs can also be true or false, and one often speaks of one belief being one's basis, reason, or ground for another belief. However, we may say a belief is true just in case the statement expressing the belief is true, and one belief is a ground for another just in case (relative to the person involved) the statement expressing the first belief is a ground or reason for the statement expressing the second belief. Thus, talk of a belief being true or being a reason can be represented in terms of a statement being true or being a reason (for the person involved). From now on we shall therefore talk primarily in terms of statements and this will largely supplant the talk of claims we have used up to now. Correspondingly, we shall often use quoted lower case roman letters like 'p' to stand for statements.

Given that P and Q are to be understood as statements, when is P a good reason for Q? Suppose a man says, "Because he is ill, he will not attend the philosophy lecture tonight." Clearly, the statement 'He is ill' is being suggested as a reason for the statement 'He won't come', and for us to accept the former as a reason for the latter, two things must obtain: (1) 'He is ill' must be true. If he isn't ill, we have been given no reasons for thinking that he won't attend. (2) There must be some sort of an evidential or ground-to-consequence relation between his illness and his absence. This can be seen by altering the example to 'Since he likes milk, he won't attend the philosophy lecture tonight'. Even if it is true that he likes milk, we feel that no reason has been given for thinking that he won't attend the lecture. On the other hand, even if it is false that he is ill, there is some sort of a ground-to-consequence relation between 'He is ill' and 'He won't attend'. Because it is so important to separate these two features of good reasons, we shall introduce the expressions 'true reason' and 'supporting reason' to mark the distinction between (1) and (2):

> (1) P is a TRUE REASON for Q just in case P is true.
> (2) P is a SUPPORTING REASON for Q just in case, whether or not one accepts P, if one is or were justified in believing P to be true, one would thereby be justified (to some degree) in believing Q to be true.

In assessing the truth of reasons, our earlier discussion of unproblematic claims as well as our discussion of analyzing arguments in Chapter 4 should be helpful. Our concern in this chapter is what makes something a supporting reason. In fact, we shall be concerned with only one kind of supporting reason, namely, the kind that is called valid or deductively valid reasons.

In order to explain the last statement, consider the following two examples:

(1) (a) He shot a bazooka point blank at the president.
    (b) The president is dead.

(2) (a) She married him and if she married him, his dream came true.
    (b) His dream came true.

Clearly the truth of (1)(a) is a compelling reason for the truth of (1)(b) today, and the same can be said of (2)(a) and (2)(b). However, there is a difference. In the future we might be able to develop some kind of electromagnetic field to surround the president's body so that any fast-moving metallic object approaching would "bounce off" this field, leaving the president unharmed. Under those circumstances, the truth of (1)(a) cannot be expected to be attended by the truth of (1)(b), and to this extent being justified in (1)(a) would not justify one in believing (1)(b). The situation with (2) is different. There is absolutely no conceivable or imaginable circumstance in which (2)(a) could be true and (2)(b) false. Of course his dream may not come true either because the marriage didn't occur or because the marriage turned into a nightmare; but in the former case 'She married him' is false and in the latter case 'If she married him, his dream came true' is false. No imaginable or conceivable development in psychology or sociology is going to make (2)(a) true and (2)(b) false. In short, the truth of (2)(a) absolutely guarantees the truth of (2)(b), and in any imaginable or conceivable circumstance, if one were justified in believing (2)(a), one would also be justified in believing (2)(b). That is, in any conceivable circumstance (2)(a) gives conclusive support for (2)(b) while this is not the case for the support of (1)(b) by (1)(a).

We shall introduce the expression *deductively valid reason,* or *valid reason* for short, to cover reasons like the one in (2). While various definitions can be given for deductively valid reasons, for our purposes, the following one is perhaps the most relevant:

> P is a DEDUCTIVELY VALID REASON for Q =
>
> There is no conceivable, imaginable, or possible world in which P is true and Q is false.

Thus, if a person reasons from A to B and A is a valid reason for B, it is impossible for the person to be led from truth to falsity. Clearly, this is a desirable feature for a supporting reason to have, and our present concern is with reasons of this type.[1]

There is one more preliminary topic requiring examination. When P is a valid reason for Q, P is typically a long statement of a form like 'q *and* r *and* s'. An example might be: 'He is going to Los Angeles or to San Francisco *and* if he goes to Los Angeles, he will see Maggie *and* if he goes to San Francisco, he will see Cecelia' is a valid reason for 'He will see Maggie or Cecelia'. When reasons become this long, it is convenient to break them up into parts. Thus, from now on we shall represent example (2) and our current example as follows:

(a) (1) She marries him.
(2) If she marries him, his dream comes true.
(3) His dream comes true.

(b) (1) He is going to Los Angeles or San Francisco.
(2) If he goes to Los Angeles, he will see Maggie.
(3) If he goes to San Francisco, he will see Cecelia.
(4) He will see Maggie or Cecelia.

Structures like (a) and (b) will be called ARGUMENTS, any statement above the line will be called a PREMISE, and the statement below the line will be called the CONCLUSION. The line itself means "therefore." We shall say an argument is a DEDUCTIVELY VALID (or simply VALID) ARGUMENT just in case: There is no imaginable, conceivable, or possible world in which *all* premises are true and yet the conclusion is false. Another way of saying the same thing is: Any imaginable, conceivable, or possible world in which the conclusion is false is a world in which *at least one* of the premises is false. Given a number of statements 'p_1', 'p_2', . . . , and 'p_n', their *conjunction* is the long statement that strings them together by putting 'and' between them—that is, the statement 'p_1 and p_2 and . . . p_n'. Clearly, an argument is deductively valid if and only if the conjunction of the premises is a deductively valid reason for the conclusion. Because it is considerably easier to work with arguments rather than with long reasons, we shall focus on arguments. The relation just stated will allow us to "translate" our results back into the jargon of reasons when the need arises.

Let us conclude our preliminary discussion of arguments with two final remarks: (i) It should be clear that the order of the premises is immaterial. We shall hence consider 'p_1, p_2 / q' to be the same argument as 'p_2, p_1 / q'. [In this horizontal notation, '/' is the same as the bar or line (meaning "therefore") in (a) and (b), and the premises are separated by commas.] Of course, switching a premise around with a conclusion results in a dif-

1. To be strictly correct we should say: P is a *deductively valid reason* for Q just in case, because of the forms of the statements involved, there is no conceivable, imaginable, or possible world in which P is true and Q is false. At this point this complication is more liable to be confusing than helpful, and we shall return to it in Section 3.2.

ferent argument; for examples, 'p_1, p_2 / q' is a different argument from 'p_1, q / p_2'. (ii) Standard terminology has it that an argument is *sound* if it is valid *and* all of its premises are true. Clearly, if we have a sound argument, the conjunction of the premises gives us an exceptionally good reason for the conclusion—that is, a reason that is true and is guaranteed to make its conclusion true.

EXERCISES—SECTION 3.1

In the following examples, assume that each alleged reason is a supporting reason. ('The president' refers to the president of the United States.) For each example, (i) determine whether the reason is a true reason; (ii) determine whether the reason is a valid reason; (iii) represent the reason and the conclusion in argument form; and (iv) determine whether the resulting argument is a sound argument.

1. 'The president jumped off the Empire State Building' is a reason for 'The president is dead or was very badly injured'.
2. 'The president is the commander-in-chief, and if the president is the commander-in-chief, the armed forces are led by a civilian' is a reason for 'The armed forces are led by a civilian'.
3. 'The president was elected, and if the president was elected, the president won his last election' is a reason for 'The president got more votes than his opponents in the last election'.
4. 'The president didn't hold his news conference standing on his head and either he held his news conference standing on his head or sitting in a hanging basket' is a reason for 'The president held his news conference sitting in a hanging basket'.

3.2 Deductive Validity: A General Informal Account

We said that an argument is valid if and only if in no possible world are all the premises true and the conclusion false. To be absolutely clear on this, we can list four possible situations that could obtain:

(1) All the premises are TRUE	and	the conclusion is TRUE.
(2) All the premises are TRUE	and	the conclusion is FALSE.
(3) At least one of the premises is FALSE	and	the conclusion is TRUE.
(4) At least one of the premises is FALSE	and	the conclusion is FALSE.

The deductive validity of an argument precludes possibility (2), but nothing else. Thus, a valid argument could be such that (1), (3), or (4) obtain. An example of a valid argument where possibility (3) obtains is:

All bachelors are women.
All women are unmarried.
___
All bachelors are unmarried.

That this is a valid argument really shouldn't be surprising. It is no more surprising than that a true belief by luck or happenstance could be based on faulty beliefs. Put in a nutshell, if you start with true premises and the argument is valid, you are bound to arrive at a true conclusion; but if a valid argument contains even one false premise, there is no telling what the truth value of the conclusion will be.

If an argument is deductively invalid, even possibility (2) isn't ruled out, and any combination of truth values may exist between the premises and the conclusion. One must not think that if the premises are all true and the argument is deductively invalid, the conclusion must be false. 'Kangaroos have long necks, Boars have short necks / Dauer teaches' is a deductively invalid argument whose premises and conclusion are all true.

The three positive relations between truth and deductive validity are:

(a) If the premises are all true and the argument is deductively valid, the conclusion must be true.
(b) If the argument is deductively valid and the conclusion is false, at least one of the premises must be false.
(c) If the premises are all true and the conclusion is false, the argument is deductively invalid.

Each of these relations has a function. Relation (a) allows you to have conclusive reasons for the conclusion and provides a means of assessing statements to be true on the basis of what you take to be unproblematic, or at least are willing to grant for the sake of the argument. Relation (b) allows you to have conclusive reasons for the falsity of *at least one* of the premises. This allows you to have conclusive reasons for the falsity of a claim or assumption *if* the truth of all the other premises and the falsity of the conclusion are unproblematic for you. Relation (c) allows you to determine that the argument is not deductively valid, in other words, that the argument is invalid. Although we shall have more to say on this topic in Chapter 4, relations (a) and (b) should give the reader some idea of why it may be helpful to know the deductive validity of arguments.

We said that an argument is valid if and only if the conclusion is true in every possible or imaginable world in which all the premises are true. Consider, then, the following valid argument:

[A] (1) If Dauer has been twice divorced, then Dauer is unhappy.
(2) Dauer has been twice divorced.
___
(3) Dauer is unhappy.

Argument [A] is constructed out of the following component sentences:

(i) Dauer has been twice divorced.
(ii) Dauer is unhappy.

Most readers presumably do not know whether or not (i) and (ii) are true (i.e., true in the possible world, which is the actual one), and hence do not know the (actual) truth values of [A](1)–[A](3). Yet most readers should be able to recognize [A] to be deductively valid. But if one doesn't know the truth values of [A](1)–[A](3) in the possible world, which is the actual one, how could one know that in *no* possible world is [A](3) false while [A](1) and [A](2) are true? Evidently, there must be some way.

Because knowledge of (i) and (ii) must turn out to be irrelevant to determining the deductive validity of [A], let us replace (i) and (ii) by blanks and see what remains:

[B] (1) If ▭, then ⬭.
(2) ▭.
―――――――――――――――
(3) ⬭.

Somehow this configuration must allow us to determine that in any possible world if all the premises are true, so is the conclusion. And this is surely the case. In any possible world where all the premises are true, [B](2) must come out true; that is, the rectangle must be filled by a statement that is true in that possible world. But then for [B](1) to come out true in that world, the oval must also be filled by something that is true in that possible world. This, however, has the consequence that [B](3) has gotten filled by something that is true in that possible world. Thus, in no possible world can the blanks of [B] be so filled that [B](1) and [B](2) both come out true while [B](3) come out false. Because [A] is one way of filling the blanks of [B], this rules out a possible world where the conclusion of [A] is false while its premises are true. The point that is now clearly suggested is this: The deductive validity of [A] is due to the configuration [B], which we shall call the LOGICAL FORM of [A].

Can we say that an argument is always deductively valid in virtue of its logical form? Strictly speaking, we can have an argument such that in no possible world is its conclusion false while its premises are true, where this crucial feature of the argument is not due to its logical form.[2] How-

2. Two kinds of cases might be listed under this heading: (i) Arguments that involve synonymous expressions. Thus, there is no possible world where the premise is true and the conclusion false in 'He is a bachelor / He is unmarried'. (ii) Arguments that involve what have come to be called *de re* necessities. Some philosophers have claimed that although it is not part of the meaning of 'gold' that it has atomic number 59, nevertheless, in no possible

ever, it is standard procedure to *define* or limit deductive validity to arguments having this crucial feature in virtue of their logical form. We shall follow this procedure and take our "official definition" of deductive validity to be given by:

> An argument is *deductively valid* =
>
> a logical form of the argument is such that in every possible world, regardless of how the blanks are filled, if all the premises come out true in that world, so does the conclusion.

Under certain plausible assumptions, the reference to possible worlds can be eliminated and deductive validity can be simply defined as: the logical form of the argument is such that, regardless of how the blanks are filled, if all the premises come out true (in the actual world), so does the conclusion. Those who find talk of possible worlds objectionably vague may adopt this definition instead of our "official" definition.

Because the notion of logical form looms large in our discussion of validity, let us look at that idea a little more closely. By logical form we shall mean expressions like [B](1), [B](2), and B[3] as well as whole configurations like [B]. Expressions like [B](1), [B](2), and [B](3) will also be called STATEMENT FORMS, while whole configurations like [B] will often be called ARGUMENT FORMS; thus, an argument form is a number of statement forms followed by a "therefore" line and one more statement form. Whether they are statement forms or argument forms, logical forms clearly have two features: (i) the blanks and (ii) the words that remain. The words that remain will be called LOGICAL PARTICLES or CONSTANTS. They are expressions like 'if . . . , then', 'not', 'and', 'or', 'some', and 'all'. To formulate the logical forms of arguments, it is generally necessary to rely on intuition about what sounds like a logical particle. A rough guide would be that logical constants or particles are words that don't pick out particular features of the actual world like 'being a bachelor', 'wearing a polka dot tie', and 'slurping wonton soup'.

As for the blanks, in going from an actual argument like [A] to a logical form like [B], (a) *all occurrences of the same sentence* (e.g., 'Dauer has been twice divorced') *must be replaced by the same kind of blank* (a rectangle in our example), and (b) *different sentences* (e.g., 'Dauer has been twice divorced' and 'Dauer is unhappy') *must be replaced by different kinds of blanks* (a rectangle and an oval in our example). Failure to abide

---

world could gold fail to have atomic number 59. If this is correct, there is no possible world where the premise is true and the conclusion false in 'This is gold / This has atomic number 59'.

by restrictions (a) and (b) will result in destroying the logical form of the argument. The form of the argument [A] is *not:*

(1) If ▭, then ▭.
(2) ⬭.
(3) ⬭.

In premise (1), both 'Dauer has been twice divorced' and 'Dauer is unhappy' were replaced by the same blank in violation of (b), and in premises (1) and (2) different occurrences of the same sentence 'Dauer has been twice divorced' were replaced by different kinds of blanks in violation of (a), and (a) is again violated in (1) and (3).

In going from a logical form like [B] to an actual argument like [A], which is an instance of that form, (a) *all occurrences of the same blank must be filled by the same expression (although it is not required that different kinds of blanks be filled by different expressions),* and (b) what replaces the blanks must be an expression of an appropriate grammatical type. Restriction (a) should be reasonably clear.[3] As for (b), it is clearly satisfied in [B] by replacing the blanks by declarative sentences. But faced with 'All ▭ are ⬭', the '▭' must be filled by a general noun phrase like 'men' and 'people who eat artichokes', and '⬭' must be filled by a general noun phrase like 'bassoon player' or by a predicate like 'mortal'.

In general, as one expands the list of logical particles to be displayed, one will be displaying more of the logical form of the argument. This increases the possibility of determining the deductive validity of the argument; however, the general procedure for showing deductive validity becomes increasingly complex as one adds to the list of logical particles. Once we realize that an argument can have a coarser and a finer structure, two things must be kept in mind: (I) If one displays less of the logical form of the argument than one could (i.e., by not displaying all the logical particles) and the argument is shown to be deductively valid, the argument *is* deductively valid. (II) If one displays less of the logical form of the argument than one could and one has filled the blanks so that all the premises come out true and the conclusion false, it does *not* follow that the argument is deductively invalid. To simplify our discussion, let us extend the notion of validity to *argument forms,* so that an argument form is valid just in case in no possible world can the blanks be so filled

3. A potentially confusing point is that different types of blanks may be filled by the same sentence. This means that

If Dauer has been twice divorced, then Dauer has been twice divorced.
Dauer has been twice divorced.
____
Dauer has been twice divorced.

is an instance of the logical form [B]. Yet, unless one violates a restriction, one can never get from this argument to [B] as one of its logical forms. This means: 'X is a logical form of the argument Y' and 'the argument Y is an instance of the logical form X' have *slightly* different meanings.

that the premises come out true and the conclusion false. (I) and (II) may then be stated as:

> (I) If a coarse form of an argument is valid, the argument is valid regardless of the finer forms it may have.
> (II) An argument may be valid even if a coarse form of the argument is invalid.

To see (I), consider:

[C] (1) If all men are rational, then some men are rational.
(2) All men are rational.
―――――――――――――――
(3) Some men are rational.

[B] is a coarse form of [C]. A more detailed logical form of [C] is given by:

[B*] (1) If all □ are ⬭, then some □ are ⬭.
(2) All □ are ⬭.
―――――――――――――――
(3) Some □ are ⬭.

The validity of the coarse form [B] guarantees the validity of [B*]: For any possible world, any way of filling the blanks of the detailed form [B*] will in effect be a way of filling the blanks of [B] in that possible world. For example, whatever the possible world may be, filling '□' by 'cats' and '⬭' by 'fish eater' in [B*] has the same effect as filling '▭' by 'all cats are fish eaters' and '⬭' by 'some cats are fish eaters' in [B]. Hence, any way of filling the blanks of [B*] in a possible world will in effect already have been considered in determining the validity of the form [B]. Statement (I) should now be obvious.

To see (II) above, consider:

[D] (1) If Dauer teaches logic, then all men are in bad shape.
(2) Some men aren't in bad shape.
―――――――――――――――
(3) Dauer doesn't teach logic (i.e., it is not the case that Dauer teaches logic).

A logical form of [D] is:

[E] (1) If ▭, then ⬭.
(2) ⬚.
―――――――――――――――
(3) It is not the case that ▭.

The invalidity of [E] is shown by:

(1) If [3 > 2], then $3 + 1 > 2 + 1$
(2) [2×2 = 4].
―――――――――――――――
(3) It is not the case that [3 > 2].

This, however, does not show [D] to be a deductively invalid argument, because the finer logical form of [D] is

[F] (1) If ▭▭▭, then all ▭ are ⬭.
(2) Some ▭ are not ▭.

---

(3) It is not the case that ▭▭▭.

and [F] is a valid argument form. To see this, consider any possible world. The only way to fill the blanks so that the conclusion is false requires filling '▭▭▭' by a true statement (in that world). But then to make (1) true, '▭' and '⬭' must be filled by 'X' and 'Y' so that all the X's are included among the Y's (in that world); otherwise, 'All X's are Y's' wouldn't come out true. (For example, 'All men are mortal' is true in our world just because all men are included among the mortals in our world.) Yet, if all the X's are included among the Y's, 'Some X are not Y' would come out false in that world; that is, the blanks of (2) wouldn't have been filled so that it comes out true in that world. Hence, in no possible world can the blanks of [F] be filled so that the premises are all true and the conclusion false. This shows that if we exhibit enough of the particles of [D], as we did in [F], we arrive at a logical form of [D] that is valid. Hence, because [E] is invalid, it doesn't follow that [D] is invalid. In short, an argument is valid as long as *at least one* of its logical forms is valid, and this is what our definition stated.

At this point, it is evident that at least in some cases, one might be able to argue for the deductive validity of an argument. That is, extract the logical form of the argument, and argue, as we have in a couple of examples, that in no possible world is there a way of filling the blanks so that the premises all come out true and conclusion false. Perhaps one more example could be given. Consider:

(1) All men are mortal.
(2) Plato is a man.

---

(3) Something is mortal.

Extracting the form of the argument, we have:

(1) All ▭ s are ⬭.
(2) ○ is a ▭.

---

(3)
Something is ⬭.

This argument form can be shown to be deductively valid by considering any possible world (except the empty world of no objects that is normally considered irrelevant for deductive validity). For (1) to come out true, '▭' and '⬭' must be filled by 'X' and 'Y' so that all the X's (if there are any) are included among the Y's in that possible world. (It should be noted that this is still compatible with there being no Y's or the class of Y's being empty in that possible world). For (2) to come out true, '○' must be filled by a name "n" so that "n" names some object n in that world; furthermore, n must be among the X's. But then, because all X's are among Y's, n must be among the Y's, and we are assured that there is at least one Y, namely, n. But this is sufficient to guarantee the truth of the conclusion that has by now gotten filled as 'Something is a Y'; that is, Y's exist in that possible world (or the class of things that are Y in that possible world is not empty). Thus, in any (nonempty) possible world, it is impossible to fill the blanks so that the premises come out true and the conclusion false, and we have shown that the argument as well as the argument form are deductively valid.

This is not a terribly practical way of showing the deductive validity of arguments, and we shall shortly introduce more practical ways. However, these more practical ways are not general; for example, they can't show the deductive validity of arguments that crucially depend on the use of 'all' and 'some'. Furthermore, the more practical way involves learning a system that might be forgotten once the reader is finished with the present course of study. *The method of extracting the logical form and arguing as we have is the most practical* **nontechnical** *way of showing arguments to be deductively valid;* it may be hoped that this will be remembered even after the methods soon to be introduced are long forgotten.

Our discussion also provides a fairly practical nontechnical way of showing arguments to be deductively invalid. In light of statement (II) above, we cannot show an argument to be deductively invalid unless we have the finest logical form of the argument on which its validity may depend. However, in practice we can often extract a logical form that exhibits *all* the particles that can plausibly be claimed to be the relevant logical particles. Although in the end one has to rely on one's nose, in most ordinary cases we have such a form if all occurrences of 'all', 'no', 'some', 'are', 'not', 'if . . . , then', 'and', 'or', and their variants are displayed as logical particles. *If we find the finest relevant form of this kind and find a clear way of filling the blanks so that all the premises come out true and the conclusion false in a possible world, we can declare the argument to be invalid* without worrying about statement (II). Because it may always be a bit unclear what is or isn't true in nonactual possible worlds, in using this method *always use the possible world that is our actual world* and fill the blanks so that the resulting statements are *clearly true or false.*

As an example, consider:

[G] (1) If the Arabs refused to sell oil to Holland, then Holland faces economic difficulties.
(2) Holland faces economic difficulties.
―――――――――――――――
(3) The Arabs refused to sell oil to Holland.

The logical form that displays all the plausibly relevant particles is:

[H] (1) If ▭, then ⬭.
(2) ⬭.
―――――――――――――――
(3) ▭ .

But [H] is an invalid form as is shown by:

[J] (1) If Caesar was guillotined, then Caesar is dead.
(2) Caesar is dead.

---

(3) Caesar was guillotined.

Because [J](1) and [J](2) are true while [J](3) is false (with reference to the actual world), [G] is shown to be deductively invalid by [J]. In this case, [J] (in connection with the actual world) is called a COUNTEREXAMPLE to the form of argument used by [G].

This way of showing an argument to be invalid by a counterexample has the following structure: [G] is a bad argument because [G] is like (or analogous to) [J] and [J] is a patently bad argument. Thus, if [G] is proposed as a valid argument, one can refute the proposal by saying: "You might as well say: Caesar was guillotined because if he was guillotined, he is dead, and he is (in fact) dead." When deductive validity is at stake, the only sense in which the two arguments [G] and [J] need to be similar is that they share the same relevant logical form [H]. However, this general method of arguing by counterexamples can be extended to informal contexts in which deductive validity is not directly at stake. *If someone proposes a suspect argument, the strategy is to present a similar argument that has true or acceptable premises and a false or unacceptable conclusion. This casts doubt on the proposed argument, and at the minimum the burden shifts back to the other person, who is now obliged to show why the apparent similarity or analogy is not genuine.* Thus, suppose someone says: "Because people spend only 5 percent of their time in parks, it is time to stop building parks." One response could be: "You might as well say: because people spend only 5 percent of their time in bathrooms, it is time to stop building bathrooms." The opponent is now obliged to point out a significant difference between parks and bathrooms. If he points out that parks aren't necessary to prevent health hazards, that is a new argument that will have to be considered; but it has been shown that 5 percent usage is not by itself a sufficient reason to stop building parks. Refuting or casting doubt on an argument by a counterexample is a powerful and often useful way of examining the legitimacy of arguments that are proposed in everyday life.

EXERCISES—SECTION 3.2

1. Letting the logical constants be limited to 'if . . . , then', 'it is not the case that', 'and', and 'or', determine the logical forms of the following statements using rectangles, ovals, etc.
   (a) It is not the case that Jackie is a popular idol.
   (b) Bob is tired of studying and Barbara is tired of studying.

(c) The president is senile or the president is lying.
(d) If she is ill or she is feeling lazy, then she will stay home.
(e) If Oscar is at home or Mary is at home, then Oscar is at home.
(f) If it is not the case that Mary is happy, then Mary will divorce her husband.
(g) It will rain tomorrow or it is not the case that it will rain tomorrow.
(h) If Jane is smart and it is not the case that Jane will marry a foolish man, then it is not the case that Jane will marry Tom.

2. For this problem, assume that the following argument forms are deductively valid:

[A] If □, then ⬭.
It is not the case that ⬭.
____
It is not the case that □.

[B] If □, then ⬭.
If ⬭, then ⬭.
____
If □, then ⬭.

Furthermore, in addition to the obvious truths you are aware of, assume that the following statements are true:

(i) If Jane lives in Texas, then Jane knows some oilmen.
(ii) Jane lives in Texas.
(iii) Jane doesn't know any Arabs.
(iv) If Jane has some mad lovers, then Jane knows some Arabs.

In each of the following examples, use one of the relations (a)–(c) that are boxed near the beginning of Section 3.2 to determine a statement to be true or false or to determine the argument to be deductively invalid.

[a] (1) If Jane lives in Texas, then Jane knows some oilmen.
(2) If Jane knows some oilmen, then Jane knows some Arabs.
____
(3) If Jane lives in Texas, then Jane knows some Arabs.

[b] (1) If Jane has some mad lovers, then Jane knows some Arabs.
(2) It is not the case that Jane knows some Arabs.
____
(3) It is not the case that Jane has some mad lovers.

[c] (1) If the French president is Belgium's head of state, then the French president is a European head of state.
(2) It is not the case that the French president is Belgium's head of state.
____
(3) It is not the case that the French president is a European head of state.

[d] (1) If Jane has some mad lovers, then Jane knows some Arabs.
(2) If Jane knows some Arabs, then Jane knows some non-Anglos.
____
(3) If Jane has some mad lovers, then Jane knows some non-Anglos.

[e] (1) If the French president is Belgium's head of state, then the French president is a European head of state.
(2) The French president is a European head of state.
____
(3) The French president is Belgium's head of state.

[f] (1) If the French president is a European head of state, the French president is Belgium's head of state.
(2) It is not the case that the French president is Belgium's head of state.
____
(3) It is not the case that the French president is a European head of state.

3. (a) Letting the logical constants be limited to 'if . . . , then', 'it is not the case that', 'and', and 'or', determine the logical forms of the following statements using rectangles, ovals, etc.
   (1) If some Italians are handsome, then some Italians are loved.
   (2) If some Italians are handsome, then some Germans are loved.
   (3) If no pig is a bird, then no bird is a pig.
   (4) If all pigs are animals, then all animals are pigs.
   (5) All Princeton students are rich or some Princeton students are not rich.
   (6) All UCLA students are beachgoers or all UCLA students are bookworms.
   (7) If all Berkeley students are smart and some smart persons are conservative, then some Berkeley students are conservative.
   (8) If every woman is a feminist and Jane is a woman, then Jane is a feminist.

   (b) Redo part (a) by augmenting the list of logical constants to include 'all', 'every', 'some', 'no', 'are', 'is a', and 'not'.

4. For each of the following, (i) extract an appropriate argument form and show the argument to be valid, *or* (ii) extract the appropriate argument form and show the argument to be invalid. [*Hint:* If you are in the dark as to whether it's valid or not, try doing (ii), and if you have no luck doing so, try doing (i), or vice versa.]

   [a] (1) If he is stupid, then it is not the case that he got elected.
   (2) He got elected.
   ---
   (3) It is not the case that he is stupid.

   [b] (1) If he lost his girlfriend, he is devastated.
   (2) He is devastated.
   ---
   (3) He lost his girlfriend.

   [c] (1) He had bad intentions or he is dumb.
   (2) It is not the case that he is dumb.
   ---
   (3) He had bad intentions.

   [d] (1) If she was a flower child, it is not the case that she avoided the drug scene.
   (2) It is not the case that she avoided the drug scene.
   ---
   (3) She was a flower child.

   [e] (1) If he is dead, his will was read.
   ---
   (2) If his will was read, he is dead.

   [f] (1) He went to Reno or he went to Las Vegas.
   (2) If he went to Reno, he lost money.
   (3) If he went to Las Vegas, he lost money.
   ---
   (4) He lost money.

   [g] (1) If Tom went to Rome, then Tom went to Italy.
   (2) Tom went to Italy or Tom went to Spain.
   ---
   (3) Tom went to Rome or Tom went to Spain.

5. Show the following arguments to be deductively valid. (*Hint:* 'Some X's are Y's' is true just in case there is at least one object that belongs both to the class of X's and the class of Y's. 'No X's are Y's' is true just in case no object belongs both to the class of X's and the class of Y's.)

[a] (1) All women are fighting for women's rights.
(2) Some women are mothers.
―――
(3) Some mothers are fighting for women's rights.

[b] (1) Tom is stupid and Tom is a man.
―――
(2) Some men are stupid.

[c] (1) All persons who marry Dartmouth men are persons who marry animals.
(2) No women are persons who marry animals.
―――
(3) No women are persons who marry Dartmouth men.

6. Show each of the following arguments to be deductively invalid.

[a] (1) All men are mortal beings.
(2) Some mortal beings are intelligent.
―――
(3) Some men are intelligent.

[b] (1) No husbands are bachelors.
(2) All bachelors are men.
―――
(3) Some husbands are men.

[c] (1) Some men are nurses or some nurses are men.
(2) Some nurses are not men.
―――
(3) Some men are not nurses.

7. Following the suggestion at the end of Section 3.2, informally criticize the following arguments by counterexamples:

[a] The time has come to change the government; four years of the present government is enough!
[b] Stop gun control; guns don't kill people, people [who use guns] do.
[c] Because efforts to eradicate prostitution have failed, we might as well legalize it.
[d] He must be a Communist because so many of his friends are Communists.
[e] I deserve a good grade because I put a lot of effort into this course.

3.3 Truth Functional Logical Forms

In Section 3.2 we saw that a finer or a coarser logical form can be assigned to an argument depending on how many of the terms are construed as logical particles to be displayed in the logical form. In this section we shall present a batch of terms to be treated as logical particles, and the resulting logical forms will be given the name "truth functional logical forms." While these logical forms are relatively coarse, the deductive validity of a large number of arguments depends only on these coarse forms. Furthermore, determining the validity of an argument with reference to these forms is a relatively easy matter. Our first task is to present the logical particles that give rise to these truth functional logical forms.

3.3.1 Truth Functional Connectives

As a first approximation, we can specify the logical particles we are interested in as:

(L) 'and', 'or', 'if . . . , then', 'if and only if', and 'it is not the case that'

as they are used to connect statements or independent clauses that are true or false. However, this specification needs several refinements.

The use of 'or' in English is ambiguous, because sometimes it means 'and/or' and sometimes it means 'or but not both'. Consider:

(1) If Statucki entered the country without a visa, Statucki is a citizen or Statucki is a spouse of a citizen.
(2) If Julia did not pay extra, Julia had soup or Julia had salad.

We would not regard (1) as false if Statucki did enter the country without a visa and it turned out that he is both a citizen and a spouse of a citizen. We might regard (2) as false if Julia had both soup and salad without paying extra. Traditionally, the 'and/or' sense is called the *inclusive* sense, while the 'or but not both' sense is called the *exclusive* sense. Thus, the natural reading of (1) is that the 'or' is being used in the inclusive sense, while at least a plausible reading of (2) is that the 'or' is being used in the exclusive sense. Given this ambiguity of 'or', in counting 'or' as a logical particle, we are counting two things as logical particles: 'or' in the inclusive sense or 'or_i' for short, and 'or' in the exclusive sense, which we'll indicate as 'or_e'.

The frequent use of statements like 'She'll come or she won't' may suggest that the most frequent use of 'or' is 'or_e'. However, there is clear evidence that someone is using 'or' as 'or_e' only if (a) there is the possibility that both parts of the 'or' statement are true, and (b) the speaker makes it clear that his statement should be taken to be false when both parts are true. Given a statement like 'She'll come or she won't', the possibility of both parts coming out true is antecedently precluded; thus, the speaker is unlikely to have made any decision as to whether his statement should be taken as true or false if she should both come and not come. In short, statements like these are precisely the ones that give no indication as to whether 'or' is being used in the sense of 'or_i' or 'or_e'. Because the logic of 'or_i' turns out to be much neater than the logic of 'or_e', the reader is well advised to construe 'or' as 'or_i' unless there are explicit indications to the contrary. If an argument turns out to depend on taking 'or' or as 'or_e', one can always add an extra premise that both parts aren't true.

It is quite possible that the particles we listed in (L) have other ambiguities. Regardless of how many senses those sentential connectives may have, for our purpose we shall be interested in one specific sense of them that we shall call the TRUTH FUNCTIONAL SENSE. That is, we shall be concerned with the sense of those connectives whereby *the truth values of the compound statements using those sentential connectives depend on only the truth values of the component statements.* The idea of the truth functional sense of a connective may be explained in somewhat greater detail as follows.

Consider:

(3) Reagan lost to Carter *and* Lyndon Johnson lived in Texas.

If 'and' is being used in the truth functional sense—that is, if the truth value of (3) depends only on the truth value of its component clauses—we should be able to replace 'Reagan lost to Carter' by any other false statement without affecting the truth value of (3); similarly, we should be able to replace 'Lyndon Johnson lived in Texas' by any other true statement without affecting the truth value of (3). And this is surely the case, because (3) is false and remains false under replacements of the kind suggested, that is, replacements like

(3′) $2 + 2 = 6$ and Santa Barbara is in California.

Thus, 'and' is being used in the truth functional sense in (3).

Now consider:

(4) America entered World War II because the Japanese attacked Pearl Harbor.

As is perhaps plausible, let us suppose that (4) and its component sentences are all true. If we replace 'The Japanese attacked Pearl Habor' by another true sentence, say 'Reno is in Nevada', we get:

(4′) America entered World War II because Reno is in Nevada.

Clearly, we have gone from truth to falsity in making this replacement. Thus, 'because' is not being used in a truth functional sense in (4), and the truth value of (4) depends on more than the truth value of the components; presumably it depends on there being some sort of a causal relationship between the attack on Pearl Harbor and our entry into World War II. While 'and' seems to be used in the truth functional sense in most contexts, it would seem that there is no such thing as a truth functional sense of 'because': the truth of '... because ______' always seems to require some sort of a ground-to-consequence relationship between ______ and ....

Having somewhat clarified the notion of a truth functional sense of a connective, our ruling was that the particles listed in (L) count as logical particles only when they are used in the truth functional sense, whereby the truth value of the compound depends only on the truth values of the components. Given this ruling, the meaning of our logical particles will be completely specified by specifying what truth values accrue to the compounds, using the particles for each combination of truth values the components may assume. Let 'X' and 'Y', then, be any two statements, and consider 'X and Y'. Letting 'T' stand for 'true' and 'F' for 'false', the possible combination of truth values the components 'X' and 'Y' may have are given by:

X	Y
T	T
T	F
F	T
F	F

The truth functional sense of 'and' is specified by specifying the truth value of 'X and Y' for each of these combinations. To introduce a bit of terminology, we say 'X and Y' is the CONJUNCTION of 'X' and 'Y', and 'X' and 'Y' are the CONJUNCTS of 'X and Y'. Now surely a conjunction is true if and only if both of the conjuncts are true. This meaning of 'and' can then be specified by the following table:

X	Y	X and Y
T	T	T
T	F	F
F	T	F
F	F	F

The meaning of the other truth functional connectives can be specified by similar tables. To abbreviate our work we shall present one grand table for all the connectives, and this grand table will be taken to supplant our initial specification of the logical constants in (L). To make the table readable, 'not' stands for 'it is not the case that' and 'iff' stands for 'if and only if'. We shall first present this grand table and then make some comments about it.

X	Y	not Y	X and Y	X or_i Y	X or_e Y	X iff Y	if X, then Y
T	T	F	T	T	F	T	T
T	F	T	F	T	T	F	F
F	T		F	T	T	F	T
F	F		F	F	F	T	T

According to standard terminology, 'It is not the case that Y' is called the *negation* of 'Y', and clearly a statement is true if and only if its negation is false; this meaning of 'it is not the case that' is found under 'not X'. The expression 'X or_i Y' is called the DISJUNCTION of 'X' and 'Y', and 'X' and 'Y' are called the DISJUNCTS of 'X or_i Y'. Clearly a disjunction is false if and only if both disjuncts are false; this meaning of 'or_i' is found on the table under 'X or_i Y'. 'X or_e Y' is just like a disjunction except that 'X or_e Y' is false when both 'X' and 'Y' are true; this meaning is exhibited under 'X or_e Y'. 'X if and only if Y' is standardly called the BICONDITIONAL of 'X' and 'Y'. It seems plausible that 'X if and only if Y' in the truth functional sense of the connective is true just in case 'X' and 'Y' have the same truth values. Thus, the meaning we assign to 'if and only if' is found on the table under 'X iff Y'.

The expression 'if X, then Y' is usually called the CONDITIONAL, and in this configuration 'X' is called the ANTECEDENT and 'Y' is called the CONSEQUENT. It's clear that a conditional is false when the antecedent is true and the consequent false. Given that we are dealing with the truth functional sense of 'if . . . , then', it may be plausible enough that the conditional is true when both the antecedent and the consequent are true. But what truth value should we assign to the conditional when the antecedent is false? Because the methods we shall be developing depend on statements being true or false, we must assign some truth values to the situations represented by the last two rows. Declaring 'if X, then Y' to be true in these cases is the only way to keep it distinct from the other statements in the table. This results in the meaning of the conditional found in the table under 'if X, then Y'.

It must be confessed that it is not entirely clear how frequently we use the connectives listed in (L) in the sense specified by our grand table, and this is especially true for 'if . . . , then' and 'if and only if'. Many of our uses of 'if . . . , then' and 'if and only if' at least appear to be non-truth functional. Consider (5) and (6):

(5) If Kennedy was assassinated, Kennedy didn't die of natural causes.
(6) If Reno is in Nevada, Kennedy didn't die of natural causes.

Clearly (5) is true. But should we therefore say that (6) is also true? If we should think not, we would have to conclude that 'if . . . , then' is not being used in the truth functional sense in (5). There is considerable debate among philosophers and linguists as to how often, if ever, the 'if . . . , then' is used in a truth functional sense.[4] However, most people agree on the following point:

As long as the particles listed in (L) are used as sentential connectives to connect declarative sentences in the indicative mood, treating them **as if** *they were used in the truth functional sense specified by the grand table causes little or no error with respect to what arguments are deductively valid and what arguments aren't.*

Thus, for the practical purpose of assessing arguments, we can generally consider the particles listed in (L) to have the sense specified by the grand table.

However, to be absolutely precise it will be convenient to have a special abbreviatory notation for the particles when they are used in the sense

4. This matter is taken up again at the end of Section 6.5.

specified by the grand table. For this purpose, we introduce the following abbreviations:

'−(X)'	for	'it is not the case that X'
'X & Y'	for	'X and Y'
'X v Y'	for	'X or_i Y'
'X v^e Y'	for	'X or_e Y'
'X ⊃ Y'	for	'if X, then Y'
'X ≡ Y'	for	'X if and only if Y'

Given this abbreviatory notation, while there might be dispute over whether or not (6) is true, there can be no debate that

(7) Reno is in Nevada ⊃ Kennedy didn't die of natural causes.

is true.

EXERCISES—SECTION 3.3.1

1. Assume the following statements to be true.
   (i) Tom went to Italy.
   (ii) Tom didn't go to France.
   (iii) Tom went to Rome.

   Determine the truth values of the following statements:
   (a) (Tom went to Italy) & (Tom went to France).
   (b) (Tom went to Italy) v (Tom went to France).
   (c) −(Tom went to Italy) v (Tom went to France).
   (d) (Tom went to Italy) v (Tom went to Rome).
   (e) (Tom went to Italy) v^e (Tom went to Rome).
   (f) −(Tom went to Italy) ⊃ −(Tom went to Rome).
   (g) (Tom went to Italy) ⊃ −(Tom went to France).
   (h) (Tom went to Italy) ⊃ −(Tom went to Rome).
   (i) (Tom went to Italy) ≡ (Tom went to Rome).
   (j) (Tom went to France) ≡ − (Tom went to Rome).
   (k) (Tom went to France) ≡ −(Tom went to Italy).

*2. Suggest how someone might urge that 'and' is not being used in the truth functional sense in 'Yvonne had a baby and Yvonne got married'. What besides the truth value of the component sentences might be urged as being needed to make 'Yvonne had a baby and Yvonne got married' true? [*Hint:* How might the statement being considered differ from 'Yvonne got married and had a baby'?]

3.3.2 Truth Functional Statement Forms

In order to facilitate an intuitive grasp of logical forms, in Section 3.2 we introduced configurations like:

If [ ], then < >.

Given our new abbreviations, we should now write this as

[ ] ⊃ < >.

However, blanks are clearly messy to deal with. This is especially the case when we have to introduce several different kinds of blanks to capture the logical form of an argument. To alleviate this problem, from now on we shall start using lower-case roman letters as blanks that are to be filled by sentences or independent clauses; when the lower-case roman letters are so used, we shall sometimes refer to them as SENTENCE LETTERS. Given this new way of writing blanks, the logical form we displayed will be written as:

p ⊃ q

This is an example of a logical form that we shall call a truth functional statement form.

At least in a rough way, truth functional statement forms may be defined as follows:

> Truth Functional Statement Forms =
>
> Blanks (sentence letters) combined with '−', '&', 'v', 'v^e', '≡', '⊃', and parentheses for grouping so that if the blanks were filled by sentences the result would be a grammatical sentence.

Thus, 'p ⊃ q' '(p ⊃ q) v −(t & u)', and 'p' are examples of statement forms. On the other hand, '≡p' and '(p v q' are not statement forms because filling the sentence letters with sentences will not result in grammatical sentences.[5]

For certain purposes it is desirable to have a somewhat more rigorous definition. To this end, we introduce Greek letters like ϕ and θ as variables ranging over statement forms and inkmark configurations in general. Although there are subtle differences, at least as a rough picture one

5. The use of parentheses discussed in this subsection is in connection with statement *forms*. When actual statements are involved, it is more perspicuous to include a set of parentheses around each independent English clause. Thus, while we write forms like 'p ⊃ (q v r)', when actual statements are involved, we shall write:

(he comes) ⊃ [(she will cry) v (she will leave)].

This seems more perspicuous than: he comes ⊃ (she will cry v she will leave).

might think of the Greek letters along the following lines: Just as 'p' and 'q' are blanks for sentences, 'ϕ' and 'θ' are blanks for statement forms (and expressions like them). Given this background, the following rigorous definition for truth functional statement forms may be offered:

(1) Any sentence letter is a truth functional statement form.
(2) If ϕ and θ are truth functional statement forms, so are $-(\phi)$, $(\phi \; \& \; \theta)$, $(\phi \vee \theta)$, $(\phi \vee^e \theta)$, $(\phi \supset \theta)$, $(\phi \equiv \theta)$.
(3) Nothing is a truth functional statement form unless its being one follows from (1) and (2).

Grouping is a matter of significance both for statements and statement forms. This can be seen by considering the following example:

(1) It is raining and Tom will go to a picnic or Jane will stay home.

This is ambiguous between (2) and (3):

(2) It is raining and either Tom will go to a picnic or Jane will stay home.
(3) Either it is raining and Tom will go to a picnic or else Jane will stay home.

If it isn't raining, statement (2) is false but statement (3) would still be true as long as Jane stays home. Clearly, grouping can make all the difference in the world. Just as (1) is ambiguous, 'p & q v r' is ambiguous between 'p & (q v r)' and '(p & q) v r'. If we supply the following truth values:

p: F, q: F, r: T

'p & (q v r)' and '(p & q) v r' end up with different truth values as the following "calculation" shows:

F & (F v T),	(F & F) v T	or
F & T,	F v T	or
F,	T.	

Thus, whether we are dealing with statements or statement forms, we must be careful to exhibit the grouping. While English allows for grouping devices like the ones indicated in (2) and (3), with logical forms and ordinary statements using abbreviating notations like 'v', parentheses become the tool for indicating the appropriate grouping. This use of parentheses is explicit in the rigorous definition of statement forms, and we shall insist (with three exceptions to be immediately noted) that grouping always be indicated in the way specified in the more rigorous definition of a statement form.

The three exceptions to showing all parentheses are these:

(i) According to the definition, 'p v q' is incorrect and should really be written as '(p v q)'. But *we shall omit the outwardmost pair of parentheses in a* **complete** *statement form* because it is always redundant.

(ii) According to the definition '−p' is incorrect and should really be written as '−(p)'. However, because the number of parentheses can quickly proliferate, let us *adopt the convention that negation governs the shortest meaningful unit and drop the parentheses made redundant by this convention.* Thus, we can write '−p', and '−p v q' will be understood as '−(p) v q'. If we want the negation to cover the entire disjunction, we shall write '−(p v q)'; the shortest meaningful unit following '−' is not '(p' because the end of a meaningful unit for a subexpression starting with '(' is not reached till the matching ')' is found.

(iii) There are two cases in which it makes no difference how expressions are grouped: a sequence of conjunctions and a sequence of disjunctions. That is, 'p & (q & r)' and '(p & q) & r' will always have the same truth value. Similarly, 'p v (q v r)' will always have the same truth value as '(p v q) v r'. Regardless of how it is grouped, the double conjunction will be true just in case all three components are true. Again, regardless of how it is grouped, the double disjunction will be false just in case all three components are false. The intuitive meaning of 'and' and 'or' should convince the reader of this; alternatively, the reader may attempt to "calculate" this result by repeatedly using the grand table with respect to '&' and 'v' for combinations of truth values the component sentence letters may assume. To avoid the proliferation of parentheses, *parentheses may be dropped within repeated conjunctions and within repeated disjunctions.* Thus, we shall allow expressions like 'p & q & r' and 'p v q v r'. It must be noted that this applies only when we have a number of conjuncts constituting an extended conjunction or a number of disjuncts composing an extended disjunction. We still cannot allow expressions like 'p & q v r', because we cannot tell whether the expression is basically a conjunction, that is, 'p & (q v r)', or a disjunction, that is, '(p & q) v r'. However, '(p ⊃ q) v (p & r) v s' will be allowed because the expression is a double disjunction and it matters not whether it is grouped as '[(p ⊃ q) v (p & r)] v s' or '(p ⊃ q) v [(p & r) v s]'.

EXERCISES—SECTION 3.3.2

1. In each of the following, supply truth values to the sentence letters so that the two statement forms finally have different truth values.

   (a) (p ⊃ q) ⊃ r, p ⊃ (q ⊃ r).

   (b) (p v q) ⊃ r, p v (q ⊃ r).

   (c) (p ⊃ q) & r, p ⊃ (q & r).

   (d) (p ≡ q) ⊃ r, p ≡ (q ⊃ r).

2. In each of the following, delete all parentheses that need not be shown:
   (a) $(((-(p) \& s) \& u) \vee r)$.
   (b) $((-(s) \vee -(u \vee t)) \vee (s \supset (p \vee r)))$.
   (c) $(((-(p) \supset (s \vee t))) \equiv ((p \& -(s \vee t)) \& u))$.
3. Show how part 2c above can be derived to be a statement form from the rigorous definition of statement forms.

3.3.3 Canonical Forms of Statements

It may have occurred to the reader that if he or she encounters 'it is not the case that he will come', its truth functional logical form can be extracted as '$-p$'; but if he or she encounters 'he won't come', the only truth functional logical form that can be extracted is 'r'. After all, 'not' as part of the verb phrase was not counted as a logical particle. Similarly, 'if he comes, then he will be happy' can be expressed as '$p \supset q$' but 'he'll be happy if he comes' can only produce 'r'. That is, while we have a way of extracting the form of the 'if X, then Y' construction, we have no way of extracting the form of the 'Y if X' construction. Clearly, this is an absurd situation. It is best to conceive the six constructions we discussed as the canonical or standard forms of statements and to convert or translate other statements into these canonical forms as an intermediary step to extracting their logical form. Thus 'he won't come' should first be translated as '$-$(he will come)' before extracting '$-p$' as the logical form of 'he won't come'. Similarly, 'he'll be happy if he comes' should be translated as 'he comes $\supset$ he'll be happy' before extracting its logical form as '$p \supset q$'.[6]

Usual cases of translation into canonical forms present no problems. No ingenuity is needed to translate 'Jane will come home or stay at the office' as '(Jane will come home) v (Jane will stay at the office)'. Nor is there any trouble in converting 'Jane and Tom will be at home' into '(Jane will be at home) & (Tom will be at home)'. However, some constructions may present problems, and we list here the canonical forms and some statements having those forms:

'$p \& q$': 'both p and q', 'p; q', 'p although q', and 'p but q'.
'$p \vee q$': '(either) p or (else) q', 'unless p, q', and 'p unless q'.
'$p \supset q$': 'if p, (then) q', 'q if p', 'p only if q', 'not p unless q', 'p is a sufficient condition for q', and 'q is a necessary condition for p'.
'$p \equiv q$': 'p if and only if q', 'p just in case q', and 'p is a necessary and sufficient condition for q'.

6. Those familiar with computer programming might conceive the six forms we have discussed as the programming language into which commands or statements must be translated; just as the rigid programming language allows computers to solve problems, so too, our rigid language of six forms allows for methods that will determine deductive validity of arguments.

In the constructions listed under the conditional, particular attention should be paid to the order. For example, 'p only if q' becomes 'p ⊃ q' and 'q only if p' becomes 'q ⊃ p'. That is, in listing 'p only if q' by 'p ⊃ q', we mean that the sentence before the 'only if' is to become the antecedent and the sentence after the 'only if' is to become the consequent.

In translating statements into canonical forms, one must be careful to preserve the correct grouping and be attentive of grouping devices in English. Punctuation is the most obvious device for grouping. But there are two other frequently used devices:

(a) The ambiguity of 'p and q or r' is often resolved by inserting 'either' (or 'else') in the appropriate place. Thus, 'either p and q or (else) r' has the grouping '(p & q) v r' while 'p and either q or r' has the form 'p & (q v r)'. The use of 'both' along with 'and' accomplishes an end similar to the use of 'either'.

(b) The ambiguity of grouping is often resolved in English by having two subject expressions with a single predicate expression or by having a single subject expression with two predicate expressions. Thus, 'Jane is sick and Tom or Mary will be home' has the form 'p & (q v r)' while 'Jane is at home or at work and Tom is playing' has the form '(p v q) & r'.

When translating complex statements into canonical forms, it is best to do it in parts starting with the outwardmost construction and successively working toward the embedded constructions. This might be called the maxim of TRANSLATING INWARD. Thus, consider:

(1) If Tom and Mary both fail to go to the hospital, then either Johnny will be upset unless the nurse plays with him or else Tim will be sad.

Trying to translate this in one step significantly increases the chances of error. Following the maxim of translating inward, the first step is to determine what the basic structure of (1) is. A moment's reflection shows the basic form of (1) to be that of a conditional. Hence, the first step of translating inward yields:

(2) [Tom and Mary both fail to go to the hospital] ⊃ [either Johnny will be upset unless the nurse plays with him or else Tim will be sad].

Along with unpacking the antecedent, the next step requires noticing that the consequent is basically a long disjunction (stretching to the end of the "or else" clause). Thus, the next step and the final obvious step are:

(3) [(Tom fails to go to the hospital) & (Mary fails to go to the hospital)] ⊃ [(Johnny will be upset unless the nurse plays with him) v (Tim will be sad)].

(4) [−(Tom goes to the hospital) & −(Mary goes to the hospital)] ⊃ [([Johnny will be upset] v [the nurse plays with Johnny]) v (Tim will be sad)].

This shows that by following the maxim of translating inward it is relatively easy to extract the logical form of a complex statement like (1) as

'$[-p \& -q] \supset [(r \vee s) \vee t]$,' or '$(-p \& -q) \supset (r \vee s \vee t)$' if we drop the needless parentheses.

The guidelines of the last few paragraphs in extracting the logical forms of statements may be summarized as follows:

(1) *Translate inward.*
(2) Beyond punctuation, rely on the following kinds of grouping clues:

$(p \& q) \vee r$	$p \& (q \vee r)$
either p and q or r	p and either q or r
x and y will F or y will G	x will F and y will F or G

EXERCISES—SECTION 3.3.3

Let the scheme of abbreviation (where sentence letters are matched with the underlined letters in the abbreviated sentences) be given by

b: The boss is working.
t: Tom is working.
s: Some other people are working.
w: The boss is watching.
p: Tom is playing.
d: The work will get done.

Using this scheme, extract the logical forms of the following sentences:

1. Either the boss is working and Tom is playing or the boss is watching.
2. The boss is working and either Tom is playing or the boss is watching.
3. If Tom is playing although the boss is watching, then the boss isn't working.
4. The boss is watching if Tom is playing; the boss is working.
5. The boss is watching if it is both the case that Tom is playing and the boss is working.
6. Tom and the boss are working or the boss is watching.
7. Tom is working and the boss is watching or working.
8. If Tom plays only if the boss is not watching, then the boss is working.
9. Tom isn't working unless the boss is working.
10. The work will get done if and only if Tom and the boss both work.
11. Unless Tom or the boss is working, the work will get done only if some other people are working.
12. Although Tom is playing, if the boss is watching and some other people are working, the work will get done.
13. Although Tom is playing, the work will get done if the boss and some other people are working.
14. Some other people are working just in case Tom and the boss working aren't sufficient for the work getting done.
15. The boss watching is a necessary condition for Tom working only if both some other people are working and the work will get done.

16. If the boss's working is a necessary condition for Tom's working, then the boss's watching is a sufficient condition for Tom's not playing.
17. If a necessary and sufficient condition for Tom working is the boss watching, then a necessary condition for the work getting done is the boss watching.
18. If Tom or the boss working is a sufficient condition for the work getting done only if some other people are working, then unless some other people are working, the work will not get done if Tom and the boss aren't both working.

3.3.4 Deductive Validity

Given our understanding of truth functional statement forms, our earlier understanding of argument forms carries over, that is, a truth functional argument form is a sequence of one or more truth functional statement forms followed by the "therefore" line and one more truth functional statement form. Deductive validity may now be defined as follows:

> A truth functional argument form is *deductively valid* =
>
> regardless of how the blanks are filled by truth values, if all the premises come out true, so does the conclusion.

As before, an invalid argument form is one that isn't valid. However, the current definition of validity requires some comments because it ostensibly differs in two respects from the general definition of validity that was given in Section 3.2.

(a) The current definition requires filling the blanks with truth values rather than sentences. The reason we can do this is that the logical particles of truth functional statement forms are truth functional connectives, that is, connectives such that the truth value of the compound depends only on the truth values of the components. It would be cumbersome to fill the blanks with actual sentences when the only thing that really matters is the truth values of the sentences filling the blanks. Hence, instead of saying, "regardless of how the blanks are filled by sentences, if the premises all come out true, so does the conclusion," we say, "regardless of how the blanks are filled by truth values, if all the premises come out true, so does the conclusion." This is an obvious simplification because there are only two truth values (true and false), instead of an infinity of sentences with which the blanks could be filled.

(b) Our earlier definition of deductive validity was in terms of "in any possible world, no matter how the blanks are filled . . . ," while our current definition has deleted references to possible worlds. Given that we are dealing with truth functional forms, this deletion is obviously justified: once we switch from sentences to truth values, in considering one way of filling the blanks with truth values, we are considering all possible worlds in which the blanks are filled by sentences having those truth values.

Given our definition for truth functional validity in terms of truth values, *showing the validity or invalidity of argument forms becomes relatively simple.* Consider [1], [2], and [3] for example:

[1]	[2]	[3]
$p \supset q$	$p \supset (q \vee r)$	$-(p \& q)$
p	$q \supset s$	$-p \supset r$
——	$r \supset s$	——
q	——	r
	$p \supset s$	

[1] of course is an example we have already discussed a number of times. Its validity may now be argued as follows: Regardless of how the blanks are filled, if we are to make all the premises true, 'p' must be filled by the value "True." But then, in order to make '$p \supset q$' true, 'q' must be filled by the value "True." Hence, any way of filling the blanks that makes all the premises of [1] true must also make its conclusion true. Thus, [1] is a valid argument form.

As for [2], it might be argued to be valid as follows: The only way the conclusion can come out false is to fill 'p' by "True" and 's' by "False." But then, the last two premises of [2] can come out true only by filling both 'q' and 'r' by "False," and this forces the first premise to come out false because 'p' is true and '$q \vee r$' now comes out false. Thus, it's impossible for the conclusion to be false and all the premises to be true, and [2] is valid.

Finally, [3] turns out to be invalid, and given our simplified definition of validity for truth functional argument forms, we only need to find one way of assigning truth values to the sentence letters so that the premises come out true and the conclusion false. This is accomplished by the following assignment:

p: T, q: F, r: F

Clearly the conclusion 'r' comes out false and the premise '$-p \supset r$' becomes '$F \supset F$' or true. The premise '$-(p \& q)$' also comes out true because under the assignment it becomes '$-(T \& F)$' or '$-(F)$'. Thus, [3] is invalid.

From our discussion of Section 3.2, it is evident that the relation between the validity of arguments and the validity of truth functional argument forms is given by:

> *An argument is valid if it has at least one truth functional argument form that is valid.*

We cannot say 'if and only if" because the validity of the argument may be due to its finer structure, which cannot be reflected in truth functional argument forms. Similarly, because an argument can be assigned a finer or a coarser truth functional argument form, we must say: an argument is valid if it has *at least one* valid truth functional argument form.

This completes our general discussion of truth functional argument forms and their validity. What remains to be done is to develop systematic methods for determining the validity of these argument forms. We shall start the presentation of the principal method of this text in Section 3.5. Section 3.4 is an optional section devoted to an alternative method for determining truth functional validity. While this alternative method does not lend itself to applications in everyday contexts, it has the advantage of deepening our theoretical appreciation of what validity amounts to. It also has the advantage of providing us with methods for determining certain logical features and relations of statements that are not covered by our discussion of deductive validity.

EXERCISES—SECTION 3.3.4

Working with the definition of valid truth functional argument forms, show the following argument forms to be valid or invalid:

[a] $$\begin{array}{l} -(p \vee q) \\ \hline -p \vee -q \end{array}$$

[b] $$\begin{array}{l} p \supset -p \\ \hline p \,\&\, -p \end{array}$$

[c] $$\begin{array}{l} p \equiv -q \\ \hline -(p \equiv q) \end{array}$$

[d] $$\begin{array}{l} p \supset q \\ q \supset r \\ \hline p \supset r \end{array}$$

[e] $$\begin{array}{l} p \vee q \\ p \\ \hline -q \end{array}$$

[f] $$\begin{array}{l} p \vee^{e} q \\ p \\ \hline -q \end{array}$$

[g] $$\begin{array}{l} p \supset q \\ -p \\ \hline -q \end{array}$$

[h] $$\begin{array}{l} p \vee q \\ -p \\ \hline q \end{array}$$

[i] $$\begin{array}{l} (p \supset q) \supset r \\ q \supset s \\ \hline (p \supset s) \supset r \end{array}$$

[j] $$\begin{array}{l} (p \vee q) \supset r \\ p \supset s \\ q \supset s \\ \hline s \supset r \end{array}$$

[k] $$\begin{array}{l} p \vee q \\ p \supset r \\ q \supset s \\ \hline r \vee s \end{array}$$

[l] $$\begin{array}{l} -(p \,\&\, q) \\ -p \supset r \\ -q \supset s \\ \hline r \,\&\, s \end{array}$$

*3.4 Other Logical Properties and Truth Table Analyses

Our discussion so far has centered on deductive validity because our principal concern is with reasoning. However, it should be clear that statements and sets of statements may have other logical properties that may be of some interest. To exemplify one such property, suppose someone tells us that she'll come to the party or she won't. This is terribly uninformative and we can see why: the logical form of the statement is such that the statement is going to be true in every possible world; thus, in asserting that she will come or she won't, nothing has been asserted

* This section is optional and may be skipped.

that would distinguish our actual world from any other possible world. Because we can determine this from the logical form of the assertion alone, we are inclined to say that the assertion is uninformative and that it is an empty tautology. Much the same can be said of statements like 'If she'll come, she'll come' and 'She'll come if and only if she comes'. Of course we could put a slightly better face on these statements by calling them "logical truths"; that is, these truths are not only true in our world but true in every possible world. This way of putting it might give these statements an aura of "supertruths," which go beyond ordinary truths that are false in some possible worlds. It is probably misleading to think of these expressions either as worthless empty statements or as some sort of supertruths. Regardless of how we think of them, *we shall say that a statement is a* TAUTOLOGY *just in case the logical form of the statement alone assures that the statement is going to be true in every possible world.*

Suppose a politician says in front of a veterans' organization that he will support increasing the military budget, and that the next day in front of a college audience he states that he will not support increasing the military budget. If we should learn of this, we should say that his statements are inconsistent. The trouble with an inconsistent set of statement like {'He will support increasing the military budget', 'He will not support increasing the military budget'} is that at least one of these statements must be false. *In general, we shall say that a set of statements* $\{S_1, \ldots, S_n\}$ *is* INCONSISTENT *just in case the logical forms of the statement preclude any possible world in which all of the members of the set come out true.* As a degenerate case, we shall say that a single statement (like 'He will come and he won't come') is inconsistent if its logical form precludes it from being true in any possible world. *A statement or a set of statements is* CONSISTENT as long as it is not inconsistent. The virtue of a consistent statement is that even if it should turn out to be false, it wasn't precluded from being true by its logical form alone. Another way of conceiving an inconsistent set of statements is that the set of statements conflict among themselves so that they can't all be true. When we insisted in Chapter 2 that the unproblematic claims must be free of any strong conflicts, what we were insisting on was that the set of unproblematic claims be consistent.

Consider now the pair of statements 'He will come' and 'It is not the case that he will not come'. In some sense we can see that these two statements assert the same thing, and to this extent we might want to call these two statements "equivalent." *What is clear about this pair of statements is that from their logical forms alone we can determine that the truth values of the two statements will agree in every possible world. Whenever two statements have this feature we shall say that the two statements have* LOGICALLY IDENTICAL TRUTH CONDITIONS. If two statements have logically identical truth conditions, in an important sense what they assert will come to the same thing.

Our discussion of the last few paragraphs may be summarized as follows:

(1) S is a *tautology* =
In virtue of its logical form, S is true in every possible world.
(2) $\{S_1, \ldots, S_n\}$ is *inconsistent* =
In virtue of the logical forms of the statements, in no possible world are all the members of the set true.
(3) $\{S_1, \ldots, S_n\}$ is *consistent* = $\{S_1, \ldots, S_n\}$ is not inconsistent.
(4) S is (in)consistent = {S} is (in)consistent.
(5) $\langle S, R \rangle$ have *logically identical truth conditions* =
In virtue of their logical forms, the truth values of S and R agree in every possible world.

Clearly, parallel notions can be defined for truth functional logical forms. Thus, understanding that the blanks of the truth functional forms are to be filled by truth values, we shall say:

(1) ϕ is a *tautology* =
However the blanks are filled, ϕ always comes out true.
(2) $\{\phi_1, \ldots, \phi_n\}$ is *inconsistent* =
However the blanks of $\phi_1, \ldots, \phi_n$ are filled, at least one member of the set comes out false.
(3) $\{\phi_1, \ldots, \phi_n\}$ is *consistent* = $\{\phi_1, \ldots, \phi_n\}$ is not inconsistent.
(4) ϕ is (in)consistent = $\{\phi\}$ is (in)consistent.
(5) $\langle \phi, \theta \rangle$ have *logically identical truth conditions* =
However the blanks of ϕ and θ are filled, ϕ and θ have the same truth value.

As with validity, some or all of the truth functional logical forms of the involved statements may be too coarse to detect that they are tautologies or are inconsistent or have logically identical truth conditions. Thus, the relationship between the two sets of definitions is given by:

(1) A statement is a tautology if at least one truth functional logical form of the statement is a tautology.
(2) A set of statements is inconsistent if at least one corresponding set of truth functional logical forms is inconsistent.
(3) A pair of statements has logically identical truth conditions if at least one corresponding pair of truth functional logical forms has logically identical truth conditions.

It should be noted that because the inconsistency of a set of statements may depend on their finer logical forms, the consistency of the corresponding truth functional logical forms allows one to draw no conclusions about the consistency of the original set of statements.

Having introduced a number of logical properties for logical forms, we can now state some relationships between these properties. Consider a logical form of the type $(\phi_1 \& \phi_2) \supset \theta$. A particular instance of it might be '[p & (p ⊃ q)] ⊃ (q v r)'. We know that a conditional is true except when the antecedent is true and the consequent is false. We also know that a conjunction is true just in case both conjuncts are true. Thus, the only way of filling the blanks that will make an instance of the type $(\phi_1 \& \phi_2) \supset \theta$ false is one that makes ϕ_1 and ϕ_2 both true and θ false. Thus, we can say that:

(A) $(\phi_1 \& \phi_2) \supset \theta$ is a tautology if and only if there is no way of filling the blanks so that ϕ_1 and ϕ_2 both come out true while θ comes out false.

Now consider the argument form $\phi_1, \phi_2 / \theta$. From our definitions we know:

(B) $\phi_1, \phi_2 / \theta$ is valid if and only if there is no way of filling the blanks so that ϕ_1 and ϕ_2 both come out true while θ comes out false.

Comparing (A) and (B), we can draw the conclusion:

$\phi_1, \phi_2 / \theta$ is valid if and only if $(\phi_1 \& \phi_2) \supset \theta$ is a tautology.

More generally, we can say that:

$\phi_1, \ldots, \phi_n / \theta$ is valid if and only if $(\phi_1 \& \ldots \phi_n) \supset \theta$ is a tautology.

Concisely stated, we may say: An argument is valid if and only if the corresponding conditional is a tautology.[7] Thus, if we can devise a method for determining tautologies, we will automatically have developed a method for determining the validity of arguments.

Similar consideration shows that having logically identical truth conditions is the validity of the corresponding biconditional: Because a biconditional is true precisely when the two parts have the same truth value, we can say that:

(C) $\theta_1 \equiv \theta_2$ is a tautology if and only if, regardless of how the blanks are filled, θ_1 and θ_2 have the same truth value.

7. When particular statements are involved, this claim must be carefully distinguished from an apparently similar but false claim that the validity of an argument is the truth of the corresponding conditional. 'Nixon was president ⊃ Kennedy was president' is true but 'Nixon was president / Kennedy was president' is invalid. Thus, the mere truth of the corresponding conditional shows nothing about the validity of the argument. What the validity of the argument requires is that 'Nixon was president ⊃ Kennedy was president' is a tautology. Precisely because this corresponding conditional is not a tautology, the argument is invalid despite the truth of the corresponding conditional.

But we also know from the definition of 'having logically identical truth conditions' that:

(D) θ_1 and θ_2 have logically identical truth conditions if and only if, regardless of how the blanks are filled, θ_1 and θ_2 have the same truth value.

Comparing (C) and (D), we have the conclusion:

θ_1 and θ_2 have logically identical truth conditions if and only if $\theta_1 \equiv \theta_2$ is a tautology.

Finally, because a conjunction comes out true just in case all its conjuncts come out true, it should be clear that:

(E) ϕ_1 & . . . & ϕ_n is consistent if and only if there is at least one way of filling the blanks so that all of $\phi_1, \ldots, \phi_n$ come out true.

From the definition of a (finite) consistent set, it is also clear that:

(F) $\{\phi_1, \ldots, \phi_n\}$ is consistent if and only if there is at least one way of filling the blanks so that all of $\phi_1, \ldots, \phi_n$ come out true.

Thus, for finite sets we can say that the (in)consistency of a set is the (in)consistency of the conjunction of its members or:

$\{\phi_1, \ldots, \phi_n\}$ is consistent if and only if ϕ_1 & . . . & ϕ_n is consistent.

This allows us to test for the (in)consistency of the entire set by simply determining whether or not there is one way of filling the blanks so that the conjunction of all its members comes out true.

What we have determined may be summarized as follows:

(1) $\phi_1, \ldots, \phi_n$ / θ is valid if and only if $(\phi_1$ & . . . $\phi_n) \supset \theta$ is a tautology.
(2) θ_1 and θ_2 have logically identical truth conditions if and only if $\theta_1 \equiv \theta_2$ is a tautology.
(3) $\{\phi_1, \ldots, \phi_n\}$ is consistent if and only if ϕ_1 & . . . & ϕ_n is consistent.

Suppose we had a method so that given any statement form ϕ we could determine whether it always comes out true, sometimes true, or never true. Such a method would then allow us to test for all the logical properties and relations we have discussed. But such a method is obviously available. All we have to do is to list all the combinations of truth values the sentence letters of ϕ may assume, and "calculate" with reference to the grand table of Section 3.3.1 what truth value accrues to ϕ for each such combination of truth values. Doing this will obviously allow us to determine whether ϕ always comes out true, sometimes true, or never true.

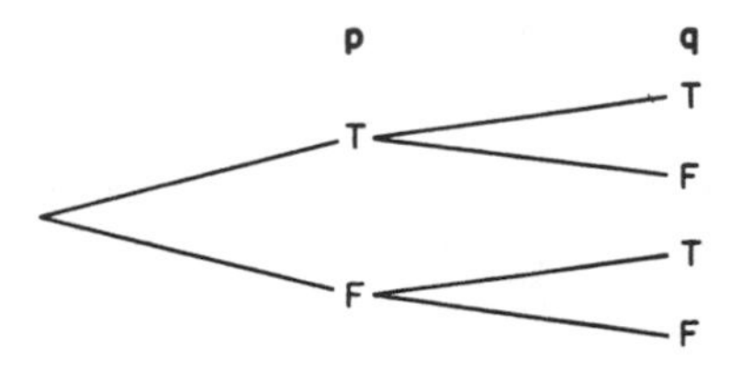

Figure 3.1.

The systematic way of doing this is called the method of TRUTH TABLE ANALYSIS, and this is the topic to which we shall now turn.

To have an example, let us suppose that we wish to test whether

S1: ([p ⊃ (q v −p)] & −q) ⊃ −p

is a tautology. The first step is to list the combination of truth values the sentence letters may assume. It should be evident that all the combinations of truth values the two sentence letters 'p' and 'q' may assume are given by the "tree" or "fan" diagram shown in Figure 3.1. That is, 'p' can be taken as 'T' or 'F', and for each way 'p' was taken, 'q' can be taken as 'T' and 'F'. Each of the four paths on the diagram displays a combination of truth values 'p' and 'q' may assume, and the four paths taken together represent all the combinations of truth values 'p' and 'q' may assume. If our statement form had a third sentence letter 'r', there would be two ways of taking 'r' for each of the ways 'p' and 'q' were taken, and a pair of branches would be added to each of the four paths on the diagram we actually displayed; the resulting diagram would then have eight paths on it. Each time we add a sentence letter, we double the number of paths or combination of truth values the sentence letters may assume. Thus, for example, if a statement form had five sentence letters, there would be 2^5 distinct paths or combinations of truth values.

Given that our diagram represents all the combinations of truth values the sentence letters 'p' and 'q' may assume, it is convenient to represent them in tabular fashion, and this would give rise to Table 3.1. The general way of arriving at such a tabular listing of the combinations of truth values should be evident: Given a statement form with n distinct sentence letters, list the letters and create 2^n rows below them; fill the column under the sentence letter farthest to the right by alternating 'T' and 'F', fill the column under the sentence letter second farthest to the right by alternating pairs of 'T's and 'F's, fill the column under the sentence letter

TABLE 3.1.

p	q	([p ⊃ (q v −p)] & −q) ⊃ −p
T	T	
T	F	
F	T	
F	F	

third farthest to the right by alternating four 'T's and four 'F's, fill the column under the sentence letter fourth farthest to the right by alternating eight 'T's and eight 'F's, and so on until the column on the far left is filled.

Using a table based on Table 3.1, and referring to the grand table of Section 3.3.1, the next task is to "calculate" what truth value accrues to the statement form for each of the rows. At least initially we can think of this "calculation" as follows: (1) fill the occurrences of the sentence letters by their truth values in that row, (2) *working from the most embedded structure outward,* successively determine the truth values that accrue to successively larger structures, and (3) continue this until the truth value for the entire statement form has been determined. The successive stages of this "calculation" for the first row in Table 3.1 is given by:

```
p    q       ([p ⊃ (q v −p)]& −q) ⊃ −p
T    T       ([T ⊃ (T v −T)]& −T) ⊃ −T
             ([T ⊃ (T v F  )]& F  ) ⊃ F
             ([T ⊃ (  T    )]& F  ) ⊃ F
             ([   T         ]& F  ) ⊃ F
             (                 F  ) ⊃ F
                                    T
```

By placing the truth value that accrues to a subexpression under the main connective of that subexpression, the above calculation can be done or represented in a single row:

```
p    q       ([p ⊃ (q v  −p)] & −q) ⊃ −p
T    T         T T  T T FT    F FT  T FT
```

Of course, to write a row like this, one can't just write it right to left, because the order of filling in the truth values under the statement form is the order that was given in the previously displayed sequence of "calculations." It should also be noted that in order to display the calculation in a single row, each subexpression must have a main connective; thus, in performing truth table analyses, we will not allow expressions like 'p v q v r'; rather, we must rewrite such an expression as '(p v q) v r' or 'p v (q v r)'. Finally, it must be conceded that the single-row calculation that was displayed is a bit difficult to read. Thus, we shall adopt two expedients: (a) Never copy the truth values to be substituted for sentence letters, because these values are already listed. (b) Box the truth value under the main connective of the entire statement form. This would result in the following simplification:

```
p    q       ([p ⊃ (q v  −p)] & −q) ⊃ −p
T    T          T    T F      F F  [T] F
```

This indicates that our statement form S1 comes out true when 'p' and 'q' are both true.

TABLE 3.2.

p	q	([p ⊃ (q v		−p)] &		−q)	⊃	−p
T	T	T	T	F	F	F	T	F
T	F	F	F	F	F	T	T	F
F	T	T	T	T	F	F	T	T
F	F	T	T	T	T	T	T	T
		5	4	1	6	2	7	3

If we repeat this process for each of the rows in Table 3.1 and box the entire column under the main connective of S1, we arrive at Table 3.2. (Disregard for the moment the numerals under the columns; these column numbers will be used in the next paragraph.) Table 3.2 gives the Truth Table Analysis of S1. It tells us that S1 is a tautology, thereby also that 'p ⊃ (q v −p), −q / −p' is valid.

Given our explanation so far, one would have written Table 3.2 in a row-by-row fashion starting with the row where 'p' and 'q' are both assigned 'T'. Although the Truth Table Analysis could be done this way, the task is significantly simplified by filling in the table columns one at a time: the numerals under Table 3.2 indicate the order in which the columns would typically be filled. Thus, columns 1, 2, and 3 are filled by simply switching around the values under 'p' and 'q'. To fill column 4, one compares the values under 'q' and '−p' and assigns a 'T' as long as at least one of the two values is 'T'. To fill column 5, one compares the values under 'p' and the 'v' and fills it by 'T' as long as the value under 'p' is 'F' or the value under the 'v' is T, otherwise by 'F', and so on.

The procedure for performing Truth Table Analyses of statement forms may now be summarized as follows:

Step 1: Given that ϕ has n sentence letters,

(a) Create 2^n rows under a listing of the sentence letters.
(b) Starting at the column farthest to the right, fill the columns under the letters by alternating 'T's and 'F's by ones, twos, fours, eights, etc.

Step 2: Determine and box the values accruing to ϕ. To do this,

(a) Refer to the grand table of Section 3.3.1.
(b) Work by columns from the most embedded structure outward.
(c) Fill in the values accruing to (sub)expressions under the main connective of that subexpression.

Let us give some additional examples of the analyses we can now perform.

TABLE 3.3.

p	q	r	A: [(p & q) ⊃ r] ≡ [p ⊃ (q ⊃ r)]		B: [(p & q) ⊃ r] ≡ [p ⊃ (q ⊃ r)]				
T	T	T	T	T	T	T	T	T	T
T	T	F	T	F	T	F	T	F	F
T	F	T	F	T	F	T	T	T	T
T	F	F	F	T	F	T	T	T	T
F	T	T	F	T	F	T	T	T	T
F	T	F	F	T	F	T	T	T	F
F	F	T	F	T	F	T	T	T	T
F	F	F	F	T	F	T	T	T	T

Suppose we want to know whether or not '(p & q) ⊃ r' and 'p ⊃ (q ⊃ r)' have logically identical truth conditions. We would form the biconditional of these two statement forms and use a Truth Table Analysis to test whether the biconditional is a tautology. This Truth Table Analysis is given in Table 3.3, in which part A indicates what the work would look like about halfway through and part B shows what the completed work would look like. Of course in practice, one would not display part A. It is displayed in Table 3.3 only for pedagogical purposes. Thus, we see that the biconditional is a tautology, and we have thereby determined that '(p & q) ⊃ r' and 'p ⊃ (q ⊃ r)' have logically identical truth conditions.

Suppose that we want to test whether or not {'p', 'p ⊃ q', '−q'} is consistent. We form the conjunction and test its consistency by a Truth Table Analysis. Because we need a main connective for each subexpression, we group the conjunction to the left, and the resulting analysis is given in Table 3.4. This table shows that the resulting conjunction is inconsistent; thus we can also conclude that the set {'p', 'p ⊃ q', '−q'} is inconsistent.

Another feature of Truth Table Analysis can be exemplified by testing for the inconsistency of the single expression '(p & q) ⊃ −(p & q)', an expression many people think to be inconsistent. The Truth Table Analysis is given in Table 3.5, and the result shows the statement form to be consistent. Thus, far from being inconsistent, '(p & q) ⊃ −(p & q)' actually comes out true in all cases except when 'p' and 'q' are both true. This result shows that a Truth Table Analysis for ϕ yields a lot more information than whether ϕ is consistent, inconsistent, or tautologous. The Truth Table Analysis shows us all the conditions under which ϕ is true and all the conditions under which ϕ is false. Thus, if one wants to

TABLE 3.4.

p	q	([p & (p ⊃ q)] & −q)			
T	T	T	T	F	F
T	F	F	F	F	T
F	T	F	T	F	F
F	F	F	T	F	T

TABLE 3.5.

p	q	(p & q)	⊃	−(p & q)	
T	T	T	F	F	T
T	F	F	T	T	F
F	T	F	T	T	F
F	F	F	T	T	F

determine the conditions under which a complex statement comes out true, the procedure would be to get its finest truth functional form and perform a Truth Table Analysis. The values of the sentence letters in the rows where the statement form comes out 'T' give us the conditions under which the statement is true. Thus, if we wanted to know the conditions under which 'He is tall and handsome only if it is not the case that he is both tall and handsome' is true, Table 3.5 tells us that this statement is true under the following three conditions: (i) he is tall and he is not handsome, (ii) he is not tall and he is handsome, and (iii) he is not tall and he is not handsome.

By giving the conditions under which a statement form comes out true, the Truth Table Analysis gives us a particularly perspicuous way of determining the variety of logical properties and relations in which we are interested. It is also a completely mechanical procedure that is guaranteed to determine for us whether or not a truth functional statement form or a (finite) set of them have the logical properties or relations in which we are interested. On the other hand, a major disadvantage of determining logical properties by a Truth Table Analysis is that because it is a "paper-and-pencil" (or computer) method, in conversational contexts it does not give us a practical method for determining whether a proposed argument is valid. And even if we use the paper-and-pencil method, if the number of sentence letters involved exceeds three or four, the analysis becomes clearly cumbersome; thirty-two and sixty-four line Truth Table Analyses may require so much paper as to endanger the trees of our forests. Another major disadvantage of using the Truth Table Analysis is that it gives us few clues on how to adjust an argument if it is invalid; that is, it gives us little clue on what missing premises may be necessary to convert the invalid argument into one that is valid. Part and parcel of this disadvantage is that it does not give us any guidelines for constructing valid arguments or reasoning deductively. Once we have an argument, a Truth Table Analysis can tell us whether or not we have a truth functionally valid argument. But it is of no use in arriving at the argument in the first place or in correcting it if the need arises; therefore, to this extent, using Truth Table Analyses is not helpful in developing and enhancing our reasoning skills. Because of these considerations, the main method of this text is the method of chain arguments, which will be presented in the next section.

EXERCISES—SECTION 3.4

1. By means of Truth Table Analyses, determine which of the following statement forms are tautologies.

   (a) $q \supset (p \supset p)$ (e) $p \supset (p \vee^e q)$
   (b) $q \supset (p \supset q)$ (f) $p \supset (p \vee q)$
   (c) $-p \supset (p \vee q)$ (g) $[(p \,\&\, q) \supset r] \supset (p \supset r)$
   (d) $-p \supset (p \supset q)$ (h) $[(p \vee q) \supset r] \supset (p \supset r)$

2. By means of Truth Table Analyses, determine which of the following argument forms of the exercise of Section 3.3.4 are valid: [d], [e], [f], [g], [h], [i], [j], [k], [l].

3. For each of the pairs given below, determine by means of a Truth Table Analysis whether it is a pair with logically identical truth conditions:

   (a) $-(p \vee q)$, $-p \vee -q$ (g) $p \equiv q$, $p \vee^e -q$
   (b) $-(p \vee q)$, $-p \,\&\, -q$ (h) $p \supset q$, $-p \vee q$
   (c) $-(-p \,\&\, -q)$, $p \,\&\, q$ (i) $p \supset q$, $p \vee -q$
   (d) $-(-p \,\&\, -q)$, $p \vee q$ (j) $-(p \,\&\, -q)$, $p \supset q$
   (e) $-(p \equiv q)$, $-p \equiv -q$ (k) $p \supset q$, $q \supset p$
   (f) $-(p \equiv q)$, $p \equiv -q$ (l) $p \supset q$, $-q \supset -p$

4. By means of the Truth Table Analysis, determine for each of (a)–(e) whether it is consistent or inconsistent. If any of (a)–(e) are consistent, specify the conditions under which the statement form, or all members of the set of statement forms, come out true.

   (a) $p \supset (q \,\&\, -q)$
   (b) $p \equiv p \supset -p$
   (c) {'$-(p \vee q)$', 'p'}
   (d) {'$-(p \,\&\, q)$', 'p'}
   (e) {'$p \supset q$', '$q \supset r$', 'p', '$-r$'}

5. Fill in the blanks of the following statements so that the resulting statement is true, *and* justify the truth of the resulting statement.

   (a) A statement form is inconsistent if and only if its negation is ____.
   (b) An argument is valid if and only if the conjunction of the premises and the negation of the conclusion is ____.
   (c) An argument is invalid if and only if ____ is consistent.

3.5 Toward a Method for Determining Deductive Validity

In this and the following sections, we shall develop a method for determining the deductive validity of truth functional argument forms.

Because the method may confuse the reader with too many items to manage at one time, we shall follow the plan of introducing the method a little at a time and present the full method is summary form at the end of this chapter. The first glimpse of this method will appear in Section 3.5.2. However, we shall have to learn that certain argument forms are deductively valid in order to use the method introduced in Section 3.5.2. Thus, we start by presenting some deductively valid argument forms in Section 3.5.1.

3.5.1 Some Deductively Valid Argument Forms

In Section 3.3.4 we showed that the following argument form is deductively valid:

[1] $p \supset q$
$\underline{p \quad\quad}$
q

This argument form has been given the traditional name of MODUS PONENS. Thus, we may take *modus ponens* (MP) to be a valid argument form. Consider now the following two argument forms:

[2] $r \supset s$
$\underline{r \quad\quad}$
s

[3] $(q \vee r) \supset (s \,\&\, t)$
$\underline{q \vee r \quad\quad\quad\quad}$
$s \,\&\, t$

Because they are constructed from different sentence letters, [1] and [2] are, strictly speaking, distinct argument forms, and in any reasonable sense of "same," [3] is not the same argument form as [1] or [2]. Yet surely the considerations that showed [1] to be valid also show [2] to be valid, and any mention of 'p' and 'q' merely has to be replaced by mention of 'r' and 's'. The same holds for [3], and with a slight variation we can restate the considerations given in Section 3.3.4: Regardless of how the blanks are filled, if all the premises of [3] are to come out true, 'q v r' must become true; but then for the first premise to come out true, 's & t' must also have been filled to come out true. Hence, any way of filling the blanks that makes all the premises of [3] true must also make the conclusion of [3] true. Because the validity of [1]–[3] depends on precisely the same considerations, it would be convenient to have a simple way of expressing the deductive validity of [1]–[3] and all argument forms of the same type.

To this end, we resort to the Greek letters we introduced in Section 3.3.2. That is, we shall use ϕ, θ, and the like as variables standing for statement forms. Given this understanding, we can list under MP any argument form having the following form:

Modus ponens (MP)

$\phi \supset \theta$
$\underline{\phi \quad\quad}$
θ

Replacing 'q v r' and 's & t' in our considerations of the last paragraph by ϕ and θ, we may take ourselves to have shown that any argument form of the type MP is deductively valid. This then constitutes the first type of argument forms that may be taken to be valid.

Similar considerations show the following two types of argument forms with the indicated names to be deductively valid:

Adjunction (Adj)	Hypothetical Syllogism (HS)
ϕ	$\phi \supset \psi$
$\underline{\theta \quad\quad}$	$\underline{\psi \supset \theta}$
$\phi \,\&\, \theta$	$\phi \supset \theta$

Argument forms of the ADJUNCTION (Adj) type are obviously deductively valid, as the reader may verify by using considerations akin to the ones we have already used. The HYPOTHETICAL SYLLOGISM (HS) is a type of argument we frequently use. For example, we might argue: "If Brian comes, Jane will be happy; but if Jane will be happy, Tom will be sad. Therefore, if Brian comes, Tom will be sad." Any argument as well as any argument form of the HS type is deductively valid. To see this, we ask if in the displayed type of argument form the blanks could be so filled as to make both premises true and the conclusion false. If the conclusion is to come out false, ϕ must become true and θ must become false. But then if ψ becomes true, the second premise would be false, and if ψ becomes false, then the first premise would be false. Hence, it is impossible to fill the blanks of an argument form of the HS type so that the premises all come out true and the conclusion false. Thus, argument forms of the HS type are valid.

In order to avoid confusion, let us be clear that the kind of consideration we have just gone through involves two levels of abstraction. At the bottom level are arguments expressed in ordinary English: the argument about Brian, Jane, and Tom was one example, and abstracting from that argument we may arrive at the argument form [4] below.

[4]		[5]		[6]	
	b ⊃ j		t ⊃ g		(m v t) ⊃ j
	<u>j ⊃ t</u>		<u>g ⊃ h</u>		<u>j ⊃ (p & h)</u>
	b ⊃ t		t ⊃ h		(m v t) ⊃ (p & h)

Argument form [4] is also the argument form of ‘if Tom will be sad, Tom’s girlfriend will be sad, and if Tom’s girlfriend will be sad, Hester will be delighted; therefore, if Tom will be sad, Hester will be delighted’. Thus, both the argument involving Brian and that involving Hester are shown to be deductively valid by showing [4] to be deductively valid. However, within a larger context, we might want to represent the argument involving Hester by the form [5]. This might be the case if we want to join this argument with the earlier one involving Brian, to draw the conclusion that if Brian comes, Hester will be delighted.

Consider now the following argument: ‘If Tom or Mary comes, Joe will be shocked; if Joe is shocked, he will perspire and his heart rate will increase. Therefore, if Tom or Mary comes, Joe will perspire and his heart rate will increase’. This argument can also be given the form [4]. But within the context of a larger argument, it may be desirable to represent this argument as having the form [6]. Argument forms [4]–[6] represent the first level of abstraction.

What we want is a uniform way of representing the argument forms [4]–[6], and this involves the second level of abstraction given in the representation of HS by means of the Greek letters. Corresponding to this second level of abstraction, we want one comprehensive way of arguing all of the argument forms of the HS type to be valid, including [4]–[6]. The discussion earlier was precisely such a comprehensive way of arguing, which avoids the need to argue individually, for the validity of [4], [5], [6], and other argument forms of the same type.

We conclude our initial batch of valid types of argument forms with two versions of an argument type called the DILEMMA. A simple version in an ordinary context might be: ‘She will divorce him or stay married to him; if she divorces him, she will be unhappy; (but) if she stays married to him, she will (also) be unhappy; so (either way) she will be unhappy’. A complex version might go as follows: ‘He will go to San Francisco or Los Angeles; if he goes to San Francisco, he will go to North Beach; if he goes to Los Angeles, he will go to the Sunset Strip; therefore he will go to North Beach or to the Sunset Strip’. Abstracting from all arguments and argument forms of this type, we arrive at the following types of argument forms:

Simple Dilemma (SDil)	Complex Dilemma (Cdil)
$\phi_1 \vee \phi_2$	$\phi_1 \vee \phi_2$
$\phi_1 \supset \theta$	$\phi_1 \supset \theta_1$
$\underline{\phi_2 \supset \theta}$	$\underline{\phi_2 \supset \theta_2}$
θ	$\theta_1 \vee \theta_2$

Any argument form of the SDil type can be seen to be valid by the following consideration: If the blanks are so filled that the conclusion θ becomes false, for the second and third premises to be true, the blanks must be so filled that ϕ_1 and ϕ_2 both come out false; but then the blanks have gotten so filled that the first premise comes out false. Hence, there is no way of filling the blanks of an argument form of the SDil type so that the premises all come out true and the conclusion false. Similar considerations show that any argument form of the type CDil is also valid.

Critical to the method of determining deductive validity, which we shall be introducing in the next subsection, is the ability to spot instances of the valid argument types we have discussed. Given a pair of lines like

(1) (s ⊃ p) ⊃ (p ⊃ q)

(2) r ⊃ (s ⊃ p)

we must be able to spot them as the premises of HS from which the conclusion 'r ⊃ (p ⊃ q)' may be inferred. This might be called *spotting the* HIDDEN GROSS STRUCTURE *of statement forms*. The crucial step to spotting these hidden structures is to ask: what is the simple or main form of (1)? Clearly the simple or main form of (1) is 'X ⊃ Y' where 'X' is 's ⊃ p' and 'Y' is 'p ⊃ q'. Given that (1) has this form, what is the simple or main form of (2)? It is a conditional whose consequent is 's ⊃ p' or 'X'; if we let 'Z' be 'r', lines (1) and (2) have the form:

(1′)	X ⊃ Y,	X: s ⊃ p,	Y: p ⊃ q
(2′)	Z ⊃ X,	Z: r	

Recalling that the order of premises makes no difference, (1′) and (2′) are the same premises as 'Z ⊃ X' and 'X ⊃ Y'. We can now see that these are the premises of HS from which we may infer the conclusion 'Z ⊃ Y' or

(3) r ⊃ (p ⊃ q)

Thus, we determine that (1) and (2) are premises of HS, from which conclusion (3) may be inferred.

A special case of spotting the hidden gross structure of statement forms involves the two dilemmas. The following are two instances of the argument type CDil:

p v q v r	p v q v r
(p v q) ⊃ (s v t)	p ⊃ s
r ⊃ u	(q v r) ⊃ (t v u)
s v t v u	s v t v u

In the first instance ϕ_1 is taken as 'p v q' and ϕ_2 as 'r'; θ_1 is 's v t', and θ_2 is 'u'. In the second instance ϕ_1 is taken as 'p' and ϕ_2 as 'q v r'; θ_1 is 's' and θ_2 is 't v u'. Because we are dispensing with parentheses in repeated disjunctions, the first premise of the displayed argument forms can be taken either as '(p v q) v r' or as 'p v (q v r)'. Again, because we are dispensing with parentheses in repeated disjunctions, we are displaying the conclusion of the two argument forms in the indicated manner rather than as '(s v t) v u' and 's v (u v t)', respectively.

We conclude this subsection with a brief discussion of how the material in Chapter 3 ties in with our ultimate goal of assessing truth claims. Suppose someone tells us: 'If he moves to Kansas, he will miss the ocean; but if he stays in Santa Barbara, he will suffer from a high cost of living; so, he will miss the ocean or suffer from a high cost of living'. Let us suppose that we know enough to be able to assess 'If he moves to Kansas, he will miss the ocean' and 'If he stays in Santa Barbara, he will suffer from a high cost of living' to be both true. Can we assess 'He will miss the ocean or suffer from a high cost of living' to be true? Suppose we add the following premise to the explicitly given reasons: 'He will move to Kansas or stay in Santa Barbara'. The resulting argument would be an instance of CDil, and the truth of the given premise and the added missing premise guarantees the truth of 'He will miss the ocean or suffer from a high cost of living'. Thus, if we have good reasons to think that he will move to Kansas or stay in Santa Barbara (perhaps because those are the only places he has been able to get a job or a job offer), we would also have good reasons for thinking that he will miss the ocean or suffer a high cost of living.

This example illustrates a general point:

We can often assess a truth claim by adding to the explicitly given reasons some missing premises that would convert the argument into a valid one.

For this reason, the ability to come up with appropriate missing premises is a highly useful skill for assessing truth claims. Although we shall be working on this skill in subsequent sections, the first step to developing this skill is obvious: It is helpful to become familiar with the valid argument types that we have studied, so that for any given type, if all but one of the premises are stated, one can quickly suggest the missing premise that will convert the argument (or argument form) into a valid one.

EXERCISES—SECTION 3.5.1

1. For each of the following sets of statement forms, (i) determine whether their hidden gross structure matches the premises of MP, HS, SDil, or CDil, and (ii) if the statement forms match these premises, then exhibit the conclusion that the instance will have.

[a] $-(s \& t)$
$-(s \& t) \supset [p \vee (q \supset r)]$

[b] $(u \supset s) \supset (t \supset u)$
$-(u \supset s)$

[c] $(p \,\&\, q) \supset r$
p

[d] $(u \vee r) \supset (p \supset q)$
$(s \vee t) \supset (p \supset q)$

[e] $(u \vee s) \supset (t \supset p)$
$(w \vee r) \supset (u \vee s)$

[f] $(s \vee u) \supset -(t \supset p)$
$(t \supset p) \supset (q \vee r)$

[g] $r \supset u$
$p \supset (q \vee r)$
$q \supset u$

[h] $(s \supset t) \supset (p \vee q)$
$(p \vee q) \supset (r \,\&\, u)$
$(s \supset t) \vee (p \vee q)$

[i] $(q \vee r) \supset s$
$p \supset s$
$p \vee q \vee r$

[j] $(p \vee q) \,\&\, r$
$p \supset s$
$r \supset t$

2. Suggest a missing premise for each of the following that will convert the argument into a deductively valid type discussed in Section 3.5.1.
   (a) If we bomb the Russians, the Russians will bomb us back. Therefore, if we bomb the Russians, we will suffer damages.
   (b) If he is the president, his assets are held in a blind trust. Therefore, his assets are held in a blind trust.
   (c) He is sick. Therefore, he won't play in the game tonight.
   (d) If it rains, I'll have fun (playing inside); if it's clear, I'll have fun (on a picnic); so, (either way), I'll have fun.
   (e) The course is either too easy or too hard. If it's too hard, there is no point in studying too much for it. So, (either way), there is no point in studying too much for it.
   (f) If he marries Grushenka, he'll have a frantic life. But if he marries Brunhilde, he'll be bored to death. So, he will either have a frantic life or he will be bored to death.

3.5.2 Introduction to Simple Chain Arguments

In Section 3.5.1 we learned a few types of deductively valid argument forms, and indeed we frequently use these types of arguments in ordinary life. However, it should also be evident that we are not going to arrive at a *general method* just by increasing our stock of valid argument types. Because there are inexhaustibly many types of valid argument forms, it is hopeless to attempt to list them all. On the other hand, if we could somehow combine the use of several valid forms to show the validity of other argument forms, perhaps a limited stock of valid argument types will be a sufficient basis for a general method of showing deductive validity. This, indeed, turns out to be the case:

By combining valid argument forms from a limited stock, we can show more complex arguments to be valid.

The idea of combining several arguments to justify a more complex argument is one we are used to in everyday life. The following example is an instance: "If Jill's stepmother hosts the reception, Jill's real mother won't be able to host the reception; (and) if Jill's real mother won't be able to host the reception, Jill's real mother will be offended [so, if Jill's stepmother hosts the reception, Jill's real mother will be offended]; (but) if Jill's real mother will be offended, Jill will be upset. Therefore, if Jill's stepmother hosts the reception, Jill will be upset." This way of arguing clearly combines two uses of HS. If we let 's', 'r', 'o', and 'u' abbreviate the stepmother hosting the reception, the real mother hosting it, the real mother being offended, and Jill being upset, the line of thought imagined may be represented in the following way:

(1) $s \supset r$ —premise
(2) $r \supset o$ —premise
(3) $s \supset o$ —from (1) and (2) by HS
(4) $o \supset u$ —premise
(5) $s \supset u$ —from (3) and (4) by HS

It should be plausible that this line of thought shows the validity of the following argument (form):

$s \supset r$
$r \supset o$
$o \supset u$
———
$s \supset u$

If combining two different instances of HS shows this argument form to be valid, we have shown the validity of an argument form that was not on the list of valid argument forms in Section 3.5.1. While this is an extremely simple example, this way of combining valid argument forms will give us a general method for determining the validity of truth functional argument forms. Furthermore, such a method will clearly reflect a natural way in which we reason, and by learning such a method we shall enhance our ability to reason in ordinary life. *The way of combining valid argument forms to show more complex argument forms to be valid is often called the method of* DEDUCTION, *but we shall use the more intuitive term, the* METHOD OF CHAIN ARGUMENT.

The simple chain argument may be understood in the following way:

Definition: if $\phi_1, \ldots, \phi_n / \theta$ is a deductively valid argument form, θ is VALIDLY INFERABLE from (or is IMPLIED BY) $\{\phi_1, \ldots, \phi_n\}$.

Definition: Let [A] be some (complex) argument form. A SIMPLE CHAIN ARGUMENT (or a DEDUCTION) for [A] is a finite sequence of lines (1), . . . , (m) such that:

(a) each line is a premise of [A] or else validly inferable from (a subset of) the previous lines in the sequence, and
(b) the last line (m) is the conclusion of [A].

Although the proof would be beyond the scope of the present chapter, it can be proved that:

> *A simple chain argument for an argument form* [*A*] *shows* [*A*] *to be a valid argument form.*

In Section 3.5.1 we arrived at an initial stock of valid argument forms, and with them, we are in a position to construct simple chain arguments to show a variety of complex argument forms to be deductively valid. In subsequent sections we shall increase the stock of valid argument forms on which we can rely in constructing chain arguments; as a result, we shall have an increasingly powerful method of chain arguments for showing the validity of various argument forms. Howcvcr, we now have enough material to see how the method of chain arguments works.

Before proceeding to some examples, it is best to standardize our work. To this end, we shall requre that, to the *right* of each line of a chain argument for [A], a *justification for that line* must be provided. In terms of the material we now have, the justification can take *one of two forms:* (i) *'Pr'*, which indicates the line to be a premise of [A], and (ii) a *list of previous line numbers* and the citation of a *valid argument form* (e.g., MP, HS, and SDil), indicating that the line in question is validly inferable from those previous lines.

To start with a fairly simple example, suppose we are trying to show the validity of the following argument form:

$p \supset q$
$q \supset r$
$p \vee s$
$\underline{s \supset r}$
r

The following simple chain argument accomplishes this end:

(1)	$p \supset q$	Pr
(2)	$q \supset r$	Pr
(3)	$p \supset r$	(1)(2)HS
(4)	$p \vee s$	Pr
(5)	$s \supset r$	Pr
(6)	r	(3)(4)(5)SDil

It is easily verified that this configuration constitutes a simple chain argument for the argument form in question. Hence, we have shown the validity of that argument form by the displayed chain. It may be again worthwhile reminding the reader at this point that the order of premises in an argument (form) is immaterial. Thus,

It matters not that (3), (4), and (5) are in an order different from the one given when we introduced SDil in Section 3.5.1.

Once a simple chain argument is presented, one can mechanically determine whether or not the configuration agrees with the definition of a simple chain argument. However, the task of constructing a simple chain argument is far more difficult. If we divide the task into tactical maneuvers to be executed and the strategies to be pursued, tactics become a matter of identifying what is validly inferable. While we shall have more to say about tactics at a later point, what matters for now is knowing the list of valid argument types (such as MP and HS), which we shall keep expanding, and being able to spot hidden gross structures so that the listed argument types can be used to infer new lines in a chain. As for strategy, the strategy to be pursued in constructing chain arguments can be broken down into three parts:

(A) Forward Strategy

Write down some of the premises, and add as new lines whatever is validly inferable from them by one of the types of argument forms you are allowed to use. If these new lines and some of the other premises allow you to infer further new lines by one of the permitted types of argument forms, write down these other premises and the second wave of new lines that can be validly inferred. Continue this process until you arrive at the desired conclusion or you reach a point where you feel that no progress is being made.

In our example above, following the forward strategy allowed us to reach the desired conclusion rather quickly. We wrote down (1) and (2) and added (3), because we could validly infer it from (1) and (2) by HS. Looking at line (3) and the remaining premises allowed us to see that SDil could be used; hence, we wrote down those premises, or "activated them," at lines (4) and (5), and validly inferred line (6) by SDil from (3), (4), and (5). In this manner we arrived at line (6), which was fortunately the conclusion we had targeted. However, constructing chain arguments is not always this simple, and sometimes one feels that no progress toward the desired conclusion is being made. In such a case, one is well advised to switch to the backward strategy.

(B) Backward Strategy

Determine what conclusion or last line you are trying to reach, and ask with reference to the permitted argument forms what intermediate line or lines would help in arriving at this conclusion.

Once you think that you have targeted a plausible intermediate line, switch to step (C).

(C) Bridging the Gap

You must now try to find a way to connect the result of the forward strategy and the backward strategy, so that you can validly infer the intermediate step revealed by the backward strategy from the result of the forward strategy, by one or more uses of the permitted types of argument forms.

This often proves to be the most difficult step. At times one may have to reapply the forward and backward strategies to get from the beginning to the end of the gap. At other times one may have to readjust the forward or backward strategy. For example, seeing what one can get from the result of the forward strategy, one may have to readjust the backward strategy so that one is aiming for a slightly different intermediate conclusion; at other times, the result of the backward strategy may indicate that one should have pursued the forward strategy in a slightly different fashion. It must be admitted that sometimes one may simply have to "brainstorm" in order to bridge the gap. On the other hand, often the gap is almost automatically bridged at the end of steps (B) and (C).

As a way of exemplifying steps (B) and (C), consider the following argument form:

r ⊃ (s ⊃ p)

(s ⊃ p) ⊃ (p ⊃ q)

r

s

(p & q) ⊃ u
___

u

Following the forward strategy, one notices that the first two premises are candidates for HS. That would give us 'r ⊃ (p ⊃ q)', and this along with the third premise would give us '(p ⊃ q)' by MP. Putting this down, we have the following lines in our chain argument:

(1)	r ⊃ (s ⊃ p)	Pr
(2)	(s ⊃ p) ⊃ (p ⊃ q)	Pr
(3)	r ⊃ (p ⊃ q)	(1)(2)HS
(4)	r	Pr
(5)	p ⊃ q	(3)(4)MP

Some readers may not feel sure of how to continue at this point; if so, it would be wise to switch to the backward strategy. We are trying to arrive at 'u' and have as a given premise '(p & q) ⊃ u'. Thus, if we could somehow get 'p & q', we could use MP to get the desired conclusion. But we can get 'p & q' from 'p' and 'q' by Adj. Thus 'p' and 'q' seem to be plausible lines to target. This use of the backward strategy may be represented by marking the last line as (*n*), because we don't know what the actual line number of the last line will be:

(*n* − 4)	p	?
(*n* − 3)	q	?
(*n* − 2)	p & q	(*n* − 4)(*n* − 3)Adj

$(n-1)$	(p & q) ⊃ u	Pr
(n)	u	$(n-1)(n-2)$MP

In actual practice, one would of course work backward from line (n), and it may be most convenient if these lines were placed in a column to the right of the column of lines representing the forward strategy.

The task is now to bridge the gap. Somehow we must get from the results of the forward strategy to 'p' and 'q'. The first thing to do in bridging the gap is to see if any of the premises have not yet been used, and if there are some that have not been used, to figure out how they may be used. In our case the premise 's' has not yet been used. Looking at line (1) we see that 's' occurs as the antecedent of the subconditional. Clearly, if we could somehow get the subconditional 's ⊃ p' alone as a separate line, 's' can be used in a step of MP to arrive at 'p', which is one of the intermediate lines we have targeted. But now we notice that line (4) is 'r' and that 'r' is the antecedent of the main conditional of (1). Thus, a use of MP will give us 's ⊃ p' as a separate line. These considerations lead to the following continuation beyond line (5):

(6)	s ⊃ p	(4)(1)MP
(7)	s	Pr
(8)	p	(6)(7)MP

Given that 'p ⊃ q' was given in line (5) as the result of the forward strategy, one more use of MP on (5) and (8) can give us 'q' at line (9), which is the other intermediate line we have targeted. Given this addition, in lines (8) and (9) we have arrived at lines $(n-4)$ and $(n-3)$ of our backward strategy. Now it is simply a matter of adjusting the line numbers in the backward strategy. Thus, the chain argument is completed as follows:

(9)	q	(8)(5)MP
(10)	p & q	(8)(9)Adj
(11)	(p & q) ⊃ u	Pr
(12)	u	(10)(11)MP

It is of course true that if one activated the premise 's' in the forward strategy, and doggedly followed the forward strategy, one could have dispensed with the backward strategy. However, in constructing chain arguments one often feels lost, and in these cases it is a good idea to switch to the backward strategy so that one has some idea of what to aim for.

The example we have gone through illustrates an important point to keep in mind in constructing chain arguments. In trying to bridge the gap, we saw that in a premise and a line the following two statement forms were available:

s

r ⊃ (s ⊃ p)

It would be a mistake to think that MP could be directly used on ‘s’ and ‘$s \supset p$’ (the consequent of the second statement form) to arrive at ‘$r \supset p$’.

> *All the valid argument forms that can be used in chain arguments apply only to* **entire lines, not** *to* **parts of lines.**

That is why we had to use MP along with the line ‘r’ to get at ‘$s \supset p$’ as a separate entire line before we could use MP along with ‘s’.[8]

EXERCISES—SECTION 3.5.2

1. Show by means of chain arguments that the following argument forms are valid. [Most of these are extremely simple exercises, and each chain will only involve one or more uses of one valid argument type.]

[a]
$(p \vee q) \supset s$
$\underline{p \vee q}$
s

[b]
$(q \vee r) \supset (s \,\&\, t)$
$\underline{(p \supset t) \supset (q \vee r)}$
$(p \supset t) \supset (s \,\&\, t)$

[c]
$-p \supset -r$
$-p \vee (q \supset r)$
$\underline{(q \supset r) \supset -r}$
$-r$

[d]
$p \supset s$
$-(q \,\&\, r) \supset t$
$\underline{p \vee -(q \,\&\, r)}$
$s \vee t$

[e]
$(p \vee q) \supset [(p \vee q) \supset r]$
$\underline{p \vee q}$
r

[f]
$(p \supset q) \,\&\, r$
$\underline{t \vee w}$
$(t \vee w) \,\&\, (p \supset q) \,\&\, r$

[g]
$p \supset q$
$-s \supset -t$
$q \supset r$
$\underline{r \supset -s}$
$p \supset -t$

[h]
$p \supset (r \vee s)$
$r \supset t$
$p \vee q$
$s \supset t$
$\underline{q \supset (r \vee s)}$
t

[i]
$s \supset t$
$p \vee q$
$r \supset u$
$q \supset s$
$\underline{p \supset r}$
$u \vee t$

[j]
$s \supset w$
$p \vee q \vee r$
$(q \vee r) \supset (r \vee s)$
$(t \vee r) \supset u$
$\underline{p \supset t}$
$u \vee w$

8. The astute reader may have noticed that ‘$s, r \supset (s \supset p) / r \supset p$’ is in fact valid. However, consider the following example: ‘$(p \supset q) \supset q, q \supset p / (p \supset p) \supset q$’. Here HS was used on the antecedent part of the conditional, and the resulting argument form is invalid as it may be checked by filling ‘p’ by True and ‘q’ by False. Clearly one cannot always use valid argument forms on parts of lines. Rather than trying to specify complicated rules as to when an argument form can be applied to parts of lines and when it can't, we make the blanket ruling that none of the argument forms can be used on parts of lines.

2. Show by means of chain arguments that the following argument forms are valid. (The use of several different argument types will typically be needed in each of the following chains.)

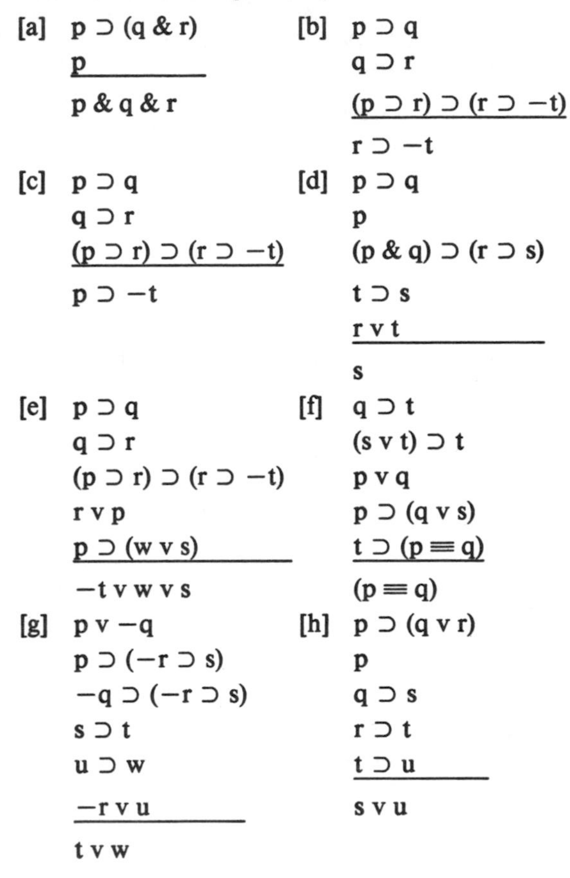

[a]
$p \supset (q \& r)$
$\underline{p}$
$p \& q \& r$

[b]
$p \supset q$
$q \supset r$
$\underline{(p \supset r) \supset (r \supset -t)}$
$r \supset -t$

[c]
$p \supset q$
$q \supset r$
$\underline{(p \supset r) \supset (r \supset -t)}$
$p \supset -t$

[d]
$p \supset q$
p
$(p \& q) \supset (r \supset s)$
$t \supset s$
$\underline{r \vee t}$
s

[e]
$p \supset q$
$q \supset r$
$(p \supset r) \supset (r \supset -t)$
$r \vee p$
$\underline{p \supset (w \vee s)}$
$-t \vee w \vee s$

[f]
$q \supset t$
$(s \vee t) \supset t$
$p \vee q$
$p \supset (q \vee s)$
$\underline{t \supset (p \equiv q)}$
$(p \equiv q)$

[g]
$p \vee -q$
$p \supset (-r \supset s)$
$-q \supset (-r \supset s)$
$s \supset t$
$u \supset w$
$\underline{-r \vee u}$
$t \vee w$

[h]
$p \supset (q \vee r)$
p
$q \supset s$
$r \supset t$
$\underline{t \supset u}$
$s \vee u$

3.6 Expanding the List of Valid Argument Types

Now that we have an idea of what simple chain arguments are, we shall continue the task started in Section 3.5 of listing valid argument types that may be used in constructing chain arguments. We shall also continue our discussion of finding missing premises that we started in Section 3.5. In Section 3.6.1 we shall deal with valid argument types involving negation and in Section 3.6.2 we shall focus on those involving conjunction and disjunction.

3.6.1 Argument Types Involving Negation

Clearly the following is an argument that should be counted as valid: "If the Earth is flat, Magellan did not circumnavigate the earth; (but) Magellan did circumnavigate the Earth; so, the Earth is not flat." Virtually identical in structure is the following obviously valid argument: "If he is in town, his car is in the garage; (but) his car is not in the garage; therefore, he is not in town." The same might be said of: "If he didn't date Jill, he is alone; (but) he isn't alone; therefore, he dated Jill." These three arguments may be given the following three logical forms:

[1]		[2]		[3]	
	$p \supset -q$		$p \supset q$		$-p \supset q$
	$\underline{q}$		$\underline{-q}$		$\underline{-q}$
	$-p$		$-p$		p

The reader may confirm that whatever truth value fills the 'p' and 'q', if all the premises come out true, so does the conclusion.

Argument forms [1], [2], and [3] are of the type traditionally called MODUS TOLLENS, or MT. It would be desirable to have one comprehensive way of representing argument forms of this type. While our use of Greek letters will help, it will not entirely suffice. Therefore we introduce the following notational convention:

> Convention: $N[\phi]$ represents $-\phi$ if ϕ is a nonnegated expression, and if ϕ is a negated expression of the form $-\theta$, $N[\phi]$ represents θ.

Thus, for example, N['q'] is '$-$q' while N['$-$q'] is 'q'. Loosely speaking, we can think of '$N[\phi]$' as switching around the positive or negative sign of ϕ or as giving us the "opposite" value of ϕ.

We can now specify the first type of valid argument forms involving negations as follows:

> Modus tollens (MT)
>
> $\phi \supset \theta$
>
> $\underline{N[\theta]}$
>
> $N[\phi]$

The general argument for the validity of MT is this: Regardless of how we fill the blanks, if the premises are all to come out true, θ must come out false so that the second premise comes out true; but then, for the first premise to come out true, ϕ must come out false. This, however, has the consequence that the blanks are so filled that the conclusion $N[\phi]$ comes out true. Hence, regardless of how the blanks of MT are filled, if all the premises come out true, so does the conclusion.

Consider now the following argument: "If Tom became a lawyer, Tom didn't go to medical school; (but) if Tom didn't go to medical school, his father didn't pay for his professional education; (and) if his father didn't pay for his professional education, Tom couldn't afford law school; (but) if Tom couldn't afford law school, Tom didn't become a lawyer. So, (it must be that) Tom didn't become a lawyer." Of course one of the premises might be false, but if they are all true, I think we can see that the conclusion has got to be true. The argument is represented in the left-hand column, and part of the chain argument for it is given in the right-hand column:

$l \supset -m$	(1) $l \supset -m$	Pr
$-m \supset -f$	(2) $-m \supset -f$	Pr
$-f \supset -a$	(3) $l \supset -f$	(1)(2)HS
$\underline{-a \supset -l}$	(4) $-f \supset -a$	Pr
$-l$	(5) $l \supset -a$	(3)(4)HS
	(6) $-a \supset -l$	Pr
	(7) $l \supset -l$	(5)(6)HS

We are in a position to finish the chain argument for the desired conclusion if '$l \supset -l$ / $-l$' is valid. The reader can quickly verify that the argument form is indeed valid. The intuitive idea behind this argument form may be stated as follows: Because even the assumption that 'l' is true leads to the conclusion that 'l' is false, 'l' can't be true and must be false. Another way of putting it might be this: Regardless of how we fill the blanks, 'l v $-l$' and '$-l \supset -l$' are always going to come out true; thus we might think of these as "free premises" that may always be invoked in determining the validity of an argument form. But then the addition of these "free" premises along with '$l \supset -l$' gives us an instance of SDil from which the conclusion '$-l$' may be inferred. Regardless of how we may conceive of it, '$l \supset -l$ / $-l$' is a valid argument form and it is an instance of the argument type called INDIRECT ARGUMENT, or IA.

Generalizing from our discussion, we may add the following two types of valid argument forms to our list:

Indirect Argument (IA)	*Reductio* (Rd)
$\underline{\phi \supset N[\phi]}$	$\underline{\phi \supset (\theta \; \& \; N[\theta])}$
$N[\phi]$	$N[\phi]$

Arguing as we have already done a number of times, the reader may verify that these two types of argument forms may be counted on for being valid. REDUCTIO is a shortened form of what is called a *reductio ad absurdum,* and the validity of this type of argument may become evident when it is expressed as:

Because the assumption that ϕ is true leads to the contradiction that θ and $-\theta$ are both true, ϕ can't be true and must therefore be false.

In Section 3.5.1 we stressed the importance of being able to detect missing premises that would convert a deductively invalid argument into one that was deductively valid. This task is relatively easy when we specify that the resulting valid argument is to be one of a few specified valid argument types; something like a process of elimination will give us the desired missing premises. However, it would be clearly arbitrary to insist that missing premises be found to convert the argument into one of those limited types of valid argument forms. The general situation is that we are given a number of premises and a conclusion, and the task is to find premises so that the resulting argument (form) can be shown to be valid by a chain argument. Given any argument form $\phi_1, \ldots, \phi_n$ / θ, there is always one missing premise that will trivially convert it into a valid argument form; that is, we merely have to add the missing premise $(\phi_1 \& \ldots \& \phi_n) \supset \theta$. In addition to lines justified by Pr, $n - 1$ steps of Adj and one step of MP will give us a chain argument showing the validity of the augmented argument form. However, when we finally come to the task of assessing actual arguments and the truth claims they allege to substantiate, this will often turn out to be unhelpful, because assessing the plausibility of that lengthy missing premise is likely to be an exceptionally difficult task. Roughly, we want a way of getting shorter missing premises.

The useful method to follow in finding such shorter missing premises is analogous to the one used in constructing chain arguments, and may be broken down to a forward strategy and a backward strategy:

(A) Forward Strategy. Start trying to construct a chain argument for the conclusion with the given premises.

If the given premises yield nothing, tentatively add one or more additional premises so that something is validly inferable from the new premises along with the old ones that were given.

Try now to finish constructing a chain argument for the desired conclusion. If this is successful, then the appropriate missing premises have been found, and with those premises added, the augmented argument (form) becomes valid. If success is not attained, one might try adding some more premises that will allow the inference of something more from the given lines or else switch to the backward strategy.

(B) Backward Strategy. Follow the backward strategy of constructing chain arguments, and locate one or more intermediate conclusions that would allow one to finish the chain for the desired conclusion.

If some of these intermediate conclusions cannot be derived from the result of the forward strategy, add them as missing premises and finish the chain, which would now show the augmented argument form to be valid. However, one should **not** *add a missing premise that would make the given premises irrelevant for establishing the conclusion.*

The last statement is in recognition of the fact that we are seeking premises to augment the given premises rather than a new argument that can dispense with the given premises.

Sometimes it may prove necessary to go back and forth between the backward and forward strategies. Unless one knows what the goals are, one doesn't know what additional premise and intermediate result are necessary as part of the forward strategy. It can also happen that one has to readjust the backward strategy. The forward strategy may yield something a little bit different from one of the intermediate conclusions that was initially targeted, and this may cause a readjustment in the other "intermediate conclusion" that one decided to add as an extra missing premise. In general, if the forward strategy yields nothing even remotely relevant to the intermediate conclusions that were targeted, one should readjust the backward strategy because the result of the forward strategy should play some role in deriving the conclusion.

Before turning to an example, several things should be noted:

(1) Of course, *if one is asked to show the validity of a given argument form by means of a chain argument, one* **cannot** *add additional premises.* What we have been talking about is entirely limited to problems in which one is trying to determine what missing premises would convert an invalid argument into one that is valid.

(2) *There is no such thing as a unique answer to a problem of finding missing premises.* There are always any number of alternative ways of adding missing premises that would convert an argument into one that is valid.

(3) In light of (2), it is somewhat artificial to find missing premises for argument forms, because one needs to know the initial argument in English in order to determine which of the alternative ways of augmenting the argument are reasonably plausible. However, one also has to know what alternatives would convert the argument into a valid one, and to develop this skill, it is useful to work on argument forms and to determine missing premises that would convert them into valid ones.

Keeping these points in mind, consider the following invalid argument form[9]:

p v q

p ⊃ r

$\underline{-(u \supset s) \supset -r}$

u ⊃ v

9. Readers may try to determine the deductive invalidity by filling the blanks with truth values so that the premises come out true and the conclusion false.

In following the forward strategy of constructing chain arguments, we reach an impasse after the first two premises. However, the addition of '$q \supset r$' would allow us to use SDil. Given that this is a problem of finding missing premises, we add this as a new premise, show the justification as '*Pr' (the asterisk indicating that this is an added premise), and continue constructing the chain argument:

(1)	$p \vee q$	Pr
(2)	$p \supset r$	Pr
(3)	$q \supset r$	*Pr
(4)	r	(1)(2)(3)SDil
(5)	$-(u \supset s) \supset -r$	Pr
(6)	$u \supset s$	(4)(5)MT

At this point it may be advantageous to switch to the backward strategy of constructing chain arguments. This would give us:

$(n-1)$	$s \supset v$	?
(n)	$u \supset v$	(6)$(n-1)$HS

Because there is no evident way of getting $(n-1)$ from the result of the forward strategy, we add this as a missing premise. [Because 'v' is entirely absent from lines (1)–(6), one should strongly suspect that no amount of work is going to give us '$s \supset v$' as a line inferable from the previous lines.] Renumbering by setting $n-1$ to 7, and justifying (7) by *Pr, we have completed the chain argument.

What does this completed chain argument show? It certainly does *not* show the original argument to be valid. What it shows is the validity of the argument form in which the conclusion is the last line and the premises are the lines which are justified by Pr and *Pr. Thus, using an asterisk to indicate the missing premises added, what is shown to be deductively valid is:

$p \vee q$
$p \supset r$
*$q \supset r$
$-(u \supset s) \supset -r$
*$s \supset v$
____
$u \supset v$

That is, we have shown that when the original argument form is augmented by adding the starred missing premises, the resulting argument form is valid.

EXERCISES—SECTION 3.6.1

1. For each of the following sets of statement forms, (i) determine whether their hidden gross structure matches the premises of MT, IA, or Rd, and (ii) if the statement forms match these premises, exhibit the conclusion that the instance will have.

   [a] $(u \supset s) \supset -(t \supset u)$
   $t \supset u$

   [b] $(s \vee t) \supset p$
   $-(s \vee t)$

   [c] $(r \vee t) \supset (r \vee t)$

   [d] $-(s \supset u) \supset [(p \,\&\, q) \,\&\, -(p \,\&\, q)]$

   [e] $q \supset [r \supset (p \,\&\, -p)]$

   [f] $-[p \supset (s \equiv u)] \supset [p \supset (s \equiv u)]$

2. Show by means of chain arguments that the following argument forms are valid. (No chain involves the use of valid argument types other than those given in Section 3.6.1.)

   [a] $-[-(s \vee t) \supset -(p \,\&\, q)] \supset -(p \,\&\, q)$
   $\underline{p \,\&\, q}$
   $s \vee t$

   [b] $\underline{-(p \supset -p) \supset (p \supset -p)}$
   $-p$

   [c] $\underline{-[-(r \,\&\, s) \supset (p \,\&\, -p)] \supset (q \,\&\, -q)}$
   $r \,\&\, s$

   [d] $-[(s \vee t) \supset -(s \vee t)] \supset (p \supset q)$
   $\underline{(p \supset q) \supset ([(s \vee t) \supset -(s \vee t)] \,\&\, -[(s \vee t) \supset -(s \vee t)])}$
   $-(s \vee t)$

3. Show by means of chain arguments that the following argument forms are valid. (The use of several different argument types from this and the previous sections will typically be needed in each of the following chains.)

   [a] $(p \supset -q) \supset -(r \vee s)$
   $r \vee s$
   $-(p \supset -q) \supset -t$
   $\underline{-s \supset t}$
   s

   [b] $p \supset (q \,\&\, -q)$
   $r \supset p$
   s
   $\underline{(-r \,\&\, s) \supset u}$
   u

   [c] $p \supset q$
   p
   $\underline{u \supset -(p \,\&\, q)}$
   $-u$

   [d] $-p \supset s$
   $-(r \supset -p) \supset -p$
   $\underline{s \supset p}$
   $-r$

   [e] $-(s \vee r) \supset (s \vee r)$
   $s \supset (t \supset u)$
   $r \supset (t \supset u)$
   $\underline{-u}$
   $-t$

   [f] $p \supset q$
   $(q \vee r) \supset (r \supset -q)$
   $-(p \vee q) \supset -(p \supset r)$
   $\underline{q \supset r}$
   $-q$

4. Add one or more missing premises to convert the following into deductively valid argument forms and show the deductive validity by a chain argument. Do not use the "trivial" missing premise described in Section 3.6.1, and be sure that all of the given premises play a role in deriving the conclusion.

[a] $p \supset q$
$\underline{(p \supset r) \supset t}$
t

[b] $p \vee q$
$q \supset (r \supset s)$
$\underline{-s}$
$-r$

[c] $p \vee r$
$p \supset (q \supset r)$
$\underline{r \supset t}$
t

[d] $-[p \supset (t \supset s)] \supset u$
$p \vee q$
$\underline{q \supset (t \supset s)}$
$t \supset w$

3.6.2 Argument Types Involving Conjunctions and Disjunctions

Among the most obviously valid argument forms are the following:

[1] $\underline{p \,\&\, q}$
p

[2] $\underline{p \,\&\, q}$
q

[3] $\underline{p \,\&\, q \,\&\, r}$
q

Argument forms of this type are called SIMPLIFICATION, or S, and it is clear that such argument forms are valid, because there is no way a conjunction could be true without each of the conjuncts being true. Argument forms that are something like notational reverses of simplification are called ADDITION, or Add, and involve forms like:

[4] $\underline{p}$
$p \vee q$

[5] $\underline{q}$
$p \vee q$

[6] $\underline{q}$
$p \vee q \vee r$

These forms are also clearly valid because there is no way a disjunction could be false as long as one of its disjuncts is true. In everyday life, we hardly notice using simplification because it is so obvious, and we would seldom have occasion to use addition; for example, if I already know that he is in Spain, why infer that he is in Spain or Timbuctu? Still, we need to include S and Add in our list of valid argument types for the technical reason that chain arguments need them to show certain argument forms to be valid.

A problem is how to represent S and Add. The conjunct that is inferred by S can be any of the conjunction's conjuncts; for example, it needn't be the first conjunct. Similarly, given ϕ, we can infer any disjunction as long as ϕ occurs somewhere as one of the disjuncts. In order to represent S and Add in their most general form, we adopt the following conventions:

Convention: $C[\phi_1, \ldots, \phi_n]$ represents a conjunction in which the conjuncts are precisely $\phi_1, \ldots, \phi_n$ **taken in any order.**
Convention: $D[\phi_1, \ldots, \phi_n]$ represents any disjunction in which the disjuncts are precisely $\phi_1, \ldots, \phi_n$ **taken in any order.**

Thus, for example, C['p', 'q'] represents 'p & q' as well as 'q & p', and D['p', 'q'] represents both 'p v q' and 'q v p'. Given these conventions, S can be taken as inferring to the first statement listed in C[ ], and Add can be taken as inferring from the first statement listed in D[ ], because it's understood that the first-listed conjunct and disjunct may occur anywhere within the conjunction and disjunction, respectively. Given these conventions, S and Add may be specified as follows:

Simplification (S)	Addition (Add)
$\underline{C[\phi_1, \ldots, \phi_n]}$	$\underline{\phi_1 \qquad\qquad}$
ϕ_1	$D[\phi_1, \ldots, \phi_n]$

Given our conventions, [1]–[3] are all instances of S and [4]–[6] are all instances of Add.

Given our C[ ] and D[ ] conventions, we can be a little more liberal in our understanding of Adj and CDil. Adjunction allowed us to form the conjunction of only two previous lines. But why not allow ourselves to form the conjunction of any number of the previous lines? A careful inspection of our prior specification of CDil shows that from the lines 'p v q', 'p ⊃ r', and 'q ⊃ s', we can validly infer 'r v s' but not 's v r'. Why not allow ourselves the liberty of inferring 's v r' as well? The liberalizations suggested are accomplished by restating Adj and CDil as follows:

Adj	CDil
ϕ_1	$\phi_1 \vee \phi_2$
.	
.	$\phi_1 \supset \theta_1$
.	
$\underline{\phi_n \qquad\qquad}$	$\underline{\phi_2 \supset \theta_2}$
$C[\phi_1, \ldots, \phi_n]$	$D[\theta_1, \theta_2]$

Unlike S and Add, the last valid argument type we shall add to our list is one with a clear everyday use. Here is an example (with the possible grounds for the premises suggested in brackets): "[Because he said so,] he went to Reno, Las Vegas, or Atlantic City; [but we found out that] he didn't go to Atlantic City; (so, it must be that) he went to Reno or Las Vegas." This is an instance of the type of valid argument called *modus tollendo ponens,* or MTP.

Given our notational conventions, MTP may be presented as follows:

Modus tollendo ponens (MTP)

$D[\phi_1, \ldots, \phi_n]$

$N[\phi_1]$

$D[\phi_2, \ldots, \phi_n]$

All the following, then, are instances of MTP:

[7] p v q v r
    −q
    ———
    p v r

[8] −p v q v r
    p
    ———
    q v r

[9] p v q v r
    −r
    ———
    p v q

That any argument form of this type is valid can be seen by asking whether it is possible to fill the blanks so that the conclusion comes out false and the premises true. If the conclusion is to come out false, the blanks must be filled so that all of $\phi_2, \ldots, \phi_n$ come out false; if all of the premises could also come out true, the blanks must be filled so that ϕ_1 comes out false; otherwise the second premise would be false. But then the blanks have already gotten filled so that the first premise comes out false in virtue of all of its disjuncts coming out false. Hence, it's impossible to fill the blanks so that all the premises come out true and the conclusion false.

Having completed our list of valid argument types, let us return again to thc task of finding "missing premises" that would convert an argument into a valid one. This time, however, we shall deal with an *actual argument in English* rather than mere argument forms. This will give us some clues about missing premises but it also creates constraints so that the missing premises will have at least an air of plausibility. Consider, then, the following piece of outrageous reasoning a scandalmonger might use: "We know someone is paying child support for Jessica's child. Because her husband never came back from a trip to India, some former lover must be the father of Jessica's child." Let us abstract the argument form by using the following abbreviations (where sentence letters are matched with the underlined letters in the abbreviated sentences):

'p': Someone is paying child support for Jessica's child.
'i': Her husband never came back from India.
'f': Some former lover is the father of Jessica's child.

We would then get 'p, i / f'. This is clearly a hopeless case for finding missing premises if we relied on only the argument form. However, given the actual argument, one can use the "gist" of the reasoning to make some headway. Evidently the scandalmonger is relying on either her husband or her former lover making the child support payments, insofar as *someone* is. Let 'h' and 'l' be given by:

'h': Her husband is paying child support payments.
'l': Her former lover is paying child support payments.

As a start, then, we can construe the argument as

p
*p ⊃ (h v l)
l
---
f

We may now start the chain as follows:

(1)	p	Pr
(2)	p ⊃ (h v l)	*Pr
(3)	h v l	(1)(2)MP
(4)	i	Pr

Using the forward strategy, we can see that adding the premise 'i ⊃ −h' would be helpful because this with (4) will give us '−h', which can then be used with (3) to yield 'l' by MTP. Because 'i ⊃ −h' (i.e., 'if her husband never came back from India, he is not making the child support payments') is something on which the scandalmonger is presumably depending, we might safely add this as an additional premise (for the atrocious piece of reasoning that we have). Doing this and continuing the chain we have:

(5)	i ⊃ −h	*Pr
(6)	−h	(4)(5)MP
(7)	l	(3)(6)MTP

At this point we might profitably switch to the backward strategy. The conclusion 'f' is easily reached if we add 'l ⊃ f' as an additional premise, which is presumably what the scandalmonger is assuming; namely, if her former lover is making the support payments, he is the father of the child. Thus, the chain may be completed as follows:

(8)	l ⊃ f	*Pr
(9)	f	(7)(8)MP

Given an actual argument, this example shows how one can rely on the "gist" of the argument to generate missing premises of the sort on which the person is likely to be depending. *Finding such missing premises can also show how shaky the apparent reasoning is.* In our example, it would seem that the scandalmonger is relying on the truth of all three of the following:

'$p \supset (h \vee l)$': If someone is making the child support payments, it is her husband or her former lover.
'$i \supset -h$': If her husband never came back from India, he isn't making the child support payments.
'$l \supset f$': If her former lover is making the child support payments, he is the father of the child.

Clearly, each of the three missing premises may well be false, because a relative may be making the payments, the husband may be sending money from India, and her former lover (if there is one) may be helping her because of his affection for her and/or the child rather than from any sense of responsibility. This kind of analysis is something we shall go into in greater detail in Chapter 4. However, presenting it here should give the reader some sense of where we are headed. It is also a good idea to start thinking in terms of finding missing premises on which an argument may plausibly be dependent.

EXERCISES—SECTION 3.6.2

1. For each of the following, determine whether or not they are instances of S, Add, the modified Adj, the modified CDil, or MTP, and for those that are, identify the type of argument it is.

[a]
$p \vee q \vee r$
———
$u \vee p \vee q \vee r \vee (s \& t)$

[b]
$(p \vee q) \& [(s \& t) \vee r]$
———
$s \& t$

[c]
p
———
$(p \& q) \vee (p \& r)$

[d]
$[p \supset (q \vee r)] \& [q \& (s \supset r)]$
———
q

[e]
$p \supset q$
p
$-q$
———
$(p \supset q) \& p \& -q$

[f]
$(p \& r) \supset s$
q
t
———
$(p \& r \& q \& t) \supset s$

[g]
$p \vee q$
$p \supset s$
$t \supset q$
———
$t \vee s$

[h]
$(p \& q) \supset (p \vee q)$
$(p \vee q) \supset (p \& q)$
$(p \& q) \vee (p \vee q)$
———
$(p \& q) \vee (p \vee q)$

[i]
$p \vee q \vee -(p \supset -q) \vee s$
$p \supset -q$
———
$p \vee q \vee s$

[j]
$(p \supset q) \vee -(r \supset s) \vee (t \supset u)$
$-(r \supset s)$
———
$(p \supset q) \vee (t \supset u)$

2. Show by means of chain arguments that the following argument forms are valid.

[a]
$$\begin{array}{l} p \,\&\, q \,\&\, r \\ t \supset -r \\ \hline -t \end{array}$$

[b]
$$\begin{array}{l} s \\ (s \vee r) \supset q \\ \hline q \end{array}$$

[c]
$$\begin{array}{l} -(p \vee r) \supset s \\ -s \\ s \vee -(p \vee r) \vee r \\ \hline r \end{array}$$

[d]
$$\begin{array}{l} (p \vee q) \supset (r \,\&\, s) \\ (-r \vee u) \,\&\, p \\ s \supset (u \supset t) \\ \hline t \end{array}$$

[e]
$$\begin{array}{l} p \,\&\, (q \vee r) \\ s \\ t \\ [(q \vee r) \,\&\, (s \,\&\, t)] \supset u \\ \hline u \vee w \end{array}$$

[f]
$$\begin{array}{l} (p \supset q) \vee r \vee -(s \,\&\, t) \\ -(s \,\&\, t) \supset (s \,\&\, t) \\ (p \supset q) \supset w \\ r \supset u \\ \hline u \vee w \end{array}$$

[g]
$$\begin{array}{l} p \,\&\, q \\ s \vee -(q \vee r) \vee t \\ \hline s \vee t \end{array}$$

[h]
$$\begin{array}{l} (-p \supset q) \,\&\, (q \supset p) \\ (p \vee w) \supset (p \supset q) \\ \hline q \end{array}$$

[i]
$$\begin{array}{l} p \vee q \vee r \\ -r \\ (q \vee r) \supset (r \vee u) \\ p \supset (w \vee r) \\ \hline u \vee w \end{array}$$

[j]
$$\begin{array}{l} p \vee q \\ p \supset q \\ q \supset t \\ p \supset -p \\ \hline t \end{array}$$

3. Add one or more missing premises to convert the following into deductively valid arguments and show the deductive validity by chain arguments. Don't use the "trivial" missing premise described in Section 3.6.1. Be sure that all of the given premises play a role in deriving the conclusion, and use the indicated scheme of abbreviation. [Bracketed material is for background only.]

(a) [The given reasons in the example concerning Douglas's alleged remark were found to be unproblematic in the exercise of Section 2.5.]

Douglas indeed attended the September 1, 1854, meeting but that day was a Friday. Public meetings do not last over twenty-four consecutive hours. But if all of this is so, Douglas did not leave the September 1 (public) meeting on Sunday morning. Therefore, at the end of the meeting Douglas did not say: "It is now Sunday morning—I'll go to church and you may go to Hell."

f: Douglas attended the September 1, 1854, meeting and that day was a Friday.
p: Public meetings do not last over twenty-four consecutive hours.
l: Douglas left the September 1 (public) meeting on Sunday morning.
s: At the end of the meeting Douglas said: "It is now Sunday morning—I'll go to church and you may go to Hell."

(b) [This example was inspired by the incident in which the Russians shot down a Korean Airlines flight that had strayed into Russian territory in the early eighties.]

If the Russians did not misidentify the Korean Airlines plane that they shot down, then they are paranoid or vicious enough to kill a planeload of innocent people. But the Russians aren't stupid and (even) the Russians aren't vicious enough to kill a planeload of innocent people. Therefore, the Russians are paranoid.

m: The Russians misidentified the Korean Airlines plane they shot down.
p: The Russians are paranoid.
v: The Russians are vicious enough to kill a planeload of innocent people.
s: The Russians are stupid.

(c) [This problem is loosely adapted from Olivia Newton John's song "Physical."]†

Knowing each other mentally is enough for her, or she wants to get physical. But he brings out the animal in her. Therefore, she wants to hear his body talk.

m: Knowing each other mentally is enough for her.
a: He brings out the animal in her.
p: She wants to get physical.
t: She wants to hear his body talk.

(d) [It will be recalled from the exercise on Dreyfus in Section 2.5 that the *bordereau* was a document in which some agent promised to deliver French military secrets. While the first court-martial judged that Dreyfus was the author, compelling evidence was presented at that court-martial that Dreyfus did not write the *bordereau.* The following is an argument that attempts to bear this out, and the reasons given were found to be unproblematic in an exercise in Section 2.5.]

Some of the documents identified and promised in the *bordereau* neither existed nor were anticipated until July 1894. We also know that the author of the *bordereau* was off to maneuvers when he wrote it. But Dreyfus was not off to maneuvers anytime on or after July 1, 1894. Thus, Dreyfus couldn't have been the author of the *bordereau.*

i: Some of the documents identified and promised in the *bordereau* neither existed nor were anticipated till July 1894.
b: The *bordereau* was written before July 1, 1894.
m: The author of the *bordereau* was off to maneuvers when he wrote the *bordereau.*
n: Dreyfus was not off to maneuvers anytime on or after July 1, 1894.
d: Dreyfus wrote the *bordereau.*

3.7 Translating Logical Forms

Constructing chain arguments is essentially a matter of writing down lines that are validly inferable from previous lines. From Section 3.5

†Adapted from "Physical," S. Kipner and T. Shaddick, Stephen A. Kipner Music and April Music Inc. (ASCAP) and Terry Shaddick Music (BMI), 1981.

onward, we have been listing frequently used types of valid argument forms. However, the astute reader may have noticed that our list contains no type of argument forms specifically involving the biconditional '≡' or the exclusive alternation 'v^e'. Similarly, faced with '–(p v q)' as a premise or line, there is nothing one can do with it unless it forms part of a hidden gross structure. We could of course keep listing more types of valid argument forms. But there is an alternative. Consider 'p if and only if q'. Surely this says simply: if p, then q, *and* if q then p. If the two things say the same thing, surely one is validly inferable from the other. This suggests allowing moves that "translate" back and forth between 'p ≡ q' and '(p ⊃ q) & (q ⊃ p)'. If we have a biconditional as a line, we could first translate it into the conjuction of conditionals and then use simplification to get two conditionals on which we can work. If we are trying to establish a biconditional, we could establish two conditionals and use a step of adjunction as a prelude to translating the result into a biconditional. In Section 3.7.1 we shall present a "dictionary" for translating logical forms. In Section 3.7.2 we shall explain the new type of valid inferences using translations and discuss the tactical maneuvers these new inferences allow us to make in constructing chain arguments.

3.7.1 Logically Identical Pairs

We may start our discussion with a definition:

> Definition: Two statement forms have logically identical truth conditions just in case there is no way of filling the blanks, so that the two statement forms have different truth values.

Thus, for example, 'p' and '– –p' have logically identical truth conditions: if 'p' is filled by the truth value True, '–p' comes out false and '– –p' comes out true. If 'p' is filled by the truth value False, '–p' comes out true and '– –p' comes out false. Thus, regardless of how the blank 'p' is filled, 'p' and '– –p' have the same truth value; hence they have logically identical truth conditions. *For brevity, we shall often refer to pairs with logically identical truth conditions as* LOGICALLY IDENTICAL PAIRS. The legitimate translations we have spoken of involve interchanging logically identical pairs. For the rest of this subsection we shall present a list of these pairs with logically identical truth conditions. This will serve as our "dictionary" for making the translations to be discussed in the next subsections.

The first batch of pairs with logically identical truth conditions may be listed as follows:

Double Negation (DN)	ϕ,	$--\phi$
Associativity (AS)	ϕ_1 & $(\phi_2$ & $\phi_3)$,	$(\phi_1$ & $\phi_2)$ & ϕ_3
AS	$\phi_1 \vee (\phi_2 \vee \phi_3)$,	$(\phi_1 \vee \phi_2) \vee \phi_3$
Idemponency (ID)	$\phi \vee \phi$,	ϕ
ID	ϕ & ϕ,	ϕ
Distribution (Dist)	ϕ & $(\theta_1 \vee \ldots \vee \theta_n)$,	$(\phi$ & $\theta_1) \vee \ldots \vee (\phi$ & $\theta_n)$
Dist	$\phi \vee (\theta_1$ & ... & $\theta_n)$,	$(\phi \vee \theta_1)$ & ... & $(\phi \vee \theta_n)$

Two general remarks are in order.

(1) Each of these types of pairs, as well as other types of pairs to be presented, can be proven to be logically identical pairs. Consider the pair ⟨ϕ & ϕ, ϕ⟩. Regardless of how the blanks are filled, ϕ comes out true or false. If ϕ comes out true, the conjunction ϕ & ϕ also comes out true and the pair have the same truth values. If ϕ comes out false, the conjunction comes out false and again the pair have the same truth values. Hence, regardless of how the blanks are filled, the pair ϕ and ϕ & ϕ have the same truth value. For some pairs, proving them to be logically identical can be more complicated; but the principle is the same and we shall hereafter omit the proofs.

(2) An instance of the first distribution pair is ⟨'p & (q v r v s)', '(p & q) v (p & r) & (p & s)'⟩. This is the intent of the '...' in the two distribution pairs and the two De Morgan pairs to be discussed shortly.

Some specific remarks about the first batch of logically identical pairs may be worth making. Given our use of the 'N[ ]' convention and the convention of deleting parentheses in a series of conjunctions and a series of disjunctions, double negation and associativity should usually be avoidable. The pairs listed under ID are seldom needed unless there is a redundant disjunct or conjunct that one wants to eliminate. In the normal course of chain arguments there will probably not be much use for the distributon pairs (although there turns out to be a theoretically interesting use of them). DN, AS, ID, and Dist are listed for the purpose of bringing certain logically identical pairs to the attention of the reader. The rest of the pairs that we shall discuss are more typically useful in constructing chain arguments.

The first two useful pairs are named after the nineteenth-century logician named De Morgan:

De Morgan's Rule (DeM)	$-(\phi_1 \text{ v} \ldots \text{v } \phi_n)$,	$N[\phi_1]\&\ldots\& N[\phi_n]$
DeM	$-(\phi_1\&\ldots\& \phi_n)$,	$N[\phi_1] \text{ v}\ldots\text{v } N[\phi_n]$

In arriving at instances of pairs involving 'N[ ]', it may be more natural to fill the Greek letters starting with the left-hand member of the pair rather than starting with the right-hand member. Two instances of the first De Morgan pair are ⟨'−(p v q)', '−p & −q'⟩ and ⟨'−(−p v −q)', 'p & q'⟩. The natural way of arriving at this second instance is to fill the ϕ_1 and ϕ_2 with '−p' and '−q' and then recognize that $N[\phi_1]$ and $N[\phi_2]$ would be 'p' and 'q'. (Of course, the pair can be filled in the other direction as long as one remembers that by the convention surrounding the use of 'N[ ]', 'p' can be represented by N['−p'], so that 'p & q' is an instance of $N[\phi_1]$ & $N[\phi_2]$ with '−p' and '−q' going in for ϕ_1 and ϕ_2.)

Beginners often think that the following pairs have logically identical truth conditions:

−(p & q) −p & − q

−(p v q) −p v −q

If 'p' is filled by the truth value True and 'q' by the truth value False, the reader can verify that the pairs do *not* have logically identical truth conditions, that is, they do not amount to the same thing. What negated disjunctions and negated conjunctions amount to are correctly given by the two De Morgan pairs:

> *To deny a disjunction (which in English can be expressed by the "neither p nor q" locution) is to claim that all the disjuncts are false. To deny a conjunction is to claim that at least one of the conjuncts is false (not necessarily that all the conjuncts are false).*

A very important pair with logically identical truth conditions is called CONTRAPOSITION, and it represents an important principle of reasoning that is often reflected in chain arguments:

Contraposition (Cont)	$\phi \supset \theta$,	$N[\theta] \supset N[\phi]$

To say, "If he went to San Francisco, then he met Cecelia," amounts to the same thing as saying "If he didn't meet Cecelia, he didn't go to San

Francisco (after all)." To say, "If he didn't avoid Jill, then he met with misery," amounts to the same thing as saying "If he didn't meet with misery, then he avoided Jill." One should become adept at going back and forth between a conditional and its contrapositive.

Beware of confusing the contrapositive with the converse. Given 'if p, then q', 'if not-q, then not-p' is its contrapositive, while 'if q, then p' is its CONVERSE. *A conditional and its converse do **not** amount to the same thing.* "If she has sex, then she had a baby" (fortunately) is not another way of saying, "If she had a baby, she had sex." On the other hand, "If she didn't have sex, she didn't have a baby" is another way of saying, "If she had a baby, she had sex." In short, if one wants to switch the antecedent and consequent of a conditional around and still say the same thing, the (affirmative or negative) sign of the components must also be switched.

The next pair worthy of attention is:

Exportation/Importation (E/I)	$(\phi \;\&\; \theta) \supset \psi$,	$\phi \supset (\theta \supset \psi)$

If one goes from left to right on the E/I pair, one is said to export a conjunct out of the antecedent into the (antecedent of the) consequent. If one goes from right to left on the E/I pair, one is said to import (the antecedent) part of the consequent into the antecedent as a conjunct. That the pairs covered by E/I amount to the same thing can perhaps be detected by the following expressions appearing to say the same things: 'If he went to Los Angeles and met Maggie, then he had a good time', 'If he went to Los Angeles and if he met Maggie, then he had a good time', and 'If he went to Los Angeles, then if he (also) met Maggie, he had a good time'.

The next three pairs basically deal with the asserting of a conditional. We list these and others without traditional names but by the translations they accomplish (e.g., the pair $\langle \phi \supset \theta, -\phi \vee \theta \rangle$ will be referred to by the notation '$\supset$/v', because it allows us to translate back and forth between a conditional and a disjunction).

$\supset$ / v	$\phi \supset \theta$,	$N[\phi] \vee \theta$
$-(\supset)$ / &	$-(\phi \supset \theta)$,	$\phi \;\&\; N[\theta]$
$-(\&)$ / $\supset$	$-(\phi \;\&\; \theta)$,	$\phi \supset N[\theta]$

If one recalls the definition of the conditional given in tabular form in Section 3.3.1, one will recognize that (a) 'p $\supset$ q' is true just in case 'p' is false or 'q' is true, and (b) 'p $\supset$ q' is false just in case 'p' is true and 'q' is false. The logically identical pair $\supset$/v essentially expresses (a) while the pair $-(\supset)/\&$ essentially expresses (b). Thinking from right to left, the pair $-(\&)/\supset$ expresses the idea that the truth of the conditional amounts to the absence of its falsification condition given by (b).

The next two pairs are concerned with ways of dealing with the biconditional.

$\equiv / \supset$	$\phi \equiv \theta,$	$(\phi \supset \theta) \& (\theta \supset \phi)$
$-(\equiv) / \equiv(-)$	$-(\phi \equiv \theta),$	$\phi \equiv N[\theta]$

The pair $\equiv/\supset$ reflects that 'p if and only q' amount to 'if p, then q, *and* if q then p'. To put it another way, to assert a biconditional is to assert the conditional and its converse. We might understand the pair designated $-(\equiv)/\equiv(-)$ as follows: '$p \equiv q$' is false just in case 'p' and 'q' have opposite truth values; but 'p' and 'q' have opposite truth values just in case '$p \equiv -q$' is true.

The following two logically identical pairs dealing with the exclusive sense of 'or' allow us to translate that sense of 'or' into other expressions with which we are now familiar.

$v^e / \equiv$	$\phi\ v^e\ \theta,$	$\phi \equiv N[\theta]$
$v^e / \&$	$\phi\ v^e\ \theta,$	$(\phi \vee \theta) \& -(\phi \& \theta)$

The pair $v^e /\equiv$ expresses that 'p or_e q' is true just in case 'p' and 'q' have opposite truth values. The pair $v^e /\&$ reflects that 'p or_e q' asserts 'p or_i q but not both p and q'.

Finally, we list three commutativity pairs:

Commutativity (Com)	$\phi \equiv \theta,$	$\theta \equiv \phi$
Com	$\phi \& \theta,$	$\theta \& \phi$
Com	$\phi \vee \theta,$	$\theta \vee \phi$

These are listed because they are useful in making translations when used in conjunction with other logically identical pairs. Thus for example, to translate '$-(p \equiv q)$' into '$-p \equiv q$', one would go through the successive translations '$-(q \equiv p)$', '$q \equiv -p$', and '$-p \equiv q$'. The first and third steps of the translation are assured by the commutativity of '$\equiv$'. Similarly, if one wanted to export the 'p' in '$(p \& q) \supset r$' into the consequent position, one would first use the commutativity of '&' to switch around the order of the antecedent prior to using E/I. Such is the dictionary or list of logically identical pairs that we shall be using in our translations.

EXERCISES—SECTION 3.7.1

For each of the following pairs, determine whether it is an instance of a type of pair that has been listed as having logically identical truth conditions, and if it is, give the name or label that has been assigned to the logically identical pairs of that type.

1.	$(p \vee q) \supset -(q \vee r)$,	$-(q \vee r) \supset (p \vee q)$.
2.	$-(p \vee q) \,\&\, -(r \vee s)$,	$-(p \vee q \vee r \vee s)$.
3.	$p \equiv (q \equiv r)$,	$[p \supset (q \supset r)] \,\&\, [(q \supset r) \supset p]$.
4.	$p \,\&\, q \,\&\, r$,	$-[(p \,\&\, q) \supset -r]$.
5.	$(r \,\&\, s) \vee (q \,\&\, t)$,	$-(r \,\&\, s) \supset (q \,\&\, t)$.
6.	$-(p \,\&\, q \,\&\, r \,\&\, s)$,	$-(p \,\&\, q) \,\&\, -(r \,\&\, s)$.
7.	$-[p \equiv -(q \equiv r)]$,	$p \equiv (q \equiv r)$.
8.	$(p \,\&\, q \,\&\, r) \supset s$,	$p \supset [(q \,\&\, r) \supset s]$.
9.	$p \,\&\, q \,\&\, (r \supset s)$,	$-[(p \,\&\, q) \supset (r \supset s)]$.
10.	$(r \,\&\, s) \vee (q \,\&\, t)$,	$(r \,\&\, s) \supset -(q \,\&\, t)$.
11.	$(p \vee s) \vee^e (p \vee -s)$,	$-(p \vee s \vee p \vee -s) \,\&\, [(p \vee s) \,\&\, (p \vee -s)]$.
12.	$p \supset -(q \vee r)$,	$-[p \,\&\, -(q \vee r)]$.
13.	$(p \supset q) \supset r$,	$p \supset (q \supset r)$.
14.	$p \equiv (q \equiv r)$,	$p \vee^e -(q \equiv r)$.
15.	$-(p \supset q) \supset (r \supset s)$,	$-(r \supset s) \supset (p \supset q)$.
16.	$-[(s \vee t) \,\&\, -(s \vee -t)]$.	$(s \vee t) \supset (s \vee -t)$.

3.7.2 Interchanging Logically Identical Pairs and the Tactics of Interchange

There is an old intuitive principle that replacing equals with equals results in equals. For example, $(3 + 2) \times 7 = 5 \times 7$ because $(3 + 2) = 5$. As far as logical forms go, at least in a metaphorical sense, pairs with logically identical truth conditions are "equals." This suggests that if we interchange pairs with logically identical truth conditons, the result should have logically identical truth conditions as the thing we started out with. That is, interchanging dictionary equivalents should give us faithful translations. More precisely, the principle suggested is this:

If ϕ_1 and ϕ_2 have logically identical truth conditions and θ_2 results from θ_1 by replacing one or more occurrences of ϕ_1 by ϕ_2, θ_1 and θ_2 have logically identical truth conditions.

A particular instance of this principle can be schematically given by:

θ_1: $\underbrace{|\ p\ |}_{\phi_1} \supset q$

θ_2: $\underbrace{|\ --p\ |}_{\phi_2} \supset q$

Because '$--$p' and 'p' have logically identical truth conditions and '$--$p ⊃ q' results from 'p ⊃ q' by interchanging the pair ⟨'p', '$--$p'⟩ (i.e., by replacing one or more occurrences of 'p' by '$--$p'), the principle claims that 'p ⊃ q' and '$--$p ⊃ q' have logically identical truth conditions. This principle concerning the interchange of logically identical pairs is indeed correct and can be proven, although the proof lies beyond the present scope.

Given the principle concerning interchange of logically identical pairs, suppose that θ_2 comes from θ_1 by interchanging a logically identical pair. In that case, regardless of how the blanks are filled, θ_1 and θ_2 cannot have different truth values. An obvious consequence is that there is no way of filling the blanks so that θ_1 comes out true and θ_2 false. Thus, the following is a legitimate principle we can use in contructing chain arguments:

If θ_2 results from θ_1 by an interchange of a logically identical pair, θ_2 is validly inferable from θ_1.

Given our list of pairs with logically identical truth conditions, we can use this principle to add lines in our chain arguments. That is, we can add a line as a translation of a previous line if it involves interchanging "dictionary equivalents" for part or all of that previous line. In order to standardize our work, we shall justify a line that comes about by a translation by citing the previous line number and the name of the "dictionary equivalent" used, that is, the name of the logically identical pairs listed in Section 3.7.1.

This extension of what is validly inferable from a previous line can now be exemplified.

Example 1:

p
p ⊃ (−q v r)
q
r ⊃ (−s ⊃ t)
(−t ⊃ s) ⊃ h
———————
h

By using the forward and backward strategies of constructing chain arguments, the steps leading to the following results should by now be reasonably familiar:

Forward Strategy:		Backward Strategy:
(1) p	Pr	
(2) p ⊃ (−q v r)	Pr	
(3) −q v r	(1)(2)MP	
(4) q	Pr	(n − 2) − t ⊃ s ?
(5) r	(3)(4)MTP	(n − 1) (−t ⊃ s) ⊃ h Pr

(6) $r \supset (-s \supset t)$	Pr	(n)h$(n-1)(n-2)$MP
(7) $-s \supset t$	(5)(6)MP	

The remaining problem is to bridge the gap between (7) and $(n - 2)$. But $(n - 2)$ simply translates (7) by contraposition. Thus $(n - 2)$ can now be added as:

(8) $-t \supset s$ (7)Cont

The chain can now be finished by simply adjusting the line numbers.

Tactics. Earlier we noted that the forward and backward strategies can be useful only if one is tactically adept at spotting what is validly inferable from what. The first tactical move is of course to see if the available lines or premises match one of the valid types of argument forms. This may be obvious or it may involve discerning the hidden gross structure of the lines as noted in Section 3.5.1. *However, if none of the available lines or premises fit the given types of valid argument forms, one can only resort to the second tactical move, which is to translate some of the available lines or premises into usable forms.* Thus, in Example 1, line (7) had to be translated to line (8), so that MP could be used on lines (8) and $(n - 1)$ to arrive at the desired conclusion 'h'. We now list some of the kinds of translations that often prove to be useful.

(1) *Translate negated expressions into usable forms.* Except for MT and MTP, none of the argument forms on our list has a negated premise. This means that quite often negated conjunctions, disjunctions, conditionals, and biconditionals must be translated into nonnegated forms. The dictionary pairs that will accomplish this are, respectively, the two De Morgan pairs: $-(\supset)/\&$, and $-(\equiv)/\equiv(-)$.

Two simple examples may be offered:

Example 2:

$-(p \& q)$

p
______

$-q$

(1) $-(p \& q)$	Pr
(2) $-p \vee -q$	(1)DeM
(3) p	Pr
(4) $-q$	(2)(3)MTP

Example 3:

$-(p \equiv q)$

p
______

$-q$

(1) $-(p \equiv q)$	Pr
(2) $p \equiv -q$	(1) $-(\equiv)/\equiv(-)$
(3) $(p \supset -q)$ $\& (-q \supset p)$	(2) $\equiv/\supset$
(4) $p \supset -q$	(3) S
(5) p	Pr
(6) $-q$	(4)(5)MP

(2) *Translate conditionals into usable forms.* Two specific tactics may be suggested under this heading. (a) *Contraposition* is often a useful prelude to *HS* and the *two dilemmas.* (b) *Exportation* is often a useful

prelude to *MP* and *importation* a useful prelude to *MT.* Example 4 exemplifies (a) and Example 5 exemplifies (b).

Example 4:

$p \supset q$
$r \supset -q$
$p \vee s$
$\underline{s \supset -r}$
$-r$

(1)	$p \supset q$	Pr
(2)	$r \supset -q$	Pr
(3)	$q \supset -r$	(2)Cont
(4)	$p \supset -r$	(1)(3)HS
(5)	$s \supset -r$	Pr
(6)	$p \vee s$	Pr
(7)	$-r$	(4)(5)(6)SDil

Example 5:

$(p \& q) \supset r$
p
$r \supset (s \supset t)$
$\underline{-t}$
$-(q \& s)$

(1)	$(p \& q) \supset r$	Pr
(2)	p	Pr
(3)	$p \supset (q \supset r)$	(1)E/I
(4)	$q \supset r$	(2)(3)MP
(5)	$r \supset (s \supset t)$	Pr
(6)	$q \supset (s \supset t)$	(4)(5)HS
(7)	$(q \& s) \supset t$	(6)E/I
(8)	$-t$	Pr
(9)	$-(q \& s)$	(7)(8)MT

Some comments about these two examples may be in order. In Example 4, it is crucial to see that given the last two premises, SDil will be effective only if we can get '$p \supset -r$'. Because HS is the only possibility that can be immediately used on two conditionals (i.e., the first two premises), we look for a use of contraposition as a prelude to HS. The essential point of HS is that the "middle term" has to match; that is, one and the same expression must be the antecedent of one conditional and the consequent of the other. Insofar as 'p' is the antecedent of what we have targeted, it is desirable to create the matching middle term by using contraposition on the second premise rather than the first (which, along with HS would only give us '$r \supset -p$': something that would have to be contraposed again to do us any good). Hence in line (3) we contrapose line (2), and the rest is clear sailing.

Example 5 is relatively straightforward, at least as it is presented. Given the first two premises, the obvious move is to export the 'q' so that we can use MP. After using MP, HS is obviously suggested given the third premise. This leads us to line (6), which, along with the remaining premise '$-t$', clearly suggests importing the 's' into the antecedent position so that we can use MT. It might be noted that using importation and MT on the last two premises leads to a chain that is far less obvious. [That would give us '$-(r \& s)$', which would have to be translated to '$r \supset -s$', so that HS could be used on it and line (4) to yield '$q \supset -s$'; this result would then have to be translated to '$-(q \& s)$'.] This illustrates an important point: *Where one has an option of doing several things, doing one thing rather than another can lead to missing out on an easy chain.* In our example, given line (4) along with the third and fourth premises, one had an option of using HS on (4) and the third premise or the option of using importation and MT on the last two premises. The first option gives rise to an easy chain, while the second option calls for a more difficult chain one may not hit upon. Thus, if one finds oneself lost, it is often useful to reconsider the matter and see if a different option could have been taken at an earlier stage.

(3) *Translate 'v^e' and '$\equiv$' into usable and reachable forms.* Because none of our listed argument forms crucially depends on these two connectives (unless the use of these connectives is incidental to the validity of the argument), each of these two connectives needs to be intertranslated with connectives that appear in the listed argument forms. Example 6 illustrates the need to translate these connectives into usable forms and Example 7 illustrates the need to translate the 'v^e' into a reachable form.

Example 6:

$p \; v^e \; q$

$\underline{p \quad\quad}$

$-q$

(1)	$p \; v^e \; q$	Pr
(2)	p	Pr
(3)	$p \equiv -q$	(1) $v^e / \equiv$
(4)	$(p \supset -q)$ & $(-q \supset p)$	(3)$\equiv / \supset$
		(4)S
(5)	$p \supset -q$	(2)(5)MP
(6)	$-q$	

Example 7:

$-r$

$p \vee q \vee r$

$\underline{(p \;\&\; q) \supset r}$

$p \; v^e \; q$

(1)	$p \vee q \vee r$	Pr
(2)	$-r$	Pr
(3)	$p \vee q$	(1)(2)MTP
(4)	$(p \;\&\; q) \supset r$	Pr
(5)	$-(p \;\&\; q)$	(2)(4)MT
(6)	$(p \vee q) \;\&\; -(p \;\&\; q)$	(3)(5)Adj
(7)	$p \; v^e \; q$	(6)v^e/&

In Example 6, first the 'v^e' had to be translated into '$\equiv$', and then '$\equiv$' into '$\supset$' before we could use our list of valid types of argument forms. Once those translations were accomplished, the rest was obvious. In Example 7, because we are aiming for '$p \; v^e \; q$', we have a choice of aiming for line (6) of Example 7 or for line (3) of Example 6. Because reaching (6) of Example 7 involves fewer transactions, we aim for it; having done so, the rest of Example 7 is straightforward.

(4) *Intertranslate connectives to suit other needs.* Various other needs of a chain argument may necessitate converting one connective into another by means of dictionary pairs allowing such translations. That is, one line or part of another often has to be translated, so that the lines can fit the hidden gross structure of one of the valid argument types on the

list. In Example 1, we needed to change a line into a form that allowed us to use MP, and Examples 8 and 9 illustrate similar needs:

Example 8:

$p \supset -(r \supset s)$
$-(r \& -s)$

$-p$

(1) $p \supset -(r \supset s)$	Pr
(2) $p \supset (r \& -s)$	(1) $-(\supset)/\&$
(3) $-(r \& -s)$	Pr
(4) $-p$	(1)(2)MT

Example 9:

$-(p \& -q)$
$-q \vee s$

$p \supset s$

(1) $-(p \& -q)$	Pr
(2) $p \supset q$	(1)$-(\&)/\supset$
(3) $-q \vee s$	Pr
(4) $q \supset s$	(3)$\supset/\vee$
(5) $p \supset s$	(2)(4)HS

In Example 8, we needed to see that the two premises would have the hidden gross structure of MT if the consequent of the first premise were translated to have the opposite value of the second premise or the second premise were translated to have the opposite value of the consequent of the first. We translated the consequent of the first premise in Example 8, but one could also have translated the second premise to '$r \supset s$' using $-(\&)/\supset$. Example 9 is admittedly more difficult. Perhaps what is needed to be seen is that nothing could probably be done with these lines unless HS could be used: The lines don't have the forms appropriate for IA, Rd, or S; because they are basically of equal length, MP, MT, MTP are out of place. The dilemmas won't work because they require three premises. Adj seems to get nowhere, and Add may be left as a last resort. Once HS is spotted as a likely argument form that could be used, it remains to translate the premises into conditionals, and hope for the best. The hope having been fulfilled in lines (2) and (4), we infer the last line by HS.

As our last example of intertranslating connectives, consider

Example 10:

$(p \& q) \supset r$
$-(p \& q) \supset -(s \& t)$
$r \supset -(s \& t)$
$(-t \& u) \supset v$

$s \supset (u \supset v)$

The steps of the forward and backward strategy are given below, but some initial comments may be in order. The second and third premises suggest that SDil could be used if we can get '$-(p \& q) \vee r$'. But translating the first premise immediately gives us that disjunction, and that constitutes the steps of the forward strategy. Turning to the backward strategy, because the consequent of the conclusion is '$(u \supset v)$', we match consequents by using E/I on the last premise. This accounts for lines $(n - 1)$ and $(n - 2)$. If '$s \supset -t$' would somehow be gotten, HS would carry us to the desired conclusion at step (n).

Forward Strategy:

(1)	(p & q) ⊃ r	Pr
(2)	−(p & q) v r	(1) ⊃/v
(3)	−(p & q) ⊃ −(s & t)	Pr
(4)	r ⊃ −(s & t)	Pr
(5)	−(s & t)	(2)(3)(4)SDil

Backward Strategy:

(n − 3)	s ⊃ −t	?
(n − 2)	(−t & u) ⊃ v	Pr
(n − 1)	−t ⊃ (u ⊃ v)	(n − 2)E/I
(n)	s ⊃ (u ⊃ v)	(n − 3) (n − 1)HS

Bridging the gap between (5) and (n − 3) turns out to be a case of translating a connective into a conditional so that HS could be used, and this is now easily accomplished by −(&)/⊃. That is, line (6) becomes

(6) s ⊃ −t (5) −(&)/⊃

and the chain is completed by adjusting the line numbers of the backward strategy.

One final point needs to be noted. We said earlier that all rules concerning what is validly inferable relate to entire lines, not parts of lines. Strictly speaking, this continues to be the case because our new rule allows us to write down a line if the line as whole is a translation of a previous line. However, because the translation often involves only an interchange of dictionary equivalents for parts of the line, in a sense the rules concerning translating previous lines can be seen as applying to parts of lines. Rules like MP and HS must of course continue to be seen as applying only to entire lines and not to parts of lines. Roughly, the difference is that rules like MP and HS involve "one-way relations" of what is validly inferable, while translations involve "two-way relations" that allow us to infer validly in both directions.

EXERCISES—SECTION 3.7.2

1. Show each of the following to be valid. Aside from the use of Pr, each chain should consist of one use of the new rule of interchange and one use of one of the previously studied inference rules.

[a]
−(−p v − q)
(p & q) ⊃ r
———
r

[b]
−(p & q)
−p ⊃ r
−q ⊃ r
———
r

[c]
q v r
p ⊃ r
p v − q
———
r

[d]
(p & q) ⊃ r
(q ⊃ r) ⊃ s
———
p ⊃ s

[e]
−p ⊃ q
r ⊃ −q
———
r ⊃ p

[f]
p ⊃ (q ⊃ −r)
r
———
−(p & q)

[g] $-(p \& q)$
$\underline{-q \supset r}$
$p \supset r$

[h] $p \equiv -q$
$\underline{r \supset (p \equiv q)}$
$-r$

[i] $p \supset (q \vee^{e} r)$
$\underline{(q \equiv -r) \supset s}$
$p \supset s$

[j] $p \vee q$
$p \supset -(r \supset s)$
$\underline{q \supset (r \& -s)}$
$-(r \supset s)$

[k] $p \vee q$
$p \supset (r \vee -s)$
$\underline{q \supset (t \vee u)}$
$r \vee (s \supset t) \vee u$

[l] $\underline{-(p \supset -q) \supset -(p \& q)}$
$p \supset -q$

2. By means of chain arguments, show the following argument forms to be valid.

[a] $-p \supset (q \vee s)$
$(q \vee s) \supset -(q \vee s)$
$-[p \& -(s \supset t)]$
$\underline{t \supset r}$
$s \supset r$

[b] $(p \equiv q) \supset -(r \equiv -t)$
$-(r \equiv t)$
$\underline{(p \equiv q) \vee [(p \& q) \supset t]}$
$(p \& q) \supset t$

[c] $-(p \vee -q)$
$p \vee s \vee -t$
$\underline{-q \vee t}$
s

[d] $(p \vee q \vee r) \supset (s \supset -p)$
$-(s \supset -p)$
$\underline{-[(-q \& -r) \& (u \supset w)]}$
$u \& -w$

3. By means of chain arguments, show the following argument forms to be valid.

[a] p
$(p \& q) \supset r$
$\underline{-r \vee s}$
$q \supset s$

[b] $p \supset -r$
$p \supset r$
$\underline{-p \supset (p \vee r)}$
r

[c] $-(p \vee q)$
$(-p \& r) \supset s$
$\underline{(-q \& u) \supset -s}$
$r \supset -u$

[d] $-(-p \& -q)$
$(s \supset r) \supset -p$
$\underline{(s \supset r) \supset -q}$
$-r$

4. By means of chain arguments, show the following argument forms to be valid.

[a] $p \vee^{e} q$
$\underline{-p}$
q

[b] $\underline{-(p \equiv q)}$
$-(p \& q) \& -(-p \& -q)$

[c] $-u \& [(p \vee q) \supset u]$
$(-p \& r) \supset s$
$\underline{(-q \& s) \supset r}$
$r \equiv s$

[d] $-(q \& -p)$
$\underline{-(p \equiv q)}$
$-(p \supset q)$

5. By means of chain arguments, show the following argument forms to be valid.

[a] $\underline{p \supset (q \supset r)}$
$q \supset (p \supset r)$

[b] $-[(p \& -q) \& -(q \equiv s)]$
$\underline{-q \equiv s}$
$p \supset -s$

[c] $(p \supset q) \supset (r \supset s)$
$-p \lor q$
$\underline{u \lor (r \,\&\, -s)}$
u

[d] $-(r \,\&\, -s) \supset (q \lor^{e} -t)$
$p \supset (r \supset s)$
$\underline{(q \equiv t) \supset u}$
$p \supset u$

[e] $(s \,\&\, t) \supset (-r \,\&\, -t)$
$r \lor t$
$-s \supset q$
$\underline{-t \supset u}$
$-q \supset u$

[f] $-u \supset w$
$w \supset -r$
$\underline{u \supset (-q \lor p)}$
$(q \,\&\, r) \supset p$

[g] $\underline{p}$
$-p \supset q$

[h] $\underline{-p}$
$-(p \,\&\, q)$

[i] $(-p \lor q) \supset (p \,\&\, -q)$
$(p \,\&\, r) \supset s$
$\underline{(s \,\&\, u) \supset q}$
$r \supset -u$

[j] $-(p \,\&\, q)$
$p \lor -q$
$\underline{q \lor r}$
r

3.8 Beyond Simple Chain Arguments

The simple chain arguments we have so far been discussing in this chapter are useful to prove a variety of argument forms to be deductively valid. However, there are certain natural ways of reasoning we use that are not covered by simple chain arguments. Furthermore, allowing ourselves these other ways of reasoning in our chain arguments will be of help in showing argument forms to be deductively valid. Thus, in Sections 3.8.1 and 3.8.2 we shall explain two additional kinds of chain arguments that prove to be useful, and in Section 3.8.3 we shall indicate how a number of chain arguments may be combined.

3.8.1 Conditional Chain Arguments

Consider the following argument:

(a) If Tom proposes to Jane, Jane will marry him or reject the proposal.
(b) If Jane marries him, Tom will be married to a person smarter than he is.
(c) If Tom is married to a person smarter than he is, then his macho image will suffer.
(d) If Tom's macho image suffers, then Tom will be unhappy.
(e) If Jane rejects the proposal, then Tom will be unhappy.
(f) If Tom proposes to Jane, Tom will be unhappy.

We might try to argue for the validity of the argument as follows: "Assume that Tom proposes to Jane. But then in virtue of (a), Jane will marry him or reject the proposal. Because he will be married to a person smarter than he is if she marries him, if she marries him, in light of (c) and (d), his macho image will suffer and he will be unhappy. On the other hand, if she rejects the proposal, he will be unhappy. So, either way, he will be unhappy. That is, the assumption that he proposes to Jane leads to the consequence that he will be unhappy. Thus, simply on the basis of (a)–(e), we may conclude that *if* he proposes to Jane, he will be unhappy." This way of arguing exemplifies that

> *We often argue for the truth of a conditional claim by assuming the antecedent and deriving the consequent from this assumption and whatever else is given; once we have done so, we can in effect cancel the assumption and claim the* **conditional** *statement simply on the basis of the other things that were given.*

Let the scheme for extracting the logical form of the argument be:

'p': Tom proposes to Jane. 'm': Jane will marry him.
'r': Jane will reject the proposal. 'u': Tom will be unhappy.
's': Tom will be married to a person smarter than he is.
'i': Tom's macho image will suffer.

[A] then represents the logical form of the argument and [A1] represents the way of arguing we have imagined:

[A]		[A1]		
$p \supset (m \vee r)$		(1)	p	As[sumption]
$m \supset s$		(2)	$p \supset (m \vee r)$	Pr
$s \supset i$		(3)	$m \vee r$	(1)(2)MP
$i \supset u$		(4)	$m \supset s$	Pr
$r \supset u$		(5)	$s \supset i$	Pr
———				
$p \supset u$		(6)	$m \supset i$	(4)(5)HS
		(7)	$i \supset u$	Pr
		(8)	$m \supset u$	(6)(7)HS
		(9)	$r \supset u$	Pr
		(10)	u	(3)(8)(9)SDil

Our example suggests the following definition:

> Definition: A CONDITIONAL CHAIN ARGUMENT for $\theta_1, \ldots, \theta_n / \phi_1 \supset \phi_2$ is a finite sequence of lines such that
>
> (a) The first line is
>
> (1) ϕ_1 As
>
> (b) All lines subsequent to (1) conform to the requirements of a simple chain argument in which the lines justified by Pr are limited to $\theta_1, \ldots, \theta_n$, and
>
> (c) The last line is ϕ_2.

What can be proven is:

A conditional chain argument for $\theta_1, \ldots, \theta_n \;/\; \phi_1 \supset \phi_2$ *shows that* $\theta_1, \ldots, \theta_n \;/\; \phi_1 \supset \phi_2$ *is deductively valid.*

Insofar as [A1] is clearly a conditional chain argument for [A], [A1] shows [A] to be deductively valid.

Beginning students of logic are often confused by conditional chain arguments and wonder how one can justify the first line by claiming it to be an assumption. It is of course true that one can't justify lines in an argument by calling it an assumption. Precisely because of this, a conditional chain argument does not in any sense establish the last line. In our example, it is certainly not established that Tom is going to be unhappy. The point of a conditional chain argument is this: If one wants to establish a *conditional* statement, one can do so by assuming the antecedent and deriving the consequent on the basis of that assumption. This establishes the *conditional,* not the *consequent.* In other words, in arguing for a conditional, one can temporarily assume the antecedent in order to derive the consequent; having derived the consequent on the assumption of the antecedent, the assumption is retracted by limiting oneself to the conditional claim that *if* the antecedent is true, so is the consequent. Thus, in our example, we have shown that Tom will be unhappy *on the assumption* that he proposes to Jane, and this amounts to showing that *if* Tom proposes to Jane, he will be unhappy; it doesn't amount to establishing the consequent that Tom will be unhappy because *that,* unlike the conditional, *does* depend on the assumption being correct.

While the applicability of conditional chain arguments is limited to showing the deductive validity of argument forms in which the conclusion is a conditional, for argument forms of that type, *conditional chain arguments characteristically make life a lot easier.* Roughly, this is so because a conditional chain argument gives us an extra line on which to work (i.e., the first line justified by As) and this allows one to have quick access to embedded structures on which rules like MP, Add, and HS can be used.

As a simple example of a conditional chain argument, let us try to show the following argument form to be deductively valid:

[B] $\underline{\text{p} \supset \text{q}\qquad}$
$\quad\;\;$ p ⊃ (q v r)

Since the conclusion is a conditional, we can attempt a conditional chain argument by assuming 'p' and trying to derive 'q v r'. But given the extra line 'p', we can immediately use MP on the premise, thereby giving us 'q'; one step of Add then gives us the desired conclusion. This conditional chain is given in [B1] and might be contrasted to the simple chain [B2] which also shows [B] to be deductively valid:

[B1]	(1)	p	As	[B2]	(1)	p ⊃ q	Pr
	(2)	p ⊃ q	Pr		(2)	−p v q	(1) ⊃/v

(3)	q	(1)(2)MP
(4)	$q \vee r$	(3)Add

(3)	$-p \vee q \vee r$	(2)Add
(4)	$p \supset (q \vee r)$	(3) $\supset/\vee$

While [B2] is just as short as [B1], the strategy involved in it is not as obvious as that of [B1]. The difficulty with the simple chain argument is that we cannot apply Add to the consequent of (1) since rules like Add apply only to entire lines and not to parts of lines. The way to get around this difficulty requires at least minimal ingenuity, while the conditional chain is entirely straightforward because we have quick access to the embedded structures.

EXERCISES—SECTION 3.8.1

Show the following argument forms to be valid by constructing conditional chain arguments:

[a] p
____
$(p \supset q) \supset q$

[b] $p \supset q$
____
$(p \& r) \supset (q \& r)$

[c] $p \supset q$
$p \supset r$
____
$p \supset (q \& r)$

[d] $p \supset (q \vee r)$
$q \supset (s \supset -p)$
$r \supset (s \supset -p)$
____
$p \supset -s$

[e] $p \supset (s \& t)$
$t \supset q$
$s \supset r$
____
$p \supset -(q \supset -r)$

[f] $(p \supset s) \vee (p \supset t)$
$-s \vee u$
$-(t \& -u)$
____
$p \supset u$

[g] $(p \& q) \supset (s \supset t)$
$-t$
____
$p \supset (q \supset -s)$

[h] $(-p \supset q) \supset (-r \supset -q)$
$-p \vee q$
____
$(p \vee q) \supset r$

[i] $q \supset (-q \vee s)$
$(r \& p) \supset -s$
____
$[(-p \vee -q) \supset (p \& q)] \supset -r$

[j] $(p \& q) \supset r$
____
$-(q \supset r) \supset (p \supset u)$

3.8.2 Reductio Chain Arguments

Sometimes when we are trying to argue for a claim ϕ (on the basis of the premises $\theta_1, \ldots, \theta_n$), we assume the negation of the conclusion ϕ and show that the assumption (along with $\theta_1, \ldots, \theta_n$) leads to a contradiction. We conclude that the assumption $-\phi$ must have been mistaken and that ϕ must therefore be true. This way of showing ϕ (on the basis of $\theta_1, \ldots, \theta_n$) is called a *reductio ad absurdum.*

As an example consider:

(a) If he went to San Francisco, he went to Pocatello.
(b) He went to San Francisco or to Reno (or both).
(c) If he went to Reno, he went to San Francisco.

(d) He went to Pocatello.

We might try to argue for the validity of this argument as follows: "Suppose that he didn't go to Pocatello. In that case, by (a), he didn't go to San Francisco. From (b) we can now infer that he went to Reno. But then (c) tells us that he went to San Francisco, and thus we have the contradiction that he both went to San Francisco and that he didn't. Hence, given that (a)–(c) are correct, our assumption that he didn't go to Pocatello must be mistaken, that is, he must have gone to Pocatello."

Let the scheme for extracting the form of the argument be:

's': He went to San Francisco.
'p': He went to Pocatello.
'r': He went to Reno.

The argument form and the way we argued for its deductive validity may then be represented as follows:

[C]		[C1]		
	s ⊃ p		(1) −p	As[sumption]
	s v r		(2) s ⊃ p	Pr
	r ⊃ s		(3) −s	(1)(2)MT
	p		(4) s v r	Pr
			(5) r	(3)(4)MTP
			(6) r ⊃ s	Pr
			(7) s	(5)(6)MP
			(8) s & −s	(3)(7)Adj

This example suggests the following definition of a *reductio* chain argument:

A *reductio* CHAIN ARGUMENT for $\theta_1, \ldots, \theta_n / \phi$ is a finite sequence of lines such that

(a) The first line is

(1) $-\phi$ As

(b) All lines subsequent to (1) conform to the requirements of a simple chain argument in which the use of Pr is limited to $\theta_1, \ldots, \theta_n$, and
(c) The last line is of the form ψ & $-\psi$.

Again, it can be shown that:

> *A reductio chain argument for* $\theta_1, \ldots, \phi_n$ / ϕ *shows that the argument form* $\theta_1, \ldots, \theta_n$ / ϕ *is deductively valid.*

Thus, insofar as [C1] is a *reductio* chain argument for [C], [C1] shows [C] to be valid.

The usefulness of the *reductio* chain is much like that of the conditional chain: By giving us an additional line on which to work (i.e., the negated conclusion on the first line "justified" by As) we attain quicker access to embedded structures on which MP, MT, and the like can be used. Furthermore, whereas the conditional chain is restricted to argument forms in which the conclusions are conditionals, the *reductio* chain can be used on any argument form. On the other hand, there is normally a problem of the chain becoming quite long. Still, a *reductio* chain often proves to be a useful "brute force" method when one runs out of ideas in trying to construct a simple chain argument.

To exemplify both *reductio* chain arguments and their tendency to become long, consider the argument form [B] from Section 3.8.1. The strategy is of course to assume the negation of the conclusion and aim for two lines of the form ψ and $-\psi$ as a prelude to using the final step of Adj to arrive at ψ & $-\psi$. Here then is a *reductio* chain for [B]:

(1)	$-(p \supset (q \vee r))$	As
(2)	$p \,\&\, -(q \vee r)$	(1) $-(\supset)/\&$
(3)	p	(2)S
(4)	$p \supset q$	Pr
(5)	q	(3)(4)MP
(6)	$-(q \vee r)$	(2)S
(7)	$q \vee r$	(5)Add
(8)	$(q \vee r) \,\&\, -(q \vee r)$	(6)(7)Adj

This derivation is twice as long as the one given in Section 3.8.1. Clearly, if one has a choice between a *reductio* chain and a conditional chain, one should always choose a conditional chain.

EXERCISES—SECTION 3.8.2

Show the following argument forms to be valid by constructing *reductio* chain arguments.

[a] $\underline{(p \supset q) \supset p}$
p

[b] $\underline{(p \supset q) \supset q}$
$(q \supset p) \supset p$

[c] $u \vee (s \supset t)$
$t \supset r$
$\underline{(s \supset r) \supset u}$
u

[d] $p \vee q$
$p \supset r$
$\underline{(-p \,\&\, q) \supset r}$
r

[e] p
$\underline{q}$
$p \equiv q$

[f] $[p \supset (p \supset -p)]$
$[q \supset (p \supset -p)]$
$\underline{q \supset p}$
$-p \,\&\, -q$

[g] $\underline{(p \supset r) \vee (q \supset r)}$
$(p \,\&\, q) \supset r$

[h] $\underline{(p \supset q) \supset (p \supset r)}$
$p \supset (q \supset r)$

3.8.3 Combining Several Chain Arguments

We now have several distinct types of chain arguments: simple, conditional, and *reductio.* In some cases, it may be desirable to combine in some fashion several different chain arguments to establish the validity of an argument form. Consider for example [D] and [D1]:

[D] $(r \supset s) \supset (s \supset t)$
$\underline{-(r \supset t)}$
$-s$

[D1] $\underline{(r \supset s) \supset (s \supset t)}$
$(r \supset s) \supset (r \supset t)$

If we can show [D1] to be deductively valid, then '$(r \supset s) \supset (r \supset t)$' is validly inferable from the first premise of [D]; this could be used in a simple chain for [D], because this result along with the second premise of [D] will give us '$-(r \supset s)$' by MT, and it would now be a simple matter to arrive at '$-s$'. [D1] can be shown to be deductively valid by a conditional chain argument, and this can be used in a simple chain for [D], as follows:

(1)	$r \supset s$	As
(2)	$(r \supset s) \supset (s \supset t)$	Pr
(3)	$s \supset t$	(1)(2)MP
(4)	$r \supset t$	(1)(3)HS

(1)	$(r \supset s) \supset (s \supset t)$	Pr
(2)	$(r \supset s) \supset (r \supset t)$	(1)[D1]
(3)	$-(r \supset t)$	Pr
(4)	$-(r \supset s)$	(2)(3)MT
(5)	$r \,\&\, -s$	(4)$-(\supset)/\&$
(6)	$-s$	(5)S

Whenever we show an argument form to be valid, we show that the conclusion is validly inferable from the premises. The requirement for a simple chain argument is that a nonpremise line be validly inferable from previous lines. Thus, whenever we show an argument form to be valid, that argument form can be used in constructing a chain argument for another argument form. In principle, we could keep a list of all the argument forms we have established to be valid and use them in constructing subsequent chain arguments. However, this tends to be counterproductive in practice, because we have to keep referring to an ever-growing list of argument forms that could be used. Thus, we shall require that a use of a valid argument form [A], which is not on our limited list of valid argument types, be accompanied by an independent chain argument showing [A] to be valid. In short, we shall extend our rules to allow the following:

> A chain argument may have a line of the form
>
> (m) ψ (i)(j) . . . (k) [A]
>
> where (i), (j), . . . , and (k) are lines prior to (m), and (i), (j), . . . , (k) / (m) is the argument form [A], which is shown to be valid by an independently displayed chain.

Our example [D] is somewhat artificial because we usually don't know ahead of time what is going to be useful in constructing a chain argument. A more useful way of using independently established argument forms is to use it as a way of *bridging the gap* after the normal strategies have been pursued. As an example, consider:

[E] (p v q) ⊃ (r ⊃ u)
(r & u) ⊃ s
―――――――――
(p v q) ⊃ (r ⊃ s)

We might start a conditional chain for [E] as follows:

[e]			
	(1)	p v q	As
	(2)	(p v q) ⊃ (r ⊃ u)	Pr
	(3)	r ⊃ u	(1)(2)MP
	(4)	(r & u) ⊃ s	Pr

Somehow we would like to get from (3) and (4) to 'r ⊃ s', or the last line of the projected conditional chain. Thus, it would be useful if [E1] were deductively valid:

[E1] r ⊃ u
(r & u) ⊃ s
―――――――――
r ⊃ s

Because [E1] itself has a conditional as a conclusion, this suggests establishing the deductive validity of [E1] by another conditional chain argument:

(1) r As

(2)	$r \supset u$	Pr
(3)	u	(1)(2)MP
(4)	$(r \,\&\, u)$	(1)(3)Adj
(5)	$(r \,\&\, u) \supset s$	Pr
(6)	s	(4)(5)MP

Having shown [E1] to be valid, the chain argument [e] for [E] may be completed by adding one last line:

(5) $r \supset s$ (3)(4)[E1]

Much of the goal in this chapter has been to divide the task of establishing validity into manageable units; combining chain arguments in the manner indicated is one more useful expedient for achieving this goal.

EXERCISES—SECTION 3.8.3

Show the following argument forms to be valid by constructing any kind of chain argument that will do this. You may combine several chain arguments if you wish.

[a] $p \supset (q \,\&\, r)$
———
$(p \supset q) \,\&\, (p \supset r)$

[b] $(p \vee q) \supset r$
———
$(p \supset r) \,\&\, (q \supset r)$

[c] $p \supset (q \supset r)$
———
$(p \supset q) \supset (p \supset r)$

[d] $p \equiv r$
$q \equiv s$
———
$(p \supset q) \supset (r \supset s)$

[c] $p \supset (-u \vee w)$
$-q \supset [(u \,\&\, w) \supset r]$
———
$-(p \vee q) \supset (u \supset r)$

[f] $p \vee q$
$(r \,\&\, p) \supset s$
$(r \,\&\, q) \supset s$
$[r \supset (s \vee t)] \supset u$
———
u

[g] $p \supset (q \vee r)$
$(q \supset s) \,\&\, (r \supset t)$
$t \supset w$
$[p \supset (s \vee w)] \supset u$
———
u

[h] $p \vee q$
$p \supset (r \supset u)$
$q \supset (r \supset s)$
$s \supset -t$
———
$t \supset (r \supset u)$

3.9 Summary and Deductive Fallacies

In the course of this chapter we successively enlarged on the kinds of moves that were allowable within a chain argument, and in the last section we introduced more complex chain arguments in addition to the simple chain arguments. So that the reader may have a concise summary of what is allowed in a chain argument, we shall give a full list of rules governing chain arguments at the end of this chapter.

Part of the plan of this text is to present frequently committed fallacies as they touch on various topics that are covered, and we shall conclude this chapter with a brief discussion of deductive fallacies. While accepting any invalid argument as deductively valid constitutes committing a deductive fallacy, three frequently committed deductive fallacies may be exemplified by the following examples:

(a) Jane must have gone back to religion, because she has found peace in her life again and that's what believing in God does for you.

(b) In Shakespeare's *Macbeth,* Macbeth is convinced by an apparition to "Fear not, till Birnam wood / Do come to Dunsinane." The enemy force camouflaged itself by walking behind branches that they cut down from Birnam wood, and being informed of their approach to Dunsinane castle, Macbeth concludes that his end can't be far off:

> ... and now a wood
> Comes toward Dunsinane. —Arm, arm, and
> out! ...
> There is nor flying hence nor tarrying here ...
> At least we'll die with harness on our back.

(c) I know that he loves me or my sister. Because he loves my sister, he must not love me.

All three examples have an air of plausibility, and the use of expressions like 'can't' and 'must' suggest that the reasoner takes the reason to be deductively valid. Yet, if we use the indicated scheme of abbreviation, their logical forms become [A], [B], and [C], respectively:

[A]	[B]	[C]
'p': Jane has gone back to religion.	'p': Birnam wood doesn't come to Dunsinane.	'p': He loves me.
'q': Jane has found tranquility.	'q': Macbeth will survive.	'q': He loves my sister.

[A]

$$\begin{array}{l} p \supset q \\ \underline{q \quad\quad} \\ p \end{array}$$

[B]

$$\begin{array}{l} p \supset q \\ \underline{-p \quad\quad} \\ -q \end{array}$$

[C]

$$\begin{array}{l} p \vee q \\ \underline{q \quad\quad} \\ -p \end{array}$$

Filling 'p' by False and 'q' by True makes all the premises of [A] and [B] true and their conclusions false. Filling both 'p' and 'q' by True results in the premises of [C] being true and its conclusion being false. This shows [A]–[C] to be invalid, and (a)–(c) are also shown to be invalid because they do not have a relevant further structure. Yet these argument forms and arguments having those forms seem to have persuasive force, no doubt in part because [A] and [B] resemble MP and MT while [C] would be valid if the inclusive 'or' were replaced by the exclusive 'or'. Because of their persuasive force, they are included in the traditional list of fallacies: [A] is called the Fallacy of Affirming the Consequent, [B] is the Fallacy of Denying the Antecedent, and [C] might be called Fallacy of Confusing the Two Senses of 'Or'.

Because these deductive fallacies are clearly inferential fallacies, we may represent them as:

AFFIRMING THE CONSEQUENT:	$(p \supset q) \& q \rightarrow p$.
DENYING THE ANTECEDENT:	$(p \supset q) \& -p \rightarrow -q$.
CONFUSING THE TWO 'OR'S:	$(p \vee q) \& p \rightarrow -q$.

Thus, the Macbeth example would be analyzed as:

Denying the Antecedent: (If Birnam wood doesn't come to Dunsinane, Macbeth will survive) and Birnam wood does come to Dunsinane → Macbeth will not survive.

Exercises on the three deductive fallacies discussed in this section will be included with exercises on other fallacies in Section 4.7.

The persuasiveness of [A]–[C] is a good reminder of the need for something more than intuitions in determining the deductive validity of arguments. If we abstract their logical form, we shall quickly be convinced that no chain is going to show them to be valid. This may lead us to attempt to fill the blanks so that the premises come out true and the conclusion false. Once we see that '$(p \supset q) \& q$' comes out true when 'p' is false and 'q' is true, we may be able to perceive that despite the truth of the statement that "If Jane has gone back to religion, she has found her tranquility," something other than religion may have allowed Jane to find her tranquility. Similarly, even accepting "If Birnam wood doesn't come to Dunsinane, Macbeth will survive," once we see that this can be true while Birnam wood does come and Macbeth survives, we should see that Macbeth panicked prematurely. Much in the same way, once we see that '$(p \vee q) \& q$' comes out true when 'p' and 'q' are both true, we can see that he may love me as well as my sister and thereby avoid the jealous conclusion that he doesn't love me. Because intuition alone can be a poor guide in determining deductive validity, we have developed in this chapter formal procedures for validity. We are now in a position to apply the methods we have learned to the central concern of this text, that is, the assessment of truth claims according to general principles. This will be the topic of the next chapter.

SUMMARY OF THE RULES FOR CHAIN ARGUMENTS

A **simple chain argument** shows $\theta_1, \ldots, \theta_n / \phi$ to be valid if and only if it is a finite sequence of lines such that the last line is ϕ and each line satisfies one of the following conditions:

(a) The line is of the form:

(m) θ_i Pr $1 \leq i \leq n$.

(b) The line is of the form:

(m) ψ (j)Y

where (j) is a line prior to (m), and line (m) results from line (j) by an interchange of the logically identical pair with the name 'Y'.

(c) The line is of the form:

(m) ψ (i)(j) · · · (k) X

where (i), (j), . . . , and (k) are lines prior to (m) and (i), (j), . . . (k) / (m) is an instance of the valid argument type with the name 'X', or shown to be valid by an independently displayed chain argument labeled 'X'.

A **conditional chain argument** shows $\theta_1, \ldots, \theta_n / \phi_1 \supset \phi_2$ to be deductively valid if and only if the first line is

(1) ϕ_1 As,

all lines subsequent to the first line conform to the above-stated requirements of a simple chain argument, and the last line is ϕ_2.

A ***reductio* chain argument** shows $\theta_1, \ldots, \theta_n / \phi$ to be deductively valid if and only if the first line is

(1) $-\phi$ As,

all lines subsequent to the first line conform to the above-stated requirements of a simple chain argument, and the last line is of the form ψ & $-\psi$.

Valid Argument Types

MP: $\phi \supset \theta$, ϕ / θ

MT: $\phi \supset \theta$, $N[\theta]$ / $N[\phi]$

MTP: $D[\phi_1, \ldots, \phi_n]$, $N[\phi_1]$ / $D[\phi_2, \ldots \phi_n]$

IA: $\phi \supset N[\phi]$ / $N[\phi]$

Rd: $\phi \supset (\theta \,\&\, -\theta)$ / $N[\phi]$

Add: ϕ_1 / $D[\phi_1, \ldots, \phi_n]$

S: $\underline{C[\phi_1, \ldots, \phi_n]}$
ϕ_1

Adj: ϕ_1
$\ldots$
$\underline{\phi_n}$
$C[\phi_1, \ldots, \phi_n]$

HS: $\phi \supset \theta$
$\underline{\theta \supset \psi}$
$\phi \supset \psi$

SDil: $\phi_1 \vee \phi_2$
$\phi_1 \supset \theta$
$\underline{\phi_2 \supset \theta}$
θ

CDil: $\phi_1 \vee \phi_2$
$\phi_1 \supset \theta_1$
$\underline{\phi_2 \supset \theta_2}$
$D[\theta_1, \theta_2]$

Logically Identical Pairs

Abbreviated Name	*Symbolic Notation*	
DN	ϕ,	$--\phi$
AS	$\phi_1 \& (\phi_2 \& \phi_3)$,	$(\phi_1 \& \phi_2) \& \phi_3$
AS	$\phi_1 \vee (\phi_2 \vee \phi_3)$,	$(\phi_1 \vee \phi_2) \vee \phi_3$
ID	$\phi \vee \phi$,	ϕ
ID	$\phi \& \phi$,	ϕ
Dist	$\phi \& (\theta_1 \vee \ldots \vee \theta_n)$,	$(\phi \& \theta_1) \vee \ldots \vee (\phi \& \theta_n)$
Dist	$\phi \vee (\theta_1 \& \ldots \& \theta_n)$,	$(\phi \vee \theta_1) \& \ldots \& (\phi \vee \theta_n)$
DeM	$-(\phi_1 \vee \ldots \vee \phi_n)$,	$N[\phi_1] \& \ldots \& N[\phi_n]$
DeM	$-(\phi_1 \& \ldots \& \phi_n)$,	$N[\phi_1] \vee \ldots \vee N[\phi_n]$
Cont	$\phi \supset \theta$,	$N[\theta] \supset N[\phi]$
E/I	$(\phi \& \theta) \supset \psi$,	$\phi \supset (\theta \supset \psi)$
$\supset$ / v	$\phi \supset \theta$,	$N[\phi] \vee \theta$
$-(\supset)$ / &	$-(\phi \supset \theta)$,	$\phi \& N[\theta]$
$-(\&)$ / $\supset$	$-(\phi \& \theta)$,	$\phi \supset N[\theta]$
$\equiv$ / $\supset$	$\phi \equiv \theta$,	$(\phi \supset \theta) \& (\theta \supset \phi)$
$-(\equiv)$ / $\equiv(-)$	$-(\phi \equiv \theta)$,	$\phi \equiv N[\theta]$
v^e / $\equiv$	$\phi \vee^e \theta$,	$\phi \equiv N[\theta]$
v^e / &	$\phi \vee^e \theta$,	$(\phi \vee \theta) \& -(\phi \& \theta)$
Com	$\phi \equiv \theta$,	$\theta \equiv \phi$
Com	$\phi \& \theta$,	$\theta \& \phi$
Com	$\phi \vee \theta$,	$\theta \vee \phi$

Analyzing Argumentative Passages

Virtually every piece of writing in nonfiction has some point to make. Of course, a lot of what we read involves nothing more than stating the point, restating the point, and embellishing it with a few rhetorical flourishes. A typical example is this letter to the editor of the *Los Angeles Times:*

> Even with my arthritis, I am writing you this letter. I am thankful for receiving my cost-of-living increase in my July Social Security check despite a President and a Smart-aleck snip of a budget director who has no compassion for the poor and elderly.

The writer is claiming that he or she is thankful for (and perhaps needs) the cost-of-living increase and that the president and his budget director are heartless when it comes to the poor and elderly. The legitimate concern of this writer is to express his or her opinion, not to argue for it. However, we often encounter passages in which the writer not only makes a point but also offers some reasons for his or her view. These passages (which may be called argumentative passages) will be the primary concern of this chapter because the reasons given provide some basis or a starting point for pursuing the activity of truth assessment. In developing a method for analyzing these passages, we shall finally fulfill the promise of blending the material covered in Chapters 2 and 3 in order to develop a method for assessing truth claims.

In our presentation, we shall adopt the second- or third-person position of analyzing an argumentative passage presented by others. However, it should be clear that we can become our own critics—as long as we have some reasons for a view that we are inclined to accept, the method developed in this chapter can be used to assess the truth or falsity of our view. To this extent, our concern is with genuine truth assessment.

Before embarking on the main concern of this chapter, we must first deal with a few preliminaries. In introducing deductively valid reasons in Chapter 3, we indicated that there are perfectly fine reasons that are nevertheless not valid reasons. Because people seldom pretend to offer valid reasons for a claim, we must discuss the several different kinds of supporting reasons one may have for a claim, and this will be our topic in Section 4.1. In that section we shall also discuss the related topic of the degrees to which one may be justified in making a claim. With reference to some of the material covered in Section 4.1, Section 4.2 will be concerned with how knowledge of deductive validity can be helpful in assessing truth claims. Given these results, Sections 4.3–4.5 form the central sections of this chapter's topic, namely, assessing argumentative passages. The optional Section 4.6 will present some auxiliary tools for analyzing argumentative passages, and Section 4.7 will deal with some of the fallacies that can be encountered in such passages.

4.1 Types of Reasons and Degrees of Justification

While deductively valid reasons give us very strong reasons for the conclusion, we often rely on reasons that aren't nearly as strong. The following three examples should give us a sense of the range of things we regard as supporting reasons—things that, if true, would give rise to some grounds for believing the conclusion:

(1) (a) Tanner beat Borg in their last match.
is a reason for
(b) Tanner will beat Borg in the upcoming Wimbledon final.

(2) (a) It is muddy outside.
is a reason for
(b) He'll get his shoes muddy if he wears them outside.

(3) (a) He is playing in the rain, and if he is playing in the rain, he will be sick.
is a reason for
(b) He will be sick.

As already suggested, one difference in these examples is the degree to which the reasons support the conclusion. While (1)(a) is a fairly weak reason for (1)(b), (2)(a) is a compelling or virtually conclusive reason for (2)(b). (3)(a) is of course a valid reason that absolutely guarantees the truth of (3)(b) in that it is impossible for (3)(a) to be true and (3)(b) to be false.

There is, however, another difference between (1) and (2) on the one hand and (3) on the other. If we were to learn that Borg "threw" the last match to Tanner in order set him up for the Wimbledon final, we may not want to consider (1)(a) to be even *a* reason for (1)(b). Certainly, we wouldn't consider (1)(a) to be a reason (even of the weakest kind) for (1)(b) if we learn that Borg had beaten Tanner in the Wimbledon final. (2)(a) is clearly an exceptionally strong reason for (2)(b) today. But if (as is perhaps likely) we should in the future fly from one place to another with jetpacks worn like backpacks, (2)(a) would cease to be a strong reason for (2)(b). On the other hand, insofar as there is no possible world in which (3)(a) is true and (3)(b) false, (3)(a)'s truth is guaranteed to yield (3)(b)'s truth whatever the circumstance may be.

What these considerations show is that, except for valid reasons, whether something is a supporting reason for something else depends on or is relative to the total evidence available to a person at a time. Although there are a number of technical complications, we can at least roughly understand a person's total evidence or his epistemic circumstance (i.e., his position with respect to various knowledge claims) in terms of the class of claims or statements that are unproblematic for him at that time. An account of supporting reasons must therefore always be understood with reference to the epistemic situation that is currently available to a person.

Taking as understood this reference to an epistemic situation, a very rough formulation of supporting reasons may be given as follows:

> X is a supporting reason for Y =
>
> [If nothing else were to incline one to believe Y,] the assumption of X makes Y somewhat more plausible than the assumption of not-X.

Leaving the bracketed qualification aside for the moment, to apply this loose definition we imagine two situations as close to our actual situation as possible: (i) a situation in which the truth of X is assumed and (ii) a situation in which the truth of not-X is assumed. X is a supporting reason for Y just in case Y is at least a bit more plausible in (i) than in (ii). The bracketed qualification can usually be ignored: It comes into play only when there are several supporting reasons for Y and one of them by itself (e.g., X*) gives one optimal confidence in Y regardless of the other supporting reasons; in such a case, to detect the support the other reasons give to Y, one must additionally assume that X* is not available.

To exemplify some normal applications of our loose definition, suppose we have just seen Borg beat Tanner in the Wimbledon final. In this epistemic situation, Tanner winning (or having won) the Wimbledon final is equally implausible whether or not we assume that Tanner beat Borg in the previous match. Hence, in this epistemic situation, (1)(a) is not a supporting reason for (1)(b). Consider now a normal situation prior to the match. Here the assumption that Tanner won the last match against Borg would make his win in the upcoming Wimbledon final at least slightly more plausible than the assumption that Tanner had lost the last match; thus, in this epistemic situation, (1)(a) is *a* supporting reason for (1)(b). It should be noted, however, that (1)(a) can be *a* supporting reason for (1)(b) even if, on balance, it is more plausible to deny (1)(b). Suppose someone knew that prior to this last match where Tanner beat Borg, Borg had beaten Tanner in all four matches. On balance, it would be more plausible for this person to believe that Borg will beat Tanner in the upcoming Wimbledon final. Still, it would be true for a person in this situation that Tanner's winning the Wimbledon final is slightly more plausible on the assumption that he at least won the last match than on the assumption that he had lost the last match as well. Thus, something can be a supporting reason for a claim without supporting the claim very strongly at all.

Our account of 'a supporting reason' is admittedly rough and stands in need of a number of refinements. One such refinement would cast the definition in terms of what a rational person would find more plausible in a given epistemic circumstance: after all, there is no telling what an irrational person would find more plausible in an epistemic circumstance. However, because this and other refinements are likely to be more confusing than clarifying for all but the advanced student, we shall rely on the reader's use of judgment in applying our loose account of supporting reasons.

It should be clear that in ordinary epistemic situations we currently encounter, (2)(a), 'It is muddy outside', is a supporting reason for (2)(b), 'He'll get his shoes muddy if he wears them outside'. However, as we noted, (2)(a) is considerably stronger reason for (2)(b) than (1)(a) is for (1)(b). To capture this difference, let us introduce the expression 'completely legitimate reason'. Again taking the reference to an epistemic situation to be implicitly understood, a loose definition is given by:

X is a completely legitimate reason for Y = If X were as good as an unproblematic claim, Y would be as good as an unproblematic claim.

If we wished to be a little more precise, we could give the following specification of 'for a person p at time t, X is a completely legitimate reason for Y':

> For a rational person in p's epistemic situation at t, if he were to accept X as unproblematic (or as justified as an unproblematic claim), this would result in Y being as justified for him as an unproblematic claim (i.e., he could count on Y's truth without any practical doubt or qualification).

Whether we rely on this account or the shorter more intuitive account, it should be clear that given our epistemic situation today, (2)(a) is a completely legitimate reason for (2)(b).

The third example of reasons we gave at the beginning of this section was one in which (3)(a) was a valid reason for (3)(b). The idea of a valid reason has been explained at great length in Chapter 3 and it would be otiose to repeat that explanation. However, it should be noted that given our account, any valid reason is also a completely legitimate reason. Of course the reverse does not hold: example (2) indicates that there are many completely legitimate reasons that are not valid reasons.

In discussing valid reasons, we found it convenient in Chapter 3 to introduce the idea of a valid argument, so that the conjunction of the premises of a valid argument is a valid reason for the conclusion of the argument. For many purposes, it is convenient to extend this idea to completely legitimate reasons that are not valid reasons. Thus, *we shall say that an argument is a* COMPLETELY LEGITIMATE NONDEMONSTRATIVE ARGUMENT *if and only if it is not a valid argument and yet the conjunction of the premises is a completely legitimate reason for the conclusion.* While the legitimacy of some nondemonstrative arguments can be understood in terms of the materials to be developed in this chapter, a full discussion of nondemonstrative arguments will be deferred until Chapter 5.

Given our discussion of different kinds of reasons, clearly reasons for a belief or conclusion can come in varying degrees. This in turn has the consequence that a belief or a claim can have varying degrees of justification for us as our epistemic situation changes. Consider again Jane's position in Chapter 1 with respect to the claim 'Professor C didn't read my paper'. Once she determined that it was unlikely that Professor C should have *distinctly* remembered having put her paper out as he claimed, she had *a* supporting reason for the statement that he hadn't read her paper. This prompted her to collect more reasons for the claim, and at some point she had enough supporting reasons for the claim to make it *more* reasonable for her to believe it than to disbelieve it. Clearly she had reached this point by the time she got the evasive answers from Professor C. Finally, when she succeeded in tripping up Professor C, Jane had a completely legitimate reason for the claim that he hadn't read her paper. This is a typical progression in many cases: We initially have one or a few supporting reason(s) for a claim Y, although on balance it may still be more reasonable to disbelieve Y. This often prompts us to find more reasons or evidence for Y, and when we do, we may reach a point where we have enough reasons to make it more reasonable on balance to believe Y than to disbelieve Y. Finally, we may sometimes be fortunate enough to have collected enough reasons for Y, so that their conjunction constitutes a completely legitimate reason for Y.

The progression just outlined emphasizes that a claim's status changes as the epistemic situation changes, and there are a number of different statuses that claims may have in any given epistemic situation. It may be useful at this point to characterize in somewhat greater detail the variety of statuses that claims can have. *The strongest status a claim C may have in an epistemic situation is that of its truth being unproblematic or as jus-*

tified as an unproblematic claim. We may say that a claim or statement is COMPLETELY JUSTIFIED *for a person at a time if it has this strong status in his epistemic situation.* Given our account of completely legitimate reasons (which include valid reasons), the class of completely justified statements can be specified as follows:

(1) Any statement that is unproblematic for a person p at time t is completely justified for p at t.
(2) If X is completely justified for p at t, and X is a completely legitimate reason for Y, then Y is completely justified for p at t.
(3) Nothing is completely justified for p at t unless its being so follows from (1) and (2).

Roughly, a statement is completely justified just in case it is free of all practical doubt. Because completely justified statements are the unproblematic statements *and* inferential conclusions drawn from them by valid or completely legitimate nondemonstrative arguments, a completely justified statement need not be an unproblematic statement of the types catalogued in Chapter 2. (See the summarizing chart on p. 188.)

The opposite extreme that a claim C may occupy in one's epistemic situation is that of the falsity of C being completely justified. These two extremes form the endpoints of a gradation on which the midpoint is the truth of C being as justified as the falsity of C, in which case C might be said to be epistemically neutral. If the truth of C is at least somewhat more justified than its falsity, we might say that C is epistemically acceptable. If the truth of C is considerably more justified than its falsity, so that its truth is almost completely justified, we might say that C is highly justified. The same gradations are mirrored in the region between C being epistemically neutral and its falsity being completely justified. The resulting gradations are summarized in the diagram given earlier.

In order to convey a sense of concreteness to the reader, a suggestive model has been placed adjacent to our summarizing chart. The idea of this model is to treat the degree of justification of C as the probability it has in the epistemic circumstance, a quantity indicated by Pr(C). The epistemic neutrality of C would then be set at Pr(C) = .5. The truth of C is being completely justified would be in the region in which Pr(C) is around 1 and its falsity being completely justified would be in the region in which Pr(C) is around 0. The exact numbers are difficult to specify even in a model, and the numbers given are merely suggestive. Remembering that the numbers are merely suggestive, "highly justified" and "merely acceptable" might be taken in the way shown. Some relations between degrees of justification seem to be correctly mirrored by the model, and the model may make the idea of "degrees of justification" more accessible to some readers. However, it should be remembered that the model is at best suggestive. Apart from the difficulties in arriving at specific numbers,it is not at all clear that degrees of justifications should ultimately be understood in terms of probabilities.

Degrees of Justification		*A Suggestive Model*
	C is *completely justified:* C is unproblematic or completely legitimized by the unproblematic.	$.95(?) < Pr(C) \leq 1.0$
C is *acceptable:* C is more justified than not-C.	C is *highly justified:* C is very much more justified than not-C.	$.80(?) < Pr(C) \leq .95(?)$
	C is *merely acceptable:* C is somewhat more justified than not-C.	$.50 < Pr(C) \leq .80(?)$
C is *epistemically neutral:* C is as justified as not-C.		$Pr(C) = .50$
	C is *merely unacceptable.* Not-C is somewhat more justified than C.	$.20(?) \leq Pr(C) < .50$
C is *unacceptable:* Not-C is more justified than C.	The *falsity of C is highly justified:* Not-C is considerably more justified than C.	$.05(?) \leq Pr(C) < .20(?)$
	The *falsity of C is completely justified:* Not-C is completely justified.	$0 \leq Pr(C) < .20(?)$

Whether or not one relies on the model, one thing that emerges from our discussion is this: While a statement is true or false, its status in an epistemic situation is not a two-valued affair. Even with the crudest classification, the epistemic status of C is a three-valued affair, that is, acceptable, unacceptable, and neutral; and within the acceptable and unacceptable ranges, there are many relevant discriminations to be made. The failure to recognize this complexity surrounding the epistemic status of a statement can lead to a variety of errors, the Fallacy of the Argument from Ignorance mentioned in Section 2.6 being one such example.

EXERCISES—SECTION 4.1

1. For each of the following pairs of statements, determine relative to your epistemic situation whether (i) is a supporting reason for (ii) and whether (ii) is a supporting reason for (i). *Justify your answer,* and if a supporting reason is exceedingly weak, indicate this fact. (If the sole reference to a person is by a personal pronoun, assume that nothing is known about that person.)
   (a) (i) He was recently playing with children who have chicken pox.
   (ii) He now has chicken pox.
   (b) (i) She is intelligent.
   (ii) She is kind.
   (c) (i) She is intelligent.
   (ii) She makes a lot of money.
   (d) (i) Carter carried at least two states in 1980.
   (ii) Carter defeated Reagan in the 1980 presidential election.
   (e) (i) John F. Kennedy was guillotined.
   (ii) John F. Kennedy is dead.
   (f) (i) Jesus performed miracles.
   (ii) Jesus is a god.
   (g) (i) Kennedy (a Democrat) won the 1960 presidential election.
   (ii) Truman (a staunch Democrat) voted for Kennedy in 1960.
   (h) (i) She gave birth to her own child on December 31, 1987.
   (ii) She had sexual intercourse or artificial insemination in 1987.
   (i) (i) (The Jewish scientist) Einstein was a genius.
   (ii) The Nazis wanted to make Einstein a German hero.
2. Which of the supporting reasons in exercise 1 are completely legitimate reasons?
3. Relative to the discussion in Section 4.1 concerning the seven different statuses a statement can have, for each of the following statements determine the status it has in your epistemic situation and justify your answer.
   (a) Los Angeles won't be decimated by an earthquake in the next ten years.
   (b) Reagan won two presidential elections.
   (c) The Florida citrus crop will be severely damaged by frost next winter.
   (d) Cleopatra had more lovers than Mark Antony.
   (e) No third-party candidate (i.e., a candidate who isn't the Republican or Democratic candidate) will be elected the president of the United States in the next twenty years.
   (f) Franklin Roosevelt never won a presidential election.
   (g) John F. Kennedy had eggs for breakfast on the day he was assassinated.
   (h) The premier of Israel and the president of Syria prepared for their bar mitzvahs together.
   (i) It will not snow in Austria next January.

4.2 Deductive Validity and Degrees of Justification

Given our discussion of different types of reasons and our account of the degrees to which a claim can be justified, we are in a position to explain how knowledge of deductive validity can help us in the activity of truth assessments. We know that if the premises of a valid argument are true, the conclusion must also be true; thus, to whatever degree the conjunction of the premises is justified (above epistemic neutrality), the conclusion is justified at least to that degree:

(i) If '$p_1, \ldots, p_n/c$' is valid and '$p_1 \& \ldots \& p_n$' is *completely justified* {*highly justified, acceptable*}, so is 'c'.

To be precise, this and subsequent relations between validity and justification should be indexed to one's epistemic situation. We shall take this to be understood so that the reader will take (i) to state, for example, that if '$p_1 \& \ldots \& p_n$' is acceptable *in one's epistemic situation,* 'c' is also acceptable in that epistemic situation.

The most obvious use of relation (i) in making truth assessments is when we have been given valid reasons that are acceptable to some degree or other. However, the use of (i) is not limited to such cases. Suppose we have been offered reasons that fail to give us a valid argument for the conclusion. In such a case one could of course criticize the argument for being invalid. But, this is not a very useful bit of criticism (unless it is a debating contest and one's opponent was claiming the argument to be valid). There are two interrelated problems with this criticism: (1) The argument may not have been intended as a valid argument; rather it may have only been intended as a completely legitimate nondemonstrative argument or perhaps even only as a set of reasons that highly justifies the conclusion or makes the conclusion acceptable. (2) One may be able to come up with a fully or highly justified missing premise that will convert the argument into a valid one. This suggests that even when valid reasons have not been offered, by finding appropriate missing premises, (i) may show us that there are good reasons for accepting the conclusion.

To clarify the situation, let us suppose that although the conjunction of the premises is completely justified, '$p_1, \ldots, p_n/c$' is invalid. If one wants 'c' to be fully or highly justified, what one is looking for is a missing premise 'q' that has two features: (a) 'q' is *strong enough* so that '$p_1, \ldots, p_n, q/c$' is deductively valid; and (b) 'q' is *weak enough* so that '$p_1 \& \ldots \& p_n \& q$' is fully or highly justified. Knowledge of what arguments are deductively valid is useful here, because without it one can't find a reasonable selection of missing premises that satisfy (a) so that one can choose one that satisfies (b) most adequately. Clearly, if one finds a missing premise 'q' that satisfies (a) and (b), 'c' is fully or highly justified. In general, by relation (i),

If one finds missing premises that convert the argument into one that is deductively valid, the conclusion is justified at least to the degree to which the conjunction of the old and new premises is justified.

Relation (i) thus gives us ways of positively assessing a claim even when the reasons offered fail to be valid reasons. This raises the question of when we can negatively assess a claim for which reasons have been offered. Suppose that '$p_1, \ldots, p_n/c$' is invalid while '$p_1, \ldots, p_n, q/c$' is valid. If 'q' is unacceptable or epistemically neutral, can we claim that 'c' is not acceptable? The answer is no. There could be an overlooked statement 'q^*' that is fully or highly justified and is such that '$p_1, \ldots, p_n, q^*/c$' is valid. But this consideration also shows that even if the offered reasons themselves are not acceptable, we cannot claim that the conclusion is not acceptable. There may be a completely different set of reasons whose conjunction is both completely justified and is a valid reason for the claim in question.

What then can be said in criticism (either of oneself or of another) when the argument presented contains premises that are not acceptable or is invalid and we can find no acceptable missing premise to convert it into a valid argument? Part of the solution lies in recognizing that there is a burden of proof on the person who is trying to make a point. If one or more of the premises are not acceptable, one can legitimately complain that grounds for accepting the conclusion have not been made evident. Similarly, if an honest attempt to find appropriate missing premises fails to unconver a (conjunctive) statement that is both acceptable and converts the argument into one that is valid, one can again legitimately complain that grounds for accepting the conclusion have not been made evident. Let us then introduce the following term of criticism:

Grounds for accepting a claim have not been made evident
(a) if the argument for the claim contains a premise that is not acceptable, or
(b) the best attempt to convert the argument into one that is valid fails to uncover an acceptable missing premise.

When missing premises are involved, it is important that an honest attempt is made to find one that is appropriate. To insist on the burden of proof without making such an honest attempt interferes with truth assessment and reduces the enterprise to a debater's game of merely scoring points. It should be clear that whether something has been made evident depends on one's own circumstance in a twofold way: the acceptability of premises is clearly relative to one's own epistemic circumstance, and the best attempt that fails is one's own attempt. To underline this, it would be best to say: The grounds for accepting the claim have not been made evident *to me.* However, for the sake of brevity, we shall sometimes take the reference to oneself to be understood.

When poor reasons are offered for a claim, typically we can only say that grounds for accepting the conclusion have not been made evident. However, there is one circumstance in which we can actually assess the claim negatively. If '$p_1, \ldots, p_n/c$' is deductively invalid, we know that there is a possible world in which all the premises are true and the conclusion false. Thus, when the argument is invalid, there is some possibly false statement 'q' such that if 'q' were false, 'c' would be false even if all of 'p_1', . . . , 'p_n' were true. If such a 'q' is *in fact* unacceptable or epistemically neutral, we can make a stronger criticism than the one that the grounds for accepting the conclusion have not been made evident:

(ii) Let 'q' be not acceptable and such that if 'q' were false, 'c' would be false even if all of 'p_1', . . . , 'p_n' were true. Then: 'c' is not acceptable and 'p_1 & . . . & p_n' is a bad reason for 'c'.

Given an invalid argument 'p_1, . . . , p_n/c', there must be some possibly false statement 'q' such that if it were false, 'c' would be false even if 'p_1 & . . . & p_n' were true. Unfortunately, there is no general method for finding such a 'q' that might easily be assessed to be less than acceptable in the actual epistemic situation. (Of course, 'if p_1 & . . . p_n, then c' is always available; but this long conditional is often useless, because it is usually difficult to gauge its degree of justification.) However, it can sometimes happen that in the search for a missing premise that would convert the invalid argument into one that is valid, one hits upon a useful 'q' of the sort specified in (ii).

As an example, let us adapt a remark of former Senator Hayakawa (to the effect that a high gas tax wouldn't affect the poor because they can't afford a car anyway). Thus, consider:

(1) If Jones is rich, he doesn't have to worry about a $1000 tax increase on his house.
(2) If Jones is poor, he doesn't have a house.
(3) If Jones doesn't have a house, he doesn't have to worry about a $1000 tax increase on his house.

---

(4) Jones doesn't have to worry about a $1000 tax increase on his house.

This argument depends on nothing more than its fairly coarse logical structure and the reader can easily ascertain that the argument is invalid. A search for missing premises to make it valid should lead to:

(5) Jones is rich or poor.

The addition of (5) as a premise would indeed convert the argument into one that is valid. However, notice: if (5) is false (because Jones is neither rich nor poor but belongs to the vast majority of middle-income home owners), (4) would be false even if (1)–(3) were all true. If one's epistemic situation contains no particular information about Jones so that (5) remains epistemically neutral or worse, in light of (ii), (4) is not acceptable and (1)–(3) constitute a bad reason for (4).

Our discussion so far has been concerned with assessing a conclusion 'c' when some reasons for it have been offered and missing premises have been provided when needed. This discussion, and the possible outcomes such an assessment can have, may be summarized by the following:

(1) 'c' is completely justified {highly justified, acceptable} if '$p_1, \ldots, p_n$/c' is valid and 'p_1 & . . . & p_n' is completely justified {highly justified, acceptable}. [relation (i)]
(2) Grounds for accepting 'c' have not been made evident if the argument for 'c'
 (a) contains a premise that is not acceptable *or*
 (b) the best attempt to convert the argument for 'c' into one that is valid fails to uncover an acceptable missing premise.
(3) 'c' is not acceptable and 'p_1 & . . . & p_n' is a bad reason for 'c' if there is a 'q' that is not acceptable and is such that if 'q' were false, 'c' would be false even if all of 'p_1', . . . , 'p_n' were true. [relation (ii)]

While this summarizes the most obvious ways in which knowledge of deductive validity can help us in making truth assessments, there are other ways in which knowledge of validity can help us in the activity of truth assessments. Suppose that the conjunction of all but one of the premises of an argument is completely justified and the remaining questionable premise makes the difference between the argument being valid or not. The validity of the argument then shows what one would be committed to if one were to accept the questionable premise. This can be clearly useful to know. If the falsity of the conclusion is completely justified, the falsity of the questionable premise is completely justified. This is precisely the relation we often use when we want to test a hypothesis or hunch 'h'. We join 'h' with a number of unproblematic claims 'p_1', . . . , 'p_n' to arrive at valid arguments for a set of conclusions, which may then be checked. In the negative situation in which we find a conclusion to be false, we have reasons against 'h'; in the positive situation when we find the conclusions to be true, we have reasons for 'h'. This kind of a "test" is covered by the following relation[1]:

(iii) Let '$p_1, \ldots, p_n$, h / c' be valid, 'h' be needed for this validity, and 'p_1 & . . . & p_n' be completely justified. Then:
 (a) '$-$c' is a completely legitimate reason for '$-$h' and
 (b) 'c' is a supporting reason for 'h' unless '$-$h' is already completely justified.

The correctness of (iii)(a) can be seen as follows: If the argument is valid, then in any conceivable world in which 'c' is false, one of the prem-

1. To cover some unusual cases, a more fully correct formulation would add the qualification: Furthermore, let nothing in one's epistemic situation preclude 'p_1 & . . . & p_n & $-$c' from being completely justified. An analogous qualification is needed for the subsequent version (iii*).

ises must be false. Thus, the falsity of 'c' is a valid reason for the falsity of at least one of the premises 'p_1', . . . , 'p_n', and 'h'. But then it also follows that in the assumed epistemic situation in which the falsity of 'c' and the truth of 'p_1', . . . , 'p_n' are completely justified, a rational person would take the falsity of 'h' to be as justified as an unproblematic claim. Hence, the falsity of 'c' is a completely legitimate reason for '$-$h' in that epistemic situation. As for (iii)(b), because the falsity of 'c' is a completely legitimate reason for the falsity of 'h', 'h' must be at least slightly more plausible for a rational person if 'c' were assumed to be true rather than false—unless of course the falsity of 'h' were already completely justified. Thus, 'c' is a supporting reason for 'h' unless '$-$h' is already completely justified. However, because *a* supporting reason can be quite weak, 'c' is seldom a valid or completely legitimate reason for 'h'.

A simple example of (iii) is the following: because 'Freud is a man, all men dream / Freud dreams' is valid and 'Freud is a man' is unproblematic, 'Freud dreams' is *a* supporting reason for 'All men dream'; on the other hand, 'Freud didn't dream' would be a completely legitimate reason for the falsity of 'All men dream'. As a very crude approximation, scientific reasoning for a hypothesis 'h' might be seen as a matter of collecting enough reasons for 'h' by the repeated use of (iii)(b) and not finding any disconfirmation of the type specified in (iii)(a). However, what constitutes a completely legitimate reason for a scientific hypothesis is a complex issue that will be discussed more fully in Chapter 5.

Other degrees of justification for the statements involved give rise to other versions of (iii). One such version is:

> (iii*) Let 'p_1, . . . , p_n, h / c' be valid, 'h' be needed for this validity, and 'p_1 & . . . & p_n' be acceptable. Then:
> (a) if 'c' is unacceptable, 'h' is unacceptable, and
> (b) 'c' is a supporting reason for 'h' unless 'h' is already unacceptable.

The correctness of (iii*) relies on much the same kind of considerations as those on which we depended earlier.

One final relation between validity and justification deserves attention. From our discussion in Section 4.1, we know that a supporting reason can be a very weak reason and that a completely legitimate reason is a very strong reason. Is there any way of gauging the strengths of reasons within this large interval? Recalling that missing premises can convert invalid arguments into ones that are valid, a rough measure of the strength of reasons is given by the following relation[2]:

2. To cover some unusual cases, a more fully correct formulation would add the qualification: Furthermore, let nothing in one's epistemic situation preclude 'p_1 & . . . & p_n & q' from being completely justified.

(iv) Let '$p_1, \ldots, p_n$, q / c' be valid, and 'q' be needed for this validity. Then the degree to which 'p_1 & . . . & p_n' supports or justifies 'c' is no less than the degree to which 'q' is justified.

Thus, given the situation stated in (iv), if 'q' is highly justified in the epistemic situation, in that epistemic situation 'p_1 & . . . & p_n' highly justifies 'c' in the sense that if 'p_1 & . . . & p_n' were completely justified, 'c' would be at least highly justified. Similarly, if 'q' is acceptable, 'p_1 & . . . & p_n' supports 'c' to the level of acceptability in the sense that if 'p_1 & . . . & p_n' were completely justified, 'c' would be acceptable. We can now see that knowledge of validity gives one tools for assessing how strongly reasons other than valid reasons support a conclusion. In this and other ways discussed in this section, although valid reasons are seldom encountered in everyday life, knowledge of deductive validity gives us tools for making a variety of assessments concerning reasons for the conclusions they support.

EXERCISES—SECTION 4.2

1. Assume the following for each of the arguments below:
   (a) The indicated missing premise is the best attempt to convert the argument into one that is valid.
   (b) The conjunction of the given premises with the missing premise is as justified as the degree to which the missing premise is justified.
   (c) The *bordereau* is a letter in which a spy promises to pass French military secrets to a German military attaché who was in collusion with the Italian military attaché, and Dreyfus is the French artillery officer accused of being that spy. (cf. Section 2.5, Exercises, problem set E. Knowledge of that problem set is not required.)
   (d) If it were not for the given and missing premises, the conclusion would be epistemically neutral in one's epistemic situation.

   Relying on relations (i) and (ii) as well as the definition of 'grounds for accepting the conclusion have not been made evident', determine for each of the arguments which of the following situations obtains:

   I. The conclusion is acceptable (and if so, to what degree); *or*
   II. Grounds for the conclusion have not been made evident; *or*
   III. The conclusion is unacceptable, and bad reasons have been given.

Justify your answers.

Note: [E]–[H] should give the reader an idea of how the material of Chapter 2 and knowledge of validity can help in truth assessments.

[A] (1) Jacques is a Frenchman.
(2) Jacques is romantic.
Missing premise: All Frenchmen are romantic.

[B] (1) If this course's text is written by Dauer, then if Dauer isn't Copi, this course's text isn't written by Copi.
(2) Dauer isn't Copi.

---

(3) This course's text is not written by Copi.
Missing premise: This course's text is written by Dauer.

[C] (1) Tom is betting a $100 that the next spin of the roulette wheel will land on a number between 1 and 9.
(2) If (1) is true and the next spin of the roulette wheel lands on one of the other numbers (between 10 and 36), Tom will lose $100.

---

(2) Tom will lose $100.
Missing premise: The next spin of the roulette wheel will land on one of the other numbers (between 10 and 36).

[D] (1) If José said that Mary and Richard live in the same dormitory, then Mary and Richard live in the same dormitory.
(2) José said that Mary and Richard live in the same dormitory.

---

(3) Mary and Richard are intimate friends.
Missing premise: If Mary and Richard live in the same dormitory, Mary and Richard are intimate friends.

[E] (1) Douglas defended his Nebraska–Kansas bill at a public meeting on September 1, 1854.
(2) September 1, 1854 was a Friday.
(3) Public meetings do not last over twenty-four consecutive hours.
(4) If (1)–(3) are true, Douglas did not leave the September 1, 1854 meeting on Sunday morning.

---

(5) At the end of the September 1, 1854 meeting Douglas did not say: "It is now Sunday morning—I'll go to church and you may go to Hell."
Missing premise: If Douglas did not leave the September 1, 1854 meeting on Sunday morning, (5) is true.

[F] (1) The handwriting of the *bordereau* is entirely that of Esterhazy.
(2) Dreyfus isn't Esterhazy.

---

(3) Dreyfus did not write the *bordereau.*
Missing premise: If (1) and (2) are true, Dreyfus did not write the *bordereau.*

[G] (1) If Dreyfus wrote the *bordereau* after June 1894, Dreyfus was off to maneuvers after June 1894.
(2) Dreyfus was not off to maneuvers after June 1894.
(3) No one could have written the *bordereau* before July 1894.

---

(4) Dreyfus did not write the *bordereau.*
Missing premise: If Dreyfus did not write the *bordereau* after June 1894 and (3) is true, Dreyfus did not write the *bordereau.*

[H] (1) The German military attaché received fortification plans of Nice from an agent he referred to by the initial "D."
(2) If (1) is true and the German military attaché was referring to Dreyfus when he referred to an agent by the initial "D," Dreyfus passed fortification plans for Nice to the German military attaché.

---

(3) Dreyfus passed fortification plans for Nice to the German military attaché.
Missing premise: The German military attaché was referring to Dreyfus when he referred to an agent by the initial "D."

[I] (1) French Intelligence knew by December 1894 that the telegram intercepted from the Italian embassy suggested lack of contact between the Italians and Dreyfus, and that the telegram did not state "Captain Dreyfus arrested. Precuations taken, emissary warned."
(2) In December 1984, French Intelligence informed the judges of Dreyfus's court-martial that the intercepted telegram stated: "Captain Dreyfus arrested. Precautions taken, emissary warned."
(3) If (1) and (2) are true, French Intelligence lied at the court-martial to the detriment of Dreyfus.

---

(4) French Intelligence was more concerned with getting Dreyfus court-martialed than with presenting truthful evidence.

Missing premise: If French Intelligence lied at the court-martial to the detriment of Dreyfus, (4) is true.

2. According to relation (iv), in which of [A]–[I] in exercise 1 do the conjunctions of the premises highly or completely justify their conclusion?
3. Let the statement or hypothesis 'h' be given by:

h: Every Japanese child has a higher IQ than all English children.
Assume that it is unproblematic that Taro is a Japanese child and that Vivian is an English child.

(a) Relying on relation (iii), propose a statement such that its truth would be a supporting reason for 'h' and its falsity would be a completely legitimate reason for the falsity of 'h'.
(b) Justify your answer in (a) by proposing and assessing an appropriate "missing premise," and producing a chain that shows the relevant argument to be deductively valid. (*Hint:* For an appropriate missing premise, fill in the blank: If h, then ______ if Taro is a Japanese child and Vivian is an English child.)

4.3 Extracting an Outline of the Argument

We now return to the main topic of this chapter, specifically, analyzing argumentative passages. These are passages in which reasons of one kind or another that were specified in Section 4.1 are offered for the point the passages are trying to make. Because our main conern is with truth assessment, in analyzing such argumentative passages it is essential to adopt what might be called the PRINCIPLE OF CHARITY: *Make out the best possible case for the view in the passage.* If one takes the stance of a debater, one may want to find as many flaws as possible in the passage. But the reward for such an effort is only to find out that the author has not made his point well. The point he is trying to make may still be correct. If we want to make some sort of an assessment of the point he or she is trying to make, we must try to make the best possible case for the view. If the best possible case is still weak, we can conclude that the reasons for accepting the author's claim has not been made evident, and in some cases we may even be able to assign the claim a low degree of justification. On the other hand, if the best possible case turns out to be strong, then we shall have discovered something valuable.

With the Principle of Charity in mind, analyzing an argumentative passage can be seen to involve three stages:

(1) Give the passage the most charitable reading possible, and extract an outline of a deductive argument from the passage. Of course many passages do not purport to give *deductive* arguments. However, three considerations are relevant:

   (a) We have just seen in Section 4.2 that the premises of an invalid argument '$p_1, \ldots, p_n/c$' may be assessed to justify its conclusion highly or completely if it is found that a highly or completely justified conjunction 'q' of statements is such that '$p_1, \ldots, p_n, q/c$' is valid.
   (b) Because we have included intuitive claims as well as general claims of science, mathematics, and common sense among our unproblematic claims in Chapter 2, we are often in the position to assess the plausibility of the missing premises needed to convert the argument into one that is valid.
   (c) The task of assessing the legitimacy of nondemonstrative argument directly (rather than by converting it into one that is deductively valid) is difficult, as we shall see in Chapter 5. Thus, for now, treating arguments as deductive arguments with missing premises is the best we can do.

(2) The argument extracted in stage (1) is almost always invalid. Thus, following the principle of charity, the second stage involves supplying missing premises that both make the argument valid and are as plausible as possible.
(3) Having gotten a valid argument for the conclusion, the third stage involves assessing the plausibility of the premises as a means to assessing the plausibility of the conclusion.

In this section we shall deal with stage (1); stages (2) and (3) will be discussed in Sections 4.4 and 4.5, respectively.

Extracting an outline of the argument may be seen to have four steps. Many of these steps will involve rewriting the passage so as to make the best possible case. It is also often true that one step cannot be done well until one has an inkling of what the later steps are going to look like. Still, as a rough guide, the four steps may be followed sequentially.

Step 1: *Isolate the Main Point(s).* There is no mechanical way to determine the main point of the passage. Typically, the main point comes either near the beginning or near the end of the passage. Near the beginning doesn't mean the first sentence, and near the end doesn't mean the last sentence. But often the main point occurs in the first few sentences or the last few sentences. Sometimes the main point is buried in the middle, but this tends to be infrequent because it is liable to confuse the reader. Because there is no specific place (like the second sentence) in which the main point has to occur, one must often get the sense of the passage to determine what the main point is. What can be helpful in this connection is to ask what the reasons offered in the passage ultimately point to; thus, in order to accomplish Step 1 one may need some sense of Step 3 (see later), in which it is determined what statements are being offered as reasons for what. Occasionally, a passage will make several separate main points; if this is detected, distinguish the several main points and treat these main points separately.

Step 2: *Edit and Rephrase the Statements.* Passages often contain rhetorical flourishes and statements irrelevant for establishing the main point. These should be edited out for the purpose of analyzing the argument in the passage. Sometimes a number of statements can be combined into one statement, and this should be done where possible. By now we also know that arguments critically depend on the same statements or independent clauses recurring in several premises. Thus, a central task of Step 2 is to rephrase the statements so that there is an optimal match among the statements that are being offered by the author. As a way of highlighting this task, it is a good idea to start assigning sentence letters to sentences in Step 2. This will also avoid rewriting a lot of long sentences and allow for an easy extraction of the argument form at a later stage.

While a central goal of Step 2 is to create an optimal match among the statements that are being offered, one must not go overboard and rephrase clearly distinct statements as the same statement. As an example consider:

> Tuition tax credits must be opposed. They will benefit the upper class and do little for the poor. Beyond this, if tuition tax credits are adopted, the government may tell the schools how religion is to be taught, and if the government does that, we will have lost our freedom of religion.

Because ‘Such and such will result in (or bring about) so and so’ can normally be treated as ‘if such and such happens, so and so will happen’, we might adopt the following scheme of abbreviation:

‘t’: Tuition tax credits are adopted.
‘u’: The upper class will be benefited and the poor will not be aided.
‘g’: The government may dictate on religious issues.

Given this scheme, ‘They [tuition tax credits] will benefit the upper class and do little for the poor’ and ‘If tuition tax credits are adopted, the government may tell the schools how religion is to be taught’ can be taken as ‘$t \supset u$’ and ‘$t \supset g$’; thus, by our use of ‘t’, we have appropriately created matching clauses in our reformulation of these two statements. However, we cannot go beyond this to create further matching clauses. In particular, two mistakes should be avoided:

(1) It would be a mistake to treat ‘Tuition tax credits must be opposed’ as ‘$-t$’: to say that tuition tax credits must or should be opposed

is quite different from the claim that tuition tax credits are not adopted. Even though tuition tax credits *must* or *should* be opposed, they may nevertheless *be* adopted, and they may not *be* adopted even if they *shouldn't* be opposed. In general, 'Such and such *is* the case' is a distinct claim from 'Such and such *should* be the case (or *must be* the case or *would be desirable*)'. Thus, a distinct sentence letter (such as 'm') has been assigned to 'Tuition tax credits must be opposed'.

(2) If we assign 'l' to the statement 'We will have lost our freedom of religion', it may be tempting to treat 'If the government does this, we will have lost our freedom of religion' as 'g ⊃ l'. This would be a mistake. Given our understanding of 'g', 'g ⊃ l' states 'if the government *may* dictate on religious issues, we will have lost our freedom of religion'. But what the author claimed was: if the government *does* dictate on religious issues, we will have lost our freedom of religion. While the government *actually* dictating on religious issues will result in the loss of our freedom of religion, the mere *possibility* of the government doing this doesn't (or doesn't as clearly) result in the loss of freedom of religion. In general, 'Such and such *is* (or will *be*) the case' is a distinct claim from 'Such and such *may be* the case (or is a *possibility* or is *likely to be* the case)'. Thus, we must choose a distinct letter (such as 'd') for 'The government will dictate on religious issues', and take 'If the government does this, we will have lost our freedom of religion' as 'd ⊃ l'.

Step 3: *Determine What Statements Are Reasons for What.* This is often the most difficult part of extracting an outline of the argument, and to a certain extent it must be combined with the final step, which extracts the argument. In particular, we must have an eye on the overall argumentative structure of the passage. Such structures fall into three kinds of cases:

[A] The simple case is where each of the edited statements (i) is a part of the direct reasons for the main point and (ii) is needed by the other statements in order to infer the main point as the conclusion of an argument.

[B] One or more edited statements in the passage are intermediate conclusions drawn from other statements, and these intermediate conclusions themselves are (part of) the reasons for the main point.

[C] Sometimes, a passage produces two or more independent arguments for the main point. This situation is detected when (i) one set of reasons has no connection with another set, and (ii) each set of reasons are reasons for the main point. In such a case, one will extract two separate arguments for the main point.

These three structures may be exemplified by the tree diagrams of Figure 4.1, where MP stands for the main point. The goal of Step 3 is to extract such a tree diagram from the passage.

A bit more then should be said about such diagrams. The bottom (of

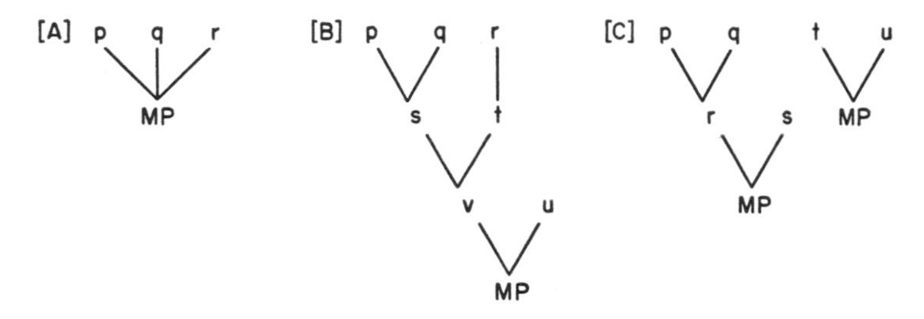

Figure 4.1.

"the main trunk") should be the main point. For all other statements in the passage there are two possibilities: (1) Either it is a direct reason for the main point or (2) it is a direct reason for an intermediate conclusion.

(1) If a statement is a *direct reason for the main point,* it should be ("a main branch") directly connected to the main point. Examples in Figure 4.1 would be 'p', 'q', and 'r' in [A], 'v' and 'u' in [B], 'r' and 's' in the first argument of [C], and 't' and 'u' in the second argument of [C].

(2) If a statement is a *reason for an intermediate conclusion,* it is either a "peripheral branch" or a "twig" connected to an intermediate conclusion, or itself an intermediate conclusion ("a middling branch") connected to another intermediate conclusion. Thus, in Figure 4.1 [B], 'p' and 'q' are twigs connected to the intermediate conclusion 's' while 'r' is a twig connected to the intermediate conclusion 't'; in the first argument of Figure 4.1 [C], 'p' and 'q' are twigs connected to the intermediate conclusion 'r'. In Figure 4.1 [B], 's' and 't' are themselves intermediate conclusions (middling branches) that are connected to (and hence are reasons for) the intermediate conclusion 'v'. Of course in a case like this, we must sooner or later reach intermediate conclusions that are (parts of) the direct reasons for (or main branches leading to) the main point; such is the case with 'v' in Figure 4.1 [B].

A general point that emerges is this: *If a statement cannot be fitted into a tree diagram in the ways indicated, it is in effect a "dangling" statement that plays no role and should have been edited out at Step 2.* Turning this point around, *if the statement does play a role, it has to be found a place in a tree diagram.*

The trick then is to find the lines of direct connection between the edited statements resulting from Step 2, so that these statements can be placed on a tree diagram. That is, we need to determine when one statement is a direct reason for another, and then indicate this relation by diagramming it on a tree diagram. The best guide for discerning what is a direct reason for what is one's intuitive sense of this as well as a sense of what is needed (as a reason) for something to be inferred. However, three auxiliary aids may be suggested:

(a) Certain words or constructions almost always indicate that reasons are being offered, and these words or constructions may be called "inference indicators." The following chart along with their obvious variations gives the most frequently used inference indicators. In the listed constructions, 'p' is typically not the sole direct reason for 'q'; rather 'p' is typically offered as a direct reason for 'q' along with other things given in the context.

p (typically along with something else) is a direct reason for q

Because (As, Inasmuch as, Since, In light of) p, q.
p. Therefore (Thus, Hence, So, As a result, Consequently, Accordingly), q.
p. We may conclude (infer, derive, deduce) q.
p proves (argues for, implies, is evidence for) q.
q because (for) p.
q follows from (is entailed by, is shown by) p.
q; otherwise p wouldn't be the case. To deny q would result in −p being the case.
p is due to (The cause of p is) q. q explains p.

Several remarks about these inference indicators are in order.

(i) Consider: "Your lawyer is sharp. Because sharp lawyers usually win, you shouldn't worry about losing." The chart clearly indicates that 'Sharp lawyers usually win' is being offered as a direct reason for 'You shouldn't worry'. But in the given context this is not the only direct reason, because clearly to infer that you shouldn't worry, it's needed that your lawyer be sharp. Thus, two direct reasons are being offered for 'You shouldn't worry'—'Your lawyer is sharp' and 'Sharp lawyers usually win'; further, on a tree diagram, these two reasons would form two branches of the branching point for 'You shouldn't worry'. This is what is meant by the parenthetical clause in 'p (typically along with something else) is a direct reason for q', for example, 'Sharp lawyers usually win' (along with something else, namely, 'Your lawyer is sharp') is a direct reason for 'You shouldn't worry'.

(ii) In constructions like 'q follows from (is entailed by) p', 'p implies q', 'q; otherwise p wouldn't be the case', and 'p is due to (is the cause of) q', *'p' must be understood to be given if 'p' is to be a reason for 'q'*. The claim 'Dauer has eight eyes' does indeed entail the claim 'Dauer has more than two eyes'; yet this wouldn't give us reasons for thinking that Dauer has more than two eyes, because it is not at all suggested that Dauer in fact has eight eyes. On the other hand the construction 'His having not arrived yet entails that he is late' takes it as given that he has not yet arrived. The use of noun phrases like 'his having not yet arrived' and 'a fire of this kind' (as in 'A fire of this kind is due to some mischief') tends to suggest, and takes it as given, that the event in question has indeed occurred. Similarly, the subjunctive in 'He must be sick; otherwise he would be here' clearly suggests, and takes it as give' , that he in fact isn't here. In using the chart, one must make certain that p is indeed taken to be given.

(iii) As already noted, in constructions like 'q (being the case) explains p (being the case)', 'p is due to q', and 'The cause of p is q', p being the case is taken to be given; 'q' then is inferred from 'p' or 'p' along with certain other things that are also taken to be given. This often indicates a nondcmonstrative argument 'p / q' (or 'p, r / q' in which 'r' is the other thing that is also taken to be given). In such cases, we should take 'p' as a direct reason for 'q', anticipating that we will eventually have to add a missing premise (perhaps 'p ⊃ q' or '(p & r) ⊃ q' in the worst case). This is, then, the function of indicators.

(b) Knowledge acquired in Chapter 3 concerning valid argument forms can sometimes help in determining what is being offered as a reason for what. For example, if $\phi_1, \phi_2 / \theta$ is valid, ϕ_1 is offered as a statement, and ϕ_2 (though unoffered) is obviously unproblematic, then it is likely that ϕ_1 is being offered as part of a direct reason for θ.

(c) Consideration of what constitutes a supporting reason for what (discussed in Section 4.1) can be of help. Normally, if 'p' is a supporting reason for 'q', 'q' is also a supporting reason for 'p'. In such a case, is 'p' being offered as a reason for 'q' or is 'q' being offered as a reason for 'p'? A useful principle of selection in many cases is this: The statement that is closer to being unproblematic is normally being offered as a direct reason for the somewhat more problematic statement.

Step 4: *Extract the Argument(s).* Given Figure 4.1 from Step 3, this becomes a fairly straightforward task. If the tree diagram is of kind [A], we merely need to collect the direct reasons for the conclusion, draw a "therefore" line, and follow it by the conclusion. Thus, given our previous diagram [A], the extracted argument becomes 'p, q, r / MP'. Faced with a type [B] diagram, we can simplify our later task by treating the arguments for the several intermediate conclusions and the main point separately. In these cases, the direct branches leading to the intermediate conclusions should be considered separate miniarguments for those intermediate conclusions. The main argument will then be taken to be the argument for the main point, in which the premises are the statements directly connected to the main point in the tree diagram. Thus, given Figure 4.1 [B], we have three miniarguments and a main argument:

$[b_1]$		$[b_2]$		$[b_3]$		[B]	
	p		$\underline{\text{r}}$		s		v
	$\underline{\text{q}}$		t		$\underline{\text{t}}$		$\underline{\text{u}}$
	s				v		MP

If we have a diagram like Figure 4.1 [C], we have two or more main arguments and possibly one or more miniarguments for each of the main arguments. In Figure 4.1 [C], the extracted arguments become:

$[c_1]$	p	$[C_1]$	r	$[C_2]$	t
	q		s		u
	r		MP		MP

As we shall see in the next subsection, if we can show the miniarguments and the main argument to be valid, it is always possible to combine the arguments into one grand argument for the main point for which the premises are the twigs on the tree diagram—that is, statements that aren't intermediate conclusions and are direct reasons for an intermediate conclusion or the main point. The accompanying chart summarizes the various steps involved in extracting an outline of the argument.

Before applying these steps to an example, one important point should be made about a facet of critical thinking skills we have not discussed. Part of that skill is the ability to write essays, proposals, assessments, and the like in a clear and cogent prose. A useful guide to achieving this goal is roughly to reverse the steps we have discussed. Start with Step 4 or perhaps the tree diagram at the end of Step 3. That is, determine the points that you wish to make, and for each of them, arrange your supporting reasons so that they will fit a tree diagram of the sort we have discussed. Continuing with reversing Step 3, add appropriate inference indicators and other devices to transform the tree diagram into prose. Having done that, perform Step 2 continuing in reverse order. That is, to avoid the utter boredom of continuously repeating the same sentence, use some variant expressions to achieve tolerable prose; however, don't overdo it to a point that the repetition of the same thought can't be recognized by a reader. For certain purposes, one may want to add rhetorical flourishes, provide background that isn't essential to the argument, or offer examples to clarify a claim or to make it vivid. If some of the reasons on the tree diagram are so obvious that they need not be mentioned explicitly, you might want to delete them as part of performing Step 2 in reverse order: in effect, you will be creating missing (but obvious) premises in your prose.

Doing Step 1 in reverse order should be a matter of looking over what you have written to make sure that your main point can be identified by the reader. Certainly, you wouldn't want the main point buried somewhere in the middle. Furthermore, if the chain of reasoning is fairly long or complex, you might want to put the main point near the beginning so that the reader knows where you are going. Of course, if your style is one of keeping the reader in suspense about the conclusion that you are going to draw, you might want to put the main point near the end; the same location of the main point may be chosen if you are using an investigative style to see what conclusion may be drawn. Whatever the style and loca-

Extracting the Argument: Summary

Step 1: *Isolate the main point.* It is normally located near the beginning or end, and the reasons in the passage point to it.

Step 2: *Edit and rephrase the statements.*

(a) Eliminate irrelevant statements.

(b) Rephrase and combine the other statements so that the assignment of sentence letters to them (i) maximizes the recurrences of the same sentence letters and (ii) minimizes the needless use of distinct sentence letters.

Step 3: *Determine what statements are reasons for what* by producing one of the three kinds of tree diagrams shown in Figure 4.2.

Principal way of determining what is a reason for what: An intuitive sense of this and what is needed to infer a claim,

Auxiliary aids for determining 'p' (along with other things) to be a direct reason for 'q':

(a) Inference indicators:

Because (As, Inasmuch as, Since, In light of) p, q.
p. Therefore (Thus, Hence, So, As a result, Consequently, Accordingly), q.
p. We may conclude (infer, derive, deduce) q.
p proves (argues for, implies, is evidence for) q.
q because (for) p.
q follows from (is entailed by, is shown by) p.
q; otherwise p wouldn't be the case. To deny q would result in −p being the case.
p is due to (The cause of p is) q. q explains p.

(b) 'p' and 'q' are given, a unoffered statement 'r' is obviously unproblematic or well justified, and 'p, r / q' is valid.

(c) 'p' fits the definition for being a supporting reason for 'q', and 'p' is closer to being unproblematic than 'q'.

Step 4: *Extract the argument(s).* Extract the argument from the tree diagram in Step 3 so that [B], for example, becomes:

[b_1] p
q
―――
s

[b_2] r
―――
t

[B] s
t
―――
MP

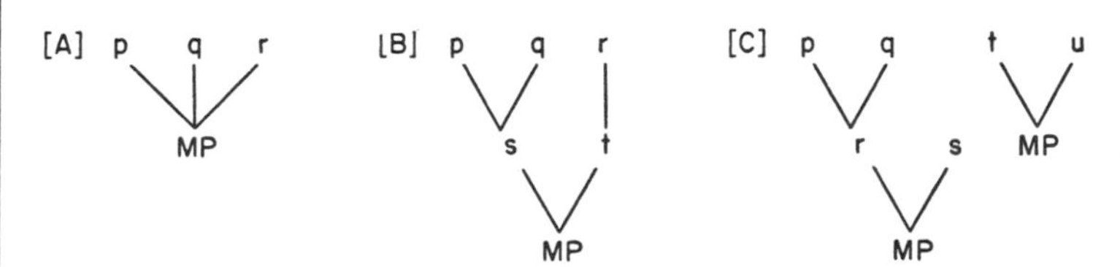

Figure 4.2.

tion chosen for the main point, you must make sure that it is easily recognizable by the reader.

Because Steps 1–4 are meant to analyze reasons in a minute way, performing these steps in reverse order is liable to give only a few paragraphs of prose at the most. Because most discursive writing tends to be a more extensive enterprise, one may wonder what should be done about an essay or proposal as a whole. Without becoming overly rigid, it would help to think in terms of reversing Steps 1–4 and take several paragraphs to be one of the branches or branching points on the tree diagram. Inference indicators are now likely to become transitional paragraphs; examples, flourishes, and background are also likely to be of paragraph size rather than of sentence size. More likely than not, paragraphs will also have to be devoted to clarifying and identifying the main points you wish to make in the essay. Such then are the lessons on prose writing to be extracted from our discussion in this section. Although no exercises on discursive writing are included in this text, the suggestions of the last three paragraphs should be kept in mind when the occasion arises outside the context of this course.

Let us now return to extracting an outline of the argument and see how Steps 1–4 are to be applied in their normal order. Consider the following letter to the editor of the *Los Angeles Times* (the sentences are numbered for reference):

> (1) I've read the *Times* article ["Marauders from Inner City Prey on L.A.'s Suburbs"] and I'm mad!
>
> (2) We can thank the criminal justice system for this! (3) How else can you explain the fact that so many repeat offenders are roaming the streets?
>
> (4) Let's face it—crime pays and it pays very well. (5) No experience necessary. (6) And the risk factor? (7) It's acceptable.
>
> (8) Let's make it unacceptable. (9) Like capital punishment or an extra 25 years sentence, in addition to the actual penalty for the crime.

Step 1 is to isolate the main point. Reading over the entire passage, (4)–(7) seem to lead naturally to (8) and (9). Thus, we seem to have a normal case in which the main point should be located near the beginning or the near the end. (3) seems to be a way of supporting (2), and nothing in the passage supports (1). Finally, (9) seems to be an elaboration of (8). All of this suggests that the main point is either (2) or (8) [as elaborated by (9)]. In (2) the author evidently finds fault with the criminal justice system, and in (8) he is urging that some steps be taken; the natural reading of this is that the fault he finds is a reason for adopting the reform he is urging. Thus, the main point of the passage is evidently (8) as elaborated by (9).

However, statement (8) stands in need of a little interpretation. The suggestion is to make the risk factor unacceptable, and one way of interpreting this is to make it harder for criminals to avoid getting caught. But this evidently is not what the author intends, because his elaboration of (8) given in (9) refers to drastically increasing the penalties. His basic idea seems to be that the (potential) cost of committing a crime should be high enough to offset the profits to be gained from crime (and the low probability of getting caught). Suspending for now the extreme aspect of his view, we might take the main point to be given by:

"We should increase the punishment for crime."

Step 2 is editing and rephrasing. It seems that we can eliminate statement (1) from our consideration, because being angry hardly seems to be a reason for the main point; it is, rather, a bit of background information.

Statement (2) that we can thank the criminal justice system for the mess (crime rate, marauders, etc.) is suggesting that some feature of the criminal justice system is responsible for the mess. From everything else he says, that feature is evidently the lax punishment the system metes out. Thus, given the abbreviation

'd': The present punishment for crime is severe enough to deter, we can take (2) as:

(2*) −d.

Given the abbreviation

'r': There is a large number of repeat offenders,

statement (3), "How else do you explain the fact that so many repeat offenders are roaming the streets?", might be taken as:

(3*) −d explains r.

Statements (4) and (5), that crime pays well and no experience is necessary, might be taken as

(4–5*) p

given the abbreviation

'p': There is easy profit in crime.

Statements (6) and (7) assert that the risk factor is acceptable, and we know the author wants to make it unacceptable. The point statements (6) and (7) are trying to make (along with the previous statements) seem to be: As long as there is easy profit in crime and the punishment isn't severe enough to deter, people can be expected to engage in crime. Because the function of this general statement is to urge making the risk factor unacceptable in the *future,* let 'f' and 'h' represent:

'f': The future punishment for crime will be severe enough to deter.
'h': The crime rate will be high.

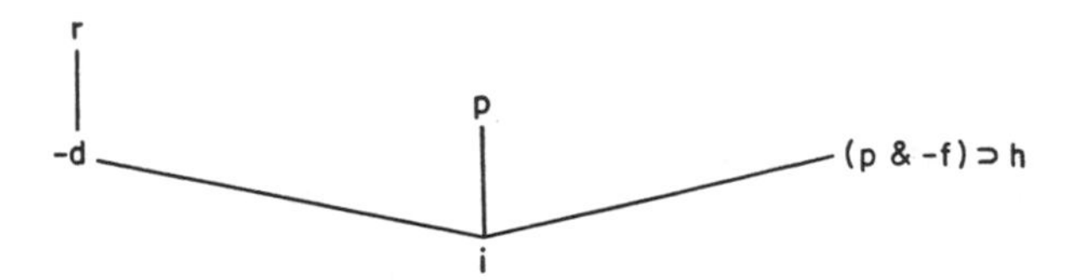

Figure 4.3.

The point of statements (6) and (7) might then be taken as this:

(6–7*) $(p \& -f) \supset h$.

Admittedly, this involves a bit of interpretation; but unless it is seen in this light, (6) and (7) ultimately repeat (2*), that is, the claim that present punishment isn't severe enough to deter.

Statements (8) and (9) have already been incorporated into the main point, which can be abbreviated as

'i': We should increase the punishment for crime.

Step 3 is to determine what is a reason for what. (2*) is '−d' ['present punishment isn't severe enough to deter'], and (3*) is '−d explains r' ['−d explains the large number of repeat offenders']. It is evident from the use of 'explains' that 'r' is the premise of a nondemonstrative argument for '−d'. Thus, we take 'r' as a direct reason for '−d' in our tree diagram. Furthermore, '−d' is evidently a reason for the main point 'i' that the punishment should be increased; thus we connect '−d' to 'i'.

Statement (4–5*) is 'p' ['There is easy profit in crime'], and this appears to be a reason for the main point. It is at least somewhat more plausible that punishment should be increased if there is easy profit in crime than if there isn't. Hence, we connect 'p' to the main point. (6–7*) is '(p & −f) ⊃ h' ['if p and future punishment isn't severe enough to deter, then the future crime rate will be high'], and there is no evident place to put it in the tree diagram except as a direct reason for 'i'. And doing this is surely correct: The assumption that (6–7*) is true makes it more plausible that punishment should be increased than the assumption that it is false, in other words, the assumption that the future crime rate won't be high despite easy profit in crime and the punishment not being severe enough to deter. Thus, we arrive at the tree diagram shown in Figure 4.3.

Step 4 is to extract the argument presented in the passage, and this can be simply "read off" from the tree diagram constructed in Step 3. Thus, we arrive at the miniargument [a] and the main argument [A]:

[a] r
―――
−d

[A] −d
p
(p & −f) ⊃ h
―――
i

This completes stage one of analyzing an argumentative passage.

EXERCISES—SECTION 4.3

Part A

Extract an outline of the argument from each of the following passages.

1. Roosevelt saved the country from the Great Depression. Because he was a Democrat, Democrats are to be trusted in times of economic woe.
2. Tommy has the chicken pox. Inasmuch as chicken pox is highly contagious, you shouldn't play with Tommy.
3. Because he is sick, he won't make it to the prize drawing. But he can't win the prize if he isn't at the drawing. We may conclude that he won't win the prize.
4. His having been on that direct flight from New York entails that he was in New York. But he denied that he was in New York. Consequently, he was lying in denying that he was in New York.
5. He is in love with Jane. Otherwise he wouldn't be spending so much money on her. But if he is in love with Jane, Mary is going to leave him. So, it looks like Mary is going to leave him.
6. The Japanese consumers will clearly benefit if their tariffs on agricultural products are reduced. Yet the Japanese government is resisting the reduction of agricultural tariffs. Why is the Japanese government resisting something that will benefit the Japanese consumer? The only explanation is that the agricultural lobby is exceptionally strong in Japan.
7. From his absence in the class, we may infer that he was ill or playing hooky from class. But he was fit as a fiddle later in the afternoon. It follows that he was not ill. Hence, was playing hooky from class.
8. His silence implies his guilt. Yet he is so far scot-free. As he has friends in high places, indictments aren't going to be forthcoming either. This proves that guilty people sometimes escape punishment.

Part B

Using the hints whenever they are provided, extract an outline of the argument from each of the following passages. Background material given in brackets is not a part of the argument to be extracted.

1. [Background: This is an excerpt from an April 2, 1982 column, "The Great Cheese Giveaway," in the *Los Angeles Times* by Ellen Haas, director of the Washington-based Community Nutrition Institute's consumer division.]

   The recent donation of 30 million pounds of government-owned cheese to needy people . . . has given the public an important opportunity to examine the interplay between federal programs that benefit special-interest industry groups and those that provide assistance to the nation's poor. The donated cheese is undoubtedly appreciated by the people who stand in line to get it. . . . Yet the fact remains that, while the Administration tosses a few million pounds of cheese to the poor, it is slashing the budget of the federal food-assistance programs. . . . Last year, funding for these combined programs was cut 14%; this year, a cut of 18% more has been proposed. At the same time, spending for the dairy price-support program has mushroomed from $270 million in 1979 to $1.3 billion in 1980 and to more than $2 billion in 1981. This year [at current levels of support] the price tag will likely be at least $2.2 billion. . . . When cuts are to be made, they must be made fairly and across the board. . . . The dairy program must be cut, and it must be cut today.

   Hint: Be prepared to edit out about half of the passage as background.

2. Pornography may be disgusting. But it takes a nitwit of a moralist not to realize that it's a waste of money to keep trying to enforce obscenity laws in southern California. As a lawyer, I can tell you that in virtually all obscenity trials in southern California, juries have acquitted defendants even when the movies shown obviously involved nothing but "hardcore explicit sexual material." The only explanation is that juries on the whole do not want to tell consenting adults what they can and can't see. But if this is the case, obscenity laws are unenforceable in southern California. Trying to enforce the unenforceable only wastes the taxpayer's money.
3. Limiting private ownership of handguns will result in a significant reduction of violence. The vast majority of murders are committed by previously law-abiding citizens committing impulsive gun murders during arguments with family members or friends. Most of these would be averted if the handgun wasn't so accessible. We can no longer tolerate the present level of violence. Because limiting the private ownership of handguns will result in a significant reduction of violence, join us in an effort to enact strong and effective handgun control legislation.
4. [Background: The following is a very loose adaptation of Judith Jarvis Thompson's sketch of the pro-life argument (that she goes on to criticize). This and subsequent references to Judith Jarvis Thompson are to her paper "A Defense of Abortion," *Philosophy and Public Affairs,* I, 1 (1971): 44–66.]

   What the pro-choice advocates often forget is a very simple general principle: one may do something only if doing it doesn't violate a right of another that is stronger than one's right to do that thing. Of course in having an abortion performed, a mother is exercising her right to determine what happens in and to her body. But she is also taking the life of a fetus. Clearly every person has a right to life, and this right is surely stronger than the right of a mother to determine what happens in and to her body. Thus, having an abortion performed violates a right of a fetus, which is stronger than the mother's right to determine what happens in and to her body. Given the general principle, it is clear that an abortion may not be performed.

5. [Background: The following is a slightly "doctored" version of a column by William Schneider, a political consultant to the *Los Angeles Times,* which appeared in that newspaper on September 26, 1982.]

   A poll taken this month by CBS News and the *New York Times* found that no less than 48% of registered voters answered yes when asked, "Is there any one issue that is so important that you would change your vote because you disagree with a candidate's position on that single issue?" High among the issues cited by these voters were abortion, busing, federal registration of handguns, and school prayer.

   Suppose a politician sees a poll showing a two-to-one majority of his constituents opposing a constitutional amendment that would prohibit abortion. What this poll does not measure is how many of the people on each side of the issue are willing to vote for or against him on the basis of that question alone. Thus, even if a politician takes the majority position (pro-choice), he may lose more votes from among the one-third of the electorate who disagree with him and who will vote against him on the basis of that issue alone, than he will gain from the two-thirds who agree with him but most of whom will not vote for him *only* because of his position on abortion.

   It follows that if a politician adopts the safe course (of doing whatever is necessary to avoid the likelihood of suffering a net loss of votes), he will not vote on such divisive issues like abortion, busing, handguns, and school prayers. Because most politicians follow the safe course in order to survive, we can expect them to do everything possible to avoid taking a congressional vote on such divisive issues.

Hint: Use only the following sentence letters:

v: There are many voters who would vote against a candidate because the candidate disagrees with them on the single issue of abortion, busing, handguns, or school prayers.
j: A politician votes with the majority on issues like abortion, busing, handguns, and school prayers.
l: There is the real likelihood that a politician will suffer a net loss of votes (in the next election).
s: A politician adopts the safe course (of doing whatever is necessary to avoid the likelihood of suffering a net loss of votes).
a: A politician will not vote on such divisive issues like abortion, busing, handguns, and school prayers.
m: Most politicians adopt the safe course of doing whatever is necessary to avoid the likelihood of suffering a net loss of votes.
p: Most politicians will do everything possible to avoid taking a congressional vote on divisive issues like abortion, busing, handguns, and school prayers.

Because only a few sentence letters are involved, be prepared to take an entire paragraph to assert a single sentence composed of one or more components suggested by the scheme of abbreviation.

6. [Background: Proposition 4 in the November 1982 California general election would have provided funding for "the purchase of property in the Lake Tahoe Basin, which is necessary to prevent the environmental decline of this unique natural resource, to protect the waters of Lake Tahoe from further degradation, and to preserve the scenic and recreational values of Lake Tahoe." The following argument against Proposition 4 was given by George E. A. White in the *Voter Pamphlet* (with numbers added for ease of reference):]

> (1) The solution to the Lake Tahoe Basin's environmental problems is a local matter. (2) State and federal interests are no greater here than elsewhere . . . (3) Acquisition of private lands and their subsequent maintenance by the state primarily benefit the remaining private properties in the basin in two ways. (4) One, by maintaining or increasing the natural beauty and economic health of the region; two, by restricting the amount of property available for development, it increases the value of the remaining properties. (5) The local economy and the local political bodies . . . have ample means to safeguard their own environmental and economic base. (6) Passage of this measure will place additional financial burdens on all Californians, not just those few who can enjoy Lake Tahoe's scenic beauty. (7a) Citizens in the rest of California are paying dearly with restrictions on their freedom and taxes to solve their own local environmental and economic problems, (7b) so why shouldn't the Lake Tahoe [citizens] pay their own way? (8) Vote AGAINST the Lake Tahoe Acquisition Bond Act unless you own property around the lake.

Hint: To a significant degree White's argument depends on urging that the problem Proposition 4 addresses itself to is a *local* environmental problem. Using the expression "The Problem" to refer to the environmental difficulties Proposition 4 is intended to solve, use the following *(partial)* scheme of abbreviation:

l: "The Problem" is a local enviromental problem of the Tahoe region.
m: The people in the Tahoe region have the means for solving their local environmental problems.

s: The people in the Tahoe region should pay for solving their local environmental problems.
f: Passage of Proposition 4 results in the people of the Tahoe region not paying for solving "the Problem."
a: You should vote against Proposition 4.
t: You own property in the Tahoe region.

Statements (1) and (5) fairly clearly become 'l' and 'm'. (7b) asks why the people around Tahoe shouldn't pay their own way, and one potential answer is that they don't have the means to do so. Because statement (5) blocks this answer, (7b) might be cast as '$m \supset s$'. Admittedly this is a somewhat charitable interpretation, but it paves a way to connect statement (5) with statement (7b). Finally, statement (6) might be taken as 'f', and this would be helpful in bringing statement (6) close to statement (7b). Part of the tree diagram for the passage may then be given by directly connecting each of 'l', 'm', '$m \supset s$', and 'f' to the *main point*.

4.4 Supplying Missing Premises

As already noted, the outline of the argument extracted from an argumentative passage is normally invalid. Having adopted the principle of charity in light of our interest in truth assessments (as well as the practice of treating nondeductive arguments as deductive ones), our next task in analyzing an argumentative passage is to supply additional premises to make the argument valid. If a passage contains one or more miniarguments for intermediate conclusions, we should first make those miniarguments valid by providing missing premises. Having done that, we should do the same for the main argument for the main point of the passage. As a final step, we should present one grand argument in which the intermediate conclusions, which are premises of the main argument, are replaced by the premises of miniarguments for those intermediate conclusions.

But how do we find the missing premises that convert the argument into one that is valid? The most useful procedure for finding missing premises (either for a miniargument for an intermediate conclusion or for the main argument for the main point) is to use the method of chain argument that was developed in Chapter 3. The idea is to construct a chain argument for the conclusion, adding missing premises as needed. Once the chain argument is completed, one can claim that the missing premises that convert the argument into a valid one have been found. Determining which missing premises should be chosen in constructing the chain argument has two aspects that might be called the "formal aspect" and the "material aspect."

The formal aspect is simply being guided by the needs of the chain argument in one's choice of a missing premise. This aspect was sufficiently covered in Chapter 3, when we discussed the forward and the backward strategies in finding missing premises. The reader may be well advised to review that material quickly at this point.

The material aspect derives from our desire to assess the conclusion and our adoption of the principle of charity. Four guidelines in choosing missing premises may be listed under the material aspect:

(a) The plausibility of the missing premises should be relatively easy to assess.
(b) The added premise should be more or less in line with the author's general outlook. In this connection, if there is a plausible statement on which the author seems to be obviously relying, it should be added as a premise with the hope that it will serve the needs of the chain argument and thereby satisfy the formal aspect.
(c) The missing premise required by the needs of the chain should be as plausible as possible.
(d) A statement should not be added as a missing premise if it renders the reasons given by the author irrelevant in establishing the conclusion. For example, we shouldn't add a statement as a missing premise if the author provides some reasons for it; adding such a missing premise would make those reasons irrelevant in "establishing" the claim for which the author was arguing.

We have already noted that any argument can be converted to one that is valid by adding the conditional in which the antecedent is the conjunction of the given premises and the consequent is the conclusion. Such a conditional satisfies the formal aspect of choosing a missing premise. However, such a choice normally fails to satisfy the material aspect guiding our choice; in particular, guideline (a) is likely to be violated. Sometimes there is no other evident alternative, but in most cases the material aspect can be better satisfied by avoiding this "trivial" missing premise.

To complete stage two of analyzing an argumentative passage, write down the complete argument starring the missing premises one has added. In doing this, replace any premise that is an intermediate conclusion by the premises of the miniargument for that intermediate conclusion. (If an intermediate conclusion C_2 depends on an intermediate conclusion C_1, first present the argument for C_2 that eliminates C_1 in favor of the premises of C_1; having done this, replace C_2 in the grand argument for the main point by the premises for C_2 revealed in the first step.) To the extent one has already shown by chain arguments that the main argument and all the miniarguments are valid, the resulting grand argument must be also be valid.

We can see this most easily from our discussion of combining several chain arguments in Section 3.8.3. Suppose chains [a] and [b] show the miniargument [A] and the main argument [B] to be valid:

[A] ϕ_1

$\underline{\phi_2}$

θ_2

[B] θ_1

$\underline{\theta_2}$

ψ

Replacing the intermediate conclusion θ_2 by the two premises of the mini-argument for it, the grand argument for the conclusion becomes:

[C] θ_1

ϕ_1

$\underline{\phi_2}$

ψ

The chain that shows [C] to be valid is just like the chain [b] that shows [B] to be valid except for the following difference: Wherever [b] appealed to Pr to put down θ_2 as a line, the chain for [C] will have the lines

(k)	ϕ_1	Pr
(k + 1)	ϕ_2	Pr
(k + 2)	θ_2	(k)(k + 1)[A]

Clearly the resulting chain shows [C] to be valid.

Stage two of analyzing an argumentative passage may be summarized as follows:

Supplying Missing Premises

(1) Convert miniarguments and the main argument into ones that are valid by supplying missing premises that satisfy the formal and material aspects:
   (a) Format aspect: The missing premises do convert the argument into one that is valid as shown and discovered by using the method of chain arguments, which adds missing premises as needed.
   (b) Material aspect:
      a. As much as possible, the missing premises should be easy to assess, be in line with the author's outlook, and be plausible.
      b. A missing premise should not make any reason given by the author irrelevant in establishing the conclusion.

(2) Present one grand argument in which the intermediate conclusions in the main argument are replaced by the premises of the miniarguments for those intermediate conclusions.

We now turn to some examples of finding missing premises, so that the procedure discussed becomes clearer. Except for the last example, in each of the following we quote the passage itself as well as the scheme of abbreviation and an outline of the argument that would emerge from stage one discussed in Section 4.3.

Example 1:

I heartily agree with your stand against tuition tax credits in your editorial. . . . Tuition tax credits are designed primarily to aid the upper-middle class, as are so many current economic suggestions. They would do little for the poor, thus fostering even greater undesirable social divisions. *(Los Angeles Times)*

Scheme:

't': Tuition tax credit is adopted.
'u': The upper-middle class will be aided and the poor will not.
'd': There will be greater undesirable social divisions.
'o': Tuition tax credits should be opposed.

Bare Argument:

(1) $t \supset u$
(2) $u \supset d$
―――――
o

Following the forward strategy, we immediately see that (1) and (2) yield '$t \supset d$' by HS. The backward strategy suggests

$(t \supset d) \supset o$

as a helpful line. Because it is at least somewhat plausible that tuition tax credits should be opposed if their adoption is a sufficient condition for greater undesirable social division, we may supply this as an additional premise. The resulting argument (form) and the chain argument showing it to be valid are:

Argument		Chain	Justification
$t \supset u$	(1)	$t \supset u$	Pr
$u \supset d$	(2)	$u \supset d$	Pr
*$(t \supset d) \supset o$	(3)	$t \supset d$	(1)(2)HS
o	(4)	$(t \supset d) \supset o$	*Pr
	(5)	o	(3)(4)MP

Example 2:

I can see no other reasonable interpretation of President Nixon's firing of Prosecutor Cox but an admission of Nixon's personal guilt and complicity in Watergate. I hope that Nixon will ultimately be exposed and dealt with appropriately through the courage of other men. If not, then our democracy is surely lost. *(Los Angeles Times)*

Scheme:

'f' Nixon fired Cox.
'a': Nixon was admitting his guilt and complicity in Watergate.
'g': Nixon is guilty of complicity in Watergate.

'h': It is to be hoped that someone will expose and prosecute Nixon.
'd': Our democracy will be lost if someone doesn't expose and prosecute Nixon.

Bare Argument:

[a]	(1) f	[A]	(1) a
	a		(2) g ⊃ d
			h

The miniargument for the intermediate conclusion can obviously be made valid by adding the premise 'f ⊃ a'. Because this is about as plausible a premise as one could provide for the author, it appears to be an appropriate premise. Thus, the miniargument [a] and the chain for it becomes:

f	(1) f	Pr
*f ⊃ a	(2) f ⊃ a	*Pr
a	(3) a	(1)(2)MP

Turning to the main argument [A], because none of the premises have matching letters, our forward strategy can't get started unless we add some premises. It seems most plausible that if Nixon admitted his guilt, he was guilty. Thus, the premise to add is:

(3) a ⊃ g

Clearly from [A](1), [A](2), and (3) we can get 'd'. Our backward strategy must somehow connect this with 'h'. Now

(4) d ⊃ h

will clearly yield the conclusion and because this seems plausible we may add it as an additional premise. The resulting argument (form) and the chain is:

a	(1) a	Pr
*a ⊃ g	(2) a ⊃ g	*Pr
g ⊃ d	(3) g	(1)(2)MP
*d ⊃ h	(4) g ⊃ d	Pr
h	(5) d	(3)(4)MP
	(6) d ⊃ h	*Pr
	(7) h	(5)(6)MP

The grand argument that is shown to be valid is simply the above argument with the first premise 'a' replaced by 'f' and *'f ⊃ a'.

Example 3:

> I heartily agree with your stand against tuition tax credit. . . . I believe separation of church and state must be absolute to protect my religious freedom. If the government were to grant tax favors to me and my favorite private school, they might later find a way to tell me how the school is to operate, how the religion is to be taught, and so on. To this, the First Amendment and I scream together loudly: Never! *(Los Angeles Times)*

Scheme:

'f': Freedom of religion will be protected.
'a': The separation of state and church will be absolute.
't': Tuition tax credit is adopted.
'g': There will be a genuine possibility of the government dictating on religious issues.
'm': The freedom of religion must be protected.
'o': Tuition tax credit should be opposed.

Bare Argument:

(1) $f \supset a$
(2) $t \supset g$
(3) m
―――――
o

Pursuing the forward strategy, we are given that freedom of religion must be protected (m) and that the absolute separation of church and state is necessary for the protection of freedom of religion ($f \supset a$). But then it would also seem that one should pursue the absolute separation of church and state. So, letting

's': The absolute separation of church and state should be pursued,

a plausible premise the author seems to be relying on is

(4) $[(f \supset a) \& m] \supset s$.

Given this premise, (1), (3), and (4) yield 's'. We are also given that the adoption of a tuition tax credit will result in the genuine possibility of the government dictating on religious issues. Clearly, the author intends that such a possibility endangers the absolute separation of state and church. Thus, letting

'd': The absolute separation of church and state will be endangered,

a premise that is at least plausible from the author's point of view is

(5) $g \supset d$.

(2) and (5) yields '$t \supset d$'.

We may now switch to the backward strategy. What would yield the result that a tuition tax credit should be opposed given that we have ‘s’ and ‘$t \supset d$’? Clearly,

(6) $[s \& (t \supset d)] \supset o$

would yield the conclusion, and it is about as plausible a premise as one can supply for the author's position.

The resulting argument (form) and the chain argument that shows it to be valid are:

Argument		Chain	
$f \supset a$	(1)	$f \supset a$	Pr
$t \supset g$	(2)	m	Pr
m	(3)	$(f \supset a) \& m$	(1)(2)Adj
*$[(f \supset a) \& m] \supset s$	(4)	$[(f \supset a) \& m] \supset s$	*Pr
*$g \supset d$	(5)	s	(3)(4)MP
*$[s \& (t \supset d)] \supset o$	(6)	$g \supset d$	*Pr
o	(7)	$t \supset g$	Pr
	(8)	$t \supset d$	(6)(7)HS
	(9)	$s \& (t \supset d)$	(5)(8)Adj
	(10)	$[s \& (t \supset d)] \supset o$	*Pr
	(11)	o	(9)(10)MP

Example 4:
Let us finally consider the example from Section 4.3. The scheme of abbreviation and an outline of the argument were:

Scheme:

‘r’: There is a large number of repeat offenders.
‘d’: The present punishment for crime is severe enough to deter.
‘f’: The future punishment for crime will be severe enough to deter.
‘p’: There is easy profit in crime.
‘h’: The crime rate will be high.
‘i’: We should increase the punishment for crime.

Bare Argument:

[a] (1) r
$\overline{\quad}$
$-d$

[A] (1) $-d$
(2) p
(3) $(p \& -f) \supset h$
$\overline{\quad}$
i

The miniargument is clearly made valid by the addition of the premise ‘$d \supset -r$’. Because this seems utterly unproblematic, we may add it as a missing premise. The resulting argument and chain are:

r	(1) r	Pr
*d ⊃ −r	(2) d ⊃ −r	*Pr
−d	(3) −d	(1)(2)MT

Turning to the main argument and pursuing the forward strategy, (2) and (3) give us '−f ⊃ h'. Because our direction from here is not evident, let us switch to the backward strategy. Because 'i' appears nowhere in the premises, we should ask what would make it plausible that we should increase punishment for crime. Given the premise '−d' ['present punishment is not severe enough to deter'], it seems plausible that if '−d' is true and future punishment should be severe enough to deter, we should increase the punishment for crime. Thus, letting

's': Future punishment should be severe enough to deter,

one useful premise toward arriving at the conclusion would be

(4) (−d & s) ⊃ i.

(4) along with '−d' and 's' would give us our conclusion. We have '−d' as a premise. Could we simply add 's' as an additional premise? This would make the author's premises concerning easy profit in crime and future crime rate irrelevant toward establishing the conclusion. Therefore, we should adopt 's' as an intermediate conclusion for which to aim and repeat the forward and/or backward strategies.

Repursuing the forward strategy with an eye toward 's', we recall from the first use of the forward strategy that (2) and (3) yield '−f ⊃ h', that is, 'if future punishment will not be severe enough to deter, then the crime rate will be high'. A plausible premise is that we want to prevent a high crime rate in the future. So, letting

'w': We want to prevent a high crime rate in the future.

we may add as an additional premise

(5) w.

(5) and '−f ⊃ h' will yield our intermediate conclusion 's' if we add the premise

(6) [(−f ⊃ h) & w] ⊃ s.

That is, if future punishment not being severe enough to deter results in a high crime rate and we want to prevent a high crime rate, then the future punishment should be severe enough to deter. Because this is probably as plausible a missing premise as we are liable to find for the author's view, let us adopt it.

The resulting main argument and the chain argument for it are the following:

$-d$	(1) p	Pr
p	(2) $(p \,\&\, -f) \supset h$	Pr
$(p \,\&\, -f) \supset h$	(3) $p \supset (-f \supset h)$	(2) E/I
$*w$	(4) $-f \supset h$	(1)(3)MP
$*[(-f \supset h) \,\&\, w] \supset s$	(5) w	*Pr
$*(-d \,\&\, s) \supset i$	(6) $(-f \supset h) \,\&\, w$	(4)(5)Adj
$\overline{}$ i	(7) $[(-f \supset h) \,\&\, w] \supset s$	*Pr
	(8) s	(6)(7)MP
	(9) $-d$	Pr
	(10) $-d \,\&\, s$	(8)(9)Adj
	(11) $(-d \,\&\, s) \supset i$	*Pr
	(12) i	(10)(11)MP

The grand argument for the main point results from the above main argument by replacing the premise '$-d$' by the premises 'r' and *'$(d \supset -r)$'.

The reader should now have some idea of how to find missing premises and to show the resulting argument to be deductively valid. While our discussion has largely been in terms of doing this for an argument someone else has presented, it should be clear that this outlined procedure provides a method for constructing arguments for one's own view. Typically if we have a view, we have (or at least can think of) *some* reasons favoring the view. To construct an argument for our own view, then, as simply a matter of finding enough plausible missing premises so that we ultimately have a deductively valid argument for our view. Precisely because we have adopted the principle of charity in order to facilitate truth assessments, there is no significant difference between considering someone else's view and considering our own view.

EXERCISES—SECTION 4.4

Part A

In each of the following, the argumentative passage and the bare argument extracted from it are given. In each problem convert the bare argument into one that is valid by supplying missing premises that adequately satisfy the formal and material aspects governing the choice of missing premises *and* show by means of chain arguments that the resulting argument is valid.

In some cases, additional sentence letters are given in the scheme of abbreviation in order to assist in choosing an appropriate missing premise.

1. The dollar is clearly headed for a significant decline against the Japanese yen. But nothing significantly curbs the American appetite for Japanese goods. So, if the Japanese keep the yen prices of their exports stable, we can expect the dollar value of American imports from Japan to rise.

Scheme:	*Bare Argument*
'd': The dollar will decline significantly against the Japanese yen.	d
'a': Nothing significantly curbs the American appetite for Japanese goods.	a
'r': The dollar value of American imports from Japan will rise.	———
'j': The Japanese keep the yen price of their exports stable.	j ⊃ r

2. If he stays at home to eat, he will have a miserable meal. But if he goes out, he will be upset over spending so much money. So, either way, he will be displeased.

Scheme:	*Bare Argument*
'h': He stays at home to eat.	h ⊃ m
'm': He will have a miserable meal.	o ⊃ u
'o': He goes out to eat.	———
'u': He will be upset over spending so much money.	d
'd': He will be displeased.	

3. If he continues smoking, his health will deteriorate. But if his continued smoking results in his work suffering, he will lose his job. Thus, if he continues smoking, unless he is independently wealthy, he will face financial problems.

Scheme:	*Bare Argument*
'c': He continues smoking.	c ⊃ h
'h': His health will deteriorate.	(c ⊃ w) ⊃ (c ⊃ l)
'w': His work will suffer.	———
'l': He will lose his job.	c ⊃ (i v f)
'i': He is independently wealthy.	
'f': He will face financial problems.	

4. It will rain or snow. But the weatherman said the temperature will not fall below freezing. If it does rain, Tony will get wet without his umbrella. So, Tony had better take his umbrella along.

Scheme:	*Bare Argument*
'r': It will rain.	r v s
's': It will snow.	f
'f': The weatherman said the temperature will not fall below freezing.	r ⊃ w
	———
'w': Tony will get wet without his umbrella.	t
't': Tony had better take his umbrella along.	

5. If nuclear weapons are eliminated, the balance of power will be determined by conventional forces. But the American and Western conventional forces are outnumbered by those of the Communist countries. It is therefore in the interest of America and the Western nations to resist the elimination of nuclear weapons.

Scheme:	*Bare Argument*
'n': Nuclear weapons are eliminated.	n ⊃ b
'b': The balance of power will be determined by conventional forces .	o
	———
'o': American and Western conventional forces are outnumbered by those of the Communist countries.	i
's': The balance of power will favor Communist countries over America and the Western nations.	
'i': It is in the interest of America and the Western nations to resist the elimination of nuclear weapons.	

Hint: Ask what will happen to the balance of power if nuclear weapons are eliminated, that is, look for an intermediate conclusion of the form 'n ⊃ ?'.

Part B

In each of the following, the bare argument extracted from an argumentative passage is given; the argumentative passage and/or the appropriate background is also provided.

In each problem, convert the bare argument into a valid one by supplying missing premises that adequately satisfy the formal and material aspects governing the choice of missing premises *and* show by means of chain arguments that the resulting argument is valid.

In some cases, additional sentence letters are given in the scheme of abbreviation in order to assist in choosing an appropriate missing premise.

1. [Background: The California general ballot of June 1982 contained Proposition 7, an initiative that would index the state income tax to the cost of living. If, for example, the 5 percent tax bracket starts at $10,000 in 1982 and the cost of living rises by 10 percent during the next year, Proposition 7 would readjust the tax brackets so that the 5 percent bracket would start at $11,000 in 1983. The argument by Howard Jarvis, a proponent of Proposition 7, is given below as it appeared in the *California Ballot Pamphlet.*]

   YES ON PROPOSITION 7! Proposition 7 will index income taxes. Indexing means inflation alone will never again increase tax rates. If Proposition 7 doesn't pass, *income tax rates for many Californians could double in just four years!* Proposition 7 will permanently end this unfair inequity in California's income tax rates.

   Scheme:
   'p': Proposition 7 will pass.
   'i': Tax rates will go up just because of inflation.
   'u': It is unfair for tax rates to go up just because of inflation.
   'v': You should vote for Proposition 7.

   Bare Argument
   p ≡ −i
   u
   ———
   v

2. [Background: Below is the argument against Proposition 7 discussed in exercise 1 as it appeared in the *Ballot Pamphlet.*]

   [Proposition 7] must be defeated. It is unfair to every taxpayer in terms of providing essential services. The state of California has suffered drastic cuts in public services. This indexing initiative [will produce] drastic revenue losses and will continue to produce increasingly larger losses in all the years to come.

   Scheme:
   's': Essential public services have already been drastically reduced.
   'p': Proposition 7 will pass.
   'r': There will be severe cuts in revenue.
   'v': You should vote against Proposition 7.
   'f': There will be severe reductions in essential public services from the present level.
   'u': There will be an unfairness to all taxpayers.

   Bare Argument
   s
   p ⊃ r
   (s & f) ⊃ u
   ———
   v

3. Proposition 9 on the November 1982 California general ballot would set up a program whereby students in private schools could borrow, free of charge, textbooks bought by the state for use in public-school classes. The following is part of an argument in favor of Proposition 9 given in the *Ballot Pamphlet.*

ALL PARENTS PAY TAXES TO PURCHASE [SCHOOL TEXTBOOKS] If children [who are attending private schools] were to enroll in public schools, it would cost the taxpayers of California over $1 billion annually. . . . vote yes on Proposition 9.

Let part of the scheme of abbreviation be:

'p': All parents pay for the state purchase of school textbooks.
'a': Private schoolchildren will attend public schools (instead).
'b': It will cost the taxpayers an additional $1 billion annually.
'm': Parents of private schoolchildren are doing more than their share to support the public-school system.
'd': Parents of private schoolchildren deserve help from the state in the form of the textbook loan program proposed by Proposition 9.
'v': One should vote in favor of Proposition 9.

A charitable interpretation of the passage is to take it as offering the following bare argument:

p
a ⊃ b
m ⊃ d
———
v

4. Reread the passage given in Part B, exercise 6 of Section 4.3. Using the scheme of abbreviation given in that exercise, take the outline of the main argument to be:

   l, m, m ⊃ s, f / a v t

5. [Background: The California general ballot of June 1982 contained Proposition 8, a tough anticrime initiative. The argument for Proposition 8 by (then Attorney General) George Deukmejian is given below as it appeared in the *Ballot Pamphlet.*]

   Crime has increased to an absolutely intolerable level. Only 5.5 percent of those persons *arrested* for felonies are sent to state prisons. Of those *convicted* of felonies, one-third go to state prisons and the remaining two-thirds are back in the community in a relatively short period of time. THERE IS ABSOLUTELY NO QUESTION THAT THE PASSAGE OF THIS PROPOSITION WILL RESULT IN MORE CRIMINAL CONVICTIONS, MORE CRIMINALS BEING SENTENCED TO STATE PRISONS. IF YOU FAVOR PUBLIC SAFETY, VOTE YES ON PROPOSITION 8.

   Scheme:
   's': There is public safety today.
   'f': The public will be safer in the future.
   'i': There will be an increased conviction rate.
   'w': One wants public safety in the future.
   'e': Proposition 8 will be passed.
   'v': One should vote for Proposition 8.

   Bare Argument
   —s
   e ⊃ i
   ———
   w ⊃ v

6. [Background: Below is the argument against Proposition 8 discussed in exercise 5 as it appeared in the *Ballot Pamphlet.*]

   Every responsible citizen opposes crime, but we should also be very HESITANT to make RADICAL changes in our Constitution. Yet Proposition 8 does just that . . . it needlessly reduces your personal liberties [or] clearly harms the true efforts to fight crime. CONSIDER THESE EFFECTS OF PROPOSITION 8:

   Takes away everyone's right to bail. Allows strip searches for minor traffic offenders. Condones the use of wiretapping. Permits spying on you in public restrooms.

Either Proposition 8 takes away your civil rights, or it is unconstitutional . . . in which case *valid criminal convictions will be thrown out.*

Scheme:
'a': Proposition 8 allows for no bail, spying on you in public restrooms, etc.
'l': Personal liberties will be reduced.
't': Valid crime convictions will be thrown out.
'h': True efforts to fight crime will be harmed.
'e': Proposition 8 will pass.
'c': Proposition 8 will be declared constitutional.
'u': Proposition 8 will be declared unconstitutional.

Bare Argument
a
e ⊃ (c v u)
(a & u) ⊃ t
———
e ⊃ (l v h)

7. Reread the passage given in Part B, exercise 4 of Section 4.3. The scheme of abbreviation and the outline of the "grand argument" for the pro-life position may be given as follows:

   Scheme:
   'l': Every person has a right to life.
   's': A person's right to life is stronger than a mother's right to determine what happens in and to her body.
   'e': In having an abortion performed, a mother is exercising her right to determine what happens to her body.
   't': In having an abortion performed, a mother is taking the life of a fetus.
   'r': One may do something only if doing it doesn't violate a right of another, which is stronger than one's right to do that thing.
   'm': An abortion may be performed.
   Bare Argument: l, s, e, t, r / −m

8. Reread the passage given in Part B, exercise 5 of Section 4.3. Using the scheme of abbreviation given in the exercise, and adding *some* of the missing premises, take the (augmented) outline of the "grand argument" to be:

   v
   *v ⊃ (j ⊃ l)
   *[s & (j ⊃ l)] ⊃ −j
   m
   *[(s ⊃ a) & m] ⊃ p
   ———
   p

   Hint: What is still missing is what happens when a politician votes with a minority on a divisive issue, and how this relates to a voting abstention. Therefore, be prepared to add one additional sentence letter.

Part C

1. Clearly, innocent people do suffer on Earth, because some are raped or murdered by evil people, and natural catastrophes like earthquakes and tornadoes cause an untold amount of suffering for innocent people. This has often been taken to show (by the so-called Argument from Evil) that the Christian belief in an omnipotent and benevolent God is false. Using the following scheme of abbreviation, construct a deductively valid argument for this conclusion:

   'c': The Christian belief is false.
   'i': Innocent people suffer on Earth.
   'o': God is omnipotent.

'b': God is benevolent.
'p': God has the power to prevent innocent suffering.

Hint: The simplest chain that would show the argument to be valid (with missing premises) is a *reductio* chain or else a conditional chain for something of the form '$-c \supset (\phi \& -\phi)$', on which Rd can be used in the main chain.

2. By the year 1985, the United States was suffering from massive trade deficits with Japan. While many called for increased tariffs on Japanese goods, the Reagan administration adopted the policy of devaluing the dollar relative to the Japanese yen. Adopting the point of view of an American, construct as plausible an argument as you can for choosing devaluation over tariffs (assuming we want to maximize the reduction of trade deficits with Japan). The argument is easiest if "the devaluation policy" is understood to be one whereby the cost of imported Japanese goods to the American consumer will be the same whether the dollar is devalued (without proposed tariffs) or the proposed tariffs are imposed (without the dollar being devalued). Bear in mind that tariffs are likely to meet with retaliatory tariffs and that a devalued dollar makes American goods cheaper in Japan.

   Hint: Let part of the scheme of abbreviation be:

   't': Tariffs are imposed on Japanese goods.
   'j': Retaliatory Japanese tariffs will be imposed on American goods.
   'd': The devaluation policy is adopted.
   'c': American goods will be cheaper in Japan.
   'a': The devaluation policy and the imposition of tariffs result in the same cost of Japanese goods in America.
   'w': We want to reduce our trade deficits with Japan as much as possible.
   's': We should choose the devaluation policy over the imposition of tariffs on Japanese goods.

4.5 Plausibility Assessments

Given the valid argument produced at the end of the second major stage of analyzing argumentative passages, the final stage is to assess the degrees of justification the premises and the conclusion have. In light of our discussion in Section 4.2, there are three possible outcomes of such an assessment:

(1) The conclusion is completely or highly justified or at least acceptable, because the conjunction of the premises is completely or highly justified or at least acceptable.
(2) The conclusion has not been made evident for us because, despite our honest attempt, at least one of the premises remains epistemically neutral or worse.
(3) The conclusion is not acceptable and the reasons are poor, because there is a statement S such that (i) if S were false, the conclusion would be false even if all the other premises were true, and (ii) the falsity of S is acceptable or epistemically neutral.

The first step in making plausibility assessments is to mark the unproblematic premises. In this connection, a writer may make an OB, PF, or

SM claim that in normal circumstances may be a candidate for unproblematic acceptance. However, there is always the suspicion that the writer may be partial in making such a claim, because he has the obvious desire to establish the main point. Furthermore, if the writer claims to be giving expert testimony, one may not be in a position to judge his or her expertise. While these factors should be kept in mind, it is often good practice to accept such a claim as unproblematic at least for the sake of the argument. One can always reraise the question of their unproblematic status later if the need arises. Having (at least tentatively) marked the unproblematic premises, one is in a position to zero in on the other premises that may be more or less problematic.

The strategy is to find the weakest links in the best case one has made for the view in the passage. To this end, one should try to find grounds for denying the premises that are less than unproblematic. The stronger the grounds one can find for denying a premise, the weaker the premise is. If these grounds make the weakest link less than acceptable, one may conclude that the reasons for accepting the conclusion have not been made evident. If the weakest link is not acceptable and is also such that if it were false, the conclusion would be false even if all the other premises were true, one can reject the reasons as bad reasons and assess the conclusion to be not acceptable.

If the weakest links are all acceptable or better, one should try to assess the degree to which the conjunction of all the premises is justified. If that conjunction has a status better than epistemic neutrality, one has correspondingly good reasons for accepting the conclusion. However, one point must be kept in mind: Even if *each* of the premises is highly justified, the conjunction of all the premises may be unacceptable. If each premise is only highly justified, there are some genuine grounds for doubt; if there is such a ground for doubt for each of the premises, there is a greater likelihood that the grounds for doubt for at least one of the premises will be realized, so that the conjunction of *all* the premises will not be true. As a simple example, suppose that there are only ten lottery tickets and that they are held by A, B, . . . , and J. Consider the argument: "A isn't going to win, B isn't going to win, . . . , J isn't going to win / No one is going to win." Each of the premises is highly justified, but the falsity of the conjunction of the premises (as well as that of the conclusion) is all but assured. A valid argument shows that the conjunction of *all* the premises is a valid reason for the conclusion. Thus, in order to be able to claim that the conclusion is acceptable to a certain degree, one must be able to claim that *all the premises taken together* are justified to that degree. However, in most cases the kind of problem raised by the lottery example need not be of too great a concern if the truth of none of the premises makes the falsity of another premise more likely.

While our main concern is with truth assessments within our own epistemic situation, the method outlined can also be helpful in clarifying disagreements. Suppose A and B disagree on some claim 'c', perhaps because of their differing epistemic situations or because some of the connected claims are unjustified opinions. Given a valid argument for 'c', A and B should disagree on one or more of the premises. If A affirms 'c' and B doesn't, the disagreement will typically center on the premises that B considers to be the weakest links. In this way, we can often isolate the source of disagreement between A and B by locating the premises on which they disagree. Doing so clarifies the disagreement over 'c' and allows A and B to appreciate their respective positions more adequately.

The recommended procedure for assessing the conclusion and clarifying a disagreement may be summarized as follows:

> Accept the unproblematic premises and determine the least justified of the remaining premises by considering possible grounds for their denial.
>
> (1) If the weakest links are acceptable, the conclusion can be assessed to be justified
>   (a) to the degree the conjunction of all the premises is justified and, typically,
>   (b) to the degree the weakest links are justified provided that the truth of no premise makes the falsity of another more likely.
>
> (2) If the weakest links are epistemically neutral or worse, the conclusion has not been made evident.
>
> (3) If any premise is epistemically neutral or worse, and its falsity would make the conclusion false, the conclusion is not acceptable.
>
> (4) If there is a disagreement over the conclusion, the source of the disagreement typically centers around the weakest links.

Evaluative Claims. In some of the examples we have considered, we encountered examples of what are sometimes called EVALUATIVE STATEMENTS, *that is, statements about what one should or ought to do, and statements about what is good or bad, beautiful or ugly.* Some philosophers have maintained that evaluative statements are neither true nor false, but rather are merely expressive of one's attitudes or are implicit commands.[3] Yet, statements as we construed them are supposed to be true or false, and the methods presented are developed within the framework of statements having truth values. This raises the question of whether the methods we are developing are applicable to evaluative statements. The short answer is: Whether or not evaluative statements have truth values, there are logical relations between them, and they are revealed by treating them *as if* they had truth values. Thus, we can bypass the question of whether they are literally true or false.

3. See Section 6.6.2 for more on this.

Connected with the problem of whether or not evaluative statements have truth values is whether any evaluative statement can be taken as unproblematic. However, recall that the notion of an unproblematic claim was always relative to a person at a time. Thus, it is probably unproblematic for most readers that one should keep one's promises and that one ought not to take human lives senselessly and indiscriminately. If these are unproblematic for a reader, he or she might take them as unproblematic INT claims. Again, for a particular person at a time 'The sunset I am seeing is beautiful' may be an unproblematic OB claim. If one has used this knife and has used a variety of knives for various purposes, the claim that this is a good knife may also be a unproblematic OB claim. Thus, to a large extent our previous notion of unproblematic claims can be applied to evaluative statements, although this will involve stretching the original intent of OB, INT, and CS claims.

Of course people can and do disagree about evaluative statements. While it is unproblematic for most of us that genocide is wrong, this was evidently not unproblematic for Hitler. Again, the sunset that one person takes to be beautiful may be garish and unappealing to another. One consequence of this is that we should not accept expert or nonexpert testimony involving evaluative statements as unproblematic. A second consequence is that it may be difficult, and in some cases perhaps even impossible, to reach agreement when evaluative statements are involved. While nonevaluative INT claims were on the whole not open to controversy, some evaluative INT claims may be controversial. Still, this need not affect one's own position as to what claims are and what claims aren't justified. Furthermore, the extent of disagreement concerning evaluative statements is often exaggerated, in that there is often a very high degree of agreement concerning what evaluative statements are unproblematic. When there is an agreement concerning evaluative statements among a group of persons, the methods developed can be used to resolve controversies just as much as in cases where the controversy is of a nonevaluative nature.

Example. To exemplify the process of assessing the plausibility of the premises, let us consider the premises of the argument we have been analyzing since Section 4.3. Of course the reader may disagree with my assessments because his epistemic situation may be different and our agreement on evaluative statements may not be complete. With this caveat, let me exemplify the process by giving my assessment of the premises. It seems to me that four of the premises in the grand argument for increasing punishment are more or less unproblematic. They are:

'r': There is a large number of repeat offenders.
'$d \supset -r$': If the present punishment for crime is severe enough to deter, there is not a large number of repeat offenders.
'p': There is easy profit in crime.
'w': We want to prevent a high crime rate in the future.

It would seem that ‘r’ is an unproblematic PF claim and that ‘$d \supset -r$’ is an unproblematic INT claim. Most of us have read many times about the high number of repeat offenders, and clearly if the present punishment were deterring, there couldn’t be such a large number of repeat offenders. While ‘p’ may be a little more questionable, if it is taken to mean nothing more than “There is some profit in activities like stealing and one is not disqualified from this ‘profession’ by the lack of previous training,” it would seem to be an unproblematic CS claim. For most of us ‘w’ would be fairly unproblematic. Thus, if we appropriately limit the reference of “we,” ‘w’ might be an unproblematic CS claim. This of course has the consequence that the conclusion is acceptable only to those who belong to the reference of the “we.”

Although the remaining three premises cannot be considered unproblematic, two of them appear to be fairly strong. Let us start with

‘$(-d \,\&\, s) \supset i$’: If the present punishment is not severe enough to deter and future punishment should be severe enough to deter, then we should increase the punishment for crime.

If we have accepted without qualification that punishment should be severe enough to deter and also that our present punishment is not deterring, how could one then deny that punishment should be increased? Two grounds may be suggested: (a) The punishment shouldn’t be increased beyond the minimum level needed to deter crime. But this could be understood to be the intent of the consequent, and if desired, the consequent could be rewritten to make this explicit. (b) Even if the antecedent is true, the consequent could be false if no increase in the punishment would be an effective deterrent, so that increasing punishment only increases suffering without any decrease in the crime rate. Certainly for some crimes (e.g., crimes of passion), it is unlikely that any increase will be fully effective in deterring. However, for certain classes of crimes (robberies, vandalism, etc.), it would seem highly plausible that at least a *drastic* increase in the punishment would have the effect of deterring crime. Thus, limiting oneself to crimes of that kind, the grounds for thinking that no level of punishment would be an effective deterrent seem highly unjustified (i.e., it’s highly justified that some level of punishment would deter). Because there appear to be no other grounds for denying the premise in question, I am inclined to assess it as highly justified as long as appropriate limitations are placed on the type of crimes involved and the level of increase in punishment is limited to the minimum amount necessary for deterring crime.

Consider now the premise

‘$(p \,\&\, -f) \supset h$’: If there is easy profit in crime and the future punishment for crime isn’t severe enough to deter, there will be a high crime rate.

Even if there is easy profit in crime and the punishment is not severe enough to deter, the crime rate might not be high under certain circumstances. For one thing, if the economic situation of potential criminals improves so that there is no need to commit crimes for profit, the crime rate might not be high despite the punishment not being severe enough to deter. Another factor that may reduce the crime rate in the absence of punishment that is high enough to deter is demographics; that is, as the number of people in the age group of 18 to 30 years declines, the amount of crime tends to decline. Of course, it may be somewhat unrealistic to think that we will decide or be able to improve sufficiently the economic lot of potential criminals, and the impact of demographics may be insufficient to reduce the "high" crime rate to a satisfactory level. Still, there are some doubts about this premise and it may be no better than merely acceptable. However, to avoid the charge of being a Pollyanna, at least for the sake of the argument we might suppose the premise to be highly justified.

The remaining premise is

'$[(-f \supset h) \& w] \supset s$': If future punishment not being severe enough to deter results in a high crime rate and we want to prevent a high crime rate, then future punishment should be severe enough to deter.

The difficulty with this premise is that even though we want to prevent a high crime rate, if this couldn't be done without increasing the punishment drastically, we might have second thoughts about having punishment that is severe enough to deter. That is, *drastic* punishment is likely to conflict with other things that we want such as the punishment matching the crime and avoiding undue hardship on minority groups with high crime rates. Thus, in the end we may prefer enduring a high crime rate to having a repressive and unjust system of punishment. Are we really willing to accept twenty-five years and two days in jail for shoplifting or writing graffiti? At least from my point of view, if the level of punishment needed is drastic and would result in a repressive society, I would prefer enduring a high crime rate over opting for the punishment that is severe enough to deter. As to whether nothing short of drastic punishment will suffice in deterring crime effectively, I simply don't know; that is, 'Drastic punishment is needed to deter crime effectively' is epistemically neutral for me. But if drastic punishment is needed, I would not seek punishment that is severe enough to deter. The upshot is that this premise as a whole is epistemically neutral for me: without knowing how drastic the punishment will have to be in order to deter, I'm not in a position to assent to or dissent from this premise. Given my epistemic circumstance, this then is the weakest link in the argument we have been considering.

The minimal result of this assessment is that because the weakest premise is not acceptable in my epistemic circumstance, it has not been made evident to me that we should increase the punishment to the level needed for effective deterrence. Though less significant in light of this assessment, it might be noted that two other premises are less than completely justified for me and that one of them may be merely acceptable for me. Furthermore, it should be noticed that two of the three premises that were less than completely justified for me were missing premises. Even the third premise that we counted as explicitly given required considerable interpretation of the author's actual statements. This is the way it often is with argumentative passages: the dubious premises or reasons are suppressed or disguised, and what is clearly stated tends toward the unproblematic side. Precisely for this reason, it is important to formulate clearly the reasons given and to uncover the missing premises.

Can we go further and claim that we have actually been given poor reasons for accepting the conclusion? That is, have we found a premise or statement S such that (a) if S were false the conclusion would be false even if all the other premises were true, and (b) the falsity of S is epistemically neutral or acceptable? It would appear that the weakest link of the argument pretty much fits this bill. Because that questionable premise is epistemically neutral, its falsity is also epistemically neutral; thus condition (b) is met. Its being false amounts to the truth of:

> Even though future punishment not being severe enough to deter results in a high crime rate and we want to prevent a high crime rate, nevertheless future punishment should not be severe enough to deter.

If future punishment should not be severe enough to deter, I see no need to increase the punishment; and if there is no need to increase the punishment, it can't be right that we should increase the punishment. Thus, the falsity of the weakest link would seem to make the conclusion false even if all the other premises were true; hence the weakest premise seems to satisfy condition (a) as well. From my point of view then, bad reasons have been offered for the conclusion, and the conclusion is not acceptable. However, it must be admitted that someone might want to say from a retributive point of view that quite independently of deterrence, criminals should suffer more and that punishment should therefore be increased. Such a person can only conclude that the reasons for increasing the punishment have not been made evident by the passage under consideration.

If someone assesses the premises the way I did, he or she should not conclude that an increase in punishment should be opposed. A modest increase in the punishment may be well worth a try. Furthermore, if our epistemic situation changes so that we have good reasons to think that a modest increase in punishment would suffice to deter crime effectively, perhaps one should increase the punishment. But the reasons offered are not in terms of trying a *modest* increase in punishment to see its effect on the crime rate; nor is our epistemic situation one in which we have been given reasons to think that a modest increase in punishment would suffice to deter crime. The argument is rather in terms of increasing punishment to the level needed for deterrence, *whatever* that level may turn out to be. In claiming that the reasons given were poor in our epistemic situation, we were only saying that because we have no grounds for thinking that the level of punishment needed is within the acceptable limits forced by our other concerns, we cannot accept the conclusion that the punishment should be increased to whatever level is needed for deterrence. That conclusion can be accepted only by someone who makes the reduction of the crime rate a top-priority item overriding virtually all other considerations; of course, such a person would find the "weakest link" we have isolated to be highly or completely justified., This result should indicate to the reader the value of analyzing argumentative passages even if total agreement cannot be attained, because it pinpoints the area of disagreement as well as where one stands on a particular issue.

EXERCISES—SECTION 4.5

1. For each of the following,
   - (i) Determine the premises that are unproblematic for you, and for those that are, specify the type of unproblematic claim it is and whether it is an evaluative claim.
   - (ii) Locate the weakest link or links among the premises by determining the degree of justification the remaining premises have, and briefly indicate why the weakest link(s) have the degree of justification they do.
   - (iii) Given your epistemic situation, assess whether the conclusion has been justified to a degree above epistemic neutrality, or is not acceptable, or has not been made evident.
   - (a) Example 1 given in the text portion of Section 4.4.
   - (b) Example 3 given in the text portion of Section 4.4. In doing this exercise, attach the following meanings to two crucial expressions in the argument:
     - Take 'absolute separation of state and church' to mean only that the government will not dictate on religious issues, rather than that there is a *no possibility* of the government doing so or that no action on their part might benefit a religious group.
     - Take 'genuine possibility of the government dictating on religious issues' to mean only that some people in the government may attempt to (pass laws that will) dictate on religious issues, not that there is a significant likelihood that such attempts will succeed.
   - (c) How would your answer in b change if we took 'absolute separation of state and church' to mean that there is no possibility of the government dictating on religious issues or of the government benefiting any religious group?
   - (d) Keeping the meaning of 'absolute separation' as specified in b, how would your answer to b change if 'genuine possibility of the government dictating on religious issues' is taken to mean that there is a significant likelihood that the government will dictate on religious issues?

2. Reread Part B, exercise 4 of Section 4.3, in which the core of a pro-life argument is sketched. Using the following scheme of abbreviation and supplying needed premises, that argument may be taken as the one given below:

   'l': Every person has a right to life.
   's': A person's right to life is stronger than a woman's right to determine what happens in and to her body.
   'e': In having an abortion performed, a woman is exercising her right to determine what happens to her body.

't': In having an abortion performed a woman is taking the life of a fetus.
'r': One may do something only if doing it doesn't violate a right of another, which is stronger than one's right to do that thing.
'm': An abortion may be performed.
'f': A fetus is a person.
's*': A fetus's right to life is stronger than the woman's right to determine what happens to her body.
'v': Having an abortion performed violates a right of a fetus that is stronger than the woman's right to determine what happens in and to her body.

l

s

f

$(l \& s \& f) \supset s^*$

e

t

$(s^* \& e \& t) \supset v$

r

$(v \& r) \supset -m$

$-m$

In response to that pro-life argument, Professor Judith Jarvis Thompson writes:

> I am inclined to think also that we shall probably have to agree that the fetus has already become a human person well before birth. Indeed it comes as a surprise when one first learns how early in its life it begins to acquire human characteristics. By the tenth week, for example, it already has a face, arms and legs, fingers and toes; it has internal organs, and brain activity is detectable. On the other hand, I think ... that a fetus is not a person from the moment of conception. A newly fertilized ovum, a newly implanted clump of cells, is no more a person than an acorn is an oak tree.
>
> ... Opponents of abortion commonly spend most of their time establishing that the fetus is a person, and hardly any time explaining the step from there to the impermissibility of abortion.... Let me ask you to imagine this. You wake up in the morning and find yourself back to back in bed with a ... famous unconscious violinist. He has been found to have a fatal kidney ailment, and the Society of Music Lovers ... found that you alone have the right blood type to help. They have kidnapped you, and last night the violinist's circulatory system was plugged into yours.... The director of the hospital now tells you, "Look, we're sorry the Society of Music Lovers did this to you—we would never have permitted it if we had known. But still, they did it, and the violinist now is plugged into you. To unplug you would be to kill him. But never mind, it's only for nine months. By then he will have recovered.... " Is it morally incumbent on you to accede to this situation? No doubt it would be very nice if you did, a great kindness. But do you *have* to accede to it? What if it were not nine months, but nine years? Or longer still? ... I imagine that you would regard this as outrageous.

(a) The supporters of the pro-life argument and Professor Thompson are likely to agree that some of the premises of the argument are unproblematic or evaluative unproblematic claims. Identify these premises.
(b) Assuming that the pro-life argument is limited to fetuses that are reasonably well advanced (say, well into the second trimester), how is Professor Thompson likely to assess the remaining premises and the argument, and how would she assess the argument's ability to establish the conclusion?

(c) Leaving aside the uncontroversial premises detected in a, and bearing in mind Professor Thompson's critique, how might the argument be defended by a strong pro-lifer, that is, a person who claims that an abortion of a fetus from the moment of conception is never justified under any circumstance?

(d) Suppose a strong pro-choicer claims that it is always permissible for a woman to have an abortion performed—even if it is an hour before the anticipated time of birth. Suppose also that the following version of 'r' is accepted:

r*: If doing something is exercising a right of a certain kind, one may do it if doing it doesn't violate any stronger right of another person.

Given this much and bearing in mind Professor Thompson's remarks about fetuses, how might a strong pro-choicer best defend the position?

3. Below is part of Ellen Haas's column "The Great Cheese Giveaway" (cf. Part B, exercise 1 of Section 4.3), which wasn't previously quoted:

> One way to compare the dairy-farmer welfare program and the federal food-assistance programs is to compare their respective costs per intended beneficiary. Using the food-stamp program as an example, the cost to the U.S. government for each of the 22 million poor Americans participating in the food-stamp program is $600 a year, while the cost to the government for each of the 200,000 commercial dairy farmers in the country is about $10,000. Yet this comparison does not tell the whole story. The dairy program also adds billions of dollars annually to the retail food costs of all Americans. . . . Moreover, in the food-stamp program the level of benefits is tied directly to the degree of need, while in the dairy program exactly the opposite is true. The Justice Department has estimated that the largest 15% of all dairy farms receive 45% of the subsidy benefits, while the smallest 50% receive only 6%. Thus, there is great hypocrisy in how the federal government runs welfare programs that benefit special business interests and how it runs those that benefit the nation's poor.

Although it is not entirely clear what the charge of hypocrisy is meant to cover, let us assume that the conclusion Ms. Haas is urging is that the more needy get less welfare assistance from the administration than some who are less needy. More precisely, let us take the conclusion as:

'h': Some classes of people who are on the average more needy get less welfare assistance from the administration than some classes of people who are less needy.

Let the scheme of abbreviation be given by:

's': The average beneficiary receives $600 per year from the food stamp program and the average beneficiary receives $10,000 per year from the dairy assistance program.

'p': The average recipient of the food stamp program is more needy than the average recipient of the dairy assistance program.

'w': The average recipient of the food assistance program receives less than $9400 in other forms of welfare aid.

'b': The largest 15 percent of all dairy farms receive 45 percent of the subsidy benefits, while the smallest 50 percent receive only 6 percent.

'l': The smallest 50 percent of the dairy farmers are more needy than the largest 15 percent.

Although this may be somewhat unfair to Ms. Haas, assume that she is providing two arguments for 'h', which become the following once appropriate missing premises are added:

[A] s, p, w, (s & p & w) ⊃ h / h   [B] b, l, (b & l) ⊃ h / h

Recall that Ms. Haas is the director of the consumer division of the Washington-based Community Nutrition Institute. Assume for the sake of this exercise that the following two claims are highly justified:

- The total welfare benefits of the average food stamp recipient was less than $10,000 in 1982.
- In 1982 the typical or average dairy farmers didn't qualify for food stamps or similar welfare benefits available to food stamp recipients.

Finally, in light of such fund-raising drives as "Farm Aid" in 1986, assume that for all you know the average dairy farms may have been on the verge of bankruptcy in the early and mid-eighties; that is, although it may be assumed that they had enough money for their day-to-day existence, take claims about the health of their business to be epistemically neutral.

(a) Perform steps (i)–(iii) of exercise 1 for arguments [A] and [B] on the assumption that X is more needy than Y if X has less money or assets than Y.
(b) Perform steps (i)–(iii) of exercise 1 for arguments [A] and [B] on the assumption that X is *as* needy (of federal assistance) as Y if X needs the assistance to avoid bankruptcy (in X's business), and Y has a similar need or needs for federal assistance to maintain minimal living standards.
(c) For the sake of this exercise, limit 'h' to be making claims only about two classes of people, that is, the dairy farmers and the recipients of food stamps. Would your assessment of the conclusion [i.e., step (iii) of the analysis] change by the shift in the meaning of 'needy' from that given in a to the one given in b?
(d) In light of your results in a and b, what is likely to be the basic difference in the points of view of the dairy farmers and Ms. Haas?

---

*4.6 Auxiliary Aids

In this section we wish to present a couple of methods that may be of some help in analyzing certain argumentative passages. Section 4.6.1 deals with the problem of determining how to proceed so as to achieve certain desired results. Section 4.6.2 presents a few logical relations that depend on the fine structure of statements that are not reflected in their truth functional logical forms.

4.6.1 Expected Utility

From Section 4.3 onward, the main example we have dealt with points out how difficult it is to determine what should be done even if there is agreement that we *want* something like a low future crime rate. The complications involved in such a determination are staggering. In order to give the reader some framework in which to conceive of the problem, we wish to present the broadest outline of a theory developed by a number of people on how such determinations might be made. Granting that our presentation is crude and oversimplified, and that the theory itself can be

*This section contains more difficult material and may be skipped.

questioned on a number of grounds, it nevertheless highlights some of the relevant considerations in determining what to do when one desires something.

Let us consider a relatively simple example: I have a disorder that is virtually certain to result in my imminent death unless something is done about it, and let us suppose that I want to live. In a situation like this the first step is to determine the options that are available to me. No doubt we can't list all of the possible options, but we might list the plausible kinds of options that are more or less readily available. Let us suppose that in our case the basic (kinds of) options are:

A1: Go to a highly reputed specialist in New York, or the Mayo Clinic, or in some similar place.
A2: Go to the local hospital.
A3: Go to a faith healer.
A4: Do nothing about it.

Given that these are my practical available options, the theory we are presenting suggests determining the "expected utility" of each of these acts, and to choose the alternative that has the greatest expected utility. That is, the theory that we'll call the *expected utility theory* suggests that 'If an act A has the greatest expected utility in a given situation among the (plausible) options, one should do A' is an unproblematic claim (perhaps of an INT variety) that can be used as a premise in an argument.

The problem then is to determine the so-called expected utility of an action or a set of contemplated actions. The first step is to form what might be called a cost/benefit space. The COST/BENEFIT SPACE might be defined as follows:

> The *cost/benefit space* for a set of contemplated actions is a set of possible outcomes $\{O_1, O_2, \ldots, O_n\}$ such that
>
> (a) each outcome specifies a possible combination of benefits and costs of at least one of the contemplated actions,
> (b) for each contemplated action, one of the outcomes $\{O_1, O_2, \ldots, O_n\}$ must occur, and
> (c) no two outcomes can both occur.

The technical jargon for conditions (b) and (c) is that the set of possible outcomes is *jointly exhaustive and mutually exclusive* (for each contemplated act).

In our example, the kinds of benefits and costs involved might be taken as 'S' (for life <u>s</u>aved), 'D' (for <u>d</u>ying), 'H' (for <u>h</u>igh-monetary expense and effort involved), 'M' (for <u>m</u>edium-monetary expenses and effort involved), 'L' (for <u>l</u>ow-monetary expenses and effort involved), and 'Z' (for <u>z</u>ero-monetary expense and effort involved). The cost/benefit space would then be given by: S & H, S & M, S & L, S & Z, D & H, D & M, D & L, and D & Z. The method employed to get at this cost/benefit space is obvious: Lump the possible benefits into mutually exclusive and jointly exhaustive classes (S and D in our case), and lump the possible costs into mutually exclusive and jointly exhaustive classes (H, M, L, and Z in our case); form the cost/benefit space by taking all combinations of possible benefits and possible costs. To lend some concreteness, we might suppose high expenses are $10,000–$30,000, medium expenses are $3000–$5000, low expenses are $200–$300, and zero expense is of course $0. Of course, to assume this, and to take the cost/benefit space to be the one given, is to claim that expenses outside of these ranges cannot occur (or at least have a negligible probability of occurring).

Given the cost/benefit space, each member of that space must be given (a) a desirability rating, and (b) a probability of being attained by each of the contemplated actions. With the desirability rating, the first step is to list the possible outcomes in the descending order of desirability. Obviously, such a ranking can vary with each individual but it is possible to limit the assessment to oneself and to those who share those preferences. In our example, the ranking should be fairly uncontroversial: S & Z, S & L, S & M, S & H, D & Z, D & L, D & M, D & H. The next and more difficult step is to assign numerical values for the degree to which these outcomes are desired. The kind of scale used is immaterial: for example, a scale of 1 to 10, a scale of -10 to $+10$, and an open-ended scale in both directions from 0, are all possible. However, the three conditions stated in the following definition must be satisfied:

> The desirability rating d(O) assigns a numerical value to each possible outcome in the cost/benefit space such that
>
> (a) if O_1 is more desirable than O_2, $d(O_1) > d(O_2)$,
> (b) the differences in the numerical values assigned roughly reflect how much more something is preferred over something else, and
> (c) for any given outcome O, d(O) is the same regardless of what action is performed to achieve O.

Thus in our example, condition (c) demands that the same scale be used to determine the expected utility of A1, . . . , A4. Obviously, such a numerical assignment cannot be made absolutely precise in most practical situations, and estimated figures will have to do. Still, we often encounter situations in which we are asked to rate variables like a teacher's effectiveness on a scale from 1 to 5; thus, it should not be impossible to come up with some estimated figures.

In our example, I might assign the following values for the degree to which the outcomes are desired:

S & Z	S & L	S & M	S & H	D & Z	D & L	D & M	D & H
150	148	140	100	−100	−100	−103	−110

It might be assumed that I might evaluate the outcomes as follows:

> Obviously the big difference is between living and dying; therefore, I'll give the worst eventuality that involves being saved the value 100 and the best eventuality accompanied by death −100. However, a debt of $10,000–$30,000 would make my life miserable for years to come, whereas a $3000–$5000 expense is something I can live with; therefore, I'll put a pretty big gap between 'S & H' and 'S & M'. The difference between $200–$300 and $0 isn't much, while the difference between $200–$300 and $3000–$5000 shouldn't be sneezed at; therefore, I'll give them some values like 140, 148, and 150. On the other hand, if I'm dead, I'm not that concerned about what happens; in fact it makes no difference to me whether or not my children inherit $200–$300 more; therefore, I'll give 'D & L' the same value as 'D & Z'. For the kids to inherit $3000–$5000 does make some difference; therefore, I'll give it a value of −103. If I end up owing $10,000–$30,000 to the doctor, my kids will probably end up inheriting nothing and that does make more of a difference. Still, their quality of life should be mostly a matter of what they earn for themselves and it doesn't bother me that much if they get no inheritance; because the kids benefiting from my hard-earned money is less important than my benefiting from it, I'll give 'D & H' a value of −110.

Given such as assignment, by our notation d(S & M) = 140, d(D & H) = −110, and so on.

The next stage in determining the expected utility of an action A is to determine the probability or chance between 0 and 1 of each possible outcome happening if A is performed. Some assessment will have to be made on the basis of one's epistemic circumstance, and it is beyond the scope of this section to go into a detailed account of probability. However, for our purposes, the requirements for $p_A(O)$—the probability that act A results in outcome O—may be stated as follows:

> For any action A, and any outcome O of the cost/benefit space, a probability $p_A(O)$ between 0 and 1 must be assigned so that (a)–(c) are satisfied.
>
> (a) The more likely outcome of A is assigned a higher probability than a less likely outcome of A.
>
> (b) For each act A and the cost/benefit space $\{O_1, \ldots, O_n\}$,
>
> $$p_A(O_1) + p_A(O_2) + \ldots + p_A(O_n) = 1.$$
>
> (c) If one takes the probability of an action A resulting in C to be x and the outcomes in the cost/benefit space including C are C & $B_1, \ldots,$ C & B_k,
>
> $$p_A(C \,\&\, B_1) + \ldots + p_A(C \,\&\, B_k) = x.$$

For practical purposes one must again rely on estimated figures. Unless required by rules (b) and (c), there is no point in giving figures like 0.738 because such precision cannot be attained; one should rather settle for figures like 0.7. Furthermore, if it is completely justifiable to think that an act A won't result in the outcome O, life is then simplified if one takes $p_A(O) = 0$; similarly, if it is completely justifiable to think that A will result in O, then one should take $p_A(O) = 1$ even if there is a small (but negligible) probability of A failing to result in O.

In our example, let us suppose that it is virtually certain that the cost of the New York or Mayo Clinic specialist is high and that the probability of the specialist saving my life is 0.9. (We are assuming that I'm suffering from an ailment that is somewhat difficult to cure.) In that case, we might take $p_{A1}(S \& H) = 0.9$, $p_{A1}(D \& H) = 0.1$, and the other outcomes to have the probability of 0. Let us suppose that the local hospital is nearly as likely to save my life (say with the likelihood of 0.85), and that although the costs can't be expected to be less than $3000, there is only a 5 percent chance that it will become very high. In this case, we might distribute the 0.85 probability of my survival and the 0.05 chances of the cost becoming high by pursuing act A2 as follows: $p_{A2}(S \& H) = 0.025$, $p_{A2}(S \& M) = 0.825$, $p_{A2}(D \& H) = 0.025$, $p_{A2}(D \& M) = 0.125$, and 0 for the other possible outcomes. Note, as required by rules (b) and (c), the probabilities of the cost/benefit space sum to 1, the probabilities of outcomes involving S sum to 0.85, and the probabilities of outcomes involving H sum to 0.05. Other ways of distributing the probabilities 0.85 and 0.05 are possible and may even be more plausible, but we need not put too fine a point on the matter.

The crude version of the theory that we are presenting may be understood through the following definition and recommendation:

(1) Given a cost/benefit space $\{O_1, \ldots, O_n\}$, the probabilities $p_A(O_i)$, and the desirability rating $d(O_i)$, the EXPECTED UTILITY U(A) of an action A is given by

$$U(A) = p_A(O_1) \times d(O_1) + \ldots + p_A(O_n) \times d(O_n)$$

(2) The (crude) expected utility theory suggests that among a set of contemplated actions one should perform the action with the greatest expected utility.

Using the formula for expected utility and our assignment of desirabilities and probabilities, we arrive at the result that $U(A1) = 79$ and $U(A2) = 102.375$. Thus, the theory in effect tells us that it is better for me to do A2 than A1. If we take the probability of being saved by doing nothing or by relying on a faith healer to be close to 0, A2 has the greatest expected utility among the contemplated actions. Thus if I rely on the theory's recommendation that I should do what has the greatest expected utility, I would conclude that I should go to the local hospital (and hope for the best). Notice, however, that if I take my living or dying to be of paramount value such that financial costs and other efforts are of no significance when life and death are at stake, I would assign all the outcomes involving S the same value, say 100, and all the outcomes involving D some identical lower value, say 0. Then the expected utility of A1 would be 90, whereas the expected utility of A2 would be 85; thus, A1 is what I should do if I assigned such a value to my life.

The theory that expected utility should be maximized is clearly a theory in which the details are both complex and controversial. Beyond that, it is possible to take exception to the idea that expected utility should be maximized. It might, for example, be urged that one must act ethically and that ethics can't be negotiated with considerations of utility. This particular objection, however, is not that telling. Suppose I want to become wealthy and that murdering my aunt is one way in which I could achieve that end. The theory doesn't tell us that the undesirability of murdering my aunt is partially (or wholly) offset by the financial gains to be achieved. For one thing, we could from the beginning rule out murdering as one of the plausible options so that the theory doesn't even touch this as one of the contemplated acts. Alternatively, murder could be treated as having a negative value against which all other values become insignificant; that is, we might treat avoiding murder in the way we treated being saved in our example, in which I placed paramount importance on my life being saved. Other objections to the theory of maximizing expected utility may be more serious. Still, the theory gives us one guideline that can be useful in determining what we should do.

To see this, let us again consider the example in Sections 4.3–4.5. The possible courses of action might be taken to be:

A1: Drastically increase the punishment.
A2: Make a modest increase in the punishment.
A3: Do nothing.

Let us take the possible benefits as D (for effectively deterring crime to a satisfactory level) and N (for not effectively deterring crime to a satisfactory level). The costs might be taken to be H (for high social cost other than the costs of a high crime rate, that is, cost to our sense of justice, hardship on minorities whose crime rate is relatively high, etc.), M (for modest social costs of the sort just mentioned), and L (for little or no additional social costs beyond that of continuing to cope with the high level of crime). The cost/benefit space would then be: D & H, D & M, D & L, N & H, N & M, and N & L.

Ranking these possible outcomes in terms of desirability is going to depend on one's priorities. But the rankings of the following two subsets are fairly uncontroversial:

(1)	D & L	D & M	D & H
(2)	N & L	N & M	N & H

Taking the highest of (2), where should it be inserted in (1)? A law-and-order person might put N & L behind D & H, showing a preference for an acceptably low crime rate at any cost over that of a high crime rate; a civil libertarian might put N & L between D & L and D & M, showing a preference for no increase in punishment whatever effect there may be on the crime rate. Suppose my own inclination is to put N & L between D & M and D & H. My partial preferences can then be simplified to:

(3)	D & L	D & M	N & L	D & H
(4)	N & M	N & H		

Now the question is whether N & M should go before D & H or after it. Suppose I prefer to cope with the present crime rate over handing out twenty-five-year jail sentences or capital punishment to vandals as the author of the letter we studied suggested. Because N & H is the worst possible outcome, the ranking becomes (5), and let us also suppose my numerical value rating to be the one given under (5).

(5)	D & L	D & M	N & L	N & M	D & H	N & H
	100	80	0	−20	−100	−200

In effect this rating involves assigning a positive value of 100 to deterring the crime rate, a negative value of −200 to the high social costs, a negative value of −20 to the moderate social costs, 0 value to little or no social costs and the unchecked crime rate, and simply adding these values. This, for example, results in the continuation of the status quo N & L having the value 0. It must not be assumed that values are always additive in these simple ways, as our earlier hospital example makes clear; however, for the sake of this example this may be good enough.

As for the determination of the probabilities of the cost/benefit space, given my epistemic situation, I can partially rely on my plausibility assessments of Section 4.5, and the virtual certainty that A1 will result in H, A2 in M, and A3 in L. Because I took it to be no more than highly justified that drastically high punishment will be an effective deterrent for crimes like vandalism, p_{A1}(D & H) might be taken as 0.9 and p_{A1}(N & H) as 0.1. Furthermore, I took it to be epistemically neutral that without drastic punishment we will have punishment that is high enough to deter. Thus, we might assign 0.5 to p_{A2}(D & M) and p_{A3}(N & M). Finally, I took it to be highly justified that doing nothing (and relying on demographics and the improvement of the economic circumstances) will not result in a satisfactory crime rate; thus, we might assign 0.1 to $p_{A3}(D \& L)$ and 0.9 to $p_{A3}(N \& L)$.

Under these assignments, the expected utilities are given by: U(A1) = −110, U(A2) = 30, and U(A3) = 10. Thus, given my preferences and assessments, it would appear that I should be urging a moderate increase in the punishment. Keeping the same probability assessments, what would happen to a law-and-order person who assigns values d(D) = 200, d(H) = −100, d(M) = −20, and d(L) = d(N) = 0, and sums these values to arrive at the value rating of the cost/benefit space? The expected utilities would then be: U(A1) = 80, U(A2) = 80, and U(A3) = 20; thus, there would still be no reason to prefer drastic punishment over moderate punishment. For a law-and-order man to be able to urge that we should have drastic punishment, he would have to assign deterrence a positive value that is more than double the social cost of drastic punishment if our probability assessments are basically correct. Granting that the analysis is highly idealized and somewhat artificial, it nevertheless gives some idea of what our values have to be if it is to be the case that we should do something.

One final point may be worth noting. In Section 4.5 I claimed that, from my point of view, if the level of punishment that is severe enough to deter is drastic, then we should not have punishment that is severe enough to deter even if we want a low crime rate. We may try to assess this conditional claim by taking $p_{A2}(N \& M) = p_{A3}(N \& L) = 1$, d(D) = 100, and asking whether future punishment should be drastic according to the expected utility theory. Given the value ratings that I have suggested and the revised probabilities, U(A1) = −110, U(A2) = −20, and U(A3) = 0. Thus, according to the theory under consideration, nothing should be done, and this accords with my claim that under the imagined circumstances we should not seek punishment that is severe enough to deter. Such then is the functioning of a theory that gives us a handle, albeit an imperfect and artificial one, on how to determine what we should do given certain desires or wants.[4]

EXERCISES—SECTION 4.6.1

1. Timmy has used up his allowance already and is thinking of asking his parents for $1 so that he can buy an ice cream cone. The relevant components of benefits and costs are: $1 (Timmy gets $1), $0 (Timmy gets no money), G (Timmy gets grounded), N (Timmy suffers nervousness), and −N (Timmy doesn't suffer nervousness). The possible actions he is contemplating are: A (ask for $1) and −A (don't ask for $1). Make the following assumptions: (1) There is some low probability of Timmy getting grounded even if he doesn't ask, but that

4. Readers wishing to pursue this subject are referred to Ellery Eells, *Rational Decision and Causality*, Cambridge: Cambridge University Press, 1982.

probability is doubled if Timmy does ask (because his parents sometimes get upset at his irresponsibility with money). (2) There is also a low probability that his parents will give him $1 if he asks, but it is three times as likely that they will give him $0 if he asks. (3) Timmy will bear the cost of N if and only if he asks. (4) There is no chance that his parents will give him $1 without him asking. (5) Take d(−N & $0) = 0. (6) Timmy attaches positive desirability to getting the $1 whether or not he bears the cost N; but even the best outcome of getting $1 has a relatively small positive desirability compared to the very high negative desirability he attaches to getting grounded.

(a) Determine the cost/benefit space for the set of contemplated action A and −A.
(b) Give a plausible ranking of the possible outcomes in the cost/benefit space from Timmy's point of view. Say enough to make the ranking plausible.
(c) Give the possible outcomes a numerical desirability rating, and say enough to make such numerical values more or less plausible (in light of the assumptions given above).
(d) For each of the two possible acts, assign more or less plausible probabilities for the various outcomes being achieved by that act. (This must be compatible with the assumptions given above and the constraints on assigning probability values given in the text.)
(e) Given a–d, what should Timmy do according to the (crude) expected utility theory given in the text?

2. The letter to the editor that we have been considering from Section 4.3 talked about making the risk factor for the potential criminals unacceptable. In light of the discussion in this section, this can be seen as urging that the expected utility for stealing be made sufficiently unattractive. To exemplify this, suppose $1000 is available for stealing by a potential criminal, and that he has two possible actions: B (be bad and steal the $1000) and N (do nothing). The outcomes in the cost/benefit space are made up of the components: $K (get $1000), $0 (get $0), P (go to prison or be punished), and F (go free because the police or the court system didn't nail him). Suppose (part of) the relevant data is given by the following chart:

Possible Outcomes	*Desirability Rating*		*Probability Given B*	*Probability Given N*
$K & F	100		z	0
$0 & F	0		0	1
$K & P	x	$(x < 0)$	$(1/3)(1 - z)$	0
$0 & P	$x + .1x$	$(x < 0)$	$(2/3)(1 - z)$	0

(a) In the chart, '$K & P' is meant to suggest that he managed to spend the stolen money or to stash it away before he was apprehended; '$0 & P' is meant to suggest that he was caught with the stolen money or in the process of stealing (with the result that the money was confiscated in addition to him being sent to prison).
  (i) Suggest why the desirability of '$K & P' might be barely more than that of '$0 & P', whereas that of '$K & F' is significantly higher than that of '$0 & F'.
  (ii) What might be the rationale for the probabilities of '$K & P' and '$0 & P' for the act B being set the way they are on the chart?
(b) Set $z = .7$ and $x = -100$, and determine U(N) and U(B).

(c) Set $z = .7$, and determine the value x^* such that if $x < x^*$, U(B) < U(N). [*Hint:* Set U(B) = U(N) and solve for x. This gives the value of x for which B and N have the same expected utility. Remember $-101 < -100$.]
(d) Set $x = -100$, and determine the value z^* such that if $z < z^*$, U(B) < U(N).
(e) Taking the case of $z = .7$ and $x = -100$, determined in b as the starting point, what do the results of c and d show about how B can be made unattractive?

3. It was suggested in Section 4.5 that the crime rate might come down if the economic circumstances of potential criminals improved. To exemplify this, suppose a job that will pay our person $1000 is there for the asking, so that in addition to the two actions considered in exercise 2, a third one is added: G (for being good and working). The outcomes in the cost/benefit space will now have two additional components: W (for the effort used in working) and −W (for no effort used in working). [To simplify, we assume that stealing the $1000 involves no more effort than doing nothing.] With essentially the same assumptions as in exercise 2, the relevant chart becomes:

Possible Outcomes	*Desirability Rating*	*Probability Given B*	*Probability Given N*	*Probability Given G*
$K & F & −W	100	z	0	0
$K & F & W	y	0	0	1
$0 & F & −W	0	0	1	0
$0 & F & W		0	0	0
$K & P & −W	x	$(1/3)(1 - z)$	0	0
$K & P & W		0	0	0
$0 & P & −W	$x + .1x$	$(2/3)(1 - z)$	0	0
$0 & P & W		0	0	0

(a) In this chart, some desirability ratings weren't filled (even with a variable). Why didn't we bother filling those spaces?
(b) Set $z = .7$, $y = 50$, and determine the value x^* such that if $x < x^*$, U(G) > U(B). (Remember $-101 < -100$.)
(c) Set $x = -100$, $y = 50$, and determine the value z^* such that if $z < z^*$, U(G) > U(B).
(d) Set $z = .7$, $x = -100$, and determine the value y^* such that if $y > y^*$, U(G) > U(B).
(e) Exercise 2b showed that when $x = -100$, $z = .7$, and G was not an option, B had greater expected utility than N. The undesirability of the punishment had to be increased or the probability of getting away with stealing $1000 reduced in order for B to cease having the greatest expected utility. Assuming that it is only twice as desirable to steal the $1000 and get away with it than to work for the $1000, how does the result in exercise 2b and c suggest that crime might be reduced without increasing the punishment or decreasing the chances of not getting caught?
(f) How might one interpret the result in exercise 3(d)?

4.6.2 Expanded Square of Opposition

In Chapter 3 we noted that because the deductive validity of an argument may depend on its fine logical structure, an argument may be deductively valid and yet incapable of being shown to be valid if we relied only on its truth functional logical forms. There is of course no effective way of overcoming this shortcoming without presenting more complex deductive systems than the elementary system of chain arguments presented in Chapter 3. However, certain very simple logical relations of a non-truth functional variety may be presented, and these relations can in turn be taken to give us some INT or SM unproblematic claims that can be added as premises in an argument. We present in this subsection those logical relations that can be displayed by the so-called square of opposition.

This square diagrams the logical relations between four types of statements that are traditionally designated as A, E, I, and O. In fact, each of these types might be taken to have three versions, and the relations diagramed by the square hold for each version (with one minor qualification). The three versions of the A, E, I, and O statements may be listed as follows:

A: (1) Being C is true of every B (i.e., all B are C, every B is C).
(2) S is necessary (or S must be true).
(3) Doing N is obligatory (i.e., one must do N).
E: (1) Being C is true of no B (i.e., no B is C, all B fail to be C).
(2) S is impossible (or S can't be true, not-S is necessary).
(3) Doing N is prohibited (i.e., abstaining from N is obligatory).
I: (1) Being C is true of some B (i.e., some B are C).
(2) S is possible (or S can or could be true).
(3) Doing N is permissible.
O: (1) Being C is false of some B (i.e., some B are not C).
(2) Not-S is possible (or S can or could be false).
(3) Failing to do N is permissible.

To make the forms of these statements more perspicuous, for an action N, let's take 'N' to stand for doing N and '−N' to stand for abstaining from (or not doing) N. Then we can represent the three versions of the A, E, I, and O statements as follows:

A: (1) *All B are* [C]
(2) *Necessarily* [S]
(3) *Obligatory to do* [N]

E: (1) *All B are* [−C]
(2) *Necessarily* [−S]
(3) *Obligatory to do* [−N]

I: (1) *Some B are* [C]
(2) *Possibly* [S]
(3) *Permissible to do* [N]

O: (1) *Some B are* [−C]
(2) *Possibly* [−S]
(3) *Permissible to do* [−N]

A final simplification can be achieved by letting 'A' stand for the italicized operators involved in the A form and 'I' stand for the italicized operators involved in the I form. In fact, we can be somewhat more liberal and allow 'A' to stand for more complex operators like '(It is) obligatory for Tom to do'. However, it must be understood that in any context of work, given an 'A' operator with a certain reading (e.g., 'necessarily' or 'obligatory for Tom to') the 'I' operator must be given the corresponding reading (i.e., 'possibly' or 'permissible for Tom to'). The A, E, I, O forms then become:

A:	$A[\phi]$	E:	$A[-\phi]$
I:	$I[\phi]$	O:	$I[-\phi]$

A = All B are, necessarily, obligatory (for P) to do.
I = Some B are, possible, permissible (for P) to do.

Given a scheme of abbreviation for 'A', 'I', and ϕ, we shall take these to be the logical forms of statements having the A, E, I, O structure.

Before proceeding to the square of opposition, we should point out that 'S is necessary' and 'S is possible' can have a number of different readings. Perhaps the most obvious is 'S is true in all possible worlds' and 'S is true in some possible worlds'. It can also be read in terms of physical or natural necessity or possibility, that is, in terms of what must happen or what can happen given our physical world (and the physical constitutions of the objects involved). Thus, 'The sun must rise' might be rendered as 'Necessarily [the sun rises]', and 'She can bear children' might be rendered as 'Possibly [she bears children]'. Another reading of 'necessary' and 'possible' involves an epistemic reading. We might take S to be epistemically necessary if given what is known, the truth of S is assured, and we might take S to be epistemically possible if the truth of S isn't precluded by what is known. Thus, given an epistemic reading of the operators, 'necessarily [S]' (or 'for P, necessarily [S]') becomes S is completely justified (for P), and 'possibly [S]' (or 'for P, possibly [S]') becomes −S (or the falsity of S) isn't completely justified (for P).

Given this background, the traditional square of opposition may be diagrammed as in Figure 4.4. Thus, I is a subalternation of A, A and O are contradictories, A and E contraries, I and O subcontraries, and so on.[5]

These names don't really matter but it's a handy way of drawing the diagram. Two statements are contraries when they can't both be true (although they might be both false), two statements are subcontraries when they can't both be false (although they might both be true), two

5. The full degree to which the traditional square of opposition can be expanded was first pointed out to me by Robert Fogelin, *Evidence and Meaning: Studies in Analytic Philosophy,* New York: Humanities Press, 1967, pp. 12–24.

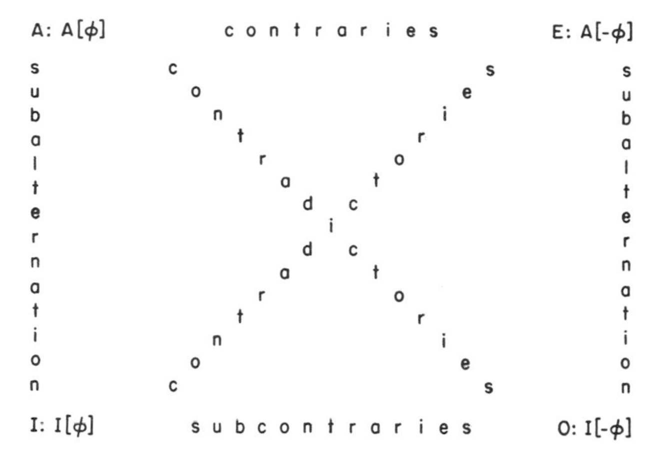

Figure 4.4. Traditional square of opposition.

statements are contradictories if one has the logically identical truth conditions as the negation of the other (and vice versa), and if 'S*' is a subalternation of 'S', 'S / S*' is deductively valid. Thus, those are the relationships given by the diagram. There is, however, one exception to the diagram that needs to be noted. For version (1) of the A, E, I, and O statements (i.e., 'All B are C', 'No B is C'), the assumption that there is at least one B is needed for the relations except for the contradictory relation, which is exceptionless. For example, 'All unicorns have one horn / some unicorns have one horn (i.e., there are unicorns with one horn)' shouldn't be deductively valid.

The relations just discussed might be summarized by saying that the statements of the following form are true in all possible worlds and may be treated as INT or SM unproblematic claims (depending on whether one can "see" that these relations have got to be right or must take the statements as expert testimony given by the text):

	From:
$A[\phi] \equiv -I[-\phi]$.	Contradictories
$A[-\phi] \equiv -I[\phi]$.	Contradictories
$[b \supset\ ]\ -(A[\phi]\ \&\ A[-\phi])$.	Contraries
$[b \supset\ ]\ -(-I[\phi]\ \&\ -I[-\phi])$.	Subcontraries
$[b \supset\ ]\ A[\phi] \supset I[\phi]$.	Subalternation
$[b \supset\ ]\ A[-\phi] \supset I[-\phi]$.	Subalternation

b: 'There are B's'.
'b ⊃ ' is needed when A is 'All B's are' and I is 'Some B's are'.

The upshot is that when we are constructing chains, we may appeal to any line of the above form by 'Pr', because we know that such a missing premise is always completely justified. Because these are special missing premises derived from the square of opposition, we shall use the notation 'Pr[S]' to justify a line that uses one of the above forms.

To exemplify this, consider the following argument:

(1) If Tom is a vegetarian, Tom is prohibited from eating meat.
(2) Tom ate meat with great delight and no guilt.
(3) If Tom ate meat with great delight and no guilt, Tom is allowed to eat meat.
(4) If Tom is a Buddhist and not a vegetarian, some Buddhists aren't vegetarians.
(5) All Buddhists are vegetarians.

---

(6) Tom is not a Buddhist.

When dealing with arguments like this, it is absolutely essential that a clear scheme of abbreviation be given, especially for the 'A' and 'I' operators and the expressions they govern. Thus, we specify a scheme of abbreviation as follows:

A1: It is obligatory for Tom to do. (I1: It is permissible for Tom to do.)
E: Eating meat.
A2: All Buddhists are. (I2: Some Buddhists are.)
V: Vegetarians.
d: Tom ate meat with great delight and no guilt.
v: Tom is a vegetarian.
b: Tom is a Buddhist.

Notice, specifying the scheme for an 'A' operator automatically specifies a scheme for the corresponding 'I' operator. Given this scheme, the argument becomes:

$v \supset A1[-E]$

d

$d \supset I1[E]$

$(b \,\&\, -v) \supset I2[-V]$

$A2[V]$

$-b$

The following chain argument shows this argument to be valid when it is augmented by the indicated missing premises:

(1)	d	Pr
(2)	$d \supset I1[E]$	Pr
(3)	$I1[E]$	(1)(2)MP
(4)	$A1[-E] \equiv -I1[E]$	Pr[S]

(5)	$(A1[-E] \supset -I1[E])$ &	
	$(-I1[E] \supset A1[-E])$	(4) $\equiv / \supset$
(6)	$A1[-E] \supset -I1[E]$	(5)S
(7)	$-A1[-E]$	(3)(6)MT
(8)	$v \supset A1[-E]$	Pr
(9)	$-v$	(7)(8)MT
(10)	$A2[V]$	Pr
(11)	$A2[V] \equiv -I2[-V]$	Pr[S]
(12)	$(A2[V] \supset -I2[-V])$ &	
	$(-I2[-V] \supset A2[V])$	(11) $\equiv / \supset$
(13)	$A2[V] \supset -I2[-V]$	(12)S
(14)	$-I2[-V]$	(10)(13)MP
(15)	$(b \,\&\, -v) \supset I2(-V)$	Pr
(16)	$-(b \,\&\, -v)$	(14)(15)MT
(17)	$b \supset v$	(16) $-(\&)/\supset$
(18)	$-b$	(9)(17)MT

Other cases go similarly except when the operators are 'all' and 'some' and we are not using the contradictory relation. In such cases, we need to add a missing premise like 'b' (for 'There are some B's') that may or may not be completely justified, so that we can use, for example, the always justified missing premise 'b ⊃ (A[C] ⊃ I[C])' in which 'A' is 'All B are'.

Modal Fallacies. The operators 'necessarily' and 'possibly' as applied to statements are called modal operators, and they are usually abbreviated by '□' and '◇', respectively. The following two fallacious inferences involving them should be noted:

[A] $\dfrac{\Box (p \supset q)}{p \supset \Box q}$ [B] $\dfrac{\Diamond p \,\&\, \Diamond q}{\Diamond (p \,\&\, q)}$

Understanding '□ p' as "p' is true in every possible world', the following example should be convincing that [A] is fallacious.

□ (Reagan is a president ⊃ Reagan is a president)
___
Reagan is a president ⊃ □ (Reagan is a president).

That the conclusion is false can be seen by the truth of statements like 'Although Reagan is a president, it is possible that he shouldn't have become a president' and 'Although Reagan is a president, he might not have been a president'. Put another way, the conclusion asserts: if Reagan is in fact a president (in our actual world), then Reagan is a president in every possible world. The premise on the other hand simply asserts 'In every possible world, if Reagan is a president (in that world), Reagan is a president (in that world)', which is obviously true. Thus, the premise of the argument is true and the conclusion false. What makes this fallacy tempting is that in the following sequence of statements, each can be heard to reassert the previous one:

(a) If Reagan is a president, it necessarily follows from this that Reagan is a president.
(b) If Reagan is a president, Reagan must be a president.
(c) If Reagan is a president, necessarily [it is a necessary truth that] Reagan is a president.

But (a) is of the form 'Necessarily (if p, then p)', whereas (c) is of the form 'If p, then (necessarily p)', and perhaps because (b) can be heard both ways, one is misled into thinking that (c) can be inferred from (a).

That the argument form [B] is fallacious should be more obvious: 'Possibly I will marry her and possibly I will not marry her' can be true, whereas the conclusion 'Possibly (I will marry and not marry her)' plainly cannot be true. Somewhat similar to this modal fallacy would be the fallacy 'Doing N is permissible and doing M is permissible / Doing N and M is permissible'. Clearly, being married to Jane at time t is permissible and being married to Jill at time t is permissible but being married to both Jane and Jill at time t is not permissible. Because the operators 'obligatory to' and 'permissible to' are sometimes called "deontic operators," this version of the fallacy might be called a "deontic fallacy." The modal and deontic fallacies discussed are clearly inferential fallacies; thus, if we let '◇' represent the modal operator 'possibly' as well as the deontic operator 'permissible to', our discussion may be summarized as follows:

MODAL FALLACY WITH □: $\Box(p \supset q) \rightarrow p \supset \Box q$.
MODAL/DEONTIC FALLACY WITH ◇: $\Diamond p \;\&\; \Diamond q \rightarrow \Diamond(p \;\&\; q)$.
◇ = possibly, permissible to

The modal operators 'necessarily' and 'possibly' as well as the deontic operators 'permissible' and 'obligatory' must be handled carefully to avoid these fallacies.

EXERCISES—SECTION 4.6.2

Part A

For each of the following arguments: (1) clearly specify a scheme of abbreviation, (2) extract the argument, and (3) by means of a chain argument show the argument to be deductively valid when augmented by missing premises derived from the square of opposition (and a missing premise concerning the existence of certain objects if needed).

1. Tom is a male chauvinist. After all, all men are male chauvinists, and if Tom isn't a male chauvinist, some men aren't male chauvinists.
2. If it is possible for her to have children, she will have had children. But she didn't have children. So, she can't have children.
3. A losing warrior in Japan wasn't prohibited from committing suicide. After all, it was obligatory for a losing warrior in Japan to commit suicide.
4. It isn't true that some children are evil. Therefore, some children are not evil.
5. It is permissible for Jane not to eat fish. After all, Jane is a vegetarian, and if she is a vegetarian, she is prohibited from eating fish.
6. [Let P be 'People have psychic powers'.] If Tom is completely justified in believing that Yayoi has psychic powers, Tom is completely justified in believing that P is true. But all people are completely justified in believing that P is false. If Tom isn't completely justified in believing that P is false, some people aren't completely justified in believing that P is false. Therefore, Tom isn't completely justified in believing that Yayoi has psychic powers.

   Hint: Use two A operators with one on 'P' and one on 'completely justified in believing that P is false'.

Part B[6]

Indicating how the modal or deontic operators are understood, analyze the modal or deontic fallacies committed in the following passages. When committing the fallacy is an intermediate step to drawing the final conclusion, briefly indicate how that final conclusion is drawn from the intermediate conclusion.

1. My vase is unbreakable, that is, it cannot be broken. After all, my vase is in perfect condition, and if it is in perfect condition, it cannot be broken.
2. Given what he has told us, we can't rule out that he was at the vault when the money was stolen, and given what we know of his character, we can't rule out that he stole the money if he was at the vault when the money was stolen. Therefore, we can't rule out that he stole the money.
3. In general, if one is to know 'p', 'p' must be true. Thus, for her to know that he loves her, he must love her. Yet it could be false that he loves her. Thus, she doesn't know that he loves her.
4. Because this is a public school, we are allowed to attend it. And surely the freedom of expression allows us to wear what we want. Therefore, the school's dress code denies what we must be allowed to do, that is, wear what we want and attend school.
5. It is true that Billy stole the car, but he can't be blamed for it. His theft of the car was caused by the poor environment in which he grew up. That is, given his background, he was bound to steal the car. In short, nothing could have prevented his theft of the car, because it was impossible for him to do otherwise. Because one can be held responsible for doing something only if one could have done otherwise, Billy can't be blamed.

---

6. Some of the exercise examples are taken from, or adapted from, a discussion by Stephen N. Thomas, "A Modal Muddle," in *Determinism, Free Will, and Moral Responsibility* (Gerald Dworkin, ed.), Englewood Cliffs, N.J.: Prentice-Hall, 1970, pp. 141–48.

4.7 Related Fallacies

In this section we wish to present a number of fallacies that often occur in the context of an argument that one is presenting, or reading or hearing from another. The six fallacies listed in this section, along with those discussed in Chapter 2 and those relating to language that will be covered in Chapter 6, constitute the most frequent fallacies committed in an argumentative context. Fallacies (1), (2), (4), and (5) of this section, as well as some of the fallacies presented elsewhere in the text, could be called fallacies of non sequitur, that is, the fallacy committed when the conclusion doesn't follow from the premises. However, precisely because non sequitur is a characterization of so many fallacies, it is a relatively useless way of analyzing what has gone wrong with an argument. Thus, the reader should always try to give an analysis that is more specific than non sequitur in analyzing a fallacy. With this background, we present the following six fallacies:

(1) Fallacy of Division. When a father learns that his son's team had a big victory, he is likely to say, "Good game, son!"—which indicates he inferred that his son played well from his team having played well. Again, a stockholder is likely to be delighted by the news that the Dow Jones went up thirty points today, which indicates he inferred that his stocks had done well from the market as a whole having done well.[7] In both of these cases, something being true of a part is inferred from that thing being true of the whole. But something can be true of the whole without being true of its parts: Although a song may have a nice melody, clearly none of its notes can have a fine melody. Similarly, the son's team may have played well without his son having played well, and the stock market as a whole (or the average price of all stocks) may have gone up without the stockholder's stocks (or the average price of his stocks) having gone up. The FALLACY OF DIVISION is said to have been committed when *something that is true of the whole is thereby taken to be true of its parts.*

The Fallacy of Division is clearly an inferential fallacy where something is mistakenly taken to be a good reason for something else. Thus, we represent it as follows:

Fallacy of Division
C is true of the whole W → C is true of the parts of W.

7. The market as a whole having gone up is itself an inference from the Dow having gone up; but we are not concerned with this inference at this moment.

Thus, faced with the argument "The average income of Americans is $20,000; therefore, the average income of black Americans is $20,000," we would analyze it as:

Division: 'having an average income of $20,000' is true of Americans as a whole → 'having an average income of $20,000' is true of the subclass of black Americans.

Another instance of this inferential fallacy might be the persistent prejudice that the only "real" Americans are Americans of European origin. At least some bigots may be committing the following fallacy:

Division: 'having an origin that can be traced back to Europe' is true of America as a nation → 'having an origin that can be traced back to Europe' is true of the people (who are the real or genuine components) of America.

(2) Fallacy of Composition. There is at least a spurious persuasiveness in the idea that ordinary things are really colorless because the atoms that make them up are colorless. Similarly, at least some people seem to have been persuaded of God's existence by the idea that because everything in the universe has a cause, the universe as a whole must also have a cause. The form of these inferences is the reverse of the inference form involved in the Fallacy of Division. That is, in our examples, something being true of the whole is inferred from that same thing being true of its parts. Clearly this reverse inference is also fallacious: although every county of California has a smaller population than the entire state, the state of California does not have a smaller population than the entire state. In general, the FALLACY OF COMPOSITION is said to be committed when *what is true of the parts of the whole is thereby taken to be true of the whole.* This inferential fallacy may thus be represented as:

Fallacy of Composition
C is true of the parts of W → C is true of W.

As an example, consider: There is not a single cell in me that is more than seven years old. Therefore, I am not more than seven years old. The fallacy committed in this argument may be analyzed as:

Composition: 'being less than seven years old' is true of each cell which is a part of me → 'being less than seven years old' is true of me.

With the "Pepsi Challenge," in which people are asked to choose between Pepsi and Coke on the basis of one sip, something akin to the Fallacy of Composition may be involved (as some ads for Coke have suggested). If Pepsi is sweeter, then a single sip of Pepsi may be preferred over a single sip of Coke by the majority of the people. But it is possible that drinking a whole bottle of Coke would be preferred on the basis of it being more refreshing, because it is not too sweet. The fallacy that seems to be implicit in the "Pepsi Challenge" may be analyzed as:

Composition: 'being tastier' is true of sips of Pepsi relative to sips of Coke → 'being tastier' is true of a whole bottle of Pepsi relative to a whole bottle of Coke.

A somewhat more subtle example of the Fallacy of Composition may be the speed with which people tend to accept Heraclitus's claim that one cannot step into the same river twice. If one day I should go into the water from the banks of the Nile, and repeat this the next day, haven't I stepped into the Nile twice? Why then does Heraclitus's claim seem so plausible? Let P1 and P2 be two adjacent places where the Nile runs, and let W1–W4 be collections of water molecules that could occupy P1 and P2. Looking at three successive moments of time t1–t3, the configuration of water at a place might be as follows:

t1:	W2	W1	t2:	W3	W2	t3:	W4	W3
	P1	P2		P1	P2		P1	P2

Here we are imagining that the river flows in the direction of P1 to P2 and that W1 is the earliest quantity of water to reach P2 while W4 is the latest. If we imagine momentary diagrams of this kind for the entire Nile, each diagram might be thought to represent a temporal stage of the Nile. The Nile, which persists through time, can then be thought to be composed of its temporal stages. Now what is clear is that one cannot step into the same temporal stage of the Nile twice because the water moves on. To conclude from this that one cannot step into the Nile twice would be to commit a fallacy that may now be analyzed as

Composition: 'not being able to step into it twice' is true of the temporal stages of the Nile → 'not being able to step into it twice' is true of the Nile.

(Presumably all that is required in order to step into the Nile twice is to step into two water–location combinations, each of which is a stage of the Nile—a river that is composed of such stages.)[8]

(3) Fallacy of Accident. Upon first hearing of Newton's first law of motion, one thinks that there must be something wrong with it. The law of motion states that if an object is moving with a certain velocity in a certain direction, it will keep moving in that direction with that velocity forever. If I let go of the accelerator on a flat road, my car soon comes to a halt; therefore, isn't Newton's first law just mistaken? To understand this kind of situation properly, we must recognize that most generaliza-

8. This analysis is derived from W. V. O. Quine, "Identity, Ostension, and Hypostasis," in *From a Logical Point of View,* Cambridge, Mass.: Harvard University Press, 1953.

tions with which we are acquainted come with explicit or *implicit* qualifications like "under normal conditions," "under standard temperature and pressure," "under white-light illumination," "in the absence of interfering or overriding factors," and "other things being equal *(ceteris paribus).*" Though normally left implicit, Newton's first law comes with the qualification 'in the absence of resistance or other interfering factors'; thus, when there is friction or air resistance, as there is on the highway, the law does not directly apply. The thought that there must be something wrong with Newton's law involved mistakenly applying the law to a case it wasn't intended to cover. Such an application of a generalization is said to commit the Fallacy of Accident, and committing the fallacy usually results from forgetting about the (often implicit) qualification that is attached to a generalization.

In general, we commit the FALLACY OF ACCIDENT when *we accept a claim on the basis of applying a generalization to a case in which the circumstances make the generalization inapplicable.* Thus, we typically commit the Fallacy of Accident when we apply a generalization to an instance when the conditions are abnormal, or interfering factors are present, or other things aren't equal. Of course, inferences from generalizations to their applications are normally reliable; however, there is also the presupposition that the case at hand is one of the intended applications of the generalization. Thus, the Fallacy of Accident is best seen as a presuppositional fallacy that may be represented as:

> Fallacy of Accident
>
> A generalization G → an application of G to an instance I; *not* {the circumstances allow G to be applicable to I}*
>
> *The inapplicability of the generalization should be explained.

Thus, our initial example would be analyzed as follows:

Accident: Newton's first law → Newton's first law applies to the car on the highway; *not* {Newtons' first law can be applied to the car}.

- Newton's first law is inapplicable to the car, because the law has the qualification that there are no interfering factors, and there is friction and air resistance to the car on the highway.

A common source of the Fallacy of Accident may be exemplified by the following example: "It's a few minutes before nine; because I promised to play bridge at nine o'clock I shouldn't stop to save this drowning child." The fallacy committed in this line of thought may be analyzed as:

Accident: One shouldn't break one's promises → I shouldn't break the promise to play bridge in order to save this drowning child; *not* {'One shouldn't break one's promises' applies to this instance where there is a drowning child}

- The general requirement that promises shouldn't be broken has a tacit qualification like "other things being equal" or "in the absence of an overriding obligation." When there is a drowning child, other things are not equal, because there is an overriding obligation to save the child.

Virtually all obligations come with some qualification like 'in the absence of an overriding obligation', and to ignore this qualification often leads one to commit the Fallacy of Accident. The oft-heard excuse of Nazi officers that they were only following the orders of their superiors is a case in point, in that although one has an obligation to obey one's superiors, this obligation is overridden by the obligation to respect the minimal human rights of other people.

(4) Fallacy of Irrelevant Conclusion *(Ignoratio Elenchi).* Most of us have probably encountered a man who claims that he is going to prove that men are superior to women, and then goes on to cite various statistics and records that indeed establish that on the average men can lift heavier things, run faster, jump higher, and so on. Faced with such an argument, it is distressing to see some women respond that Martina Navratilova can beat a lot of men in tennis, that few men can keep up with Mary Decker, and so on, as if the point would have to be conceded if it turned out that men were physically stronger than women in most respects. A far better response is to admit that he may have established that men are stronger than women in many or most ways, and then point out that this does nothing to prove the announced conclusion because this conclusion is far from being decisively relevant to establishing the superiority of men. *The* FALLACY OF *Ignoratio Elenchi or Irrelevant Conclusion is committed when a claim that is irrelevant to the conclusion is argued.*

From this account, it is evident that the Fallacy of *Ignoratio Elenchi* is a fallacy of relevance. The problem with the general characterization of the Fallacy of Irrelevant Conclusion is that any fallacy of relevance can be seen as the Fallacy of Irrelevant Conclusion. It is therefore best to give a narrower characterization of the fallacy, so that it can be distinguished from the other fallacies of relevance like *Argumentum ad Populum* and Emotional Appeals. For our purpose, then, we shall understand the Fallacy of Irrelevant Conclusion or *Ignoratio Elenchi* as follows:

Fallacy of Irrelevant Conclusion

$C^o \rightsquigarrow C$: C^o is argued and C isn't, 'C if C^o' is implausible when made explicit*, and C and C^o have a superficial similarity*.

*One should explain why the conditional is implausible and what the similarity between C and C^o consists in.

In this definition the clause "'C if C°' is implausible when made explicit" expresses C° being an irrelevant conclusion, and the fallacy is trading on never making this implausible conditional explicit. The material after the colon in this and other representations of fallacies indicates additional specifications that have to be met for something to be an instance of the fallacy. Correspondingly, analyzing a passage to commit the fallacy should indicate that these additional specifications are met.

Given this understanding of *Ignoratio Elenchi,* the example with which we started may be analyzed as follows:

Irrelevant Conclusion: Men are physically superior to women (C°) ⇝ Men are superior to women (C).

- C° is argued for while C isn't.
- C if C° is implausible once made explicit; after all, being physically superior doesn't amount to being a superior human being.
- C and C° are superficially similar because both talk about superiority.

I once heard a lecture by a man from a TV advertising agency in which he tried to convince the audience that *The Beverly Hillbillies* was a classy TV show; he rested his case after having produced data on the relative longevity of the show, the average Nielsen ratings over the years, and so on. The fallacy he committed may be analyzed as:

Irrelevant Conclusion: The Beverly Hillbillies was one of the most popular TV shows (C°) ⇝ It was a classy show (C).

- C° is argued for while C isn't.
- C if C° is implausible once made explicit; we know all too well that being popular is insufficient for having class.
- C and C° are superficially similar because both involve positive evaluations.

Aside from the superficial similarity between C and C° and never explicitly stating 'C if C°', these examples exemplify another feature of the psychological dynamics that often accompanies the *Ignoratio Elenchi;* that is, because a great deal of argumentation or data is presented to establish the irrelevant conclusion C°, by the time the listener has gone through all of this, he or she has half forgotten what was supposed to be established. Perhaps this is the reason the listener often argues about C° instead of pointing out that the Fallacy of Irrelevant Conclusion has been committed.

(5) Fallacy of *Argumentum ad Hominem.* When an admiral argues for the need to have a strong navy, pacifists as well as air force generals may reject the argument out of hand just because an admiral is proposing the argument. Even when perfectly good reasons have been proposed, an audience can be led to reject the conclusion when someone points out that the speaker is a Communist, or an ex-con, or a member of the Moral Majority. In rejecting someone's view on such a basis, one is said to commit the Fallacy of *Argumentum ad Hominem,* or the fallacy of arguing against the person rather than the view espoused. After all, despite his interest in the navy, the admiral may have a good argument for our need to have a strong navy, and even a Communist, or an ex-con, or a member of the Moral Majority can have a sound view or decent argument on some particular matter; their arguments or views should not be rejected without examination.

We shall define the FALLACY OF *Argumentum ad Hominem* as one in which *a view or an argument of an opponent is rejected on the basis of features of the opponent that are not decisively relevant to the correctness of the view or argument proposed.* Clearly, this is again a fallacy of relevance and we shall represent it as follows:

Fallacy of *Argumentum ad Hominem*
Person P has feature F ⇝ rejection of P's view or position V.

Thus if a pacifist rejects the admiral's view by saying, "But he is part of the war machine," the fallacy would be analyzed as:

Ad Hominem: The admiral is part of the war machine ⇝ rejection of the admiral's view that we need a strong navy.

If the air force general rejects the admiral's view by saying, "But of course he's interested in advancing the navy," the fallacy would be analyzed as:

Ad Hominem: The admiral is interested in the navy's cause ⇝ rejection of the admiral's view that we need a strong navy.

Perhaps the most frequent type of *ad Hominem* fallacy involves abusing one's opponent with such appellations as male chauvinist pig, or ultraconservative, or son of a bitch. Among these abusive types of *ad Hominem* fallacies are two kinds of cases that should be distinguished. Sometimes the trait about the opponent cited is quite irrelevant to the view involved. To reject (or urge rejecting) the view that we should have competent teachers, because an ultraconservative or a son of bitch urged it, would be to reject a view on utterly irrelevant criteria. However, often the trait cited about the opponent consists of a certain prejudice or a clear advantage to be gained by the opponent if his view is adopted. For instance, suppose a male chauvinist, known for the virulence of his stance, proposes an argument against affirmative action; this predisposition of the person may not be entirely irrelevant to the issue involved. His prejudice should perhaps be grounds for being extra careful with his proposed argument, so that a clever maneuver isn't effective. However, to reject his argument on the basis of his known predisposition is to commit the Fallacy of *Argumentum ad Hominem,* because such a predisposition doesn't preclude the possibility that he has produced an effective argument and as such this prejudice isn't decisively relevant to the correctness of the argument. Of course we are all short of time, and given a certain past history of the advocate, one may not bother with the argument on the basis of the assumption that this argument will most likely contain an unwarranted prejudicial step. This, however, is a very dangerous move; one should be very careful to acknowledge that to use such a shortcut in daily life is in effect to postpone an examination of the argument under the pressures of time rather than rejecting it on the solid grounds of reason.

Not all forms of the *ad Hominem* fallacy are of the abusive kind. If X presents a view C, one might reject it or urge others to reject it because X also accepts the view C*, and C* is incompatible with C. For example, if a Republican advocates strict federal laws on pornography, one might argue that the suggestion should be rejected because, as a Republican, he believes in reducing the federal bureaucracy (and federal laws on pornography would have the opposite effect of increasing the role of the federal government). To argue in this fashion is to commit the *ad Hominem* fallacy, which may be analyzed as:

Ad Hominem: The Republican believes in reducing the federal bureaucracy $\rightsquigarrow$ the federal bureaucracy should be reduced (and his position on pornography be rejected because it would increase the bureaucracy).

If it is really true that the role of the federal government should be reduced, this would be a reason for rejecting the proposed pornography law. The argument as presented simply relies on the Republican believing in a minimal federal role; but the truth of the matter may be that the pornography law should be adopted and the blanket view on a minimal federal role be rejected. Another closely related form of the *ad Hominem* fallacy would be to dismiss the criticism by some person O of me for doing N on the grounds that O does the same sort of thing. Again, the truth of the matter could well be that I shouldn't do N and that O shouldn't do the same sort of thing either. Thus, the feature about the opponent to which we point in order to reject his view or argument could be the opponent's own actions or other views. But as long as the actions or the other views could be incorrect, we lack decisive reasons for rejecting the opponent's currently proposed view or argument.

Of course the nonabusive form of the *ad Hominem* fallacy indeed constitutes a legitimate criticism that an opponent doesn't practice what he preaches or that the totality of his views are inconsistent. But to go from this criticism to the conclusion that his current view or argument should be rejected is to commit the *ad Hominem* fallacy, in which one is arguing against the person rather than the view or argument currently presented by the opponent. On the other hand, the sound criticism that the totality of the opponent's views is inconsistent or that he doesn't practice what he preaches can be a legitimate invitation to investigate whether the current view of the opponent should be rejected or his other views or practices be altered.

(6) Fallacy of Begging the Question. Suppose in the context of a discussion about the relative merits of various baseball players someone argues: Because no one else was nearly as good a hitter as Babe Ruth, Babe Ruth was clearly the greatest hitter. This piece of reasoning is not very likely to convince someone who was urging that Ty Cobb was the greatest hitter. Muhammad Ali's colorful statements of the past like, "I'm going to whup Frazier because I am the greatest," were unlikely to reassure those who had doubts about his chances of winning. If we spell out these arguments, they become:

[1] No one else was nearly as good a hitter as Babe Ruth.
―――――――――――――――
Babe Ruth was the greatest hitter.

[2] Ali is the greatest boxer.
If Ali is the greatest boxer, Ali will beat Frazier.
―――――――――――――――
Ali will beat Frazier.

There is no doubt that the two arguments are deductively valid. What then is wrong with these arguments? The person who is urging that Ty Cobb was the greatest hitter will complain that the premise of [1] simply assumes the very point of contention in favor of Ruth. As for [2], although his doubters would have granted that Ali would beat Frazier if he was the greatest, they had doubts as to whether Ali (still) was the greatest; thus the first premise of [2] simply assumed that their doubts about the conclusion were unfounded.

[1] and [2] are examples of the FALLACY OF BEGGING THE QUESTION, and at least the general idea of this fallacy is that *the argument assumes in one of the premises the correctness of the very point that is to be established.* Other names for this fallacy are "The Fallacy of *Petitio Principii*" and "The Fallacy of (presenting) a Circular Argument." Under whatever name, clearly an argument that commits this fallacy is defective, in that it is powerless to convince those who aren't already convinced of the conclusion, and it is typically useless for those already convinced of the conclusion because it fails to provide them with any additional reasons for accepting the conclusion.

Postponing for a moment a more exact specification of the Fallacy of Begging the Question, we should first note what kind of a fallacy it is. Because (as in the case of [1] and [2]) an argument committing the fallacy is typically valid, it is neither an inferential fallacy nor a fallacy of relevance. In some vague sense it might be thought of as a presuppositional fallacy; however, our understanding of a presuppositional fallacy is that an argument committing it would have been legitimate if the unsatisfied presupposition could have been added as a missing premise. Because [1] and [2] are valid, the problem with them is not a matter of missing premises; rather, the problem centers on being able to accept one of the given premises, that is, the premise that begs the question. Let us therefore introduce the fourth and final category of fallacies, or the FALLACIES OF

SUBSTANCE. If we think of the issues of validity and support as having to do with the form of the argument, we can think of the issues surrounding the truth and acceptability of the premises as having to do with the matter or substance of the argument. A fallacy of substance then *involves some flaw that in the context of the argument undermines the plausibility or acceptability of the premises.* Fallacies of substance and their abbreviating diagram may generally be understood as follows:

> Fallacies of Substance
>
> $R_1, \ldots, R_n$ / c The argument fails to establish its conclusion
> └── F because in the context of the argument flaw F undermines the plausibility or acceptability of the premises.

Given 'I'm going to whup Frazier because I am the greatest', at least as a first shot, we would analyze the fallacy as follows:

Begging the Question:

Ali is the greatest boxer.
If Ali is the greatest boxer, Ali will beat Frazier.
———
Ali will beat Frazier.
└── The first premise simply assumes that any doubt about the conclusion is unfounded.

Although the general idea of the Fallacy of Begging the Question should by now be fairly obvious, its precise specification is rather difficult. In our examples of *petitio principii,* the argument is valid or easily becomes valid with the addition of some missing premise; this must be generally true when one begs the question, because to beg the question is to assume the correctness of the very conclusion to be established. On the other hand, in any valid argument, if all the premises are true, the conclusion must be true; thus, in some sense, the conclusion is contained in all the premises combined and one can't accept all the premises without accepting the conclusion. Yet it is clear that not all valid arguments beg the question. The upshot is that some valid arguments beg the question and others don't, and the difficulty is to characterize the Fallacy of Begging the Question in such a way that genuine cases are picked out without condemning all valid arguments to be instances of begging the question.

Certainly a central feature of begging the question is that some *single* premise of the argument assumes the correctness of the conclusion to be established. This has led some people to suggest the following definition:

(i) An argument begs the question if and only if the conclusion is one of the premises of the argument.

Certainly any argument that begs the question by this account would intuitively be regarded as begging the question. For example, 'Ruth is the greatest hitter / Ruth is the greatest hitter' clearly begs the question. However, by this account, neither argument [1] above nor 'Ruth is the greatest hitter and hit sixty home runs in one season / Ruth is the greatest hitter' begs the question. Strictly speaking, both 'No one else was nearly as good a hitter as Ruth' and 'Ruth is the greatest hitter and hit sixty home runs' are distinct from 'Ruth is the greatest hitter'. Thus, the single premises of the two arguments are distinct from their conclusions, and (i) is too narrow an account of begging the question.

To circumvent the difficulty, one might try the account:

(ii) An argument begs the question if and only if one of its premises is a deductively valid reason for the conclusion.

This will take care of the counterexamples of the last paragraph. But by this account the question is not begged by either argument [2] or

[3] (1) Capitalism embraces a free-enterprise economy and communism supports a state-controlled economy.
(2) If (1) is true, capitalism is preferable to communism.
―――――――――――――――――――――――
(3) Capitalism is preferable to communism.

In both [2] and [3] no single premise is a valid reason for the conclusion, because both premises are needed in order to have a valid reason for the conclusion. But if the conjunction of the premises being a valid reason for the conclusion is taken to be the grounds for [2] and [3] begging the question, then all valid arguments would be condemned as begging the question. Clearly, we have to get back to the idea that a *single* premise begs the question. However, what complicates the matter is that while [2] and [3] both have the same structure of *modus ponens,* [2] seems to beg the question in its first premise ('Ali is the greatest') and [3] seems to beg the question in the second premise.

To isolate the question-begging premise, it is best to think of the argument as being presented in a context in which one is arguing with a person who holds a conflicting view and thereby denies the conclusion. Someone who thought that Frazier was going to beat Ali was not questioning that *if* Ali were the greatest, Ali would beat Frazier. Given this agreement, the claim that Ali was the greatest amounted to, or was tantamount to, denying the opposing view that Frazier was going to beat Ali. In the case of [3], a communist and a capitalist are not going to disagree about premise (1), because that premise is unproblematic for both. Given this agreement, the communist is going to complain that premise (2) amounts to a denial of his view that communism is better than capitalism. Thus, we can try to understand the matter as follows: In the context of an argument with a conflicting view C^o, the question-begging premise amounts to a denial of C^o. At least as a rough guide we can understand P "amounts" to a denial of C° as: P along with unproblematic claims accepted by the participants to the debate constitute deductively valid reasons for not-C°.

There is, however, one final complication to be faced. Suppose A asks, "Why should I respect the human rights of my enemies?", thereby suggesting that perhaps they need not be respected. Suppose in response B says: "Because you should respect the human rights of every human being." The argument of B is:

[4] One should respect the human rights of every human being.
―――――――――――――――――――――――――――
One should respect the human rights of one's enemy.

Clearly, the premise of this argument denies the conflicting view that one needn't respect the human rights of one's enemy, and thus the premise begs the question against the opposing view. Yet A might respond, "I guess you are right, human rights of all human beings, including one's enemies, need to be respected," and thereby be convinced by the argument. No fallacy seems to be committed in being so convinced, and indeed, no one is likely to have a better reason for respecting the human rights of one's enemies than the reason that human rights of all human beings need to be respected: indeed, it is for this reason they are *human* rights. On the other hand, A might complain that the argument of B just begs the question, and this complaint seems to have some legitimacy too. Well, does the argument of B commit the Fallacy of Begging the Question or not?

In the end, I think there is no simple answer, because whether or not an argument commits the Fallacy of Begging the Question depends on whether or not the participants to the dispute recognize that there are more reasons for accepting the potentially question-begging premise than there are for accepting the conflicting view. If A thinks that there is more reason to accept the premise of [4] than to accept the view that an enemy's human rights needn't be respected, the Fallacy of Begging the Question is not committed in the context of the dispute. On the other hand, if A remains unconvinced and complains that there is no more reason to accept the premise of [4] than to accept the opposing view on the matter, one would have to concede that in this context argument [4] commits the Fallacy of Begging the Question and that one needs to argue for the premise of [4].

Much the same point emerges with argument [3]. Certainly in the context in which a capitalist is arguing with a communist, premise (2) begs the question. Premise (2) amounts to the denial of the communist position, and the communist is likely to claim that his ideal of the distribution of wealth according to need requires that people be denied the freedom to accumulate as much wealth as they can. Yet the freedom to accumulate wealth with minimal governmental interference may be someone's reason for preferring capitalism over communism. Thus, while [3] commits the Fallacy of Begging the Question as an argument against the communist, to be persuaded by [3] need not involve the Fallacy of Begging the Question.

Our account of the Fallacy of Begging the Question thus becomes this:

> Fallacy of Begging the Question
>
> $R_1, \ldots, R_n$ / C
>
> In the context of the argument, *(a) a premise R amounts to the denial of a conflicting view C°, and *(b) no more reasons have been given for accepting R than for accepting C°.
>
> *Both points (a) and (b) should be explained in analyzing a passage as committing the Fallacy of Begging the Question.

However, there is the complication that unless we know the details of the context, it will be difficult to determine what is accepted (for the sake of the argument) as unproblematic; moreover, without this knowledge, it will be difficult to determine which premise "amounts" to affirming C and denying C°. Similarly, without knowing the details of the context, we cannot determine what reasons have been given or accepted by the participants to the dispute. For the sake of exercises, unless the context has been specified, we shall take it that (a) premises other than the one that is most likely to be controversial is accepted as unproblematic, and (b) no reasons have been given or accepted for or against the controversial premise or the view C° that conflicts with the conclusion C. Given this understanding, let us conclude with a few sample analyses.

(1) "I'm going to whup Frazier because I'm the greatest."

Begging the Question:

(1) Ali is the greatest boxer.
(2) If Ali is the greatest boxer, Ali will beat Frazier.
―――――――――――――――
(3) Ali will beat Frazier.

(a) Because the second premise is relatively uncontroversial, we take it as unproblematic. But then in this context (1) amounts to the denial of
C°: Frazier will beat Ali.

(b) Because we are to assume that no reasons for or against (1) and C° have been given or accepted, in this context there is no more reason to accept (1) than there is reason to accept C°.

(2) The "Babe Ruth is the greatest hitter" example. Assume that the person disputing the conclusion thinks that Ty Cobb is the greatest hitter;

furthermore, assume that every reason for Ruth being the greatest hitter (e.g., that he hit more home runs) is matched by Cobb being the greatest hitter (e.g., that he had more hits) and that every reason against Cobb being the greatest hitter is matched by a reason against Ruth being the greatest hitter.

Begging the Question:

(1) No one else was nearly as good a hitter as Babe Ruth.

(2) Babe Ruth was the greatest hitter.

(a) Clearly to accept (1) is to deny the conflicting conclusion C°: Cobb was the greatest hitter.

(b) Because every reason favoring (1) is matched by a reason favoring C° and every reason against C° is matched by a reason against (1), in this context there is no more reason to accept (1) than C°.

(3) The philosopher David Hume[9] raised doubts about whether we can know anything about the future. Part of the basis for his doubts about the possibility of future knowledge may be put like this: "The justification of any claim about the future depends on assuming the truth of:

(F) The future will be like the observed past.

As such, one cannot have reasons for any claim about the future until one has established (F), and any reason for a future claim is reason that is based on reasons for (F). But how is one to establish (F)?" To see part of the force of Hume's doubts, let us assume that the considerations put forward by Hume are accepted and that in the context of trying to establish (F) we put ourselves in a position in which there are no reasons for or against (F) and other claims about the future that conflict with (F) unless there are independent reasons for each of the premises of the argument for (F). Given this context, consider the following attempt: "Surely there is no problem in justifying (F). In all our observations we have found that what was the case continues to be the case." This will not do in our context of meeting Hume's doubts because it commits the Fallacy of Begging the Question:

Begging the Question:

(1) In all observed cases (F) was true.

(2) If in all observed cases (F) was true, (F) is true.

(3) (F) is true.

(a) Because (1) is obviously (close enough to being) true, we may take it to be unproblematic. Thus, (2) amounts to the denial of the conflicting conclusion
C°: The future will be unlike the observed past.

9. David Hume, *A Treatise of Human Nature*, Oxford: Oxford University Press, 1888, Book I, Part iii, section 6.

(b) Clearly (2) is a claim about the future; thus by Hume's considerations that are accepted in the context, any reason for (2) is a reason that is based on reasons for (F). In other words, any reason for (2) is a reason that is based on reasons for (3). C° is also a claim about the future. Thus, in the argumentative context assumed, there are no reasons for or against (3) or C° unless there are independent reasons for (2). But there are no independent reasons for (2) because any reason for (2) is a reason based on reasons for (3). Thus, there are no reasons for or against (3) or C°, and hence also none for (2). But then there is no *more* reason for (2) than C° in the context of the argument and the proposed argument commits the Fallacy of Begging the Question.

This result seems to have rather unsettling consequences. It would seem that any valid argument for (F) will ultimately beg the question; moreover, it is difficult to see how a valid argument for a claim about a future will avoid among its premises a claim about the future. If our knowledge about the future is not to be threatened, evidently something about the context for the argument must be rejected, that is, we must deny Hume's claim that reasons for any claim about the future depend on reasons for (F) and that there can be no reasons for a such a claim until an argument establishes (F). How such a denial is to be plausibly accomplished is no easy matter and has been the source of much philosophical debate.

EXERCISES—SECTION 4.7

Part A

Analyze (in the manner indicated in the text) the fallacies that are explicitly or implicitly committed in the following passages. The fallacies covered include the six fallacies covered in this section and the three deductive fallacies discussed in Section 3.9.

In analyzing a nonabusive Fallacy of *ad Hominem,* indicate in parentheses the conclusion the author goes on to draw after having committed the fallacy.

In analyzing the Fallacy of Begging the Question, assume that the context of the argument is one in which (a) premises other than that which is most likely to be controversial are accepted as unproblematic, and (b) no reasons have been given or accepted for or against the controversial premise or the view C° that conflicts with the conclusion C that is drawn in the passage.

The material in brackets is background material.

1. Knowing that if his wife's car broke down, she will be hours late, Tom concludes that her car must have broken down because she should have been home hours ago.
2. [On the November 1982 California ballot was a nuclear weapons initiative, Proposition 12. If it passed (as it did by a wide margin) it required the governor to inform the president of the United States and other officials that

Californians are concerned about the nuclear arms race and urge the United States and the Soviet Union to agree to a mutually verifiable ban on testing, construction, and deployment of such weapon by the two countries. The following is part of the argument against Proposition 12 in the *Ballot Pamphlet,* and assume that it is a successful argument for the claim that a Brezhnev-type unilateral freeze will not reduce the danger of nuclear war.]

> A YES vote on the freeze initiative will not reduce the danger of nuclear war. That danger comes from the Soviet Union, now engaged in the largest nuclear weapons buildup in history. . . . On March 16, Soviet President Leonid Brezhnev announced a unilateral Soviet freeze on the deployment of SS-20 intermediate range missiles. . . . Then we learned that between mid-March and July 1 the Soviet Union deployed 45–50 more SS-20 missiles. It's dangerous to trust a Brezhnev-type freeze. . . . Send Brezhnev a message. Vote NO on Proposition 12.

3. My client is innocent of the charge of murdering her husband because she did not kill her husband.
4. Because it is cruel to kill animals, it was cruel for farmer Jones to kill his lame horse that could no longer stand.
5. Because she will miss her period if she is pregnant, she must be pregnant because she has missed her period.
6. [Because a city is always changing,] you can't visit the same city twice.
7. [Proposition 6 on the November 1982 California ballot allows for less conservative investments of public employees' pension funds. Opponents argued in part in the *Ballot Pamphlet:* "The California Public Employees' Retirement System is having a difficult enough time generating sufficient earnings on investments. In these difficult and fluctuating economic times, we hardly need to allow the imposition of questionable fiscal practices." The rebuttal in the *Ballot Pamphlet* in part states the following:]

   > Even the opponents of Proposition 6 acknowledge that public pension funds are having a hard time earning money on their investments. Other jurisdictions have adopted the practices outlined in Proposition 6, and private pension funds have used these investments to make more money for years. Why should California's public pension funds be restricted to earning less?

8. We know that he saw Mario or Vito. Because he was going to see Mario or Vito if he went to New York, he must have gone to New York.
9. Every action has some goal or meaning; therefore, life as a whole must have some goal or meaning.
10. We just found out that he didn't get into Harvard or Yale. If he was going to Harvard or Yale, he will have been going to one of the best universities in the country. But now he must abandon his hope of going to one of the best universities in the country.
11. [Proposition 10 in the November 1982 California ballot would have unified municipal and superior courts for the sake of an alleged efficiency. Opponents mainly urged that this is a hidden salary increase for municipal court judges because they would receive the salary of superior court judges. The rebuttal to these arguments in the *Ballot Pamphlet* stated:]

    > For the most part, those opposed to Proposition 10 are those who wish to maintain the status quo because they have learned how to "play the system," seeking delays and postponements, and thus preventing a swift and sure delivery of justice.

12. [The bottle deposit initiative (Proposition 11) on the November 1982 California ballot would have made deposits on beverage containers mandatory.

This was for the sake of cleaning up litter, conserving natural resources, etc. In arguing against the opponents, the proponents urged in the *Ballot Pamphlet:*]

> Opponents of Proposition 11 are mainly the large industries who make more money by selling wasteful throwaway containers. They claim all kinds of undesirable things will happen to our state if Proposition 11 passes.

13. Going by what Tom said, either he eats cannelloni when he goes to Italian restaurants or he eats Moo Shi pork when he goes to a Chinese restaurant. Because we found out that he eats cannelloni when he goes to Italian restaurants, it must be false that he eats Moo Shi pork when he goes to Chinese restaurants.
14. [An ad for Six Flags Movieland:]

    > Movieland Wax Museum is one museum where you just can't be bored. You can't be bored being trapped in the sinking ship Poseidon or speeding through space abroad the Starship *Enterprise* or shivering through a Russian winter with Dr. Zhivago. So, come and spend hours being face-to-face with 256 of the greatest stars.

15. [In the November 1982 *California Ballot Pamphlet* members of the Libertarian party opposed a bond issue to build more county jails. In part they urged reducing the number of inmates by eliminating laws against certain voluntary sexual activities, gambling, and other aspects of personal life—the category of victimless crimes; they also urged other arguments against the bond issue such as its high cost and its tendency to drive up interest rates for private borrowers. The following is part of the rebuttal in the *Ballot Pamphlet.* Treat the rhetorical question as a statement to the effect: One should not give much weight to. . . .]

    > How much weight should you give to recommendations on crime issues by ANY group saying we can solve jail overcrowding by just releasing all those charged with what they term "victimless" crimes?

16. [Argument in the November 1982 *California Ballot Pamphlet* for a bond act to purchase undeveloped land in the Lake Tahoe region:]

    > For each Californian the cost of this bond issue amounts to pennies—an average of 39 cents a year. Surely this is a small, but wise, investment to protect a California resource that is truly one of a kind.

17. I can't understand how so many professors with moderate salaries can afford to buy houses in Montecito, which is known to be an expensive area.
18. Because you like carrot cake, you should enjoy the tray of carrots I've prepared.
19. This substance will ignite in the presence of a flame because it is inflammable.
20. Knowing that our daughter Karen has been dating her professor or her classmate John, we were relieved by her confession last night that she had been seeing John. Thank goodness she isn't dating that older man.
21. The traditional definition of man as a rational animal is ridiculous. A baby can hardly engage in rational reasoning activities at birth.
22. His future with the company can no longer be assured. If he married the boss's daughter, his future was assured, but he stupidly didn't marry her.
23. [Veterans Bond Act of 1982 provided for issuing state bonds to provide mortgage aid for California veterans, thereby creating more money for the California veteran mortgage program. The following is part of the argument against it in the November 1982 *California Ballot Pamphlet,* and assume that the author has successfully argued that we shouldn't create more money by printing press money.]

All the benefits of the proposed bill are pale in comparison with their adverse effect on THE SINGLE GREATEST ISSUE OF OUR TIME: the vanishing value of our currency. Printing press money is one of the signs of a civilization near collapse, like our own.

24. [Proposition 15 on the November 1982 California ballot was a modest gun control initiative requiring the registration of handguns and freezing the number of handguns in California at the present level. Among the various contested issues, the proponents stated in the *Ballot Pamphlet* that passage of Proposition 15 will help in reducing the number of gun-related crimes. In their rebuttal, the opponents claimed:]

    Everyone knows that criminals are going to ignore this initiative.

    [Assume that the author is claiming that potential criminals will ignore the initiative rather than making the trivial point that people in the future who will have committed a gun-related crime (with an unregistered gun) will have ignored the initiative.]
25. I know that he is going to buy a TV or a stereo. Because he bought a TV, he must have abandoned the idea of buying a stereo.
26. Because water boils at 100 degrees centigrade, this kettle of water in Tibet will boil at 100 degrees centigrade.
27. Because it was a close election, it must have been close in Los Angeles.
28. If she is willing to sacrifice her career for me, she really loves me. But because she isn't willing to sacrifice her career for me, she can't really love me.

Part B

In analyzing the following instances of the Fallacy of Begging the Question, in addition to the assumed context that is given, assume that premises other than that which is most likely to be controversial are accepted as unproblematic.

1. Surely we would object if the Russians tried to interfere with the actions of the American government. The plain fact is that no foreign country has the right to interfere with the actions of a legitimately constituted government. Therefore, we have no right to interfere with the actions of the South African government.

    Assume: The context of the argument is such that (a) every reason for the legitimacy of the South African govermment (e.g., there being a constitution) is matched by a reason for its illegitimacy (e.g., the blacks lacking a vote), which in turn is a reason for America's right to interfere; and (b) that the reasons against America's right to interfere are canceled by reasons against the legitimacy of the South African government.
2. Hitler's orders must be followed, because he ordered that his orders be followed.

    Assume: (i) In the context of the argument, there are no reasons for or against the conclusion or its denial unless there are independent reasons for each of the premises of the argument for the conclusion. (ii) Any reasons for following any particular order of Hitler is a reason that is based on a reason for following his orders in general.

5

Nondemonstrative Arguments

Suppose '$e_1, \ldots, e_n$ / H' is a nondemonstrative argument. The method of adding missing premises discussed in Chapter 4 suggests: if there is a 'q' such that (a) '$e_1, \ldots, e_n$,q / H' is a valid deductive argument, and (b) 'q' is completely justified, then '$e_1, \ldots, e_n$ / H' is a completely legitimate nondemonstrative argument. Condition (a) can always be trivially satisfied by taking 'q' as '(e_1 & . . . & e_n) ⊃ H'. However, determining that condition (b) is satisfied for this long conditional statement is often at least as difficult as the direct evaluation of the nondemonstrative legitimacy of '$e_1, \ldots, e_n$ / H'. This is particularly the case when 'e_1', . . . , 'e_n' are potentially unproblematic OB or PF claims, and 'H' is either a general statement (e.g., a scientific hypothesis) or another particular statement (like 'The butler killed her') that isn't directly based on an observation or (expert) testimony in one's epistemic situation. In this chapter we shall be concerned with the direct assessment of nondemonstrative legitimacy.

In Section 5.1 we shall give an overview of our approach, which conceives nondemonstrative legitimacy in terms of the conclusion being the best explanation of the premises. Section 5.2 will present a general method for assessing nondemonstrative legitimacy, and in Sections 5.3–5.5 we shall indicate some differences among the kinds of arguments that can be assessed, directly or indirectly, by the method developed in Section 5.2. However, it should be stated at the outset that the procedure we shall outline for determining nondemonstrative legitimacy only provides rough guidelines, which need to be filled in with strong doses of sound judgment. Unlike the case of deductive validity, there is no known rigid procedure (like that of chain arguments) for determining the legitimacy of nondemonstrative arguments, and it is unlikely that this deficiency will ever be overcome.

One additional preliminary remark is in order. In this chapter we need to rely on the deductive validity of certain (forms of) arguments in which the validity cannot be understood in terms of their truth functional structure alone. The validity of most of these arguments should be intuitively evident, and readers who want to check on their intuitions should refer to the general account of validity given near the beginning of Chapter 3.

5.1 Nondemonstrative Legitimacy as the Inference to the Best Explanation

To see what is involved in legitimate nondemonstrative arguments, let us consider three relatively simple examples:

(a) We have observed 200 ravens and observed them to be all black. As long as our sample can be presumed to be fairly representative, we should have fairly strong grounds for saying that all ravens are black. Schematically, the nondemonstrative argument that is suggested is:

[A] (e) All observed ravens are black.
____
(H) All ravens are black.

Notice in this example that if all ravens are black, then clearly each of the observed ravens is black. That is, the following is a valid argument:

(H) All ravens are black.
____
(e) All observed ravens are black.

Thus, we see: the conclusion of [A] is the premise of a valid deductive argument for the premise of [A]. At least in a very weak sense of 'explains' we might thus say: the conclusion that *all* ravens are black explains the observed ravens being black.

(b) Two robbers got away on a motorcycle during a rainy night on a muddy road. The next day, when we followed the tracks left by the motorcycle, we noticed that beyond a certain point the tracks became shallower; we also noted that the consistency of the dirt road did not change at this point. We concluded that someone got off the motorcycle at that point. Schematically, the nondemonstrative argument is:

[B] (e) The tracks become shallower.
(a_1) The consistency of the road is uniform.
____
(H) Someone got off the motorcycle at this point.

Given the background condition provided by (a_1), in a fairly obvious sense of 'explains', the conclusion that someone got off explains the crucial premise that the tracks became shallower. This explanatory relation can again be seen in terms of a reverse deductive relation. Given the background (a_1) and the unproblematic CS or SM claim concerning the tracks being shallower if there are fewer people on the motorcycle, we can deductively conclude that the tracks are shallower from that point. More explicitly, we have the following valid argument:

(H) Someone got off the motorcycle at this point.
(a_1) The consistency of the road is uniform.
(a_2) If someone got off the motorcycle at this point and the consistency of the road is uniform, the tracks become shallower at this point.

(e) The tracks become shallower at this point.

Again, the conclusion of [B] augmented by completely justified claims is a deductively valid reason for the crucial premise of [B].

(c) Was Frenchy playing at the Sing-Along Bar last night? Suppose that nine impartial witnesses seem to remember seeing him. Because they only *seem* to remember, and were drinking in any case, we might suppose that 'Frenchy was (seen) playing' isn't an unproblematic (transmitted) observation claim in our situation. Still, that nine of them seem to remember seeing him appears to be good reason for thinking that he was playing at the bar last night. Schematically, we have the following nondemonstrative argument:

[C] (e) Eyewitnesses one to nine seem to remember seeing Frenchy playing the piano at the Sing-Along Bar last night (as its piano player).

(H) Frenchy was playing the piano at the Sing-Along Bar last night.

Here again, Frenchy playing the piano last night at the bar explains the eyewitnesses who seem to remember seeing him play. However, the reverse deductive validity in this case is more complex because (H)/(e) is not valid, and the addition of no plausible premise is likely to render this argument valid. The problem is this: If Frenchy played the piano at the Sing-Along Bar (as its piano player), we can fully expect that a number of people will seem to remember seeing him play; but we cannot expect any particular eyewitness to remember this. Such a person might have been too drunk or too amorously involved with his date, and the ways he may fail to remember seeing Frenchy seem too numerous to list. Thus, no fully justified auxiliary premise together with (H) would constitute deductively valid reasons for a claim like (e).

To account for (H) explaining (e) in terms of deductive validity, we may first note: if 'Frenchy was playing the piano at the Sing-Along Bar (as its piano player)' is augmented by a plausible missing premise, we would have deductively valid reasons for a number of people who seem to remember seeing him. That is, the following is a valid argument:

(H) Frenchy was playing the piano at the Sing-Along Bar (as its piano player) last night.
(a) If (H) is true, a number of eyewitnesses (will) seem to remember seeing him play.

(v) A number of eyewitnesses (will) seem to remember seeing Frenchy playing the piano at the Sing-Along Bar last night.

Because (a) appears to be completely justified, [C]'s conclusion (H) seems to explain (v) on the model of explanations seen in example (b). Notice next that one way in which (v) can be true is that eyewitnesses one to nine seem to remember seeing him. Let us introduce the term INDETERMINATE VARIANT, so that (v) is an indeterminate variant of (e). We shall use this term so that 'Something is F' is an indeterminate variant of 'x is F' and 'x is F and y is F'; 'Some F are G' is an indeterminate variant of 'x is both F and G' and 'x is both F and G and y is both F and G'; 'A number of F's are G's' is an indeterminate variant of 'x is both F and G, and y is both F and G, and z is both F and G'; and so on. Given this somewhat loose terminology, we can understand the nondemonstrative legitimacy of [C] in terms of its conclusion (H) along with the completely justified auxiliary premise (a) being deductively valid reasons for an indeterminate variant of the evidence (e).

In our three examples of (fairly) legitimate nondemonstrative arguments, we have seen that there is an explanatory or reverse deductive relation from the conclusion to the premises. In order to have a model by which to assess nondemonstrative arguments let us therefore say:

> 'H' strongly [weakly] explains 'e' =
>
> 'H / e' *or* 'H, a / e' *or* 'H, a / v' is deductively valid
>
> where 'a' is an available auxiliary premise that is completely [highly] justified and 'v' is an indeterminate variant of 'e'.

This is a slight simplification, and several things should be kept in mind in using this definition:

(i) 'H' must play an essential role for the deductive validity of the arguments. Otherwise 'Reagan is a president' explains 'The sun will rise tomorrow' insofar as 'Reagan is a president, the sun always rises / the sun will rise tomorrow' is a valid argument.

(ii) An auxiliary premise 'a' may not always be needed for the validity of 'H, a / v'; thus if 'H / v' is valid and 'v' is an indeterminate variant of 'e', 'H' explains 'e'.

(iii) To be more correct, we should have said, "'H' explains 'e' for a person P at time t," and indexed the justification of the auxiliary premises to P at t. From now on, where the person and time parameters are obvious, we shall leave it to the reader to provide them.

With these qualifications or emendations, the intent of the definition of 'explanation' should be clear enough.

In Chapter 4 we noted that if 'a' is completely justified and 'H, a / e' is valid, 'e' is *a* supporting reason for 'H'. Although there are some differences in detail, at least roughly, if 'H' strongly explains 'e', 'e' is *a* supporting reason for 'H'. This consideration as well as our examples suggest the following necessary condition for the legitimacy of nondemonstrative arguments:

> *If* '$e_1, \ldots, e_n$ / H' *is a legitimate nondemonstrative argument* (except for premises that play an auxiliary or background role), *'H' must explain the premises* 'e_1', . . . , 'e_n' (or conjunctions of them).

Can we convert this necessary condition for nondemonstrative legitimacy into a sufficient condition as well? That is, can we say '$e_1, \ldots, e_n$ / H' is a legitimate nondemonstrative argument if and only if 'H' explains the premises 'e_1', . . . , 'e_n'? No is the answer.

To see why not, consider [A] again, in which we observed 200 black ravens: If we recast 'All observed ravens are black' as 'Ravens 1–200 are black', we can have the following nondemonstrative argument that goes from the same observations to a different conclusion:

[A*] (e) Ravens 1–200 are black.

(H*) Some ravens are black but others are not.

(H*) strongly explains (e) because (H*) is a valid reason for 'Some ravens are black' and 'Some ravens are black' is an indeterminate variant of (e). But we surely don't want to say that [A] and [A*] are both legitimate because this would force a rational person who has observed the 200 ravens in question to accept as justified both the conclusion that all ravens are black and the conclusion that some of them aren't black. Similarly, consider:

[B*] (e) The tracks got shallower at this point.

(H*) One of the robbers managed to decrease the depth of the tracks at this point by willpower alone (rather than by getting off).

Clearly (H*) strongly explains (e) because (H*) along with the completely justified conditional linking (H*) to (e) constitute valid reasons for (e). But surely we don't want to say that [B] and [B*] are both legitimate nondemonstrative arguments.

What these considerations show is that given an argument '$e_1, \ldots, e_n$ / H' of the type we are discussing, in addition to 'H', any number of competing hypotheses 'H_1', . . . , 'H_k' may explain 'e_1', . . . , 'e_n'. For '$e_1, \ldots, e_n$ / H' to be a legitimate nondemonstrative argument, 'H' must be the *best* available explanation for 'e_1', . . . , 'e_n'. Consider a simple case: We see that Smith is dead at the bottom of a cliff. Given this much there may be three potential explanations.

'H_1': Smith died of natural causes (such as a heart attack).
'H_2': Smith had an accident (such as falling off the cliff).
'H_3': Smith was murdered.

If we know Smith to have been healthy and there is evidence that his body fell from the top of the cliff, 'H_2' and 'H_3' seem to be better explanations than 'H_1' for all of the available evidence. Suppose we also find some evidence of a scuffle at the top of the cliff, for example, some footprints indicating a scuffle, bits of torn clothing, and some blood. This would be explained somewhat better by 'H_3' (now taking the form that Smith was shoved off the cliff by the killer). Still, there is considerable room for doubt about 'H_3', and to this extent 'H_2' still seems to be a live hypothesis. As we collect more and more evidence, 'H_2' may be eliminated (along with 'H_1') for all practical purposes. It is at this point that we might be said to have completely legitimate reasons for 'H_3'.

This should make it plausible that a legitimate nondemonstrative argument is one in which the conclusion is *the best* available explanation of the premises. However, the example of the last paragraph suggests that not all "best explanations" are of equal status, that is, some may be the best explanation by a wide margin while others are only marginally better than their competitors. We shall reserve the term 'completely legitimate nondemonstrative argument' for those arguments in which the conclusions are *by far* the best explanations of their premises; we shall also demand that in such an argument the conclusion *strongly* explain the premises, and that most of the evidence in favor of the conclusion be included among the premises.

By placing these strong constraints on *completely* legitimate nondemonstrative arguments, we can be a bit more liberal in what counts as a legitimate nondemonstrative argument in that we shall only require of them that the conclusions be the best explanations of the premises. Thus, we shall allow that in some legitimate nondemonstrative arguments, the conclusions may only be somewhat better explanations than their competitors. As might have been expected, the legitimacy of nondemonstrative arguments come in degrees, and our focus will be on legitimate nondemonstrative arguments in general. It will then be largely a matter of judgment whether a legitimate nondemonstrative argument is completely legitimate in virtue of its conclusion being "by far" the best explanation of the premises. Thus, the central notion of interest to us is captured by:

> '$e_1, \ldots, e_n$ / H' is a legitimate nondemonstrative argument =
> 'H' is the best available explanation of 'e_1', . . . , 'e_n'.

In applying this definition, it should be borne in mind that those premises that play the role of providing the relevant background (e.g., 'The consistency of the road was uniform') need not be explained by the conclusion 'H'.

EXERCISES—SECTION 5.1

1. Let 'h' be given by

   'h': Tom killed Jane in her house last night.

   Show by means of appropriate chain arguments that 'h' explains each of the following statements:

   (a) Jane didn't come to class today.
   (b) Tom was near Jane's house last night.
   (c) A duplicate key of Jane's house was found on Tom (i.e., having a duplicate key is a method of entry to Jane's house that was available to Tom).

2. In each of the following nondemonstrative arguments, (i) show that the conclusion explains the premise, (ii) suggest another explanation that would also explain the premise, and (iii) show that the explanation suggested in (ii) does explain the premise.

   (a) The birthrate in America has declined dramatically since the sixties. Americans must therefore be sexually far less active than they used to be.
   (b) When one examines the conditions of city streets, it becomes evident that streets in the more expensive neighborhoods are kept in a better condition than those in the slums. One can only conclude that the city officials involved are more interested in pleasing the rich than the poor.

5.2 Determining the Best Explanation

Having identified legitimate nondemonstrative arguments as ones in which the conclusions are the best explanations of the premises, we should like to have a procedure for selecting the best explanation. While there is no simple or mechanical procedure for making such a selection, there are clear guidelines for determining the best explanation. The purpose of this section is to formulate and order these guidelines, so that we have something like the rough outlines of a general procedure in choosing the best explanation. This procedure won't automatically or mechanically select the best explanations; rather, it outlines the kinds of considerations one should go through in attempting to determine the best explanation.

5.2.1 Initial Phase

Given a nondemonstrative argument '$e_1, \ldots, e_n$ / H', the first step is to reject all explanations of 'e_1', . . . , 'e_n' that are initially utterly implausible, and in some cases this may result in rejecting 'H' itself. Thus, the first step might be given as:

> *Step 1:* If completely justified statements are deductively valid reasons for '−H', condemn 'H' as a poor explanation.

Of course, if all alternative explanations of a body of evidence are also condemned, we shall have to rethink some of the statements we took to be completely justified with an eye to rehabilitating some of the condemned explanations. But in the absence of such an extreme circumstance, we should condemn explanations that conflict with unproblematic CS and SM claims as well as other completely justified general claims; we should also condemn explanations that conflict with what is normally considered evidence, that is, unproblematic OB and PF claims.

In the robber example, the explanation that one of the robbers managed to make the tracks shallower by willpower alone conflicts with the unproblematic CS or SM claim that no one can do this; in other words, that no one can do this is a completely justified claim that is a deductively valid reason for the robber not having done this. Thus, the "willpower" explanation of the tracks becoming shallower is rejected. It can also happen that the very conclusion of '$e_1, \ldots, e_n$ / H' may be rejected by this step and the argument thereby be shown to be an illegitimate nondemonstrative argument. Thus, with respect to argument [C] concerning Frenchy, suppose that the police records show that they booked him at four o'clock yesterday afternoon, interrogated him all night, and didn't release him until this morning. If I was one of the police officers who interrogated Frenchy last night, at least in my epistemic situation, there is an unproblematic OB claim that conflicts with the conclusion in [C] that Frenchy played at the Sing-Along Bar last night. That is, the unproblematic OB claim 'Frenchy was at the police station last night' along with the unproblematic INT claim 'If he was at the police station, he wasn't playing at the Sing-Along Bar' constitute deductively valid reasons for 'He wasn't playing the piano at the Sing-Along Bar last night.' Thus, the conclusion in [C] is rejected as an initially implausible explanation, and [C] is rejected as an illegitimate nondemonstrative argument—at least for someone in my epistemic situation. Of course if all attempts to find an explanation for the premises of [C] fail, I may have to rethink the situation and consider such remote possibilities as Frenchy having an identical twin.

Step 2 is to determine the best explanation of 'e_1', . . . , 'e_n' among the explanations that survived Step 1. However, Step 2 has many complications and we shall be able to specify it only at the end of Section 5.2. We start with the following definitions:

> If 'd' is at least highly justified,
>
> 'd' is positive evidence for 'H' if 'H' explains 'd', and
> 'd' is negative evidence for 'H' if 'H' explains '−d'.
>
> 'H' 's data base = positive and negative evidence for 'H' and its competitors.

Clearly, to ascertain the best explanation, we need to determine which of the hypotheses or explanations fits best with the totality of available evidence that is relevant, that is, with the data base. To this end, we shall list preference rules that are relevant to making this determination, or rules that might be called "Rules of Fit." However, one should remember that preference rules typically do not dictate that one thing is better than another; rather, they merely give one consideration for preferring one choice over another. "Hire the smarter candidate" may be a preference rule with which employers work; yet if the smarter person has a known drinking problem, one might hire someone who is not quite as smart. In part, this is because there is another preference rule, "Hire the more dependable candidate." In general, preference rules are of the form 'Other things being equal, X is better than Y', and judgment has to be used in applying the rules to arrive at what is the best. Our preference rules, then, are all of the form "Other things being equal, H is a better explanation than H* if . . . ," and we shall abbreviate this as: 'H > H* if . . .'.

Given this background, and taking the reference to the data base of H as understood, the RULES OF FIT may be stated as follows:

H > H* if

(1) H has more positive evidence than H*.
(2) H more strongly explains the positive evidence of H than H* explains that of H*.
(3) H has less negative evidence than H*.

Of course rules 1 and 3 have to be taken somewhat intuitively because we have not defined what counts as a unit of evidence to which we can refer in talking about more or less. Still, in most cases the intuitive idea should be clear enough.

The most obvious point of rule 1 is that one prefers hypotheses with more positive evidence. For example, suppose that Ed Morrow, a three-pack-a-day smoker, died of lung cancer. The hypothesis 'Smoking caused his death' is preferable to the (tobacco industry) hypothesis 'Factors other than smoking caused his death', because there is more positive evidence for the smoking hypothesis. Rule 1 also has the effect that a more general explanation that explains a variety of phenomena is preferable to a batch of specific explanations in which the applications are limited. Thus, with respect to the relation between pressure and volume of gases, Boyle's law (which merely specifies inverse proportionality) is less preferable to the explanation in terms of molecular motion, because the latter has wider applicability and hence greater positive evidence.

As an example of applying rule 2, suppose that I have no recollection of listening to a lecture by Professor Dull. Yet my friend claims that I was at the lecture and suggests that I may have forgotten because it was a very boring lecture indeed. Two hypotheses and the auxiliary premises that each hypothesis needs to account for the evidence (namely, I don't recollect attending the lecture) are:

'H': I did not attend Professor Dull's lecture.
'a': If I did not attend Professor Dull's lecture, I will not remember attending it.
'H*': I attended the very boring lecture by Professor Dull.
'a*': If the lecture by Professor Dull that I attended was very boring, I will not remember attending it.

There is no doubt that the auxiliary hypothesis 'a' is more justified than 'a*' even if we assume that 'a*' is highly justified. To this extent, 'H' explains the evidence 'e' more strongly than 'H*'. Hence, by rule 2, 'H' is preferable to 'H*'. Rules 1 and 2 are so obvious that saying more would be to belabor the obvious.

Rule 3 is also an obvious rule: a hypothesis or explanation that has less negative evidence is to be preferred. As we shall see shortly, negative evidence is very damaging to a hypothesis. Therefore, this rule should normally be given far greater weight than the other two rules. Because of this importance attached to negative evidence, and because of the complexities negative evidence introduces, we devote a separate subsection to the problem of coping with negative evidence.

5.2.2 Coping with Negative Evidence: Supplemental Hypotheses

To investigate the situation in which there is negative evidence, let us concentrate on the example involving the robbers on a motorcycle, and stipulate our epistemic situation to contain the following completely justified statements:

(i) The police chased the two robbers on the motorcycle until they got to the muddy road where the police car got stuck.
(ii) There was only one set of tracks on the road the next morning.
(iii) The change in the depth of the tracks on the road at the point in question allowed forensic experts to determine that about 150–200 pounds of weight was eliminated at that point.
(iv) There are no inhabitants along the road between the point in question and the edge of the nearby village of Middleton.

Let us suppose that after eliminating the initially implausible hypotheses, in light of (iii), the two remaining hypotheses are[1]:

'R': One of the robbers got off the motorcycle at the point in question.
'E': At the point in question, the robbers discarded some heavy equipment.

1. Because these abbreviations will have to be remembered for a number of pages, in this and the following, abbreviating letters are matched with the underlined letters in the abbreviated sentences.

Let us now suppose that the data base contains:

'w': Two eyewitnesses claim that they saw a motorcycle with two riders enter Middleton on the dirt road last night.
'n': There was no heavy equipment found around the point in question.

'w' is negative evidence for 'R' and 'n' is negative evidence for 'E'. This can be seen as follows: Given (i), (ii), and (iv), 'a_1' below is highly justified, and given (ii) and (iv), 'a_2' below is highly justified.

'a_1': $R \supset -w$. 'a_2': $E \supset -n$.

Clearly, '$R, R \supset -w$ / $-w$' and '$E, E \supset -n$ / $-n$' are valid. Thus, we have a situation in which both competing hypotheses or explanations have negative evidence in the data base.

The typical case in which 'd' is negative evidence for 'H' involves 'H, a / −d' being valid, and 'a' and 'd' being at least highly justified. If 'a' and 'd' were both completely justified, 'H' would have been rejected as initially implausible in Step 1 and the issue of coping with the negative evidence would not have arisen. (It should of course be remembered that if all hypotheses were rejected by Step 1, we would have had to rethink the situation and perhaps rehabilitate 'H' by taking 'a' or 'd' to have been no more than highly justified.) Thus, when 'H' survives Step 1 despite the negative evidence, at least one of 'a' and 'd' is at most highly justified. Still, it should be clear that as long as the data base contains negative evidence for 'H', 'H' cannot be a very good explanation. The problem is that if 'H' has negative evidence, it is only minimally better than hypotheses rejected as initially implausible. The only difference is between 'a' and 'd' both being completely justified and at least one of 'a' and 'd' being only highly justified. While 'R' and 'E' in our example may both be better explanations than the one in terms of willpower, in light of the negative evidence, the difference isn't much.

Faced with negative evidence, a hypothesis must somehow defuse or *explain away* the negative evidence if the argument for it is to have any significant degree of legitimacy. Where 'd' is negative evidence due to the validity of 'H, a / −d', the auxiliary premise 'a' or the negative evidence 'd' is no more than highly justified. This means that there must be some genuine grounds for doubt concerning 'a' or 'd'. Thus, the task for a supporter of 'H' is to increase the grounds for doubting 'a' or 'd', so that at least one of them will no longer be even highly justified. Let us therefore introduce the following definitions:

Where 'd' is negative evidence for 'H' with 'a' as an auxiliary premise, 'S_H' is a supplemental hypothesis for 'H' if it doesn't conflict with 'H' and its truth could make 'a' or 'd' less than highly justified.

A supplemental hypothesis for 'H' is strong if it explains 'd' (in conjunction with 'H') or highly justifies '−d' independently of 'H'.

The task for a supporter of 'H' is to propose a supplemental hypothesis and to gather enough evidence for the supplemental hypothesis, so that it is justified to a point in which 'a' or 'd' ceases being highly justified. If this is accomplished, 'd' will cease being negative evidence for 'H'. To make this clearer, we shall first consider the types of supplemental hypotheses that may be offered, and defer to the next subsection the discussion of how supplemental hypotheses are justified.

In our example, two possible supplemental hypotheses for 'R' might be:

'L_R': The two witnesses were lying and trying to make it appear that both robbers entered Middleton.

'D_R': The two witnesses were drunk and their testimony is unreliable.

Clearly, the auxiliary premise that makes 'w' negative evidence for 'R' (i.e., '$R \supset -w$') is highly justified only because of the presumption that the eyewitnesses were reporting what was there to be seen. Thus, if 'L_R' or 'D_R' were highly justified, the grounds for accepting the auxiliary premise '$R \supset -w$' would virtually vanish.

Furthermore, 'L_R' explains the negative evidence 'w' because

$$L_R \supset w$$

is highly justified, and '$L_R, L_R \supset w / w$' is deductively valid. On the other hand, 'D_R' doesn't explain 'w' because no highly justified statement can be conjoined with it to give a deductively valid reason for 'w'; that is, because they were drunk and are unreliable hardly guarantees along with some other plausible statement that they were bound to misdescribe the motorcycle as having two riders. In effect, if 'D_R' were sufficiently justified, it would reduce the justification of the auxiliary premise '$R \supset -w$', so that '$-w$' would be eliminated from the data base with the result that the negative evidence of 'R' would be eliminated. The strong supplemental hypothesis 'L_R' would not only eliminate the negative evidence of 'R' but explain it. Thus, if it were accepted, it would convert 'w' into positive evidence for the combined theory composed of both 'R' and 'L_R'.

A supplemental hypothesis that might be proposed for 'E' is:

'P_E': Someone came along and picked up the heavy equipment that was left around the point in question.

Because 'P_E' would explain the negative evidence 'n' (i.e., the absence of equipment around the point in question), it is a strong supplemental hypothesis for 'E'.

In the scheme in which 'd' is negative evidence for 'H' because '$H, a / -d$' is deductively valid, we have so far seen supplemental hypotheses that, if justified, would discredit 'a'. To see an example in which 'd' is made less than highly justified, let us reconceive the negative evidence for 'R' by letting 't' be given by:

't': Two riders entered Middleton on the motorcycle.

Clearly, 'R, R ⊃ −t / −t' is valid. The auxiliary premise 'R ⊃ −t' is highly justified, and we might take 't' to be highly justified by the testimony of the two eyewitnesses. Thus, 't' is negative evidence for 'R'. When the negative evidence of 'R' is conceived in this way, we can still see 'L_R' and 'D_R' as supplemental hypotheses for 'R'. Because the testimony of the two eyewitnesses highly justifies 't' only because it was unlikely that the eyewitnesses were mistaken, if 'L_R' or 'D_R' were sufficiently justified, it would discredit the eyewitnesses; 't' would then no longer be highly justified and it would be eliminated from the data base.

In this kind of case, we cannot expect 'L_R' or 'D_R' to be strong supplemental hypotheses by explaining 't' because the point of the supplemental hypothesis is to suggest that 't' may be false. Thus, in this situation a supplemental hypothesis is strong if its being highly justified would highly justify the falsity of the alleged negative evidence. In this sense 'L_R' is strong because if it were highly justified (i.e., if it were highly justified that the witnesses were lying and trying to make it appear that two riders entered Middleton), it would be highly justified that there weren't two riders entering Middleton; that is, '−t' would be highly justified. This would then have the consequence that '−t' enters the data base as positive evidence for R. On the other hand, 'D_R' is not strong because its being highly justified would not result in '−t' being highly justified. This should give the reader some idea of how supplemental hypotheses would explain away the negative evidence if they were justified. We now turn to the justification of supplemental hypotheses.

5.2.3 Justifying Supplemental Hypotheses, Changing Epistemic Circumstances, and Preference Rules for Negative Evidence

Let us recall that 'd' is negative evidence for 'H' in an epistemic circumstance C when 'H, a / −d' is valid and both 'd' and 'a' are highly justified in C. A supplemental hypothesis 'S_H' was such that if it were sufficiently justified, 'a' or 'd' would not be highly justified. It should be clear that because 'a' and 'd' were highly justified in C, 'S_H' cannot be sufficiently justified in C. Thus, for the supplemental hypothesis to have the effect of actually defusing the negative evidence of 'H' or 'd', the epistemic situation must change from C to another one. The new epistemic situation results by collecting new evidence for the supplemental hypothesis and/or reassessing the justification of various statements relevant to 'H' and its alternatives. Because we saw that a hypothesis 'H' cannot be a very good explanation if the data base contains negative evidence for 'H', often the legitimacy of a nondemonstrative argument is the final result of a process in which the epistemic situation and the data base change. The deductive validity of an argument could be seen statically because time and epistemic situations don't affect validity. On the other hand, the legitimacy of nondemonstrative arguments must often be seen dynamically in which its legitimacy in an epistemic situation is due to that epistemic situation having had a certain history from which it evolved, that is, a history in which the negative evidence was successively defused.

In our example, let C_1 be the epistemic circumstance in which 'w' is negative evidence for 'R', 'n' is negative evidence for 'E', and 'L_R' and 'P_E' were proposed. Let C_2 be the subsequent circumstance in which we discover that regarding the point in question, there are no signs of someone having carted off the equipment: the area is muddy but there are no footprints beyond the one set leading away from the point (and none coming toward the point); also, there are no marks of heavy equipment or of someone having dragged it away. The effect of this is that the supplemental hypothesis 'P_E' is virtually eliminated by considerations involved in eliminating initially implausible hypotheses. That is, the premises of the following valid argument seem to be virtually completely justified:

(1) [(P_E) & (the area is muddy but not muddy enough to eliminate all traces)] $\supset$ [there will be traces of someone having picked up the equipment].
(2) The area is muddy but not muddy enough to eliminate all traces.
(3) There are no traces of someone having picked up the equipment from the point in question.

---

(4) $-P_E$

Furthermore, because the falsity of the supplemental hypothesis 'P_E' is almost completely justified in C_2, the auxiliary premise '$E \supset -n$' that gave rise to the negative evidence of 'E' ('n') now seems close to being completely justified. Thus, in the epistemic circumstance C_2, 'E' becomes a very poor explanation, and should probably be rejected as an initially implausible hypothesis in this revised epistemic situation.

How does 'R' fare in C_2? Two elements can be noted:

(i) 'E' is now (virtually) eliminated and new evidence for 'R' was found in the footprints leading away from the point in question. In C_2, 'R' seems to be just about the only possible explanation for the change in the depth of the motorcycle tracks and the new positive evidence of the footprints. Indeed, 'R' seems to be the best explanation by far for the available data in C_2.
(ii) The evidence of the two eyewitnesses from Middleton that was negative evidence in C_1 still remains, and no direct evidence for 'L_R' or 'D_R' has emerged. Certainly, nothing in C_2 justifies 'L_R' or 'D_R'.

However, another supplemental hypothesis that will do as well for 'R' is:

'M_R': The eyewitness reports are mistaken; that is, what the two eyewitnesses reported wasn't there to be seen.

Given that 'w' is highly justified and that 'R' is just about the only possible explanation of what happened, there seems to be fairly strong grounds for accepting 'M_R'. In C_2, I think we should be willing to say that the truth of 'M_R' is considerably more justified than its falsity, and this is enough to make the auxiliary premise '$R \supset -w$' less than highly justified. Hence, 'w' is no longer negative evidence for 'R' (because it will no longer be in the data base).

Still, there is no direct evidence for 'M_R', because the only ground for it is that without it, the otherwise plausible hypothesis 'R' would come close to being condemned by the negative evidence for 'R'. To deal with this kind of situation let us introduce the following definition:

> A supplemental hypothesis for 'H' is ad hoc =
>
> There are no positive grounds for the supplemental hypothesis beyond its ability to defuse the negative evidence of 'H'.

Clearly, ad hoc supplemental hypotheses are not very attractive because they can be used to save bad explanations or hypotheses from disconfirmation and outright falsification by the available evidence. By invoking enough (implausible) ad hoc hypotheses, it may even be possible to save the "hypothesis" that the Earth is flat. In general, we should not give much credence to a hypothesis 'H' that requires ad hoc supplemental hypotheses to save it from the negative evidence. The only exception is when 'H' is virtually the only available explanation for the available data and there is no negative evidence or other strong reason against the ad hoc supplemental hypothesis (beyond its failure to have positive evidence). Thus, while 'M_R' is an ad hoc supplemental hypothesis, in C_2 we should be justified in accepting it to defuse 'w', the negative evidence of 'R'.

Finally, to bring our story to a happier end, let us suppose that the following evidence emerges in the epistemic situation C_3 that is subsequent to C_2: In the house of the two eyewitnesses from Middleton, we find some of the stolen money and some of the tools used in the robbery. Furthermore, witnesses at the bank where the robbery occurred have identified the robbers as Tricky Dick and Slippery Jim. Finally, we learn that the two "eyewitnesses" from Middleton were involved in previous robberies with Tricky Dick and Slippery Jim. In C_3 we now have positive evidence for 'L_R'. Combining this revelation with the capacity of 'L_R' to eliminate the negative evidence for the hypothesis that is virtually the only one possible, 'L_R' is now at least highly justified and 'R' seems to be completely justified.

We can now state some additional *rules for the preference of one explanation over another; such rules might be called* RULES CONCERNING NEGATIVE EVIDENCE. We shall state these rules with reference to the final epistemic situation in which the negative evidence has been explained away.

In these rules, 'supplemental hypotheses of H' should be understood as: supplemental hypotheses H needs to explain away evidence that was negative evidence in prior epistemic situations.

H > H* if

(4) H needs fewer poorly supported supplemental hypotheses than H*.
(5) The supplemental hypotheses of H are more justified than those of H*.
(6) H has proportionately more strong supplemental hypotheses than H*.
(7) H has fewer ad hoc supplemental hypotheses than H*.

Given our discussion, the rationale for these rules should be fairly obvious.

Let us now consider some applications. Suppose that in C_3 we try to save the hypothesis 'E' and its supplementation P_E by invoking the ad hoc supplemental hypothesis 'D' that the traces of the equipment being carted off *somehow* disappeared. Comparing 'E' to 'R', 'E' requires more poorly supported supplemental hypotheses; these are less justified than the supplemental hypotheses of 'R'; and 'E' has more ad hoc supplemental hypotheses than 'R'. Thus, Rules 4, 5, and 7 would give preference to 'R' over 'E' in C_3. Comparing 'R' in C_2 to 'R' in C_3, in C_2 'R' had more poorly supported supplemental hypotheses, and this supplemental hypothesis was less justified, failed to provide a strong explanation for the negative evidence, and was an ad hoc supplemental hypothesis as well; hence, by all the Rules 4–7, 'R' is a better hypothesis in C_3 than it was in C_2. A slightly more delicate comparison is between 'R' and 'E' in C_2 if the supporters of 'E' and 'P_E' proposed the ad hoc supplemental hypothesis 'D' that traces of the equipment having been carted off somehow disappeared. Rule 7 gives preference to 'R' because while 'R' needed only one ad hoc supplemental hypothesis, 'E' needed two. Rule 6 gives preference to 'E': the supplemental hypothesis of 'E' ('P_E') explains the missing equipment, while the supplemental hypothesis of 'R' that the witnesses were mistaken doesn't explain what they said. Rule 4 gives preference to 'R' because 'E' had to appeal to two poorly supported supplemental hypotheses: 'P_E' and 'D'. Rule 5 also gives preference to 'R' on two counts: first, 'P_E' has the negative evidence of the missing traces; and second, the general presumption that traces don't just disappear in this kind of a case is a reason against 'D' even if it isn't strong enough to condemn 'D' unconditionally. Thus, on balance, 'R' is preferred over 'E' in C_2. It should not be thought that this is just a matter of counting up the rules in favor of 'R' and 'E', because consideration has to be given to the generally greater importance of Rules 4, 5, and 7 over the lesser importance of Rule 6.

These examples may suggest that there is a certain redundancy in Rules 4, 5, and 7. But Rules 4 and 5 are clearly needed in addition to Rule 7: There can be supplemental hypotheses that have some measure of support but not much. In these cases both the number of such supplemental hypotheses needed as well as their comparative support become relevant. Rules 4 and 5 combined may make Rule 7 redundant. But ad hoc supplemental hypotheses are very undesirable, and this should be separately highlighted: Two marginally supported supplemental hypotheses are likely to be better than one ad hoc supplemental hypothesis, and the combined effect of Rules 4 and 5 may be insufficient to make this clear. However, because Rule 7 may be logically redundant, it is clear that the preference rules are not necessarily meant to be independent of each other. They are also dependent on each other in the sense that applying any of the rules for coping with negative evidence requires having previously applied the rules of fit.

5.2.4 Extratheoretical Considerations

Finally, there are a number of *rules that do not make a direct reference to the data base,* and for this reason they are often called extratheoretical considerations. Letting it be our understanding that H and H* include the supplemental hypotheses they need, the central considerations of this kind may be encapsulated by the following four EXTRATHEORETICAL PREFERENCE RULES:

H > H* if

(8) H coheres better with other justified statements than H*.
(9) H is simpler than H*.
(10) H is a causal explanation (preferably involving substructures) and H* is a mere observed regularity or correlation.
(11) H has a greater predictive power than H*.

Rule 8 concerning the fit with other statements may be exemplified as follows: Suppose it were the case that Oriental children were more docile and adaptive to their environment than Caucasian children who were more rebellious and intent on changing their surroundings. Because so many behavioral differences of this kind have been explained in terms of upbringing rather than genetic differences, other things being equal, an explanation of the difference in terms of learned behavior is preferable to one in terms of genetic differences in the races. Another consequence of this rule is that it is very difficult to dislodge scientific theories that have been accepted for some time. In virtue of being the accepted theory, they are highly or completely justified, if not outright unproblematic. Any competitor would therefore automatically run afoul of Rule 8. While this "principle of conservativism" may seem repugnant to the young at heart, it embodies a sound principle: Accepted scientific theories that have achieved comprehensiveness and refinement over a period of time should not be discarded unless there is a clearly better substitute for them.

The most dramatic use of Rule 9 concerning simplicity was the initial choice of the sun-centered Copernican theory over the Earth-centered Ptolomaic theory. In terms of the positive and negative evidence in the data base, there was not much to choose between these theories. However, the Copernican theory of planetary motion was far simpler than the Ptolomaic theory. In this connection, it is true that the rule of simplicity concerning supplemental hypotheses (i.e., Rule 4) also had a role. To explain the sun and the other planets revolving around the Earth, the basic Earth-centered hypothesis needed a number of supplemental hypotheses in terms of epicycles within the basic orbits of the sun and the planets. (Roughly, epicycles were smaller circular paths superimposed on the basic orbit and the celestial bodies departed from the basic orbits along these epicycles.) But beyond the need for epicycles, the Ptolomaic theory as a whole was enormously cumbersome and complex, and it is in this respect that Rule 9 comes into play most clearly.

The preference for causal explanations stated in Rule 10 should be clear. While we might accept the hypothesis that all ravens are black on the basis of all observed ravens being black, we would clearly prefer an explanation in terms of genetic coding in the DNA molecules. Similarly, the explanation in terms of molecular motion is preferable to Boyle's law, which merely inversely correlates the volume of a gas to its pressure.

Finally, Rule 11 concerning the greater predictive strength of preferred hypotheses may be exemplified by the following trivial example. Consider the hypothesis that some ravens are black but others aren't. We noted earlier that this hypothesis explains all observed ravens being black. However, as the number of observed ravens increases and it is observed that all are black, it becomes increasingly difficult to explain why there have been observed no ravens that are not black. Indeed, 'If two million ravens are observed under varied conditions in all five continents, then if some ravens are not black, some observed ravens are not black' seems highly justified. Thus, 'All observed ravens are black' becomes negative evidence for 'Some ravens are black but others aren't'. Suppose that the hypothesis is now changed to 'All easy to observe ravens are black but some difficult to observe ravens aren't black'. If this hypothesis isn't rejected by Rule 7 because of the ad hoc nature of the supplementation or by Rule 9 because of its complexity, Rule 11 constitutes yet another consideration against it. If 'difficult to observe raven' is defined as one that will never be observed, the second half of the hypothesis allows no prediction. Even if 'difficult to observe raven' isn't so defined, this hypothesis allows less determinate predictions than the hypothesis that all ravens are black, because when exactly is a raven "difficult to observe"? Because predictive power is to be measured in terms of the number of predictions and the determinateness of the predictions, in one way or the other, Rule 11 gives a reason against the hypothesis. Rule 11 might also be seen as a reason why mathematically formulated scientific hypotheses are preferable to ones that are qualitatively formulated, because the mathematical formulations allow more determinate or precise predictions.

A philosophical question that can be raised about these extratheoretical considerations is what they may have to do with truth. The rules of fit and the rules for coping with negative evidence have a clear or plausible bearing on the truth of a hypothesis. But what does simplicity or predictive power, for example, have to do with truth? Obviously, a number of different answers may be proposed. Some may simply have faith that nature is manageably simple, predictable, and coherent, so that the extratheoretical considerations give us the best shot at the truth; of course, it remains unclear how such a faith is to be ultimately justifed. Others may believe that there are no "hard facts" beyond observational evidence, so that truth simply is what is described by the most preferable theory fitting the data in which preferability is a function of the extratheoretical preference rules; but it is of course highly controversial that the relation between truth and the extratheoretical considerations can be established by a fiat of the kind urged by such a "pragmatic" theory of truth. Yet others may claim no direct tie between truth and the extratheoretical considerations and claim: because the rules relating directly or indirectly to evidence will not dictate a choice among a number of competing theories, one needs some convenient principle of choice, and the convenient choice is the one dictated by the extratheoretical preference rules. Whatever the ultimate rationale may be for appealing to extratheoretical considerations, a clear fact of scientific practice, and inferential practice in general, is that they are guided by these considerations. Within the scope of this text, we cannot hope to settle the deeper philosophical issues underlying this practice.

5.2.5 The Best Explanation and Nondemonstrative Legitimacy

Step 2 of the procedure for selecting the best explanation can now be formulated as:

> *Step 2:* Arrive at the best among the explanations surviving Step 1 by collecting more evidence if necessary and applying the Rules of Fit 1–3, the Rules Concerning Negative Evidence 4–7, and the Extratheoretical Preference Rules 8–11.

Nondemonstrative Legitimacy: Summary

'e_1, . . . , e_n / H' is a [completely] legitimate nondemonstrative argument

Other than the premises that play a background or auxiliary role, 'H' is [by far] the best available explanation of the premises (as determined by Steps 1 and 2), and the premises include most of the positive evidence of 'H'.

Step 1: If completely justified statements are deductively valid reasons for '−H', condemn 'H' as a poor explanation.

Step 2: Arrive at the best among the remaining explanations by collecting more evidence if necessary and applying the Rules of Fit 1–3, the Rules Concerning Negative Evidence 4–7, and the Extratheoretical Preference Rules 8–11.

RULES OF PREFERENCE: H > H* if

1. H has more positive evidence than H*.
2. H more strongly explains the positive evidence of H than H* explains that of H*.
3. H has less negative evidence than H*.
4. H needs fewer poorly supported supplemental hypotheses than H*.
5. Supplemental hypotheses of H are more justified than those of H*.
6. H has proportionately more strong supplemental hypotheses than H*.
7. H has fewer ad hoc supplemental hypotheses than H*.
8. H coheres better with other justified statements than H*.
9. H is simpler than H*.
10. H is a causal explanation (preferably involving substructures) and H* is a mere observed regularity or correlation.
11. H has a greater predictive power than H*.

Definitions of crucial terms

a. 'H' strongly [weakly] *explains* 'e' =
'H / e' *or* 'H, a / e' *or* 'H, a / v' is deductively valid, where 'a' is an available auxiliary premise that is completely [highly] justified and 'v' is an indeterminate variant of 'e'.

b. When 'd' is at least highly justified,
'd' is *positive evidence* for 'H' if 'H' explains 'd', and
'd' is *negative evidence* for 'H' if 'H' explains '−d'.

c. Where 'd' is negative evidence for 'H' with 'a' as an auxiliary premise, 'S_H' is a *supplemental hypothesis* for 'H' if it doesn't conflict with 'H' and its truth would make 'a' or 'd' less than highly justified.
A supplemental hypothesis for 'H' is *strong* if it explains 'd' or highly justifies '−d' independently of 'H'.

d. A supplemental hypothesis for 'H' is ad hoc = there are no positive grounds for the supplemental hypothesis beyond its ability to defuse the negative evidence of 'H'.

Given Steps 1 and 2 of our procedure, we can restate our account of nondemonstrative legitimacy given in Section 5.1 as follows:

> An argument for H is a (completely) legitimate nondemonstrative argument if Steps 1 and 2 result in H being (by far) the best explanation and most of the positive evidence for H is included among the premises.

The reason for the last clause is this: Suppose we have observed innumerable ravens and observed them all to be black. If we construe all but one of these observations as background given in the epistemic situation, 'This raven is black / All ravens are black' might become a legitimate nondemonstative argument. Because this would stretch our intuitive idea of what a legitimate nondemonstrative argument is, we require that the premises of such an argument incorporate most of the positive evidence in the data base. A full summary of the material covered in this section is given on the boxed chart on page 289.

In Chapter 4 we took a completely legitimate nondemonstrative argument to be one in which the conclusion is completely justified if the conjunction of the premises are completely justified. The account just given should approximate this if we come down sufficiently hard on the qualification "*By far* the best explanation," by requiring, among other things, that the conclusion strongly explain the premises. However, it should be clear that there can be fairly strong nondemonstrative arguments in which the conclusions would be at least highly justified if the conjunction of the premises were completely justified. Those arguments would be legitimate nondemonstrative arguments, albeit not completely legitimate because the conclusions aren't *by far* the best explanations of the premises. At least roughly, the degree of legitimacy to be attached to a nondemonstrative argument, and the degree to which the premises of such an argument justify the conclusion, is the degree to which the conclusion is a better explanation of the premises than the other available competing explanations. Such then is our general account of nondemonstrative legitimacy.

EXERCISES—SECTION 5.2

In all of the exercises, claims of deductive validity need to be made to justify the claim that something is positive or negative evidence. To avoid redundancy of work, the chains need not always be provided. However, enough should always be said so as to leave no room for doubt that the chain could be produced on demand. Thus, for example, it would suffice to say things like, "Two uses of MP and S show the validity of . . . ," and "Aside from steps of S and Adj, three uses of MP and a use of HS, show the validity of . . ." If an argument form has been shown to be valid by such a statement or a chain, subsequent uses of the same form need not be justified within the same problem set. *Furthermore,* provide auxiliary premises as needed and indicate them to be at least highly justified. *Finally,* unless explicitly asked to assess whether a supplemental hypothesis is sufficiently justified to defuse the negative evidence, assume that once a supplemental hypothesis is proposed, it defuses the negative evidence so that the assessment shifts from Rule 3 to the other rules, especially Rules 4–7.

Problem Set A

1. Assume

   'd': America lost the war in Vietnam to a second-rate military power.

   to be completely justified. This may be taken to substantiate the communist hypothesis

   'c': American military power is a paper tiger (i.e., is not at all what it's cracked up to be).

   Let the Reagan hypothesis be

   'r': America is a great first-rate military power.

Problem a: Show that 'd' is positive evidence for 'c' and negative evidence for 'r'.

Problem b: Suggest a supplemental hypothesis 's[r]' that would defuse the negative evidence against 'r' if 's[r]' were sufficiently justified.

2. Reread the story for problem 1 of Problem Set D in Section 2.5 (Chapter 2). Use the following scheme of abbreviation:

   'c': Cutts is correct in saying: upon looking at his watch, Douglas left the September 1 meeting telling the crowd, "It is now past midnight and it is Sunday morning—I'll go to church and you may go to Hell."
   't': The September 1 meeting did not last over twenty-four hours.
   'f': September 1 was a Friday.
   'p': The September 1 meeting came to a close at 10:30 P.M.

   Assume 't' is highly justified, 'f' completely justified (by the perpetual calendar), and 'p' highly justified (by the reports in the Detroit and Chicago papers).

Problem a: Show that 'f' and 'p' are negative evidence for 'c'.

Problem b: Suggest a supplemental hypothesis consistent with all the assumptions of the problem and (i) show that it would defuse the evidence if it were sufficiently justified, and (ii) assess whether it is sufficiently justified.

3. Reread the story of Problem Set C of Section 2.5 (Chapter 2) and subtract from it Jane's scribbled message that Tom was her murderer. Let 'k' and 'e' be given by:

   'k': Tom killed Jane between 10:00 and 11:30 P.M.
   'e': Tom was at his home at least every half an hour between 10 P.M. and midnight.

Problem a: Put yourself in the narrator's position before the revelations about the participants' problems of gauging time after they left Tom's party. Taking 'e' to be highly justified on the basis of the participants' testimony, explain why 'e' is negative evidence for the hypothesis 'k'. (Do not complicate the problem: just one highly or completely justified auxiliary premise will do.)

Problem b: Given the revelations about the participants' problem with time judgments, take

   's1': The participants' judgment of time during the party is unreliable.

as a supplemental hypothesis for 'k'. Explain how 's1' would defuse the negative evidence for 'k' if it were sufficiently justified, and assess whether it is sufficiently justified (given the revelations about the problems the participants had with time judgments).

Problem c: Given the revelations about the participants' time judgment after the party, consider the supplemental hypothesis:

> 's2': Tom surreptitiously set the clock at the party one hour behind (so that *n* o'clock on that clock really was $n + 1$ o'clock), and the testimony of the participants was based on this clock.

Explain how 's2' would defuse the negative evidence for 'k' if it were sufficiently justified, and assess whether it is sufficiently justified (given the revelations about the problems the participants had with time judgments).

Problem d: Is either supplemental hypothesis a strong supplemental hypothesis? Justify your answer, and if a supplemental hypothesis is strong, fully justify the claim that it explains the relevant thing. (Recall that the participants did testify that Tom was gone between nine and ten in the evening. Take the fact of this testimony to be completely justified.)

Problem Set B

Chubby, a new hamburger chain, has decided to compete in the Bay Area of California with McDonald's. To this end, they have built a number of stores in the Bay Area so that the following is highly justified:

> 'a': Availability, service, locations, and the physical attractiveness of the stores are virtually identical for the Chubby and McDonald's chains in the Bay Area.

The owners of the Chubby chain believe that their hamburgers are better than McDonald's in the sense that their hamburgers are (or would be) preferred in taste by most consumers (if they tried both kinds of hamburgers). Let their hypothesis then be given by:

> 'h': Chubby hamburgers are better than McDonald's hamburgers.

Critical to the success of the new chain is the need to get customers to try their hamburgers; therefore, let us suppose that shortly after they open they engage in an advertising campaign, and consider the following three possible outcomes in the Bay Area:

(A) The sale of Chubby hamburgers goes up significantly with the advertising campaign, and it stays at that higher level.
(B) The sale of Chubby hamburgers goes up significantly with the advertising campaign, but soon drops off to the former low level despite the continued advertising campaign and despite the lack of any new advertising campaign or gimmicks from McDonald's.
(C) The advertising campaign has no effect on the sale of Chubby hamburgers at all, and throughout the period, the sale of Chubby hamburgers remains at the low level it was before the advertising campaign started.

A successful advertising campaign would at least get people to try Chubby hamburgers, and thus we can think of a trial period in which customers try Chubby hamburgers, and let us suppose that it is highly justified that virtually everyone who tries Chubby hamburgers has tried McDonald's hamburgers. Use the following scheme of abbreviation:

> 't': A significant number of people have tried both Chubby and McDonald's hamburgers.

'u': The sale of Chubby hamburgers in the posttrial period is significantly higher than during the pretrial period.
'c': The sale price of Chubby hamburgers is the same as that of McDonald's hamburgers.

Problem 1: For each of the possible outcomes (A), (B), and (C) above, assume that 'c' and the described outcome are completely justified, and determine whether there is positive, negative, or no evidence for or against 'h'.

Problem 2: In the outcome(s) where problem 1 yielded negative evidence for 'h', suppose the owners of the Chubby chain propose the supplemental hypothesis S that it is difficult to change consumer habits of buying products with long-established brand names.

(a) Explain how S would defuse the negative evidence of 'h' if S were sufficiently justified.
(b) What would be needed if S is not to be an ad hoc supplemental hypothesis?
(c) Suppose we take 'h' and S to be combined into one hypothesis and compare it to the competing hypothesis that McDonald's hamburgers are better. Restricting oneself to data of the sort provided by (A) and (B), would preference Rule 11 favor one hypothesis over the other?

Problem 3: In the outcome(s) where problem 1 yielded negative evidence for 'h', suppose that a few of the Chubby stores, unlike most, continued to have significantly higher sales during the posttrial period (when compared to the pretrial period).

(a) Suggest a supplemental hypothesis based on this finding and explain how this supplemental hypothesis would defuse the negative evidence against 'h' if it were sufficiently justified.
(b) Assume it is completely justified that the gains of these few Chubby outlets were matched by losses in the nearby McDonald's outlets, and that at the other outlets, the customers returned to McDonald's outlets in the posttrial period. To make things concrete and also simple, suppose that there are 100 McDonald's outlets and 100 Chubby outlets in the Bay Area, and that they can be paired so that, for example, customers at McDonald's store #4 as well as Chubby's store #4 choose only between McDonald's store #4 and Chubby's store #4. Adjust our scheme of abbreviation as follows:

'm': McDonald's hamburgers are better than Chubby hamburgers.
'a1': Availability, service, location, and the physical attractiveness of McDonald's store #1 and Chubby's store #1 are virtually identical.
't1': A significant number of people frequenting McDonald's store #1 have tried hamburgers at Chubby's store #1.
'u1': The sale of hamburgers at Chubby's store #1 in the posttrial period is significantly higher than during the pretrial period.
'r1': Most customers at McDonald's store #1 who tried hamburgers at Chubby's store #1 returned to become customers at McDonald's store #1 in the posttrial period.

'a2', 't2', etc. would be the same with store #2 instead of store #1, and so on. Assume 't1'–'t100' to be highly justified, and that at least initially so are 'a1'–'a100'. Assume 'u1'–'u3' and '−u4' to '−u100' to be completely justified. Similarly take '−r1' to '−r3' and 'r4'–'r100' to be completely justified.

Problem: Assuming that both Chubby's and McDonald's propose to defuse the negative evidence in the way suggested in problem #3(a), how would 'h' and 'm' fare according to the Preference Rules 1, 2, and 4–7?

Problem 4: Assume that an outcome of problem 1 that provides positive evidence for 'h' in fact occurs. Now the owners of the Chubby chain want to find out whether consumers are willing to pay fifteen cents more for Chubby hamburgers than the McDonald's hamburgers. What would give them positive evidence that virtually all customers are willing to pay the extra fifteen cents and what would give them negative evidence for this hypothesis?

Problem Set C

Mary's husband Joe has often been coming home quite late recently, and Mary has begun to worry because he also started losing romantic interest in her at about the same time. Her suspicions seemed somewhat confirmed when she called Joe at his office around eight in the evening a number of times when he was late returning; she never got an answer, and on those days he came home quite late despite his office being no more than a half an hour away. Let 'W' and 'L' be two hypotheses Mary forms:

'W': Joe is just working late at his office these days and is not being unfaithful.
'L': Joe has a lover on the sly these days with whom he is spending the evenings.

Let the scheme of abbreviation be given by:

'd1': Joe has often been coming home late these days.
'd2': Joe has recently lost romantic interest in Mary.
'd3': On the number of times Mary called Joe around eight in the evening, Joe never answered his office phone.
'v1': On some occasions when Mary calls, Joe does not answer the phone.

Assume 'd1'–'d3' are completely justified items of data for Mary. Assume also that Mary is highly justified in believing that Joe is a monogamous sort of person who finds himself incapable of being romantically inclined toward two women at the same time. Finally, assume that 'L ⊃ v1' is highly justified.

Problem 1: Relative to 'd1'–'d3', which hypothesis (if any) would be preferred by the Rules of Fit?

Being a careful person, Mary considers the possibility that Joe may be going out to eat around eight, and asks him, "Don't you ever get hungry working so late at the office?" Joe replies that he goes out for a bite around eight every night. She calls Joe on many evenings in the following days (at times other than eight) and finds him to be always there.

[By shifting the time reference, there is a problem about which days 'these days' refers to in the data statements. Perhaps 'L' was true but Joe broke up with her, or perhaps the lover is away on a trip for a couple of weeks. Assume that these complications can be ignored. Perhaps Joe shows no signs of distress and Mary knows Joe well enough to be highly justified in believing that if he broke up with a lover or was separated even for a few days from her, he would show signs of extreme distress. In any event, assume that we can simplify our problem by allowing 'these days' to cover the entire period so that, *in the absence of evidence or considerations to the contrary,* what was valid evidence for or against 'W' or 'L' at one time is also valid evidence at other times.]

Extend the scheme of abbreviation as follows:

'd4': Joe always answered his office phone on the many evenings Mary called him (at times other than eight).
'v2': Joe often answered his office phone when Mary called him in the evenings.

Take 'd4' to be a completely justified item of data for Mary and assume that 'W ⊃ v2' is highly justified.

Problem 2: What supplemental hypothesis for 'W' did Mary consider, and how would it defuse the negative evidence if it were sufficiently justified? Is it a strong supplemental hypothesis? If so, show it to be one.

Problem 3: Including an assessment of whether the supplemental hypothesis proposed for 'W' is sufficiently justified to defuse the negative evidence, relative to 'd1'–'d4', which of 'W' and 'L' (if any) is on balance the better hypothesis?

When Mary mentions the matter to her friend, her friend suggests: "Maybe Joe was lucky, because whenever you called him, he was away from his lover and happened to be in his office to answer your call."

Problem 4: What supplemental hypothesis has been proposed for 'L' and how would it defuse the negative evidence if it were sufficiently justified? Is it a strong supplemental hypothesis? If so, show it to be one.

Problem 5: Given that the suggested supplemental hypotheses were proposed for 'W' and 'L', relative to 'd1'–'d4', which of 'W' and 'L' (if any) is on balance the better hypothesis according to Rules 1–7?

Problem 6: Suppose that the supplemental hypothesis proposed by Mary's friend is extended to something like this: "Joe is extremely clever and will arrange things so that whatever attempt Mary or anyone else makes to discover his dalliance, they will always fail because he will show up at the right place at the right time." Suppose that this is incorporated as part of the "theory" 'L'. Would any extra-theoretical considerations favor 'W' over 'L'?

Problem Set D

Consider the findings by a team of astronomers (headed by Turner) that was reported in the following article in the May 19, 1986, issue of *Time:*

> The Kitt Peak telescope had been aimed at what appeared to be two quasars. . . . Gathered by the telescope's parabolic mirror, the light from each of the quasars was converted into a spectrum, from which a quasar's characteristics and even its distance can be determined. . . . The two spectra recorded at Kitt Peak were virtually identical. This meant that if each were from a different quasar, the two objects would not only have identical chemical properties and temperature but also would be the same distance . . . away—a highly unlikely coincidence. [This suggested that there is only one quasar.] How does one quasar produce two images? The answer, astronomers say, lies in a "gravitational lens," an immense object with a powerful gravitational field located somewhere between the quasar and the earth. As light from the quasar approaches the object, it is diverted from its original path by the intense field and produces what earthbound observers see as a multiple image.

[A diagram is provided by *Time* that is like the one given in Figure 5.1. On that diagram the solid line is the path of light predicted by the gravitational-lens hypothesis, and the dotted line (and the part of the solid line it joins) is the path that would be followed by the light rays if there were two quasars. The article continues:]

> As long ago as 1915, Albert Einstein predicted that as a consequence of his general theory of relativity, light rays would be bent if they passed through the intense gravitational field of a massive object. That prediction was confirmed by British astronomer Arthur Eddington in 1919. . . . Then in 1979, two Britons and an American working at Kitt Peak observed the first lensing phenomenon. . . . Since then, five other examples of quasar multiple images have been observed, and intervening lens galaxies found for three of them.

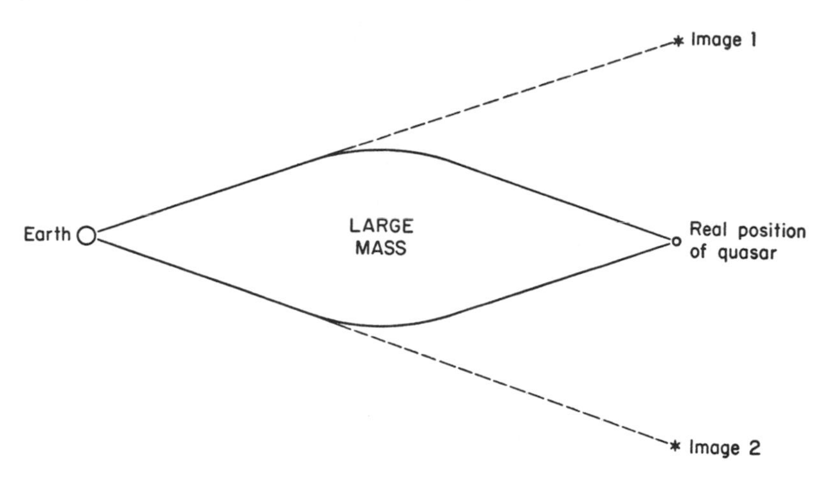

Figure 5.1.

Let two hypotheses be given by:

'T': There are two quasars at locations corresponding to the positions of images 1 and 2 in Figure 5.1.
'O': There is one quasar at the location corresponding to "real position of quasar" in Figure 5.1, and there is a massive body at the location corresponding to "large mass" on the diagram.

Use the following scheme of abbreviation:

'd1': Two quasar images are observed at Kitt Peak as described in the article.
'd2': The recorded spectra of the two quasar images are virtually identical.
'i': The quasars (producing the two quasar images) have (virtually) identical properties.

Take 'd1' and 'd2' to be completely justified items of data, and let 'd2 ≡ i' be one of the highly or completely justified auxiliary premises. You should also take 'O ⊃ i' as trivially and completely justified. Finally, the second part of the article that was given should be taken to justify completely one of the auxiliary premises you need.

Problem 1: With reference to the Rules of Fit, determine which of the two hypotheses 'T' and 'O' is better relative to the data presented.

The article continues as follows:

> While none of these previous multiple images were separated in the sky by more than seven arc seconds, the latest dual quasar images are 157 arc seconds . . . apart. In order to bend light that much, the lens must have the mass of a thousand galaxies. . . . So far, however, it is an invisible elephant. Says . . . Schmidt, the Caltech astronomer, "The fact that we do not see anything there makes it rather challenging. It is difficult to hide an appropriate cluster of mass between us and the quasar." Rising to the challenge, Turner's team suggests another possible source of the powerful gravitational lens: a black hole at least a thousand times as large as the Milky Way galaxy. . . . Still, astrophysicists find it difficult to explain how so tremendous a black hole could have formed. . . . Another intriguing possibility for the lens effect [has been suggested]: the cosmic string. This weird one-dimensional creature was derived . . . by physicists pondering the events that occurred in the first fraction of a second after

> the Big Bang created the universe... Although infinitesimally thinner than the nucleus of an atom, those that have survived should have formidable gravitational fields. Each mile of length could contain a mass equivalent to the earth.... Turner has reservations. "I give the cosmic string theory less than a fifty–fifty chance of being the answer.... But if it is, it would be extremely exciting. Just think, we would be looking at a fossil of the Big Bang."

Extend the scheme of abbreviation as follows:

'd3': We have difficulty in finding the large mass between us and the quasar.
'b': The large mass is a black hole.
's': The large mass is a cosmic string.
'c': Although it was unlikely, in fact the two distinct quasars have virtually identical properties.

Let 'd3' be a completely justified item of data.

Problem 2: Show how 'd3' can be taken as negative evidence for 'O'.

Problem 3: Show how 'b v s' is a supplemental hypothesis for 'O' and how 'c' is a supplemental hypothesis for 'T'. If any of these are strong supplemental hypotheses, show that they are.

Problem 4: Assume that because of the negative evidence neither 'O' nor 'T' has been accepted. Is 'c' an ad hoc supplemental hypothesis? Is 'b v s' an ad hoc supplemental hypothesis?

Problem 5: In light of the previous problems, how would you rate 'O' and 'T' according to the Rules Concerning Negative Evidence?

5.3 Varieties of Nondemonstrative Arguments

Our discussion in Section 5.2 essentially shows legitimate nondemonstrative arguments to be inferences to the best explanation. This characterization has the crucial advantage of giving a uniform account of *all* legitimate nondemonstrative arguments. This advantage, however, has a certain price: it tends to gloss over certain differences between various different kinds of nondemonstrative arguments. In this section we shall broadly divide nondemonstrative arguments into several kinds.

We have been concerned with nondemonstrative arguments in which legitimacy cannot be easily assessed by the method of converting them into valid deductive arguments by adding appropriate "missing premises." This means we are primarily concerned with nondemonstrative arguments in which the premises are essentially particular statements, that is, arguments in which the particular premises cannot be augmented by plausible general statements to convert them into ones that are deductively valid. We may now divide these arguments, which we may call "essentially" nondemonstrative arguments, into those having particular conclusions and those having general conclusions.

The example of one of the robbers getting off the motorcycle can be taken as characteristic of nondemonstrative arguments with *particular conclusions.* A crucial feature of arguments of this type is that the explanation of the particular premises by the particular conclusion implicitly or explicitly depends on some *general statements* that are accepted as completely or highly justified in the epistemic circumstance. Without such a dependence, it is difficult to see how one particular statement can explain another particular statement. In our example, we relied on the statement 'If someone got off the motorcycle at this point and the consistency of the road is uniform, the tracks become shallower at this point'. In its explicit formulation, this statement is particular, because it doesn't explicitly say anything about *all* vehicles and their tracks. However, we accept the statement about this particular motorcycle and its tracks only because we know that objects having greater weight exert greater force on the surface on which they rest. We may have difficulties in the precise formulation of the general statement on which we are relying. Still, we are at least in the position to take it as completely or highly justified that "things like this" generally behave "like that." In this sense, nondemonstrative arguments from particular premises to particular conclusions always rely *at least tacitly* on general statements that are accepted as highly or completely justified in the epistemic circumstance.

Nondemonstrative arguments with particular premises and general conclusions may roughly be divided into two kinds depending on whether the conclusion is a "descriptive generalization" or an "explanatory generalization" relative to the premises. Several things should be said about this distinction in a preliminary way.

(1) By an inference of a descriptive generalization I mean the inference of a generalization that is couched in a vocabulary that is of the same sort as, or pretty close to, the vocabulary used in the premises that state the data. Suppose one wonders whether the failure to study hard enough or the failure to get sufficient sleep accounts for a poor performance on college exams. If such a person tests the insufficient-sleep hypothesis by sleeping more before exams and finds good test performances to follow well-rested nights, he or she may conclude that insufficient sleep was the cause of poor test performance. Except for the term 'cause' (which makes the conclusion a tacitly general one), the conclusion is couched in the same sort of terms as the data: 'sleep' and 'poor test performance'. Similarly, suppose the data record the amount of pressure applied to a gas and the volume of the gas, and the generalization claims the relation to be inversely proportional (Boyle's law). Again the vocabulary of the premises describing the data and the vocabulary of the generalization are essentially the same; hence the inference is an inference of a descriptive generalization. On the other hand, if the data are stated in terms of the volume and pressure of gases and the generalization is in terms of the molecular motion, the vocabulary is very different. The inference of the generalization in terms of molecular motion is an instance of an inference of an "explanatory generalization." While more adequate ways of distinguishing inferences of descriptive and explanatory generalizations may be available, a useful and simple way of distinguishing them is in terms of

whether or not (with the exception of the term 'cause') the generalization is couched in the same kind of vocabulary as the data or evidence.

(2) It would be an oversimplification to suppose that generalizations (as opposed to inferences of generalizations) break into two neat categories of descriptive and explanatory generalizations. In fact, there is something like a continuum between 'All ravens are black' on the one hand and quantum mechanics on the other. Boyle's law and low-level scientific claims in general differ only marginally from commonsense generalizations that are couched in the vocabulary of ordinary observations. Thus, for example, consider:

Given a stimulus S and several patterns of responses, positive reinforcement of a response pattern enhances that response to S and negative reinforcement suppresses that response to S.

For any commodity C, if other things are equal, the price of C varies inversely with the supply of C.

Certainly the vocabulary of positive and negative reinforcements is different from the vocabulary of 'the rat was given food' and 'the rat was given an electric shock of five volts'. On the other hand, the distance between 'cheese' and 'positive reinforcement' is relatively small; correspondingly, we consider the crude generalizations of early psychology and economics to be pretty close to commonsense generalizations. The situation is quite different even with Newtonian physics. The distance between 'It took the two cylinders the same amount of time to go down the inclined plane' and the theoretical statements of Newtonian physics is significant; for example, aside from the concept of mass, which is quite different from that of weight (which is understood as force), Newtonian physics requires concepts of differential calculus to arrive at the concept of "velocity at an instant," which can't be understood in terms of distance covered over a unit of time. By the time we arrive at twentieth-century physics, the ultimate vocabulary is very far removed from ordinary observational vocabulary, and correspondingly we have a sense of the paradigm of an advanced science.

(3) Taking the ordinary vocabulary of observations and their commonsense generalizations (which may involve the additional term 'cause') as our starting point, the continuum we have just noted can roughly be conceived in terms of each new level of generalization requiring an inference of an explanatory generalization, which carries with it a new vocabulary relative to the previous level. Within any given level, we can often rely on inferences of descriptive generalizations in which the vocabulary is of the same kind as that of the evidence or data (usually because the evidence has been redescribed using the vocabulary of that level); but to advance to a new level in the first place, an inference of an explanatory generalization with an essentially new vocabulary is needed.

Perhaps we can see this in a simple way as follows: Our ordinary vocabulary of observations such as 'The needle on the meter moved' or 'The

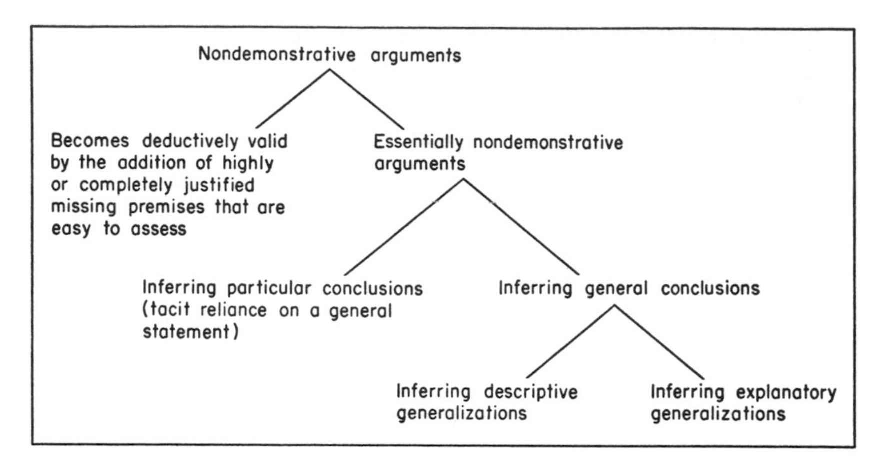

Figure 5.2. Summary of the types of nondemonstrative arguments.

finger pressure of squeezing a balloon increased' might allow us to say, 'Squeezing the balloon (or increasing the finger pressure on the balloon) made it (caused it to become) smaller'. But this would not allow a precise formulation of Boyle's law; thus, the concept of the amount of force on a unit area of surface has to be introduced to formulate Boyle's law. Given Boyle's law and a way of measuring pressure in the laboratory, the meter readings obtained can be explained. Thus, relative to the crude vocabulary of ordinary observations, the inference of Boyle's law (along with statements linking pressure to meter readings) may be seen as an inference of an explanatory generalization. On the other hand, once the concept of pressure and the experimental methods of measuring pressure are given, the data can be described in terms of pressure and volume, so that within this background the inference of Boyle's law can be seen as a descriptive generalization. However, no set of inferred descriptive generalizations couched in the vocabulary of pressure and volume is going to allow us to infer an explanation or generalization in terms of molecular motion; that would require another inference of an explanatory generalization that is couched in a new vocabulary. Once we have the theory of molecular motion, this can explain Boyle's law as well as what Boyle's law explained; and for certain purposes it may be convenient to redescribe increasing pressure on a gas as decreasing the distances between the molecules composing the gas. Thus, although descriptive generalizations may be used within any given level of generalization that is achieved, the crucial development of a science can roughly be seen in terms of successive inferences of explanatory generalizations in which the vocabularies move further and further away from our ordinary observational vocabulary.

The broad division of nondemonstrative arguments is summarized in Figure 5.2. Given our discussion of Chapter 4 and Section 5.2, what remains to be discussed in greater detail are inferences of explanatory generalizations and inferences of descriptive generalizations. These will be the topics of the next two sections.

EXERCISES—SECTION 5.3

In each of the following examples identify the argument as one of the following types: (i) an argument that becomes deductively valid by the addition of a highly or completely justified missing premise; (ii) an essentially nondemonstrative argument that infers a particular conclusion; (iii) an essentially nondemonstrative argument that infers a descriptive generalization; or (iv) an essentially nondemonstrative argument that infers an explanatory generalization. In case (i) identify the missing premise needed, and in case (ii) identify a general statement on which one is at least tacitly relying.

1. The inference *from* 'the measurement of blood alcohol levels of people and their general behavior' *to* 'people lose significant control when their blood alcohol level reaches .01 percent'.
2. The inference that could have been made in the early part of Problem Set D in Section 5.2 *from* the data that were presented there *to* the claim that there was only one quasar that was the source of the multiple quasar images.
3. Inference *from* a person's breath reeking of alcohol *to* that of his having been drinking.
4. Inference *from* the known and apparent location of a star (observed by Eddington during a total eclipse) *to* 'Light bends when it passes through an intense gravitational field'. [Assume that nothing theoretically sophisticated is needed to determine the known and apparent positions of a star.]
5. Inference *from* 'the fingerprints on the gun match those of Jones' *to* 'Jones touched the gun'.
6. The inference Mary might have made in the early part of Problem Set C in Section 5.2 *from* Joe's loss of romantic interest, his late returns home, and his failure to answer his office phone *to* Joe has a lover with whom he is spending the evenings.
7. The inference *from* such phenomena as the room becoming uniformly heated if a hot object is placed in one part of it *to* the law of thermodynamics that entropy increases in cases like these.
8. The inference *from* massive data correlating people and their fingerprints *to* no two people have identical fingerprints.

5.4 Inferring Explanatory Generalizations

We have seen that inferring explanatory generalizations is central to the progress of science. This is a natural consequence if we understand science as aiming for the most general explanations of phenomena. If we rely on our ordinary vocabulary for describing observations, we quickly reach an upper bound to the generality we can attain. When we ignite a piece of paper, we may observe that it is reduced to ashes. We may then infer the descriptive generalization that burning paper causes (or is always attended by) the paper's being reduced to ashes. Observing that a piece of iron left in air results in its becoming rusty, we may again infer the descriptive generalization that air causes iron to rust. But can we somehow find a generalization or an explanation that would account for both the burned paper being reduced to ashes and iron rusting in air? In terms of the ordinary vocabulary that is (or was) available, there seems to be no way of doing this and we have reached an upper bound of the generality we can attain by inferring descriptive generalizations.

Early attempts to find a common explanation for the two phenomena introduced the notion of phlogistons: both paper and iron contained phlogistons that separated away in the process of burning the paper and leaving the iron in air. Somewhat later it was found that a certain gas increased this activity, and that gas was called dephlogisticated air; because the air was lacking in phlogistons, the phlogistons from the iron and the paper filled that vacuum of phlogistons that much more quickly. Various quantitative experiments, however, produced increasingly more negative evidence against the phlogiston theory. It was finally abandoned when Lavoisier produced an alternative theory that explained the available data: the dephlogisticated air was renamed "oxygen," and the burning paper and the rusting iron were accounted for in terms of oxygen combining with the elements in paper and iron. In this way both phenomena were conceived as instances of oxidation—combustion being an instance of rapid oxidation.

What this example shows is generally true. The use of ordinary concepts and inferences of descriptive generalizations based on them quickly lead to an upper bound of generality that can be attained; greater generality can only be attained by reconceptualizing our world in terms of new concepts and new entities these new concepts usher in. Phlogiston and oxidation are new concepts that allowed formation of hypotheses of sufficient generality to explain both the process of the burning paper and that of the rusting iron. Science is often said to give us the underlying explanation of observable phenomena, and we can now see why this is correct. Observational concepts or terms are disparate, and must be so if they are to pick out different aspects of experience. If we are to have a general explanation for phenomena that are separately identified by the observational terms, a new vocabulary must be found that would unite these phenomena and allow a general explanation to be formulated. Because of its use of the new uniting vocabulary, the explanation will be seen to give us the "underlying" explanation.

The crucial step from common sense and low-level science to an advanced science is taken by the formation of new concepts, and in terms of these new concepts explanatory generalizations can be formulated and justified as being the best explanation of the observable phenomena. More than anything else, the formation of new concepts through which new general hypotheses may be formulated is the act of scientific genius for which there can be no rules or recipes. However, once the vocabulary is available and the hypotheses are formulated, our account of nondemonstrative arguments in terms of the inference to the best explanation can again be applied. But how are we to justify a new theory by reference to observations if a new theory is couched entirely in terms of new concepts that are distinct from observational concepts? A feature of a set of explanatory generalizations that constitutes a theory is that some of them will be hypotheses framed entirely in the new vocabulary, while others will relate such hypotheses back to the observational vocabulary. It is through these "bridge laws" that the entire set of explanatory generalizations that constitute the theory can be justified as the best explanation of the observable phenomena.

Before exemplifying the justification of an explanatory theory, one further general remark about the advanced sciences may be in order. We have noted that the aim of science is generality. To the extent that we conceive of physics, biology, and chemistry as distinct sciences, this aim of generality is not fully achieved. It is therefore natural that there should be a drive to unify all the distinct sciences by means of a single vocabulary and a single theory composed of relatively few laws or hypotheses stated in that ultimate vocabulary. The prospects of achieving this to a significant extent now seem to be in sight. That is, it appears increasingly that physics may take on the role of the universal science. Fundamental chemical laws can be seen to be explained by basic principles of physics. Significant portions of phenomena traditionally studied by biology can now be explained in chemical terms, and neurophysiology seems to provide the best prospects for explaining a variety of psychological phenomena. Given the successes we have had, we can anticipate a continued preference for physical explanations over other kinds of explanations.

Let us conclude this section by giving an example of explanatory generalizations that are inferred as the best explanation of the available data. As our example, I select Mendel's pioneering work in genetics. A monk and abbot of the Augustinian order, Mendel carried out a series of experiments in the monastery garden with the culinary pea. He concentrated on a variety of factors in the pea such as the form of the seed, color of the unripe pods, the stem length. For each such factor, the peas displayed two alternative characteristics—the seed form was round or wrinkled, the color of the seeds was gray or white, the stem lengths were tall or dwarf. Mendel took a generation of peas (generation g[0]) and crossed the two alternative characteristics to form the next generation g[1]. Thus, with respect to stem length, each member of g[1] had one tall parent and one dwarf parent. As it turned out, tall members outnumbered dwarf members among g[1] (although the actual ratio turns out to be irrelevant). With respect to the color of the seed, each member of g[1] had one gray parent and one white parent, and in g[1] gray seeds outnumbered white seeds. Generation g[2] was formed by self-fertilizing the members of g[1]. With respect to stem length, members of g[2] that came from dwarf parents were all dwarf, while those that came from tall parents divided into

787 tall and 277 dwarf offspring; that is, the split was 74 to 26 percent in favor of the tall offspring. With respect to the color of the seed, all members of g[2] that had white parents were white, while members of g[2] that came from gray parents divided 76 to 24 percent in favor of gray. Each of the various factors Mendel studied displayed the same pattern.

To account for the data he accumulated, Mendel introduced the concept of a gene and formulated hypotheses in terms of it that accounted for the data. The hypotheses he developed are explanatory generalizations using this new concept, and the meaning of the concept (or the nature of the entity to which the concept refers) can only be understood in terms of Mendel's explanatory hypotheses. For our purpose, these hypotheses may be taken in the following way:

The first hypothesis involves the postulation of genes and their states:

H_1: For each factor, there is a corresponding gene, and each alternative characteristic of the factor corresponds to alternative states of the gene. [Somewhat aberrantly, I will say a gene *in* one of these alternative states is an allele.]

Thus, there is a gene that corresponds to the factor of stem length, and the gene is either in a state corresponding to the characteristic of being tall or to the characteristic of being dwarf. A gene in the state corresponding to tall would be an allele according to my usage, as would a gene in a state corresponding to dwarf. Clearly H_1 is also a bridge law because it links observational concepts like tall to the new concept of a gene.

The next three hypotheses relate to how genes are passed on from one generation to another.

H_2: For each factor, an individual has two alleles (which may or may not be of the same type), and each of the individual's gametes (sex cells) has one of the two genes (or alleles), which is randomly chosen.

If we let 'T' and 'd' stand for alleles corresponding to tall and dwarf stems, an individual pea has one of the following three combinations of alleles: ⟨T,T⟩, ⟨T,d⟩, ⟨d,d⟩. Given H_2, gametes of individuals with alleles ⟨T,T⟩ and ⟨d,d⟩ will, respectively, have the alleles T and d. H_2 and obvious probabilistic considerations highly justify roughly 50 percent of the gametes of an individual of type ⟨T,d⟩ having T and the remainder having d.

H_3: Fertilization of a maternal and paternal gamete is random.

H_4: The fertilized egg and the individual resulting from it have a pair of alleles for each factor, one coming from the maternal gamete and one coming from the paternal gamete.

H_3 claims that there is no tendency of a gamete with a certain allele to fertilize with a gamete having the same or opposite allele.

The last hypothesis may be expressed by means of a definition:

Definition: For any factor and its alternative characteristics X and x, X is the dominant characteristic if and only if offspring having X outnumber offspring having x when parents having X are crossed with parents having x. If an allele corresponds to the dominant characteristic of a factor, the allele is also called dominant. A characteristic or allele alternative to the one that is dominant is called recessive.

H_5: Given H_1 and H_2, an individual exhibits a recessive characteristic if and only if it has two alleles corresponding to that characteristic; an individual exhibits a dominant characteristic if and only if it has at least one allele corresponding to that characteristic.

Clearly, H_5 functions as another bridge law.

It can be shown that the explanatory hypotheses H_1–H_5 explain the data Mendel collected. To indicate this, we shall only consider the stem lengths of the peas, which are tall and dwarf. Because the derivation of the data from the hypotheses and background premises is reasonably complex, the reader is advised to follow the tree diagram in Figure 5.3. The branches act as deductively valid reasons for what is below, and the extremities (or twigs) are deductively valid reasons for the data d_1 and d_2 found at the base of the tree.

Let us start with the derivation of d_1. Two background statements that are completely justified are:

a_1: All members of the generation g[1] are offspring of one tall parent and one dwarf parent.

a_2: There are more tall members of g[1] than dwarf members.

Given a_1, a_2, and the definition of dominant and recessive, tall is dominant and dwarf is recessive. Thus, by the postulation of genes [H_1], there being two alleles per factor in an individual [H_2], and the bridge law [H_5] about what gets exhibited, all dwarf members of g[1] have ⟨d,d⟩ allele pairs. Obviously, H_2 and H_4 constitute deductively valid reasons for: If both parents are of the type ⟨d,d⟩, the offspring will be of type ⟨d,d⟩. A completely justified auxiliary premise is

a_3: The members of the generation g[2] result from self-fertilization of the members of g[1].

Given this premise, as well as dwarfs of g[1] having ⟨d,d⟩ and the offspring of ⟨d,d⟩ being ⟨d,d⟩, we may conclude the members of g[2] coming from dwarf parents have the allele pair ⟨d,d⟩. Using the bridge law H_5 about what gets exhibited, we have the conclusion

d_1: All members of g[2] who come from dwarf members g[1] exhibit dwarf stems.

Collecting the premises at the extremities of the tree diagram (Figure 5.3), we have it that 'H_1, H_2, H_4, H_5, a_1, a_2, a_3 / d_1' is deductively valid. From

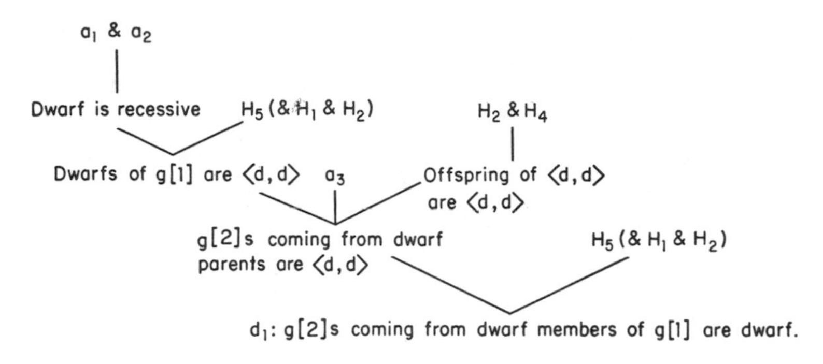

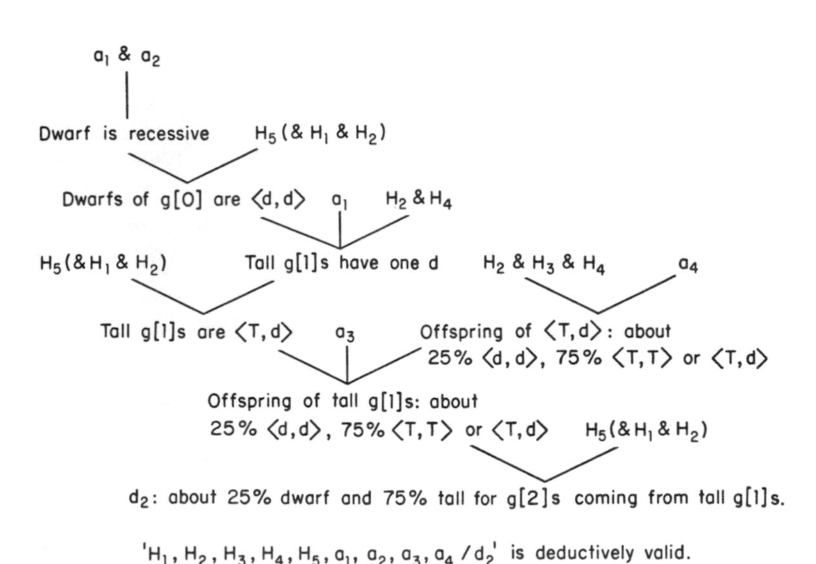

Figure 5.3. Explanation of data by Mendel's theory.

H_1: Genes and alleles correspond to factors.
H_2: For each factor characteristic, two alleles per individual, one randomly chosen allele per each individual's gamete.
H_3: Fertilization of gametes is random.
H_4: Offspring have one allele from each parental gamete.
H_5: Given H_1 and H_2, recessive feature is displayed if and only if both alleles are recessive.
a_1: g[1] members have one tall parent and one dwarf parent.
a_2: g[1] has more tall members than dwarf members.
a_3: g[2] members come from g[1] members by self-fertilization.
a_4: If H_2–H_4, offspring of ⟨T, d⟩ are about 25 percent ⟨d, d⟩ and 75 percent ⟨T, T⟩ or ⟨T, d⟩.

the initial description of Mendel's experiment, d_1 is part of the data that are completely justified. Thus, because the auxiliary premises a_1–a_3 are completely justified, we see that the hypotheses H_1, H_2, H_4, and H_5 jointly explain d_1, and d_1 is positive evidence for Mendel's theory.

Turning to the derivation of d_2, the same reasoning as before allows us to conclude that the dwarf members of g[0] have the allele pair ⟨d,d⟩. According to a_1 these members are crossed with tall members of g[0] to form g[1], thus all tall members of g[1] have one d allele (by H_2 and H_4); because these tall members exhibit tallness, (by H_5) the tall members of g[1] have at least one T allele. Thus, we have the result that all tall members of g[1] have the allele pair ⟨T,d⟩. A little bit of probability theory has the effect of highly justifying the following auxiliary premise:

a_4: If H_2–H_4 are all true, approximately 75 percent of the offspring of parents who are both of type ⟨T,d⟩ will have at least one T allele, while the remaining offspring will be of the type ⟨d,d⟩.

Given that g[2] results from g[1] by cross-fertilization according to a_3, and that the tall members of g[1] have the allele pair ⟨T,d⟩, a_4 and H_2–H_4 give us the result that the offspring of tall members of g[1] roughly divide into 25 percent with ⟨d,d⟩ alleles and 75 percent with ⟨T,T⟩ or ⟨T,d⟩ pairs. Thus, given H_5 concerning what characteristic is displayed, we have the conclusion

d_2: Approximately 75 percent of the members of g[2] who come from tall members of g[1] exhibit tall stems, and the remaining 25 percent exhibit dwarf stems.

Again, collecting the premises at the extremities of the tree diagram in Figure 5.3, we have it that 'H_1, H_2, H_3, H_4, H_5, a_1, a_2, a_3, a_4 / d_2' is deductively valid. Because the auxiliary premises are at least highly justified and d_2 belongs to part of Mendel's data, we again have it that Mendel's theory explains d_2 and that d_2 is positive evidence for the theory.

Thus, we may conclude that Mendel's explanatory generalizations explain the data he collected about tall- and dwarf-stemmed peas. Similar considerations show that his theory explains the data he collected on the other characteristics of the pea. Was his theory the best explanation of the data? At the time Mendel's work, his theory was the *only* explanation of the data, and therefore the best. It is true that there were other speculations concerning heredity, and these assumed that inherited characteristics somehow mixed in the individual and the individual passed on the resulting mixture to the next generation. But these conjectures were hardly precise enough to lead deductively to any notable observable consequences and hence could not be said to explain much of anything. Mendel's results, however, do support his so-called law of separation or segregation that alleles do not mix in an individual: how else could two tall parents give rise to a dwarf offspring? To this extent, Mendel's results provided negative evidence for the prevailing competing "theory" or speculation. Without doubt, Mendel offered by far the best explanation at that time and the inference of his conclusions might be said to be completely legitimate, and the conclusion completely justified. (Unfortunately, little attention was paid to Mendel's work by his contemporaries and he may have been alone in making the completely legitimate nondemonstrative inference.)

Mendel's theory provides a good example of inferring an explanatory generalization. The inferred generalization does involve a new conceptualization of the phenomena, and hence the vocabulary of the data and the generalization are different. To allow the generalizations to be empirically tested, the generalizations taken as a whole included bridge laws H_1 and H_5. In giving a general account of the observed phenomena by introducing the new vocabulary of genes, we inevitably get the sense of having been given an underlying explanation of the phenomena. It might also be noted that no single hypothesis among H_1–H_5 was individually tested, but rather the inference was to the entire set of hypotheses that Mendel proposed. And this is generally true of inferences to explanatory generalizations; that is, what explains and is inferred is a set of generalizations that together constitute a theory. The ability of our general discussion of nondemonstrative inferences to account for inferences in the sciences is further evidence that inference to the best explanation is *the* form of nondemonstrative or nondeductive inference.

One complication in our account should be noted: When an explanatory theory has been accepted, there is a tendency to redescribe the data in terms of the new vocabulary that the explanatory theory has introduced. Thus, pointing to a dwarf pea, one may describe the pea as a pea with the alleles ⟨d,d⟩. Once this is done, the inference of explanatory generalizations can become indistinguishable from inferences of descriptive generalizations. Indeed, we pointed out in Section 5.3 that once an explanatory generalization is accepted, this creates a level of descriptions in which inferences can be seen as descriptive generalizations. However, what matters is the initial acceptance of the explanatory generalization, and two points may be noted:

(a) Even if one tends to describe the data in terms of the new vocabulary, to a large extent, one can describe the data independently of the new vocabulary. Certainly this was the case in our example.
(b) Except for the inference of the explanatory theory, there are no grounds for describing the data in terms of the new vocabulary. In effect, to accept the new description of the data is to accept the explanatory theory.

If describing the data in terms of the theoretical vocabulary is inevitable, as some philosophers of science have proposed, we may isolate the initial inferences of explanatory generalizations that crucially advance a science as follows: these are inferences of generalization in which one cannot clearly distinguish between the description of the data and the acceptance of the inferred generalization.

The subsequent development of the gene theory may be seen to have two aspects. (i) In terms of the function of the gene in determining inherited characteristics, a number of supplementary hypotheses (and in some cases actual modification) had to be made to account for negative evidence that arose. For example, insofar as certain characteristics like skin color seemed to be a blend of the parents' skin color, skin color had to be seen as the result of the joint action of a number of genes in order to preserve Mendel's law of segregation of the genes. Though far more complex, this was the sort of process we described in the discussion of negative evidence in Section 5.2. (ii) The second development was the determination of the physical basis of the gene. As proposed by Mendel, the gene was not given a physical basis. Such so-called hypothetical constructs are perfectly legitimate in a scientific enterprise. However, given the drive toward the unification of the sciences under the auspices of physics, science tends to insist on a physical identification of "hypothetical constructs." By the close of the last century, biologists had identified chromosomes in sex cells and had inferred that hereditary characteristics that were transmitted from one generation to the next were carried by the chromosomes. Once Mendel's neglected work was rediscovered around the turn of the century, the hypothesis was created that the genes were carried or located in the chromosomes. This hypothesis received massive confirmation in time, and with the discovery of the DNA molecule, we have determined alleles to be chemically encoded in that genetic material. This entire process can be seen as the incorporation of Mendel's gene theory first into biology and then into chemical biology, and as such it now forms a part of our very general physical theory. In a sense it gains positive evidence from all the positive evidence for the physical theory of which it is now a part, and it in turn provides positive evidence for the general physical theory by adding to its positive evidence the evidence that is derived from phenomena of heredity.

Such then is a brief account of the scientific enterprise and the inferences of science. It is in a sense just one more instance of inferences to the best explanation. However, we have seen that it is an instance with very special characteristics, that is, the drive for generality, the creation of new concepts to achieve generality, and the hope to amalgamate all science under physics.

EXERCISES—SECTION 5.4

For any claim of something being positive or negative evidence, follow the directions for the exercises in Section 5.2 concerning showing the deductive validity of arguments, providing auxiliary premises as needed, and indicating them to be at least highly justified. As in Section 5.2, assume again that once a supplemental hypothesis is proposed, it defuses the negative evidence so that the assessment shifts from Rule 3 to the other rules, especially Rules 4–7.

Problem Set A

This problem is based on an article by T. G. R. Bowers in *Scientific American.* According to most traditional theories of how we come to perceive the world around us, the quality of solidity belongs to the sense of touch in the same way that the quality of color belongs to the sense of vision or the quality of pitch to the sense of hearing. The ability to identify solid objects visually is the result of learning to associate visual clues with tactile impression according to the traditional theories. More recent theories suggest that there is an innate unity of the senses whereby, for example, we expect tactile consequences of visual impressions independently of learning. Let the following two hypotheses be the two plausible competing hypotheses:

L: The expectation of tactile consequences of visual stimuli is learned.
U: The expectation of tactile consequences of visual stimuli is innate.

Let 'E', which will act as an intermediary hypothesis, be given by:

E: Infants expect tactile consequences of visual stimuli by the age of two weeks.

Our discussion will focus on three experiments that we shall call experiments 1, 2, and 3. Let 'e[1]', 's[1]', 'd[1]' be given as follows:

e[1]: The infants in experiment 1 expect tactile consequences from visual stimuli.
d[1]: The infants in experiment 1 exhibit defensive behavior to visual stimuli of approaching objects.
s[1]: The infants in experiment 1 see the visual stimuli of approaching objects.

Let 'e[2]', 'e[3]', etc. be the same abbreviations with 'experiment 2' and 'experiment 3' replacing 'experiment 1'.

Assume that the following are completely or highly justified:

E ⊃ e[*n*] for $n = 1, 2$, and 3.
s[*n*] ⊃ (e[*n*] ⊃ d[*n*]) for $n = 1, 2$, and 3.

Experiment 1

Bowers describes experiment 1 as follows: "We took infants in their second week of life, placed them on their back, and moved objects toward their face. We used objects of a wide variety of sizes and a wide variety of speeds. All of this was to no avail. The infants, more than 40 of them, did not even blink."

Problem 1: What negative evidence did experiment 1 produce for E?

Problem 2: Assume that as a result of experiment 1, '−E' is highly justified. Let 'P' be given by

P: There is a period of infancy in which tactile consequences of visual stimuli are not expected.

Assuming that if '−E' is highly justified, 'P' is highly justified, show that there is positive evidence for 'L' and negative evidence for 'U'.

Problem 3: Let 's[E]' be given by

s[E]: Two-week-old infants lying on their back are never fully awake.

Show how 's[E]' is a supplemental hypothesis that would defuse the negative evidence against 'E' if 's[E]' were sufficiently justified.

Experiment 2

This experiment was conducted by Bowers after he learned from Prechtl that 's[E]' appears to be indeed true. "We repeated the experiment with infants of the same age who were held in an upright or semiupright position. With this modification the results were totally different. The infants clearly showed a defensive response to an approaching object."

Problem 4: What positive evidence for 'E' do Bowers's experiments 1 and 2 provide? Assuming that 's[E]' has been proposed, given Prechtel's findings, how does 'E' fare with respect to Preference Rules 4 and 7?

Problem 5: The intermediate hypothesis E could be questioned as to whether the infants exhibited defensive behavior to *visual* stimuli of the approaching objects. Let 's[−E]' be given by

s[−E]: The approaching visual objects in experiment 2 had accompanying air pressure.

Explain how 's[−E]' would eliminate positive evidence for 'E' that experiment 2 provided if 's[−E]' were sufficiently justified.

Experiment 3

Bowers writes: "In order to rule out the possibility that [air] pressure changes were the effective stimulus, we had a group of infants view an approaching virtual object produced by a shadow-caster. An object behind a translucent screen was moved away from the infant toward a projector. When the infant is placed at the same distance in front of the screen as the projectors are behind it, a shadow on the screen produces an image on the infant's retina that is identical with the image produced by a real object moving toward the baby, without the displacement of air and other nonvisual changes that accompany the movement of a real object. The results were that seven out of seven infants in their second week of life exhibited defensive behavior when they saw the approaching virtual object."

Problem 6: Assuming that as a result of experiment 3, 'd[2]' is highly justified, what positive evidence is there for E as a result of experiments 1–3?

Problem 7: Bowers states, "In our culture it is unlikely that an infant less than two weeks old has been hit in the face by an approaching object, so that none of the infants in the study could have been exposed to situations where they could have learned to fear an approaching object and expect it to have tactile qualities." Let 'I' be given by:

I: Infants learn to expect tactile consequences of visual stimuli during their first two weeks of life.

and assume that '−I' is highly justified. Assuming 'E' to have been highly justified by Bowers's experiments, show how 'E' is positive evidence for 'U' and negative evidence for 'L'.

Problem Set B

This set of problems concerns the debate between the phlogiston theory and Lavoisier's oxygen theory. The problems are in part derived from James Bryant Conant, ed., *Case 2: The Overthrow of the Phlogiston Theory, the Chemical Revolution of 1775–1789,* Harvard Case Histories in Experimental Science, Cambridge: Harvard University Press, 1953. Also consulted were the *Encyclopaedia*

Brittanica, 14th edition Vol. 3, Chicago: Encyclopaedia Brittanica Inc., 1939, and H. Gilman McCann, *Chemistry Transformed: The Paradigm Shift from Phlogiston to Oxygen*, Norwood, N.J.: Ablex Publishing Corporation, 1978.

Throughout this extended problem set, consider all items of data to be completely justified.

The intuitive background of the phlogiston theory is this: When we burn a substance like a metal, something seems to depart from the metal into the air leaving a residue that is called *calx*. Also if we take metallic ore (also a calx) and heat it, a pure metal results, suggesting that some "metallizing agent" was added to the ore. *Phlogistons* were proposed as entities that departed the burning of metal and acted as the metallizing agent in the heating of ore. Thus, in combustion, the phlogistons separate from the metal leaving calx, and upon heating the calx, a metal is produced by the acquisition of phlogistons.

Given this background, a simplified version of the phlogiston theory may be taken as a theory P, which has the following hypotheses as parts:

P1: Metal = ⟨calx + phlogiston⟩.
P2: Heating ⟨calx + phlogiston⟩ results in a decomposition that phlogisticates the air and leaves a residue of calx.
P3: Charcoal contains a high degree of phlogistons, and heating calx in the presence of phlogistons results in phlogistons combining with the calx and the remainder (if there is a remainder as there is when the calx is heated with charcoal) phlogisticating the surrounding air.
P4: Phlogisticated air is incapable of supporting combustion or animal respiration.

The following may be taken as data:

d1: Upon heating "red powder" (a calx of mercury) with charcoal, a metal (mercury) is formed and the air immediately surrounding becomes incapable of supporting combustion or animal respiration.
d2: When mercury (a metal) is heated (in the presence of ordinary, common air), a calx (called "red powder") is formed and the air immediately surrounding becomes incapable of supporting combustion or animal respiration.

Let a scheme of abbreviation be given by:

C(r): "Red powder" is a calx.
HC(r): "Red powder" is heated with charcoal.
mf: A metal is formed.
pa: The immediately surrounding air is phlogisticated.
i: The immediately surrounding air is incapable of supporting combustion or animal respiration.
M(m): Mercury is a metal.
H(m): Mercury is heated (in the presence of ordinary, common air).
c: A calx is formed.

The data may then be taken as:

d1: HC(r) ⊃ (mf & i).
d2: H(m) ⊃ (c & i).

Three of the several completely justified auxiliary premises may be taken as:

A1: M(m)
A2: C(r)
A3: [P1 & P3 & C(r)] ⊃ [HC(r) ⊃ (mf & pa)]

Hereafter by 'P' we shall mean the conjunction of 'P1'–'P4' or any part of that conjunction.

Problem 1: Show that 'd1' and 'd2' are positive evidence for P.

Problem 2: Given that phlogistons are not directly observable, which part of P is most clearly a "bridge law"?

• • •

By the late eighteenth century the following terminology was used: "common air" is the air around us that we breathe [now known to be about 20 percent oxygen and 80 percent nitrogen]. A gas called "fixed air" [now known to be carbon dioxide] had been isolated and found to be incapable of supporting combustion or respiration. [This feature of "fixed air" may be taken as completely justified.] As a very slight fictionalization of Lavoisier's theory, let us take "pure air" as the gas most capable of supporting combustion and respiration. The resulting very slightly fictionalized version of Lavoisier's theory may be given as follows:

L1: Calx = metal + pure air.
L2: Upon heating a metal in common air, the metal combines with the pure air in the common air and the common air is deprived of pure air.
L3: Upon heating the compound ⟨metal + pure air⟩, the metal remains as a residue, pure air is released, and if the compound was heated with charcoal, the released pure air combines with charcoal to form fixed air.
L4: The presence of pure air is necessary for combustion and respiration.

Hereafter, let L be the conjunction of 'L1'–'L4' or any part of that conjunction. Let additions to our scheme of abbreviation be given by:

ff: Fixed air is formed in the immediate surroundings.
npa: There is no pure air in the immediate surroundings.

Two of the several additional completely justified auxiliary premises may be taken as:

A4: ff ⊃ npa
A5: [L1 & L2 & C(r)] ⊃ [HC(r) ⊃ (mf & ff)]

Problem 3: Show that 'd1' and 'd2' constitute positive evidence for L.

• • •

Experiments by Lavoisier and others produced the following results: when mercury is heated, the resulting red powder (a calx) weighs more than the mercury that was heated; furthermore, when the surrounding common air was enclosed in a receptacle, the air was measured to lose weight in the process of heating mercury to produce red powder. Augment the scheme of abbreviation as follows:

G(c,m): The resulting calx weighs more than the mercury that was heated.
L(a): The immediately surrounding air loses weight.
PL(c,m): The resulting calx is the mercury less its phlogistons.
PG(a): The immediately surrounding air gains phlogistons.

Taking 'H(m)' to be one of the completely justified auxiliary premises, the data may then be formulated as:

d3: G(c,m).
d4: L(a).

Problem 4: Show that 'd3' and 'd4' are negative evidence for P and positive evidence for L.

• • •

Lavoisier also performed an experiment in which the calx "red powder" was heated without charcoal. This resulted in the metal mercury being formed, the surrounding air increasing in weight and supporting combustion and respiration to a higher degree than common air.

Extend our scheme of abbreviation as follows:

HWC(r): "Red powder" is heated without charcoal.
G(a): The immediately surrounding air gains weight.
R(pa): Pure air is released to the immediately surrounding air.
s: The immediately surrounding air supports combustion and respiration to a higher degree (than common air).

Take 'HWC(r)' as a completely justified auxiliary premise. The data Lavoisier produced may then be formulated as:

d5: mf
d6: G(a)
d7: s

Refine L4 to:

L4*: The presence of pure air is necessary for combustion and respiration, and the more pure air there is, combustion and respiration are supported to a higher degree.

Problem 5: Show that 'd5'–'d7' constitute positive evidence for L.

Problem 6: If we take the relevant data base to be restricted to 'd5', why would preference rule 1 (Section 5.2.1) prefer L over P?

• • •

Priestley performed the same "red powder" experiments as Lavoisier under more careful conditions and was able to isolate the gas that was released as red powder was heated (without charcoal) to produce mercury. This gas that Priestley isolated was exceptionally capable of supporting combustion and respiration. Lavoisier immediately interpreted this gas as the "pure air" for which he was looking, and eventually named it oxygen. Being a subscriber to the phlogiston theory, Priestley called this gas "dephlogisticated gas"—the result of removing all phlogistons from common air. Add 'P3°' to the phlogiston theory P and refine its 'P4' to 'P4*':

P3°: Common air contains some phlogistons (though not enough to prevent combustion or respiration).
P4*: (Significantly) phlogisticated air is incapable of supporting combustion or animal respiration, and the fewer phlogistons there are in the air, the higher degree of combustion and respiration is supported.

Let 'HWC(r)' again be one of the completely justified auxiliary premises, and extend the scheme of abbreviation by

PL(a): The surrounding air loses phlogistons.

Problem 7: Show that 'd5' and 'd7' become positive evidence for (the augmented) P but that 'd6' remains negative evidence.

• • •

One of the supplemental hypotheses proposed for P was the following:

S[P]: Phlogistons have negative weight so that when phlogistons are removed from [added to] any substance, the substance increases [decreases] weight.

Problem 8: Show that 'S[P]' is a strong supplemental hypothesis for P relative to 'd3', 'd4', and 'd6' in the extended sense that when it is conjoined with P, it can explain this data which was previously negative evidence.

Problem 9: Assume no independent positive evidence is found for 'S[P]', and let P be supplemented by the supplemental hypothesis 'S[P]'. Taking the data base to consist of 'd1'–'d7', which of the preference rules 1–11 (Sections 5.2.1–5.2.4) favors L?

Problem 10: Given that Lavoisier was able to point to his oxygen (the gas Priestley had isolated), is there any reason to think that Lavoisier's theory had a clearer physical basis than the phlogiston theory?

• • •

Lavoisier's theory, however, did not win immediate acceptance, mostly because there was some evidence concerning acids and salts that constituted negative evidence for Lavoisier's theory and positive evidence for the phlogiston theory.

It was universally accepted that a salt is a compound of a calx and an acid. Furthermore, by the time of the controversy, a gas called "inflammable gas" (now known to be hydrogen) had been identified, and data emerged showing that when a metal is dissolved in acid, a salt is formed and inflammable air is released. These data could be accounted for by the phlogiston theory once P was augmented by the following additional hypothesis:

P5: A phlogiston is in part (or all) inflammable gas.

To show this, use the following scheme of abbreviation:

A6: Salt = calx + acid.
C(p,c,a): Phlogistons, calx, and acid are combined.
D(m): A metal is dissolved in acid.
sf: A salt is formed.
R(ig): Inflammable gas is released.

Take 'D(m)' to be a completely justified auxiliary premise. The data can then be formulated as:

d8: sf
d9: R(ig)

Take 'A6' above and 'A7' below to be completely justified:

A7: [C(p,c,a) & A6 & P5] ⊃ [sf & R(ig)].

['A7' is justified because the calx and the acid form a salt and the phlogiston is (or combines with something else to form) inflammable gas.]

Problem 11: Show that 'd8' and 'd9' constitute positive evidence for P by showing that their conjunction is positive evidence for P.

• • •

Lavoisier, on the other hand, had the following hypothesis concerning acids, which we shall consider added to L:

L5: Acid = oxygen + a nonmetallic substance.

The problem for Lavoisier was twofold: (a) When a metal was dissolved in acid, no compound of an acid and calx could be formed because the oxygen needed for the calx was already used up in the acid. (b) No combination of a metal, oxygen, and a nonmetallic substance would release inflammable gas.

Augment the scheme of abbreviation as follows:

ao: There is an additional source of oxygen within the experimental setup of dissolving a metal in an acid.
f(ac): A compound of acid and calx is formed in the experimental setup of dissolving a metal in an acid.
C(o,nms,m): Oxygen, a nonmetallic substance, and a metal are combined.
aig: There is an additional source of inflammable gas within the experimental setup of dissolving a metal in an acid.

Along with 'A6', take the following to be among the completely justified:

A8: [L1 & L5 & D(m)] ⊃ [ao v −f(ac)]
A9: C(o,nms,m) ⊃ [aig v −R(ig)]

Furthermore, take

A10: −(ao)
A11: −(aig)

to be highly justified, and continue to take 'D(m)' to be completely justified by the experimental setup.

Problem 12: Show that 'd8' and 'd9' are negative evidence for L.

• • •

Cavendish, another supporter of the phlogiston theory, was able to produce an experiment that resulted in water when inflammable gas (hydrogen) was burned in dephlogisticated air (oxygen). Given this result, Cavendish augmented P by adding

P6: Water = phlogistons (which are all or part of inflammable air) + dephlogisticated air.

Lavoisier, on the other hand, augmented L by adding

L6: Water = oxygen + inflammable gas.

He now altered L5 to

L5*: Pure acid = oxygen + nonmetallic substance.

and proposed the supplemental hypothesis

S[L]: Common acids used in the experiment of dissolving metal in acids are dilutions of water and pure acids.

Problem 13: Why would 'S[L]' defuse the negative evidence 'd8' and 'd9' against L if 'S[L]' were sufficiently justified?

• • •

Let the scheme of abbreviation be altered and augmented as follows:

D(m): A metal is dissolved in a common acid.
f(ac): A compound of pure acid and calx forms in the experimental setup of dissolving a metal in common water.
C(ow,m): The oxygen in the water and the metal combine.
cf: A calx is formed.
rw: The residue from the water is inflammable gas.

In addition to what was previously taken to be completely justified, take the following to be completely justified:

[L6 & S[L] & D(m)] ⊃ [C(ow,m) & (cf ⊃ f(ac)) & rw].

Problem 14: Relative to 'd8' and 'd9', show that 'S[L]' is a strong supplemental hypothesis for L in the extended sense that when it is conjoined with L, it can explain the conjunction of 'd8' and 'd9'.

• • •

The discovery that water can be produced from inflammable gas (hydrogen) and dephlogisticated air (oxygen) was the "critical experiment" that won the day for Lavoisier's theory. Yet this very discovery allowed the phlogiston theory to revise its hypotheses in a systematic way that would dispense with its ad hoc claim about negative weight. The revised phlogiston theory may be formulated as follows:

P1*: Metal = ⟨pure earth + phlogiston⟩; calx = ⟨pure earth + water⟩.

P2*: Common air contains water and heating ⟨pure earth + phlogiston⟩ in common air is a process whereby

⟨pure earth + phlogiston⟩ + water + rest of common air

is transformed into

⟨pure earth + water⟩ + rest of common air + phlogistons.

P3*: Given P6, heating calx [in common air] is a process whereby

⟨pure earth + water⟩ [+ common air]

is transformed into

⟨pure earth + phlogiston⟩ + dephlogisticated air [+ common air].

P4*: (Significantly) phlogisticated air is incapable of supporting combustion or animal respiration, and the fewer phlogistons there are in the air, the higher degree of combustion and respiration is supported.

P5*: Phlogiston = inflammable gas.

P6: Water = phlogistons + dephlogisticated air.

The revised theory will continue to account for the positive evidence that the phlogiston theory had. To assure ourselves of this, let us take 'd2', 'd5', and 'd8 & d9' as characteristic. A brief reminder of this data is given below:

d2: $H(m) \supset (c \,\&\, i)$

'd2' concerned heating mercury in common air to produce calx and air incapable of supporting combustion and respiration, where 'M(m)' ('Mercury is a metal') was a completely justified auxiliary premise.

d5: mf

'd5' concerned heating red powder without charcoal to produce metal, in which 'C(r)' ('Red powder is a calx') and 'HWC(r)' were completely justified auxiliary premises.

d8 & d9: sf & R(ig)

'd8 & d9' concerned dissolving a metal in common acid (which is pure acid diluted with water) to produce salt and released inflammable gas. 'D(m)' ('a metal is dissolved in common acid') and 'A6' ('salt = calx + acid') were completely justified auxiliary premises. Furthermore, given the scheme

C(pe, ph, w, ac): Pure earth, phlogistons, water, and pure acid are combined.
C(pe + w, ac): The compound ⟨pure earth + water⟩ is combined with acid.
R(ph): Phlogistons are released.

take the following auxiliary premise as completely justified:

$C(pe, ph, w, ac) \supset [C(pe + w, ac) \,\&\, R(pf)]$

Finally, assume that by this time 'S(L)' (common acid is a mixture of water and pure acid) is at least highly justified.

Problem 15: Show that 'd2', 'd5', and 'd8 & d9' are positive evidence for the revised phlogiston theory P* composed of 'P1*'–'P5*' and 'P6'.

• • •

The principal negative evidence against the original phlogiston theory was 'd6', 'd3', and 'd4'. The revised phlogiston theory P* needs no supplementary hypotheses concerning negative weights to explain 'd6', 'd3', and 'd4'; thus they become positive evidence for P*. A brief reminder of the data is given below:

d6: G(a)

This again is the experiment of heating red powder without charcoal to produce a metal with the result that the air gained weight. 'C(r)' and 'HWC(r)' were completely justified auxiliary premises, and to facilitate the work use the following abbreviation:

R(dpf): (Metal is formed and) dephlogisticated air is released from the water that was in the calx.
d3: G(c,m).
d4: L(a).

'd3' and 'd4' concerned heating mercury in air to produce a calx with the result that the produced calx had greater weight than the mercury and that the surrounding air lost weight in the process. 'M(m)' and 'H(m)' were taken to be completely justified. Let the scheme abbreviation be extended as follows:

WC: The weight of the resulting calx = [the weight of the mercury − the weight of the mercury's phlogistons + the weight of the water the calx acquired].
WA: The weight of the surrounding air after the experiment = [the weight of the air before the experiment − the weight of the water given to the resulting calx + the weight of the phlogistons released by the mercury].
LPM: The weight of the phlogistons in a metal is less than the weight of the water acquired by the calx when the metal is converted to calx by heating.

Take the following as completely justified:

[P1* & P2* & M(m)] ⊃ [H(m) ⊃ WC].

[P1* & P2* & M(m)] ⊃ [H(m) ⊃ WA].

Finally, because it's completely justified that oxygen (dephlogisticated air) weighs more than hydrogen (phlogistons), take it as completely justified that

[P1* & P2* & P6] ⊃ LPM.

Problem 16: Show that 'd6', 'd3', and 'd4' are positive evidence for P*.

• • •

Given the results so far, it would seem there is not much to choose between Lavoisier's theory and the revised phlogiston theory relative to the data 'd1'–'d9'. In terms of the three chemical reactions we have discussed, there is a strong symmetry. Using the following abbreviations:

e: pure earth P: phlogistron M: metal pa: pure acid
D: dephlogisticated gas O: oxygen W: water A: air H: hydrogen

the three chemical reactions studied may be diagrammed as follows:

(I) Metal + Common Air → Calx + Decreased Air
P*: ⟨e + p⟩ + W + (A − W) → ⟨e + W⟩ + (A − W + p)
L: m + O + (A − O) → ⟨m + O⟩ + (A − O)

(II) Calx + Common Air → Metal + Increased Air
p*: ⟨e + ⟨p + D⟩⟩ + A → ⟨e + p⟩ + (A + D)
L: m + O + A → m + (A + O)

(III) Metal + Common Acid → Salt + Inflammable gas
P*: ⟨e + p⟩ + (pa + ⟨p + D⟩) → ⟨pa + ⟨e + ⟨p + D⟩⟩⟩ + p
L: m + (pa + ⟨H + O⟩) → ⟨pa + ⟨m + O⟩⟩ + H

What L and P* predict or claim about (II) and (III) are exactly the same. With (I) there is a difference, but only this: whether metal contains p (hydrogen), whether water (hydrogen + oxygen) or oxygen alone is taken from the common air, and whether the calx contains p in addition to dephlogisticated air (oxygen). Because hydrogen (or phlogiston) is the lightest element, assume that these differences between P* and L were undetectable at the time when L became generally accepted.

Problem 17: Is there any reason to prefer L over P* so that L could be claimed to be the best explanation when it became generally accepted?

5.5 Mill's Methods and Inferring Descriptive Generalizations

Inferring explanatory generalizations is largely the task of science—a task most of us do not confront in our everyday life. Thus, inferences of descriptive generalizations are likely to be more central to our daily concerns. The overall account of nondemonstrative inferences given in Sections 5.1–5.2 remains the most helpful general guide to any inference that is essentially nondemonstrative. However, there is some value in the methods discussed by almost every critical-thinking text: Mill's methods of experimental inquiry, the five methods claimed by John Stuart Mill to be complete methods for the discovery and demonstration of causes of phenomena. These methods are typically criticized for being neither a complete method of discovery nor a method of demonstration. While these and other criticisms are just, the methods often provide useful guidelines for arriving at inferences to the best descriptive generalizations and can be seen as special instances of the general account given in Sections 5.1–5.2.

Because Mill's methods are designed for inferring causes and effects of phenomena, to this minimal extent the conclusions go beyond the typical observational vocabulary of the premises. While we allowed such minimal departures from the vocabulary of the premises in our account of inferring descriptive generalizations, something needs to be said about the meaning of 'cause'. Clearly, if X is to be the cause of P, X should occur no later than P and X should be spatiotemporally close to P (or there should at least be a spatiotemporal path of cause–effect relations leading from X to P). We shall assume throughout that these requirements are satisifed. Furthermore, 'X causes P' should be understood as the general statement 'All instances of X cause P (in the absence of interfering factors)', and this in turn can be taken to entail 'All instances of X are attended with P (in the absence of interfering factors)'. Thus, as long as the spatiotemporal conditions are satisfied, positive and negative evidence for 'All instances of X are attended with P' will be positive and negative evidence for 'X causes P'.

Given this much, we can consider one of Mill's methods both in order to understand its limitations and to highlight the need for further clarification of the notion of cause. His Method of Agreement comes to this:

If the several instances of P have only one circumstance (or antecedent) X in common, X is a cause of P.

Even if this statement is true, it is useless. In no single instance of P can we hope to produce a finite list of *all* attendant circumstances or antecedents, and without a finite list we can never claim that X is the *only* circumstance the various instances of P had in common; that is, we may have overlooked or failed to have thought of Z, which may also have attended all the examined instances of P. If the method of agreement is to be useful, we must have a finite list of *relevant* circumstances attending the several instances of P. But what constitutes a relevant circumstance can never be decisively demonstrated, and hence we are never in a position to demonstrate X to be the cause of P. Such is a standard criticism of Mill's Method of Agreement, and similar criticisms (which won't be repeated) apply to his other methods.

To appreciate the difficulties involved in a concrete way, consider the following simple example: I ignite a piece of paper by striking a match on one occasion and by focusing sun rays with a magnifying glass on another. If we make a chart of the data in which '+' indicates the presence of the phenomenon, or factor, we would have Table 5.1. The method evidently would ask us to declare the presence of oxygen as a cause of the paper's ignition, and as far as this method goes, the flame (of the match) and the focused sun rays would be ignored. It is true that oxygen is indispensable for igniting the paper, while neither the flame nor the focused sun rays are. On the other hand, the presence of oxygen is not by itself sufficient to ignite the paper. This example illustrates two points:

(i) Even assuming that we have a relevant vocabulary at hand (e.g., our ordinary observational vocabulary), much depends on how that vocabulary is used to pick out the factors. If we took the disjunctive factor "flame or focused sun rays" as one, it would have appeared as one of the common antecedents; the same result would have been attained by choosing "intense heat" as one of the factors. Because the possible ways of combining the vocabulary to pick relevant factors are infinitely many, in using Mill's methods we are always forced to function within the working assumption that the list of factors we have chosen to aid in our investigation contains the cause of the phenomenon in question.

(ii) While we often tend to think in terms of a single cause for a single phenomenon, a cause sufficient for the effect often involves combinations of factors, and in some cases there can be a number of different causes, each sufficient for the effect in question. Let us introduce some terminology to sort out the complications (where =df means "is another way of saying"):

X is a sufficient factor for P =df Whenever X is present, so is P.

X is a causally relevant part of P's sufficient factor C =df While C is sufficient for P, C without its part X is not a sufficient factor for P.

X is a total cause for P =df X is a sufficient factor for P and each subfactor of X is a causally relevant part of the sufficient factor for P.

X is the sole cause for P =df X is the only total cause for P.

TABLE 5.1.

Instance	*Oxygen*	*Flame*	*Focused Sun Rays*	*Ignited Paper*
1	+	+	−	+
2	+	−	+	+

To be more accurate, we should probably have prefixed each of these definitions with some clause like 'in the absence of interfering factors', because any statable candidate for a sufficient factor is likely to be defeated by some interfering factor like a sudden wind. Keeping this in mind, we might say: A flame in the presence of oxygen in Santa Barbara is a sufficient factor for igniting the paper. Being in Santa Barbara is not a causally relevant part of this sufficient factor while the presence of oxygen and the flame are. Thus, a flame in the presence of oxygen is a total cause of igniting the paper, as is focusing the sun rays in the presence of oxygen. Neither of these total causes is the sole cause for igniting the paper, while sufficient heat in the presence of oxygen might be taken as the sole cause of igniting paper.

It should be reasonably evident that we seek total causes of phenomena. Notice, if X is a total cause of P, the concomitance of observed X's and P's is explained, as is a single occurrence P by the presence of an X. That is, if we substitute our definitions for 'total cause', both of the following are deductively valid arguments in which the premises explain their conclusions:

X is a total cause of P.
____
All observed X's are attended with P's.

An instance X is present.
X is a total cause of P.
____
An instance of P is present.

Furthermore, these explanations have the virtue of simplicity by not containing any irrelevant factor insofar as a total cause results from a sufficient factor by stripping away all causally irrelevant sub-factors. Thus, it is clear that we are interested in inferring general statements of the form 'X is a total cause of P'. While the sole cause of a phenomenon is the most desirable end of our investigations, often we have to settle for total causes, especially when we are working with our ordinary observational vocabulary.

In order to state Mill's methods, we shall make two simplifications.

(a) While Mill's methods are designed to discover causes as well as effects, we shall state them as methods for determining causes of phenomena. Determining the effect can be treated in a parallel manner.
(b) We shall assume potentially relevant factors to be positive factors so that a total cause is a conjunction of one or more such factors. Of course disjunctions of factors as well as the absence of factors can

be parts of a total cause; we shall assume, however, that for purposes of simplification such factors have been formulated as single positive factors.

Given this much in terms of background and simplification, we now turn to Mill's five methods.

(1) Method of Agreement. This method can now be formulated as follows:

METHOD OF AGREEMENT: *If all observed instances of a phenomenon P have a (combination of) antecedent factor(s) X in common,*

(1) there is positive evidence that X is part of every total cause of P, and
(2) negative evidence that the other factors are parts of every total cause of P.

Thus, in our example of igniting the paper, there is positive evidence that the presence of oxygen is part of every total cause of paper igniting, and negative evidence for flames and focused sun rays being parts of every total cause of such an ignition. Because a diagrammatic summary is likely to be more useful than any circumlocution, we shall summarize the Method of Agreement as follows:

	Factors			*Phenomenon*
Instance	*X1*	*X2*	*X3*	*P*
(1)	+	+	+	+
(2)	+	−	+	+

Positive evidence for: X1 + X3 is part of every total cause of P.

Negative evidence for: X2 is part of every total cause of P.

It should be evident that the Method of Agreement is simply an application of the general method of inferring the best explanation. Clearly, the following is a valid argument with a completely justified second premise:

(1) X is part of every total cause of P.
(2) If (1) is true, all observed P's are attended by X.
____
(3) All observed P's are attended by X.

Thus, all observed P's being attended by X is positive evidence for X being a part of every total cause of P. By the same token, a failure of all observed P's to be attended by X would constitute negative evidence for (1). In fact, if such a failure is completely justified, (1) should simply be condemned forthwith.

While the Method of Agreement is simply an application of the general method, in a limited sense it does provide a method of discovery. In its standard use, we would of course be collecting many more instances than indicated in the summarizing diagram (which presents the "bare logical structure" of the method). In collecting the many instances of P it can indeed emerge that there is a common factor, and we may thereby have discovered a factor necessary for any occurrence of P. Furthermore, the Method of Agreement can also be a way of tentatively isolating potentially relevant factors. By collecting various instances of P one is likely to have varied a number of factors in the process. If some factor is found to be often, though not necessarily always, present with P, this would give some indication that it may be a relevant factor. For example, although striking a match is not always present when paper is ignited, their frequent concomitance should suggest that striking a match may be a causally relevant factor for igniting paper. Thus, although the basic vocabulary to describe the factors must be antecedently given and complicated combinations of factors will not be evident, to a limited degree the Method of Agreement can be a method for discovering (potential) relevant factors.

(2) Method of Difference. Mill's account of this method is in effect: If the presence and absence of P correlates with the presence and absence of X *while all other circumstances remain the same,* X is a cause (or causal factor) of P. It is of course impossible to keep *all* the other circumstances constant. Thus, to apply this method, we need at least a working hypothesis as to what the potentially relevant factors are. For our purposes, we may reformulate this method as:

METHOD OF DIFFERENCE:

(1) *If the presence of P correlates with the presence and absence of X while the other relevant factors remain the same, there is positive evidence that X is a causally relevant part of that sufficient factor for P.*
(2) *If the presence and absence of P isn't correlated with the presence or absence of X while the other factors remain the same, there is negative evidence for X being a causally relevant part of that sufficient factor for P.*

The diagrammatic summary then is:

	Factors			*Phenomenon*
Instance	*X1*	*X2*	*X3*	*P*
(1)	+	+	+	+
(2)	−	+	+	−
(3)	+	−	+	+

(1) and (2) are positive evidence for: X1 is a causally relevant part of the sufficient factor X1 + X2 + X3.

(1) and (3) are negative evidence for: X2 is a causally relevant part of the sufficient factor X1 + X2 + X3

As a simple illustration of how the method works, suppose a laboratory wants to test the effectiveness of a drug D in curing a disease. One exper-

TABLE 5.2.

Possible Outcomes	*Given D*	*Other Factors*	*Cured*
(1) Test group	+	+	+
Control group	−	+	−
(2) Test group	+	+	+
Control group	−	+	+

imental group of people suffering from the disease are given D. A second control group is matched with the first group as closely as possible except for not having been given D. The two possible outcomes of such an experimental setup are shown in Table 5.2. Outcome 1 gives positive evidence for D having been a causally relevant factor in the cure of the test group (and thereby negative evidence for the other factors having been sufficient). Outcome 2, on the other hand, gives negative evidence for D having been a causally relevant factor in the cure of the test group (and thereby positive evidence for other factors having being sufficient for the cure). While this is a highly oversimplified example (which lumps all factors other than being given D as "other factors"), it illustrates the importance of the Method of Difference and the control group it prompts; that is, without the control group one cannot distinguish between outcome 1 in which the drug is effective and outcome 2 in which it isn't.

It should be evident that the relations stated by the Method of Difference are again instances of the general method of inferring the best explanations. The following is a valid argument with a completely justified second premise:

(1) X is a causally relevant factor in X + Y for the production of P.
(2) If (1) is true, P is not produced by Y alone.

---

(3) P is not produced by Y alone.

Thus, if P is not produced by Y alone, there is positive evidence for X being a causally relevant factor in X + Y. On the other hand, if P is produced by Y alone, there is negative evidence for X being a causally relevant factor in X + Y. Again, if the failure of (3) is completely justified, (1) should be condemned forthwith. Thus we see what we saw earlier: Although the Method of Difference is an application of a general method, it provides a limited method of discovery; given a case in which P is produced, successively vary the factors to isolate those that are causally efficacious.

(3) Joint Method of Agreement and Difference. Given a set of factors $X_1, \ldots, X_n$ and the phenomenon P, the Method of Agreement and the Method of Difference are both ways for determining the relations between P and $X_1, \ldots, X_n$ by varying some factors while keeping other things fixed; more specifically, the Method of Agreement keeps P fixed and varies the X factors while the Method of Difference varies one X factor while keeping the other factors fixed to check the result on P. It is therefore natural to combine the two methods by systematically varying the factors involved. This is precisely the crux of Mill's Joint Method of Agreement and Difference.

A somewhat more determinate formulation of the Joint Method may be given as follows:

JOINT METHOD OF AGREEMENT AND DIFFERENCE:

Step A: By independent considerations (or by collecting many instances of P and finding factors frequently conjoined with P), determine a list of factors which are likely to be potentially relevant for P. Collect (more) data by varying the potentially relevant factors as much and as systematically as possible.

Step B: Based on the data collected in Step A, (1) list each combination of (positive) factors (e.g., X + Y + Z) that was attended by P, and (2) if the list contains two combinations of factors which are exactly alike except that one factor is omitted in the second combination, cancel the first combination with the extra factor (e.g., given X + Y + Z and X + Y on the list, cancel X + Y + Z). Repeat step (2) until no further combination of factors can be eliminated.

Step C: If an incoherent result is obtained (such as all factors having been deleted or one and the same factor being both sufficient and insufficient), start the procedure over again with a different set of potentially relevant factors.

Step D: If the data from Step A are sufficiently rich to assure that the combinations of factors remaining after Step B cannot be further reduced (e.g., if X + Y remains after Step B and Step A included cases of X without Y and Y without X), *relative to the factors considered to be relevant in Step A, the best explanation of the data given in Step A is that each combination of factors remaining after Step B is a total cause of P* (and if only one combination of factors remains after step B, it's the sole cause of P).

In a more abbreviated form, the method is:

A. Determine potentially relevant factors and collect data by varying these factors.
B. (1) List combinations of factors attended by P.
   (2) Eliminate combinations with causally irrelevant parts.
C. If an incoherent result is obtained, restart the procedure with a new set of potentially relevant factors.
D. If the data are rich enough to foreclose a combination M being further reduced, relative to the factors and the data, 'M is a total cause of P' is the best explanation.

To see that the Joint Method as described is covered by our more general discussion, suppose X + Y is isolated as being one of the total causes.

Given the definition of 'total cause', *relative to the data and the factors considered to be relevant,* there can be only two kinds of alternative hypotheses:

(a) X + Y is insufficient for P. But there is positive evidence that X + Y is sufficient for P because we were able to reduce the combination to X + Y in step B; furthermore, that process (which applies the Method of Difference) indicates negative evidence for the other factors being causally relevant.
(b) X + Y contains causally irrelevant factors. But Step D required that the data be sufficiently abundant that X without Y and Y without X were considered. Because Step B didn't cancel X + Y in favor of X or Y, the Method of Difference gave positive evidence that both X and Y are causally relevant factors.

Thus, X + Y being a total cause of the P is the best explanation relative to the data and the factors considered to be relevant.

Can we conclude that the explanation produced at Step D is the best explanation of all the available data? The answer obviously depends on two considerations:

(a) Are there available data that should have been considered in Step A but weren't? If there are new data that we have not yet considered, we may not be in a position to claim that we have considered all of the relevant data.
(b) Are there grounds for taking a different set of factors as relevant? Such grounds would exist if there is an alternative hypothesis that conceives the data in a different way.

However, if the answers to (a) and (b) are negative, we would have the best available explanation. Of course it is important to remain vigilant for new data that may constitute negative evidence or make the results incoherent (and thereby force a selection of new factors at Step C.)

To illustrate the Joint Method, let us alter our earlier paper ignition example by supposing that instances 1 and 2 both occurred in Santa Barbara. Let 'O', 'F', and 'R' abbreviate the presence of oxygen, a flame, and focused sun rays, and let 'B' abbreviate the location of Santa Barbara. Following Step A of the Joint Method, let us vary at least some of the factors so that we finally have the data summarized in Table 5.3. Of course this table is a simplification because Step A asks us to consider numerous instances of ignited paper. Part of this is an innocent simplification because we can assume each listed instance to summarize numerous instances of a similar kind. What is less innocent is that only the factors listed should have emerged as potentially relevant. Smoldering cigarettes, rubbing sticks, and the like are likely to have emerged as potentially relevant factors as well; furthermore, even those listed factors haven't been sufficiently varied. However, let us stay with these data to exemplify Steps B–D.

TABLE 5.3.

Instance	*O*	*F*	*R*	*B*	*Ignited Paper*
1	+	+	−	+	+
2	+	−	+	+	+
3	−	+	−	+	−
4	+	−	−	+	−
5	+	+	−	−	+

The combinations that are sufficient may be listed as O + F + B, O + R + B, and O + F. We would cancel the first of these combinations and arrive at O + R + B and O + F at the end of Step B. Because the result isn't incoherent, we ask (at Step D): are the data adequate to assure us that O + F can't be further reduced? The answer is yes. If O alone is sufficent, O + B should have been sufficient; but it isn't, as instance 4 shows. If F alone is sufficient, F + B should have been sufficient; but it isn't, as instance 3 shows.[2] Thus, at Step D we can say that the best explanation for the data includes F + O being a total cause for paper igniting. How does O + R + B fare? The data are not sufficient to assure us that this combination can't be further reduced, because there are no data showing how O + R would behave in the absence of B. Thus, we cannot conclude that O + R + B is a total cause, because O + R + B may contain irrelevant factors. It must not be thought that because B was irrelevant in the combination O + F + B, it is irrelevant in O + R + B; after all, the sun rays *in Santa Barbara* may be particularly propitious for igniting paper.

What would be needed to conclude that relative to the data and the chosen factors, O + R is a total cause for paper igniting? (1) We need an instance of focused sun rays and oxygen outside Santa Barbara being attended by paper igniting. That would allow us to get to O + R at the end of Step B. We know from instance 4 (in which O + B were insufficient) that O alone isn't sufficient; thus, R can't be canceled. But we do not have a case of R without O on our chart that would assure us of the relevance of O. Thus, we also need: (2) an instance of focused sun rays without oxygen failing to be attended by the paper igniting. Given the addition of (1) and (2), we can conclude at Step D that relative to the data and the factors considered to be relevant, the best explanation includes O + R being a total cause of paper igniting. Such then is the use of the

2. Of course this assumes, for example, that B doesn't defuse the power of O to produce the effect. But if B were such a factor, O + (absence of B) would be a relevant combination. Because we stipulated at the beginning that all factors are to be specified as positive factors, we can discount this possibility. Of course what the conclusion in Step D allows is relative to those chosen factors being the ones relevant; thus, if the absence of B were relevant, presumably sooner or later Step C would come into play: O will emerge as sufficient (in the absence of B) and insufficient (in the presence of B), and we would be enjoined to restart with a new set of potentially relevant factors.

Joint Method. We now turn to Mill's last two methods, both of which have more limited applications.

(4) Method of Concomitant Variation. Mill's version may be stated as: When a variation in X is correlated with a variation in P, X is the cause or at least a causal factor of P. Thus, noting that increasing the pressure on the accelerator is correlated with increasing the speed of the car, we are enjoined to conclude that stepping on the accelerator is the cause or a causal factor in the car moving.

Clearly, if P has degrees and X is a total cause of P, we should expect variations in the degree of P to be matched by variations in the degree of some factor that is part or all of X. That is, the following deductively valid argument has a highly or completely justified second premise:

(1) P has degrees and X is a total cause of P.
(2) If (1) is true, variations in the degree of P are matched by a variation in the degree of some factor of X.

---

(3) Variation in the degree of P is matched by a variation in the degree of some factor of X.

Thus, given that P has degrees, failure of (3) is negative evidence for X being a total cause of P. Furthermore, if we should discover that (3) is an indefinite variant of a bit of data (e.g., if we should discover that X* is a factor of X in which variations in degree are matched by variations in the degree of P), this bit of data would be positive evidence for X (containing X*) being a total cause of P. The method may therefore be reformulated as follows:

METHOD OF CONCOMITANT VARIATION: *Suppose P is a phenomenon that has degrees. Then:*

(1) If variations in the degree of X are matched with variations in the degree of P, there is positive evidence for 'X* is at least part of a total cause of P'.*
(2) If variations in the degree of P aren't matched by variations in the degree of (a factor of) X, there is negative evidence for 'X is a total cause of P'.

Letting '<', '=', and '>' represent decrease, constancy, and increase in the degrees of the factors involved, the method may be given in the following summarizing diagram:

	Factors			*Phenomenon*
Instance	*Y1*	*Y2*	*Y3*	*Q*
(a)	>	=	<	>
(b)	=	>	=	=
(c)	<	=	>	<

Positive evidence for: Y1 is part of a total cause of Q.
Positive evidence for: Y3 is part of a total cause of Q.
Negative evidence for: Y2 is a total cause of Q.

Notice that there is positive evidence not only for Y1, but also for Y3, being part of a total cause of Q. That is, the "match of variations" can be in the reverse order; for example, decrease in the distance between the gas pedal and the floor is matched by an increase in the speed.

(5) Method of Residue. This method is of a rather specialized nature and may be described as follows:

> METHOD OF RESIDUE: *Let it be given as background that x_1 is a total cause of p_1 and that P is the compound phenomenon $p_1 + p_2$. Whatever positive and negative evidence there is for the compound $x_1 + x_2$ being (part of) a total cause of P is positive and negative evidence for x_2 being (a part of) a total cause of p_2.*

Put in a slightly abbreviated form, we have what follows:

> Let $P = p_1 + p_2$, $X = x_1 + x_2$, and x_1 be a total cause of p_1.
>
> Evidence for or against $x_1 + x_2$ being (part of) a total cause of P =
> Evidence for or against x_2 being (a part of) a total cause of p_2.

As a simple illustration of this method, suppose I know the weight of an empty bowl to be one pound; that is, the bowl alone causes the scale to register one pound. If I fill the bowl with some cherries and the scale registers two pounds, there is positive evidence for ⟨the bowl + the cherries⟩ causing the scale to indicate ⟨1 + 1⟩ pounds. By the Method of Residue, this positive evidence can be taken as positive evidence for the cherries causing the scale to indicate the additional pound, that is, for the cherries weighing one pound. Given the specialized and limited nature of this method, perhaps nothing more needs to be said beyond noting that in our example, given the background of the bowl weighing one pound, the cherries weighing one pound clearly explains the scale registering two pounds for the bowl of cherries.

The accompanying boxed chart (p. 330) summarizes Mill's methods. Let us then conclude our discussion of these methods by giving a genuine example of their application. In the middle of the nineteenth century, the French silk industry was on the verge of being destroyed by a disease afflicting its silkworms. The French minister of agriculture commissioned Pasteur to study this disease, which was generally called *pebrine.* Starting with the eggs, the life cycle of the silkworm consists of thirty-five days as a worm, which ends with the building of a cocoon; following a fifteen-day period in the cocoon in which the transformation from worm to moth occurs, the moth lays 600–800 eggs. The grower smothers most of the cocoons for silk, leaving a few to become moths and to lay eggs for the next year's harvest. Pebrine caused most worms to die before they created a cocoon, and the few cocoons that were created were of poor quality. One among the many complications was that, even among the viable

Summary of Mill's Methods

Sample Data

Instance	*Factors* X1	X2	X3	*Phenomenon P*
(1)	+	+	+	+
(2)	−	+	+	−
(3)	+	−	+	+
(4)	+	−	−	−

Instance	*Factors* Y1	Y2	Y3	*Phenomenon Q*
(a)	>	=	<	>
(b)	=	>	=	=
(c)	<	=	>	<

METHOD OF AGREEMENT: Instances (1)–(4) are

Positive evidence for: X1 + X3 is part of every total cause of P.
Negative evidence for: X2 is part of every total cause of P.

METHOD OF DIFFERENCE:

Instances (1) and (2) are positive evidence for: X1 is a causally relevant part of the sufficient factor X1 + X2 + X3.
Instances (1) and (3) are negative evidence for: X2 is a causally relevant part of the sufficient factor X1 + X2 + X3.
The Method of Difference also applies to (3) and (4).

JOINT METHOD:

A. Determine potentially relevant factors and collect data by varying these factors.
B. (1) List combinations of factors attended by P: X1 + X2 + X3, X1 + X3.
   (2) Eliminate combinations with causally irrelevant parts: remainder = X1 + X3.
C. If an incoherent result is obtained, restart the procedure with a new set of potentially relevant factors.
D. If the data are rich enough to foreclose a combination M being further reduced, relative to the factors and the data, 'M is the total cause of P' is the best explanation: X1 + X3 is a total cause of P.

CONCOMITANT VARIATION: Instances (a)–(c) are

Positive evidence for: Y1 is part of a total cause of Q.
Positive evidence for: Y3 is part of a total cause of Q.
Negative evidence for: Y2 is a total cause of Q.

RESIDUE: Let $P = p_1 + p_2$, $X = x_1 + x_2$, and x_1 be a total cause of p_1.

Evidence for or against $x_1 + x_2$ being (part of) a total cause of P = Evidence for or against x_2 being (a part of) a total cause of p_2.

TABLE 5.4.

Broods	*Parent Moths Lacking Corpuscles (%)*	*Other Factors*	*Healthy Offspring (%)*
A	$>$	=	$>$
B	$<$	=	$<$

cocoons that survived to become moths, the next year's offspring from these eggs were often afflicted by pebrine. It took three years of intermittent study by Pasteur to diagnose the essential features of the disease, and the full study took over ten years. A somewhat simplified account of his investigations in the first three years may be given as follows.[3]

In 1865 Pasteur noted what others had noted before, namely, that the worms or moths afflicted by pebrine were often attended by small corpuscles. The evidence for the significance of corpuscular presence was confusing and mixed. Nevertheless, Pasteur ended his first year of investigation by recommending that moths be studied for corpuscular presence and that eggs of only corpuscle-free moths be kept for next year's crop.

In 1866 Pasteur experimented with a large number of broods and was able to correlate pebrine with corpuscular presence in virtue of the kind of data given in Table 5.4. The Method of Concomitant Variation gives positive evidence that being born of corpuscle-free parents (and hence of corpuscle-free eggs) was at least part of a total cause for being healthy offspring (which produced good cocoons), and that being born of corpuscular parents was part of the total cause for failing to be healthy offspring. Another commercially significant fact that was discovered by Pasteur was that even broods largely infested with corpuscles occasionally produced worms without any corpuscles; this allowed for the regeneration of a healthy strain of silkworms.[4]

By 1877 Pasteur had significant numbers of corpuscle-free eggs and was able to experiment by infecting worms born of such eggs with inoculations of live corpuscles from other silkworms. Conducting these inoculations at various stages of the worm's development, the kinds of results shown in Table 5.5 were obtained on worms born from corpuscle-free parents.

Suppose we redo Table 5.5 in terms of corpuscular presence *by* day 5, day 35, and the egg-laying stage, that is, corpuscular presence any time prior to day 5, prior to day 35, and so on. Suppose also that to the data of 1867 is added a refinement of part of the data from 1866. In particular,

3. Most of this material is adapted from Emil Duclaux, *Pasteur, the History of a Mind,* Erwin F. Smith and Florence Hedges, trans., Philadelphia: W. B. Saunders Co., 1920.
4. Careful readers will notice that this constitutes some negative evidence for corpuscular parents producing unhealthy offspring. Some supplemental hypothesis is needed to defuse this evidence. After it was eventually determined that the corpuscles were parasites, the supplemental hypothesis was that in a few cases the parasites were not transmitted from parents to egg.

let's add a brood D that was free of corpuscles prior to making cocoons but was infested by the egg-laying stage, with the result that the offspring were unhealthy at birth. Finally, taking the "effect" as "being unhealthy or having offspring unhealthy at birth," we arrive at Table 5.6.

Taking C[5], C[35], O, and C[E] to abbreviate the factors, we list the sufficient combinations as Step B of the Joint Method enjoins:

C[5] + C[35] + O + C[E]	C[35] + O + C[E]	O + C[E]
C[5] + C[35] + C[E]	C[35] + C[E]	C[E]

The deletion part of Step B results in C[E] being the sole survivor on the list. (This kind of case makes it clear that the Joint Method is so designed as to give the same result as the Method of Agreement, with the added bonus of knowing which of the other factors (if any) are causally relevant.) Because there is no incoherence in the result, we ask: Are the data good enough to assure us that the sole remaining factor C[E] is relevant (and can't itself be deleted)? Yes, the behavior of brood C assures us that the effect of being unhealthy or having unhealthy offspring isn't forthcoming without C[E]. Thus, relative to the factors taken to be relevant, the best explanation of the data is that corpuscular presence by the egg-laying stage is the sole cause of pebrine in the organism or its offspring at birth. And this was indeed Pasteur's conclusion in 1867.

A further result is indicated by the data of 1867. If the data are recast with the factors as "corpuscular absence in days 1–5," "corpuscular absence in days 6–35," and "other considered factors," the Joint Method will indicate that corpuscular absence in days 1–5 is the sole cause of the worm making good cocoons. This indicates that it takes thirty days for the corpuscles to take their toll on the infested organism. This explains why apparently healthy cocoons can produce offspring that are unhealthy; that is, the organism is already infected but the effect shows up only in the moth stage or in the offspring that came from the infested eggs.

In this way, pebrine was determined to be an attack on the silkworms by the corpuscles, which are parasites. The parasite can be transmitted from parent to offspring through the egg as well as from one silkworm to another through scratching, ingestion of excrement, and the like. How-

TABLE 5.5.

Brood	*Inoculation During Days 1–5*	*Inoculation During Days 6–35*	*Other Considered Factors*	*Made Good Cocoon*	*Prior Death of Corpuscular Moth*
A1	+	–	+	–	+
A2	+	–	–	–	+
B1	–	+	+	+	+
B2	–	+	–	+	+
C1	–	–	+	+	–
C2	–	–	–	+	–

TABLE 5.6.

Brood	*Corpuscles Present by Day 5*	*Corpuscles Present by Day 35*	*Other Considered Factors*	*Corpuscles Present by Egg Laying*	*Disease in Self or in Offspring*
A1	+	+	+	+	+
A2	+	+	−	+	+
B1	−	+	+	+	+
B2	−	+	−	+	+
C1	−	−	+	−	−
C2	−	−	−	−	−
D1	−	−	+	+	+
D2	−	−	−	+	+

ever, Pasteur also discovered the parasites to be short-lived outside the body of a host organism. Thus, by starting the cycle with corpuscle-free eggs, one could be assured of having good cocoons except for the small possibility of the worm being infected during the first five days by parasites that found a host organism other than the silkworm. For all practical purposes, the French silk industry was saved, except for one additional problem that came to light in 1867.

In 1866 Pasteur sent to various growers samples of corpuscle-free eggs produced by corpuscle-free moths. While the resulting worms were largely successful in 1867, in some instances whole broods were wiped out by disease despite variations in circumstances of place, time, and climate. It was at this point that Pasteur realized that there were two diseases: pebrine and a second disease sometimes called *flacherie* but confused with pebrine up to that point. Short of a careful separation of the symptoms (which Pasteur was so far untrained to perform), without having determined pebrine to be caused by the corpuscles, this realization woud have eluded Pasteur.

To see this, letting E1 and E2 be the broods afflicted with flacherie, and combining these data with the initial data of 1867, we would have the array of data shown in Table 5.7. Listing of the various sufficient factors enjoined by Step B of the Joint Method gives us:

C[5] + C[35] + O	C[35] + O	O
C[5] + C[35]	C[35]	"Zero Factor"

When we start deleting combinations that contain irrelevant factors, we ultimately have nothing at the end of Step B. That is, brood E2 seems to show that both C[35] and "other considered factors" are causally irrelevant for the disease. Given this result, Step C enjoins one to restart by changing the set of potentially relevant factors (rather than accepting the silly conclusion that the disease is without cause).

While this new evidence greatly perturbed Pasteur, based on the massive evidence that he had previously accumulated, by 1867 Pasteur

TABLE 5.7.

Brood	*Corpuscles Present by Day 5*	*Corpuscles Present by Day 35*	*Other Considered Factors*	*Organism or Offspring Diseased*
A1	+	+	+	+
A2	+	+	−	+
B1	−	+	+	+
B2	−	+	−	+
C1	−	−	+	−
C2	−	−	−	−
E1	−	−	+	+
E2	−	−	−	+

believed himself to be justified in concluding that the corpuscles were the sole cause of pebrine and that there was a second disease. In effect, what he changed was the "phenomenon factor" P rather than one of the antecedents of P: the phenomenon was recast from "having a disease" to "having pebrine" and "having a second disease."[5]

In any event, given the conclusion that the corpuscles are the sole cause of pebrine and the recasting of the phenomenon as "pebrine" and "a second disease," the Method of Residue can be seen to yield a conclusion. The data of the corpuscle-free brood E may be taken as positive evidence for ⟨no corpuscles + other unconsidered factors⟩ being a sufficient factor for ⟨no pebrine + some other disease⟩. Because the absence of corpuscles is sufficient for the absence of pebrine (in that the corpuscles are the sole cause of pebrine), the Method of Residue (extended from total causes to sufficient factors) yields: the behavior of brood E is positive evidence for the unconsidered factors being sufficient factors for the other disease. Much of the research in the succeeding years was devoted to identifying a more determinate factor X such that ⟨no corpuscles + X⟩ could be taken as the total cause of ⟨no pebrine + flacherie⟩. Any positive evidence for that causal relation would, by the Method of Residue, be positive evidence for X being a total cause of flacherie. By 1868 Pasteur identified "offspring of worms that languished or belonged to broods with a high mortality rate" as such a factor X, and later X was determined to be the presence of a certain bacillus in the digestive tract of the parent worms. (The exact functioning of the bacillus turned out to be quite complicated. Roughly, being attacked by the bacillus weakened the parent and created a hereditary feebleness in the offspring to attacks by that bacillus; the bacillus is fairly common in the environment but is resisted in normal exposure by worms free of the hereditary weakness.)

5. Nothing in Mill's methods or other methods shows that claiming a second disease (or even a second total cause for the one disease) is the right assumption to make in the absence of having identified a potential causal factor for the unhealthy brood E. This is the kind of case in which a successful scientist takes the right turn instead of the wrong one—which in this case would be that the corpuscles after all have nothing to do with the disease.

Our discussion of Mill's methods may be summarized as follows:

(1) Properly reformulated, they turn out to be special instances of features involved in the inference to the best explanation.
(2) In certain specialized kinds of cases they provide useful recipes for collecting and assessing evidence for hypotheses or explanations.
(3) Except for the use of the term 'cause', Mill's methods couch the data and the inferred generalization in the same vocabulary.

This last point shows that the applicability of Mill's methods is limited to inferring descriptive generalizations from the data. Indeed, in the extended example we considered, Mill's methods would only allow inferences to such generalizations as 'Corpuscular presence is the sole cause of pebrine' and 'Presence of a certain bacillus in the parent is (part of) a total cause of flacherie'. While such inferences are helpful in arriving at explanatory generalizations, unless the data are redescribed using such terms as 'parasites' and 'hereditary susceptibility', Mill's methods and methods essentially similar to them will not allow inferences to such explanatory generalizations as 'Pebrine is caused by the attack of the organism by a *parasite*' and 'Attacks of flacherie cause a *hereditary weakness* in the offspring that makes them *susceptible to a common bacillus* that causes such attacks'. Such are the limitations of Mill's methods and the inferences of mere descriptive generalizations.

EXERCISES—SECTION 5.5

1. In the discussion of Pasteur's investigations of pebrine, it was claimed that the initial data of 1867 indicated that corpuscular absence during days 1–5 was the sole cause of the worm making good cocoons. Justify this claim by the Joint Method.
2. A well-known fact is that meat, vegetables, and other dead organisms putrefy and become infested with bacteria of various kinds. A question in the eighteenth and nineteenth centuries was the cause of this activity. One popular view was that of spontaneous generation; that is, dead organic matter spontaneously generated new life (i.e., various microbes) by coming into contact with air. Opponents insisted that the "new" life was nothing more than germs in the air infesting the dead organic matter. The geneal idea of testing these theories is fairly clear: take some putrefiable matter (i.e., dead organic material), heat it in a solution so that all living organisms in the dead organic material and the surrounding air are killed, and see what happens. (Of course one heats it in a solution so that the dead organic matter doesn't burn up.) Needham, an Irish priest, constructed an experiment to support the spontaneous-generation view: He put some putrefiable matter into a corked flask, heated it to kill all the germs, and observed microscopic organisms a few days later: these organisms must have spontaneously generated. Spallanzani countered that Needham had not sufficiently heated the flask, and by heating the flasks to higher temperatures, he obtained the result of the substance remaining sterile for weeks. Supporters of spontaneous generation countered that heating

the flask either destroyed some inorganic element in the air that was a needed catalyst for spontaneous genration or else damaged some genetic power in the dead organic substances. The debate raged for years, and it was Pasteur who finally disabused the scientific community of the idea of spontaneous generation. The repeatability of his experiments, their care and accuracy, and a certain amount of showmanship contributed to Pasteur's success. We briefly describe here two of his experiments.

Experiment 1

This consisted in two parts, the first being a version of Spallanzani's. (a) The long neck of a flask was bent ninety degrees and connected to a platinum rod that could be heated. By heating the flask containing the putrefiable substance in a liquid, all the substance's germs were killed; when cooled, the liquid's vapors condensed and new air entered the flask through the platinum rod, which was heated to kill all germs in the air. Then the flask was sealed by fusing the neck with a blowpipe. With no possibility of germs entering, the substance remained sterile indefinitely. (b) In the presence of sterilized air, a piece of cotton soiled by germs was later introduced into the neck of one of the flasks. Because the germs were trapped in the cotton, the putrefiable substance remained sterile. (c) Finally, by tilting the flask, the cotton was dropped into the liquid. Within twenty-four hours bacteria started developing.

Experiment 2

This time a flask with a long neck in the shape of an S lying on its side was used. (a) The flask was heated as before, and when the vapors condensed and new cool air came in, the condensation on the neck cleaned the air and the force of gravity additionally prevented the germs in the air from traveling up and down the S course. Left in this state in which there was a constant supply of new air that continued to be cleaned by the neck, the substance remained sterile indefinitely. (b) Subsequently, the neck was cut off so that the liquid was in contact with air that didn't go through the cleansing action of the S-shaped neck. In a short time, the dead organic substance was infested with microbes.

(a) Let the experimental cultures be 1a, 1b, 1c, 2a, and 2b; let the factors be "environmental germs," "dead organic substance + air," and "cool air"; and let the phenomenon be "microbes develop in the culture." Make a chart of the data provided by experiments 1 and 2.

(b) Using the Joint Method (and the background assumption that the dead organic substance and air cannot be eliminated to produce microbes in the dead substance), determine that the compound "environmental germs + the dead organic substance and air" is the sole cause of the microbes developing in the cultures.

(c) What part of the answer in (b) constitutes negative evidence for the spontaneous-generation view?

(d) One of the supplemental hypotheses of the spontaneous-generation view was that by heating the air a needed inorganic catalyst for spontaneous generation is destroyed. How does this supplemental hypothesis fare in light of Pasteur's experiment?

(e) Suggest a supplemental hypothesis still available for the spontaneous-generation view. Given this suggestion along with the experiments of Pasteur, how would you judge the spontaneous-generation theory? (Refer to considerations from Section 5.2.)

3. In 1865, the first year of his investigation into pebrine, Pasteur examined various broods for corpuscles. Part of the data he collected might be taken to involve three broods X, Y, and Z. Microscopic examinations showed the fol-

lowing: Brood X had corpuscles in all three stages (worm, cocoon, and moth), and yet they produced good cocoons. Brood Y showed no corpuscles until the cocoon and moth stages and yet failed to produce good cocoons. Brood Z had corpuscles in the worm stage and died during that stage.

(a) Make a chart of this evidence using the categories "corpuscles in the worm stage," "corpuscles in the cocoon stage," and "corpuscles in the moth stage" for the factors and "failure to produce good cocoons" for the phenomenon. Use "dead" when "+" or "−" seems inappropriate for a factor but always use "+" or "−" for the phenomenon.

(b) Explain how the Joint Method would be applied to this case.

Faced with the puzzling evidence, Pasteur conjectured that the corpuscles were tardy or late symptoms of a constitutional disease in the silkworm (which explains Y and Z), and X was explained away by the ad hoc hypothesis that in some cases of the disease was not sufficiently strong to prevent decent cocoons. This is certainly one way of recasting the factors, and he held on to this conjecture much longer than any of his assistants. When early and less complete versions of the experiments of 1867 were conducted in 1866, Pasteur held on to his conjectures while the assistants were convinced of pebrine being caused by the corpuscles. Duclaux, one of the assistants, writes: "Here we behold a spectacle rare in the life of Pasteur: an experiment the full and complete meaning of which he does not immediately comprehend."[6] Before criticizing Pasteur too quickly, consider problem (d) below.

(c) Given hindsight of Pasteur's investigations presented in the text, what is the likeliest conjecture concerning the behavior of broods X, Y, and Z?

(d) The news Pasteur received in 1867 concerning the failure of some broods coming from corpuscle-free eggs led him to the conclusion that there is a second disease: flacherie. Why was this move less plausible in 1865?

4. It is known that certain species of birds always start their annual northward migration on a specific date (such as March 22). Treating the date of departure as a phenomenon capable of having degrees and using the Method of Concomitant Variation, researchers quickly eliminated the availability of food and the temperature as total causes of the date of departure. To explain this use of the method, make the following assumptions: (i) The species S always starts their northward migration on March 22. (ii) In the wintering location of S, in 1921 there were fifty grams of food available per bird per day around March 22 and the mean temperature of the week prior to March 22 was sixty degrees fahrenheit.

   (a) Specify sample data for 1922 and 1923 that might have been obtained that would justify the elimination of food and temperature as total causes of the departure date by the Method of Concomitant Variation.

   (b) Justify your answer in (a) by using the Method of Concomitant Variation to eliminate food and temperature as total causes of the departure date.

5. Researchers studying the migratory habits of birds quickly conjectured that the number of daylight hours was part of every total cause of the specific date being the departure date. Further evidence for this was collected by placing birds in aviaries with artificial light sources and manipulating the amount of daylight hours. Make the same assumptions as in exercise 4.

   (a) Informally (i.e., without charts, etc.) explain how the Method of Agreement indicates the conjecture the researchers quickly reached.

6. Duclaux, *Pasteur,* p. 167.

(b) Suggest an experimental setup that, in light of the Method of Concomitant Variation, would give positive evidence for the number of daylight hours being part of the total cause of the departure date (or negative evidence for the daylight hours being a total cause of the departure date).

(c) Specify sample data you might obtain in your experimental setup that, if obtained, would give by the Method of Concomitant Variation positive evidence for the number of daylight hours being part of a total cause of the departure date. (These data need not be put into a chart form, although it will have to be translated to a chart form in (d) below.)

(d) Justify your answer in (c) by supposing the specified data were obtained and using the Method of Concomitant Variation.

6. Suppose a mountain climber records the amount of heat it takes to boil water as he is at various altitudes and produces the following chart:

Altitude in Feet	*Degrees Centigrade Needed*
15,000	85
10,000	90
7,500	92
5,000	95
2,000	98
0 (= sea level)	100

(a) The phenomenon of water boiling can be taken to have degrees in the sense of the amount of heat it takes to boil water. What may be concluded from the mountain climber's records by the Method of Concomitant Variation?

(b) Let

x = the amount of distance between, and velocities of, water molecules produced by 100 degrees centigrade of heat in the absence of other influences.

y = the amount by which distances between, and velocities of, water molecules are decreased so that water boiling at sea level is the compound effect ⟨x + (the negative factor) y⟩.

Suppose the atmospheric pressure at sea level is measured to be 14.7 pounds per square inch and that applying 100 degrees centigrade of heat to water at sea level results in water boiling. What can you conclude by the Method of Residue?

(c) Suppose the altitude in the mountain climber's chart is rewritten in terms of decreasing atmospheric pressure. Let (P) be given by:

(P) = Decrease in atmospheric pressure increases the distances between, and the velocities of, water molecules.

(1) Given the vocabulary of the revised chart, could P be an inference of a descriptive generalization (by methods like Mill's)?

(2) What explanatory generalizations would have had to be inferred before P could have been seen as an inference of a descriptive generalization (by methods like Mill's)?

7. Toward the middle of the nineteenth century the difficulty of accounting for the path of the planet Uranus became apparent. This led to the discovery of Neptune, which may be described very crudely as follows: In 1845 Leverrier tackled the problem, and by a number of complex calculations concerning forces exerted on Uranus, determined that an unknown planet of a certain

mass in a certain orbit in conjunction with the behavior of the known celestial bodies would account for the peculiar path of Uranus. He therefore postulated the existence of such an unknown planet, and in September 1846 the planet (later to be called Neptune) was found at the predicted place by the German astronomer Galle. This discovery of Neptune is often cited as an application of the Method of Residue, and to a certain extent it might be so considered.

Let x_1 be an unknown postulated planet of mass m on a path p. Let x_2 be the known celestial bodies with the set of masses M and set of paths P. Use the following scheme of abbreviation:

e: Uranus follows the path p*.
a: x_2 is a total cause of forces f_2 acting on Uranus.
H: The combination of x_1 and x_2 is a total and sole cause of all the forces acting on Uranus.
f: The forces acting on Uranus are exactly f_1 and f_2.

Assume the following:

(a) 'e', 'a', 'H $\supset$ f', and 'f $\supset$ e' are completely justified.
(b) In light of 'H $\supset$ f' being completely justified, any positive evidence for 'H' is positive evidence for '$x_1 + x_2$ is a total cause of $f_1 + f_2$ which is the sum of all the forces acting on Uranus'.

Relying in part on the Method of Residue, show that 'e' is positive evidence for an unknown postulated planet of mass m and path p being a total cause of forces f_1 acting on Uranus.

[*Hint*: By the method of Section 5.2, show 'e' is positive evidence for 'H' and use assumption (b).]

*8. Assume it is completely justified that the phenomenon P is the compound phenomenon "p_1 & p_2" and that x_1 is a total cause of p_1. Assume also for the sake of this problem that 'E' is positive evidence for 'H' if and only if 'E' is at least highly justified and there is a set of highly or completely justified statements $A_1, \ldots, A_n$ such that 'H, $A_1, \ldots, A_n$ / E' is deductively valid. Partially justify the Method of Residue by producing an argument for the claim: any positive evidence for the compound $\langle x_1 + x_2 \rangle$ being a total cause of P is positive evidence for x_2 being a total cause of p_2.

6 Language and the Levels of Meaning

A proper appreciation of the language we use can be crucial to truth assessment. In Chapter 1 we saw that Jane was able to uncover the failure of Professor C to read her paper by paying attention to the evasiveness of his answers and his use of the word "distinctly." We have postponed our discussion of the use of language to this late chapter for two reasons: (i) To a large extent, attentiveness rather than a set of rules is what is needed for one's mother tongue. (ii) Philosophers of language as well as linguists disagree significantly about how language exactly (or even broadly) functions, and there is nothing like an established set of rules for determining the meaning of expressions. Still some discussion of how language functions is likely to serve as a consciousness-raising device even for native speakers, and if not too fine a point is put on the rough picture to be presented, perhaps it won't be found to be too contentious or controversial.

While language is indispensable for formulating and communicating our thoughts, it is also the source of a large number of fallacies and confusion. For this reason, rather than lumping the language-related fallacies together at the end of the chapter, we shall make them integral to the main text discussion. Indeed, a secondary aim of this chapter is to warn readers of various fallacies and pitfalls related to our use of language.

Finally, even a cursory discussion of language can at times involve complications that may not be of great interest to everyone. Rather than completely omitting complications that a decent discussion requires, this chapter is sprinkled with starred paragraphs that may be skipped by readers not inclined to pursue somewhat advanced topics.

6.1 Introduction and Use/Mention Confusions

In studying the nature of language, there are a number of interrelated concerns of possible interest. Suppose in my presence Jane utters the words,

"What a bore you are!" With this statement we might say that she made a comment, expressed her disgust, and issued an insult. Clearly, there are many things we can do with words, and the primary focus of an inquiry could be an examination of what might be called speech acts, that is, the kinds of acts that are performed in using words. Another focus could view language as the primary instrument that allows speakers to make statements, express approval, issue insults, and so on. Central to such an interest might be the grammar or syntax of language and the semantics or meaning of words. Yet a third concern might be an analysis of the end product, that is, the statement made or the question asked or the insult issued. And of course the list could go on, with etymology and phonetics, just to mention two.

Because our interest in the context of critical thinking is to assess truth claims, it would seem that our primary goal should be the clarification and analysis of the end product of a speech act that results in a statement being made. Yet to a large extent, what is conveyed is a function of the other features of language we have mentioned such as syntax, semantics, the circumstances of the speaker's act, and the act performed by the speaker; furthermore, truth claims may be conveyed or suggested, or be otherwise relevant even when the principal speech act is not that of making a statement. Inevitably, then, we must look at the various influences that contribute to the total impact of an utterance.

At least in a rough way our discussion of contributing influences will be in ascending order; that is, typically contribution of one influence will depend on the contributions of the others already having been determined. Specifically, assuming that we have a sequence of phonetically correct sounds or correctly spelled written words, we shall discuss in order: grammar, semantics or the meaning of words, speech acts or the use of meaningful sentences by speakers in particular circumstances, conversational implications or the unasserted claims or suggestions made by speech acts, and finally, certain special features of some particular uses of language. Each of these will be seen to contribute a level of meaning. Before embarking on our examination of language and the levels of meaning, we conclude this section by discussing one kind of confusion or fallacy that can arise when one talks about language.

Confusing Use and Mention. Once we start talking about language, it is evident that words can play a dual role, as in the following example:

(1) Jabbar is a short name.
(2) Jabbar is a tall basketball player.

In (1) we are using 'Jabbar' to talk about a word and not about a basketball player, while the reverse is the case in (2). The pair of terms 'use' and 'mention' is used standardly to distinguish these two functions an expression can have; that is, an expression is being *mentioned* when we are talking about the linguistic expression itself, whereas an expression is being *used* when we are talking about what the expression names (or talks about) in the world. Thus, 'Jabbar' is being mentioned in (1) because we are talking about the word itself, while 'Jabbar' is being used in (2) because we are talking about the person named by the word 'Jabbar' (the center of the Los Angeles Lakers who dominated the league for years) rather than the name itself.

When words play this dual function of being used and mentioned, the possibility of confusion arises: Is it or is it not true that Jabbar is short? Well, the word is short but the person isn't. In order to avoid confusion it is important that we introduce a name for the *name* so that we can have separate words depending on whether we are talking about the basketball player or his name. We could do this, for example, by introducing '!' as the name for the name 'Jabbar' and reserving 'Jabbar' as the name for the basketball player. In that case we would rewrite (1) and (2) as:

(1*) ! is a short name.
(2*) Jabbar is a tall basketball player.

Given this convention,

Jabbar is (a) short (name)

would be false. Obviously something like this should be done; on the other hand, it would be tedious to learn a whole new set of names for words. Thus, we shall use the usual convention of quoted expressions being a name for the linguistic expression inside the quotes; to put it another way, when an expression is being mentioned, rather than used, we enclose the expression within quotation marks (single or double depending on one's taste). Given this convention, (1) is now strictly speaking false, and the true statement is:

'Jabbar' is (a) short (name).

If one abides by this convention of using quotation marks, there is little danger of confusing use and mention. However, if one forgets about the convention or in other ways confuses use and mention, we shall say that a Use/Mention Fallacy has been committed. More specifically: One commits a USE/MENTION FALLACY

> *(a) when things that are true of linguistic expressions are thereby attributed to what those expressions talk about,* **or** *(b) when features of things in the world are thereby attributed to linguistic expressions for those things.*

An example of mistakenly going from features of linguistic expressions to what they talk about might be: "The name of my date tonight is 'Horatio.' Boy, he must be old-fashioned!" That 'Horatio' is an old-fashioned name is a poor reason for thinking that Horatio himself is old-fashioned: he might be one of the wildest swingers in southern California. An example in the opposite direction is the following "puzzle" of ancient Greek origin: "You can't say the word wagon because whatever you say must come through your mouth; but a wagon is far too big to come through your mouth."

Let '(. . .)' and '(. . .)°' be two linguistic contexts that are the same except for some parenthetical additions. An example of such a pair of contexts would be 'is (an) old-fashioned (name)' and 'is old-fashioned'. Given this understanding, the two versions of the inferential fallacy we have discussed may be represented as follows:

> Use/Mention:
> . . . 'X' . . . → . . . X . . .°
> . . . X . . . → . . . 'X' . . .°
> ['(. . .)' & '(. . .)°' the same except for parenthetical additions.]

The examples of the last paragraph may then be analyzed as follows:

Use/Mention: 'Horatio' is (an) old-fashioned (name) → Horatio is old-fashioned.
Use/Mention: (A) wagon cannot come out of one's mouth → (The word) 'Wagon' cannot come out of one's mouth.

These are of course silly and simplistic examples of Use/Mention Fallacies. Perhaps only slightly less silly is the amount of money companies spend on finding a right name for themselves or their products. When 'Esso' was found to be too tame a name (for the tiger one puts in the tank), the company spent millions of dollars to come up with 'Exxon.' The enlarged second 'X' in the logo made the word look especially powerful, and no doubt the company is banking on the customers committing the Use/Mention Fallacy to conclude that the gas would be powerful as well. Readers seeking more subtle examples might continue reading the rest of this section.

★ ★ ★ ★

Here then are some examples of Use/Mention Fallacies that are somewhat more subtle:

(1) "The ratios (or rational numbers) 2/3 and 5/3 have the same denominator." The most likely source of this false claim is that one is confusing a fraction (a notational device for naming a ratio or a rational number) with the ratio named. The ratio or the rational number itself has no such thing as a denominator, as should be evident from the realization that '2/3', '4/6', '100/150', and '0.66666 . . . ' are all different expressions for the same ratio. The parallel Use/Mention Fallacy is committed in the opposite direction when one says: "The fraction 2/3 is the same as the

fraction 4/6." This is much like saying, "The name Marilyn Monroe is the same as the name Norma Jean Baker," or, "The numeral IV is the same as the numeral 4."

(2) "Identity is a relation between two names." Statements of the form 'A = B' are indeed true if and only if 'A' and 'B' name the same thing. But the statement 'Marilyn Monroe = Norma Jean Baker' asserts the identity of Marilyn Monroe herself with Norma Jean Baker herself. This identity of the person with herself does not depend on the existence of any names, and the statement of identity certainly doesn't assert the identity of 'Marilyn Monroe' with 'Norma Jean Baker.' Given our scheme, we would analyze the most likely source of the false claim as:

Use/Mention: 'A = B' (is true if and only if there) is a relation between 'A' and 'B' (namely, of their naming the same thing)[1] → A = B is a relation between 'A' and 'B'.

(3) "That is a false fact." If we allow that there are such things as facts, facts simply are and are neither true nor false. What can be true or false are statements about the world (or beliefs expressed by statements about the world). While beliefs and statements can be true or false of the world, the world itself is neither true nor false. Thus, if we are thinking about 'Texas is small' being a false fact, the likely source of the mistaken claim is the fallacy of

Use/Mention: 'Texas is small' is false → (The fact that) Texas is small is false.

(4) "Experience itself cannot be mistaken; it is therefore certain." This statement doesn't commit the Use/Mention Fallacy and might even be true if an experience is understood to involve having a belief that one is experiencing such and such. However, the Use/Mention Fallacy is committed if one thinks that a statement or belief about experience is certain because the *having* of the experience (the felt headache itself) is something that cannot be wrong. Of course the having of an experience can be neither right nor wrong. However just because *what* the belief or claim is about cannot be wrong (or right for that matter), it does not follow that the belief or statement about it cannot be wrong. Thus, we should analyze the fallacy as:

Use/Mention: (The fact that) I have a headache cannot be mistaken → (Belief in) 'I have a headache' cannot be mistaken.

One commits the Use/Mention Fallacy in the opposite direction when it is suggested that the having of the experience is certain. Our beliefs or claims about having an experience can be certain or uncertain, but the very having of the experience itself can be neither certain nor uncertain.

1. For this "premise" to be true, the first parenthetical addition may not be deleted.

Thus, the throbbing pain I feel in my temples is neither certain nor uncertain, although my claim or belief that I have such a headache might be.

While the average reader might have little occasion to commit Use/Mention Fallacies of the kind just listed, they do show that when one starts philosophizing, one must be very careful in the language used. The field is in a sense ripe for linguistic confusion, the Use/Mention Fallacy being one prominent example.

★ ★ ★ ★

EXERCISES—SECTION 6.1

In each of the following, analyze the fallacy that is the most likely source of the mistaken or questionable claim. [In exercises 5–7, π is the number (with the decimal representation '3.1415 . . . ') that gives the circumference of the circle when it is multipled by the circle's diameter.]

1. Love is a four-letter word.
2. If you keep your name Smith, you are going to continue being an ordinary person.
3. She must be of French origin because her name is Michelle.
4. [An ad for a fabric softener:] SNUGGLE—snuggly softness that's less expensive! (*Caution:* 'Snuggle' as the name for the fabric softener is a different term from the verb 'snuggle' and its variants like 'snuggly'.)

*5. π is the name of a number.

*6. π begins with the numeral '3'.
[To analyze the fallacy involved, be prepared to consider a name for π that is other than 'π', and thereby for a slight deviation from the pattern (. . . 'X' . . .) → (. . . X . . .)°.]

*7. 'π' is a number referred to by a Greek letter.

*8. It's a dubious fact that the president still possesses all of his powers.

*9. It is in virtue of the meaning of the words that this husband has a wife.

6.2 The Level of Syntax

If one wishes to analyze the contributing elements to the meaning or impact of an utterance, the natural place to begin is the contribution of grammar or syntax. In this section we shall discuss the role of grammar in a general way (6.2.1), suggest some methods for analyzing ungrammatical sentences (6.2.2), and present some linguistic fallacies related to our discussion of grammar (6.2.3)

6.2.1 The Role of Grammar

A mere set of words can have no meaning as a whole. The meaning of the whole emerges only when the words are arranged in one or another of the ways that are permitted by the grammar of the language. Consider the four words 'did', 'Tom', 'Jane', and 'hit'. Some of the possible permutations of these four words are: (1) Tom Jane hit did. (2) Did hit Jane Tom. (3) Tom did hit Jane. (4) Jane did hit Tom. (5) Did Tom hit Jane. We can see that (1) and (2) are ungrammatical expressions that (barring special circumstances) convey nothing meaningful; (3) and (4) have the form of declarative sentences that can be used to make statements, although different statements would be made by them. Except for the dispensable aid provided by punctuation, (5) is an interrogative sentence that can be used to ask questions. In this way, the grammar of the language determines whether we can attach (normal) meaning to a sequence of words, and if we can, what kind of meaning is to be attached.

The kinds of meaning grammar is able to convey are well exhibited in the first two lines of Lewis Carroll's *Jabberwocky:*

> 'Twas brillig, and the slithy toves
> Did gyre and gimble in the wabe:

Except for the grammatical particles, the words are unknown to us. And yet three kinds of minimal meanings are conveyed to us by the grammar of English that the sentence displays:

(1) Because of the grammatical positions they occupy, each of the nonsense words are assigned some minimal meaning. 'Brillig' must be a word for something like the climatic condition or a period of time; 'toves' presumably is the plural form of 'tove', and a tove is a kind of creature or thing capable of action. 'Gyre' and 'gimble' stand for some kind of action that can be performed without the the presence of an object toward which the action is directed; that is, they are verbs with an intransitive use. Finally, 'wabe' must refer to a location or a period of time or be a description of such a location or time. " 'Twas night and the chilly winds did blow and howl in the dark" would be of the same grammatical form, as would "'Twas high noon and the lusty cowboys did drink and sing in the bar." Thus, we can see that part of the meaning of the word is the grammatical category (or the "syntactic marker") assigned to the word, and the rules of grammar stipulate that this or that grammatical position can only be occupied by words of certain grammatical categories.

(2) In addition to the minimal word-meaning conveyed by the grammar, the grammar also conveys a minimal sentence-meaning. In the lines of the poems, in effect we are told that in a certain period of time or under certain climatic conditions, things called toves that are said to be "slithy" performed certain actions in a place, time, or circumstance of a certain kind. 'The toves in the wabe did slithly gimble' would convey a different minimal sentence-meaning, namely, that things called toves in a certain kind of place performed some action in a manner said to be 'slithly'.

(3) Finally, the grammar gives some indication of the type of speech act performed (or at least attempted). The two lines of the poem we have

considered presumably attempt to make a statement. Different grammatical constructions would indicate different speech acts; for example, 'Did the toves gyre and gimble(?)' would be an attempt to ask a question while 'How slithy the toves are(!)' would be an attempted exclamation.

It is sometimes claimed that syntax is only concerned with structure and that meanings always belong to the domain of semantics. In its extreme form such a claim would be mistaken. Linguistics attaches the syntactic marker "animate noun" to 'tiger', and to this extent part of the meaning of 'tiger' is construed to be part of its grammar. Complete words like 'a' and 'the' might be called grammatical particles because their entire meanings are taken to be in the domain of grammar. The distinction between syntax and semantics is not precise and has to do with a difference in generality. Syntax incorporates those meanings, whether it be part or all of a word's meaning, in terms of which general rules of wide-ranging applicability can be formulated for the normality and abnormality of sentences. Thus, grammar should include enough of the meaning of words to account for the normality of grammaticalness of 'The tiger ran' and the aberrance or ungrammaticalness of 'The house ran'. In contrast, consider 'His polka-dot tie had no circles'. No doubt this sentence is deviant or aberrant, but the rules needed to determine that it is deviant would be rather specific to the meaning of 'polka dot'. Hence, the rules and meanings involved in determining 'His polka-dot tie had no circles' to be deviant and 'His polka-dot tie had red circles' to be normal are relegated to the level of semantics.

The contribution of grammar to our understanding of what is conveyed is so ubiquitous that it often goes unnoticed. By stripping away much of the meanings we are accustomed to receiving, *Jabberwocky* exhibits grammar's contribution in a stark way. However, encounters with ungrammatical or grammatically aberrant sentences are the more usual reminders of grammar's role. Yet what role grammar plays in such a case may be less than obvious. Admittedly grammar indicates the sentence to be aberrant. But what conclusion should one draw from a sentence being ungrammatical? It might be thought that being grammatical is a precondition for managing to convey any meaning, so that a use of an ungrammatical sentence fails to convey meaning. One might even think that if this were not so, there would be no role for grammar to play. However, such a view of grammar's role would seem to be mistaken.

Poetry and ordinary conversations make it obvious that meanings can be conveyed by sentences that are ungrammatical by any ordinary standards. How, then, should we construe the role of grammar?[2] The plausible answer construes it as establishing a *norm* for conveying meaning.

2. The following discussion of normality and aberrance relies heavily on Hilary Putnam, "Some Issues in the Theory of Grammar," in *Mind, Language, and Reality: Philosophical Papers*, Vol. 2, London: Cambridge University Press, 1975.

The norm is not necessarily the statistically most frequent. Rather, for something to be a norm, it must satisfy the following three conditions:

(i) No *special* explanation is needed for anything that satisfies the norm.
(ii) Any deviation from the norm must be attributable to some interfering factor.
(iii) What departs from the norm must be explicable partly by the interfering factors and partly by the norm; that is, in some form the norm must be reflected in the aberrant instance so that part of its full explanation refers back to the norm.

Perhaps the most vivid example of a norm is Newton's first law of motion as it relates to moving bodies:

> Every body continues in its state . . . of uniform motion in a right line, unless it is compelled to change that state by forces impressed upon it.[3]

In other words, the norm for a body moving in a certain direction with a certain velocity is that it will forever keep moving in that direction with that velocity. If something accords with this norm, no special explanation of its behavior is required, because it is behaving precisely as it should according to Newton's first law. Of course virtually nothing that we know of behaves in the way described by this norm; as such, behavior according to the norm is hardly the statistically most frequent. Most bodies we know of depart from the norm as a result of interfering influences—resistance being an obvious example. Yet the behavior of something that is slowing down because of resistance is in part accounted for by the norm. The gradual deceleration of the body is explained as a compound effect of the velocity with which it was moving and the interfering force that decelerates its motion.

In claiming grammar as establishing a norm for conveying meaning, we are then claiming three things:

(i) No *special* explanation is needed for why a grammatical sentence manages to convey meaning; that is, to be grammatical is precisely to be so constructed that it will convey meaning.
(ii) On the other hand, the use of grammatically deviant sentences to convey meaning requires special explanatory mechanisms that prevent the utterances from conveying nothing. The most general mechanism that allows something to be conveyed by the use of ungrammatical sentences (and deviant sentences in general) is the Principle of Charity, a principle that, unless the circumstance absolutely precludes the possibility, a serious use of words by an adult

3. *Sir Isaac Newton's Principles of Natural Philosophy & his System of the World* (A. Motte, trans. [1729], F. Cajori, ed.), Berkeley and Los Angeles: University of California Press, 1934, p. 13.

speaker conveys something informative and appropriate (however inept the execution may appear to be).[4]

(iii) The grammatical norms for conveying something meaningful should in some fashion be reflected in the total impact of the use of a deviant sentence. This means that even in uses of grammatically deviant sentences, grammar contributes to the meaning conveyed. This role of grammar will become more evident in the next subsection, in which we shall suggest some methods for determining what is conveyed by the use of ungrammatical sentences.

The only real alternative to this way of coping with sentences that are apparently deviant but still manage to convey meaning is to construe them as being nondeviant and normal, according to an expanded conception of grammar. Unfortunately this has two negative consequences. (a) The explanation of the conveyed meanings becomes more complex by having to postulate an increasing number of rules of grammar for constructing nondeviant sentences. By the same token, the explanatory power of the rules we normally recognize is reduced, in that they will no longer play a role in explaining what is conveyed by what once counted as deviant sentences. (b) There is a strong likelihood that no sentence could be declared deviant because even for the most deviant-looking sentences, one can with ingenuity probably think of circumstances in which their use will manage to convey some meaning. While 'Did hit Tom Jane' cannot be used to convey meaning in normal circumstances, in some circumstance it might be used to convey what might be conveyed by "Did hit Tom—(that) Jane. [She sure did!]" Regardless of how ungrammatical a sentence is, given a serious use by an adult speaker, the Principle of Charity is likely to allow us to attribute some meaning to what was said. Thus, the grammatical aberrance of a sentence should not be taken as its incapacity to be used for conveying meaning, and grammar is best seen as establishing a norm along the lines already indicated.

EXERCISES—SECTION 6.2.1

1. The third and fourth lines of Lewis Carroll's *Jabberwocky* are as follow:

   All mimsy were the borogoves
   And the mome raths outgrabe.

   (a) Specify the minimal meanings assigned by syntax to the words 'mimsy', 'borogoves', 'mome', 'raths outgrabe'.

4. This principle and more specific versions of it engender a number of implications that we shall see (in Section 6.5) to belong to the domain of pragmatics. That something is conveyed by grammatically aberrant sentences thus belongs to this area of pragmatics. On the other hand, as we shall see shortly, syntax plays a role in specifying what is conveyed by use of ungrammatical sentences.

(b) On the basis of (a), suggest several meaningful lines of the same grammatical form as the two lines of *Jabberwocky* cited in this exercise.
(c) On the basis of (a), specify the minimal sentence-meaning syntax assigned to the lines cited in this exercise.
(d) A later line of *Jabberwocky* is 'O frabjous day! Callooh! Callay!' What type of speech act is performed or at least attempted by this line?

2. Suggest something that might be conveyed in a special circumstance by the ungrammatical expression 'Milk me coffee'.

6.2.2 Deviant Sentences and Some Methods for Analyzing Them

We have just suggested that uses of deviant sentences can convey meaning and that grammar accounts for part of what is conveyed. To exemplify this and to give readers some tools for dealing with deviant sentences, we shall present three methods for analyzing the various meanings conveyed by the use of such sentences. However, it should be understood that these methods are of only limited value. First, native speakers normally have an intuitive grasp of what is said. As such, most of the time we need not rely on any method for appreciating what is conveyed. On the other hand, analyzing why an utterance conveys what it does can give us an added appreciation of our language and in some cases may even shed further clarity on what was conveyed. Second, as with almost everything we say in this chapter, the methods must be used with caution. The methods are by no means foolproof and they certainly do not work in all cases. Finally, the three methods to be presented hardly exhaust the methods for determining what is conveyed by uses of deviant sentences. Indeed it is unlikely that one can ever have such a complete list; our aim is only to present some methods that apply to a significant number of cases.

To introduce the first method, consider the Dylan Thomas line: "A grief ago, I saw him there."[5] This sentence is grammatically aberrant, in that the construction 'A ______ ago' requires the blank to be filled by a term measuring time such as 'year' or 'week'; we have a grammatical aberration on our hands precisely because 'grief' is not a term of that kind. Given the Principle of Charity and the circumstance that this is a poetic line, suppose we make the following hypothesis: the line is suggesting that grief has features in common with referents of terms that would be grammatical in the construction 'A ______ ago'. Because years and weeks are ways of measuring time, we may hypothesize the line to be suggesting: the griefs one endures form a way of measuring time (or what time measures such as one's life span). Given that this makes tolerable sense of the poem's line, we tentatively include among the conveyed suggestions the one that a person's life can be measured not only

5. The analysis of this line is borrowed from Putnam, "Some Issues in the Theory of Grammar," pp. 89–90.

by the years survived but also by the griefs endured. This suggestion was conveyed precisely because syntax requires 'A ______ ago' to be filled by a measure of time; in this way, even in a use of an aberrant sentence, grammar plays a role in the meaning conveyed. Here and elsewhere, our attribution of what is conveyed is tentative because decisiveness concerning the meaning of aberrant sentences seems to be often elusive. Given this introduction, we may specify the first method for analyzing what is conveyed by a grammatically deviant sentence as follows:

Method of Nondeviant Substitutions

(a) Given ' . . . E . . . ' with 'E' as the isolated source of the aberrance, find some nondeviant substitutions ' . . . X . . . ', ' . . . Y . . . ', . . . , and
(b) Identify a feature ϕ of X, Y, . . . , and if plausible, hypothesize that ' . . . E . . . ' conveys that E has feature ϕ.

Another example for the Method of Nondeviant Substitutions can be gleaned from Putnam's analysis of a Lawrence Durrell line:

> Durrell writes: "And I, my selves, observed by human choice" (Durrell, 1960). . . . First, 'selves' is a peculiar plural (apart from such constructions as 'them-selves'). Second, 'choice' is used as if it were an animate noun. So we have *invention* even at the grammatical level. . . . By treating one's choices (or 'choice' in the abstract) as an observer, Durrell makes the . . . point that I must often find out what I feel by seeing what I choose—but with a startling inversion: my choice is thought of as observing me, to see what I am. And the pluralization of 'self' denies, in effect, the idea of a unitary 'person' behind all of my choices.[6]

Concentrating on 'observed by human choice', the Method of Nondeviant Substitutions yields the following two-step analysis:

(a) 'Human choice' is the source of aberrance and some of the nondeviant substitutions are 'observed by one's analyst' and 'observed by a telescope'.
(b) Being someone who can observe or being an instrument of observation are features of analysts and telescopes. Because it is plausible, we hypothesize that the line conveys that human choice is (like) someone who can observe, or that one's choices are means of observing, the sort of person one is.

We now turn to a method of analyzing what is conveyed by a deviant utterance that can also be used when no aberrance is involved. What

6. Putnam, "Dreaming and Depth Grammar," in *Mind, Language, and Reality,* p. 313.

underlies this method is what might be called the Principle of Linguistic Specificity: Work on the assumption that even the slightest variation in an utterance results in a variation in what is conveyed. Although it's only a working assumption, the principle suggests that at least with respect to the total impact of an utterance, there are no synonymies that are interchangeable. (Of course, this is compatible with there being synonymies that are interchangeable without any variation in truth values in any possible world, because the truth claimed by an utterance is after all only part of the utterance's total impact.) A method based on this principle may be stated as follows:

Method of Alternatives

(a) Given '... E ...', find alternatives '... X ...', '... Y ...', ... in which 'X', 'Y', ... are expressions similar to or contrasting with 'E'.
(b) Determine what makes '... E ...' specifically different from '... X ...', '... Y ...', ..., and take these specific differences to be conveyed by '... E ...'.

As an example of using this method, consider: "I, my selves, observed by human choice." Applying the method on 'my selves', which we take as the source of the aberrance, we should have:

(a) The most clearly relevant alternative to 'I, my selves, observed by human choice' is 'I, myself, observed by human choice'.
(b) The specific difference between the original and the alternative is a grammatical distinction between a singular and a plural; because it is plausible, we hypothesize that the original lines convey that a person is not a unitary self but something composed of many selves.

To consider an example in which the Method of Alternatives is applied to a nondeviant case, suppose Jane says, "He isn't without flaws." Taking 'E' as 'isn't without flaws', we would have:

(a) Some alternatives to 'He isn't without flaws' are:

    (1) He has many flaws.
    (2) He has (some) flaws.

(b) The contrast with (1) suggests that perhaps he does not have too many flaws. The specific difference with (2) suggests that 'He is flawless' is being denied, because perhaps someone claimed that he is flawless or he himself has an overinflated opinion of himself or others are overly admiring of him. Thus, because it is plausible, we may hypothesize that what Jane's utterance conveys is that, although he may not have too many flaws, what he or his admirers tend to overlook is that he certainly has some flaws.

Unlike the Method of Nondeviant Substitutions, the Method of Alternatives requires some understanding of the original utterance. It is primarily a method of fine-tuning what is conveyed. The third and final method we shall present can be of help (like the Method of Nondeviant Substitutions) in cases in which we come close to drawing a blank on first encountering an utterance. To introduce this method, consider Romeo's often-discussed line, 'Juliet is the sun'. This is ungrammatical because the subject and predicate noun fail to be of a compatible grammatical category. Locating 'the sun' to be the principal source of the aberrance, we might form a list of what is plausibly or obviously true of the sun, and see if any of these things might be attributed to Juliet. The list might include such items as: 'the brightest thing I know', 'the warmth of my world', 'the day begins with it', 'only with its nourishment can onc grow', and 'everything is lit by it'. Because paraphrasing 'the sun' by these things that are true of the sun yields plausible renditions of the things conveyed by 'Juliet is the sun', we may tentatively take Romeo's line to convey something like: Juliet is the brightest thing I know and everything is lit by her, she is the warmth of my world, my day begins with her, and only with her nourishment can I grow.[7] Given this introduction, we may specify the third method as follows:

> Method of Paraphrase
>
> Given the aberrant utterance '... E ...' with 'E' as the located source of aberrance,
>
> (a) find 'X', 'Y', ... that are plausibly true of (something that is) E, and
> (b) if '... X ...', '... Y ...', ... are plausible partial renditions of '... E ...', take them to be part of what is conveyed by '... E ...'.

It should be noted that most of the paraphrases of 'Juliet is the sun' are themselves aberrant or at least false on a straightforward reading (e.g., the sun, rather than Juliet, is still the brightest thing Romeo knows). It is indeed doubtful that metaphors can be completely paraphrased into nonmetaphorical utterances, and that is not the purpose of the Method of Alternatives. The point of the method is rather to shed some light on what is conveyed by a deviant utterance when one intially draws a blank. It might also be noted that in this example grammar plays a fairly minimal role in accounting for what is conveyed. The role seems to be limited

7. The paraphrases and the method behind them were suggested to me entirely by Stanley Cavell's "Aesthetic Problems of Modern Philosophy," in *Must We Mean What We Say,* New York: Charles Scribner's Sons, 1969; and Ted Cohen's "Notes on Metaphor," *The Journal of Aesthetics and Art Criticism,* **34,** 3 (Spring 1976).

to being able to derive 'N1 (Juliet) is A (the brightest thing Romeo knows)' from 'N1 (Juliet) is N2 (the sun)' and 'N2 (the sun) is A (the brightest thing Romeo knows)'. In general, the Method of Paraphrase is helpful when the bulk of the meaning conveyed is due to what is generally known to be true of the thing to which the aberrant expression refers. Finally, it may be noted that trying to use the Method of Nondeviant Substitutions on 'Juliet is the sun' yields nothing. Using that method, we would consider expressions like 'Juliet is the lover of Romeo', 'Juliet is a woman', and so on. Could it be Romeo's suggestion that the sun is like a woman or a lover? Because attributing such a suggestion to his utterance would hardly be in keeping with the Principle of Charity, another method of analysis was required.

★ ★ ★ ★

So far we have analyzed what is conveyed by the use of a grammatically aberrant sentence. However, there are also grammatically aberrant uses of (grammatical) sentences. We have seen that grammar indicates what kind of speech act is normally to be performed by a sentence of a certain type, that is, stating or asserting with declarative sentences, questioning or requesting with interrogative sentences, ordering with imperative sentences, and so on. However, it should be clear that one can order with an interrogative sentence, ask with a declarative sentence, and so on. Grammar contributes to what is conveyed by such grammatically aberrant uses of grammatical sentences, and part of what is conveyed can be analyzed by methods similar to those we have already discussed.

To consider an example, imagine a self-satisfied San Franciscan arriving in Los Angeles and uttering with snobbish disgust one or the other of the following:

(a) Is *this* a *city?*
(b) *This* is a *city?*

Context clearly makes the use of the interrogative grammatically aberrant. Testing situations aside, a normal prerequisite for asking a question is that the questioner doesn't know the answer. In the straightforward sense of 'city', the snob can be expected to know that Los Angeles has an population large enough to count as a city. Even in the extended sense of 'city', in which only places approximating the model of Paris, New York, and San Francisco can count as cities, the tone and accompanying gestures we can imagine make it clear that the speaker doesn't entertain any doubts about the status of Los Angeles. Because context rules out the utterance being a question, we have a grammatically aberrant use of the interrogative.

Because the Principle of Charity enjoins one to take the speaker to be making an appropriate conversational contribution, one may surmise that instead of asking a question, the speaker is making some comment that could (roughly) be expressed by declarative sentences like 'This doesn't count as a city', 'This can't be called a city', or 'This place is a dump'. However, intuitions of the kind involved in the Method of Alternatives suggest that the speaker's use of the interrogative conveys something that is lost in the use of the declarative sentence. What then is conveyed by the use of the interrogative that isn't conveyed by the declarative sentence? A way of determining this distinction is to rely on a slightly modified version of the Method of Nondeviant Substitutions:

Modified Method of Nondeviant Substitutions

(a) Given that the utterance U is an aberrant use of the grammatical type T, find some nondeviant uses U*, U**, . . . of type T.
(b) If plausible, hypothesize that what U conveys is, or is related to, some identified feature ϕ of U*, U**, . . .

Applying this method, nondeviant uses of the interrogative are questions like "Is this the way to the baggage claim area?" and "How does one get to the center of the city?" An identifiable feature ϕ of these interrogatives is:

ϕ: They call for an answer.

What is conveyed by the snob's use of the interrogative can be seen to be related to this feature ϕ. For, how is the Angelino to respond to the call for an answer? The problem is that while the interrogative grammatically calls for an answer, the context makes it clear that no answer is requested, because the snob is making a comment and (thinks he) already knows the answer. Any attempt to answer the question would show the Angelino to be dull-witted: they would ridicule him in Nob Hill clubs for failing even to appreciate the force of the utterance. In short, the Angelino is silenced and cannot do what is grammatically requested by the snob's remark without appearing dull-witted. Precisely because interrogatives call for an answer and the context rules out an answer, we may hypothesize that the snob's remark conveys something like: It is beyond dispute that Los Angeles isn't a city. Furthermore, because the Angelino is prevented from doing what the interrogative requires, the snob's remark has the force of an effective slight that is lacking in the straightforward declarative sentence. An unequivocal assertion like 'This is a dump' or 'This can't count as a city' almost invites the Angelino's protest, and the use of such a declarative sentence would thereby lose the contemptuousness and cutting edge that the snob's use of the interrogative conveys.

To exemplify further the Modified Method of Nondeviant Substitutions, let us compare the two alternative remarks we have imagined for the snob: (a) 'Is *this* a *city?*' and (b) '*This* is a *city?*' The construction (b) is somewhat unusual for an interrogative: instead of inverting the word order as in (a), (b) transforms a declarative sentence into an interrogative by merely adding a question mark or a rising pitch at the end.[8] A non-deviant use of such an interrogative construction is:

A: I *heard* that Jane is going to marry Tom.
B: Jane is going to marry *Tom?*

A feature of ϕ of such an interrogative may be identified as:

ϕ: It questions or raises doubts about the truth of what was just asserted by someone else.

Thus, by the Method of Nondeviant Substitution, we may surmise that remark (b) has a feature that is at least related to raising doubts about someone's assertion that Los Angeles is a city. While (b) is not a response to anyone's actual assertion, the claim 'Los Angeles is a city' is in the offing somewhere in the background, and presumably if anyone would make the claim, it is the Angelino. Thus, part of what (b) conveys is that it is a response to the claim the Angelino can be expected to make, and the response raises doubts about the Angelino's judgment in considering this to be a city. Hence, the aberrant use of the interrogative (b) conveys contempt that is more openly directed at the Angelino and not just his city. Because the normal use of the straight interrogative (a) doesn't require someone's assertion that Los Angeles is a city, the snob's use of (a) conveys contempt that is more obviously directed to the city and less openly to its inhabitants. Thus, the subtle difference between (a) and (b) is that (b) is more openly combative than (a) in expressing contempt at the Angelino, and what accounts for this difference is shown by features related to the normal uses of the interrogative constructions of types (a) and (b).

★ ★ ★ ★

EXERCISES—SECTION 6.2.2

1. Using the Method of Nondeviant Substitutions on the underlined words, explain what might be conveyed or suggested by the following expressions.

8. One could consider construction (b) as a grammatically aberrant use of a declarative sentence. If so, the Modified Method of Nondeviant Substitutions would indicate that what is conveyed by the question must be related to some feature of the normal use of declarative sentences. A feature of such a use is that an assertion is made. Thus, one may surmise that what is questioned by construction (b) is someone's explicit or implicit assertion. Because the grammaticalness of (b) isn't entirely clear, I have opted for the easier exposition in which (b) is taken to be a grammatical use of an interrogative rather than a way of raising a question by a grammatically aberrant use of a declarative sentence, in which the raising of the question in turn ends up being a way of making a comment rather than asking a question.

Bracketed portions are for background only, and in some cases notes by literary scholars are included for information.

(a) The Moon doth with delight
Look around her [when the heavens are bare;]
(from Wordsworth, *Ode. Intimations of Immortality from Recollections of Early Childhood*)

(b) [My one and noble heart has witnesses
in all love's countries, that will grope awake;]
And when blind sleep drops on the spying senses,
[The heart is sensual, though five eyes break.]
(From Dylan Thomas, *When all my five and country senses see*)

[*love's countries:* the senses, in which love lives as well as in the heart. *is sensual:* feels, passionately. *eyes:* senses. *break:* fail.]

(c) Nativity, [once in the main of light,]
Crawls to maturity, [wherewith being crowned,
Crooked eclipses 'gainst his glory fight,
And time that gave doth now his gift confound.]
(From Shakespeare, *Sonnet* 60)

[*Nativity:* newborn infant. *main of light:* full of day: *eclipses:* eclipses that portend bad times. *confound:* destroy.]

(d) last line of (c) on 'time'.

2. Using the Method of Alternatives on the underlined words, explain what might be conveyed or suggested by the following expressions.

(a) He isn't without means.

(b) [He saw her from the bottom of the stairs . . .]
She took a doubtful step and then undid it
[To raise herself and look again.]
(From Robert Frost, *Home Burial*)

(c) [Let us go through certain half-deserted streets,]
The muttering retreats
[Of restless nights in one-night cheap hotels
And sawdust restaurants with oyster-shells:]
(From T. S. Eliot, *The Love Song of J. Alfred Prufrock*)

3. Using the Method of Paraphrase on the underlined words, explain what might be conveyed or suggested by the following expressions.

(a) Is she not pure gold, my mistress?
(From Robert Browning, *Dramatic Lyrics*)

(b) [To-day I shall be strong,
No more shall yield to wrong,
Shall squander life no more;]
Days lost, [I know not how,]
I shall retrieve them now.
(From A. E. Housman, *How clear, how lovely bright*)

*4. Suppose the chancellor writes to a department chair: "Will you submit your budget by next Monday?"
   (a) Locate features of the context that make the chancellor's use of the interrogative grammatically aberrant.
   (b) Using the Principle of Charity, determine what is the most likely speech act the chancellor is performing by his use of the interrogative, and what the grammatically appropriate form of that speech act would be.
   (c) Using the Modified Method of Nondeviant Substitutions, explain what might be conveyed or suggested by the chancellor's use of the interrogative that would not have been conveyed by using the grammatically appropriate form for the speech act the chancellor was performing.

*5. Consider the conversation:

   A: The Lakers won the playoffs.
   B: The Lakers won?

   Assume that B accepts A's statement and that B's utterance has a rising pitch with a stress on 'won'; this would indicate a deviant use of an interrogative that makes an exclamation. Using the Modified Method of Nondeviant Substitution, determine what is expressed by the exclamation.

6.2.3 Related Fallacies

We conclude this section with a short discussion of two fallacies that are related to our discussion of grammar.

(1) Fallacy of Amphibole. We all have occasion to make or hear ambiguous utterances. Typically, the ambiguity is due to a term in the utterance having several meanings or senses that can be located in a dictionary. Some ambiguities, however, are of a grammatical nature, and these are the ambiguities with which this section is concerned. Irving Copi cited a wartime poster that read: SAVE SOAP AND WASTE PAPER.[9] This is clearly grammatically ambiguous between '(SAVE SOAP) AND (WASTE PAPER)' and 'SAVE (SOAP AND WASTE PAPER)'. One of the problems with an ambiguous expression of any kind is that one may unwittingly shift from one meaning of the expression to another, and doing so typically involves a fallacy; the Fallacy of Amphibole is said to be committed when the ambiguity is grammatical.

At the most general level, then, the Fallacy of Amphibole is committed when one illegitimately shifts from one disambiguation[10] of a grammatically ambiguous expression to another. Of course, it may be possible that during the course of an argument, one fails to notice that one has made such a shift. But this must be a rare occurrence because grammatical shifts tend to be dramatic and noticeable, and it is unlikely that one unwittingly confuses saving waste paper and wasting paper. The Fallacy of Amphibole occurs most frequently when a reason R for some conclu-

9. Irving Copi, *Introduction to Logic,* 5th ed., New York: Macmillan, 1978, p. 112.
10. In accordance with the usage that is now fairly frequent, attaching one of its several possible senses to an ambiguous expression will be called "disambiguating" an expression; "disambiguation" stands for the act or product of disambiguating an expression.

sion is accepted on someone's authority, and one disambiguates R in an unintended way. Thus, for our purpose, we shall usually understand the FALLACY OF AMPHIBOLE as follows: *If being legitimately persuaded of a conclusion requires disambiguating a grammatically ambiguous premise in a certain way, and the basis for accepting the ambiguous premise is that someone else has said it, one commits the Fallacy of Amphibole when one disambiguates the premise in a way that may not have been intended.* Because this fallacy involves a flaw that undermines the plausibility or acceptability of the premises, we shall class it as a Fallacy of Substance and represent it as follows:

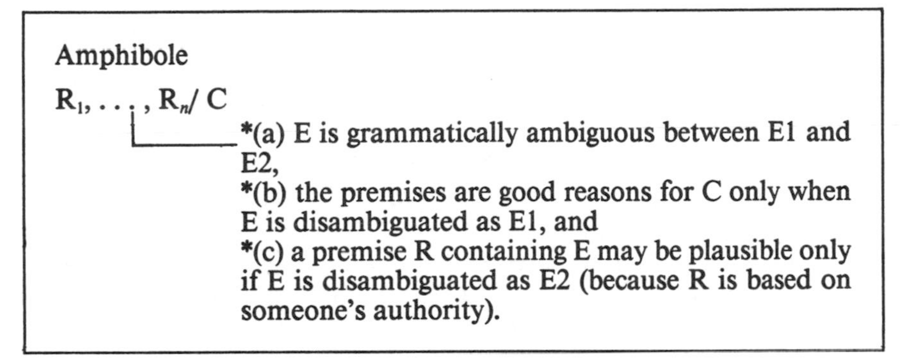

Amphibole

$R_1, \ldots, R_n/$ C

*(a) E is grammatically ambiguous between E1 and E2,
*(b) the premises are good reasons for C only when E is disambiguated as E1, and
*(c) a premise R containing E may be plausible only if E is disambiguated as E2 (because R is based on someone's authority).

As usual, the starred items need to be explained in the analysis of the fallacy. We give two examples in analyzing the Fallacy of Amphibole:

(A) "How stupid for the government to urge people to save soap and waste paper. Why should we waste paper?!"

Amphibole:

(1) The government urged people to save soap and waste paper.
(2) It is stupid to waste paper.
(3) If (1) and (2) are true, the government is stupid.

---

(4) The government is stupid.
(a) The sentence E is ambiguous between E1 and E2:
E: The government urged people to save soap and waste paper.
E1: The government urged people to save (soap and waste paper).
E2: The government urged people to (save soap) and (waste paper).
(b) (3) is plausible only if E is taken as E2, and thus we have good reasons for the conclusion only if E is taken as E2 throughout the argument.
(c) But (1) is based on the government poster, and because the government may well have meant E as E1, premise (1) may well be plausible only when E is disambiguated as E1.

(B) "She said she went to hear Mr. Travel talk about his summer holidays in Oxnard. Boy, is she going to be bored. Oxnard is about as boring a place for holidays as one can imagine!"

Amphibole

(1) She went to hear Mr. Travel talk about his summer holidays in Oxnard.
(2) If (1) is true, she is going to be bored.

---

(3) She is going to be bored.
(a) The sentence E is ambiguous between E1 and E2:
  E: She went to hear Mr. Travel talk about his summer holidays in Oxnard.
  E1: She went to hear Mr. Travel talk about his Oxnard summer holidays.
  E2: She went to Oxnard to hear Mr. Travel talk about his summer holidays.
(b) Because (2) is plausible only if E is disambiguated as E1, we have good reasons for (3) only if E is taken as E1 throughout the argument.
(c) Because (1) is based on her having said no, and because she may well have intended E as E2, (1) may be plausible only if E is disambiguated as E2.

(2) Fallacy of Complex Question. When someone poses a rhetorical question, the interrogative form is being used to make an assertion or a comment rather than to ask a question. However, the use of an interrogative can also ask a question and make a comment without in any sense being a rhetorical question. A question of this sort is "Have you stopped beating your wife?"—the standard example of the Fallacy of Complex Question. The respondent cannot answer the question without acquiescing to the potentially controversial claim that he did beat his wife in the past: if he answers "No," he admits that he did indeed beat his wife (and continues to do so), and if he answers "Yes," he still admits that he did beat his wife. We shall say: In asking a question one commits the Fallacy of Complex Question if the question cannot be answered without presupposing the truth of some claim that is likely to be problematic or controversial in the context.

The Fallacy of Complex Question does not neatly fit into any of our four fallacy categories. Because it seems closest to the Fallacy of Substance category, we shall represent it as:

Complex Question Any answer to question Q / C └ Any answer to Q commits one to claim C, which is potentially controversial in the context.

Thus, the standard example would be analyzed as:

Complex Question:

Any answer to "Have you stopped beating your wife?"

You did beat your wife.

Any answer to the question commits one to having beaten one's wife, and this is potentially controversial in the context.

Before accusing someone of committing the Fallacy of Complex Question, it is important that the context be considered. If it is generally known that I am a chain smoker, it would be ridiculous to suppose that some fallacy is committed in asking, "Have you stopped smoking?" On the other hand, even when everyone knows that Jablonsky committed the murder, the attempt to trap her into admitting her guilt by asking "Why did you kill him?" commits the Fallacy of Complex Question. The Fallacy of Complex Question is a standard ploy of interrogators in attempting to get a confession or some information from a person.

EXERCISES—SECTION 6.2.3

Analyze the fallacies in the following passages.

1. I can't understand why you didn't marry her. How could you let such a wonderful woman slip away?
2. *Professor:* I will give no more extensions on your term papers in the future.
   Student: I'm glad that you are going to give the same extensions in the future as you have given up to now.

   To get you started, here is the first step of the analysis:

   (1) The professor will give no more extensions in the future.
   (2) If (1) is true, the professor will give the same extensions in the future as he has given up to now.

   (3) The professor will give the same extensions in the future as he has given up to now.
3. Is the integer for which the square equals -1 a negative or nonnegative number?
4. Proponents of Proposition 14 call this reform. Whom are they kidding? (From *California Ballot Pamphlet,* November 1982)
5. My mom is pretty sharp and she told me that all men are not nice. But then, if no man is nice, Jack can't be nice either.

   To get you started, here is the first step of the analysis:

   (1) All men are not nice.
   (2) If all men are not nice, no man is nice.
   (3) If no man is nice, Jack isn't nice.

   (4) Jack isn't nice.
6. How can you say that your son's Transformer is a stupid boy's toy? Your son isn't a stupid boy.

6.3 The Level of Semantics

Semantics is commonly considered to be conceived with the meaning of words, and it is at best an area of considerable controversy. Many philosophers have even denied that there are any such things as meanings. All the same, it is obviously useful in many contexts to perform the activity we ordinarily call "considering the meaning of the words." So something should be said about this difficult topic. We start with a general discussion of meaning as a prelude to more specific topics.

6.3.1 A General Account of Meaning

It is useful to get into the discussion of meaning by first considering the so-called *extension* of a linguistic expression. 'Reference' and 'denotation' are often used instead of 'extension', but I will most frequently use the term 'extension'. Very roughly, the extension of an expression is what the expression names or talks about in the world. The linguistic intent of a singular term like 'Lincoln' or 'the sixteenth president of the United States' is to name or select a unique object, and the exension of such a term is simply the object named or selected—in this case Lincoln, that very person who was the sixteenth president of the United States. When we come to a general term like 'giraffe', it can't be said to talk about any particular giraffe, that is, the term applies to any giraffe, and it could even function if there were no giraffes (as the usage of the general term 'unicorn' shows). If we are to relate any single entity to 'giraffe' as its extension, it is most convenient to take its extension as the class of all (past, present, and future) giraffes in the world—many of whose members (did, do, or will) live in Africa, the others being scattered in the various zoos of the world. Put another way, we shall take the extension of 'giraffe' to be the set of objects of which the expression 'is a giraffe' is (tenselessly) true. Given a term like 'red', its extension is the class of (past, present, and future) objects in the world that are red. That is, it is the set of objects of which the expression 'is red' is (tenselessly) true. Given a term like 'unicorn', its extension will simply be the empty or null class because there is no object in our world of which 'is a unicorn' is true.

A diagram may help to make the notion of extension more perspicuous. In diagramming extensions, one normally lets an area stand for or represent specified classes of objects. Thus, in Figure 6.1, the rectangle represents the various things that are plants (or nonanimate living things); we can then think of the rectangle as representing the extension of 'plant' as well as those of 'nonanimate living things'. In a case like this, we normally say that the two terms 'plant' and 'nonanimate living things' are coextensive, meaning that they have the same extension. Thus, 'tree' and 'plant with trunk' are also coextensive. Included in the class of plants is the class of trees; thus, the outer oval representing the extension of 'tree' is included within the area representing plants. In the same way,

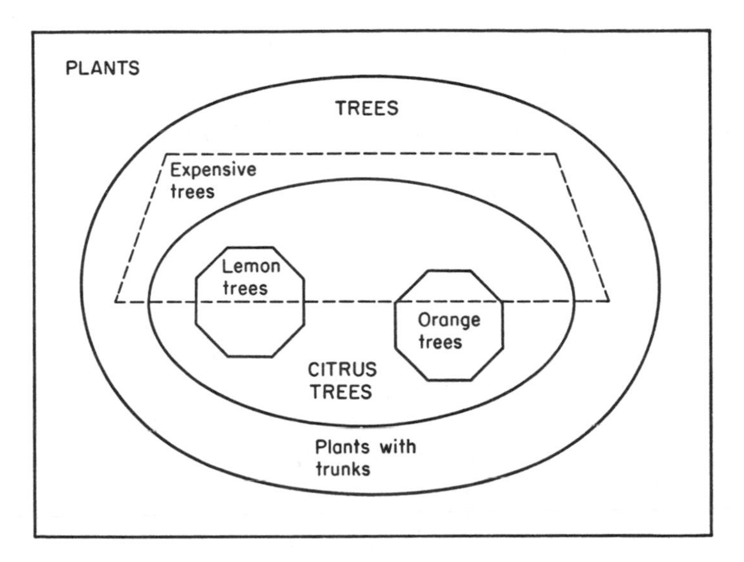

Figure 6.1.

insofar as the class of citrus trees is included in the class of trees, the inner oval representing the class of citrus trees (or the extension of 'citrus tree') is within the area representing the class of trees (or the extension of 'tree'). The two octagons represent the class of lemon trees and orange trees, and because both classes are part of the class of citrus trees, the octagons are included inside the area of the inner oval; on the other hand, because nothing is both a lemon tree and an orange tree, the two octagons don't overlap. Finally, the trapezoid represents the class of expensive trees, that is, those that were (are, or will be) expensive at nursery stores. The diagram as given represents some (but not all) trees, citrus trees, orange trees, and lemon trees being expensive trees.

When we turn to relational expressions like 'loves' or 'is a mother of', the notion of their extension becomes more complicated. Roughly, we want to say that what belongs to the extension of 'loves' is not a single individual but pairs of individuals, like the pair comprising Mark Antony and Cleopatra. However, we all know that much of human heartache is due to the possibility of A loving B while B doesn't love A. Thus, the extension of a term like 'loves' is not just a pair but a pair taken in a certain order or direction. This leads to the idea of an ordered pair, usually represented by a notation like '⟨A, B⟩'. Thus, we might say: ⟨Antony, Cleopatra⟩, ⟨Cleopatra, Antony⟩, and ⟨Søren Kierkegaard, Regina Olsen⟩ belong to the extension of 'loves' while (as far as we know) ⟨Regina Olsen, Søren Kierkegaard⟩ does not because Regina didn't return Søren's love. For a complete sentence like 'Dauer teaches logic' or 'Reagan is the Santa Barbara County Dog Catcher', its extension is standardly taken to be the truth value of the sentence. Thus, the extension of the first sentence is True while that of the second is presumably False. This is admittedly somewhat artificial but there is rationale behind this usage. (The rationale is the idea that if one interchanges parts of a sentence by expressions having identical extensions, the extension of the sentence should remain the same. For most sentences, this idea is satisfied only by taking their extension to be their truth value.) For most purposes of this chapter, we can avoid these complicated or artificial extensions and stick with the straightforward type discussed in the previous paragraphs.

At least roughly, the meaning of an expression is that in virtue of which one can determine the extension of that expression. Given a red thing x and a white thing y, the meaning of 'red' should be that in virtue of which x belongs to the extension of 'red' while y doesn't. This seems intuitive enough but what about the meaning of a term like 'or' which doesn't have an extension? A fairly natural answer is: the meaning of 'or' is that in virtue of which we can determine the extension of a sentence using 'or' provided that the extensions of the other parts of the sentence are given. Seen this way, we can think of the truth value table for 'or' given in Section 3.3 as exhibiting the meaning of 'or'.

Given this background, let us understand the meaning of an expression 'E' as

> *whatever it is such that, given any possible world, it determines what in that world belongs to the extension of 'E' in that world* [or determines what the extension of sentences using 'E' are in that world, given the extensions the other parts of the sentences have in that world].

I have purposely not specified what kind of entities meanings are by using the phrase 'whatever it is such that'. In order to have some concreteness, I will often think of meanings as rules of some kind that determine extensions. But readers may supply their own favorite account of what sort of entities meanings are. Perhaps some would rather think in terms of ideas or abstract forms intuited by the mind's eye. And of course there are other possibilities as well.[11]

What are some of the relationships between meaning and extension? If we accept a fairly commonsensical view of meaning, three traditional relations emerge:

(i) *If the meanings of two terms are identical, the extensions of the two terms are identical in all possible worlds.* If the rule for determining the extension of 'X' is the same as the rule for determining the extension of 'Y', obviously the two terms must always have the same extension. Thus, if we think that the meanings of 'nonanimate living thing' and 'plant' are

11. Followers of G. Frege think in terms of senses while those of the UCLA school of Montague and Kaplan might think in terms of abstract functions or mapping from possible worlds to the extensions of the expressions in those worlds.

the same, in no possible world will the extensions of these two terms diverge.

(ii) It seems plausible to say that the meaning of 'citrus tree' includes the meaning of 'tree' as a part, and if we refer to Figure 6.1, we see that the extension of 'citrus tree' is included in the extension of 'tree'. What we mean by "one meaning includes (or contains) another" is this: The meaning of 'citrus tree' contains or includes the meaning of 'tree', because the rule for determining the extension of 'citrus tree' requires that the rule for determining the extension of 'tree' be satisfied. Seen in this way, we can also say that the meaning of 'orange tree' includes the meaning of 'citrus tree' as well as the meaning of 'tree' and 'plant'. This has the effect that in every possible world the extension of 'orange tree' is included in the extensions of 'citrus tree', 'tree', and 'plant'. These relations we have just seen generally hold:

If the meaning of 'X' contains the meaning of 'Y', in every possible world the extension of 'X' is contained in the extension of 'Y'.

(iii) It is sometimes intuitive to think in terms of greater or lesser meaning, and this can be done in certain cases. Let us say the meanings of two terms are comparable if the meaning of one is contained in the meaning of the other. Thus, the meaning of 'expensive tree' is comparable to that of 'tree' because the meaning of 'tree' is contained in the meaning of 'expensive tree'; similarly, the meaning of 'citrus tree' is comparable to that of 'lemon tree' because the latter contains the former. Of course, the meanings of most pairs of terms are not comparable. Thus, although the meaning of 'orange tree' and 'lemon tree' have a common part, they are incomparable according to the usage introduced because the meaning of neither is contained in the other. If we have terms that have comparable meanings in the sense defined, we can speak of greater or lesser meaning. Thus, we might think of 'tree', 'citrus tree', 'orange tree', and 'expensive orange tree' as having increasingly greater meaning. Our discussion of the previous paragraph indicates that in this situation, 'tree', 'citrus tree', 'orange tree', and 'expensive orange tree' have successively smaller exensions. This then suggests the following loosely stated relationship: the greater the meaning, the smaller the extension. More precisely stated:

Where the meanings of 'X' and 'Y' are comparable, if the meaning of 'X' is greater or equal to that of 'Y', the extension of 'X' is less or equal to that of 'Y'.

This is sometimes called the inverse rule between meaning (or intension—another term for meaning) and extension. It simply reflects the fact that the more precisely one specifies something, a correspondingly smaller class of things is selected (as the extension).

The relations (i)–(iii) just outlined should be taken with reservation, because in many cases it may be difficult or impossible to determine in any significant way the relations of meaning identity and meaning inclusion. Still, in some cases these relations seem to have some applicability and can act as a measure of the content. For statements of the form 'A is X', the greater the meaning or intension of 'X', the greater the content or (potential) information that is conveyed by 'A is X'. If someone says, "A is an entity," he has said virtually nothing. Because the meaning of 'entity' is included in virtually every meaning, it has a small meaning: correspondingly, the extension of 'entity' is very large, and pointing out that A belongs to this large class says very little. Somewhat similarly, if someone says, "He has a plant," this is not terribly informative; saying that he has a tree would be somewhat more informative. Saying that he has a citrus tree is fairly informative, and saying that he has an orange tree would be quite informative. Saying that he has an expensive orange tree is even more informative, because the meaning of 'expensive orange tree' is quite large and the extension relatively small; thus, saying that he has something belonging to this small class says quite a bit in terms of distinguishing what he has from other things in the world.

It should be evident that identity of extension for two terms does not imply the identity of meaning. It is true in our world that 'being a hearted creature' and 'being a kidneyed creature' have the same extension. And yet in some possible worlds we would expect the extension of the two terms to be different. Thus, the rules for determining the extensions of the two terms must be different, so that they can yield different results in those worlds. Hence, the meanings of the terms are different even though the extensions of the terms are the same in our world. Could we then say that the meanings of two terms are the same if the extensions of the two terms are the same in every possible world? It would appear not. The rule for determining the extension of 'is a three-sided (Euclidean) figure' seems to be different from the rule for determining the extension of 'is a figure in which the internal angles add up to 180°'; yet the extension of the two terms is presumably identical in every possible world. Perhaps the same could be said of 'tree' and 'plant with a trunk', whose extension is represented by the large oval in Figure 6.1.

The notion of semantic aberrance can now perhaps be explained as follows:

> *The rules for determining the extensions of the terms preclude the sentence from being true or being successfully used for the speech act for which it is designed.*

As an example, consider: "Find me an adult who is a child!" The rule for determining the extension of 'adult' precludes anything belonging to that extension also belonging to the extension of 'child'. Thus, nothing can be both an adult and a child, and there is no possibility of fulfilling the order. Yet for the imperative sentence to succeed as an order, it must not preclude the possibility of the order being fulfilled. The imagined sentence is semantically deviant precisely because it precludes this possibility. The same terms would be involved in the semantically deviant sentence 'That adult is a child', which is precluded from being true. If we were to try to determine what is conveyed by such a semantically deviant utterance, we can resort to the methods suggested in Section 6.2, and the most useful one for dealing with semantically deviant sentences is the Method of Paraphrase. Thus, applying that method on 'child' in 'That adult is a child' would yield the following result:

(i) 'Irresponsible', 'self-centered', 'playful', 'can't be trusted to take care of himself', and so on, are plausibly true of children.
(ii) Because these substitutions seem plausible, we hypothesize that part of what is conveyed is: that adult is an irresponsible, self-centered, playful person who cannot be trusted to take care of himself.

Aside from the obvious use of '=' to represent identity, let '$x \subseteq y$' stand for x is contained in y, '$x < y$' for x is less than y, and '$x \leq y$' for x is less than or equal to y. Using these abbreviations and letting M(X), E(X), and I(X) stand for the meaning of X, the extension of X, and the information or content conveyed by X, the various and sundry relations we have discussed in this section may be summarized as follows:

(1) If $M(X) = M(Y)$, then in all possible worlds $E(X) = E(Y)$. [The converse is not generally true.]
(2) If $M(Y) \subseteq M(X)$, then in every possible world $E(X) \subseteq E(Y)$.
(3) Where M(X) and M(Y) are comparable, that is, $M(X) \subseteq M(Y)$ or $M(Y) \subseteq M(X)$,
    (a) If $M(X) \geq M(Y)$, then $E(Y) \geq E(X)$. [The Inverse Law]
    (b) If $M(X) > M(Y)$, then $I(X) > I(Y)$.
(4) S is semantically aberrant: the meanings of the terms in S preclude S from being true (or succeeding in the speech act for which S was designed).

Related Fallacies. We conclude this section with a discussion of fallacies involving words having "opposite" meanings. 'Good' and 'bad' have opposite meanings and yet it would be a mistake to suppose that they exhaust all possibilities, because many things are neither good nor bad. For example, a dinner may be neither good nor bad but satisfactory or adequate. Forgetting about the intermediate possibilities or the shades of gray leads one to commit what is called the BLACK AND WHITE FALLACY. *The Black and White Fallacy is committed in giving or accepting an argument if the legitimacy of the argument requires a pair of terms S and T to exhaust a relevant class of objects or states of affairs* **without residue** *and in fact S and T do* **not** *so exhaust the class.* Thus, for example, the Black and White Fallacy is committed when one reasons that the dinner must have been bad because it wasn't good. The failure of S and T to exhaust all the possibilities can be seen as a failure of the argument's presupposition being satisfied. Thus, we shall count this as a Presuppositional Fallacy and represent it as:

Black and White
R → C; NOT {S and T exhaust all the relevant possibilities}.

Thus we shall analyze the good and bad dinner example as:

Dinner was not good → Dinner was bad; NOT {'Good dinner' and 'bad dinner' exhaust all the relevant possibilities}.

Black and White Fallacies often involve opposite or polar words like 'good' and 'bad,' 'beautiful' and 'ugly', 'happy' and 'unhappy', and 'friend' and 'foe'. Clearly with each of these pairs, there is at least a third alternative. For example, it's perfectly possible to be neither happy nor unhappy; one might certainly be neither happy nor unhappy about driving home, and even for extended periods of time we might just muddle through without being either happy or unhappy. Another frequent source of Black and White Fallacies are opposites of the following form (in which doing not-X should be understood as refraining from doing X):

$$P \left\{ \begin{array}{l} \text{believes} \\ \text{ought to do} \\ \text{knows} \\ \text{is justified in} \\ \quad \text{believing or doing} \\ \text{affirms (states)} \end{array} \right\} \text{not-X.} \qquad P \left\{ \begin{array}{l} \text{believes} \\ \text{ought to do} \\ \text{knows} \\ \text{is justified in} \\ \quad \text{believing or doing} \\ \text{affirms (states)} \end{array} \right\} \text{X.}$$

Clearly, one could suspend judgment on the truth or falsity of X with the result that one neither believes X nor believes not-X. Again, in typical circumstances, 'One ought to have a glass of water' and 'One ought to refrain from having a glass of water' may both be false because it is a matter of (moral or prudential) indifference whether or not one has a glass of water.[12]

Some examples of the Black and White Fallacy and their analyses are:

(1) "Because he is not a theist (a believer in God), he must be an atheist (a person who believes that God doesn't exist)."

12. If we think of 'P ought to do X' and 'P ought to make it true that P does X', and if we let 'ϕ' stand for 'believes that', 'ought to make it true that', 'is justified in making it true that', and so on, all the examples from this paragraph have the form 'P ϕ q' and 'P ϕ $-$q'. While 'P ϕ q' and '$-$(P ϕ q)' do exhaust all the relevant possibilities, 'P ϕ q' and 'P ϕ ($-$q)' do not. This shows that '$-$(P ϕ q)' and 'P ϕ ($-$q)' are not the same thing, and Black and White Fallacies often involve failing to see this difference in the parsing or the "scope" of the negation—that is, the expression governed by the negation sign.

Black and White: He doesn't believe God exists → He believes God doesn't exist; NOT {'believes God exists' and 'believes −(God exists)' exhaust all the relevant possibilities}.

(2) "Because the alleged rape victim didn't tell him to stop, she (in effect) told him not to stop."
Black and White: She didn't tell him to stop → She told him not to stop; NOT {'telling him to stop' and 'telling him not to stop' exhausts all the relevant possibilities}

(3) "Mr. Mitchell doesn't remember telling Mr. Dean to pay off Hunt; therefore, Mr. Dean was lying when he said that Mr. Mitchell told him to pay off Hunt." Even assuming that (a) 'remembering −p' implies that 'p' is false and that (b) if 'p' is false, Mr. Dean was lying in saying 'p', the conclusion still would not follow because a fallacy is committed at an earlier step:
Black and White: Mr. Mitchell doesn't remember . . . → Mr. Mitchell remembers −(. . .); NOT {'remembering p' and 'remembering −p' exhaust all the relevant possibilities}.

A topic somewhat related to the Black and White Fallacy involves pairs of terms S and T such that they describe the extremes of a continuous gradation. 'Fat' and 'skinny', 'tall' and 'short', and 'thick-haired' and 'bald' are obvious examples. Of course, to conclude that someone is skinny because he isn't fat is to commit the Black and White Fallacy. But these somewhat vague terms present additional difficulties with which it is not easy to deal. The difficulties may be exemplified in two ways: (i) It seems plausbile to accept the statement, 'If Tom is skinny and he gains one pound, he will still be skinny'. But clearly, if we use this as a premise often enough in an argument that begins with 'Tom is skinny', we can ultimately arrive at the absurd conclusion that Tom will still be skinny if he gains 250 pounds. This has sometimes been called the paradox of the sorites. (ii) While we would not expect 'fat' and 'skinny' to exhaust all possibilities, we might expect 'fat' and 'not-fat' to exhaust all possibilities. Yet it would seem that there is a gray region between being fat and non-fat, and it would seem arbitrary to impose a sharp boundary like 160 pounds (for someone six feet tall) as the dividing line between being fat and non-fat.

It is not entirely clear how one is to deal satisfactorily with the problems raised by vague terms describing the extremes of a continuous gradation. However, two points may be made with relative certainty: (i) With terms for the extremes of a continuous gradation, one must not repeatedly use a premise like 'If Tom is skinny and he gains one more pound, he will still be skinny'. The repeated use of such a premise has sometimes been called the Fallacy of the Slippery Slope. (ii) One should not conclude that the terms for the extremes of a continuous gradation are illegitimate or that there is no difference between the extremes just because there seems to be no nonarbitrary dividing line (even if the terms for the extremes are 'X' and 'not-X'). Even if we cannot specify an exact dividing line between being fat and non-fat, 'fat' can be legitimately used; there is a difference at the extremes, and of two people A and B at or near the extremes it can be true that A is fat while B is not fat.

EXERCISES—SECTION 6.3.1

1. Rank the following expressions from the one with the smallest meaning (intension) to the one with the largest, allowing for ties when the meanings are identical:
   (a) Blond bachelor
   (b) Living organism
   (c) Animal
   (d) Unmarried male adult human
   (e) Mammal
   (f) Living organism that isn't a plant
   (g) Human being
   (h) Bachelor
2. Relying on the inverse law between meanings (or intensions) and extensions, the extensions of which terms in exercise 1 are greater than or equal to that of 'mammal' in every possible world?
3. With which of the terms in exercise 1 is 'tiger' comparable? State the meaning identity or meaning inclusion relation 'tiger' has to the comparable terms in exercise 1. Which terms in exercise 1 have an extension greater than or equal to that of 'tiger' in every possible world?
4. Relying on the meanings involved, order the following statements in terms of decreasing content or information conveyed:
   (a) She is smarter than some.
   (b) She is exceptionally intelligent.
   (c) She is not stupid.
   (d) She has an above average intelligence.
5. Relying on the meanings involved, which statements in exercise 4 have less content than 'She is smarter than average but not by a big margin'?
6. Are the meanings of 'buffalo nickel' and 'Indian nickel' the same? Why? [At one time the United States minted a five-cent coin that pictured a buffalo on one side and an Indian on the other; these were the only nickels minted by the United States that pictured a buffalo or an Indian.]
7. Can 'is lonely' and 'is lonely and sick or is lonely and not sick' have different extensions in any possible world? Do they have the same meaning? Why?
8. For each of the following, (i) explain why they are semantically deviant, and (ii) suggest by the method of paraphrase (on the underlined word) what might be conveyed by them:
   (a) Ever since his divorce, Mary's ex-husband has been a <u>housewife</u>.
   (b) Jane's husband is a <u>bachelor</u>.
   (c) He has <u>breakfast</u> just before going to sleep at midnight.
9. Analyze the Black and White Fallacy committed in each of the following:
   (a) You don't like her?! I don't understand how you could dislike her.
   (b) If he isn't for me, he's against me.

(c) Because you didn't see him in class, you must have noticed that he was absent.
(d) Because I have no obligation to see him, I ought to avoid seeing him.

10. Explain what is wrong with the following arguments or lines of thought:
    (a) I think it's ridiculous for you to go around labeling some people as rich and some people as poor. Is someone who makes $35,000 a year rich? Does $50,000 make him rich? Does $28,000 make a person poor? There just are no clear dividing lines for rich and poor.
    (b) [A man ordering at a restaurant:] Now I must order a cheap dinner. Ah, here is a $5.95 chicken dinner. But wait, for a dollar more I can have a pork dinner that I prefer much more; so, I'll have the $6.95 pork dinner. Wait a moment, $6.95 is basically $7, and for only a $1.50 more, I can have a sirloin steak. So, I'll take the $8.50 sirloin dinner. Goodness, look at that! Steak *and* shrimp is only a dollar more. That's a bargain. But I really love lobster; if I'm already spending $9.50, why not go all the way to the $11 steak and lobster? And for an additional 50¢ I can have bernaise sauce. So, I'll have steak and lobster with bernaise sauce.

6.3.2 Ambiguity

It is of course well known that words are typically ambiguous. The word 'bank', for example, might mean the sides of a river or a financial institution; that is, there is one rule for determining the extension that deals with determining the object to be a side of a river and another rule for determining the extension that has to do with the object being a repository for money. While this is a standard example, it is a relatively rare instance of a genuine homonym in which two completely different meanings are assigned to a word; in fact, in some ways it seems more natural to consider this as a case of two words having the same pronunciation and spelling.

More typical cases of ambiguity center around the different and related senses of a single word. Consider some of the different senses of 'street': (a) any thoroughfare, large or small, (b) a thoroughfare and its adjacent buildings, trees, and so on, as in 'He lives on such and such a street', (c) a medium-sized thoroughfare as distinguished from alleys and lanes on the one hand and avenues and boulevards on the other, and (d) the inhabitants of a street, as in 'The whole street was in an uproar over the proposed zoning laws'. Clearly I might use the same word in different senses at different times, and you and I might at the same time use a word in differing senses. In short, the multiplicity of senses that words have paves the way for confusion in thought and conversation. Yet, despite the overwhelming magnitude of ambiguity, we manage tolerably well. Context and the Principle of Charity go a long way; for example, if someone says, 'He lives on Maple Street', we discount the possibility that he leads a dangerous life of living on the pavement of the street. Still, breakdowns do occur, and we cite two kinds of breakdowns in this section.

(1) Verbal Disputes. Sometimes we find ourselves arguing with one another, only to discover that there were no substantive differences of opinion. To take a trivial example, suppose I claim that the banks of the Congo are risky, and you claim that the Congo is no longer a backward area where one has to worry about dangerous natives and crocodiles. I may agree that it's not as backward as it used to be but that the banks are still risky. It could emerge that I was talking about the risks of investing in the financial institutions of the Congo, where 'the Congo' was used as a name of the region, while you were talking about riverbanks of the Congo, where 'the Congo' was being used as the name of the river. We might both agree that a riverboat ride is now fairly safe but that investing in the financial institutions of the region would be risky at best. Here we have an example of a 'mere' verbal dispute; there are no substantive issues on which we disagree. For each meaning of 'bank' and 'the Congo', we agree on whether or not the extension of 'the banks of the Congo' is a part of the extension of 'risky (things)'.

In general, we may understand a verbal dispute as follows:

> The dispute between A and B over S is a verbal dispute:
>
> A and B attach different meanings S[A] and S[B] to S, and A and B can both be expected to agree about S[A] and S[B].

In analyzing something to be a verbal dispute, we should specify the disputed sentence S, and say enough about the meanings each person attaches to the critical terms in S to arrive at the meanings attached to S. Thus, given the account of the different meanings attached to 'bank' and 'the Congo' in our example, we would have:

S: The banks of the Congo are risky.
S[you]: The banks of the Congo River are risky.
S[I]: The banking institutions of the Congo region are risky.

To complete the analysis of our example, we need to point out that both of us agree that S[you] is false and S[I] is true.

We have a substantive dispute if given the same meaning (or the same rule for determining the extension of the term), we disagree on whether something fits that extension or whether something fitting that extension also belongs to the extension of another term. For example, we may agree that we are talking about financial institutions and that 'safe' means having a low probability of failure. We may also agree on what constitutes a low probability of failure in this kind of context. If despite these agreements, you should think that the banks of the Congo are safe while I think that they are risky, we have a genuine dispute on whether or not the banks of the Congo belong to the extension of 'safe (things)'. You judge the probability of failure to be low enough and I judge it to be too high.

It should not be thought that disputes are either verbal or substantive (in the exclusive sense of 'or'). Many disputes are an admixture of both. If we alter our example again, we might both agree that the probability of failure of a financial institution in the Congo region is around 5 percent. I may say that these banks are risky while you say that they are safe. Our dispute is partially due to our attaching different meanings to 'safe' and 'risky'. On the other hand, there is probably a genuine dispute as well, because I think that it's foolish to invest in banks with a 5 percent probability of failure while you think it's a sound practice. This highlights the need for putting verbal disputes out of the way so that one can identify and focus on the areas of genuine dispute.

(2) Fallacy of Equivocation. This fallacy is the semantic version of the Fallacy of Amphibole, and in its most general sense it is committed when one illegitimately shifts from one meaning or sense of a term to another. What distinguishes it from the Fallacy of Amphibole is that the ambiguity is a semantic ambiguity rather than an ambiguity of grammar. As a trivial example that exemplifies a frequent form of the fallacy, consider the following argument:

(1) All women are men.
(2) All men are nonchildbearers.
___
(3) All women are nonchildbearers.

At first appearance, the argument certainly appears valid. Is it also sound; that is, are the premises true? (1) is obviously true when 'men' is understood in the gender-neutral sense of 'human being', and (2) is obviously true when 'men' is understood as 'male human beings'. But the conclusion is clearly false. What has happened? The validity of the argument crucially depends on the terms being univocal or having the same meaning within the context of the whole argument. Thus, if the argument is to be valid, the term 'men' must be used univocally. But if we take 'men' in the gender-neutral sense, while (1) is true, (2) is false; if we take 'men' in the gender-specific sense, (2) is true but (1) is false. Thus, there is no way the argument can be sound if it is to be valid.

Because this example exemplifies a significant and perhaps most serious type of Fallacy of Equivocation, for our purpose we shall characterize the Fallacy of Equivocation as follows: *In being persuaded by an argument one commits the* FALLACY OF EQUIVOCATION *if the validity of the argument depends on taking a term T univocally and if taking the argument to be sound or the premises to be plausible depends (or may well depend) on using T equivocally.* A special instance of this fallacy occurs in the following kind of case: Suppose an argument uses T in premises (1) and (2), and (2) is plausible only if T is disambiguated as T2; in other words, of the two meanings assignable to T, (2) is plausible only if we assign it the meaning T2. If (1) is accepted on the basis of a (reliable) person's statement, the plausibility of (1) depends on disambiguating T in the way intended by the person. If it is an open possibility that the person intended T as T1 rather than T2, it may very well be the case that both premises can be taken to be plausible only if T is used equivocally. Thus, in this kind of case one has committed the Fallacy of Equivocation as we have defined it if one hasn't been careful to disambiguate the other person's claim in the intended way.

The Fallacy of Equivocation is clearly a Fallacy of Substance; hence we shall represent it as:

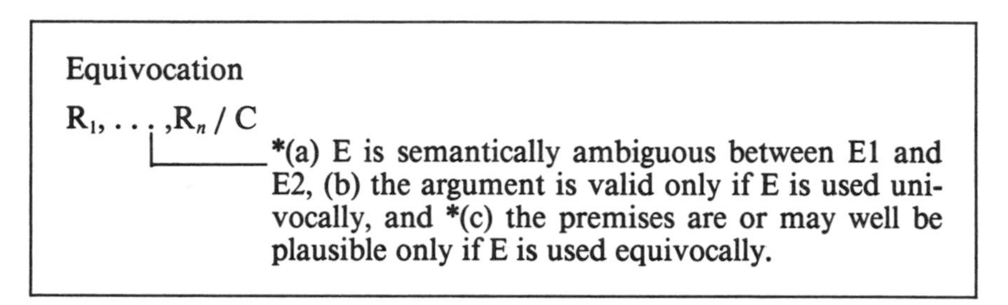

Equivocation

$R_1, \ldots, R_n$ / C

*(a) E is semantically ambiguous between E1 and E2, (b) the argument is valid only if E is used univocally, and *(c) the premises are or may well be plausible only if E is used equivocally.

As usual, the starred items (a) and (c) need to be explained in analyzing someone as having committed the Fallacy of Equivocation.

As an example, consider: "The free election of a president is a fine moment for any country. Because there can be no doubt that Nixon was freely elected in 1972, it was a good thing we elected Nixon." The analysis would be as follows:

Equivocation:

(1) The election of Nixon as the president in 1972 was a fine moment for our country.
(2) If the election of Nixon as the president in 1972 was a fine moment for our country, it was a good thing we elected Nixon.

---

(3) It was a good thing we elected Nixon.
(a) 'The election of Nixon' (E) is ambiguous between the process of electing Nixon (E1) and the result or product of the process of electing Nixon (E2).
(b) The validity of the argument requires that E be used univocally.
(c) Given the Watergate fiasco, (1) is plausible only if E is understood as E1. But (2) is plausible only when E is taken as E2, that is, only if the result rather than the process of having elected Nixon is a fine moment would it be plausible that it was a good thing we elected Nixon (rather than McGovern). Thus, the premises are plausible only if E is used equivocally.

A variation of this example would be if we accepted (1) on the authority of a political science professor. In that case, the analysis under (c) would become:

(c) Premise (2) is plausible only when E is taken as E2. But (1) is accepted on the political science professor's authority, and because she/he may well have intended E as E1, premise (1) may well be plausible only when E is taken as E1. Thus, the premises may well be plausible only if E is used equivocally.

EXERCISES—SECTION 6.3.2

1. In each of the following, (i) show that the dispute is at least in part a verbal dispute, and (ii) suggest the substantive disagreement that may persist after that verbal dispute has been cleared away:
   (a) *A:* We no longer have a free country in the United States.
   B: Why would you say that?
   A: I tried to add an extra room to the house I own, and city hall wouldn't allow it.
   B: That hardly makes our country into a country like Russia, where everything is controlled by the government and one has no freedom of speech, no freedom of movement, no freedom of opportunity, and so on.
   A: We are not controlled by the government?! I can't keep all the money I make, because the government takes away a big chunk of it without my approval. The highway patrol closed down the road I wanted to use last month, and when I told the officer where he could go, I got a fat fine as well. When my company wanted to drill for oil in the channel, the courts stopped us.
   B: But every country has to finance the public good and some controls are always needed.
   A: See?! You admit that we no longer have a free country.
   B: Not at all.
   (b) *A:* You have stocks in a company that invests in South Africa?! I don't want to have anything to do with a racist like you.
   B: Wait a moment! Don't call me a racist! I have nothing but contempt for Hitler and his actions—I fought in World War II. I've supported the civil rights movement; I contributed to NAACP, Southern Christian Leadership, Jesse Jackson's Operation Breadbasket, and so on. Sure I have stocks for my retirement. That the company does a little business in South Africa doesn't make me a racist.
   A: Say what you will. You are a racist and you know it!
2. Analyze the Fallacy of Equivocation that may be committed in the following examples:
   (a) I'm surprised to hear that Tom didn't get angry with you when he found out that you were dating his girl. Tom must have changed a lot, because when I knew him years ago in college, he would get furious when someone so much as tried to talk to his girlfriend.

Here is a partial analysis—the presentation of the argument used:

(1) If Tom is still the jealous type, he will be angry if he knows that you are dating his girl.
(2) Tom isn't angry and he knows that you are dating his girl.

(3) Tom is no longer the jealous type.

(b) No one would seriously try to compare Leonardo da Vinci to Mozart. It follows that Mozart is a better artist than Leonardo.

(c) A great work of art must be beautiful. Distorted pictures of mangled and mutilated human beings are hardly beautiful, and yet Picasso's *Guernica* is just such a picture. Picasso's *Guernica* is not a great work of art.

Hint: One of the premises is 'If distorted pictures of mangled and mutilated human beings aren't beautiful and Picasso's *Guernica* is such a picture, Picasso's *Guernica* is not beautiful'.

(d) Dauer claims that he is a teacher but he is wrong. We went to his class every day but he didn't teach us anything.

Hint: One of the premises is 'If Dauer claims that he is a teacher, he is wrong if he isn't a teacher.'

6.3.3 Definitions

The ambiguities of words can lead us into verbal disputes and committing the Fallacy of Equivocation, so it may seem desirable to define the meaning of the terms we are using. Indeed we have often given or heard the injunction: "Define your terms!" And of course if we do not know the meaning of a term, a definition might be useful.

However, the importance of definitions (in any strict sense of the term) is exaggerated. As for learning the meanings of terms, we seldom learn them by definitions, and we certainly did not do so when we first learned our language. A mother would hardly propose to teach her child the meaning of 'mother' by giving some sort of a definition. In many cases she simply points to the object and says the word. One is sometimes said to be giving an ostensive definition in doing this sort of a thing. But to call such a simple activity "giving a definition" is misleading at best. If it really is a definition, there should be no ambiguity as to what is being pointed at, yet pointing inevitably involves massive ambiguities. To eliminate the ambiguity, the mother would have to say to her child something like, "The color of the object I am pointing to (as opposed to its shape or its use, for example) is called 'red'." Clearly it would be ridiculous to suppose that this is how a mother teaches her child the various color words. Typically the child is only given a few samples along with the word and he miraculously starts using the word correctly, perhaps because of a shared innate biological structure. With other words like 'and' and 'not', pointing is more or less out of place and we tend to teach a child the meaning of such words by giving him a number of true sentences using those words. In short, we did not initially learn our language by being told rules for determining the extensions of terms or rules for determining the extensions of sentences using the terms to be learned. Rather we are given scant samples of the members of the extension or sentences that truly (or falsely) use the term in question. If such a meager basis were not sufficient and we had to rely on definitions in any strict sense of that term, it would be doubtful that we could ever learn our first language.

The situation is not much improved when an adult speaker tries to clarify or specify the meaning of the terms he or she is using. Wittgenstein[13] pointed out the virtual impossibility of defining the word 'game'. If one thinks that winning and losing or a competition is essential, one has the difficulty of including Ring-around-the-Rosie; besides, wars can be won and lost as well as games. To think that playfulness is essential to the definition of a game would be folly because poker may be anything but playful for a professional gambler. Skill or talent is important for many games, but one would have to wonder about the skill involved in playing bingo. For all the difficulties involved in defining 'game', there is no doubt that we know its meaning sufficiently well to use it correctly. Even with less difficult examples, the best we can often do is cite some examples, point out some characteristics that may be relevant in determining the extension of the term, and give examples of plausibly true sentences (or plausibly false sentences) in which the term is used. Indeed, a dictionary often doesn't do much more. Such abbreviated explanations are of course useful both for learning the meaning of words and for clarifying the meanings of words we already know. But they clearly fall short of definitions or complete rules for determining extensions.

Still, sometimes we can give adequate or nearly adequate definitions, and this can be helpful in making our meanings precise. If we really do get down to the business of providing definitions, the one important point to remember is to avoid *circular defintions,* that is, a definition of a term that uses the very term to be defined or its cognates in such a way that if one didn't already understand the term to be defined, one could not understand the definition. Even granting that the point of defining a word is not so much to teach its meaning to the untutored but to clarify the meaning satisfactorily, if one uses the very term to be defined, the achievement of clarity would depend on its meaning already having been clear. Given this warning about definitions, we may single out three types of definitions or strategies for defining a term. The second and third require a bit more effort to understand than the first and may be skipped by the less adventurous.

(1) The Explicit Definition. An explicit definition for a term 'T' gives an expression 'E' such that in no possible world will interchanging 'T' and 'E' in a sentence result in the sentence having different truth values. The definition of 'bachelor' by 'unmarried man' or 'vixen' by 'female fox'

13. Ludwig Wittgenstein, *Philosophical Investigations,* 2nd ed., Oxford: Basil Blackwell, 1963, Part i, Section 66ff.

would be such examples. The example in Section 6.3.1 of 'a three-sided figure' and 'a figure in which internal angles add up to 180°' suggests that if 'triangle' is defined by one of these expressions, the defined and defining expressions may not have the same meaning. However, it would seem that the word 'triangle' can be defined equally well by either of the two expressions; thus, the identity of meaning may not be necessary for a definition as long as it satisfies the condition suggested. It should be noted that if 'T' and 'E' are terms having extensions, the suggested condition is satisfied as long as the rule for assigning the extension of 'T' can never diverge from the rule for assigning the extension of 'E'.

Following Plato, Aristotle suggested that terms be defined in terms of species and differentia. To define 'T', the idea is to find a species or a larger class S such that the extension of 'T' is part of S, and then to specify a differentia 'D' that distinguishes T's from all other S's. His classic example was the definition of 'man' as a 'rational animal'. The class of men is a part of the species or class of animals, and what differentiates men from other animals is our rationality; that, anyway, was the idea. Following this method, one might define 'pistol' as 'bullet-shooting firearm that is of such a size that it is normally shot by holding it in one's hands'.

A curious feature of the definition of 'man' as a 'rational animal' is that even if a man is a rational animal in every possible world, in some worlds there may be rational animals that are not men. Still, to the extent the class of rational animals is exhausted by men in the actual world, the definition doesn't seem entirely useless. This suggests that for some purposes we should weaken the requirements for a definition and say: some clarification is given if 'T' and 'E' are coextensive in the actual world and in every possible world the extension of 'T' is a part of the extension of 'E' or the other way around. Of course, the ultimate weakening of the requirement is that 'T' and 'E' be coextensive so that 'man' might be defined as 'featherless biped'. Such a definition might be called an extensionally adequate definition. There is no need to be dogmatic and insist that every definition must be of the ideal type initially specified. As long as we make explicit the limitations and weaknesses of the definitions, we can avail ourselves of definitions of 'T' by 'E' even when the two terms have differing extensions in some possible worlds. After all, definitions are hard to come by and we should be thankful for whatever elucidation we may receive.

★ ★ ★ ★

(2) Recursive Definitions. To get the idea of this kind of a definition, consider the following definition of 'natural number' in terms of '0', '+', and '1':

(a) 0 is a natural number.
(b) If x is a natural number, $x + 1$ is a natural number.

(c) Nothing is a natural number unless (a) and (b) determine it to be a natural number.

It should be evident that this does define the extension of the term 'natural number'. That is, it should be clear that something belongs to the extension of 'natural number' just in case it can be generated through the rules (a) and (b). The strategy in this kind of a definition of a term 'T' is to list one or more 'seeds' or starting T's, to specify generation rules for getting new T's from other T's, and then to have a closure statement that nothing is a T unless it can be generated from the seeds by the iterated use of the generation rules. Two things should be noted about such a definition: (1) Despite the use of the very term to be defined (e.g., 'natural number') in the definition, it is not circular. It would of course be circular if the first clause specifying the seeds were omitted; but as long as we have a clause that gives the seeds, it does determine the extension without a prior understanding of the term. (ii) At least in the form given, there is no evident way to convert the definition of 'natural number' into an expression 'E' such that 'E' can replace occurrences of the defined term. In this way, recursive definitions differ from the more standard explicit definitions. Clearly, 'even number' can be given a recursive definition in terms of 2 being an even number and any even number plus 2 also being an even number. This differs from the explicit definition 'is a number divisible by 2', which can replace any occurrence of 'is an even number'. (It is true that by advanced logical maneuvers a recursive definition can be converted into one that is explicit, but the adequacy of recursive definitions was recognized long before the logical maneuver was discovered.)

When the extension of a term 'T' can be seen to be well ordered by generation rules from starting seeds, a recursive definition often proves to be the easiest way to define 'T'. In the course of this text we had at least two occasions to use recursive definitions. One was in Chapter 3, in which we defined truth functional logical forms in terms of sentence letters that acted as the seeds, and elementary operations of juxtaposition or concatenation that acted as the generation rules. The second instance was in Chapter 4, in which we defined completely justified statements with reference to unproblematic claims that acted as the seeds, and the relation of 'is a completely legitimate reason for' that acted as the generation rule. It is difficult to see how those terms could have been easily defined except with the help of recursive definitions.

(3) Contextual Definitions. Suppose we have a term 'T' that we wish to define and a scheme of translation such that (a) every sentence containing 'T' gets translated into a sentence that doesn't contain 'T', and (b) in every possible world, the sentence containing 'T' has the same truth value as its translation. Under such circumstances, 'T' has been defined (or perhaps "defined away") by the translation scheme and the translation scheme is called a contextual definition. Obviously any explicit definition automatically gives us such a translation scheme: specifically, simply replace 'T' in all contexts by its explicit definition. Thus, if we wished, we could think of an explicit definition as a special kind of contextual definition; however, we shall reserve 'contextual definition' for cases other than explicit definitions. Again, as in our discussion of explicit definitions, we might want to relax the standards a bit so that in the limiting case we only require that sentences containing 'T' and their translations have the same truth value in the actual world.

A simple example might be the following contextual definition of the logical particle 'if and only if':

p if and only if q: (if p, then q) and (if q then p).

Clearly, this will allow us to translate away any use of a biconditional in favor of a conjunction of two conditionals. Perhaps somewhat more interesting is the traditional definition of '=' in terms of class membership. If *x* and *y* are identical, they obviously must belong to the very same classes; also if they aren't identical, there is at least one class *x* belongs to (i.e., the class composed of *x* alone) to which *y* doesn't belong. For two classes *A* and *B*, their identity is simply their having the same members. Understanding '*A*' and '*B*' to be variables for classes and '*x*' and '*y*' to be variables for individual things, we can propose the following translation scheme:

A = B: For any *x*, *x* belongs to *A* if an only if *x* belongs to *B*.
x = y: For any *A*, *x* belongs to *A* if and only if *y* belongs to *A*.

It should be evident that by this translation scheme, we can translate any sentence containing '=' into one that doesn't. Notice that, as in the case of the biconditional, there is nothing in the translation that can be identified with '='; thus, we have not given an explicit definition of '='. We have only given a method for paraphrasing any sentence using '=' into one that doesn't. That meaning can sometimes be exhibited only in this way has led some philosophers to say that in many (or all) cases the smallest unit of meaning is not the word but the entire sentence.

The obvious advantage of a contextual definition is that it gives some hope for a definition when an explicit or recursive definition seems hopeless. The example of '=' may make this evident. To consider an example that hasn't been worked out, suppose one wanted to define a mental state like 'pain' in terms of some brain state B. Expressions like 'He has a pain in the leg' seem to make an explicit definition hopeless because that would yield the obvious falsehood that he has a brain state B in the leg. Somewhat more hopeful would be a translation scheme like

He has a pain in location L: He has a brain state B that was brought about by neurophysiological processes in location L.

Of course this is only a sketch of a program for providing a translation scheme, because we certainly haven't given a translation scheme for translating away all sentences containing 'pain'. Still, the idea of a contextual definition might give one hope that mental states can be defined in terms of brain states.

★ ★ ★ ★

While we have presented some stragegies for defining the meaning of words, it must be remembered that being able to give a definition is not a necessary condition for having attached a clear meaning to one's words. Perfectly adequate definitions are as a rule not easy to come by and may often be impossible. On the other hand, the strategies suggested can prove helpful in giving approximate meaning. The method of species and differentia may get one fairly close to the extension one assigns to a term without giving us a perfect match. [Citing a few seeds and some generation principles may give the gist of the sort of thing meant when those rules generate a significant part of the term's extension (and no significant part outside the term's extension). Again, citing a partial translation scheme may go toward attaching some meaning to the term in question.] An obsession with perfect definitions is out of place in ordinary contexts in which critical thinking takes place.

EXERCISES—SECTION 6.3.3

1. What is wrong with the following definitions?
   (a) 'Being' may be defined as something having being.
   (b) 'Beautiful' may be defined as having beauty.
2. (a) Give an explicit definition of 'x is an uncle of y' in terms of 'parent' and 'brother'.
   (b) Give an explicit definition of 'x is a brother-in-law of y' in terms of 'spouse', '(natural) brother', and '(natural) sister'.
3. In each of the following definitions (provided by Aristotle),[14] (i) state the species, (ii) state the differentia used (there may be several), and (iii) give an example of something of the same species that is excluded by the differentia.
   (a) A sentence is a significant portion of speech, some parts of which have an independent meaning.
   (b) Fear may be defined as a pain or disturbance due to a mental picture of some destructive or painful evil in the future.
   (c) Shame may be defined as pain or disturbance in regard to bad things, whether present, past, or future, that seem likely to involve us in discredit.
   (d) Kindness may be defined as helpfulness toward someone in need, not in return for anything, nor for the advantage of the helper himself, but for that of the person helped.

14. Example (a) from *On Interpretation;* (b)–(d) from *Rhetoric;* (e) from *Poetica.*

   (e) The ridiculous may be defined as a mistake or deformity not productive of pain or harm to others.
4. Using the species "vehicles," give a definition of 'passenger car (automobile)' by providing enough in the way of differentia.
*5. Give a recursive definition of 'is an ancestor of y' in terms of 'is a parent of'.
*6. Give a recursive definition of 'is a grammatical sentence constructed entirely from "Tom loves Mary," "Mary is disgusted," and the truth functional connectives "–" and "v" '. (Note: For a sentence to be entirely constructed from a set of expressions doesn't require that all of those expressions be used.)
*7. Assume that we have a complete list of permissible immediate inferences. Suppose we want to say something like: reasonable beliefs based on a set of statements S are beliefs in the members of S and beliefs in results of sequences of permissible immediate inferences that ultimately start with members of S. Sharpen this idea by proposing a recursive definition of 'is a reasonable belief based on the set of statements S'.
*8. Suggest a contextual definition of '⊃' in terms of '–' and '&'.
*9. Suppose, we want to define the number 3 as the property common to all sets that can be put into a one-to-one correspondence with the set {a,b,c}. Suggest a contextual definition for '3' that will be adequate for contexts of the form 'There are 3 X's' (e.g., 'There are 3 houses on the street').

6.3.4 The Semantic Contributions of Context

We have been understanding the meaning of a term as a rule that determines the extension of the term. In many cases, it would seem that given the meaning of a term and an object in a world, a suitably knowledgeable person could determine whether or not the object belongs to the extension of the term. However, there are some obvious exceptions that need to be noted: Regardless of how knowledgeable a person may be about the various individual objects in the world, if the sentence 'I am sick' is taken out of context, the knowledgeable person will not know whether a given person belongs to the extension of 'I' (i.e., whether the given person is the referent of 'I') and hence also not know the extension or truth value of 'I am sick'. In one perfecly good sense of 'meaning', such a person *does* know the meaning of 'I', that is, that 'I' picks out the author of the utterance as its referent. This rule will allow the listener to determine the reference or extension of 'I' but only if given the context in which someone uses the word. If Jill is speaking to Tom and says, "I am sick," that context along with the rule surrounding the use of 'I' will allow the determination of the reference of 'I' as Jill. This way in which the context of utterance can help determine the reference or extension of an expression might be called the semantic contribution of context.

What holds for 'I' also holds for terms like 'now', 'here', 'you', 'this', 'there', and so on. For 'I', 'now', and 'here', the only part of the context needed to determine the reference is the speaker along with the place and time of utterance. 'You' requires also knowing to whom the utterance was addressed in the context, and 'this' and 'there' requires knowing what was pointed to (e.g., by a gesture). Whenever tenses are used, the reference or extension cannot be determined independently of the context of utterance, which determines the present. 'Dauer finished writing the book' is false in contexts prior to his completion of the book and true thereafter, while 'Dauer will finish writing the book' is true prior to his completion but false thereafter.

To appreciate these semantic contributions of context, it is important to remember that distinction between an expression like 'Some person (or other)' that is not intended to pick out a particular person, and expressions like 'I' and 'he' that are intended to pick out a particular person. Thus, the content of 'I'm sick' isn't just that some person is sick, but rather that the particular person picked out as the referent of 'I' is sick. To consider a slightly more complicated case of this type, consider:

(a) He was sick at least one of the times when she visited him.
(b) He was sick when she visited him.

For us to be able to determine the truth value of (a), context must fix the referent of 'he', 'she', and the time of utterance before which at least one of the sicknesses and visits are supposed to have occurred. To determine the truth value of (b), the context must allow us to fix all of this *and* the specific time at which the visit is supposed to have occurred; that is, (b), unlike (a), is talking about a specific visit.[15]

Definite descriptions of the form 'the so and so' can also make greater and lesser demands on the context to fix the referent. No semantic contribution of context is needed to fix the referent of 'the lightest chemical element'. To fix the reference of 'the song he is singing', the context must fix the referent of 'he' and the time of utterance when the singing is supposed to be occurring. Even more needs to be fixed by the context to fix the referent of 'the song he sang'. Context must clearly fix the referent of 'he' and the time of utterance before which the singing was supposed to have occurred. But because we can expect him to have sung many songs in the past, the context must also determine which of these songs is being referred to, and this might be done by having the context fix the specific time in which the song was supposed to have been sung.

Another area in which context helps to determine reference is our use of proper names. In a discussion of ancient philosophy, 'Aristotle' may be used to refer to the famous Greek philosopher who was the student of Plato. Yet in another context we may be using 'Aristotle' to talk about the twentieth-century Greek shipping magnate who married a widow of an American president. There is no doubt that context is helpful in determining the person referred to by using sounds or inkmarks like 'Aristotle' and 'Bill Smith'.

15. The analysis of statements involving tense can become very complicated, and complications that are well beyond the scope of the present text are discussed in Nathan Salmon, *Frege's Puzzle*, Cambridge, Mass.: MIT Press, 1986, Chapter 2.

★ ★ ★ ★

What is less clear is the correct account of proper names. Some have claimed that in any given context the use of a name like 'Aristotle' is in fact a use of a contextually engendered description like 'the twentieth-century Greek shipping magnate who married a widow of an American president'. Seen in this way, 'Aristotle' is indefinitely ambiguous, and context determines what meaning or description is to be attached to the use of the name, and the attached meaning or description will disambiguate and determine the reference. Other have suggested that a proper name directly refers to a person without any such meaning being attached to it: Unlike inkmarks, a *name* is identified through a chain of transmissions going back to the initial baptism of a person by that name. As such, the different uses of 'Aristotle' we have imagined are uses of different names. Seen in this light, each name has a unique reference attached to it and the context (of being in a certain chain of transmissions) determines which name is being used. Regardless of how we look at the matter, in the case of sounds or inkmarks like 'Aristotle' and 'Bill Smith', it is clear that context helps us in determining to whom we are referring.

★ ★ ★ ★

Beyond these examples in which context is needed to identify what individual is the referent of a referring expression, context can be significant for determining the meaning of ordinary descriptive words. Words may be given a special meaning in a context and they can also be uttered with a particular tone or accent that slightly shifts the meaning. An interesting example is the following portion of a Robert J. Samuelson column in the *Los Angeles Times*:

> This reporter spent much of his apprenticeship in the chambers of the City Council of Cambridge, Mass. At the end of a debate he lost, a mayor named Ed Crane said, "I don't get shook up over these things. The city won't blow up, the sun won't rise in the west." President Reagan won a triumph over the fiscal 1982 budget. Many journalists have already created a number of myths concerning the Reagan triumph. But the sun won't rise in the west. The first myth is that. . . .

It would be a mistake to think that the second use of 'the sun won't rise in the west' is an unproblematic claim of science or common sense. In this context it means something like: It's not going to be a disaster, things aren't going to change that much, and so on.[16] If the Reagan budget had

16. It could be suggested that this meaning is only a pragmatic or conversational implication of the utterance (along the lines of Section 6.5) and that what is literally asserted concerns sunrises. It remains unclear to me that we would want to say Samuelson's statement is true in any sense if the Reagan budget had turned out to be very different from what he expected.

turned out to be a disaster and things had turned out to be very different from the way they were, the extension or truth value of Samuelson's statement 'the sun won't rise in the west' is false even if we should continue to look for sunrises in the direction of the east. Such then are some of the semantic contributions of context.

Related Fallacies. Suppose a term is used in a context in which the context makes a semantic contribution. If we think of semantics as dealing with what determines extensions or referents, the semantic contributions of context will have to be seen as part of the semantics of the term as it is used in that context. This in turn has the result that, for example, if the context engenders some ambiguity as to who the referent of 'he' is, the use of 'he' in that context is semantically ambiguous. Because the Fallacy of Equivocation centers around the semantic ambiguity of our words, it should be evident that some instances of the Fallacy of Equivocation will be contextually engendered by the ambiguity surrounding the semantic contribution of the context. This is indeed the case, and we give two examples of the Fallacy of Equivocation that are contextually engendered:

(1) "Tom must be lying. He said he visited Mary when he went to San Francisco. But Mary was visiting me last weekend." Let us suppose that there is no doubt about 'Mary' referring to the same person. The fallacy would then be analyzed as follows:

Equivocation:

(1) Tom said he visited Mary when he went to San Francisco.
(2) Mary was visiting me last weekend.
(3) If Tom said he visited Mary when he went to San Francisco and Mary was visiting me last weekend, Tom is lying.

---

(4) Tom is lying.

(a) The use of 'when he went to San Francisco' (E) is ambiguous between E1 and E2:
  - E1: Picking last weekend as the time referent of 'when he went to San Francisco'.
  - E2: Picking some time other than last weekend as the time referent of 'when he went to San Francisco'.

(b) The validity of the argument requires that the uses of 'when he went to San Francisco' univocally pick the same time referent.

(c) Premise (3) is plausible only when E is understood as E1. But because (1) is based on Tom's statement, and because he may well have used E as E2, premise (1) may well be plausible only when E is taken as E2. Thus, the premises may well be plausible only when E is used equivocally.

(2) In ancient Greece, Croesus went to the Oracle of Delphi to consult about his prospects should he wage war with Persia and its leader Cyrus. The Oracle said: "If Croesus goes to war with Cyrus, he will destroy the mighty kingdom." Based on this, Croesus went to war and his kingdom was quickly wiped out by Cyrus and the Persians. When he returned to Delphi to complain, the Oracle pointed out that indeed the mighty kingdom had been destroyed by him, namely his own. Croesus's fallacious attempt to refute the Oracle may be analyzed as follows:

Equivocation:

(1) The Oracle said that Croesus will destroy the mighty kingdom if he goes to war with Cyrus.
(2) If the Oracle said . . . and the Oracle was right, Croesus will have been the victor if he went to war with Cyrus.
(3) Croesus went to war with Cyrus and Croesus was not the victor.
(4) The Oracle was not right.
(a) 'The mighty kingdom' (E) is ambiguous between E1 and E2:
E1: The mighty kingdom of Persia.
E2: Croesus's own mighty kingdom.
(b) The validity of the argument requires that 'the mighty kingdom' be used univocally.
(c) Premise (2) is plausible only if E is disambiguated as E1. But because premise (1) is based on the Oracle's statement, and because the Oracle may well have intended E as E2 (as indeed it later did claim), premise (1) may well be plausible only if E is disambiguated as E2. Thus, the premises may well be plausible only if E is used equivocally.

To accuse poor Croesus of committing the (contextually engendered) Fallacy of Equivocation on top of everything else that happened to him may seem a bit cruel; on the other hand, ambiguity was the Oracle's stock in trade, and Croesus should have been more cautious in his disambiguation (which led him to go to war with Cyrus).

Beyond the semantic contribution of context to determine the referent of a term, we have also seen that ordinary descriptive terms can acquire a special meaning in a context. One way in which context can alter the meaning of such descriptive words is by the particular tone or accent with which they are used. The written equivalents of tone and accent are made by indications like italics and the use of quotation marks that we sometimes call "scare quotes." In a broad sense, the FALLACY OF ACCENT *occurs when accented expressions are treated as unaccented or as accented in a different way*. For our purposes we shall single out a central form of this fallacy that may be treated as a Fallacy of Substance and specify it as follows:

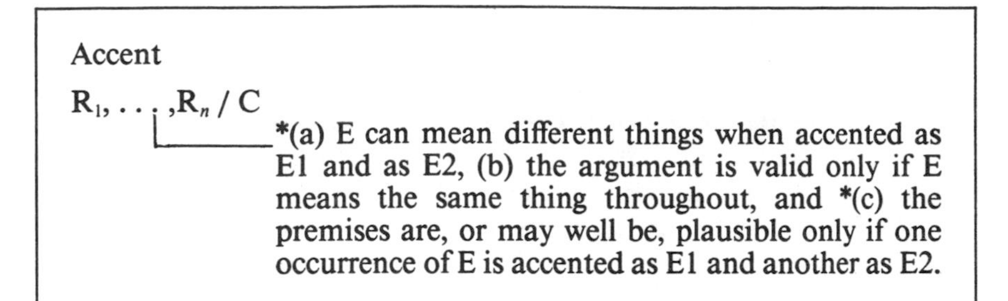

As usual, the starred items (a) and (c) need explanation in the analysis. What the Fallacy of Accent amounts to may be exemplified by the following two examples:

(1) "Tom should go to work because he isn't really sick. If he were *really* sick, he would have a very high temperature; but he doesn't."

Accent:

(1) If Tom is really sick, he has a very high temperature.
(2) Tom doesn't have a very high temperature.
(3) If Tom isn't really sick, Tom should go to work.

---

(4) Tom should go to work.
(a) 'Really sick' (E) can mean different things when accented as E1 and E2:
E1: '*really* sick': very sick
E2: 'really sick': actually sick as opposed to faking it
(b) The argument is valid only if E means the same thing throughout.
(c) Premise (1) is plausible only if E is accented as E1. Premise (3), on the other hand, is plausible only when E is accented (or unaccented) as E2. Thus, the premises are plausible only when the several occurrences of E are accented differently with the result that they mean different things at those occurrences.

(2) "Am I going to have a boring date! He said he fixed me up with a 'nice' girl, and we all know 'nice' girls are boring."

Accent:

(1) My date is a nice girl.
(2) If my date is a nice girl, I'm going to have a boring date.

---

(3) I'm going to have a boring date.
(a) 'Nice girl' (E) can mean different things when accented as E1 and E2:
E1: "Nice girl": a straightlaced, unadventurous girl
E2: 'Nice girl': a pleasant girl

(b) The argument is valid only if E means the same thing throughout.

(c) Premise (2) is plausible only when E is accented as E1. But because premise (1) is based on someone's assertion, and because the person may well have intended E to be accented (or unaccented) as E2, (1) may well be plausible only when E is accented as E2. Thus, the premises may well be plausible only when E is accented differently in its several occurrences, which would make them mean different things at those occurrences.

Perhaps in its most general characterization, the Fallacy of Accent occurs when one pays insufficient attention to the context that might be making a semantic (or syntactic) contribution. In this most general form, the fallacy is committed when people or texts are quoted out of context or are misquoted by the deletion of verbal or written accents, with the result that semantic or syntactic meanings different from those intended are attached. Whenever making a citation, one should be very careful to avoid this most general form of the Fallacy of Accent.

EXERCISES—SECTION 6.3.4

1. Assuming that the referents of the proper names used are fixed, in each of the following, determine the minimum semantic contribution of context that is needed in order for the uttered sentence to have a truth value.
   (a) Texas is larger than my state of birth.
   (b) I am twice divorced.
   (c) The man Reagan shook hands with is now dead.
   (d) You used to love me.
   (e) He wasn't there when she phoned him.
   (f) He was here when she arrived tonight.
2. Suggest two different contexts for using "'Love' is a four-letter word" so that different things are conveyed by it in those two contexts.
3. Analyze the fallacies involved in the following passages.
   (a) "I'm not bothered by your criticism that I say *nothing* eloquently. You at least admit that even when I say nothing, I do so eloquently."

      Hint: One of the premises is, "If I say nothing eloquently, even when I say nothing, I do so eloquently."
   (b) *A:* Now you broke my computer! That's "great."
      B: I'm glad that you are pleased.
   (c) "It's amazing how the fortune-teller knew I would marry Jill. Years before I moved into the condo and met Jill who was living next door, the fortune-teller told me that I would marry the girl next door."
   (d) *She:* It's that time of the month. I'm suffering from "the Curse."
      He: I didn't know that you were superstitious.
   (e) "Tom, Uncle Sam was lying when he said that he wants you. After all, Tom, when you tried to volunteer last year, he turned you down."

*6.3.5 A Pair of Semantic Subtleties

The topic of this subsection is somewhat advanced and the average reader might wish to skip it. We point out here two features of language that are fairly pervasive without being universal, and warn against errors that result from the failure to recognize their lack of universality.

(1) Extensional and Intensional Contexts. Consider the following inferences:

'Tom' and 'Mary's dull-witted husband' refer to the same person (are coextensive terms). Tom left the motel at 3 A.M. / Mary's dull-witted husband left the motel at 3 A.M.

'Starter of the Union High basketball team' and 'person who raped Jill's mother' refer to exactly the same persons (i.e., are coextensive terms), because it turns out that Jill's mother was raped by precisely those starters. A starter of the Union High basketball team had a car accident / A person who raped Jill's mother had a car accident.

'Hearted creature' and 'kidneyed creature' refer to exactly the same things (are coextensive terms). A fox is a hearted creature / A fox is a kidneyed creature.

All of these inferences are perfectly legitimate, and what underlies these inferences is the apparent correctness of

E: If 'X' and 'Y' are coextensive, then '. . . X . . .' and '. . . Y . . .' have the same true value

where '. . . Y . . .' results from '. . . X . . .' by interchanging 'X' and 'Y'. Is E always correct so that we can rely on any inference of the form: 'X' and 'Y' are coextensive; . . . X . . . / . . . Y . . . ?

If we can, we would have to count the following inference as correct:

'Starter of the Union High basketball team' and 'person who raped Jill's mother' are coextensive; Jill hopes that she will have a date with a starter of the Union High basketball team / Jill hopes that she will have a date with a person who raped her mother.

Suppose it really is the case that it was the starters of the basketball team who raped Jill's mother, but that Jill is ignorant of this. Surely we can suppose that Jill does hope that she will have a date with a starter and yet be truthful in claiming that the last thing she would hope for is a date with one of her mother's rapists. In the imagined circumstance, the inference evidently leads from truth to falsity. As a result, E is not universally correct, because in our example, although 'starter of the Union High basketball team' and 'a person who raped Jill's mother' are coextensive, the truth value will not remain the same, as these terms are interchanged in the context 'Jill hopes that she will have a date with _____'.

* This section contains more difficult material and may be skipped.

Our examples suggest that in some linguistic constructions the truth of what is being claimed is sensitive to the referring expressions used and not just the objects that happen to be selected as the referents of those expressions. Evidently, 'she hopes that she will have a date with ______' is such a construction, while '______ left the motel at 3 A.M.' and '______ had a car accident' are not. As a way of distinguishing these two types of constructions, standard terminology has it that a context '. . . ______ . . .' (such as '______ left the motel at 3 A.M.' or 'she hopes that she will have a date with ______') is an *extensional* context when E holds for that context, and *intensional* otherwise. In other words,

> '. . . ______ . . .' is an *extensional* context: '. . . X . . .' and '. . . Y . . .' have the same true value if 'X' and 'Y' are coextensive.
> '. . . ______ . . .' is an *intensional* context if it isn't extensional.

In short, while the interchange of coextensive terms can be relied upon to preserve truth values in an extensional context, this is not so in an intensional context.

The jargon 'extensional context' thus derives from the idea that an extensional context gives rise to a sentence in which the truth value depends only on the extensions of its component expressions. Given an intensional context '. . . ______ . . .', it is not entirely clear what must be true of 'X' and 'Y' for '. . . X . . .' and '. . . Y . . .' to have the same truth value; but it has sometimes been suggested that the needed condition is that 'X' and 'Y' have the same meaning or intention, hence the jargon of 'intensional context'. Sometimes the distinction between extensional and intensional contexts is couched in the terminology of 'referentially transparent' and 'referentially opaque' contexts. Seen within this terminology, transparent contexts engender sentences in which the truth values depend only on what is referred to regardless of the referring expressions used, and opaque contexts give rise to sentences in which the truth values depend not only on the referents but also on the referring expressions used. The idea of the terminology is thus clear: if we think of referring expressions as windows to the referents and think of truth values as what is seen, in transparent contexts the "windows" do not affect what is seen while in opaque contexts they do.

It is probably true that most sentences we encounter are engendered by extensional contexts. But this is clearly not universally true, as our example of Jill's hopes for a date shows. Two frequent sources of intensional contexts are (a) words indicating attitudes one may have about statements such as 'believes' and 'wants (it to be true that)', and (b) modal expressions such as 'must', 'necessarily', and 'possibly'. If we think of statements expressing beliefs and desires as somehow involved in the belicf and desire, it is not surprising that 'believes', 'wants', and their near relatives give rise to intensional contexts that are sensitive to the referring expressions used. 'Jill hopes that she has a date with _____' proved to be an intensional context because hoping for something is closely associated with wanting that thing, and both hoping and wanting something tend to vary with the description of the thing even if the descriptions happen to be coextensive. As for the modalities, if we think that some necessities (like that of all hearted creatures being hearted creatures) derive from certain statements (such as 'All hearted creatures are hearted creatures') being true in virtue of the meaning of the terms, it is again not surprising that modal sentences can give rise to intensional contexts that are sensitive to the linguistic expressions employed.

Despite the frequency of extensional contexts, some sentences are engendered by intensional contexts. Thus we can say that a fallacy is *committed when an intensional context is treated as extensional,* that is, as one that allows for inferences of the sort underwritten by E. Let us call this the FALLACY OF IGNORING INTENSIONAL CONTEXTS; we can classify it as a Presuppositional Fallacy and represent it as follows:

> Ignoring Intensional Contexts
>
> Extension of 'X' = Extension of 'Y' & . . . X . . . → . . . Y . . . ; NOT {' . . . _____ . . .' is an extensional context}.

Thus, our initial example would be analyzed as:

Ignoring Intensional Contexts:
Extension of 'a starter of the Union High basketball team' = extension of 'a person who raped Jill's mother', and Jill hopes that she will have a date with a starter of the Union High basketball team → Jill hopes that she will have a date with a person who raped her mother; NOT {'Jill hopes that she will have a date with _____' is an extensional context}.

Two more examples of this fallacy may be given:

"How could he believe that Lincoln is the seventeenth president of the United States? Because Lincoln is the sixteenth president of the United States, this is as ridiculous as believing that the sixteenth president of the United States is the seventeenth president."

Ignoring Intensional Contexts:
Extension of 'Lincoln' = extension of 'the sixteenth president of the United States', and he believes that Lincoln is the seventeenth president of the United States → He believes that the sixteenth president of the United States is the seventeenth president of the United States; NOT {'He believes that _____ is the seventeenth president of the United States' is an extensional context}.

"It is a necessary truth that all hearted creatures are hearted creatures. Because the hearted creatures are precisely the kidneyed creatures, it is a necessary truth that all hearted creatures are kidneyed creatures."

Ignoring Intensional Contexts:
Extension of 'hearted creature' = extension of 'kidneyed creature', and it is a necessary truth that all hearted creatures are hearted creatures → It is a necessary truth that all hearted creatures are kidneyed creatures; NOT {'It is a necessary truth that all hearted creatures are ______' is an extensional context}

Such then is the nature of the Fallacy of Ignoring Intensional Contexts.[17]

(2) *De Re* and *De Dicto* Uses. Consider:

It has sometimes been suggested that were circumstances a bit different, Kennedy's assassin might not have assassinated Kennedy. But this is clearly false. To say A might not have done D if the circumstances were different is to say that in a possible world (close to ours) in which the circumstances are appropriately different, A did not do D. But in no possible world could someone be Kennedy's assassin and fail to assassinate Kennedy whatever the circumstances may be in that world.

Something seems to be awry in this line of reasoning, but what?

To investigate the matter, let us limit our discussion to statements of the form 'X is Y' and their variants. Let us also limit our attention to expressions 'X' in which the meaning can be taken to specify a (complex) property P such that an object belongs to (or is) the extension of 'X' just in case it has the property P. In this case we shall say that P is the property associated with the meaning of 'X'. Let us also note that given a statement of the form 'X is Y' there is a conveyed content that is typically true in some possible worlds and false in others. Thus, for example, the conveyed content of 'Reagan is president' is false in some possible worlds and true in others including our actual world. The question that needs to be asked is: How does the property associated with the meaning of 'X' partake in the content that is conveyed by 'X is Y'?

Typically, the property associated with the meaning of 'X' is part of the content conveyed by 'X is Y', so that the content is true or false depending on whether or not the object having the associated property is Y. As an example, consider the utterance 'Bachelors are sloppy'. We might take being an unmarried male adult as the property associated with the mean-

17. Admittedly, some have suggested that 'He believes that the sixteenth president is the seventeenth president' should be given an extensional reading and be understood as 'Of the sixteenth president, he believes that he is the seventeenth president'; the latter presumably is true as long as he believes that Lincoln is the seventeenth president. If this suggestion were correct, the Fallacy of Ignoring Intensional Contexts would not have been committed in the way suggested in the text. However, it seems to me that at best 'He believes that' (as well as certain other attitude expressions) are ambiguous between intensional and extensional readings; thus, if the premise is given an intensional reading, the fallacy would have been committed in the way discussed in the text.

ing of 'bachelor'; that is, something belongs to the extension of 'bachelor' just in case it has the property of being an unmarried male adult. The conveyed content of 'Bachelors are sloppy' is true or false in a possible world depending on whether or not objects having the property of being unmarried male adults are sloppy in that world. At least in a loose way, the use of an expression is said to be a *de dicto* use if what the expression contributes to the content of the statement using that expression is the meaning of that expression. Applying this idea to the kinds of cases in which we are interested, let us provisionally say: the use of 'X' in the utterance 'X is Y' is a *de dicto* use just in case the content of 'X is Y' is true or false depending on whether or not the object that has the property associated with the meaning of 'X' is also Y. The use of 'bachelors' in 'Bachelors are sloppy' is therefore a *de dicto* use. Certainly most uses of expressions we encounter are *de dicto* uses. Are there then any uses of expressions that aren't *de dicto* uses?

Consider the utterance 'I am sick'. The meaning of 'I' specifies that someone is the referent (or the extension) of 'I' just in case that person is the speaker. Bringing in the semantic contribution of context, we can say the referent (or extension) of this particular use of 'I' is the person who has the property of being the speaker at the time and place of the utterance. So, suppose I said 'I am sick' at midnight in Santa Barbara, or more precisely, at midnight of a specified date D at a specified location L in Santa Barbara. The referent (or extension) of my use of 'I' is then the person who has the property of being the speaker at midnight in Santa Barbara. Can we then say that the content of my utterance is that the midnight speaker in Santa Barbara is sick (at midnight)?

The answer appears to be negative. What I convey by saying 'I am sick' is that I, Francis Dauer, am sick at midnight (on the precise date D). This is something that might have been false; that is, in a possible world I might have avoided the cold so that I am fit as a fiddle at midnight (on the precise date D) and am enjoying a weekend in Las Vegas. On the other hand, in that world Nathan might be sick and say at midnight (on date D at location L) in Santa Barbara, "I am sick." Assuming Nathan to have spoken truthfully, in this possible world it is true that the midnight speaker in Santa Barbara is sick (at midnight). Thus, if the conveyed content of my actual-world utterance 'I am sick' were that the midnight speaker in Santa Barbara is sick, the conveyed content of my utterance would be true in the imagined possible world. But it is clear that what I conveyed by my actual-world utterance, 'I am sick', is false in the imagined possible world. Thus, the conveyed content of my utterance is not that the midnight speaker in Santa Barbara is sick, and my use of 'I' in 'I am sick' is not a *de dicto* use; that is, the property associated with the meaning of 'I' that fixes me as the referent of 'I' in the utterance 'I am sick' is not part of the conveyed content of the utterance. The same point can be made more dramatically by switching the example to 'I am speaking'. Presumably what is conveyed by this utterance could be false, in that there are possible worlds in which I, Francis Dauer, am not speaking at midnight; but there seems to be no possible world in which the midnight speaker in Santa Barbara is not speaking (at midnight). Clearly, then, the conveyed content of my utterance 'I am speaking' is not that the midnight speaker in Santa Barbara is speaking.

How then should we conceive the conveyed content of my utterance 'I am sick'? A natural answer is to think of myself, this very person, as being part of the content of 'I am sick' because the truth or falsity of what is conveyed by my utterance in a possible world is to be gauged by whether or not I, Francis Dauer, am sick in that world.[18] In this kind of case, the standard terminology has it that the use of 'I' is a *de re* use. In Latin, *'dicto'* means speech while *'re'* means thing. Thus, the idea is this: given a *de dicto* use of 'X' in an utterance U, the semantic contribution of 'X' to the conveyed content of U is the meaning or associated properties of X; given a *de re* use of 'X', its semantic contribution to the conveyed content of U is the very object that is fixed as the referent of 'X' by U and its surrounding context.

To put the matter a little more precisely for the kinds of cases in which we are interested, let us understand *de dicto* and *de re* uses as follows:

The use of 'X' in the actual-world utterance 'X is Y' is a

De dicto use: The content of the actual-world utterance is true or false in a possible world W depending on whether or not the object that in W has the property associated with meaning of 'X' is also Y in W.

De re use: The content of the actual-world utterance is true or false in a possible world W depending on whether or not the very object that is the referent of 'X' in the actual world is Y in W.

A consequence is that if the use of 'X' in the utterance 'X is Y' is a *de re* use, the content of the utterance is to be understood in terms of the referent of 'X' being fixed for all possible worlds as the actual-world referent of 'X'; if the use is a *de dicto* use, the content is to be understood in terms of the referent of 'X' varying from world to world as the objects having the property associated with the meaning of 'X' vary from world to world.

18. This conclusion of David Kaplan and other "direct reference theorists" is a more extreme version of Kripke's more modest official view that the semantic contribution of certain words cannot be understood in terms of the meanings (if any) that those words may have. [Cf. Saul Kripke, *Naming and Necessity,* Cambridge, Mass.: Harvard University Press, 1980]. For an excellent discussion of the (often unpublished) views of Kripke, Kaplan, and others, see Nathan Salmon, *Reference and Essence,* Princeton, N.J.: Princeton University Press, 1981.

Seen in this way, while most expressions can be given a *de dicto* use, it is doubtful that indexicals like 'I', 'here', and 'now' have anything other than *de re* uses.

Let us now return to 'Kennedy's assassin might not have assassinated Kennedy'. Could what is conveyed by 'Kennedy's assassin assassinated Kennedy' have been false? It certainly can't if we assign a *de dicto* use to 'Kennedy's assassin'. The property associated with the meaning of 'Kennedy's assassin' is presumably the property of having assassinated Kennedy. Thus, if the use of 'Kennedy's assassin' in the utterance is a *de dicto* use, the conveyed content of the utterance is to be assessed to be true or false in a world W depending on whether or not the person who assassinated Kennedy in W assassinated Kennedy in W. Thus understood, it is clear that the conveyed content of 'Kennedy's assassin assassinated Kennedy' cannot be false in any possible world. But 'Kennedy's assassin' can also be given a *de re* use. Seen in this way, the conveyed content of 'Kennedy's assassin assassinated Kennedy' is true or false in a world W depending on whether or not the very person who assassinated Kennedy in our actual world (Lee Harvey Oswald himself) assassinated Kennedy in W. Because there presumably are possible worlds in which Oswald did not assassinate Kennedy, the conveyed content of 'Kennedy's assassin assassinated Kennedy' could be false in a possible world as long as we take 'Kennedy's assassin' to have a *de re* use. Given the utterance, "If circumstances were a bit different, Kennedy's assassin might not have assassinated Kennedy', the Principle of Charity would enjoin us to take 'Kennedy's assassin' to have a *de re* use so that what is conveyed by the utterance has a chance of being true.

Given the prevalence of *de dicto* uses, there is the danger, as our Kennedy example shows, of ignoring *de re* uses of expressions. To ignore such a use might be called the FALLACY OF IGNORING *DE RE* USES, a presuppositional fallacy that may be represented as:

> Ignoring *De Re* Uses
>
> The conveyed content of 'X is Y' is true in world W → the object that in W has the property associated with the meaning of 'X' is Y in W; NOT { the use of 'X' is a *de dicto* use in 'X is Y'}.

Thus, the fallacy committed in the example that started our discussion of *de dicto* and *de re* uses might be analyzed as:

Ignoring **De Re** *Uses*:

The conveyed content of 'Kennedy's assassin didn't assassinate Kennedy' is true in world W → the person who in W assassinated Kennedy didn't assassinate Kennedy in W; NOT {'Kennedy's assassin' is a *de dicto* use in 'Kennedy's assassin didn't assassinate Kennedy'}.

Interestingly enough, the same fallacy is committed in: "'My wife is ill' cannot have the same conveyed content as 'The speaker's wife is ill'." The two utterances could have the same content if 'the speaker's wife' and 'my wife' are both given *de re* readings.

EXERCISES—SECTION 6.3.5

1. To construe the connective 'if/then' as a truth functional connective (Cf. Section 3.3) comes to the same thing as construing the context 'if . . . , then _____' as an extensional context. Explain why this is so.
2. Let U be the actual-world utterance 'The sixteenth president is believed by Joe to be the seventeenth president'.

   Assume '_____ is believed by Joe to be the seventeenth president' is an extensional context, and that Lincoln is believed by Joe in our actual world to be the seventeenth president. Furthermore, assume that the following is true in a possible world W: (i) Lincoln remained an unknown who never went into politics with the result that nothing is believed about Lincoln by Joe, (ii) Stephen Douglas is the sixteenth president, and (iii) Stephen Douglas is believed by Joe to be the seventeenth president. Answer the following questions and justify your answer in each case.
   (a) Is the conveyed content of U true in our actual world when 'the sixteenth president' is given a *de dicto* use?
   (b) Is the conveyed content of U true in our actual world when 'the sixteenth president' is given a *de re* use?
   (c) Is the conveyed content of (the actual-world utterance) U true in W when 'the sixteenth president' is given a *de dicto* use?
   (d) Is the conveyed content of (the actual-world utterance) U true in W when 'the sixteenth president' is given a *de re* use?
3. In each of the following passages, analyze the fallacy that is committed or is likely to have been committed in the reasoning that led to one of its claims. If something is analyzed to commit the Fallacy of Ignoring *De Re* Uses, precede the analysis by an informal but full presentation of the argument on which the passage is (likely to be) relying.
   (a) Despite what she says, she isn't scared that the murderer they are discussing in the papers will come to her house. Although she may not know it, her son is that murderer, and we know that she isn't scared of her son's visits.
   (b) It is plainly false to suggest that the rod in Paris by which the length of one meter is defined might have been less than one meter long.
   (c) She is clearly delighted that her son is a friend of all the rich students in his class. Because the rich students in his class are precisely the children of Mafia parents, I guess she is delighted that her son is a friend of all the Mafia children.
   (d) There are no wild tigers in Africa. Therefore, if 'he is hunting wild tigers in Africa' is true, so is 'He is hunting square circles'.

(e) In no possible world can the cause of A fail to cause A. Thus, if B is the cause of A, in no possible world can B fail to cause A. (Identify the fallacy as the fallacy that is likely to have led to the claim that in no possible world can the cause of A fail to cause A.)
(f) In no possible world can the cause of A fail to cause A. Thus, if B is the cause of A, in no possible world can B fail to cause A. (Identify the fallacy as the one that is committed in drawing the inference 'Thus . . .')

6.4 The Level of Illocutionary Forces

We noted from the outset of this chapter that there are a number of different things we may be doing in uttering words or sentences. The syntactic classifications of sentences into such types as declarative, interrogative, imperative, and exclamatory point to some of the different things we can do in uttering a sentence. Because our main concern is with assessing truth claims, we should of course concentrate on declarative sentences that are the typical vehicles for making truth claims or assertions or statements. However, the pioneering work of John Austin has shown that in uttering a declarative sentence we are often doing something other than making an assertion or a claim. He coined the term "illocutionary force" for the sorts of things we may be doing in uttering a sentence, and the point just made can be recast as:

> *Stating is not the illocutionary force of many utterances involving declarative sentences. Furthermore, even when stating is part of the illocutionary force of an utterance, it is often only part of the force, and what is more, the statement made may not be what the syntax and semantics might lead us to expect.*

The principal task of this section is to make a little clearer the different kinds of illocutionary forces a declarative sentence may have so that we can isolate the claim or statement involved in an utterance.

In order to highlight illocutionary forces of utterances, we start in Section 6.4.1 with so-called performative utterances, which at first glance appear to be completely devoid of the illocutionary force of stating, claiming, or asserting. In Section 6.4.2 we shall discuss illocutionary forces in general. While this material is entirely from Austin, it is simplified and to a certain extent distorted for ease of presentation; thus, fidelity to Austin's subtle work is not being claimed.

6.4.1 Performative Utterances

Austin introduced the idea of a performative utterance in the following way:

> I want to discuss a kind of utterance which looks like a statement . . . and yet is not true or false. They will be perfectly straightforward utter-

> ances, with ordinary verbs in the first-person singular present indicative active. . . . Furthermore, if a person makes an utterance of this sort we should say that he is *doing* something rather than merely *saying* something. Suppose, for example, that in the course of a marriage ceremony I say, as people will, "I do"—(sc. take this woman to be my lawful wedded wife). Or again suppose that I tread on your toe and say "I apologize." Or again, suppose that I have a bottle of champagne in my hand and say "I name this ship the *Queen Elizabeth.*" Or suppose I say "I bet you sixpence it will rain tomorrow." In all these cases it would be absurd to regard the thing that I say as a report of the performance of the action that is undoubtedly done—the action of betting, or christening, or apologizing. We should rather say that, in saying what I do, I actually perform that action. When I say "I name this ship the *Queen Elizabeth,*" I do not describe the christening ceremony, I actually perform the christening; and when I say "I do" (sc. take this woman to be my lawful wedded wife), I am not reporting on a marriage, I am indulging in it.[19]

Performative utterances then have two interconnected features:

(1) They are not true or false. Change the tense or person, and we do have a statement or report that is true or false. 'I named the ship *Queen Elizabeth*' and 'He is betting that it will rain tomorrow' are both clearly true or false; they purport to describe the act performed by the utterance of the first-person present-tense version. The utterance of the first-person present-tense version itself, on the other hand, is not a description of the act.

(2) In uttering a performative one performs an action rather than stating something to be the case, or at least one does something different from stating or asserting something to be true. Typical of performative utterances is that the saying so makes it so. To say 'I bet' is to bet and to bring about the bet; to say 'I name' is to name and to bring about the naming, and so on.

This last point isn't quite correct, because things can go wrong and the performative might fail in a number of ways. If I am already married, my saying 'I do' doesn't bring about the marriage. If it's already raining, my saying 'I bet you it will rain today' will not bring about a bet; further, my saying 'I bet' will also fail if you don't take me up on the bet. These things that can go wrong don't make the performative utterance false but in some sense they make the utterance, in Austin's terms, "unhappy" or "infelicitous." This then brings us to the third point about performatives:

(3) Performative utterances are happy (felicitous) or unhappy (infelicitous). As an incomplete classification of the types of infelicities to

19. John Austin, "Performative Utterances," in *Collected Philosophical Papers,* J. O. Urmson and G. J. Warnock, ed., Oxford: Clarendon Press, 1961, p. 222.

which performative utterances are susceptible, Austin proposed the following.[20]

(A) Misfires. In one form or other, the act fails to occur, as in the above examples of the marriage and the bet that didn't come off. Among misfires, Austin listed two major subdivisions:

(i) Misinvocations. Two fairly obvious conditions must be satisfied for a performative to succeed: (A) There must exist an accepted conventional procedure to bring about a conventional effect by the utterance of some words by certain persons in certain circumstances. (B) The particular person and circumstance for invoking the procedure must satisfy the conditions specified by the conventions for that procedure. A misinvocation occurs when either (A) or (B) isn't satisfied [and Austin used the term "misapplication" for the failure of (B)]. A failure of (A) might be an attempt of a gay couple to be legally married by saying 'I do'. Our society at large accepts no such convention. On the other hand, within a subculture where some such conventional procedure has been accepted, some appropriate conventional effect might be brought about by saying 'I do'. (B) is violated if I say to another woman 'I do' in an appropriate ceremony when I am already married, because I fail to satisfy a condition specified by the procedure. Even if I'm not married, the circumstance of my utterance is inappropriate, and (B) is again violated, if I say 'I do' in the presence of someone who is not authorized to marry me.

(ii) Misexecutions. For the performative to succeed, the procedure must be executed by all participants correctly and completely. If the justice of the peace fails to sign the appropriate document, despite the performatives by the participants, the marriage fails to occur. My saying 'I bet' fails to come off when you don't take me up on the offer. Both of these would be instances of misexecution.

(B) Abuses. Even when a performative utterance comes off, it can still be unhappy in other ways. Often performatives carry with them a linguistic or conventional expectation that the speaker has certain thoughts or feelings, and in many cases performatives are designed for bringing about certain further actions. The utterance of 'I promise' carries with it the linguistic expectation that the speaker intends to keep the promise, and the performative is designed to bring about the promised action. An abuse occurs in these cases when the person fails to have the expected thoughts or feelings or when the course of action the convention is designed to bring about fails to be performed. Austin labeled the abuse of not having the expected thoughts or feelings an "insincerity." Thus, if I say 'I promise' while having no intention of keeping the promise, there is an abuse that is an insincerity. Even if I intended to keep the promise, there is an infelicity under the category of abuse if I ultimately break the

20. Austin, *How to Do Things with Words: The William Japnes Lectures Delivered at Harvard University in 1955,* J. O. Urmson, ed., Oxford: Clarendon Press, 1962, pp. 13–18.

promise. However, unlike a misfire, an abuse does not have the consequence that the performative failed to come off. Saying 'I promise' does bring about the promise whether or not the performative is abused in one form or another. It would indeed be convenient for promise breakers if they could claim that no promise was made because none was intended (or fulfilled).

Austin pointed out that this classification of infelicities will not capture all infelicities and that a particular infelicity might with equal justice be assigned to two different categories:

> Suppose that you are just about to name the ship, you have been appointed to name it, and you are just about to bang the bottle against the stem; but at that very moment some low type comes up, snatches the bottle out of your hand, breaks it on the stem, shouts out "I name this ship the *Generalissimo Stalin,*" and then for good measure kicks away the chocks. Well, we agree of course on several things. We agree that the ship certainly isn't now named the *Generalissimo Stalin,* and we agree that it's an infernal shame and so on and so forth. But we may not agree on how we should classify the particular infelicity in this case. We might say that here is a case of a perfectly legitimate and agreed procedure which, however, has been invoked in the wrong circumstances, namely by the wrong person, this low type instead of the person appointed to do it. But on the other hand we might . . . say that this is a case where the procedure has not as a whole been gone through correctly, because part of the procedure for naming a ship is that you should first of all get yourself appointed as the person to do the naming and that's what this fellow did not do.[21]

In this kind of case, it doesn't really matter whether one calls it a misinvocation or misexecution as long as reasons are given for classifying it that way.

Performative utterances begin to show the variety of illocutionary forces that utterances can have. Marrying, betting, apologizing, naming, and promising are examples of illocutionary forces. Doing these things is a very different thing from making a statement or expressing an opinion. While the First Amendment protection of freedom of speech clearly protects the free expression of opinion, it does not give a blanket protection of free speech that would allow one to say 'I do' when already married or 'I name the ship *Generalissimo Stalin*' in the circumstances recently imagined. Clearly, it is important to realize that speaking can be a way of acting, and performatives in general create a gray region between the expression of opinion that is protected by the freedom of speech and the performance of actions that may be legitimately limited by the government.

21. "Performative Utterances," pp. 226–27.

Our discussion of performative utterances may be summarized as follows:

Performative Utterances

(1) They aren't reports or descriptions and are neither true nor false.
(2) In uttering them one performs an action rather (or other) than stating something to be the case.
(3) They can be "unhappy" in one or more of the following ways:
  (A) *Misfires:* The act fails to come off.
    (i) *Misinvocation:* The procedure is absent for the person invoking it because (a) the procedure simply does not exist or (b) the person or circumstance doesn't satisfy the condition specified by the procedure.
    (ii) *Misexecution:* The procedure is not executed by all participants correctly and completely.
  (B) *Abuses:* Conventional expectations are frustrated.
    (i) *Insincerity:* The speaker lacks the conventionally expected thoughts or feelings.
    (ii) *Other abuses.*
(4) In the absence of misfires, the saying so makes it so.

EXERCISES—SECTION 6.4.1

In each of the following, identify and explain the infelicity involved as one of the two types of misinvocation, as misexecution, or as one of the two types of abuses:

1. An umpire (paid by the gambling mob) calls a pitch "Strike!" when he clearly sees that it is outside the strike zone.
2. Of a watch that doesn't belong to me I say to my child: "I make you a present of this watch."
3. Frank Fink secretly hates Mary Smart who has always outdone him in classes. When he learns that her mother has died, he says to Mary: "You have my full sympathy."
4. Unknown to Dolt and the chancellor, Dolt failed his last course and doesn't have enough units to graduate. He is at the graduation ceremony, and the chancellor says to Dolt: "By the authority invested in me by the Regents of the University of California, I confer upon you the degree of Bachelor of Arts."
5. At the graduation ceremony, the provost says to the parents of the graduating seniors: "By the authority invested in me by the Regents of the University of California, I confer upon you the title of Supporter of College Student Emeritus."
6. Riverboat Jack is out of money (or chips) in a poker game and says: "I raise you $200."
7. In all sincerity Joe College said on the phone to the alumni representative: "I pledge $50 for this year's Alumni Drive." But when the time comes, he doesn't pay.

8. To someone who has banged into my car, I say "I thank you. I needed that about as much as a hole in the head."
9. The department chair writes to a visiting speaker: "The department thanks you for your magnificent lecture last week." To the chair's surprise, it later turns out that the rest of the department found the lecture horrible and wanted, if anything, to have a letter of protest written.

6.4.2 Illocutionary Forces and Truth Assessments

Language would be nice and neat if speech acts could be divided into performative utterances that are neither true nor false but happy or unhappy, and the making of assertions, claims, and statements that are true or false. However, Austin was led to realize that nothing in life or language is quite that simple. The problems with the simple distinction are two in kind.

(1) If I say, "I warn you: there is a bull behind you," I have uttered a performative. Assuming that the performative is happy, to say 'I warn' is to warn. Furthermore, whether or not there is a bull behind you, the utterance cannot be said to be true or false. Of course the utterance could be unhappy in a number of ways: If I didn't look at the person (or in other ways make it clear to whom I was talking), we might consider it a misexecution, in that I did not correctly go through the procedure of warning. The statement could also be a misinvocation: If you are a matador and I shout out this statement to you at your moment of triumph, where you customarily turn your back on the bull, the circumstances for invoking the procedure of warning are inappropriate. Again, even if there is a bull behind you, if I falsely believed that there is no bull behind you (and only wanted to scare you), my performative would be unhappy by being an abuse (of the procedure).

But suppose I just said: "There is a bull behind you." Surely, in saying this I could be warning you, even though I didn't preface my utterance with 'I warn you:' the addition that would have made my utterance an explicit performative. My utterance 'There is a bull behind you' could still be happy or unhappy in the ways imagined. But the problem is that my utterance can now be said to be true or false as well. It now seems that an utterance can have a happiness/unhappiness dimension as well as the straightforward truth/falsity dimension that is due to the syntax and semantics of the expression. Even with the explicit performative, while 'I warn you: there is a bull behind you' perhaps cannot said to be true or false because the issuance of a warning cannot be true or false, nevertheless it falls under a dimension of criticism in which the truth or falsity of 'There is a bull behind you' is of central concern.[22]

22. Cf. Lectures V–VI, *How to Do Things with Words.*

(2) 'I state that he will come' appears to be as much a performative as 'I bet that he will come'. To say 'I state' is to state, and in saying 'I state' I am doing something. The utterance can be happy or unhappy in the same sorts of ways a performative can be. If I have not managed to specify the referent of 'he', we seem to have a misinvocation; that is, the circumstance or condition for making a statement is not satisfied. Again, if I meant to say, "I state: *she* will come," but by a slip of the tongue ended up saying, "I state: he will come," we seem to have a misexecution; that is, in a good sense I didn't state that she will come because due to the slip of the tongue I didn't correctly go through the procedure for making a statement. Finally, it is obvious enough that despite my utterance I may believe that he will not come, and we would have an abuse (of the procedure of making statements) that is an insincerity.

So far, 'I state: . . .' appears to be a performative. Is it also the case that 'I state: . . .' is neither true nor false? Certainly, the utterance 'he will come' is true or false. But the illocutionary force of 'I state: he will come' seems to be identical to that of 'He will come'. In saying 'he will come', I am making a statement, and the statement made appears to be identical to the one made in saying 'I state: he will come'. Thus it would seem that what is said by 'I state: he will come' can be true or false. It would be difficult to maintain that the performative utterance of making a statement can't result in a statement that is true or false.[23]

The upshot of both considerations would appear to be that for most utterances, there are two dimensions of criticism or assessment: (1) The happiness/unhappiness dimension that relates to the illocutionary force of the utterance. This is a level of meaning beyond syntax and semantics that we discussed in earlier sections of this chapter. (2) The dimension of criticism or assessment that is distinct from the utterance's happiness or unhappiness, and yet is prompted by the illocutionary force of the utterance and involves the assessment of truth or falsity. For some illocutionary forces such as asserting or stating, this second dimension of assessment will be the very statement made by the utterance. In other cases such as warnings, it will not be the statement made (because there is none) but one that is closely related and is relevant to the warning being correct or sound (e.g., is it true or false that there is a bull behind you?). In yet other cases, such as promising, the statement to be assessed for truth or falsity may be further removed and relate to the prudence or appropriateness of making such a promise. Because this level of assessment involves such a variety, let us call these assessments T-assessments of the utterance, understanding that such assessments are (a) truth assessments of (b) statements closely tied to the utterance's illocutionary force, and yet (c) are independent of assessments of the utterance's felicity.

23. Cf. Lecture XI, *How to Do Things with Words.*

Given this much, the method for analyzing speech acts may be specified as follows:

> Method for Analyzing Speech Acts
>
> *Step A:* Identify the illocutionary force or forces of the utterance.
> *Step B:* Identify the statements that are pertinent to the T-assessment of the utterance.

In performing Step B, care must be taken not to include the particle(s) that signal the illocutionary force as part of the statement to be T-assessed. For example, it would be an error to suppose that even if he doesn't come, what I stated in saying 'I state: he will come' is true insofar as it can't be denied that I did state that he will come. In saying 'I state: he will come', what I stated and what is to be T-assessed is 'He will come', because 'I state' is playing the role of indicating the illocutionary force of stating.

To facilitate this kind of an analysis we give part of Austin's listing of illocutionary forces.[24] These forces may be conveyed with or without particles like 'I warn' that would be needed for explicit performatives. Along with the listing of the various illocutionary forces, we make suggestions concerning statements that would be relevant for the corresponding T-assessments. We follow Austin's grouping of the illocutionary forces into five categories, and present the categories roughly in the order of increasing distance between the utterance and the statements to be T-assessed.

(I) Stating, affirming, denying, describing, reporting, arguing, concluding, and so on. These forces make some claim or give an exposition of a claim (Austin calls them EXPOSITIVES). The relevant statements to be T-assessed are the statements or claims that are stated, reported, argued, and so on. In the case of arguing and concluding, one should also T-assess whether the conclusion is correctly or legitimately drawn.

(II) Assessing, estimating, grading (e.g., a restaurant to be a three-star restaurant), and ruling (e.g., the judge might rule in favor of the defense). These forces involve some sort of a verdict (Austin calls them VERDICTIVES). These things are typically done on the basis of some evidence or reasons, and the relevant T-assessments are concerned with whether the estimate was accurate, the ruling or grading was correct, good, sound, or legitimate. In some cases of grading or ruling, grading it or ruling it makes it so, for example, if the grader rates the restaurant as a three-star restaurant, it is a three-star restaurant; but even in these cases, one can still T-assess the grading to involve good or bad judgment.

24. Cf. Lectures XI–XII, *How to Do Things with Words.*

(III) Naming (a person or ship), ordering, bequeathing, protesting, warning, urging, advising, and so on. These forces involve a person exercising a position or special relation to a person or thing (Austin calls them EXERCITIVES). For example, one must be appointed to name, have authority to order, and possess the object to bequeath it. Warning tends to require a position of superior knowledge, protesting seems to involve an inferior position in some pecking order or another, and advising may require a position of superior knowledge and/or a special relation to the one being advised. What distinguishes these illocutionary forces from those listed in (II) is that while advising, protesting, and warning are typically done on some basis of reason or evidence, they aren't verdicts, findings, or assessments of (or based on) the evidence. With advising, protesting, warning, and so on, the T-assessments would be concerned with whether there is a sound basis for the advice, protest, or warning. With naming, ordering, and bequeathing, the statements to be T-assessed seem to be further removed and might involve claims as to whether or not it was well advised.

(IV) Apologizing, thanking, sympathizing, criticizing, commending, deploring, and so on. These relate in one form or other to our interactions with one another (and are called BEHABITIVES by Austin, perhaps from "behavior" and an obsolete sense of "habitude" meaning manner of being with relation to something else). These illocutionary forces typically require certain appropriate feelings or thoughts if they are to be happy. Yet the apology given in saying "I am sorry" may only require that one feels or thinks that feeling sorry would be fitting on the occasion; it may not actually require feeling sorry or repentant. T-assessments may be expected to be concerned with whether the criticism or commendation was merited or deserved, and whether the apology or sympathy was appropriate or in order.

(V) Promising, contracting, vowing, betting, consenting, and so on. These acts typically commit one to some further acts (and are called COMMISSIVES by Austin). That is, one is committed to such things as keeping the promise, collecting on the bet, allowing an act previously consented to, living in a condition consented to (in the marriage vow). In these cases, the T-assessments might be concerned with whether the promising, betting, or consenting was ill advised or not.

The variety of illocutionary forces we have listed and the associated statements to be T-assessed are summarized in Table 6.1.

There are a number of actions we perform in or by using words that are not covered by Austin's listing of illocutionary forces. In locating illocutionary forces, a guiding principle for Austin was that there be some illocutionary particle that could be used to utter an explicit performative with that force. Thus, for example, while one can insinuate that someone isn't too bright, there is no performative utterance like "I (hereby) insinuate: he is not so bright." Thus, insinuating is not counted as an illocu-

TABLE 6.1.

Austin's Term	*Illocutionary Forces*	*Object of T-Assessment*
Expositives	Stating, affirming, denying, describing, reporting, etc.	Claim stated, affirmed, etc.
	Arguing, concluding, etc.	Claim argued or concluded, and legitimacy of the argument.
Verdictives	Assessing, grading, ruling, estimating, etc.	The assessment, grade, etc. is accurate, good, sound, or legitimate.
Exercitives	Protesting, warning, urging, advising, etc.	The basis for the protest, warning, etc. is sound.
	Naming, ordering, bequeathing, etc.	The naming, ordering, etc. is well or ill-advised.
Behabitives	Criticizing, commending, deploring, etc.	The criticism, commendation, etc. is deserved.
	Apologizing, thanking, sympathizing, etc.	The apology, appreciation, etc. is appropriate.
Commissives	Promising, contracting, vowing, betting, consenting, etc.	The promise, the bet, etc. is well or ill advised.

tionary force by Austin. Somewhat similar remarks apply to expressing or evincing feelings or emotions. One can express one's disgust by saying, "He is disgusting." But there doesn't seem to be a performative like "I express my feelings: I find him disgusting," or "Here are my feelings: He is disgusting." If anything, these utterances seem to be reports of one's feelings or assessments of his nature. It would seem best to leave illocutionary forces along the lines suggested by Austin, and to try to account for these features at other levels of meaning.

Given this background, let us consider an example with several parts:

> (1) The base runner slides into third base, and the umpire yells out: "You are out." (2) The runner stands up and yells back to the umpire, 'I wasn't out!', at which time (3) the umpire tells the runner: "I promise you, I'll kick you out of the game if you yell at me again." The third-base coach comes over to the runner and says, "(4) The ump said you are out. (5) So, you are out," and (6) adds, "Look, I'll buy you a steak dinner if you'll shut up." (7) With a chagrined look, the runner mumbles to the umpire: "I'm sorry I yelled at you." (8) Upon returning to the bench, the manager says to the runner, "I'm sorry that he called you out," and (9) adds, "But I'm pretty sure that you were out." (10) The runner replies, "Well, *I* at least still think I was safe."

Adding additional expository comments as they seem to be called for, the analysis of the speech acts involved in this example might proceed as follows:

(1) Illocutionary Force: A call or ruling (that he is out, and his saying so makes it so).

Statement to be T-assessed: this was a good or sound or correct call—'The runner was tagged prior to his touching the base'.

(2) Illocutionary Forces: Protesting the call (that he was out) and making an assessment (that he wasn't out, although this assessment has no official standing).

Statement to be T-assessed: The statement on which the protest and the assessment is based—'The runner wasn't tagged prior to touching the base'.

The runner is obviously not denying that he was called out. The protest is not to be judged ill-founded just because he is out insofar as the umpire called him out. Thus, the relevant statement to be T-assessed is that he wasn't tagged before he reached the base.

(3) Illocutionary Force: threatening and thereby committing himself (to throwing him out if the runner yells again).

Statement to be T-assessed: statements concerning whether the threat was well advised—'What the runner said deserved the threat as a response', 'He was well advised to commit himself to throwing the runner out if he yelled again', and so on.

The umpire's utterance, "I promise you, I'll kick you out of the game if you yell at me again," is an aberrant utterance. While the use of 'promise' indicates the illocutionary force of promising, part of the conventions surrounding promising is that what is promised must be at least thought to be advantageous to the one who is promised. Thus, seen as an attempted act of promising, it misfires by being a misinvocation. In general, we might say that an utterance is ILLOCUTIONARILY DEVIANT

if the context or the rest of the utterance ensures a misfire as long as the utterance is taken to have the illocutionary force it ostensibly has.

Thus, (3) is illocutionarily deviant: the ostensible illocutionary force is that of promising and yet what is promised ensures a misfire. However, as with other deviant utterances we have considered, the Principle of Charity enjoins us to make some sense of what is said if that is at all possible. Applying this principle, it's fairly obvious that we should construe the utterance's illocutionary force as that of making a threat. This, then, leads to the analysis given for utterance (3).

(4) Illocutionary Force: Reminding (the runner what the ump said).

Statement to be T-assessed: 'The ump called him out'.

Reminding has the illocutionary force that is in the same ballpark as stating, describing, etc.

(5) Illocutionary Force: Concluding (that he is out).

Statement to be T-assessed: 'He is out' and the inference of this from the umpire having called him out.

(6) Illocutionary Force: Promising (to buy him a steak dinner if . . .).

Statements to be T-assessed: Statements relating to whether the coach was well advised to make this promise, and this will involve statements like 'It is likely to calm down the runner', 'The coach can afford to stake the runner to a steak dinner', and so on.

(7) Illocutionary Force: Apologizing (for having yelled at the ump).

Statement to be T-assessed: 'An apology was appropriate (called for)'.

Given the chagrined look and the mumbling, it's doubtful that this is a report of his inner feeling of repentance. Furthermore, the apology need not be insincere as long as the runner at least felt that an apology or a feeling of repentance would be fitting.

(8) Illocutionary Force: Sympathizing (for the runner having been called out).

Statement to be T-assessed: Statements relating to whether or not the sympathy was merited or called for—'It was a close call', 'It was a good attempt to reach third base', and so on.

(9) Illocutionary Force: Making a statement or assessment that the runner was out.

Statement to be T-assessed: 'The runner was tagged before he reached third base'.

'I believe', 'I'm pretty sure', and so on, typically have the illocutionary force of making a statement. In contrast to 'I'm sure that' and a definite assertion, the use of 'I believe' and similar devices signals the illocutionary force of somewhat qualifying the statement or assessment; that is, in making the statement one isn't fully vouching for the statement made. It would be a misreading to take 'I'm pretty sure that . . . ' as a report or statement of his inner conviction. Thus, whether it's a statement or an assessment, the relevant T-assessment centers around 'You were out' rather than 'I'm pretty sure that you were out', and because the umpire calling him out is not at issue, the relevant T-assessment concerns the grounds for the umpire's call.

(10) Illocutionary Force: Reporting (on his own assessment of the matter) and secondarily stating (that he was safe).

Statements to be T-assessed: 'The runner assesses that he wasn't tagged before he reached the base' and secondarily, 'He wasn't tagged before he reached the base'.

Given the insertion of 'I at least' with a stress on the 'I', the runner's utterance 'Well, *I* at least still think I was safe' might be taken as a report of his own assessment and the relevant T-assessment would be whether or not he assess that he was safe.[25] Of course the utterance seems to be doing double duty of making an assessment as well, and in that case, as in (1), (2), and (9), a relevant T-assessment involves the grounds for that assessment.

Such then is an analysis of the interplay between the illocutionary forces and the T-assessments of the truth or falsity of related sentences in a speech act situation. Having isolated in a speech act situation the statements or sentences that are the appropriate targets for truth assessment, we revert to statements that are true or false as the primary focus of our interest. However, before doing so, we discuss a fallacy that is loosely connected to an extended notion of illocutionary force.

Fallacy of an Appeal to the Imagination. While we have concentrated on the illocutionary force of individual utterances, entire passages or stretches of speaking, as well as special contexts, can signal that something special is being done with one's sentences or utterances. As a simple example, consider the following political cartoon by Paul Conrad at the time when Nixon appointed Gerald Ford as vice-president: It showed Nixon next to a Ford automobile along with the caption, "Get-Away Car." Because it is a cartoon, Conrad was doing something less than stating that Nixon appointed Ford so that he could be pardoned if things should turn out badly for him. In an extended sense of illocutionary force, the illocutionary force of a political cartoon protects the author from having to substantiate the suggestion or being otherwise responsible for its truth or falsity.

Similarly, we might think of an extended piece of writing as having the illocutionary force of a satire. An example might be the following *Los Angeles Times* column by David Broder during the Nixon era (which we shall discuss in greater detail in Section 6.6):

> [T]he guardians told him: It's all right now, Mr. President, those nasty men won't bother you any more. You can go back to drawing peace plans on your yellow pads. . . . They told the President: You've turned it around, sir. The polls show you've surged from 27% support all the way up to 29% . . . You know how important momentum is, Mr. President; just like football.

The column as a whole makes it clear that the illocutionary force of the individual sentences is not that of reporting or opining; rather the column as a whole should be taken to have something like the illocutionary force of presenting a satire. What makes this "illocutionary force" evident is that many of the statements are humorous and incredible as literal reports of what happened.

25. In this kind of case in which we have a first-person report or statement about how it is with the first person, the relevant T-assessment comes very close to the assessment of sincerity. But in principle it might be possible that the runner believes that he assesses himself to be safe (and hence his report is sincere), and yet (in his heart) he doesn't really assess himself to be safe (so that the T-assessment of 'he assesses himself to be safe' is false).

Of course, talking about illocutionary forces of political cartoons and satires departs from Austin's account in two ways: (a) There seems to be no illocutionary force indicator like 'I hereby make a political joke' or 'I satirize' that converts the utterance into a performative. (b) Illocutionary forces in the strict sense were engendered by individual utterances rather than by stretches of talk or special contexts. Still, recognizing that an entire book or column is a satire, or that a sentence occurs within the context of a political cartoon, has a decisive bearing on one's understanding of what is being done with the use of those words.

Allowing ourselves this loose use of 'illocutionary force', *the illocutionary force of a political cartoon or a piece of satire has the effect of prefacing the entire passage with the sign "This is not (or may not be) entirely true." An effect is of course that we turn off our critical-thinking faculties; but the result can be that we ultimately accept a lot of the suggestions (subconsciously). Being so persuaded might be called the* FALLACY OF AN APPEAL TO THE IMAGINATION. This fallacy is clearly a Fallacy of Relevance and may be represented as:

> Appeal to the Imagination
>
> C is suggested or stated in the story* S ⇝ C.
>
> *Explain why S is a story.

By 'explain why S is a story', we mean that an indication should be given of why S should be taken as a story or a fiction rather than a straight report of what is the case. Thus, the Conrad cartoon would be analyzed as:

Appeal to the Imagination: The Conrad cartoon suggests that Nixon appointed Ford to get a pardon if he needed one ⇝ Nixon appointed Ford to get a pardon if he needed one.
A political cartoon comes with an "illocutionary force" of 'This is a story'.

Similarly, the Broder column would be analyzed as:

Appeal to the Imagination: The Broder column suggests that Nixon is a childlike figure who needs to be pampered by guardians ⇝ Nixon is a childlike figure who needs to be pampered by guardians.
What is "reported" is too incredible to be intended or taken as a report of what actually transpired.

We could have listed this fallacy in Chapter 2 as one kind of the Fallacy of Appealing to Emotions. However, clarity seems to be shed on how this fallacy works by thinking of it in terms of "illocutionary forces" of entire passages or special contexts. It goes without saying that many TV advertisements have an illocutionary force that in effect prefaces the advertisement with something like: "This, of course, isn't strictly or really true."

EXERCISES—SECTION 6.4.2

1. In doing this exercise, take statements like 'The paper is a good one' and 'The paper is poor' to be statements that can be T-assessed and form the basis of assessments like 'This is a B paper' and 'This is a D or F paper'.

   For each of the following numbered utterances, state the illocutionary force or forces involved and indicate the relevant statement(s) to be T-assessed.

   Upon being asked about what grade he would be given on the term paper, (1) the professor says, "It's a C paper." (2) The student replies: "Aw come on prof! This is at least a B paper." (3) The professor replies, "As it is I gave you a pretty generous grade." (4) He says, "You misquoted Plato, got his points wrong, didn't provide a single argument for your views, and many of the sentences were ungrammatical and unintelligible," and (5) adds: "That's surely enough to make it a poor paper." (6) The student replies, "I spent a lot of time on that paper," and adds, (7) "The effort alone should make it a B." (8) The professor replies: "That you spent a lot of time on it is indeed commendable." A long conversation follows on whether effort counts toward a grade, the value of expressing opinions, the point of writing philosophy papers, and so on. Finally, (9) the professor says: "You really should try to take in the criticism instead of arguing with the grade," and adds: (10) "Look, I'll give you a chance to rewrite the paper, and (11) give you a higher grade for the term paper if your rewrite is better."

*2. G. E. Moore first pointed out the paradoxical nature of utterances like the following two:

   M1: Todd isn't there but I believe that Todd is there.
   M2: Todd is there but I don't believe that Todd is there.

   Something is clearly wrong with these utterances, and yet at the level of syntax or semantics it seems doubtful that there is any contradiction. Certainly replacing 'I' by 'Dauer' produces a perfectly satisfactory statement that may be true, and the semantic rule for determining the reference of 'I' seems unlikely to account for the aberrance [the way in which it along with the rule for 'here' might account for 'I'm not here' being deviant].

   (a) Explain how M1 and M2 are both illocutionarily deviant.

   [*Hints:* (a) The act of making a statement is performed correctly only if one doesn't make and withdraw (or refuse to make) the same statement in the same context. (b) The illocutionary force of 'I don't believe . . . ' might be taken as refusing to state that. . . .]

   (b) Assume that the speaker doesn't believe both that Todd is there and that Todd isn't there. Show that if one took 'I believe' and 'I don't believe' as reports of how it is with the speaker, M1 as well as M2, has the feature of being felicitous only if it is false.

(c) Which of the two accounts given (i.e., a or b) better explains what's wrong with uttering M1 and M2?
(*Hint:* Consider what's wrong with saying, "I don't feel that an apology is even called for but to make everyone happy I'll say it: I apologize.")

3. In each of the following the Fallacy of an Appeal to the Imagination would be committed if, on the basis of what was said (done or drawn), one ultimately accepted the claim one is tacitly being asked to accept. Analyze the fallacy that would be committed.
   (a) [An old TV advertisement for a hair cream:] To burlesque-house type music, a gorgeous woman slowly comes out of a tube of Brylcream, and starts caressing an ordinary-looking man. A male announcer's voice says: "Rumor has it that Brylcream contains some magical new ingredient. But, look men, nothing could be further from the truth. . . . As far as any fringe benefits . . . well." By this time the woman is kissing the man; she then looks up and says in a sultry voice: "Are you man enough to try it?"
   (b) [Background: In 1985 Rev. Jerry Falwell, the leader of the Moral Majority, visited South Africa; he stated that he too (like Bishop Tutu) was a man of the cloth and went on to say complimentary things about the South African government.] The Conrad cartoon with the caption "I too am a man of the cloth" shows Falwell wearing a Klu Klux Klan robe.

6.5 The Level of Pragmatics

Syntax and semantics give us the first two levels of meaning, and the level of illocutionary force gives us the level of meaning having to do with what is done in saying something as well as what are the appropriate statements or sentences to assess as true or false. However, what is conveyed in or by saying something is not limited to what is conveyed by the syntax and semantics involved and the kind of illocutionary force the utterance has. "Pragmatics" has often been used for the level of meaning that accounts for what is conveyed by something other than syntax and semantics. Discussion of illocutionary forces is sometimes included under pragmatics, but I have separated it from pragmatics because under the heading of pragmatics I shall be dealing with the kinds of information or suggestions conveyed rather than the kinds of acts performed.

This additional level of meaning can be easily seen from an example or two: If she says, "There is a peach or a plum in the refrigerator," she conveys that she doesn't know whether it is a peach or a plum that is in the refrigerator. If a professor's letter of recommendation for a student is limited to the single sentence "Mr. Jones has excellent penmanship," the professor conveys that he doesn't think very well of the student's abilities. In these cases, there seems to be no hope of accounting for what is conveyed in terms of the syntax, semantics, or the illocutionary forces of the utterances. How then is this level of conveyed meaning to be explained? How are the obvious suggestions or implications to be accounted for?

The most authoritative research in pragmatics has been done by Paul Grice, and in what follows, we shall give a very sketchy account of the theory he has developed, so that the reader can get basic exposure to the level of pragmatics.[26] As with Austin, strict fidelity to Grice's view is not being claimed.

Grice's theory centers on the idea that with other things being equal, speakers should be expected to observe the COOPERATIVE PRINCIPLE: *Make your conversational contribution in the manner required, at the stage at which it occurs, by the accepted purpose or direction of the conversational exchange in which you are engaged.*[27] What we have called the Principle of Charity (a serious use of words by an adult speaker conveys something informative and appropriate) can be seen as the hearer's presumption that the speaker is observing the Cooperative Principle (to whatever extent possible under the circumstance). At least roughly, we can then identify the level of meaning conveyed by PRAGMATICS, that is, the pragmatically or conversationally implicated, as follows:

> *In saying, 'p', one conversationally or pragmatically implicates 'q' if the Principle of Charity (or the presumption that the speaker is observing the Cooperative Principle) requires that in uttering 'p' the speaker thinks that q.*[28]

Substance is added to this general account of pragmatic implications or implicatures[29] by Grice's specification of specific maxims of conversation that must be followed (to the maximal extent possible in a given circumstance) if one is to be observing the Cooperative Principle. Conversational implicatures are typically derived by showing that unless the speaker things that q, such and such a maxim would be violated by his

26. The material of this section is largely derived from Paul Grice, "Logic and Conversation," in *Syntax and Semantics,* Vol. 3, *Speech Acts,* Peter Cole and Jerry L. Morgan, eds., New York: Academic Press, 1975, pp. 41–58. Some of the material is drawn from (my imperfect memories of Grice's) lectures and seminars.
27. Ibid., p. 45.
28. Grice adds two other conditions: (a) Nothing in the circumstance prevents one from presuming the speaker to be observing the Cooperative Principle. (b) The speaker thinks (and would expect the hearer to think that the speaker thinks) that it's within the hearer's competence to grasp that the speaker's thinking that q is required for his utterance of 'p' to observe the Cooperative Principle. While additional requirements like these seem to be needed, we simplify our discussion because these requirements can be assumed to be satisfied in normal circumstances.
29. Hereafter I shall use Grice's term 'implicature' and its verbal form 'implicate', whose meanings are close to the ordinary meanings of 'implication' and 'imply'. In logical and philosophical circles 'implication' is typically restricted to logical or deductive implication. 'Implicature' is intended to be a broader term covering logical implications as well as other implications (in the ordinary sense). Conversational implicatures are implicatures that are not implications in the logician's sense.

or her utterance of 'p'. While admitting that I(B) below may be disputable, the main specific maxims suggested by Grice are the following:

Maxims of Conversation

I. The Maxims of Quantity:
   (A) Make your contribution as informative as is required (for the purpose of the exchange).
   (B) Do not make your contribution more informative than is required.

II. The Maxim of Quality: Try to make contributions that are true. Two specific maxims under this heading are:
   (A) Do not say what you believe to be false.
   (B) Do not say something for which you lack adequate evidence.

III. The Maxim of Relation: Be relevant.

IV. The Maxim of Manner: Be perspicuous.

The ways in which these maxims engender conversational implicatures is divided by Grice into three categories, and we might indicate each of these three ways:

(i) Implicatures engendered by utterances in which no maxim is even apparently violated. Perhaps the most obvious example is that in making any statement one conversationally implicates that one believes that the statement is true. Unless the person takes himself to believe that the statement he is making is true, he would be violating the Maxim of Quality that one should try to make conversational contributions that are true. Hence, the presumption that the speaker is observing the Cooperative Principle engenders the conversational implicature that he believes what he is saying. Another obvious example would be:

Guest: I would really like to have some beer.
Host: The kitchen is through that hallway.

The host conversationally implicates that there is some beer in the kitchen because, unless he thought this, he would be violating the Maxim of Relation to be relevant. Because of the same maxim, he also implicates that the guest will have to get the beer himself.

At least in some cases, the expression of one's feelings might be understood in terms of conversational implicatures of this kind. Suppose Julie says, "He is disgusting." In this kind of case it would seem that the speaker has inadequate evidence or basis for making the claim unless the speaker personally found him to be disgusting. The testimony of even the most reliable witness would seem to be insufficient unless the claim is watered down to 'He is said to be disgusting' or the testimony consisted of a straight description of what the person did and one's reaction as the hearer was to find a person doing such a thing disgusting. If this is right, Julie is observing the Maxim of Quality (Have sufficient evidence!) only if she personally found him to be disgusting. Thus, the presumption that she is observing the Cooperative Principle engenders the conversational implicature that she found him disgusting. Because the idea of expressing a feeling (as opposed to reporting or stating one's feelings) is that one's feelings are conveyed without actually stating them, it would seem that in saying 'He is disgusting' Julie is expressing disgust; that is, what she said doesn't literally say anything about her feelings and yet it is pragmatically conveyed that she was disgusted by him.

(ii) Implicatures that are engendered because (although a maxim is violated) the violation is to be explained by the supposition of a clash with another maxim (so that the implicature is a result of the speaker being taken to be observing the Cooperative Principle to the greatest degree possible in the circumstance). The first example of this section (in which the woman says that there is a peach or a plum in the refrigerator) is an example of this type if, as is plausible, one takes the Cooperative Principle to give priority to the Maxim of Quality (Have sufficient evidence!) over the Maxim of Quantity (Be appropriately informative!). The utterance that there is a peach or plum fails to be as informative as is required (or desired). Saying that there is a peach or that there is a plum would have better satisfied the Maxim of Quantity. Thus, if we are to take the speaker to be observing the Cooperative Principle to the greatest extent possible, we must presume that she opted for the less informative statement because the more informative statement would have violated the Maxim of Quality. Therefore, it is conversationally implicated that the speaker has insufficient grounds for saying that it is a plum or that it is a peach; that is, there is a conversational implicature that she doesn't know whether it is a plum or a peach.

(iii) Implicatures engendered by blatantly violating a maxim at the level of what is explicitly said (despite the absence of a clash with another maxim). These implicatures differ from the prior two types in two respects: (a) At the level of what is explicitly said, the utterance indeed violates the Cooperative Principle of abiding with the maxims to the greatest extent possible. (b) The presumption that the speaker is abiding with the Cooperative Principle at the level of total impact, or the hearer's adherence to the Principle of Charity, indicates that something informative and appropriate is being conveyed. However, unlike type (i) and type (ii) conversational implicatures, the maxims themselves will not typically indicate what is being implicated: some additional factor or aid is normally required to account for what is implicated. Thus, covered under these implicatures are all the deviant utterances considered earlier in the chapter. At the level of what is explicitly said, the Maxim of Manner (Be perspicuous!) is violated by grammatically deviant utterances, and the Principle of Charity (or the presumption that the speaker is observing the Cooperative Principle) leads us to seek what may be conveyed. In such a

case, as we saw, methods like the Method of Nondeviant Substitutions can aid us in determining what is conveyed. Again, at the explicit level, a semantically deviant utterance (like 'That adult is a child') violates the Maxim of Quality that one should try to avoid making false statements. In these cases, we found that the Method of Paraphrase is often a useful aid in determining what is conveyed.

To unify the other cases, let us say that an utterance is PRAGMATICALLY DEVIANT if:

> *at the explicit level it violates the Cooperative Principle and the utterance is not grammatically, semantically, or illocutionarily deviant.*

A simple example might be 'Boys will be boys'. At the explicit level this is an uninformative tautology, and as such its utterance violates the Cooperative Principle by violating the Maxim of Quantity to be suitably informative. The Principle of Charity enjoins the hearer to seek some appropriate contribution, and the Method of Paraphrase may help in determining what is conveyed: Paraphrasing the second occurrence of 'boys' with descriptions that are obviously, plausibly, or stereotypically true of boys, we would have it conveyed that boys (typically) act in such and such ways. This result, along with the Maxim of Manner (Be relevant!) and the context (which isolates a particular boy), leads to the presumption that the speaker intends the generalization to apply to the boy in question. Finally, given the concerns of the context, we would end up with conversational implicatures like 'It's not surprising that this boy will do the sort of things he did' and 'Don't worry, there is nothing abnormal about your boy doing such a thing'.

Consider now the professor's letter of recommendation that was limited to praising the student's penmanship. Clearly, the Maxim of Quantity to be suitably informative is violated, and there can't be a clash with the Maxim of Quality because the professor presumably has enough evidence to say more. In this kind of case the conversational implicature is isolated by adopting the Principle of Charity and identifying the most plausible explanation of why the speaker made the deviant utterance. By presuming that the professor is observing the Cooperative Principle, we take it that the professor is trying to convey something relevant about the student's abilities. The most plausible explanation of the deviant utterance is that the professor didn't want to say explicitly anything negative about the student. Putting these two points together we have it that the professor is conveying that he or she can't find anything positive to say about the student beyond his penmanship. Thus, the professor has conversationally implicated that the student isn't very good, and we might say that through this pragmatic implicature the professor has insinuated that the student is not very good.

A couple of additional examples from Grice may be sufficient to indicate the nature of conversational implicatures brought about by pragmatically deviant utterances. The first deviant utterance violates the

Maxim of Relation (Be relevant!) and the second violates the Maxim of Manner (Be perspicuous!):

> At a genteel tea party, A says *Mrs. X is an old bag.* There is a moment of appalled silence, and then B says, *The weather has been quite delightful this summer, hasn't it?* B has blatantly refused to make what HE says relevant to A's preceding remark. He thereby implicates that A's remark should not be discussed, and perhaps more specifically, that A has committed a social gaffe.[30]
>
> Compare the remarks:
>
> (a) *Miss X sang "Home Sweet Home."*
> (b) *Miss X produced a series of sounds that corresponded closely with the score of "Home Sweet Home."*
>
> Suppose that a reviewer has chosen to utter (b) rather than (a). . . . Why has he selected that rigmarole in place of the concise and nearly synonymous *sang?* Presumably, to indicate some striking difference between Miss X's performance and those to which the word *singing* is usually applied. The most obvious supposition is that Miss X's performance suffered from some hideous defect.[31]

In the first example, the best explanation of the deviant utterance of B is that B thought the remark of A shouldn't be discussed. In the second example, we might see something like the previously discussed Method of Alternatives at work in discerning what was implicated.

Adopting the Principle of Charity and taking the speaker to be following the Cooperative Principle, the method for determining what is conversationally implicated may be summarized as follows:

Determining Conversational Implicatures

(1) When no maxim appears to be violated, an utterance conversationally implicates that each maxim is followed, and whatever it takes to follow them in the context.
(2) If an apparent violation of a Maxim M1 (often the Maxim of Quantity) is plausibly explained as being required to abide by a more stringent maxim M2 (typically the Maxim of Quality), an utterance conversationally implicates that the speaker can abide by M2 only by violating M1, and whatever this involves in the context.
(3) If the utterance is blatantly deviant by violating a maxim in the absence of a need to abide by a more stringent conflicting maxim, what the utterance conversationally implicates is determined by using the Principle of Charity and (a) applying one of the methods for analyzing deviant utterances or (b) identifying what is the most plausible explanation of why the deviant utterance is made.

30. Ibid., p. 54.
31. Ibid., pp. 55–56.

We conclude with some additional discussion of conversational implicatures that may be skipped by readers who are in a hurry.

★ ★ ★ ★

An essential feature of conversational implicatures or what is conveyed at the level of pragmatics is that what is so conveyed need not be true for the truth of what is explicitly asserted or stated. If this were not so, the implicature would have to be construed as what is conveyed at the level of semantics because semantics deals with rules that determine the truth and falsity of sentences. Grice has suggested two tests for showing that what is conveyed is at the level of pragmatics rather than syntax or semantics. Although what is conversationally implicated will not typically satisfy both tests, they will typically satisfy one or the other. Furthermore, the tests make it evident that if what is implicated does satisfy one or the other of these two tests, the implicature is conveyed by the level of pragmatics rather than the level of syntax or semantics. The two tests are:

(1) Cancellability. Can one add the denial of the conversational implicature to the utterance without creating a contradiction or aberrance? If so, what was conversationally implicated is not needed for the truth of what was explicitly stated in the original utterance; as such, the implicature arises not from the level of semantics but from the level of pragmatics. Applied to one of our earlier examples, it would seem that the woman could say: "There is a plum or peach in the refrigerator. I know which fruit it is but I'm not going to tell you so that it will be a surprise for you." There is nothing deviant about this statement and this shows that what was implicated (namely, her ignorance as to whether it's a peach or a plum) is not needed for the truth of what was explicitly stated (namely, there is a plum or a peach in the refrigerator). The implicature must therefore have been at the level of pragmatics rather than semantics. Similarly, there is nothing linguistically deviant about the professor saying, "He has excellent penmanship. I don't mean to imply that he isn't good in other respects. In fact, he is outstanding in every respect." As Grice has stated, one may wonder why the professor places such high value on penmanship, but there is nothing linguistically deviant about this cancellation of the conversational implicature.

(2) Detachability. Is there another way of making the same assertion or statement that doesn't have the implicature? If so, then the truth of the implicature was not required for the truth of what was stated, and hence the implicature was not conveyed by the level of semantics. If someone says, "He will come home today," the implicature that the speaker has sufficient evidence for the claim does not seem cancellable. That is, there is something linguistically odd or deviant about 'He will come home today but I have no reason for thinking that he will'. However, 'I guess (or suspect) that he will come home today' might be seen as a qualified way of making the same assertion, and this utterance doesn't have the implicature that I have sufficient reasons for thinking that he will come home. Hence the implicature of the original statement is detachable and thereby shown to be conveyed at the level of pragmatics.

Let us conclude the topic of pragmatics by touching on a topic we left unresolved in Chapter 3. It was there that we said it was not clear whether the '⊃' meant the same thing as 'if . . . , then'. The principal reason for thinking that it doesn't is that the ordinary use of the conditional seems to carry with it the suggestion that there is some sort of a ground-to-consequence relationship between the antecedent and the consequent that would preclude it from being treated as a truth functional connective. Thus, one might argue that the statement 'He'll be happy if she comes' isn't true if all we have is that she does come and that he is happy, because the truth of the conditional requires that her coming *made* him happy. If this is right, even if the component clauses are both true, the compound would have different truth values depending on the existence or nonexistence of this ground-to-consequence relation; but this would mean that the 'if . . . , then' is not being used in the truth functional sense in 'He'll be happy if she comes'. It must be admitted that it is not entirely clear whether or not this line of thought is correct, that is, whether or not it is part of the semantic meaning of the typical use of 'if . . . , then' that there be a ground-to-consequence relation. Whatever the correct answer to this issue may be, Grice has been able to show that any use of '⊃' will convey the presence of a ground-to-consequence relation between the antecedent and the consequent at the level of pragmatics. At least in a simplified and schematic form that leaves many details to be filled in, the argument runs as follows:

Anyone uttering a statement of the form 'p ⊃ q' conversationally implicates that he doesn't know 'p' to be true: For, if such a person did know 'p' to be true, he could satisfy both the Maxim of Quality (Have sufficient evidence!) and the Maxim of Quantity (Be appropriately informative!) by making the more informative statement 'q', which is deductively inferable from 'p' and 'p ⊃ q'. Thus, because he stated 'p ⊃ q' rather than 'q', this conversationally implicates that he doesn't know 'p' to be true. He also conversationally implicates that he doesn't know 'p' to be false because he would seem to be violating the Maxim of Relation (Be relevant!) if he already knows 'p' to be false. (Why say, 'It's raining ⊃ I'll be sad' if I know it isn't raining?) The speaker also implicates that he doesn't know 'q' to be false because if this were known, one should make the more informative statement '−p' by the Maxim of Quantity or shouldn't assert 'p ⊃ q' by the Maxim of Relation concerning relevance. If the speaker knows 'q' to be true, one should assert the stronger 'q' rather than the weaker 'p ⊃ q'. Thus, in asserting 'p ⊃ q', one implicates that one doesn't know the truth values of the components.

But by the Maxim of Quality one also implicates that there is sufficient evidence or reason for thinking 'p ⊃ q' to be true. Because the speaker has already implicated that his reason for thinking that 'p ⊃ q' isn't his knowing the truth values of 'p' or 'q', his only reason for thinking that 'p ⊃ q' must be his thinking that there is a ground-to-consequence relation between 'p' and 'q'. Because his thinking this is required for taking him to be observing the Maxim of Quality, the utterance of 'p ⊃ q' brings about the conversational implicature that there is a ground-to-consequence relation between 'p' and 'q'. Thus, stating 'p ⊃ q' conveys the presence of a ground-to-consequence relation between the antecedent and the consequent at the level of pragmatics. This alone doesn't show that 'p ⊃ q' means 'if p, then q'; however, it does show that whatever differences there may be between the two expressions, 'p ⊃ q' manages to convey all that 'if p, then q' does once the level of pragmatics is taken into account.

Grice actually continues the argument to suggest that 'p ⊃ q' does mean the same as 'if p, then q', and that the use of the 'if . . . , then' locution has a general conversational implicature of a ground-to-consequence relation between the antecedent and the consequent. Such generalized implicatures differ from the examples we have previously considered that depend on the use of expressions in particular conversational contexts. While Grice's full argument is beyond our present scope, it might suffice to note the following: (a) He finds some uses of the 'if . . . , then' that contextually cancel the implicature (thus indicating one sense of the 'if . . . , then' in which the ground-to-consequence relation is not conveyed at the level of semantics). (b) Given (a) and that the ground–consequence relation can be seen to be conversationally implicated by '⊃', he urges that the Principle of Simplicity (cf. Chapter 5) be applied to linguistics in the form: Do not multiply the senses of a word needlessly.

★ ★ ★ ★

EXERCISES—SECTION 6.5

1. In each of the following examples, (i) suggest the most obvious or striking conversational implicature the utterance of B is likely to bring about, and (ii) explain how this conversational implicature can be determined by reference to the specific maxim that either is presumed to be observed or is blatantly violated (in case of pragmatically deviant utterances).

   (a) *A:* I would like to meet some interesting women.
       B: Oscar's nightclub seems to be a lively spot.
   (b) *A:* I find college awfully difficult.
       B: Well, you are no longer in high school.
   (c) *A:* Professor B, why is it that you are so mean? Is it because you don't get enough loving from your wife at night?
       B: Well, let's get back to your term paper, shall we?
   (d) *A:* I wonder why George isn't at the party tonight.
       B: I saw him with a new girlfriend last night.

(e) *A:* We sure had some lulus in our critical-thinking class.
B: I wonder what ever happened to Tom?

(f) *A:* Is Tom studying this afternoon?
B: Well, he did take a route from here that led him into the library.

2. In each of the following explain with reference to the specific maxims of conversation how the statement within '⟨ ⟩' may be determined to be conversationally implicated by the utterance. The material in '[ ]' is meant to provide background information (of which the hearer may be assumed to be aware).

   (a) [She says:] Mario is such a darling! ⟨She likes Mario.⟩
   (b) [A wonders where George was last night, and B says:] He wasn't at my house. ⟨B doesn't know where George was last night.⟩
   (c) [A number of people are discussing Tom's mental capacities, and one person says:] Well, I wouldn't say that he isn't stupid. ⟨Tom's stupidity is an open possibility.⟩
   *(d) He isn't dating both Sally and Mary. ⟨There are reasons to think that there is some conflict in his dating of both Sally and Mary.⟩

*3. Add additional clauses to each of the utterances considered in exercises 1(a), 1(d), 2(b), and 2(c) that would cancel the conversational implicature. Find an alternative expression for the utterance in exercise 1(f) that detaches the conversational implicature.

*4. 'She married Tom and had a baby' (as opposed to 'She had a baby and married Tom') conveys that she married Tom first and then had the baby. Suggest a maxim that may be included under the Maxim of Manner, which would have the consequence that even the use of the truth functional sense of 'and' would conversationally implicate that she married Tom first and then had a baby.

*5. Consider again M1 and M2, the two utterances mentioned in exercise 2 of Section 6.4 concerning Moore's paradox.

   (a) Show that each of M1 and M2 has the feature that a part of the utterance in effect denies what is conversationally implicated by the other part.
   (b) Would the feature uncovered in (a) be a good explanation of the paradoxical nature of the utterances M1 and M2?

6.6 Two Additional Dimensions of Meaning

Certain uses of words can carry dimensions of meaning that we have not yet discussed, and the purpose of this section is to discuss two such dimensions. In the first half of the twentieth century many philosophers of language thought that these two dimensions of meaning provided a general theory of meaning. While their general theory of meaning is now largely discredited, they were pointing to something important about our understanding or use of language. Unfortunately, specifying the important grain of truth they were pointing to is no easy task. Our strategy will be to present their view as a general theory of meaning, point out the deficiencies of such a general theory, and attempt to formulate a qualification of their views that may be seen as directing our attention to certain dimensions of meaning. Again, readers disinclined toward abstract discussions may skip the starred elaborations and criticisms of the discredited theories. In Section 6.6.1 we shall discuss the dimension of empirical meaning and in Section 6.6.2 we shall discuss the dimension of evaluative meaning.

6.6.1 The Dimension of Empirical Meaning

The American pragmatists claimed that the truth or falsity of a statement must make some difference on the kinds of experiences or observations we would have; if the truth or falsity of an alleged statement made no detectable difference in the experiences we would have, the statement is without any "cash value," without any meaning. The same point was essentially made by a number of empiricists who insisted that a meaningful sentence must be verifiable; that is, we must be able to assign some actual or possible observations that would verify (or confirm or act as evidence for) the sentence and some actual or possible observations that would falsify or disconfirm it. (Logical and mathematical truths were exempt from this requirement because they were thought to be vacuously true in virtue of the meaning of the terms involved.)

★ ★ ★ ★

Given the basic assumption that the truth or falsity of a sentence is essentially tied to the verifiable difference between its truth and falsity, it would seem to follow that a sentence is meaningful only if it is verifiable. For the meaning of S is that in virtue of which the truth or falsity of S (i.e., the extension of S) is fixed in any possible world. Therefore, if the truth or falsity of S is essentially tied to a verifiable difference, it would seem that the meaning of S must fix for every possible world the verifiable difference of the truth or falsity of S; if such a verifiable difference were not fixed, no meaning would have been assigned to S.

An even more extreme version of the theory was that the very meaning of a statement is its method of verification. Thus, the meaning of 'The cat ate the mouse' would be those observations and experiences that would verify it and those that would falsify it. Sometimes this was put by saying: the meaning of a sentence (or a term) was the operations that had to be performed in order to determine its truth or falsity (or determine whether or not something belonged to the extension of the term). A definition that specified the needed operations was called an operational definition, and the demand was that an operational definition be given for all terms.

This theory, which was sometimes called the verification theory of meaning, has few supporters today, and no doubt with good reason. The more extreme theory that the meaning of an expression is its method of verification is almost certainly false. We saw in Chapter 5 that a hypothesis faces experience along with the other hypotheses that compose the theory and a number of auxiliary premises. What would verify or confirm a statement will vary as the other hypotheses and auxiliary premises are abandoned in favor of better ones; yet the meaning of the fixed hypothesis needn't change with these background changes.

Even the milder theory that a meaningful sentence must be verifiable seems to be untenable because the assumption on which it is based (i.e., the truth or falsity of a statement must make a verifiable difference) seems to be wrong. Put in a nutshell, there seems to be no essential connection between a statement being true and our ability to find this out. A standard example is the sentence 'Everything in the universe is expanding at a uniform rate'. It may be that this would be impossible to confirm or disconfirm because rulers and other measuring devices for determining size would also be expanding. Yet it would seem that the statement could be true, and it certainly seems to have meaning. It is precisely because it has meaning that we can detect the difficulties in verifying or falsifying it. Thus, it would seem that the verification theory of meaning is mistaken.

★ ★ ★ ★

Although the verification theory seems to be mistaken as a general theory of meaning, it does seem to be pointing toward something that is reasonable. If someone tells me that by 'The Absolute' he means the profound reality underlying all appearances, and then goes on to tell me that The Absolute is a perfect sphere, in a fairly good sense I don't seem to understand what he is talking about. One wants to ask things like: How would one recognize The Absolute when one came into contact with it (or It)? What might show The Absolute to be spherical rather than cubical? If he can answer no questions of this type, it *is* tempting to think that he isn't making very good sense and might be just talking nonsense. What then shall we say about the verification theory, granting that it isn't a general theory of meaning?

Let us recall that a large number of claims in which we are interested are what might be called empirical claims, that is, claims that are directly or more tenuously connected to observations and experiences that go toward confirming them (in conjunction of course with other statements we accept). In this broad sense of empirical, unproblematic OB, PF, and the nonmathematical SM claims discussed in Chapter 2 are empirical claims, as are the "best explanations" discussed in Chapter 5. If someone makes a claim as an empirical claim (a claim to be supported directly or indirectly by experience or observation), it is not unreasonable to ask what observations would go toward showing it to be true or false assuming that the other things we accept or know are kept fixed. If this question cannot be answered, there are clear difficulties in treating the claim as an empirical claim.

Let us then introduce the term "empirical meaning" in such a way that a statement is said to have (or have been given) an empirical meaning if and only if some actual or possible observations count (or are specified) as going toward showing the statement to be true and others count (or are specified) as going toward showing the statement to be false, again assuming that various other things we accept or know are taken to be fixed as background. It must be kept in mind that "empirical meaning" isn't semantic meaning as discussed in Section 6.3. Keeping this in mind, the point we seem to have reached may now be stated as: *An empirical claim must have some empirical meaning assigned.* In making use of this principle, two points should be remembered.

(A) Judgment must be used in determining what counts as specifying empirical meaning. The need for good judgment may be exemplified by two examples:

(1) If empirical meaning has been assigned to 'The cat ate the mouse', what goes toward confirming or disconfirming this statement would also confirm or disconfirm 'The cat ate the mouse and The Absolute is perfectly spherical'. Yet good judgment should tell us that empirical meaning hasn't been assigned to the whole conjunction insofar as none has been assigned to the second conjunct.
(2) Whether Cleopatra ate figs on her last day is no doubt beyond confirmation or disconfirmation today. Still, she presumably did have the relevant observations and others could have had it if they were there. Thus, we should count 'Cleopatra ate figs on her last day' as having empirical meaning. On the other hand, 'Everything in the universe is expanding' shouldn't be thought to have been given empirical meaning by saying, "If we could step out of the universe, we could observe it expanding." Good judgment is needed to determine what is and what isn't in principle possible to observe.

(B) The principle that empirical claims must have empirical meaning tells us nothing about a statement that doesn't have empirical meaning. Given any statement that is to be assessed for truth and falsity, often it may be useful to start by asking for its empirical meaning. If one is specified, fine; it's an empirical claim and in a sense we know what to do with it. But if it doesn't have any empirical meaning, we should ask what sort of a statement it is, and some of the possibilities are:

(1) Because of its syntax and the semantics of its component terms, it might be a perfectly good statement like 'Everything is expanding at the same rate', which nevertheless cannot be confirmed or disconfirmed by any possible experience. In such a case, we should recognize that as far as our practical concerns go, it would be idle for us to spend time worrying about its truth or falsity. After all, we are never going to find out and its truth or falsity is not going to make any difference on what we shall experience or observe.
(2) It might be something like the intuitive claims discussed in Chapter 2—that is, claims like those of logic, mathematics, or spatiotemporal relations that are so central to our conceptual scheme that denying them (in the absence of a fully worked-out alternative) makes it virtually impossible for us to think about the world. For such a statement we would not be able to specify any experience that would falsify it, and it would be somewhat odd to count all observations as verifying it.

(3) It might be a definitional statement like 'Bachelors are unmarried'. If I say that nothing can falsify 'Bachelors are unmarried', you might take my statement as definitive of what I mean by 'bachelor'.
(4) It might be a semantically deviant expression like 'This adult is a child', in that no experience could verify it because whatever would verify that the person is an adult would also falsify that the person is a child.
(5) It might be a staetment that is intended as an empirical claim but one for which no empirical meaning has been given. In that case, one should suspect that for all practical purposes the speaker may be just babbling.

As an example of an analysis concerning empirical meaning, suppose someone says that no profound thought can be communicated. We should of course be puzzled. We reply: "Well, Einstein had a number of profound thoughts. Weren't those ideas perfectly well communicated to the scientific community?" Suppose he tells us that that's not what he means by a profound thought. We might then try asking him about the thoughts of Christ, Buddha, Tolstoy, or Gandhi. We can imagine three continuations:

(a) If he tells us that none of them had profound thoughts, we may well begin to wonder what shows that none of them had profound thoughts. We might ask him (i) what falsifies 'Christ had profound thoughts' and (ii) what would have verified it if He had profound thoughts. Suppose he tells us that (i) what falsifies 'Christ had profound thoughts' is His thoughts having been communicated in the Bible, and (ii) nothing could verify the statement because verifying a thought to be profound would presuppose the thought having been communicated, and its having been communicated disqualifies it from being profound. At this point a fair assessment would seem to be that 'No profound thought can be communicated' is for him a definitional truth, and whatever he may mean by 'profound' and 'communicate', it is not what we ordinarily mean by those terms. If he resists this move by claiming that we are making a joke of what he has learned by experience, it is time to suspect that he is just babbling.

(b) Suppose he admits that Christ, Buddha, Tolstoy, and Gandhi did have profound thoughts, but that they just didn't communicate them to anyone. We should now begin to wonder what falsifies 'Tolstoy communicated profound thoughts in *War and Peace*' and what would have verified it if it were true. Suppose he tells us that what falsifies the statement is that when he read *War and Peace* in his youth he got nothing out of it; after many years of living, he enjoyed it upon rereading it, but that was only because he had experienced and developed those thoughts himself—it wasn't news to him any more. If he says something like this, we begin to understand what he means. He means something like: one cannot just be told a profound thought, but must make it one's own through personal experience. While things are still somewhat vague, at least roughly what verifies 'No profound thought can be communicated' is no one becoming wise by just reading the thoughts of another, and what would falsify it would be if people did become recognizably wise by just reading a book.

(c) He tells us that he doesn't know that much about the lives of Gandhi, Tolstoy, Christ, and so on. Rather, he says that he has met a number of people who were "born again" or went through Zen meditations or other such things. In each case their lives changed significantly and they attained a level of tranquility and serenity seldom found. He takes this to be a sign that they attained some profound thoughts. Yet in each of these cases, he tells us, he could not appreciate or make full sense of what they were trying to tell him when they tried to explain what constituted their enlightenment or new vision. This, again, gives us some idea of what would verify and falsify 'No profound thought can be communicated': Find people who attained serenity through some sort of a conversion and see if others can understand their explanations of the enlightenments they achieved.

These examples should make it plausible that asking for the empirical meaning can often be helpful in understanding what is meant by someone's otherwise puzzling statement. Of course such a pursuit can sometimes result in the assessment that a person is uttering a definitional truth (involving a redefinition of ordinary terms) or that he is coming close to babbling.

★ ★ ★ ★

One final point should perhaps be made about empirical meaning. Levels of meaning tend to carry with them utterances that are deviant with respect to that level of meaning. The dimension of empirical meaning is no exception. Let us say that a sentence is *verificationally* deviant if it is impossible for there to be any confirming evidence for the sentence. Clearly any semantically deviant sentence (e.g., 'This adult is a child') will be verificationally deviant. However, there are verificationally deviant sentences that are not semantically deviant. 'Everything is expanding at a uniform rate' is such an example.

As another example, suppose someone claims, "The natives on that island believe that contradictory statements of the form 'p and not-p' are often true." Presumably the grounds for attributing a belief of this kind to the natives involve their assent to statements of a certain kind that are taken to express their beliefs. What then is the statement that expresses a belief of theirs of the form 'p and not-p'? Let us suppose it is 'p ka da-p'. The attribution of a belief in the contradiction clearly depends on the adequacy of translating 'ka' by 'and' and 'da' by 'not'. But what shows or confirms a translation E of a native sentence X to be correct? Roughly, the answer seems to be: Their assent and dissent to X match our assent and dissent to E under varying circumstances. For example, under varying conditions of pointing and looking, whenever we are inclined to say 'This is a tree', they assent to X, and when we are inclined to dissent to 'This is a tree', they dissent to X. This would be the empirical basis for translating X as 'This is a tree'. But now, insofar as we don't assent to contradictions and they evidently assent to 'p ka da-p', this would be empirical grounds for condemning the translation of 'p ka da-p' by 'p and not-p'. The upshot is: the grounds for attributing to them a belief of the form 'p and not-p' (i.e., their assent to 'p ka da-p') are grounds for denying that 'p ka da-p' means 'p and not-p'; but in that case, the grounds for attributing a belief of the form 'p and not-p' have vanished. Because it is impossible for anything to verify or confirm "They have beliefs of the form 'p and not-p'," the sentence is verificationally deviant. As a consequence, even if we think that the sentence could somehow be true, it makes no sense to say: "It was empirically discovered that they have beliefs of this form."[32]

★ ★ ★ ★

Our discussion of empirical meaning may be summarized as follows:

(1) Empirical meaning of P = observations O+ and O− that one could at least in principle have had, where O+ would be evidence for P and O− would be evidence against P.
(2) An empirical claim must have some empirical meaning assigned.
(3) If P is without empirical meaning,
   (a) P may be meaningful because of its syntax and semantics,
   (b) P may be an INT claim or what can be derived from INT claims,
   (c) P may be a definitional statement incorporating the standard or abnormal meaning attached to a component term,
   (d) P may be a semantically deviant statement, or
   (e) The speaker is babbling in claiming P if she/he intends P to be an empirical claim.
(4) Analyzing the empirical meaning of a statement P:
   (a) Determine the empirical meaning of P or specify one of the possible outcomes for statements lacking empirical meaning.
   (b) If needed for (a), determine the aberrant or unusual (empirical) meaning given to an expression in P.
(*5) P is verificationally deviant if it isn't semantically deviant and it is impossible that there should be confirming evidence for P.

32. I loosely borrow this example from W.V.O. Quine, *Word and Object*, Cambridge, Mass.: MIT Press, 1960, Chapter 2.

EXERCISES—SECTION 6.6.1

1. For each of the following suggest at least part of the empirical meaning O+ and O−.

    (a) Jack killed Sissy last night in her bedroom.
    (b) Horatio is a nice person.
    (c) Tom loves Mary.
    (d) Yuba City (California) is a miserable city in which to live.
    (e) For most people, it is more satisfying to live in a democratic society than an autocratic society.

2. For each of the following, suggest (i) one continuation in which some empirical meaning is attached to the underlined claim of A, and (ii) one continuation in which consideration of the empirical content of the claim of A leads to the conclusion that the underlined claim of A lacks empirical meaning. In (i) specify what empirical meaning is attached to the claim of A and in (ii) specify what kind of claim the underlined claim of A is.

    (a) *A:* Goodwill toward others is just a dream. There is no such thing as an unselfish generous act.
    B: I don't see how you can say that. Look at people who have donated millions to charitable institutions! Don't people sometimes help others who are stranded on highways? Haven't Boy Scouts saved lives of drowning people?
    A: Don't be naive. People donate money to charitable institutions for tax deductions and for looking good in the eyes of others. Sure, some people help others who are stranded on highways, but that's because they expect some favor in return; Boy Scouts probably wouldn't be saving lives if there wasn't a big medal attached to it. Besides, an act is generous only if one wants to help the others; if one doesn't want to do it and it's done just out of a sense of duty or obligation, it shouldn't be called a generous act. But if you want to help others, you take some pleasure in doing so, and it turns out to be a selfish act after all.
    B: I grant that an act is generous only if one wants to help others. But the rest of what you say doesn't wash. Let's start with your claims about Boy Scouts, contributors, and so on.

    (b) *A:* I never know what someone else is really feeling.
    B: How can you say that? Don't you know that Tom who has just crashed his hang glider is in pain? Don't you know that Jane who was just accepted to Harvard Law School is delighted?
    A: But I don't feel the pain Tom does, and I don't experience the delight Jane has.
    B: How could that be relevant to your original claim?

    [*Hint:* For (ii), think in terms of knowing a feeling requiring having the feeling, and that any feeling I have is *my* feeling and not someone else's.]

*3. Show how each of the following might be argued to be verificationally deviant.

    (a) The natives of Samoa believe that the ocean surrounding them is coconut juice. (Would it make any difference if the Samoans used the same word for what we call coconut juice and what we call ocean water?)
    (b) I am awake and not dreaming that I have evidence that I am awake.

*4. Assuming the arguments given in exercise 3 are accepted, how should one respond to someone who claimed that he had empirically determined (a) and (b) of exercise 3 to be true? Are (a) and (b) of exercise 3 semantically deviant?

6.6.2 The Evaluative Dimension of Meaning

A frequent companion of the verification theory of meaning in the first half of the twentieth century was a theory of meaning that may at least be caricatured along the following lines:

> There are two kinds of meanings a term may have: descriptive and evaluative or emotive. The descriptive meaning is that in virtue of which one determines a term's extension. The evaluative or emotive meaning, on the other hand, is a component of a word's meaning that doesn't play a role in determining the extension of the term, but rather its role is to evaluate or express a pro or con attitude toward something included in the term's extension. Thus, for example, while the descriptive meaning of 'statesman' is something like 'government leader', its emotive meaning is either something like 'worthy person' or else the word's capacity to express approval. In general, there are three categories of expressions: value-neutral expressions or expressions having only a descriptive meaning, purely evaluative expressions like 'good' that have an evaluative meaning but no descriptive meaning, and mixed terms like 'statesman' that have both evaluative and descriptive meanings. Any sentence that contains a term having some evaluative meaning is an evaluatively or emotively charged sentence, and to avoid fallacies and confusions, one should replace such a sentence by a purely descriptive sentence, so that one does not mistakenly accept the distinct evaluative component merely on the basis of having accepted the value-neutral content.

★ ★ ★ ★

The account just outlined is likely to be mistaken in virtually all of its claims. The main problem with the view sketched is that the distinction between evaluative and descriptive meaning cannot be made out in the way imagined. Consider again the term 'statesman': it is not true that its descriptive meaning is exhausted by 'government leader'. The descriptive meaning itself specifies additional characteristics like "puts the interest of the country ahead of his or her own interest," "has directly or indirectly benefited the country," "has served the country for many years." Because each of these characteristics is relevant for determining whether or not someone is to be included in the extension of 'statesman', they form part of the descriptive meaning. Let us therefore take the descriptive meaning of 'statesman' to be something like "a government leader who puts the interest of the country above his or her own and has served the country for many years benefiting it in a number of direct and indirect ways." But to describe a person in these ways is already to evaluate the person positively. Similarly, it's difficult to see what could be the descriptive meaning of 'stupid' that doesn't already negatively evaluate a person in some respect. Thus, the descriptive meanings of 'statesman' and 'stupid' are by themselves sufficient to play the role of evaluating a person positively or negatively, and there is no room or need for separate evaluative meanings for 'statesman' and 'stupid'.[33]

In a few cases, it does seem possible to distinguish the evaluative and the descriptive meanings in the way initially imagined. Given a term of abuse like 'wop', 'Italian' is clearly a part of the descriptive meaning. Let us suppose the evaluative component is something like "a person unworthy of respect." Could this evaluative component be seen as a second aspect of the descriptive meaning for 'wop'? This would have the result that some Italians are wops (namely those who are unworthy of respect) while most Italians would not be. This doesn't seem to be the right account of the meaning of 'wop'. 'Wop' seems to be applicable to any Italian, and one uses that term instead of 'Italian' when one wants to express disrespect; for anyone using 'wop', it's not that some Italians aren't wops but rather that he wouldn't use that term for Italians he doesn't want to abuse. Thus, it may be plausible that being Italian is the complcte descriptive meaning of 'wop', while being unworthy of respect is a separate emotive or evaluative meaning of 'wop' that doesn't make a contribution to determining extension. While there are examples like this, for most terms that carry an evaluation, the distinction between evaluative and descriptive meaning fails because the descriptive meaning that determines extension includes an inextricable evaluative component.

Beyond this, we should not endorse the theory's account of terms like 'good'. If such a term is purely evaluative and has no descriptive meaning, presumably 'good' has no extension (because only descriptive meanings are supposed to determine extension). Thus, to say that 'good' has no descriptive meaning seems to commit one to the idea of it not being strictly true or false that anything is good. This is pretty clearly a philosophical theory that we have no business endorsing in a text on reasoning.

★ ★ ★ ★

While the original theory seems untenable, it seems pretty clear that in using words sometimes we are evaluating something to be good or bad in

33. It will not help to say "even if a government leader puts the interest of the country above his own, . . . I still might evaluate him as a bad person; thus the genuine evaluation must be assigned to a separate evaluative meaning of 'statesman'." If there is a "genuine" evaluation that can be separated from the descriptive meaning of 'statesman' in the way imagined, it becomes dubious that any meaning of 'statesman' includes such a "genuine" evaluation.

certain respects, and at other times we are relatively disengaged from making such an evaluation. It is doubtful that there is any sharp dividing line between evaluating and describing without evaluating. Nor is it always clear whether the evaluation is part of the meaning of the term or merely associated with our typical uses of the term. For example, suppose we say that he *withheld* some information. Withholding information seems close to concealing information, and concealing information seems close to some form of deception; the meaning of 'deception' certainly seems to carry with it a negative evaluation (which of course might be overridden when other factors are considered). There seems to be little point in trying to determine whether the (descriptive) meaning of 'withholding information' already carries a negative evaluation or merely suggests or tends to lead to a negative evaluation as a matter of course. A further complication is that the use of a term can be relatively free of evaluation in some contexts and yet be loaded with an evaluation in others. Consider the word 'American': perhaps in most contexts of its use there is little in the way of evaluation. Yet in the context, "You can't expect any better from him; after all he's an American," the use of the term 'American' seems to carry the evaluation involved in saying, 'He is rich, arrogant, and uncultured."

In light of all these complications, let us say:

> *The use of an expression E in a context C is evaluatively charged if to use E in C is to evaluate something positively or negatively in some respect or to use E in contexts like C tends to lead to such an evaluation as a matter of course.*

A term like 'wop' seems to be evaluatively charged in virtually all contexts because it seems to have something that is identifiable as its evaluative meaning. Terms like 'statesman' seem to be evaluatively charged in virtually all contexts because the meaning that determines the extension seems to include an inextricable evaluative component. Perhaps 'withholds information' is evaluatively charged in most contexts only because its use in such contexts tends to lead to an evaluation as a matter of course. 'American' is evaluatively charged in the context recently considered because to describe him as an American in such a context is to evaluate him negatively.

Part of the theory with which we started our discussion was that, faced with a sentence using evaluatively charged expressions, we should find a value-neutral expression retaining the same descriptive meaning. Given the difficulties with the initial theory, this is not feasible. However, given the use of an evaluatively charged expression, we can try to list the various elements of what is conveyed by the use of that expression in such a context, and try to separate out the relatively neutral components that are more or less free of evaluation and those that seem to involve an evaluative charge. Given a fairly typical context for 'He is a statesman', we might list the things conveyed as follows:

(a) He is a government leader.
(b) He has served the country for many years.
(c) He benefited the country in various ways.
(d) He puts the interest of the country above his own.

Given such a listing, we might take (a) and (b) as the components that are relatively neutral and (c) and (d) as the evaluatively charged components.

Two things must be remembered about this procedure:

(1) There is no suggestion that only the components that are free of evaluation are relevant for determining the extensions of the terms involved. Thus, we are not suggesting that (a) and (b) exhaust the descriptive meaning of 'He is a statesman'.
(2) We are not suggesting that a relatively neutral component is completely devoid of evaluation.

One might claim: To say that he is a government *leader* is already to evaluate and as such instead of (a) the evaluation-free component should be taken as

(a*) He occupied a position near the top of the government organization chart.

Similarly, one might claim: Because to say that he *served* the country is to evaluate, instead of (b) the neutral component should be taken as

(b*) He was employed by the government for many years.

If we could be assured of being able to reach the ideal of specifying a component that is completely free of evaluation, perhaps we should worry whether the asterisked or unasterisked versions of (a) and (b) should be listed as neutral. But it is doubtful that such an ideal can be reached. If (a) is evaluatively charged, who is to say that (a*) isn't? Could not (b*) be evaluatively charged (at least for some people)? The prudent course is to give up on the ideal of components that are completely free of evaluation; rather, we settle for those that are *relatively* neutral or free of evaluation when compared to the others. Given this outlook, we might as well settle on (a) and (b) as relatively neutral when compared to (c) and (d).

The sound idea behind the advice of the old theory that one should find a neutral alternative when faced with an evaluatively loaded statement was that accepting the neutral component of the statement should not automatically lead one to accept the evaluative component. We might now translate this idea as follows: Given the separation of what is conveyed by a statement using evaluatively charged expressions into the relatively neutral and relatively charged components, separately assess the acceptability of those components along the lines suggested in Chapter 4. For example, suppose that 'He is a statesman' is said of Nixon. In such a case, one might determine (at least from a personal perspective) that (a) and (b) are completely justified, (c) is acceptable or highly justified and (d) is unacceptable. If one were talking about Lincoln, one might assess all of (a)–(d) to be completely justified. Breaking up a statement in this way is an essential part of critical thinking, especially when dealing with evaluatively charged expressions. We now turn to a somewhat more precise account of how passages using evaluatively charged expressions should be approached.

Analyzing Evaluatively Charged Passages. Given what we have already said, the task of analyzing such passages may be divided into four stages:

(A) Isolate expressions in which the use in the passage is evaluatively charged. Normally this is not too difficult because it is pretty easy to spot expressions that are evaluatively charged. When in doubt, follow the Method of Alternatives suggested in Section 6.2.2; that is, substitute some other similar or contrasting expression for the expression in question to see if there is some detectable difference in the evaluative force conveyed. As a special instance of the Method of Alternatives, if it is grammatically possible, try deleting an adjectival or adverbial modifier to see if that brings about a detectable difference in the evaluative force.

(B) Using the Method of Alternatives, separate what is conveyed into the relatively neutral and evaluatively charged components. Trying various different similar or contrasting alternatives to the charged expression in question should allow one to determine what is specifically conveyed by the use of the charged expression.

(C) Find a way of restating the passage so that the relatively neutral components (if any) remain the same and the evaluative ones are given an opposite or different charge. This step is particularly useful if Step B revealed no component that was relatively neutral. For example, given a statement like 'He is immoral', there is unlikely to be any discernible neutral component of any interest. Thus, as Step C one should propose statements like 'He is amoral' and 'He is moral'.

(D) Assess the neutral and evaluative components separately, and in this process determine if the original statement or the one produced in Step C (or neither) are close to the truth. This step involves applying the material already discussed in Chapters 2 and 4.

Because the central concern of the present discussion is with Steps A–C, we may streamline our work by relying on the following procedure for determining the relatively neutral and evaluatively charged components:

> Procedure for Determining Neutral and Evaluatively Charged Components
>
> (1) Rewrite the sentence, underlining and numbering for reference the expressions that give rise to evaluatively charged components.
> (2) Extract the relatively neutral component (if any) from the sentence.
> (3) Extract the evaluatively charged components, and by using the numbering from Step 1 for cross reference, combine the charges into one or more statements.
> (4) Present a statement with an opposite or different evaluative charge from that found in Step 3 that nevertheless has a neutral content that approximates the one found in Step 2.

To exemplify this procedure, consider 'He made love with the daughter of that elegant Italian man'. We would rewrite the sentence as:

He <u>made love with</u> [i] the daughter of that <u>elegant</u> [ii] Italian man.

The relatively neutral component N, the evaluatively charged component E, and the oppositely or differently charged version O may taken as:

N: He had sexual intercourse with the daughter of that Italian man.
E: The act was an expression of emotional attachment and concern and not a crass act of mere physical satisfaction [i] and her father was an elegant person [ii].
O: He screwed the wop's daughter.

As another example, consider:

Last night the president finally informed the nation of the magnitude of America's involvement in Central America.

The procedure for determining the evaluative and neutral components might be applied as follows:

Last night the president <u>finally</u> [i] informed the nation of the <u>magnitude</u> [ii] of America's involvement in Central America.

N: Last night the president informed the nation of the degree of America's involvement in Central America.
E: The president has withheld information about our involvement until last night (and to this extent was being deceptive) [i], and the American involvement turns out to be quite significant [ii].

O: Given the increasing magnitude of America's involvement in Central America, despite political and military considerations to the contrary, the president last night informed the nation of America's involvement in Central America.

The use of 'magnitude' instead of 'degree' indicating a significant involvement should perhaps be treated as one of the relatively neutral components; however, because it affects the negative evaluation attached to the president having withheld the information up until now, it was included among the evaluative components. As for the opposite or differently charged version, it at best *approximates* the neutral content but nothing better seems to be obviously available. This example indicates that in determining the relatively neutral and evaluatively charged components, one need not put too fine a line on the division and or insist on an alternative version with exactly the same neutral component.

As an example of a slightly longer passage, consider a portion of David Broder's column in the *Los Angeles Times* during the Watergate scandals in the Nixon administration. Sentences are here numbered for subsequent reference.

> (1) Every time the Nixon administration seems to be veering dangerously close to contact with political reality, you can count on one of the president's nannies to tug him safely back to dreamland. (2) This mission was entrusted to H. R. Haldeman and John Ehrlichman in the first term. (3) For four turbulent years, they kept the "Do Not Disturb" sign firmly in place on the Oval Office door.[34]

The application of our procedure might proceed as follows:

(1) Every time the Nixon administration seems to be veering dangerously close [i] to contact with political reality, you can count on one of the president's nannies [ii] to tug him safely back to dreamland [iii].

N: When the Nixon administration came close to contact with political reality, his aides shielded Nixon from it.

E: Nixon had a policy or set course of avoiding political reality (from which one might veer), and he considered it dangerous to come into contact with it [i]. He needed aides who would mother him [ii], and because he could not cope with reality he had to be allowed to live in his dream world [iii].

O: Every time the Nixon administration was harassed by this or that piece of petty politics, one could depend on the presidential aides to shield him so that the president could discharge the duties of his office.

34. This is part of the column considered in Section 6.4 in which we discussed the "illocutionary force" of a satire. Although the column is a satire, we can still separate the relatively neutral and the evaluatively charged components.

(2) This mission was entrusted to H. R. Haldeman and John Ehrlichman in the first term.
  N: The task of shielding Nixon from the political reality was assumed by Haldeman and Ehrlichman during Nixon's first term.
  E: (Because of the high-sounding 'mission was entrusted' instead of 'the task was assigned':) The welfare of our country depended on someone assuming the duty of mothering Nixon and letting him live in his dreamland.
  O: This unpleasant but needed task (of shielding the president from petty politics) was assumed by Haldeman and Ehrlichman in the first term.

(3) For four turbulent [i] years, they kept the "Do Not Disturb" sign [ii] firmly in place on the Oval Office door.
  N: During that first term, they prevented people from seeing Nixon.
  E: Nixon slept and dreamt through (did not pay any attention to) [ii] important issues and crises [i] during his first term.
  O: For four years of political bickering and strife, they kept a variety of self-serving politicians from distracting the president.

It would seem clear that the components under E negatively evaluate Nixon and his administration and that there is a significant gap between these components and the relatively neutral ones given under N. Correspondingly, accepting the claims under E requires a lot more justification than accepting the relatively neutral components given by N. Obviously, a very different picture emerges under O, which attaches differing evaluative components to relatively neutral components that are virtually identical. As is so often the case, the relatively neutral components are uncontroversial while those that are evaluative are anything but uncontroversial. Does the Broder version or the alternative version given under O (or some other version) give the true picture of the situation? Whatever assessment one makes, the need for separating components that are evaluatively charged from the relatively neutral ones should be clear.

Fallacy of Illicit Redefinition. We conclude this section with a discussion of a fallacy in which the most pernicious instances typically involve the use of evaluatively charged terms. We start, however, with a general characterization of the fallacy. While expressions have ordinary or standard meanings, there is nothing wrong with attaching a new meaning to the term for a particular purpose. Sometimes a person will introduce the new meaning he or she is attaching by explicitly saying something like: "For our purpose, we shall understand 'X' to mean. . . . " At other times a person will use a term in such a way that the Principle of Charity will force us to assume that the person has attached a new or nonstandard meaning to the term; in such a case we might say that the person has implicitly redefined the term. There is nothing wrong with redefining a term implicitly or explicitly. But something does go wrong when the person equivocates back and forth between the standard meaning and the redefined meaning. By the FALLACY OF ILLICIT REDEFINITION we shall understand *a special instance of the Fallacy of Equivocation in which one occurrence of the critical term must be understood in the ordinary sense and another occurrence of the term must be understood in the new way in which one is explicitly or implicitly proposing to use the term.* Thus, except for one of the senses that is involved being the new or redefined meaning attached to the term, the summarizing diagram for the Fallacy of Illicit Redefinition is identical to that of the Fallacy of Equivocation:

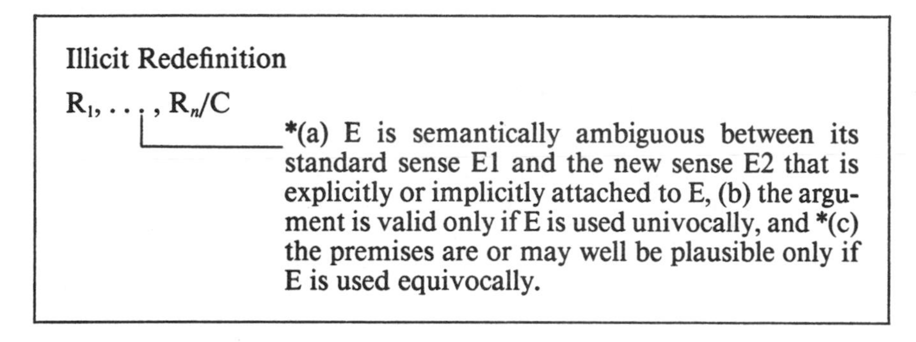

As always, the starred items need to be explained in analyzing a passage to commit the Fallacy of Illicit Redefinition.

A relatively simple example (similar to one that was proposed by the physicist Eddington) is this: "People have been wrong in believing tables to be solid. If we examine a table closely, we will find that there is a great deal of empty space between the millions of molecules making it up." If we spell out the argument, we would get something like this:

Illicit Redefinition:

(1) There is a great deal of space between the millions of molecules making up a table.
(2) If (1) is true, tables are not (cannot be said to be) solid.
(3) If tables are not solid and most people believe that tables are solid, most people are wrong in believing tables to be solid.
(4) Most people believe that tables are solid.

---

(5) Most people are wrong in believing tables to be solid.
(a) 'Solid' is ambiguous between its ordinary meaning, according to which a solid thing is something one can pound, bump into, and so on, and a newly introduced sense in which it means not having any space between the molecules making it up.
(b) The argument is valid only if 'solid' is used univocally.
(c) In the ordinary sense of 'solid', (4) is highly plausible but (2)

seems to be outright false. In the redefined sense, while (2) is plausible, (4) is highly implausible. Because the premises are plausible only if one equivocates on 'solid' and one of the senses is a newly introduced sense, the Fallacy of Illicit Redefinition is committed.

An example directly relevant to the discussion of this section is:

To extinguish the life of something that would become a full human being if left alone is to commit murder. Because contraception by means of an IUD extinguishes the life of a fertilized egg by preventing it from staying attached to the womb, people who practice birth control with the IUD are murderers. Therefore, people who use the IUD for contraception are despicable.

The analysis of the fallacy that is commited would be:

Illicit Redefinition:

(1) To extinguish the life of something that would become a human being if left alone is to commit murder.
(2) Contraception by means of the IUD extinguishes the life of something that would become a human being if left alone.
(3) If (1) and (2) are true, people who avoid conception with the IUD are murderers.
(4) If people who avoid conception with the IUD are murderers, they are despicable.

---

(5) People who avoid conception with the IUD are despicable.
(a) 'Murderer' is ambiguous between the ordinary sense of someone who intentionally kills another human being without being authorized by the law to do so and the tacitly introduced new sense in which it means extinguishing the life of something that would become a human being if left alone.
(b) The validity of the argument requires using 'murderer' univocally.
(c) Premise (4) is certainly plausible if 'murderer' is understood in the ordinary sense, but in this sense (1) is false. On the other hand, if 'murderer' is given the tacitly introduced new sense, while (1) is now clearly true, (4) in effect states:

> If people who avoid conception with the IUD extinguish the life of something that would become a human being if left alone, they are despicable.

But this claim is far from obvious or plausible.[35] Thus, we have a form of the Fallacy of Equivocation that depends on

35. Of course one might say that the new sense of 'murder' is something like 'the vicious and unwarranted extinguishing of life of something that would have become a human being if left alone'. In that case, while (4) might be plausible, (1) would not.

equivocating between the ordinary and the redefined sense of 'murderer'; that is, we have a Fallacy of Illicit Redefinition.

This example is an instance of what frequently occurs: People take a term like 'murderer' that is evaluatively charged and attach a new meaning to it. When this is done, there is absolutely no reason to think that evaluative component of the old meaning carries over to the new meaning of the term. Yet the groundwork is laid for a Fallacy of Illicit Redefinition in which, unless extreme caution is exercised, one can unwittingly be led to attach the evaluative component of the old meaning to the redefined term. What is particularly pernicious about this fallacy can be exemplified in our example. Someone proposing the argument is likely to omit premise (4) and simply conclude that users of the IUD are murderers. It is thereby left for the reader to commit the Fallacy of Illicit Redefinition and to evaluate the users of the IUD negatively by attaching the evaluative component of the old meaning to the newly defined term. This kind of Fallacy of Redefinition was given the name "persuasive definition" by C. L. Stevenson.[36] Within the context of the theory stated at the beginning of this section, it was defined as changing the descriptive meaning while keeping the evaluative meaning the same. It was called a *persuasive* definition because it was an attempt to persuade the reader to evaluate positively or negatively items picked out by the (new) descriptive meaning. While we have cast doubt on the machinery underlying this account, the danger remains the same: When someone redefines an evaluatively charged term, be careful not to carry over unwittingly the evaluative component of the old meaning to the new meaning.

EXERCISES—SECTION 6.6.2

Part A

Follow the procedure for determining the relatively neutral and evaluatively charged components for each of the numbered statements in the following three passages. The bracketed material is for background only.

A. [During the spring of 1974, Republicans lost most of the special elections for vacant seats in Congress. Some of these losses came in traditional Republican districts. Some commentators thought that these Democratic victories represented a vote against Nixon and his involvement in the Watergate scandal. One of these special elections was held in the district covering Santa Barbara county, and Lagomarsino (a Republican) won the election.] (1) The party that perpetrated the Watergate scandal got a badly needed shot in the arm from the sleepy resort town of Santa Barbara. (2) Most residents were too busy enjoying the southern California weather, and the few who did stumble into

36. Cf. Charles L. Stevenson, *Ethics and Language,* New Haven, Conn.: Yale University Press, 1944.

the voting booths obviously hadn't heard that the rest of the country was sending Nixon a message. (3) The morning after the day before, Santa Barbara found itself having elected a Republican to Congress.

B. [The Broder column considered in the text continues as follows: Regrettably, the Watergate affair—one of those minor disturbances that the guardians assured Mr. Nixon was beneath his notice—carried those good servants off, and made it necessary to find someone new to chase trouble from the White House doorstep. . . .] (1) They told the president: You've turned it around, sir. The polls show that you already surged from 27% support all the way up to 29%, and your momentum will carry you the rest of the way. You know how important momentum is, Mr. President; just like football. . . . (2) This is Fantasyland, and here are your friendly guides, Ron and Al. (3) Forget your troubles; forget the real world's woes, and come journey with us down the River of Dreams. . . . (4) He will play in Fantasyland until a new jolt of reality shakes the White House again. [Ron and Al are Ron Ziegler and Al Haig who replaced Haldeman and Ehrlichman as Nixon's close advisors after the latter two were forced to resign because of their involvement in the Watergate coverup.]

C. [The events mentioned in this passage are: (i) America having limited the Little League World Series to American teams after the team from Taiwan won the Little League World Series for a number of years consecutively. (ii) America's withdrawal from the Vietnam war. (iii) The cutoff of oil to the United States in the early seventies by a number of Arab nations, and the Yom Kippur War in which, after Israel had penetrated deep into Egypt, America had a role in the cease-fire that included the Israeli pledge to retreat to prewar positions; America did describe this role as the American Peace Initiative.] (1) The indefatigable American spirit to be second to none has now degenerated to a point where we think we can succeed by a series of evasions. (2) This can be seen in our underhanded maneuvers with respect to the Little League World Series. (3) When those little yellow punks from Taiwan beat us five straight years, we chickened out and limited the Little League Championships to teams from our own little pond. (4) Our lily-livered success formula can be seen elsewhere. (5) When things got a little harder in Indochina, we quit and rationalized that it was their war, not ours. (6) When the Arabs made things a bit inconvenient for us, the country we helped to father was urged to raise the white flag. (7) Instead of considering it to be the betrayal it was, we called it part of the great American Peace Initiative. (8) With "successes" like these, our friends are beginning to worry. (9) So should we.

Part B

Analyze the Fallacy of Illicit Redefinition committed in each of the following:

1. If two people live together, give each other financial support, and are intimate in other ways, they are married. Therefore, gay couples can file a joint tax return.

   [One of the premises is: If gay couples live together, give each other financial support, and are intimate in other ways, gay couples are married couples.]

2. Alcohol is a drug, and anyone who sells a drug is a drug peddler. Therefore, liquor store owners should be sent to jail.

   [To simplify, take one of the premises as: If liquor store owners sell alcohol, liquor store owners are drug peddlers.]

3. "Wabbly, goo goo da" is a typical piece of meaningless nonsense. But so are many sentences uttered by philosophers and theologians. If a sentence is mean-

ingful, there must be some actual or possible observations that would confirm it and some actual or possible observations that would disconfirm it. Philosophers and theologians admit that their statements often are not subject to confirmation or disconfirmation by observation. Therefore, many of their statements deserve no more attention than meaningless nonsense like "Wabbly, goo goo da."

[Two of the premises are: (i) Many philosophical and theological statements are not subject to confirmation or disconfirmation by observation. (ii) If many philosophical and theological statements are nonsense, many philosophical and theological statements deserve no more attention than meaningless nonsense like "Wabbly, goo goo da."]

4. Whenever one's aim is to kill people of a particular nationality or race, one is committing genocide. When the Americans fought the Germans in World War II, the American aim was to kill Germans. The Americans therefore committed genocide, and insofar as the Germans are to be condemned for committing genocide in their attempt to exterminate the Jews, Americans must also be condemned for genocide in World War II.

   [Two of the premises are: (i) If the American aim in World War II was to kill Germans, Americans committed genocide in World War II. (ii) If the Germans are to be condemned for committing genocide, and the Americans committed genocide in World War II, Americans must also be condemned for committing genocide.]

7

Glimpses Beyond Critical Thinking

In this book we have tried to present reasonably accessible rules and maxims that can guide our ordinary activity of truth assessments. That is to say, we have avoided all but the most elementary symbolic or formal techniques that can aid our reasoning. However, some aspects of reasoning call for more advanced formal techniques that are essentially beyond the scope of an introductory text in reasoning. This chapter is intended to give the interested reader a glimpse of a more advanced study of reasoning. Furthermore, the material in this chapter can be used in certain situations to enhance or augment the techniques that were investigated in Chapters 2–6.

We have known since Chapter 3 that the validity of arguments can depend on logical forms that are more refined than the truth functional logical forms on which we have concentrated. Section 7.1 is intended to familiarize readers with the finer logical structures of statements and arguments. While a very limited method for determining the validity of some of these arguments will be presented, the general method for determining the validity of these arguments will have to be a topic of a more advanced text.

A glaring omission in Chapters 2–6 has been their failure to discuss reasoning involving probabilities. In much of our lives we face probabilities rather than certainties, and some familiarity with this notion seems essential to any thinking person. Unfortunately, probability theory is a complicated subject more appropriate for an advanced text. However, in order not to leave the reader completely in the dark, Section 7.2 presents some of the rudiments of probability theory that can be useful in at least certain situations. In sum, the two topics covered in this chapter are intended to fill some gaps and to whet the reader's appetite for a further study of reasoning.

7.1 The Finer Structure of Statements

While relatively coarse, the truth functional logical forms discussed in Chapter 3 have a wide range of applications. Furthermore, the method of chain arguments studied there reflects ordinary reasoning processes in a clear manner. In a sense the method merely articulates how we ordinarily think, and becoming more adept with the method can be seen as a way of improving our ordinary reasoning abilities. When we turn to methods for dealing with the validity of arguments depending on the finer structure of statements, the matter is somewhat different: The easy methods are limited in application and the general method involves complexities that students typically forget when they finish the text. Thus, the ultimate practical value of the methods beyond those developed in this text can be doubted. On the other hand, what is indubitable is that one often becomes clear on what a statement asserts if one can discern the fine logical form of that statement. Thus, the principal practical aim of this section is best seen as an attempt to make the reader fluent with the finer logical structures of statements. Starting with relatively unrefined forms in Section 7.1.1, we shall present a way of delving quite deeply into the structures of statements in Section 7.1.3. Section 7.1.2 is a short section that presents a method for determining the deductive validity of the limited class of arguments called syllogisms.

7.1.1 Venn Diagrams and the A, E, I, O Structures

Aristotle identified and analyzed four different kinds of finer structures that propositions can assume, and these structures have been given the traditional names "A," "E," "I," and "O."[1] These structures can be exemplified by the following four statements:

A: All pigs fly.
E: No pig flies.
I: Some pigs fly.
O: Some pigs do not fly.

The choice of the letters "A," "E," "I," and "O" may now be explained: The Latin words for affirming and denying are "affirmo" and "nego." The A and I statements both affirm while the E and O statements deny; thus, the affirming A and I statements take the first two vowels from 'affirmo', while the denying E and O statements take the vowels from 'nego'. The first vowel is used for the universal "all" or "no" statement, while the

1. Readers of Section 4.6.2 will recognize these as one version of the A, E, I, and O structures discussed there. The treatment of this version of these structures in this section differs somewhat from the earlier treatment (in which the aim was to present structural similarities between several versions of the A, E, I, O structures).

second vowel is used for the so-called existential "some" statements. While this may sound terribly amateurish by modern standards, a surprisingly large number of statements do have one of these A, E, I, or O structures. Thus, these structures form a good starting point for analyzing the finer logical forms of statements.

The meanings traditionally assigned to the A, E, I, and O statements can be explained by reference to diagrams called Venn diagrams in honor of the English logician Venn. In Figure 7.1 the area covered by the rectangle U is intended to represent all the things that exist in the universe. The area covered by the circle P represents all the pigs in the universe, and the area covered by the circle F represents all things in the universe that (naturally) fly. The areas 1, 2, 3, and 4, respectively, represent pigs that don't fly, pigs that do fly, flying things that aren't pigs, and things that are neither pigs nor flying things.

Given this understanding of Figure 7.1, the A statement that all pigs fly can be understood as saying that pigs are included among the things that fly. Alternatively, it could be understood to say that nonflying pigs don't exist. Let us adopt the following convention:

> *The diagram of a statement S shades out an area just in case S asserts that the class of objects represented by that area is empty.*

Thus, the Venn diagram for the A statement considered would shade out area 1, that is, the area representing nonflying pigs. The effect of this (as can be seen below) is that the class of pigs has now been included in the class of flying things—just the thing we wanted for the A statement. The E statement that no pigs fly can be understood as asserting that flying pigs don't exist, in other words, that the class of pigs that fly is empty. Thus, the Venn diagram for our E statement would shade out area 2 in Figure 7.1. These results are summarized in Figure 7.2, which gives the Venn diagrams for each of the A, E, I, and O statements.

The I statement that some pigs fly has traditionally been understood to assert that there is at least one flying pig, in other words, that the class each of whose members is both a pig and a flyer is nonempty. Similarly, the O statement that some pigs don't fly is traditionally understood to

Figure 7.1.

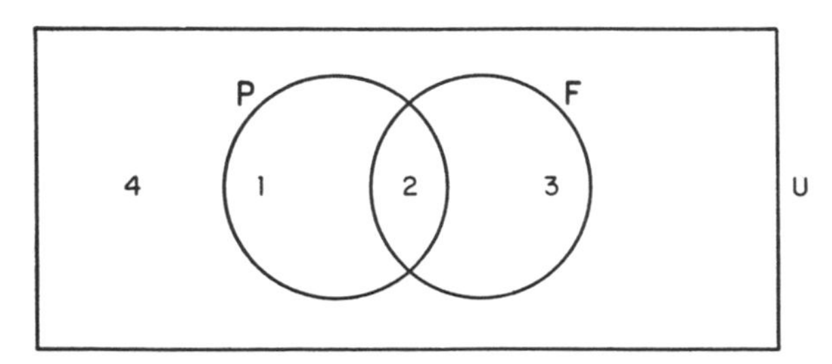

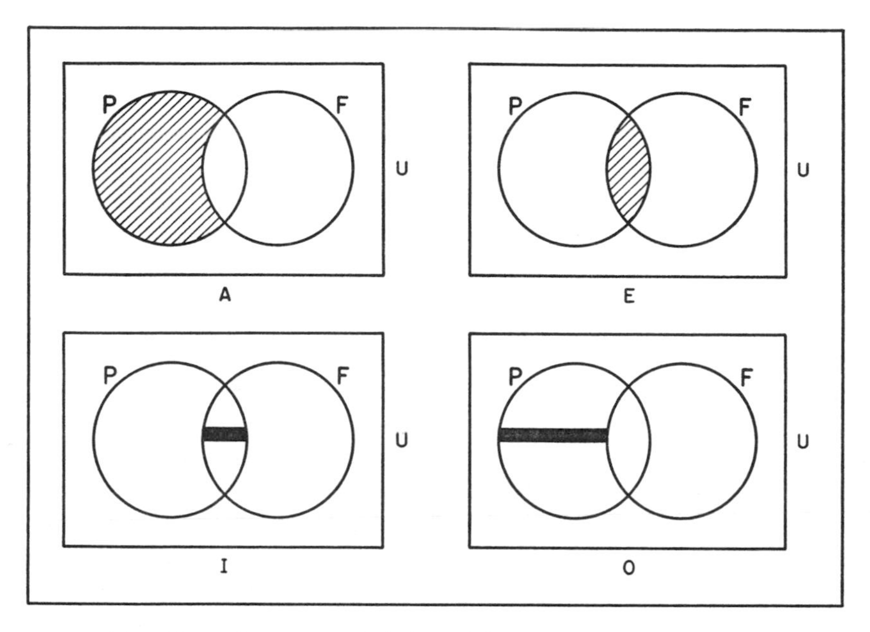

Figure 7.2. Venn diagrams for A, E, I, and O statements.

assert that the class of pigs that fail to fly has at least one member, in other words, is nonempty. Let us adopt the following convention:

The diagram of a statement S has a solid bar going through (all subareas of) an area but not extending beyond that area just in case S asserts that the class of objects represented by that area is nonempty.

Given this convention, the Venn diagrams for our I and O statements are given in Figure 7.2, which gives a perspicuous representation of all the A, E, I, and O statements.

The first step to appreciating the finer structure of statements is to develop the ability to spot the A, E, I, O structures when one encounters them. While the standard A statement is of the form 'All men are animals', the second term can be an adjectival expression or a verb phrase. Thus, 'All men are mortal' and 'All men eat grains' are A statements asserting that all men are mortal beings and that all men are eaters of grain. In general, the second term in any of the A, E, I, O structures may be a noun phrase, a verb phrase, or an adjectival phrase. Often the term 'All' is dropped in an A statement, and sometimes it is phrased in the singular as well. 'Men are sinners' and 'Man is a sinner' presumably both state that all men are sinners. A more complicated example might be 'Tom loves sorority girls'. This presumably states something like 'All sorority girls are persons Tom loves (to meet)'. On the other hand, 'Sorority girls love Tom' presumably states something like 'All sorority girls are persons who love Tom'. Interestingly, many temporal statements can

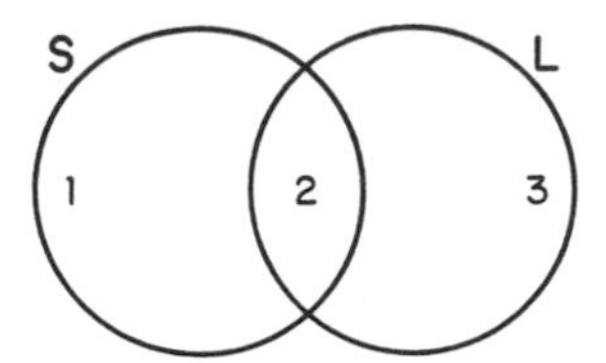

Figure 7.3.

also be seen to have A, E, I, O structures. Thus 'I met him before' is an I statement that some moments before the present moment are moments at which I met him; similarly, 'I never met him' is an E statement that no moment (prior to the present one) is a moment at which I met him.

These examples suggest that there is not going to be any simple general formula for spotting the A, E, I, and O structures. While some translation schemes for the A, E, I, and O structures will be given in Section 7.1.3, when things are not straightforward, one is often best advised to rely on the meanings of the A, E, I, and O structures as represented by the Venn diagrams. We suggest two such ways of thinking about the matter in terms of the example 'Tom loves sorority girls':

(1) Imagine or draw a Venn diagram involving sorority girls and persons Tom loves (to meet) (Figure 7.3). What relation between the representing areas is claimed by 'Tom loves (all) sorority girls'? Nothing specific is said about area 3, the area for people Tom loves who aren't sorority girls. Area 2, the area for sorority girls Tom loves (to meet), is evidently being claimed to be the area where the sorority girls are to be found. That is, the area for sorority girls is being claimed to be included in the area for the persons Tom loves (to meet). But this means that area 1, the remaining potential area for sorority girls, must be shaded out. Doing this precisely gives us the Venn diagram for 'All sorority girls are persons Tom loves (to meet)'.

(2) Ask what would be the *precise* falsification of 'Tom loves sorority girls'; in other words, ask for a condition C such that the statement is false if *and only if* C obtains. The precise falsification for our statement would presumably be the existence of one or more sorority girls not loved by Tom, that is, a bar in but not going beyond area 1. Thus, the precise *verification* condition must deny this; in other words, area 1, the area representing sorority girls not loved by Tom, must be empty or shaded out in the Venn diagram. Thus, we are once again led to the Venn diagram for 'All sorority girls are (persons) loved by Tom'. A good way of checking one's intuitions is to try out both the direct way (1) and the indirect way (2) to confirm the same result. Beyond this, there is no substitute for practice.

EXERCISES—SECTION 7.1.1

Take the A, E, I, and O forms to be 'All F are G', 'No F are G', 'Some F are G', and 'Some F are not G'. For each of the following, determine which of the A, E, I, and O forms it has *and* specify what 'F' and 'G' would be.

1. All philosophers are tiresome.
2. Some kids aren't nice.
3. No friend of Tom is a friend of Jane.
4. Some doctors are crooks.
5. Rock singers are thrilling.
6. Tom hates to eat tamales.
7. There are some stupid Harvard men.
8. He is unloved by some.
9. There are no winged horses.
10. She is not without admirers.
11. Not all of her friends are rich.
12. Only the rich attend Princeton.
13. John never kissed Mary.
14. He has eaten haggis before.
15. Blessed are the poor.
16. She doesn't stand for fools.
17. He has nights without a date.
18. People in Kentucky are happy when the sun shines.
19. She visited Paris in the spring.
20. He isn't always happy.

7.1.2 Syllogisms

Not only do Venn diagrams give a perspicuous representation of the meanings of the A, E, I, and O statements; they can also be used to determine the validity of a limited set of argument forms that are called syllogisms (as well as some minor variations of syllogisms). A SYLLOGISM is an argument having the following three features: (1) It has precisely two premises and a conclusion. (2) Each premise as well as the conclusion has an A, E, I, or O structure. (3) The number of terms (e.g., pigs, flyers) in the premises and the conclusion combined are precisely three. Thus, for example, 'All pigs fly, Some flyers eat corn / Some pigs eat corn' is a syllogism composed of the three terms pigs, flyers, and corn eaters.

The Venn diagram method of testing the validity of syllogisms has three stages:

(*I*) *Draw the Venn diagram for the three terms involved.* Thus, letting P, F, and C stand for pigs, flyers, and corn eaters, the Venn diagram for these three terms or classes is given by Figure 7.4. For the purpose of testing the validity of syllogisms, we can disregard the rectangle representing the universe. Furthermore, it is a matter of indifference which of the three circles is taken to represent which of the three terms involved

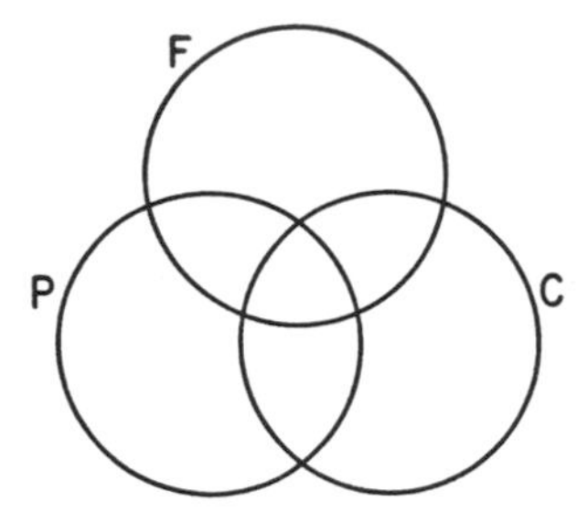

Figure 7.4.

in the syllogism. Obviously, except for the labeling of the circles, the first step of the Venn diagram test is identical for all syllogisms.

(*II*) *Diagram each of the two premises on the Venn diagram* (Figure 7.4) *given in Step* (*I*). Because we are mixing universal and existential statements, one point needs to be noted: the two diagrams given in Figure 7.5 are equivalent. Both Figure 7.5a and b superimpose two statements: 'Pigs exist (or there are some pigs)' and 'All pigs fly (or are flyers)'. As far as the first statement goes, we know that there is at least one thing in the class represented by the circle P, but we are not told whether that one thing is a flying pig or a nonflying pig. The second statement asserts that the class of nonflying pigs is empty. The effect of conjoining the two statements is precisely that the class of nonflying pigs is empty and the class of flying pigs is nonempty. It is immaterial whether we use Figure 7.5a or b to represent this combined effect. Figure 7.5a first diagrammed 'Pigs exist' (hence the bar extends to the entire P area) and then superimposed 'All pigs fly' on that diagram. Figure 7.5b first diagrammed 'All pigs fly', and then noting that the area of nonflying pigs is empty, limited the bar for 'Pigs exist' to the unshaded area of P. While Figure 7.5a and b are equivalent, clearly Figure 7.5a is messier. To simplify our diagrams, we adopt the following procedures:

> *When diagramming a syllogism,* (*1*) *diagram the universal premise before any existential premise, and* (*2*) *in diagramming existential premises, do not extend the bar to subareas that are already shaded out.*

Figure 7.5.

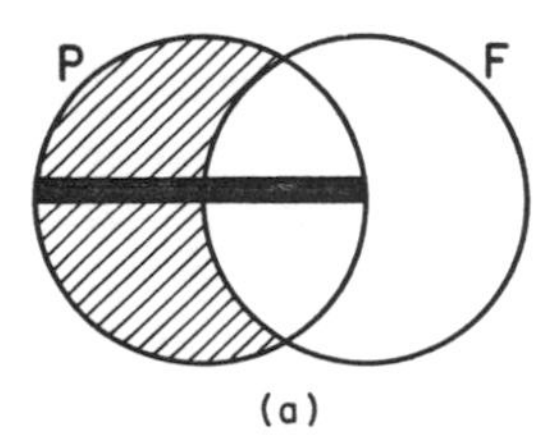

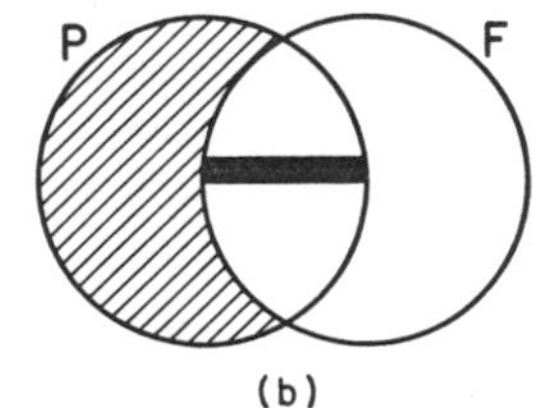

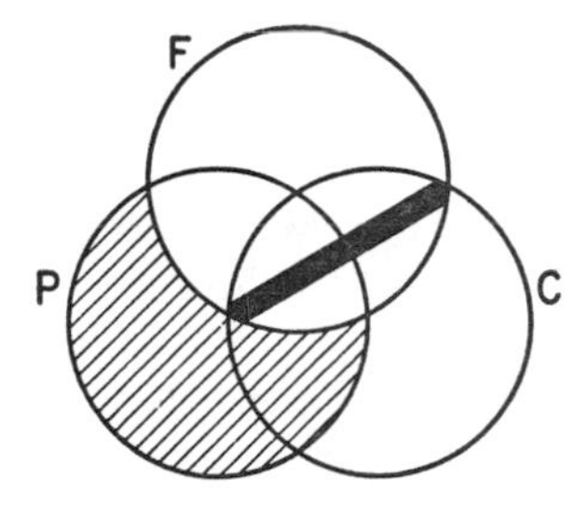

Figure 7.6.

Diagramming the premises of the syllogism 'All pigs fly, some flyers eat corn / some pigs eat corn' gives us Figure 7.6.

(III) Determine the syllogism to be valid or not by determining whether or not the diagram for the conclusion is contained in the diagram resulting from step (II). Specifically this means the following for the four possible conclusions:

A: All F are G: The area representing F's that aren't G's must be completely shaded (although other areas may be shaded as well).
E: No F are G: The area representing things that are both F and G must be completely shaded (although other areas may be shaded as well).
I: Some F are G: There must be a bar somewhere in the area representing F's that are G, *and that bar must not extend beyond that area.*
O: Some F are not G: There must be a bar somewhere in the area representing F's that aren't G, *and that bar must not extend beyond that area.*

Notice that for I (and O) conclusions, it is not required that the bar extends to all subdivisions of the area representing F's that are G (F's that aren't G). This is because if it's already given that some subclass of F's that are G is nonempty, the entire class of F's that are G must also be nonempty. For example, if it's already given that the class of rich American widows is nonempty, the class of American widows must also be nonempty. This means that there is a slight difference between diagramming an I statement and reading an I statement as a conclusion. In diagramming 'Some Americans are widows' one can't assume which subclass of American widows is nonempty (unless some other subclass has already been shaded out); thus, the bar must extend to all unshaded subareas of the area for American widows. But in reading 'Some Americans are widows' as a conclusion, it suffices that there is a bar somewhere in the area for American widows (such as the area for rich American widows), *as long as the bar doesn't extend beyond the area for American widows.*

Our sample syllogism given in Figure 7.6 is not valid because the conclusion 'Some pigs eat corn' is not contained in the diagram resulting from Step (II). As we just remarked, the trouble is not that the solid bar doesn't extend to the (shaded) area representing nonflying, corn-eating pigs. As long as there is a solid bar somewhere within the area representing corn-eating pigs, the conclusion would be contained *provided that the solid bar doesn't extend beyond the area representing corn-eating pigs.* What prevents our syllogism from being valid is precisely that the solid bar extends beyond the area representing corn-eating pigs. That is, the diagram tells us that there is at least one corn-eating flyer, but it doesn't tell us whether this corn-eating flyer is a pig or not.

To apply the method of Venn diagrams to a slightly different syllogism, consider 'No pig flies, some flyers eat corn / some corn eaters are not pigs'. The result of Step (II) would give us Figure 7.7. This diagram assures us there is at least one corn eater that is not a pig because there is a solid bar in the area representing nonpig corn eaters *and the bar doesn't extend beyond this area.* (As noted earlier, it is immaterial that the bar doesn't extend to the area for corn eaters that are neither pigs nor flyers.) Thus, the diagram for the conclusion 'Some corn eaters are not pigs' is contained in the diagram that results from diagramming the premises (Figure 7.7), and the syllogism is deductively valid.

Such is the Venn diagram method for testing the validity of syllogisms, which may be summarized as follows:

(1) Draw a diagram of three circles with labels for the syllogism's three terms.
(2) Diagram the premises according to the following rules:
  (a) Diagram A and E statements before diagramming I and O statements.
  (b) In diagramming I and O statements, extend the bar to all unshaded subareas of the area in question.
(3) The syllogism is valid if and only if the conclusion can be read off from the diagram.

Reading an I or O statement requires that the bar occurs somewhere within the area in question and does not extend beyond the area in question.

This method can be extended to arguments slightly more complex than syllogisms as long as there are only three terms. With enormous effort, one can extend it to arguments containing four terms. The effort is in making a Venn diagram for four terms that would involve sixteen subareas; this requires a very careful drawing of four ovals. It is geometrically impossible to draw a Venn diagram for five terms in two dimensions, and

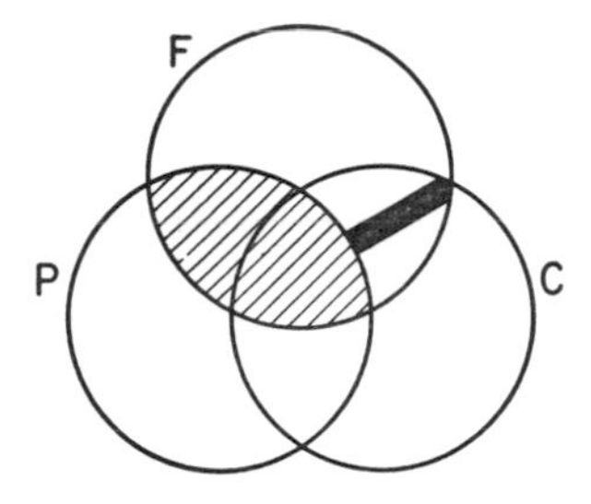

Figure 7.7.

this represents an essential limitation to the method of Venn diagrams for testing the deductive validity of arguments.

EXERCISES—SECTION 7.1.2

Using Venn diagrams, determine whether or not the following syllogisms are valid:

1. All Japanese eat fish, all fish eaters are healthy / all Japanese are healthy.
2. No tiger is scared, some tigers are zoo dwellers / some zoo dwellers are not scared.
3. All Americans are proud, some proud people are vain / some Americans are vain.
4. All her boyfriends are intelligent, some Stanford men are not intelligent / some Stanford men are not her boyfriends.
5. All murderers are vicious, all criminals are vicious / all murderers are criminals.
6. Some women are mothers, some mothers have sons / some women have sons.
7. All women are intelligent persons, no intelligent person has too many children / no woman has too many children.
8. No Republican is a Democrat, no Democrat is an independent / no Republican is an independent.
9. No friend of Jane is a friend of Tom, some friends of Mary are not friends of Jane / some friends of Mary are not friends of Tom.
10. All Italians love the opera, some Italians are Mafia members / some lovers of opera are Mafia members.

7.1.3 Quantificational Structures

In this section we shall present a general way of arriving at a large class of fine-grained logical forms. These logical forms are called quantificational logical forms and they involve taking 'all' and 'some' as logical constants in addition to the truth functional connectives considered in Chapter 3.

Consider again the Venn diagram for an A statement, for example, 'all horses are mammals' (Figure 7.8):

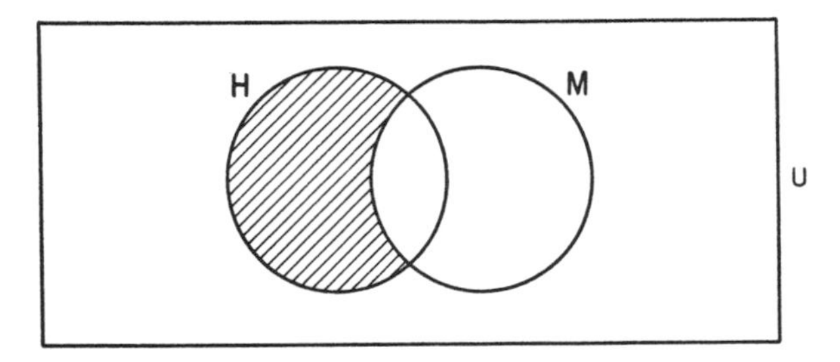

Figure 7.8.

From this diagram we can see that the A statement asserts that everything in the universe fails to be both a horse and a nonmammal. Let us introduce 'x', 'y', 'z', etc. as symbols that (ambiguously) stand for or name various individual things in the universe. The A statement 'All horses are mammals' can then be understood as asserting:

Everything x in the universe is such that x fails to be both a horse and a nonmammal.

Let us abbreviate 'everything x in the universe is such that', 'everything y in the universe is such that', and so on, by '(x)', '(y)', etc. Recalling our abbreviations for truth functional connectives like 'and' and 'not', the A statement can be successively seen to assert:

(x)[x fails to be both a horse and a nonmammal]

(x)[−(x is a horse & x is a nonmammal)]

(x)[−(x is a horse & −[x is a mammal])]

Recalling that '−(p & −q)' and 'p ⊃ q' have logically identical truth conditions, our A statement can be seen to assert:

(x)(x is a horse ⊃ x is a mammal).

This last statement is the standard way of displaying the QUANTIFICATIONAL STRUCTURE of the A statement 'All horses are mammals'. In this structure, the term '(x)' is called the UNIVERSAL QUANTIFIER, and its usual short reading is 'for all x'.

The Venn diagram for an E statement shows that the E statement 'no pigs fly' asserts that everything in the universe fails to be both a pig and a flyer, that is,

(x)[x fails to be both a pig and a flyer]

Going through the same kind of considerations as in the last paragraph, we end with the standard display of an E statement's quantificational structure:

(x)[−(x is a pig & x is a flyer)]

(x)[x is a pig ⊃ −(x is a flyer)]

Turning to the I statement that some philosophers are dull, its Venn diagram makes perspicuous that the statement asserts:

There is at least one x in the universe such that x is both a philosopher and dull.

Let us abbreviate 'there is at least one x in the universe such that', 'there is at least one y in the universe such that', and so on, as '(∃x)', '(∃y)', etc. The I statement that some philosophers are dull can then be taken to assert

(∃x)(x is a philosopher & x is dull).

This is the standard way of displaying the quantificational structure of an I statement. The term '(∃x)' is called the EXISTENTIAL QUANTIFIER, and it is usually read as 'there is (or exists) an x such that'. Similar considerations show that the quantificational structure of the O statement that some athletes are not dumb can be displayed as:

(∃x)[x is an athlete & −(x is dumb)]

Let us use 'F', 'G', and so on to abbreviate terms like 'pig', 'corn eater', 'dull being', and so on. What we have so far said about the quantificational structure of statements can then be summarized by Table 7.1. Under the column "ordinary formulation" we have listed the most obvious formulation of the statement type in question. We shall shortly give some translation schemes that will help in translating other formulations into the "canonical forms" listed under the "quantificational structure" column.

Let us now note that the use of quantifiers along with truth functional connectives allows us to display far more than the A, E, I, O structures of statements. To see this, consider

S: Every blond boy has a mother who is blond.

TABLE 7.1.

Statement Type	*Ordinary Formulation*	*Quantificational Structure*
A	All F's are G's.	(x)(x is an F ⊃ x is a G)
E	No F is a G.	(x)[x is an F ⊃ −(x is a G)]
I	Some F's are G's.	(∃x)(x is an F & x is a G)
O	Some F's are not G's.	(∃x)[x is an F & −(x is a G)]

The coarsest structure of S is that of an A statement. Thus, S can be rewritten as

(x)(x is a blond boy ⊃ x has a mother who is blond)

However, this structure can be further analyzed by analyzing 'x is a blond boy' and 'x has a mother who is blond' in terms of truth functional connectives and other quantifiers. Thus, to say that x is a blond boy is surely to say that x is both blond and a boy. This suggests that the finer structure of 'x is a blond boy' is given by

x is blond & x is a boy.

To say that x has a blond mother is to say that there is some entity y in the universe such that y is a mother of x and y is blond. Thus, the finer structure of 'x has a mother who is blond' is given by

(∃y)(y is a mother of x & y is blond).

Putting all of this together, the finer quantificational structure of S is displayed by formulating S as:

(x)[(x is blond & x is a boy) ⊃ (∃y)(y is a mother of x & y is blond)].

This example shows how the use of truth functional connectives along with quantifiers allows us to display complicated logical structures of statements. To arrive at such structures, one should follow the PRINCIPLE OF TRANSLATING INWARD—that is, the principle of successively displaying the finer structures of statements. At least in a rough way, the process of translating inward can be seen to have four stages:

(1) Get the truth functional structure of the statement, although sometimes the truth functional structure is simply 'p' (as in our last example). The discussion of Section 3.3.3 should be sufficient for this stage.

(2) Get the coarse quantificational structure of the statement or substatement. This usually means getting the expression into one of the A, E, I, or O forms. Occasionally one may have to resort to structures like '(x)(x is an F)' or '(∃x)(x is an F)'. This would be the case with statements like 'Everything is a substance or mode' and 'There are giraffes', which would respectively become '(x)(x is a substance or mode)' and '(∃x)(x is a giraffe)'.

As for determining the relevant A, E, I, or O structure, we have already seen in Section 7.1.1 that the Venn diagram is often a helpful tool in determining which of these structures is asserted by a statement. As an auxiliary, we list below some of the more frequent ways in which the A, E, I, and O structures may be expressed. Any formulation listed under "A" should be treated to have the quantificational structure '(x)(x is an F ⊃ x is a G)', and the corresponding structure applies for the listings under the other three statement types.

A: Every (any, each) F is a G. Only G's are F's. Being an F is sufficient for being a G. Being a G is necessary for being an F. F's are G's.	E: There are no FG's. (e.g., There are no flying pigs.) Nothing is an FG.
I: There are FG's. FG's exist.	O: Not all F's are G's. All F's are not G's.

One word of caution is in order concerning the A, E, I, O structures: Structures of the following type are almost always incorrect formulations of statements occurring in ordinary language:

(x)(x is F & x is G)

(∃x)(x is F ⊃ x is G).

The first structure asserts that everything whatsoever in the universe is both an F and a G; however, this is an extraordinarily strong statement that is false as long as there is at least one thing that isn't an F or one thing that isn't a G. Thus, for example, it certainly isn't the structure of 'all horses are animals'. The second displayed structure is an extremely weak statement that is true as long as there is at least one thing that isn't an F or at least one thing that is a G. This can be seen by noting that 'p ⊃ q' and '−p v q' have logically identical truth conditions; thus, the second displayed structure amounts to the same thing as '(∃x)[−(x is F) v x is G]. This is certainly not the structure of 'Some men have five eyes'; if it were, it would be true because there is at least one thing in the universe that isn't a man.

(3) Get the finer truth functional structure of the expressions involved. Thus, for example, faced with 'x is a substance or a mode', this should be analyzed as 'x is a substance v x is a mode'. Much of this is obvious. Perhaps not quite so obvious is the translation scheme:

x is F & x is G:	x is an FG, x is an F which (that, who) is G.

Thus, both 'x is a flying pig' and 'x is a pig which (that, who) flies' have the structure 'x is a pig & x flies'.

(4) Get the finer quantificational structure of the expressions involved. The finer quantificational structure usually involves an embedded expression of the A, E, I, O forms. The following examples are typical

of frequently occurring patterns, with the A, E, I, O type being indicated in brackets:

x loves everyone:	$(y)(y \text{ is a person} \supset x \text{ loves } y)$	[A]
everyone loves x:	$(y)(y \text{ is a person} \supset y \text{ loves } x)$	[A]
x loves no one:	$(y)[y \text{ is a person} \supset -(x \text{ loves } y)]$	[E]
x hates someone:	$(\exists y)(y \text{ is a person} \ \& \ x \text{ hates } y)$	[I]
x eats beans:	$(\exists y)(y \text{ is a bean} \ \& \ x \text{ eats } y)$	[I]
x is a head of a horse:	$(\exists y)(y \text{ is a horse} \ \& \ x \text{ is a head of } y)$	[I]
x doesn't like some women:	$(\exists y)[y \text{ is a woman} \ \& \ -(x \text{ likes } y)]$	[O]

Three things ought to be noted about displaying the finer quantificational structures:

(a) When a quantifier is introduced as part of the finer structure, choose a quantifier in a different variable from the variables with which one has been working. Thus, in the above example, the quantifier was chosen in 'y' because we were working with the variable 'x'.

(b) In order to get the finer A, E, I, O structure, one should ask two questions: (i) Is the expression positive or negative? If it's positive, the A or I statement is suggested, whereas an E or O statement is suggested if it is negative. (ii) Is the expression making some universal (all type) claim or only an existential (some type) claim? If it's universal, an A or E statement is suggested, whereas an I or O statement is suggested if it is only an existential claim. Thus, because 'x loves everyone' is both positive and universal, an A statement is its formulation; because 'x loves no one' is negative and universal, an E statement is its formulation. As for 'x eats beans', it is clearly positive, but is it universal or existential? That is, is it claiming that x eats at least some things that are beans or that x eats all things that are beans? Surely 'x eats beans' doesn't mean to suggest that x eats everything in the universe that is a bean; hence, it's a positive existential or an I-type statement. Similarly, because 'x is a head of a horse' doesn't claim that x is the head of every horse in the universe, 'x is a head of a horse' is a positive existential or I-type statement.

(c) Occasionally, the finer quantificational structure is not in one of the A, E, I, O forms. Two such patterns may be cited:

x loves x: x loves himself.

$(\exists y)(x \text{ is a mother of } y)$: x is a mother.

While 'x is a mother' could be treated as 'Fx', it is often more perspicuous to treat it as asserting that there is something of which it is a mother.

If one follows stages (1)–(4) in order, surprisingly complex structures can be displayed with relative ease. To have another example, let us consider a variation on a famous example by De Morgan. We simply display the successive stages of translating inward and put the results all together at the end:

If all sows are pigs, all heads of sows are heads of pigs.
All sows are pigs ⊃ all heads of sows are heads of pigs.
  All sows are pigs: (x)(x is a sow ⊃ x is a pig).
  All heads of sows are heads of pigs: (x)(x is a head of a sow ⊃ x is a head of a pig).
    x is a head of a sow: (∃y)(x is a head of y & y is a sow).
    x is a head of a pig: (∃y)(x is a head of y & y is a pig).
(x)(x is a sow ⊃ x is a pig) ⊃ (x)[(∃y)(x is a head of y & y is a sow) ⊃ (∃y)(x is a head of y & y is a pig)].

Beginners often think that there is an error in this translation, because the variable 'x' is used for sows and pigs in the antecedent, while in the consequent 'x' is used for heads and 'y' for pigs and sows. The plain fact of the matter is that once the mate of the open parenthesis following a quantifier is reached, one is free to use the variable again in any way one wishes.

Having found a way of displaying the quantificational logical structure of a statement, the next step is to abstract the logical form. Roughly, this is a matter of introducing blanks for expressions other than the logical particles. For the sake of visual ease and variety, in Chapters 4 and 5 we allowed ourselves the luxury of occasionally using expressions involving capital letters like 'H' and 's[E]' to represent sentences. However, with the advent of quantificational structures, we need to abstract from sentences as well as predicates like 'is a pig'. Thus, we revert to limiting sentence letters to lowercase roman letters and we shall use capital roman letters 'F', 'G', and so on as blanks for expressions like 'is a pig' and 'loves'. Such letters will be called *predicate letters* in order to keep them distinct from sentence letters. To clarify the matter, let us return to our recent example about pigs and sows. As before, the logical form of this statement is extracted by specifying a scheme of abbreviation. However, a scheme will now take the following form:

S: ⟨1⟩ is a sow.
P: ⟨1⟩ is a pig.
H: ⟨1⟩ is a head of ⟨2⟩.

A scheme of this type is to be understood as follows: Given any unquantified expression like 'x is a pig', the variable that is in the location of '⟨1⟩' is to be placed immediately after the predicate letter in abstracting the logical form. Thus, given the above scheme, 'x is a sow' and 'y is a sow' are to be respectively abbreviated by 'Sx' and 'Sy'. Given a scheme like the one for 'H', the understanding is that faced with an expression like 'x is a head of y', the variable in the position of '⟨1⟩' is to be placed immediately after the predicate letter and the variable in the position of '⟨2⟩' is to be placed in the second position after the predicate letter. Thus, given the above scheme, 'x is a head of y', 'z is a head of x', and 'x is a head of z' would respectively be abbreviated as 'Hxy', 'Hzx' and 'Hxz'. Thus, with the indicated scheme of abbreviation, the quantificational logical form of our statement becomes:

(x)(Sx ⊃ Px) ⊃ (x)[(∃y)(Hxy & Sy) ⊃ (∃y)(Hxy & Py)].

Consider now another example:

If Ken is a child of a Japanese-American, all of Ken's children are Japanese-Americans.

Following our strategy of translating inward, we would have:

Ken is a child of a Japanese-American ⊃ all of Ken's children are Japanese-Americans.
Ken is a child of a Japanese-American: (∃y)(Ken is a child of y & y is a Japanese-American).
All of Ken's children are Japanese-Americans: (x)(x is a child of Ken ⊃ x is a Japanese-American).

Let us take the scheme of abbreviation as:

J: ⟨1⟩ is a Japanese-American.

We would then have:

(∃y)(Ken is a child of y & Jy) ⊃ (x)(x is a child of Ken ⊃ Jx).

This is not very satisfactory because we still have the expressions 'Ken is a child of y' and 'x is a child of Ken'. Clearly, we would like to use something like 'C' for '⟨1⟩ is a child of ⟨2⟩' in order to extract more of the form. But what are we to do with 'Ken'? 'Ken' is meant as a name of a particular person, and thus treating it as a variable is a bit awkward. Let us therefore introduce constants in addition to variables, and use lower-case letters of the first part of the alphabet for constants and the lower-case letters of the tail end of the alphabet for variables. What this means is that schemes of abbreviation have to include abbreviations for names and singular terms in general. Doing this, we might augment our scheme as follows:

a: Ken
C: ⟨1⟩ is a child of ⟨2⟩.

The logical form of our statement then becomes:

(∃y)(Cay & Jy) ⊃ (x)(Cxa ⊃ Jx).

This should suffice to give the reader a fairly decent understanding of how to determine the deep logical structures of statements. We conclude our discussion of the finer structure of statements with a glimpse of what is involved in a further study of quantification theory.

Having arrived at quantificational logical forms, we have in effect also arrived at quantificational argument forms like:

$\underline{(x)Fx}$	$\underline{Fa}$
Fa	$(\exists x)Fx$

Roughly, to say that such an argument form is valid is to say: Regardless of how we fill the blanks and whatever nonempty universe we choose, if all the premises come out true, so does the conclusion. (We exclude the empty universe because it is of no interest to us.) It should be fairly evident that the above two argument forms are valid: If '(x)Fx' comes out true, everything in the universe is an F with the result that whatever 'a' may name in the universe, it too must be an F. Similarly, if 'Fa' comes out true, there is at least one thing in the universe that is F (namely, a), and thus '(∃x)Fx' comes out true. These two argument forms are, respectively, instances of inference rules called UNIVERSAL INSTANTIATION and EXISTENTIAL GENERALIZATION, and the method of chain arguments is enhanced in quantification theory to allow lines to be put down by these inference rules.

What complicates life in quantification theory is that the parallel Existential Instantiation and Universal Generalization fail to be deductively valid. We can see this in the following instances:

$\underline{(\exists x)Fx}$	$\underline{Fa}$
Fa	$(x)Fx$

Let 'a' be filled by 'Ronald Reagan'. The first form leads from truth to falsity when 'F' is filled by '⟨1⟩ is a dog catcher for Santa Barbara County'; the second leads from truth to falsity when 'F' is filled by '⟨1⟩ is a president of the United States'. Getting around these difficulties is what complicates quantification theory. It is precisely these complications that are beyond the scope of this text, and thus further discussion of quantification theory must await a more advanced text.

EXERCISES—SECTION 7.1.3

1. Determine the quantificational forms of the following statements using the scheme of abbreviation indicated:
   (a) No friend of Tom is a friend of Jane.
   [F: ⟨1⟩ is a friend of ⟨2⟩; a: Tom; b: Jane.]
   (b) He is unloved by some (persons).
   [P: ⟨1⟩ is a person; L: ⟨1⟩ loves ⟨2⟩; a: he.]

(c) She is not without male admirers.
[M: ⟨1⟩ is a male person; A: ⟨1⟩ admires ⟨2⟩; a: she.]
(d) Only the rich attend Princeton.
[R: ⟨1⟩ is a rich person; A: ⟨1⟩ attends ⟨2⟩; a: Princeton.]
(e) No nun is a daughter of a nun.
[N: ⟨1⟩ is a nun; D: ⟨1⟩ is a daughter of ⟨2⟩.]
(f) Among teachers only scientists are rich.
[T: ⟨1⟩ is a teacher; R: ⟨1⟩ is rich; S: ⟨1⟩ is a scientist.]
(g) Unless some philosopher is a king, no king is admired by a philosopher.
[P: ⟨1⟩ is a philosopher; K: ⟨1⟩ is a king; A: ⟨1⟩ admires ⟨2⟩.]
(h) People in Kentucky are happy when the sun shines (in Kentucky).
[L: ⟨1⟩ is a person living in ⟨2⟩ at ⟨3⟩; S: ⟨1⟩ is a moment at which ⟨2⟩ shines in ⟨3⟩; H: ⟨1⟩ is a moment at which ⟨2⟩ is happy; a: the sun; b: Kentucky.]
(i) He who eats beans is not admired by anyone who admires a Pythagorean philosopher.
[P: ⟨1⟩ is a person; E: ⟨1⟩ eats ⟨2⟩; B: ⟨1⟩ is a bean; F: ⟨1⟩ is a Pythagorean philosopher; A: ⟨1⟩ admires ⟨2⟩.]
(j) Anyone who drives a car while drunk is insane.
[P: ⟨1⟩ is a person; D: ⟨1⟩ is a moment of time at which ⟨2⟩ is drunk; C: ⟨1⟩ is a moment of time at which ⟨2⟩ drives a car; I: ⟨1⟩ is insane.]

2. Which of the following are true and which are false? Give reasons for your answers.
(a) '(x)Fx, (x)Gx / (x)(Fx & Gx)' is deductively valid.
(b) '(∃x)Fx, (∃x)Gx / (∃x)(Fx & Gx)' is deductively valid.
(c) '−(x)Fx / (x)−Fx' is deductively valid.
(d) '−(x)Fx / (∃x)−Fx' is deductively valid.

7.2 Probabilities

The aim of this section is to acquaint readers with some rudimentary relations governing probabilities. We start with an introductory discussion on the meaning of 'probability' before entering into some of the probability relations established by probability theory.

7.2.1 Introduction: What Are Probabilities?

While we all use the term 'probability' in our daily lives, the intuitive meaning of the term is both unclear and subject to controversy. However, because it would be pointless to pursue any discussion of probability without giving the reader some sense of what 'probability' might mean in a concrete way, we start with two idealized (and somewhat inaccurate) accounts of how that term might function in our ordinary life.

Let p state that this die will land showing six spots, and let 'Pr(p) = 1/6' abbreviate 'The probability that p is true is 1/6'. One way of trying to explain the intuitive notion of probability is to explain what it might mean to say: Pr(p) = 1/6 for (a person) A. This latter statement might be taken to express the degree of confidence A has in the truth of p measured from 0, which indicates absolute confidence in the falsity of p, to 1, which indicates absolute confidence in the truth of p; .5 would indicate no confidence in either the truth or falsity of p. The level of confidence A has in p might in turn be understood in terms of how much A is willing to wager that p is true. Thus, we might understand the 1/6 level of confidence that A has in p in terms of $1 being the maximum A is willing to put into a betting pool that will pay him back $6 if p should turn out to be true. Somewhat more generally, we might try to explain the term 'probability' by saying: Pr(p) = n/m for A if and only if $$n$ is the maximum A is willing to put into a betting pool that would pay him $$m$ back if p should turn out to be true. Thus, if we recast our example as Pr(p) = .17 for A, insofar as .17 = 17/100, $17 is the maximum that A is willing to put into a betting pool that pays him back $100 if p should turn out to be true. The particular examples show that some qualifications must be made concerning A having sufficient money to enter the pool, his willingness to enter into wagers at all, and so on. Furthermore, the interpretation is likely to be inaccurate in assuming that $2x is always twice as desirable or valuable for A as $x. Still, it gives some sort of intuitive meaning to the notion of probability. To have a term, we might call this the subjective interpretation of probability.

One can to an extent "objectify" the subjective interpretation by relativizing probabilities to what a perfectly rational gambler with sufficient money would wager in an epistemic circumstance. Under this idealization, one might say Pr(p) = n/m in an epistemic situation E if and only if $$n$ is the maximum an ideally rational gambler in E is willing to put into a betting pool that would pay him $$m$ if p should turn out to be true. (This account makes the possibly questionable assumption that all ideally rational gamblers in the same epistemic circumstance would give a statement the same probability.)

Another useful interpretation of our intuitive notion of probability is the so-called frequency interpretation. Recalling that p stated that this die will land showing six spots, we might interpret 'Pr(p) = 1/6' as: If a die just like this one were rolled sufficiently often, the side with six spots turns up in approximately one-sixth of the total number of rolls. To make the matter a little more precise, we can imagine the die rolled 10 times, 100 times, 1000 times, and so on. Let n be the number of times the die is rolled. The idea in our example is that as n increases, we should get closer and closer to one-sixth of the total rolls coming up on the side with six spots. Let f(p;n) be the frequency or ratio of the die coming up on a side with six spots in n rolls. Thus, if the die is rolled 100 times and it comes up on a side with six spots 20 of the 100 times, f(p;100) = .2. The statement 'Pr(p) = 1/6' might then be taken as: f(p;n) = $1/6 \pm r$, such that as n increases r decreases and as n increases toward infinity r converges toward (or gets closer and closer to) 0. Clearly, this interpretation involves a considerable amount of idealization; that is, we have to think in terms of this die or a die *just like this one* being rolled indefinitely. Nor is it clear how to apply this interpretation in some cases; for example, are we to understand the probability of *me* getting a divorce from *her* as a statement about the frequency with which an infinite number of persons just like me will get divorced from women just like her? Still, the frequency interpretation seems to capture some aspects of our intuitive understanding of probability.

In contrast to these intuitive notions of probability, probability theory is a pure mathematical theory that says nothing about frequencies or betting behaviors. It leaves its central term 'probability' undefined except for the structural constraints imposed on it by the axioms of probability theory. Given its axioms, a number of theorems can be derived in the sense that the theorems are conclusions of deductively valid arguments in which the premises are the axioms of probability theory. The axioms and theorems of probability theory constitute the "statements" of pure probability theory. Some have suggested that 'probability' be given a "logical" interpretation, whereby probabilities are whatever the pure mathematical theory "says" they are. However, this fails to give us any clear way in which probability relations may be applied in ordinary circumstances. Furthermore, if we give the term 'probability' either the subjective or the frequency interpretation suggested, the axioms of probability theory will turn out to agree fairly well with our intuitive notion of probability. Thus, our approach will be this: While probability theory will be seen as a pure mathematical theory, we shall think of it as being interpretable in either the subjective or the frequency sense we have indicated.

A consequence of this approach is that the mathematical theory of probability *under interpretation* (in either of the two ways) can be seen to be a systematic articulation of our intuitive notion of probability and the inferences it licenses. For example, in probability theory, a "fair coin" is defined as one in which the probability of landing heads is 1/2 and in which the probability of landing tails is 1/2 on any given toss of the coin. Rounded off to the closest thousandths, it is a theorem of probability theory that Pr(the number of heads in 100 tosses of a fair is greater than 60) = .033. Now suppose you have a coin C and take it be a "fair" one in the frequency sense; in other words, as the number of tosses of C is increased, the ratio of heads will get closer and closer to 50 percent. One can then interpret the theorem as stating: In approximately 3 percent of times will tossing C a hundred times result in more than 60 heads. Alternatively, one might interpret a fair coin as one on which one is willing to bet even money that it will come up heads on any given toss. One could then interpret the theorem as stating: If one were a rational bettor with enough money, $33 is the maximum one would be willing to put into a betting pool that pays one $1000 if the next 100 tosses of the coin result in more than 60 heads.

Given this background, we turn to an intuitive presentation of certain rudimentary aspects of probability theory. It is an "intuitive" presentation in two senses: (1) While some axioms (or definitions incorporating the axioms) and theorems will be stated, the theorems will not be proven in any rigorous manner from the axioms. Although a sketch of a proof is typically provided, we shall also be relying on the reader's intuitions. (2) Both as a way of making intuitive sense of what the theory says and as a way of applying the results of the theory, we shall assume a background in which the term 'probability' is given one or the other of the intuitive interpretations. The basic aim of this section is to familiarize the reader with some basic probability relations and their applications.

EXERCISES—SECTION 7.2.1

1. Let Pr(p) = n/m for an ideally rational gambler in a certain epistemic situation. Assume that in such a case $$(m - n)$ is the maximum such a gambler is willing to put into a pool that pays him $\$m$ if '−p' is true. On this assumption show that Pr(−p) is 1 − Pr(p) for such a gambler. [*Hint:* what would the Pr(p) and Pr(−p) add up to?]
2. *Odds* are given by ratios like 1:6 and 3:2 and the meaning is this: the odds L:W is being offered for the truth of 'p' if and only if the ratio of the amount a bettor will lose to the amount the bettor will win by betting for the truth of 'p' is L/W. Thus, if you are offered 1:6 odds that a certain horse will win, a $2 bet will result in you losing your $2 if the horse doesn't win, and you getting back $14 if your horse does win (i.e., the $2 you put in plus the $12 you won). Odds are said to be fair if the [L × Pr(−p)] = [W × Pr(p)], that is, when the ratio or odds L/W equals the ratio Pr(p)/Pr(−p).
   (a) Suppose that Pr(p) = 0.3 for an ideally rational gambler (in a certain epistemic situation). Will he or she accept 1:2 odds in favor (i.e., for the truth) of 'p'?
   (b) Given the same assumptions about the gambler as in (a), what would he or she take to be fair odds for the truth of 'p'?
3. Flip a coin twenty-five times and take 'p' to be 'The coin lands heads'. Record f(p;5), f(p;10), f(p;15), f(p;20), and f(p;25).

7.2.2 Probability Spaces and Elementary Theorems

Probability theory will not allow us to speak of probabilities except with reference to what I will call a probability space. Probability spaces can in turn be understood with reference to what are normally called possibility spaces or sample spaces. But before explaining these notions, it will be useful to introduce a handy bit of logic terminology. The deductive validity of ϕ/θ was understood in terms of θ being true in every possible world in which ϕ is true; this circumstance can also be described by saying ϕ implies or entails θ. Although logicians generally dislike this idea, we can introduce the notion of *relative entailment.* The idea is that ϕ entails θ relative to D if in every possible world in which D is true, θ comes out true whenever ϕ comes out true. Clearly, ϕ entails θ relative to D just in case D, ϕ / θ is valid. Two notions we have had no occasion to introduce until now (except in the optional Section 3.4) are "logical truth" and "logical falsehood" (or inconsistency): A statement is logically true if it is true in every possible world and a statement is logically false if it is false in every possible world. Again, we can relativize these notions: ϕ is logically true (false) relative to D just in case in every possible world in which D is true, ϕ is true (false). Clearly, ϕ is logically true relative to D if and only if D / ϕ is valid, and ϕ is logically false relative to D just in case D/$-\phi$ is valid. Given this much, we turn to an account of possibility spaces.

Possibility spaces can be understood either in terms of possible events or states of affairs or else in terms of statements that talk about such events or states of affairs. It should be intuitively plausible that the possibility space for a single throw of a die consists in six possible events:

s_1: The die turns up with one spot.
s_2: The die turns up with two spots.

. . .

s_6: The die turns up with six spots.

Alternatively, we could say the possibility space for a single toss of the die is described by the statements 'the die turns up with one spot' [or statement 's_1' for short], 'the die turns up with two spots' ['s_2'], . . . , 'the die turns up with six spots' ['s_6']. It is convenient for us to be able to go back and forth between these two ways of thinking of the elements of a possibility space.

An essential feature of a possibility space is that the set of events that composes it are mutually exclusive and jointly exhaustive. To say that the events or states $s_1, \ldots, s_6$ are mutually exclusive is to say that only one of the six possible events or states can actually happen (or be realized); to say that the six events or states are jointly exhaustive is to say that at least one of them must happen (or be realized). Using our recently introduced terminology, this amounts to: relative to the description of the space—'a toss of a die'—'s_i & s_j' is logically false when $i \neq j$ (mutual exclusiveness) and 's_1 v s_2 v . . . v s_6' is logically true (joint exhaustiveness). Possibility spaces can be finite (have a finite number of possible events in them) or be infinite. We shall concentrate on finite possibility spaces because probability theory for infinite possibility spaces is complex and requires significant knowledge of mathematics. For our purpose, then, a POSSIBILITY SPACE can be defined as follows:

> *A finite possibility space consists of a finite number of possible events* $\{s_1, \ldots, s_n\}$ *described by statements* 's_1', . . . , 's_n' *that are mutually exclusive and jointly exhaustive (relative to the description of the space).*

A probability space, as I will use the term, is simply a possibility space plus an assignment of probabilities to each member of the possibility space. Thus, a probability space for a single toss of a die might assign the probability 1/4 to each of s_2, s_4, and s_6, and the probability 1/12 to each of s_1, s_3, and s_5. Such a probability space would be a probability space for a toss of a die that is biased in favor of turning up with an even number of spots, and we shall write, for example, $Pr(s_2) = 1/4$, to indicate that the probability space assigns 1/4 to the event s_2. The probability space for a single toss of a fair die would assign the probability 1/6 to each of the six possible events in the possibility space, that is, $Pr(s_i) = 1/6$ for all i. Two features are essential for a probability space:

(1) The probability assigned to a possible event must be between 0 and 1 (inclusive).
(2) The probabilities assigned to the members of the possibility space must add up to 1.

These two requirements can be seen as fundamental axioms of probability theory. We shall incorporate these axioms as part of our definition of PROBABILITY SPACE:

A finite probability space consists of a possibility space $\{s_1, \ldots, s_n\}$ *and an assignment of a probability* $Pr(s_i)$ *to each member of the possibility space such that*

(i) $0 \leq Pr(s_i) \leq 1$ for all i, and
(ii) $Pr(s_1) + Pr(s_2) + \ldots + Pr(s_n) = 1$.

In an intuitive way the possibility space may be understood to give us the basic events relative to the purpose at hand. A probability space then assigns probabilities to the events that are basic in its possibility space. Although the probabilities assigned to the basic events need not be known or specified, probability theory allows us to talk meaningfully of a probability of an event only relative to some probability space that is taken to have *some* assignment of probabilities to the basic events.

Let us then suppose that we have the probability space for a single toss of a fair die, that is, one in which each basic event $s_1, \ldots, s_6$ is assigned the probability 1/6. What is the probability that the toss of a die will result in an even number of spots turning up? Obviously it should be 1/2. The question is: how do we get this probability? Roughly, the answer is: the event that an even number of spots turns up can be realized by three basic events s_2, s_4, and s_6 in the probability space; adding the probabilities of these basic events, we get $1/6 + 1/6 + 1/6$, or 1/2. We may take it as an axiom of probability theory that the probability of an arbitrary event, relative to a probability space, is the sum of the probabilities of the basic events that realize that arbitrary event. This axiom and the foregoing discussion may be expressed in terms of the following definition:

For an arbitrary event or state p, a basic event s in the probability space S realizes p just in case if s occurs p must occur (i.e., 's' entails 'p' relative to S). Let T(p,S) be the set of basic events in S that realize p. Relative to the probability space S, Pr(p) = the sum of the probabilities of the members of T(p,S).[2]

In the above definition, " 's' entails 'p' relative to S" is meant to be shorthand for: 's' entails 'p' relative to the description of the possibility space of S. T(p,S) might be thought of as the truth set for 'p' in S, that is, the set of basic events in S that make 'p' true.

Taking the relativization to the description of the possibility space as tacit, the definitions so far developed may be summarized or abbreviated as follows:

> Finite Probability Space =
>
> (1) A set of basic events $\{s_1, \ldots s_n\}$ that are mutually exclusive and jointly exhaustive, and
> (2) An assignment of probabilities between 0 and 1 to each of $s_1, \ldots, s_n$ so that the assigned probabilities sum to 1.
>
> In a probability space S, Pr(p) = sum of the probabilities of the basic events in S that realize p.

Given our definitions, certain theorems follow. For convenience, a listing of all the significant definitions and theorems is given at the end of Chapter 7. Each of our theorems should be understood to be prefixed by the clause "Whatever probability space S Pr(p) is taken to be relative to." An obvious theorem is

> **T1:** $0 \leq \text{Pr(p)} \leq 1$.

For any space S, Pr(p) is sum of the probabilities of the events in T(p,S). Clearly the probabilities of each member of S are between 0 and 1 and the probabilities of all the members of S add up to 1. Thus, insofar as T(p,S) is a subset of S, Pr(p) must be between 0 and 1.

2. This definition and the axiom it incorporates will have counterintuitive results if the event p has realizations outside of the probability space S. For example, relative to the probability space for a single toss of a fair coin, Pr(the sun rises tomorrow v the side with six spots turns up) = 0 + 1/6 = 1/6. We could avoid this result by limiting the last clause of the definition to a probability space S that is appropriate for p in the sense that any possible realization of p is included in S. Rather than formulating cumbersome definitions for a probability space appropriate for p, the basic theorems of probability theory are formulated so that they come out correct whatever probability space the quantity Pr(p) is taken to be relative to. As the consequence, the basic probabilistic relations we shall establish are *ipso facto* correct for probability spaces appropriate for p. Of course, to avoid counterintuitive results in specific cases, we must choose a probability space appropriate to the specific event in question.

Let us take expressions like 'is logically true (relative to S)' to mean: is logically true or at least logically true relative to S. Another obvious theorem is then given by

T2: If ϕ and θ have logically identical truth conditions (relative to S), $Pr(\phi) = Pr(\theta)$.

If ϕ and θ have logically identical truth conditions (relative to S), any basic state that realizes the truth of ϕ will also realize the truth of θ and vice versa. Thus, $T(\phi,S) = T(\theta,S)$. Because relative to S $Pr(\phi)$ and $Pr(\theta)$ are the sums of the probabilities of the members of $T(\phi,S)$ and $T(\theta,S)$, respectively, $Pr(\phi) = Pr(\theta)$.

The next two theorems concern logically true and false statements:

T3: If ϕ is logically true (relative to S), $Pr(\phi) = 1$.
T4: If ϕ is logically false (relative to S), $Pr(\phi) = 0$.

Intuitively these theorems state: if ϕ is logically true (relative to S), because every basic event of S realizes ϕ, $Pr(\phi) = 1$; if ϕ is logically false (relative to S), because no basic event of S realizes ϕ, $Pr(\phi) = 0$. Somewhat more rigorously we may say: If ϕ is logically true (relative to the description D of the possibility space of S)—that is, if ϕ can't be false (given the possibility space)—any statement will entail ϕ (relative to D). Thus, all statements stating the basic events of S will entail ϕ (relative to D); hence $T(\phi,S) = S$. Because the sum of the probabilities of all members of S must add up to 1, $Pr(\phi) = 1$. As for theorem 4, we have been understanding a possibility space S to include *only possible* events; that is, a statement stating a basic event of S is true in some world in which the description D of the space S applies. Because no statement that is possibly true can entail a statement that can't be true, if ϕ is logically false (relative to D), no statement stating a basic event of S space will entail ϕ (relative to D). Hence, $T(\phi,S)$ is the null class, and the sum of the probabilities of 0 members is evidently 0.

A highly useful theorem is given by

T5: $Pr(p \vee q) = Pr(p) + Pr(q) - Pr(p \,\&\, q)$.

The easiest way to see this is to draw a Venn diagram of an arbitrary probability space S (see Figure 7.9). Pr(p) sums the probabilities of basic

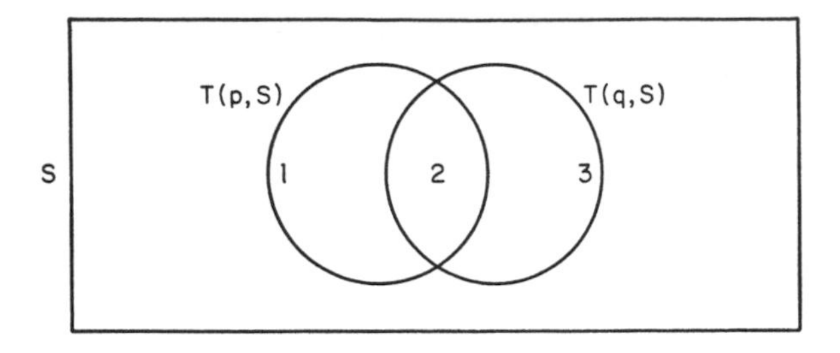

Figure 7.9.

events in the areas 1 and 2, while Pr(q) sums the probabilities of the basic events in areas 2 and 3. Thus, Pr(p) + Pr(q) sums the probabilities of the events in areas 1 and 3 once and the probabilities of events in area 2 twice. On the other hand, Pr(p v q) sums the probabilities of events in areas 1, 2, and 3 once. Clearly, Pr(p v q) should equal Pr(p) + Pr(q) *minus* the second summing of the probabilities in area 2. But summing the probabilities in area 2 simply is Pr(p & q). Hence, the formula given in theorem 5 must be correct for any probability space.

T5 yields two immediate results:

> **T6:** If 'p & q' is logically false (relative to S), Pr(p v q) = Pr(p) + Pr(q).
> **T7:** Pr(−p) = 1 − Pr(p).

As for T6, if 'p & q' is logically false (relative to S), then by T4, Pr(p & q) = 0. Thus, by T5, Pr(p v q) simply is Pr(p) + Pr(q). As for T7, because 'p v −p' is a logical truth, by T3, Pr(p v −p) = 1. Because 'p & −p' is logically false, by T6, Pr(p v −p) = Pr(p) + Pr(−p). Thus, we may conclude Pr(p) + Pr(−p) = 1, and T7 follows.

Let us now try to apply some of these theorems to simple cases. Suppose we have two tosses of a coin. Letting, for example, ⟨t,h⟩ represent the outcome in which the first toss resulted in tails and the second in heads, the possibility space for two tosses of the coin would be: ⟨t,t⟩, ⟨t,h⟩, ⟨h,t⟩, ⟨h,h⟩.[3] If we take this to be an *equiprobable space*—that is, a probability space in which each basic event has the same probability—

3. It may be wondered: How can ⟨t,h⟩, for example, be a *basic* event because it is composed of two events, that is, the first toss resulting in t and the second toss resulting in h? It must be remembered that our use of 'basic' does not carry with it any ultimate physical or metaphysical sense. As we are using the term, an event is considered basic in a situation relative to *the purpose at hand.* For our present purpose of analyzing two tosses of a coin, it is most convenient to treat each possible sequence like ⟨t,h⟩ to be basic. The only requirement is that basic events constituting the possibility space are mutually exclusive and jointly exhaustive. Because our example satisfies this requirement, there can be no objection to treating the basic events in the manner we have.

each of the four basic events would have the probability of 1/4. In that case, Pr(at least one heads turns up) = 3/4: Because ⟨h,h⟩, ⟨h,t⟩, and ⟨t,h⟩ are the basic events that realize at least one heads turning up, summing their probabilities gives 3/4.

To consider a slightly more complex example, consider the game of craps. The game may be described as follows:

> Each play involves a player throwing two dice and the number of spots showing on the two dice are added together. The first play has three possible outcomes: (1) The play results in a 7 or an 11; in this case the player WINS. (2) The first play results in 2, 3, or 12, in this case the player LOSES (craps out). (3) The first play results in 4, 5, 6, 8, 9, or 10; in this case the game continues to the second play with whatever number the player threw becoming "his number." The game continues then with as many plays as necessary for outcome (a) or (b) below to be realized, the game terminating with whichever outcome occurs first: (a) A play results in the player's number (determined in the first play), and the player WINS. (b) A play results in a 7, and the player LOSES.

Assuming that tosses of two dice result in an equiprobable space of thirty-six basic events (e.g., 6 and 3, 3 and 6, 1 and 4), what is the probability that the player wins on the first play? Clearly this is given by Pr[(the player throws a 7) v (the player throws an 11)]. Because the disjuncts are mutually exclusive (i.e., because the conjunction of the two disjuncts is logically false), the answer involves simply adding Pr(the player throws a 7) and Pr(the player throws an 11). Letting, for example, ⟨3,4⟩ represent the first die turning up with three spots and the second die turning up with four spots, the basic events that realize the player throwing a 7 are: ⟨6,1⟩, ⟨1,6⟩, ⟨5,2⟩, ⟨2,5⟩, ⟨4,3⟩, ⟨3,4⟩. Because each of these events has the equal probability of 1/36, Pr(the player throws a 7) = 6/36. The basic events that realize the player throwing an 11 are ⟨6,5⟩ and ⟨5,6⟩, and Pr(the player throws an 11) = 2/36. Thus, the probability of the player winning on the first play is 8/36 or 2/9.

Another class of problems involving equiprobable spaces is the class of random selection problems. The concept of RANDOM SELECTION is precisely defined in probability theory as follows:

The selection of an item from a total population S is random = Every member of S has an equal probability of being selected.

Suppose one draws one card at random from a fifty-two-card bridge deck; this means that each card has an equal probability of being selected. Thus, the probability that one draws a king is 4/52, because four basic events (corresponding to the four kings in the deck) realize drawing a king. Suppose now that one has drawn a king and then draws a second card. What is the probability that the second-drawn card is a king? The answer depends on whether the selection occurs with or without replacement. If it occurs with replacement—that is, if the first card is put back in deck and one draws at random from the fifty-two-card deck, the probability of drawing a king the second time is again 4/52. On the other hand, if the selection occurs without replacement—that is, if the first card isn't put back in the deck—the probability of drawing a king on the second draw reduces to 3/51: The population or deck of cards has reduced to fifty-one items, giving rise to a fifty-one-membered equiprobable space, and three of these basic events will realize drawing a king.

To consider a slightly more interesting case, suppose you have been dealt 7, 8, 9, and 10 of hearts and a 2 of spades in draw poker; you discard the 2 of spades and draw a card at random. What is the probability that you will end up with a straight flush [i.e., five cards in consecutive order (a straight) and five cards of the same suit (a flush)]? The population in this case should be taken to have forty-seven cards. It's determined that one isn't going to get any of the five cards that were initially dealt. Any other card has an equal probability of being drawn (because it isn't specified what cards were randomly dealt to the other players). Clearly, only two basic events—the jack of hearts and 6 of hearts—will realize a straight flush. Thus, the probability of drawing a straight flush is 2/47.

Such are some of the applications of the elementary theorems we have developed. However, although we have talked about coins and bridge decks, the reader should remember that our discussion is in the mathematical theory of probability. Applying our results to real coins and decks of cards involves interpretation. Although the mathematical definition of randomness can be carried over to the real world by interpreting 'probability' in the usual ways, neither the frequency sense nor the subjective sense is likely to allow us to determine in a useful way that a selection was random. In fact, how we empirically determine that a selection was random is a most difficult question to which there is no obvious solution. In cards we assume that the selection is random if the cards are sufficiently shuffled and we know the dealer to be a fairly honest person. When an election poll selects a sample class, it takes certain precautions that the selection is random. But there is no way of assuring a random selection, and the failure of a random selection is often conjectured in the postmortems that surround an election when the poll's predictions go awry. Still, the kinds of results we obtained and shall obtain can be applied as long as we are in a fairly good position to presume that the selection is random.

EXERCISES—SECTION 7.2.2

1. Assume that Pr(p & q) = .3 and Pr(p & −q) = .2. What is Pr(p)? Justify your answer with reference to the elementary theorems. [*Hint:* 'p' and 'p & (q v −q)' have logically identical truth conditions.]

2. Determine the following probabilities for the game of craps (assuming the dice are fair):
   (a) The probability that the player loses on the first play.
   (b) The probability that the game goes on to the second play.
   (c) Assuming that the game has gone on to the second play, the probability that the player doesn't lose on the second play.
3. Let a "worthless" hand in draw poker be a hand lacking flushes, straights, straight flushes, and two or more cards of the same kind. Assume that you drew Q, J, 10, and 9 of spades and a 2 of diamonds. If you discard the 2 of diamonds and draw one more card at random, what is the probability that you will end up with a "worthless" hand?

7.2.3 *Conditional Probability*

A highly important notion in probability theory is given by its abbreviatory definition of the quantity Pr(p/q), called the conditional probability of p given q. Where Pr(q) ≠ 0, this quantity is defined as:

$$\Pr(p/q) = \Pr(p \,\&\, q) \,/\, \Pr(q).$$

Clearly, probability theory can define anything in any way it pleases. Furthermore, because the definition is merely an abbreviatory definition, probability theory is entirely expressible without a notation for conditional probability. However, there is every reason to think that a highly useful concept has been isolated by the definition. It seems to correspond very well to our intuitive idea of the probability of an event p given that we have found out that (or are interested in cases in which) q is true.

Both as a way of making this evident, and as a way of further explaining the defined notion of a conditional probability, suppose we have a population of 200 that breaks down as in Table 7.2. If we select one person at random, the probability that the person is rash is clearly .5. If we are only interested in the population of women and select a woman at random, the probability that the person is rash is .4. Thus we should expect that Pr(a person is rash / the person is a woman) = .4. The definition tells us that this is so:

Pr(the person is rash & a woman) / Pr(the person is a woman)

$$= \frac{(40/200)}{(100/200)} = .4.$$

TABLE 7.2.

	Men	*Women*
Sensible	40	60
Rash	60	40

It should be clearly noted that Pr(p/q) is a different quantity from Pr(q ⊃ p). Pr(q ⊃ p) = Pr(−q v p) = Pr(−q) + Pr(p) − Pr(−q & p). Letting 'q' be 'the (selected) person is a woman' and 'p' be 'the (selected) person is rash)', Pr(q ⊃ p) = .5 + .5 − .3 = .7.

One of the most important uses of the idea of conditional probability is that it gives us an intuitively plausible way of defining probablistic or statistical independence. Consider again our imaginary population of men and women who are rash and sensible, and suppose we select a person from this population at random. Pr(the selected person is rash) = .5. On the other hand, we saw that the conditional probability Pr(the selected person is rash / the selected person is a woman) = .4. Under this condition, there is some sort of a probabilistic or statistical dependence between the selected person being rash and the selected person being a woman. On the other hand, suppose we select two people from the population with replacement. If the selection is random, we should think the result of the first selection has no effect on the result of the second selection (because we are selecting with replacement). This idea that there is a probabilistic or statistical independence between the two selections is naturally expressed by saying: Pr(the second-selected person is a woman / the first-selected person is a woman) = Pr(the second-selected person is a woman). Such appears to be the intuitive idea of statistical independence. In any event, the formal definition of STATISTICAL OR PROBABILISTIC INDEPENDENCE in probability theory is given by:

> Two events p and q are statistically (probabilitistically) independent $=_{df}$ Pr(p/q) = Pr(p).

Given this much, we turn to a few theorems concerning conditional probabilities. It can be shown that conditional probabilities given q form an altered probability space, mainly the one that results from the original by adding to the specification that 'q' is true. This means that all of the theorems for unconditional probabilities we established earlier apply to conditional probabilities. For example, Pr[(p v r) / q] = Pr(p/q) + Pr(r/q) − Pr[(p & r) / q]. We can summarize this fact by the following theorem:

> **T8:** Theorems T1–T7 apply to conditional probabilities.

It is often easier to determine conditional probabilities than unconditional probabilities. Thus, the definition of conditional probabilities allows us a way of assessing the probabilities of conjunctions. That is, $Pr(p \& q) = Pr(p/q) \times Pr(q)$. Applying this formula twice gives us:

$$\begin{aligned} Pr(p \& q \& r) &= Pr(p / q \& r) \times Pr(q \& r) \\ &= Pr(p / q \& r) \times Pr(q / r) \times Pr(r). \end{aligned}$$

Generalizing to *n* terms, we have:

T9: $Pr(p_1 \& p_2 \& \ldots \& p_n) = Pr[p_1/(p_2 \& \ldots \& p_n)] \times Pr[p_2 / (p_3 \& \ldots \& p_n)] \times \ldots \times Pr(_{pn-1}/p_n) \times Pr(p_n)$

This is often referred to as the multiplication theorem of the probability calculus. Given that $Pr(p \& q) = Pr(p/q) \times Pr(q)$, if p and q are statistically independent, $Pr(p \& q) = Pr(p) \times Pr(q)$. Thus, we have an immediate theorem:

T10: If p and q are statistically independent, $Pr(p \& q) = Pr(p) \times Pr(q)$.

Sometimes, T10 is used as the definition of statistical independence [in which case it will be a theorem that if p and q are statistically independent, $Pr(p/q) = Pr(p)$]. Because the mutual independence of many events is messy to specify in terms of conditional probabilities, it is sometimes defined as:

> *A set of events is statistically* MUTUALLY INDEPENDENT *if and only if the probability of any conjunction of the events is the product of the probabilities of the conjuncts.*

In any event, we shall take it that T10 has an expansion to *n* terms.

We present one final theorem relating to conditional probabilities that is of general interest. From the definition of conditional probabilities, we know:

$$Pr(p/e) = Pr(e \& p)/Pr(e).$$

Because 'p v −p' is logically true, 'e' and 'e & (p v −p)' ultimately have logically identical truth conditions; thus, 'e' and '(e & p) v (e & −p)' also have logically identical truth conditions (cf. the logically identical pair Dist Section 3.7). Thus, by T2 and T5, $Pr(e) = Pr[(e \& p) \vee (e \& -p)] =$

Pr(e & p) + Pr(e & −p). Using the definition of conditional probability three times, the displayed formula for Pr(p/e) becomes:

$$\textbf{T11:}\quad Pr(p/e) = \frac{Pr(e/p)Pr(p)}{Pr(e/p)Pr(p) + Pr(e/-p)Pr(-p).}$$

Theorem 11 is a simplified version of what is called Bayes' theorem. What it does is to give the correct relation between "probabilistic converses"—Pr(p/e) and Pr(e/p). If we suppose 'e' is some bit of evidence and 'p' something we want to infer from 'e', T11 is often helpful because we might know Pr(e/p).

As an application of T11, suppose we have a disease D afflicting 5 percent of our total population and that a test T for it has been developed. Let 'd' and 't' be given as

d: Person A has disease D.
t: Test T performed on A indicates he has D.

Suppose the accuracy of test T is given by the following probabilities:

$Pr(t/d) = .95 \qquad Pr(t/-d) = .05$

Let A be a randomly selected person from the total population. What is the conditional probability Pr(d/t)? By T11:

$$Pr(d/t) = \frac{Pr(t/d) \times Pr(d)}{[Pr(t/d) \times Pr(d)] + [Pr(t/-d) \times Pr(-d)]}$$
$$= \frac{(.95) \times (.05)}{[(.95) \times (.05)] + [(.05) \times (.95)]} = .5$$

Initially the test sounded pretty good, because it had something like a 95 percent accuracy rate. Yet when an arbitrary person tests positive, there is only a 50/50 chance that the person has D. In a sense, the problem is that the disease is too rare. If 50 percent of the population was afflicted by it, Pr(d/t) becomes what we should expect: .95. But there aren't too many diseases afflicting half the population. It would appear that if the disease is reasonably infrequent, we would want the Pr(t/−d) to be very low before urging that everyone be tested for it by T.

To see the same problem in another way, let us say that a person is "odd" if he or she is pensive, impractical, socially inept, and likely to overtheorize. Suppose that 99 percent of the philosophers are odd and that only 1 percent of nonphilosophers are odd. If you happen upon an odd person, isn't it a near certainty that he or she is a philosopher? Application of Bayes' theorem shows otherwise. Even with the generous estimate that 1 person in 100 is a philosopher, the probability of an odd person being a philosopher is only .16; that is, the probability of an odd person *not* being a philosopher is .84. The difficulty again is that the base rate of philosophers, or the antecedent probability of a randomly selected person being a philosopher (whether or not the person is odd), is too low. Because it was very tempting to think that the odd person was virtually certain to be a philosopher, we might single out this error as the FALLACY OF IGNORING ANTECEDENT PROBABILITIES. It is an inferential fallacy that may be diagrammed as:

> Ignoring Antecedent Probabilities:
> Pr(e/h) is high & Pr(e/−h) is low → Pr(h/e) is high.

It has often been remarked that it is dangerous to make inferences on the basis of stereotypes. Let 'h' be some conclusion based on someone satisfying a certain stereotype, and let 'e' be the statement that the given person satisfied the stereotype. Often the stereotypes are unreliable in the sense that Pr(e/h) (the probability of a philosopher being odd) is not that high or Pr(e/−h) (the probability of a nonphilosopher being odd) is not that low. But even if we assume that the stereotypes are reliable (as we suppose quite implausibly with respect to philosophers and oddness), the inference is still dangerous because the antecedent probability Pr(h) (the probability that any person is a philosopher whether or not he fits the stereotype) may be quite low. It is this danger involved in making inferences on the basis of stereotypes that is brought to the foreground by the Fallacy of Ignoring Antecedent Probabilities.

EXERCISES—SECTION 7.2.3

1. Suppose two fair dice A and B are thrown. Determine the following conditional probabilities:
   (a) The probability that both dice come up with four spots, given that die A has come up with four spots.
   (b) The probability that both dice come up with four spots, given that one die has come up with four spots.
   (c) The probability that both dice come up with an even number of spots, given that one die has come up with four spots.

   Hint: 'One die has come up with four spots' means: A has come up with four spots v B has come up with four spots.
2. Suppose you have a group composed of 100 college graduates and 100 who aren't college graduates. Assume also that all 200 have been married at least once. Let 'p' be 'a randomly selected person is divorced at least once' and let 'q' be 'a randomly selected person is a college graduate'.
   (a) Suggest a breakdown of the 200 people that would make 'p' and 'q' statistically independent.

(b) Suggest a breakdown of the 200 people that would make Pr(p/q) > Pr(p).
(c) Suggest a breakdown of the 200 people that would make Pr(p/q) < Pr(p).

3. Suppose a man (whom we'll call the chicken sexer) is found in Australia who is remarkably good at distinguishing male chickens by merely looking at them from a distance. Let 'm' and 's' be given by:

   'm': The chicken checked by the chicken sexer is male.
   's': The chicken sexer claims that the chicken is a male.

   For a randomly selected chicken from the population checked by the chicken sexer, assume that Pr(s/m) = .95 and that Pr(s/−m) = .10. For each of the following assumptions about the population of chickens checked by the chicken sexer, determine Pr(m/s) for a randomly selected chicken from the population:

   (a) The population divides into 50 percent males and 50 percent nonmales.
   (b) The population divides into 90 percent males and 10 percent nonmales.
   (c) The population divides into 10 percent males and 90 percent nonmales.

4. There is a group of 100 people composed of engineers and lawyers, so that if a person is not an engineer, he is a lawyer. You are given the following personality profile[4]:

   > Jack is a forty-five-year-old man. He is married and has four children. He is generally conservative, careful, and ambitious. He shows no interest in political and social issues and spends most of his free time on his many hobbies, which include home carpentry, sailing, and mathematical puzzles.

   Suppose that 80 percent of the engineers in the group fit this personality profile and that only 20 percent of the nonengineers (the lawyers) fit this profile. For each of the assumptions (a) and (b) below, determine the probability that a randomly chosen person from this group fitting the profile is an engineer.

   (a) The group consists of seventy engineers and thirty lawyers.
   (b) The group consists of thirty engineers and seventy lawyers.

   Postscript: In Kahneman and Tversky's experiment, the subjects were not given the "80 percent–20 percent reliability" of these profiles (a rate that is merely assumed in our problem). However, one group of subjects was told (a) and the other group was told (b). Both groups gave the virtually identical probability of the person being an engineer given that he fits the profile. This is fairly dramatic evidence that the Fallacy of Ignoring Antecedent Probabilities (or Base Rates) is quite common.

5. Consider the following argument:

   > Because God is by definition omnipotent, omniscient, benevolent, and so on, given the assumption that He exists, it would be certain that our universe would be orderly. On the other hand, given the assumption that God doesn't exist, the probability of our universe being orderly would be quite low. Given that our universe *is* orderly, it's most probable that God exists.

   Assume for the sake of the argument that Pr(universe is orderly / God doesn't exist) = .01. Criticize the argument by showing that the premises could be true and yet the conclusion false.

---

4. This problem is partially derived from experiments by Kahneman and Tversky, reported in Nisbett and Ross, *Human Inference,* pp. 143–44.

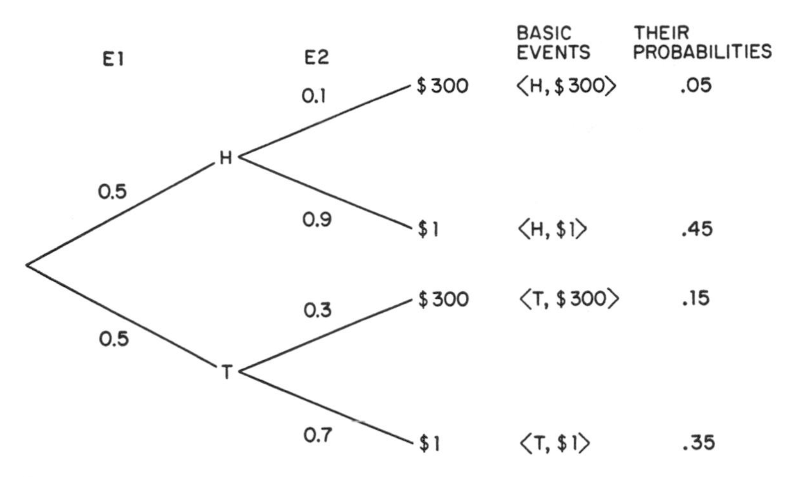

Figure 7.10.

7.2.4 Multiple-Stage Processes

The multiplication theorem T9 (and its special instance T10 for statistically independent events) allows us to analyze a large number of probability problems involving sequences of events, trials, or experiments. To exemplify this, consider the following sort of a game: A player first flips a coin; if he gets heads, he picks a prize from urn one; if he gets tails, he picks a prize from urn two. Urn one has one \$300 prize and nine \$1 prizes; urn two has three \$300 prizes and seven \$1 prizes. Assuming that the toss of the coin is a random selection from {heads, tails}, and that the pick of a prize is a random selection from the prizes in the urn, how might we determine the probability that the player gets a \$300 prize?

Notice first that we can conceive of this game as involving two stages, experiments or acts:

E_1: Flipping the coin with possible outcomes heads and tails.
E_2: Choosing a prize from an urn with the possible outcomes of a \$300 prize and a \$1 prize.

Figure 7.10 presents a tree diagram of this game. The possible outcomes of the game, corresponding to complete paths on the diagram are ⟨H,\$300⟩, ⟨H,\$1⟩, ⟨T,\$300⟩, and ⟨T,\$1⟩, in which '⟨H,\$300⟩', for example, is an abbreviation for 'E_1 = H and E_2 = \$300' or 'E_1 resulted in heads and E_2 resulted in a \$300 prize'. Because these outcomes are mutually exclusive and jointly exhaustive, they form a possibility space. Thus, if we know the probability of each of these four outcomes, we can determine the probability of winning \$300 by summing the probabilities of the possible outcomes that realize a \$300 winning.

What is the probability, for example, of the outcome ⟨H,\$300⟩? It is $Pr(E_1 = H \& E_2 = \$300)$, and by the multiplication theorem this quantity is evidently $Pr(E_2 = \$300/E_1 = H) \times Pr(E_1 = H)$. Thus, we can calculate the probability of ⟨H,\$300⟩ if we have $Pr(E_1 = H)$ and $Pr(E_2 = \$300/E_1 = H)$, that is, if we have the probability of the branch leading to H and the probability of the branch leading from H to \$300. More generally, if we know the probabilities on each branch on the tree diagram, by the multiplication theorem, the probability of any basic outcome of the whole process will be the product of all the branch probabilities on the complete path corresponding to that basic outcome.[5] Given the description of our game, we have:

$Pr(E_1 = H) = .5$ $Pr(E_1 = T) = .5;$

$Pr(E_2 = \$300 / E_1 = H) = .1$ $Pr(E_2 = \$1 / E_1 = H) = .9$

$Pr(E_2 = \$300 / E_1 = T) = .3$ $Pr(E_2 = \$1 / E_1 = T) = .7$

Having placed these values on the branches in Figure 7.10, use of the multiplication theorem T9 allows calculation of the probability of the basic outcomes of the game; these calculations are also given in Figure 7.10. Finally summing the event that realized a \$300 winning, we determine that the probability of winning \$300 in the game is .20.

The just-described procedure for analyzing multiple or *n*-stage processes may be summarized as follows:

(1) Conceptualize the process as a tree diagram.
(2) Assign probabilities to each branch B emanating from a branching point P so that:
 (a) The probabilities of the branches emanating from P sum to 1 and
 (b) The probability assigned to branch B is the probability of the process following branch B given that the process has followed the path up to the branching point P.
(3) (a) The probability of a complete path is the product of the branch probabilities on it, and
 (b) Each such complete path is a basic event of the entire *n*-stage process.
(4) To determine the probability of any statement ‘p’ about the entire process, sum the probabilities of the basic events of the *n*-stage process that realize ‘p’.

5. This account is a simplification, and it in effect relies on the following unproven theorem: A probability space of the basic outcomes of the entire process can be specified by specifying miniprobability spaces at the various branching points (on the tree diagram) and stipulating those probabilities to be conditional probabilities relative to the main space of the entire process.

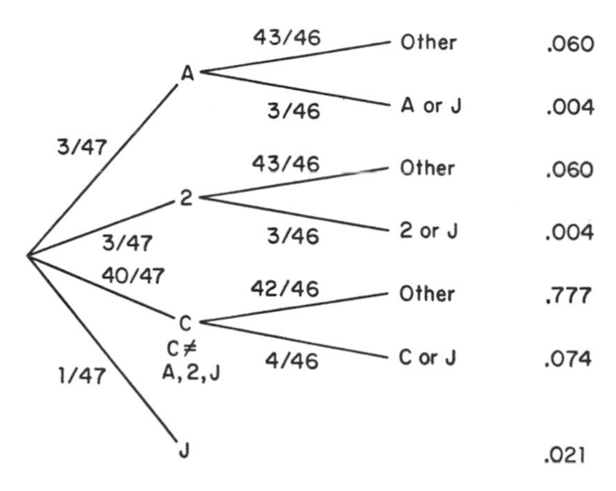

Figure 7.11.

We now exemplify the method in a number of other cases.

(1) A fair coin with outcomes that are statistically independent of all previous outcomes is tossed ten times. What is the probability that these ten tosses result in exactly one heads? We can conceive of this as a ten-stage process in which each stage has the two possible outcomes h and t. Furthermore, because the outcomes are statistically independent of previous outcomes and the coin is fair, the conditional probability of heads (tails) on any given branch is equal to the unconditional probability .5. Thus, the probability of a complete path or basic outcome for the entire process multiplies these branch probabilities and has the value of $.5 \times .5 \times \ldots$ (ten times), that is, $(.5)^{10}$. How many of these complete paths will realize exactly one heads turning up in the ten tosses? Well, the lone occurrence of the heads can occur on the first toss or on the second toss or. . . . Thus, there are exactly ten basic outcomes that realize exactly one heads coming up in the ten tosses. The answer we are looking for then is $10 \times (.5)^{10}$.

(2) Suppose one is dealt three jacks, an ace, and a deuce in draw poker; one has a choice of discarding the deuce and drawing one card or just keeping the jacks and drawing two cards. Which is more likely to improve one's hand, when the possible improvements are a full house (three of a kind and a pair) and four of a kind? If one keeps the ace, there are one jack and three aces in the remaining forty-seven cards; thus, the probability of increasing the value of the hand is 4/47 or .085.

When we draw two cards, we have a two-stage process (see Figure 7.11). The probabilities of the branches are calculated as follows: For the first draw, one is drawing from a population of forty-seven cards and in that population there are three aces, three deuces, and a jack left. Thus, the probability of drawing an ace and that of drawing a deuce are both 3/47, while the probability of drawing a jack is 1/47. The probability of drawing some other card C is 1 minus the probability of drawing an ace, deuce, or jack, that is, 40/47. Because we can't improve the hand after drawing a jack, we don't further analyze the last branch. On the second draw, the population is forty-six cards. Consider the branches leading away from having drawn an ace the first time. Because there are now two aces and a jack left, the probability of improving the hand is 3/46, while the probability of drawing some other card that won't improve the hand is 43/46. The branches leading from deuce and from C are similarly analyzed.

Multiplying the branch probabilities on each complete path, we arrive at the probabilities for the basic events of the two-stage process. They are listed beside the complete paths on the tree diagram (Figure 7.11). The probability of improving the hand is the sum of the probabilities of the basic events that would improve the hand, and this is

$$.004 + .004 + .074 + .021 = .103$$

Because the probability of improving the hand by keeping the ace and drawing only one card was .085, one has a better chance of improving one's hand by discarding the ace and drawing two cards.

(3) Suppose we have thirty people in the room and wonder how likely it is that at least two people in the room have the same birthday (such as April 1). To simplify, we forget about February 29 and assume that a person's birthday is a random selection from the remaining 365 days of the year. The easiest way to solve this problem is to think of it as a thirty-stage process in which the outcomes of each stage i is whether or not the ith person asked matches the birthday of some previous person asked. The number of paths where there is some match is obviously staggering; but there is only one path where each person's birthday fails to match that of any earlier person asked, and that path will give us the probability of '—(at least two people in the room have the same birthday)'. The probability we are looking for is 1 minus this quantity.

So, what we have to do is to determine the probabilities on the branches of the path where there is no match at all. The first person's birthday obviously fails to match that of any other earlier person asked; thus, the first branch has the probability of 1. In this kind of case, it is often more natural to think of the process as one that starts in earnest with the second person asked; the first person is, as it were, a "wild card" that has the probability of one. Regardless of how we think of the first branch probability, the probability that the second person fails to match the birthday of the first person is 364/365; that, then, is the probability on the second branch. Given that the first two individuals didn't match, the probability of the third person's birthday matching one of the first two is 2/364; that is, of the 365 equally probable days on which he might have been born, two will match those of the previous two people asked (given that those two didn't match), and 363 will fail to match either of the two previous birthdays. By now, it should be evident that the probabilities on the branches of the path that fail to produce any match are: 1 (or 365/365), 364/365, 363/365, 362/365, ... Multiplying these thirty terms on that complete path gives the figure .294, which is the probability that there are no matching birthdays among the thirty people. Thus, the probability that there is at least one match of birthdays among the thirty people is .706.

This figure is a surprisingly high number. The consequence is that if the random selection of birthdays is justified, a rational gambler should be willing to put in up to $7.06 into a betting pool that will pay him or her $10 if at least two people in the room of thirty have the same birthday. (Given unwitting participants, one should be able to get quite handsome odds.) In fact, given the assumptions, as long as the room has more than twenty-three people in it, it's more probable than not that at least two people share birthdays. We conclude our section on multiple-stage processes with a discussion of the so-called Gambler's Fallacy.

A person is usually said to commit the GAMBLER'S FALLACY when he or she reasons in the following ways:

(a) "Because red came up ten times in a row on this roulette table, there is a good chance that it will come up black the next time [black is overdue, black is bound to come up.]"
(b) "Because I've gone without a car accident for five years, I better expect one soon [my number is just about up]."

As long as we understand the outcome of any given spin on a roulette wheel to be statistically independent of previous spins, the conclusion of (a) is clearly false even if the reason offered is true. If we take the result of each driving day relative to having an accident to be statistically independent of the results of prior driving days, the conclusion of (b) would be similarly mistaken.

The existence of statistically independent processes shows the invalidity of an argument like: "It's improbable that ten tosses of the coin should result in heads; thus, given that nine tosses have resulted in heads, it's probable that the tenth toss won't." When the process is statistically independent, it is indeed improbable that ten tosses of a fair coin should all result in heads. But once nine heads have turned up, in a loose sense of "the improbable," the improbable has for all practical purposes already happened; given normal assumptions, on the average it happens about twice in 1000 times of tossing a coin nine times. Given that the improbable has already happened, the result of the tenth toss turning up heads is no greater than the probability of any other toss turning up heads. Of course, 'All ten tosses turn up heads' is twice as improbable as 'nine tosses all turn up heads'; but this is precisely accounted for by taking the probability of the tenth toss turning up heads to be 1/2.

It should be clear now that if the tosses are statistically independent of each other, one reasons from truth to falsity when one reasons from the improbability of ten tosses being heads to the improbability of the tenth toss being heads given that the first nine tosses were heads. But the gambler presumably thinks that spins on the roulette wheel (or on the highway) are in fact statistically dependent. In that case, has any fallacy or mistake been committed? The answer is yes, because they are making an empirical error about the nature of certain processes. For any reasonably balanced roulette wheel, its behavior is better explained by the hypothesis of statistical independence than the gambler's hypothesis. That is, the actual frequencies with which such roulette wheels behave come pretty close to the frequencies projected by the assumption of statistical independence, and certainly far closer than those projected by the gambler's hypothesis.

To exemplify this sort of a point, let us suppose that on day 1 the probability for me to have a car accident is 1/3650. Letting '$E_i = S$' stand for 'Day *i* is accident free', the probability for me not to have a car accident by the end of day 30 is given by

$$Pr(E_{30} = S \,/\, E_1 = S \,\&\ldots\&\, E_{29} = S) \times \ldots$$
$$Pr(E_2 = S \,/\, E_1 = S) \times Pr(E_1 = S)$$

On the assumption that for me to have a car accident on any given day is statistically independent of whether or not I had an accident on prior days, each of these factors would be 3649/3650 and the probability for me not to have an accident by the end of day 30 would be $(3649/3650)^{30}$ or approximately .976. Suppose, on the other hand, that each safe day of driving reduces my chances of having another safe day so that

$$Pr(E_i = S \,/\, E_{i-1} = S \,\&\ldots\&\, E_1 = S) = \frac{3650 - i}{3650}$$

In that case, the probability for me to avoid an accident by the end of day 30 would be

$$\frac{(3649)(3648)\ldots(3620)}{(3650)^{30}} = 0.323$$

Given any reasonable basis for taking the probability for a person to have an accident on day 1 to be 1/3650 (such as the person having had one accident over the last ten years), it is simply false that of every 1000 such people, around 677 of them would have an accident in the succeeding one month. To this extent, the "gambler's hypothesis" of the kind we have imagined is out of accord with the empirical facts. Obviously, there can be processes in which the failure in the past makes success in the future more likely; for example, if I draw cards from a deck without replacement, my failure to get a king in the first forty-seven draws makes it very likely that I will get one on the next draw, and after forty-eight failures I am assured of drawing a king. On the other hand, this is not the way spins on roulette wheels and highways behave.

Our discussion may be summarized by treating the Gambler's Fallacy as the following presuppositional fallacy:

Gambler's Fallacy:	Prior outcome X → [in,de]creased probability of Y; NOT {X and Y are statistically dependent}*.

Whether it is due to the empirical behavior of coin flips or the conceptualization of the problem, when the presupposition of statistical dependence cannot be presumed, one commits the Gambler's Fallacy in inferring the decreased probability of 'the next toss will be heads' on the basis of the prior nine tosses having been heads. The '*' of course indicates that in analyzing someone as having committed the Gambler's Fallacy, one should explain why the presupposition of statistical dependence can't be presumed.

EXERCISES—SECTION 7.2.4

1. Assume that you throw a fair die ten times. What is the probability that fewer than two 6's will turn up in these ten tosses?
2. Suppose you drew three cards at random from a bridge deck without replacement. What is the probability that you get cards of three different suits?
3. (a) In drawing the first set of five cards (at random) in draw poker, what is the probability of drawing a flush?
   (b) In drawing the first set of five cards (at random) in draw poker, what is the probability of drawing two or more cards of the same kind(s), that is, a pair or two pairs of three of a kind or full house or four of a kind?
4. Suppose you drew two jacks, an ace, a deuce, and a three in draw poker.
   (a) If you keep the jacks and the ace and draw two new cards (at random) from the remaining forty-seven cards, what is the probability that you will get a full house or four of a kind?
   (b) If you only keep the two jacks and draw three new cards (at random) from the remaining forty-seven cards, what is the probability that you will get a full house or four of a kind?
5. Suppose we have four people in the room. Assuming birthdays are randomly distributed by months, what is the probability that at least two people have birthdays in the same month?
6. In poker if two players have a pair, a pair of aces beats a pair of kings, a pair of kings beats a pair of queens, and so on. The same applies to three of a kind and four of a kind. If two players have two pairs each, the one with the higher ranking pair wins, and if two players have a full house, the higher ranking three of a kind wins. In five-card stud poker, one card is dealt face down to each player and the remaining four cards are dealt face up. However, each time after a face-up card is dealt to all the players, there is a round of betting before the

next set of face-up cards are dealt. Suppose you are playing five-card stud with one opponent and the cards were dealt randomly.

(a) After all the cards are dealt, you show a pair of kings, a 2, and a 3, and your concealed card is a 7. Your opponent shows a pair of jacks, a 7 and a 6. What is the probability that you have the winning hand?
(b) Make the same assumptions as in a. Suppose your opponent will continue betting if he has two pairs or three of a kind. On the other hand, if he is beaten by your face-up cards, there is a probability of .9 that he will fold (i.e., concede the game and pot to you) and a probability of .1 that he will bluff and continue betting. Given that your opponent continues betting, determine the conditional probability that you have a winning hand.
(c) Redo b with the following change: If your opponent is beaten by your face-up cards, there is a .7 probability that he will fold and a .3 probability that he will bluff.

7. Suppose A is playing "Old Maid" with three other people. (In "Old Maid" a deck of cards is equally divided among the four players, and one designated card—often the queen of spades if a bridge deck is used—is called the "old maid." Subsequent play of the game doesn't matter for this problem, but the idea is that whoever gets stuck with the "old maid" at the end loses.)

(a) If the several deals of the cards in Old Maid are statistically independent of each other and each player has the equal probability of being dealt the old maid, determine:

Pr(A is dealt the old maid two deals in a row)
Pr(A is dealt the old maid precisely once in two deals)
Pr(A avoids being dealt the old maid twice in a row)
Pr(A is dealt the old maid three times in a row)
Pr(A is dealt the old maid the next time / A was dealt the old maid three times in a row)

(b) Let 'O(*i*)' be 'A is dealt the old maid in the *i*th deal'. Assume Pr(O(1)) = 1/4, Pr(O(2)/O(1)) = 1/8, and Pr(−O(2)/−O(1)) = 3/8. Determine the following probabilities:

Pr(A is dealt the old maid on both of the first two deals)
Pr(A is dealt the old maid precisely once in the first two deals)
Pr(A avoids being dealt the old maid in the first two deals)

(c) Suppose A has been dealt the old maid in the first deal, and thinks: "Well, this at least makes it more likely that I'll avoid it the next time." Analyze the fallacy in his thinking.

7.2.5 Random Variables, Mean, Variance, and Standard Deviation

In this final section we provide the conceptual mechanism for giving a quick description of what is likely to occur in an uncertain situation. To get into this topic, suppose player A plays a game of flipping a fair coin three times in which he wins \$1 each time heads comes up and loses \$1 each time tails comes up. From a tree diagram of this game, we can easily tabulate the possible outcomes, their probabilities, and his winnings or losses. This is given in Table 7.3. Suppose we let $\mathbf{W}^{\circ}$ be the amount in dollars that A wins or loses; thus for example, if he wins \$1, $\mathbf{W}^{\circ} = 1$, and

TABLE 7.3.

Outcomes	*Their Probability*	*Winnings/Losses*
⟨H,H,H⟩	1/8	+\$3
⟨H,H,T⟩	1/8	+\$1
⟨H,T,H⟩	1/8	+\$1
⟨H,T,T⟩	1/8	−\$1
⟨T,H,H⟩	1/8	+\$1
⟨T,H,T⟩	1/8	−\$1
⟨T,T,H⟩	1/8	−\$1
⟨T,T,T⟩	1/8	−\$3

if he loses \$3, $\mathbf{W}^\circ = -3$. It should be noted that this has the effect of assigning a numerical value to each basic event of the probability space. Given this specification of $\mathbf{W}^\circ$, we can now ask questions like: What is the probability that $\mathbf{W}^\circ = 1$? The answer is evidently the sum of the probabilities of the basic events that realize $\mathbf{W}^\circ = 1$. Thus, the answer is 3/8. The probability of his wins and losses can now be represented by Table 7.4. $\mathbf{W}^\circ$ is an example of what is called a random variable, and Table 7.4 is a probability distribution for that random variable.

The notion of a random variable and its probability distribution may be generally understood as follows:

> A random variable $\mathbf{X}^\circ$ on a probability space S
>
> (a) Assigns a number to each basic event of S, and
> (b) $\Pr(\mathbf{X}^\circ = x)$ = sum of the probabilities of the basic events in S that have been assigned the number x.
>
> The probability distribution of a random variable $\mathbf{X}^\circ$ is the set of probabilities $\Pr(\mathbf{X}^\circ = x)$ for all the values that $\mathbf{X}^\circ$ may assume.

$\mathbf{W}^\circ$ in our example assigned 3 to the basic event ⟨H,H,H⟩, 1 to ⟨H,H,T⟩, ⟨H,T,H⟩, and ⟨T,H,H⟩, and so on. $\Pr(\mathbf{W}^\circ = 3)$ is the probability of ⟨H,H,H⟩ and $\Pr(\mathbf{W}^\circ = 1)$ is the sum of the probabilities of ⟨H,H,T⟩, ⟨H,T,H⟩, and ⟨T,H,H⟩. In most of our examples, the numbers assigned by a random variable are integers but they could also be real numbers like 3.21454343. . . .

The probability distribution of $\mathbf{W}^\circ$ was displayed in Table 7.4. An examination of that table should make it evident that in general the prob-

TABLE 7.4.

$\Pr(\mathbf{W}^\circ = -3) = 1/8$	$\Pr(\mathbf{W}^\circ = 3) = 1/8$
$\Pr(\mathbf{W}^\circ = -1) = 3/8$	$\Pr(\mathbf{W}^\circ = 1) = 3/8$
$\Pr(\mathbf{W}^\circ = x) = 0$ for all x other than -3, -1, 1, and 3.	

ability distribution of a random variable $\mathbf{X}^{\circ}$ (on a probability space S) itself forms a probability space. Clearly the different values $\mathbf{X}^{\circ}$ takes on are mutually exclusive and jointly exhaustive; furthermore, the probabilities must add up to 1 because every basic event in the original space S realizes one and only one event of the form $\mathbf{X}^{\circ} = x$. In our example, the random variable $\mathbf{W}^{\circ}$ forms a probability space in which the basic events are $\mathbf{W}^{\circ} = n$ for integer values of n; all the basic events of this derived space have a probability of 0 except for $\mathbf{W}^{\circ} = -3$, $\mathbf{W}^{\circ} = -1$, $\mathbf{W}^{\circ} = 1$, and $\mathbf{W}^{\circ} = 3$. Because basic events with the probability of 0 are of no interest, we could alternatively say that $\mathbf{W}^{\circ}$ can only assume the values -3, -1, 1, and 3. In this case $\mathbf{W}^{\circ}$ forms a space of four basic events: $\mathbf{W}^{\circ} = -3, -1, 1$, and 3.

To consider a slightly more complex example, suppose you are dealt the first two cards of a new deck in a game of blackjack. (In this game, 10's and face cards count as 10, the ace can count as 1 or 11 depending on the player's choice, and the other cards have the values of the spots; the object of the game is to get the highest value less than or equal to 21.) We can now introduce a random variable $\mathbf{P}^{\circ}$ that is equal to the point count of the two cards that were dealt, assuming that the value of the ace is optimized (i.e., it counts as 11 in all cases except when one is dealt two aces, in which case one is counted as 1 and the other as 11). To exemplify determining the probability distribution of $\mathbf{P}^{\circ}$ or the probabilities of the basic events in the derived space (derived from that of the original space involving the dealing of two cards), consider $\Pr(\mathbf{P}^{\circ} = 18)$, that is, the probability of the new basic event $\mathbf{P}^{\circ} = 18$. The combination of two cards that realize $\mathbf{P}^{\circ} = 18$ are:

$\langle 10,8\rangle, \langle 8,10\rangle, \langle 9,9\rangle, \langle A,7\rangle, \langle 7,A\rangle,$

in which '10' represents a 10 or a face card. In a deck there are sixteen cards with the value 10, and four cards with the value 8. Thus, $\Pr(\langle 10,8\rangle) = (16/52)(4/51)$. $\Pr(\langle 8,10\rangle)$ is identical except that the numerators are switched around. Similar reasoning makes it evident that $\Pr(\langle A,7\rangle) = \Pr(\langle 7,A\rangle) = (4/52)(4/51)$. $\Pr(\langle 9,9\rangle)$ can be seen as follows:

$$\begin{aligned}\Pr(\langle 9,9\rangle) &= \Pr(\text{second card} = 9 \,/\, \text{first card} = 9) \times \Pr(\text{first card} = 9)\\ &= (3/51)(4/52)\end{aligned}$$

Thus, $\Pr(\mathbf{P}^{\circ} = 18) = (1/52)(1/51)[(2)(16)(4) + (2)(4)(4) + (3)(4)] = .0649$. The probability distribution for $\mathbf{P}^{\circ}$ (or the derived probability space) is given by the Table 7.5 (in which the probability of the unlisted values is 0).

Given any probability distribution for a random variable, the most detailed information we can have about it is to have the complete probability distribution of $\mathbf{X}^{\circ}$. Thus, the most detailed information about the probability distribution for $\mathbf{P}^{\circ}$ is Table 7.5. However, in order to have something easier to manage, for many purposes we should like to have a shorter description of the likely outcome. This can be accomplished by

TABLE 7.5.

$Pr(P^o = 4) = .0045$	$Pr(P^o = 13) = .0965$
$Pr(P^o = 5) = .0121$	$Pr(P^o = 14) = .0890$
$Pr(P^o = 6) = .0166$	$Pr(P^o = 15) = .0845$
$Pr(P^o = 7) = .0241$	$Pr(P^o = 16) = .0769$
$Pr(P^o = 8) = .0287$	$Pr(P^o = 17) = .0724$
$Pr(P^o = 9) = .0362$	$Pr(P^o = 18) = .0649$
$Pr(P^o = 10) = .0407$	$Pr(P^o = 19) = .0603$
$Pr(P^o = 11) = .0483$	$Pr(P^o = 20) = .1026$
$Pr(P^o = 12) = .0935$	$Pr(P^o = 21) = .0483$

specifiying the mean or expected value of the random variable $\mathbf{X}^o$ as long as the so-called variance is reasonably small. We now turn to a clarification of these notions, which is the central purpose of this subsection.

The idea of average, mean, or expected value is given by the following definition:

> Where the nonzero values of $\mathbf{X}^o$ are $x_1, \ldots, x_n$, the mean or expected value of $\mathbf{X}^o$ is given by the formula
>
> $$M[\mathbf{X}^o] = x_1 Pr(\mathbf{X}^o = x_1) + \ldots + x_n Pr(\mathbf{X}^o = x_n).$$

In the game of flipping the coin three times in which the probability distribution for $\mathbf{W}^o$ was given in Table 7.4, the mean or expected wins $M[\mathbf{W}^o]$ for a player is:

$$(3)(1/8) + (1)(3/8) + (-1)(3/8) + (-3)(1/8) = 0$$

We might express this fact by saying things like: on the average the player will win \$0 or his mean or expected winning is \$0. In any fair game, the expected winning should be \$0; if it is more than \$0, it is favorable and if it is less than \$0, it is unfavorable. Using the same method of calculation, the mean or expected point value $\mathbf{P}^o$ for the blackjack game is 14.57. It should be clear that the idea of a mean requires numerical values that can in some sense be "averaged." Precisely because random variables take on numerical values, this kind of numerical averaging is possible for probability spaces that are probability distributions for random variables. Hence our interest in random variables and their probability distributions.[6]

6. Readers who read Section 4.6.1 on expected utility of an action can now see how that formula was derived. For a given action A, the cost/benefit space is a possibility space describing the basic events that are the possible outcomes of A. This is converted to a probability space by assigning probabilities of the action A resulting in those outcomes. Finally, the function d that assigned desirability values or ratings to the possible outcome is in effect a random variable $\mathbf{D}^o$. The expected utility of the action A then is simply the expected value of this random variable $\mathbf{D}^o$.

When we say things like a person's expected winnings is $0, or that the mean or expected point value of the dealt blackjack hand is 14.57, it is natural to assume that this or something reasonably close to it is what is most likely to happen. This is not always true. Suppose we have a single toss of a die. Let $\mathbf{X}^o$ be the number of spots that turns up, and consider three cases:

(a) The die is fair and $M[\mathbf{X}^o] = 3.5$. But there is no greater likelihood of $\mathbf{X}^o$ being around 3.5 than around 2 or 5.
(b) The die is biased so it comes up with 50/50 chance on 3 or 4 and no chance of landing with the other spots up. In this case $M[\mathbf{X}^o]$ is again 3.5, and this time it is most likely that $\mathbf{X}^o$ will be around 3.5.
(c) The die is biased so that it comes up 1 or 6 with 50/50 chance and no chance of landing with the other spots up. $M[\mathbf{X}^o]$ is once again 3.5. This time it is least likely that $\mathbf{X}^o$ should be around 3.5.

It is clear that sometimes the most likely outcome for $\mathbf{X}^o$ is around the mean of $\mathbf{X}^o$ and sometimes the most likely outcome for $\mathbf{X}^o$ isn't around the mean of $\mathbf{X}^o$ at all. When do we have the first case, and when do we have the latter situation?

One way of trying to determine this is to find the average deviation from the mean. If we do this in the three cases of the last paragraph, we get the following results:

(a) Each of the six sides has 1/6 probability of landing, and the mean was 3.5. Thus, there is a 1/6 probability that six spots show up and that the deviation from the mean is 2.5, 1/6 probability that one spot shows up and that the deviation from the mean is again 2.5, 1/6 probability that five spots show up and that the deviation from the mean is 1.5, and so on. Thus, the average deviation from the mean is

$$(2.5)(1/6) + (1.5)(1/6) + (0.5)(1/6) + (0.5)(1/6) + (1.5)(1/6) + (2.5)(1/6) = 1.5$$

(b) When the die is loaded in favor of 3 and 4, the average deviation is $(0.5)(1/6) + (0.5)(1/2) = .5$.
(c) When the die is loaded in favor of 1 and 6, the average deviation is $(2.5)(1/2) + (2.5)(1/2) = 2.5$.

Inspection of these figures clearly shows what we should have expected: When the average deviation from the mean is greater, the mean is a less reliable measure of what is likely to happen; conversely, when the average deviation from the mean is smaller, the mean is a more reliable measure of what is roughly likely to happen. In our coin-tossing example the average deviation of 1.5, and although the mean of 0 is not an exceptionally bad indicator of what is likely to happen, it is not a very good one either; if the coin were tossed more often, the mean would become a better indicator.

Our discussion in the previous paragraph clearly suggests that the mean is a fairly reliable indicator of what is most likely to happen if the average deviation from the mean is small. We would like to have a nice formula for the average deviation, or something like it, as a gauge of how good an indicator the mean is for the likely outcome. A formula that may be suggested by our discussion is $M[\mathbf{X}^o - M[\mathbf{X}^o]]$. However, this turns out to be something other than what we want, because in case (c), for example, we would get $(6 - 3.5)(1/2) + (1 - 3.5)(1/2) = 0$. The problem is that some values of $\mathbf{X}^o$ are greater than the mean and some values of $\mathbf{X}^o$ are less than the mean and we don't want these to cancel out. We could try to frame the formula in terms of the absolute value of the distance from the mean, but absolute values are messy to use. The other route is to take the square of the distance from the mean because multiplying two negative quantities together produces a positive quantity. Thus, if we use the formula $M[(\mathbf{X}^o - M[\mathbf{X}^o])^2]$ we would get in cases (a)–(c) the figures $35/12 = 2.92$, $1/4 = .25$, and $50/8 = 6.25$. Although the numbers are a little different, their order is certainly what we want as a gauge on how much we can rely on the mean to tell us the likely outcome. This quantity is called the VARIANCE. Because the variance involves squaring the distance from the mean, sometimes it is desirable to have less exaggerated figures; for this purpose the (positive) square root of the variance is taken, and it is called the STANDARD DEVIATION. Although this figure is usually not the average deviation from the mean (which we worked with a paragraph ago), it is close to it. In examples (a)–(c), the standard deviations are 1.71, 0.5, and 2.5.

Our discussion of the previous paragraphs can be combined into the following definition:

> Where the nonzero values of $\mathbf{X}^o$ are $x_1, \ldots, x_n$, the variance of $\mathbf{X}^o$ ($V[\mathbf{X}^o]$) and the standard deviation of $\mathbf{X}^o$ ($D[\mathbf{X}^o]$) are given by:
>
> $$V[\mathbf{X}^o] = (x_1 - M[\mathbf{X}^o])^2 Pr(\mathbf{X}^o = x_1) + \ldots + (x_n - M[\mathbf{X}^o])^2 Pr(\mathbf{X}^o = x_n)$$
> $$= [x_1^2 Pr(\mathbf{X}^o = x_1) + \ldots + x_n^2 Pr(\mathbf{X}^o = x_n)] - M[\mathbf{X}^o]^2$$
> $$D[\mathbf{X}^o] = \text{SQUARE ROOT of } V[\mathbf{X}^o]$$

Thus, if $\mathbf{X}^o$ assumes the values $x_1, \ldots, x_n$ with probabilities $p_1, \ldots, p_n$, and $m = M[\mathbf{X}^o]$,

$$V[\mathbf{X}^o] = (x_1 - m)^2 p_1 + \ldots + (x_n - m)^2 p_n$$
$$= (x_1^2 p_1 + \ldots + x_n^2 p_n) - m^2$$

The second part of the definition of the variance given actually incorporates a theorem that we shall not prove in this context. It is included here in order to make the calculation of the variance a bit easier.

TABLE 7.6. Ten Independent Tosses of a Coin with Probability .6 of Landing Heads[a]

Probability distribution for H°

Pr(H° = 0) = .000	Pr(H° = 6) = .251
Pr(H° = 1) = .002	Pr(H° = 7) = .215
Pr(H° = 2) = .011	Pr(H° = 8) = .121
Pr(H° = 3) = .042	Pr(H° = 9) = .040
Pr(H° = 4) = .111	Pr(H° = 10) = .006
Pr(H° = 5) = .201	

M[H°] = 6 V[H°] = 2.4 D[H°] = 1.55

Pr(5 ≤ H° ≤ 7) = .666 Pr(3 ≤ H° ≤ 9) = .982

[a]H° = Number of heads resulting from ten tosses.

```
Pr. = .25                           X
                                    X
                                    X
                                    X
                                    X   X
Pr. = .20                       X   X   X
                                X   X   X
                                X   X   X
                                X   X   X
                                X   X   X
Pr. = .15                       X   X   X
                                X   X   X
                                X   X   X
                                X   X   X   X
                            X   X   X   X   X
Pr. = .10                   X   X   X   X   X
                            X   X   X   X   X
                            X   X   X   X   X
                            X   X   X   X   X
                            X   X   X   X   X
Pr. = .05                   X   X   X   X   X
                        X   X   X   X   X   X   X
                        X   X   X   X   X   X   X
                        X   X   X   X   X   X   X
                    X   X   X   X   X   X   X   X   X
------------------------------------------------------
H°:         0   1   2   3   4   5   6   7   8   9   10
                             <------ M ------>
                           -1D             +1D
                        <---------- M ---------->
                      -2D                       +2D
```

[a]H° = Number of heads resulting from ten tosses.

We give a couple of examples to make these ideas more concrete. Suppose we toss a coin that is slightly biased toward heads, so that the probability of it landing on heads on any toss is .6; we continue to assume that the outcome of any toss is statistically independent of previous outcomes. Let H° be the random variable that gives the number of the heads in the ten tosses. The probability distribution for H° and a "graph" for it is given in Table 7.6. $M[H°] = 6$, and the variance and standard deviation are, respectively, 2.4 and 1.55. These are nice low figures, and indeed the probability of the value of $H°$ being close to the mean is fairly high, namely, $Pr(5 \leq H° \leq 7) = .667$. Consider now the blackjack example. In this case, the mean for the point value $P°$ was 14.57 and the variance and the standard deviation can be calculated to be 16.45 and 4.07, respectively. These figures are significantly worse than in the coin-tossing case, and it is not all that likely that an outcome is going to be very close to the mean. The reason is evident if we look at the "graph" of the probability distribution for $P°$ given in Table 7.7. The distribution peaks at two points $P° = 20$ and $P° = 13$, and the mean is somewhere in between. Noticing that $Pr(5 \leq H° \leq 7) = .667$ and $Pr(11 \leq P° \leq 19) = .687$, we see that a much wider range from the mean has to be included before the probability of $P°$ being in that range reaches a high .6 level. Hopefully, these examples make it fairly clear that being told the mean may not be that informative; in fact it can be outright misleading if the variance or standard deviation is large. Thus, when one hears about means and expected values, one should also inquire into the standard deviation before jumping to any conclusions.

One final result for which the proof is well beyond our scope may be stated as follows: Suppose we have an n-stage process in which the outcome of each stage is statistically independent of the outcomes of the prior stages. Suppose also that the random variable $X°$ sums the outcomes of the various stages (such as the number of heads turning up in stages 1 through n combined or the number of dollars won or lost in stages 1 through n combined). The CENTRAL LIMIT THEOREM states that as n approaches infinity, the graph of the distribution for $X°$ approaches the "bell curve" (as indeed the distribution of $H°$ given in Table 7.6 already approaches that curve with $n = 10$). A consequence of the Central Limit Theorem is this: If n is reasonably large, the probability of $X°$ being within plus-or-minus one standard deviation approximates .682 and the probability of $X°$ being within plus-or-minus two standard deviations approximates .954. Table 7.6 shows that for $H°$ these figures are already approximated with $n = 10$.[7]

7. The blackjack example given in Table 7.7 shows that the probabilities for $P°$ being within one or two standard deviations of the mean approximate the figures just given. However, this case is not covered by the Central Limit Theorem as should perhaps be evident from the graph for the distribution of $P°$ which is not at all close to the bell curve. There are two reasons this case does not fall under the Central Limit Theorem: (a) It is not a statistically independent process [although it is nearly so because independence fails only in relatively few cases involving only small deviations from probabilities of an independent process; that is, the deviation occurs only when two cards of the same kind are dealt and in these cases the probabilities are off by 1/(52)(51) from those of an independent process]. (b) The process covers only two stages: the first card dealt and the second card dealt. As such, we only have $n = 2$ and there is no obvious way to increase n. The nature of the problem is clearly changed if we consider the number of deals with p points (or the average number of points per deal) for n deals of two cards. These latter cases would be covered by the Central Limit Theorem.

TABLE 7.7. First Two Cards Dealt in Blackjack[a]

Probability distribution for P^o

$Pr(P^o = 4) = .0045$	$Pr(P^o = 13) = .0965$
$Pr(P^o = 5) = .0121$	$Pr(P^o = 14) = .0890$
$Pr(P^o = 6) = .0166$	$Pr(P^o = 15) = .0845$
$Pr(P^o = 7) = .0241$	$Pr(P^o = 16) = .0769$
$Pr(P^o = 8) = .0287$	$Pr(P^o = 17) = .0724$
$Pr(P^o = 9) = .0362$	$Pr(P^o = 18) = .0649$
$Pr(P^o = 10) = .0407$	$Pr(P^o = 19) = .0603$
$Pr(P^o = 11) = .0483$	$Pr(P^o = 20) = .1026$
$Pr(P^o = 12) = .0935$	$Pr(P^o = 21) = .0483$

$M[P^o] = 14.57$ $V[P^o] = 16.45$ $D[P^o] = 4.07$

$Pr(11 \leq P^o \leq 19) = .686$ $Pr(7 \leq P^o \leq 21) = .967$

[a]P^o = Point value of the two cards (optimized).

```
                                                          X
Pr. = .10                                                 X
                                     X                    X
                                  X  X                    X
                                  X  X  X                 X
                                  X  X  X  X              X
Pr. = .08                         X  X  X  X              X
                                  X  X  X  X  X           X
                                  X  X  X  X  X  X        X
                                  X  X  X  X  X  X        X
                                  X  X  X  X  X  X  X     X
Pr. = .06                         X  X  X  X  X  X  X  X  X
                                  X  X  X  X  X  X  X  X  X
                                  X  X  X  X  X  X  X  X  X
                               X  X  X  X  X  X  X  X  X  X  X
                               X  X  X  X  X  X  X  X  X  X  X
                            X  X  X  X  X  X  X  X  X  X  X  X
Pr. = .04                X  X  X  X  X  X  X  X  X  X  X  X  X
                         X  X  X  X  X  X  X  X  X  X  X  X  X
                      X  X  X  X  X  X  X  X  X  X  X  X  X  X
                   X  X  X  X  X  X  X  X  X  X  X  X  X  X  X
Pr. = .02          X  X  X  X  X  X  X  X  X  X  X  X  X  X  X
                X  X  X  X  X  X  X  X  X  X  X  X  X  X  X  X
             X  X  X  X  X  X  X  X  X  X  X  X  X  X  X  X  X
             X  X  X  X  X  X  X  X  X  X  X  X  X  X  X  X  X
          X  X  X  X  X  X  X  X  X  X  X  X  X  X  X  X  X  X
-------------------------------------------------------------------
      P°: 4     6     8     10    12    14    16    18    20 21
                                 <---------- M ---------->
                               -1D                  +1D
                     <------------------- M -------------------->
                   -2D                                      +2D
```

[a]P^o = Point value of the two cards (optimized).

EXERCISES—SECTION 7.2.5

1. Let the first two cards from a new deck be dealt (at random) in blackjack, and let $\mathbf{P}^{o}$ be the random variable for the point count of the two cards (in which the value of the ace is optimized). Explain how $\Pr(\mathbf{P}^{o} = 16)$ can be determined to be .0769.
2. Two fair dice are thrown and let $\mathbf{S}^{o}$ be the random variable for the combined number of spots that come up. Determine (a) the probability distribution for $\mathbf{S}^{o}$, (b) the mean or expected value of $\mathbf{S}^{o}$, and (c) the standard deviation for $\mathbf{S}^{o}$.
3. Each play of the game costs $1 to enter and involves betting on a number between one and six. On each play two fair dice are thrown. If your number doesn't come up, you lose your $1; if your number comes up once, you win $1; if your number comes up twice, you win $2. Let $\mathbf{G}^{o}$ be the number of dollars you win or lose in two plays of the game (expressed as positive or negative integers). Determine (a) the probability distribution for $\mathbf{G}^{o}$, (b) the mean or expected value for $\mathbf{G}^{o}$, and (c) the standard deviation for $\mathbf{G}^{o}$. [*Hint:* Get the probability distribution for $\mathbf{G}^{o}$ in two stages: (a) a tree diagram for one play of the game in which branches are matching your number and not matching your number, and (b) a tree diagram for two plays of the game in which branches are the amount of money you win or lose on each play.]
4. Let the tree diagrams for three tosses of a (peculiar) coin be as shown in Figure 7.12. Let $\mathbf{H}^{o}$ be the random variable for the number of H(eads) in the three tosses. Determine (a) the probability distribution for $\mathbf{H}^{o}$, (b) the mean or expected value of $\mathbf{H}^{o}$, and (c) the standard deviation for $\mathbf{H}^{o}$.
5. Repeat exercise 4 with the probabilities at each branching point reversed.
6. Repeat exercise 4 on the assumption that the probability of heads is always 1/2.
7. (a) Let A be a person who believes that an ordinary coin behaves in the way given in exercise 4 and let B be a person who believes that an ordinary coin behaves in the way given in exercise 5. Which of these people adopts something like a "gambler's hypothesis" discussed in connection with the Gambler's Fallacy? Which of the people adopts what might be called a "streak hypothesis"?
   (b) Given what you have discovered about the means and variances in exercises 4–6, how would you characterize the "gambler's hypothesis" and the streak hypothesis relative to the "normal hypothesis" given by exercise 5?

Figure 7.12.

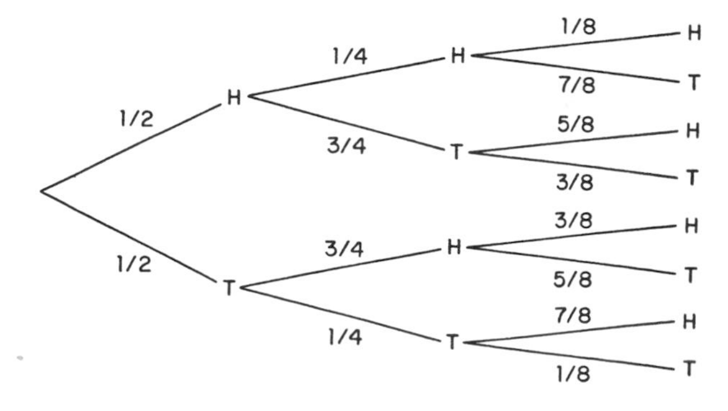

(c) Letting the mean of $\mathbf{H}°$ be given by m, based on your work in exercises 4–6, determine for each of the three hypotheses

$$\Pr(m - .5 \leq \mathbf{H}° \leq m + .5)$$

If we assign a frequency interpretation (cf. Section 7.2.1) to these figures and suppose the mean to be 1.5, we would get statements to the effect: If the number of times the coin is tossed three times is sufficiently large, roughly N percent of the tosses will result in one or two heads.

Perform three tosses of a coin ten times, and record the number of times you got three heads, two heads, one heads, and zero heads. Although ten trials may not be large enough, if we suppose that it were, which of the three hypotheses would your data tend to support?

Note: This kind of inference tends to be dangerous unless one takes into account the margin of error, which is a topic of statistics that is beyond our scope.

SUMMARY OF SECTION 7.2

Definitions

D1. Finite Probability space =

(1) A set of basic events $\{s_1, \ldots s_n\}$ that are mutually exclusive and jointly exhaustive, and
(2) An assignment of probabilities between 0 and 1 to each of $s_1, \ldots, s_n$ so that the assigned probabilities sum to 1.

D2. In a probability space S, Pr(p) = sum of the probabilities of the basic events in S that realize p.
D3. The selection of an item from S is random = every member of S has an equal probability of being selected.
D4. Conditional Probability: Pr(p/q) = Pr(p & q)/Pr(q).
D5. p and q are statistically independent: Pr(p/q) = Pr(p)
D6. A random variable $\mathbf{X}°$ on a probability space S

(a) Assigns a number to each basic unit of S, and
(b) $\Pr(\mathbf{X}° = x)$ = sum of the probabilities of the basic events in S that have been assigned the number x.

The probability distribution of a random variable $\mathbf{X}°$ is the set of probabilities $\Pr(\mathbf{X}° = x)$ for all the values that $\mathbf{X}°$ may assume.

D7. Where the nonzero values of $\mathbf{X}°$ are $x_1, \ldots, x_n$, $M[\mathbf{X}°]$ (the mean or expected value of $\mathbf{X}°$), $V[\mathbf{X}°]$ (the variance of $\mathbf{X}°$), and $D[\mathbf{X}°]$ (the standard deviation of $\mathbf{X}°$), are given by:

$$M[\mathbf{X}°] = x_1\Pr(\mathbf{X}° = x_1) + \ldots + x_n\Pr(\mathbf{X}° = x_n)$$

$$V[\mathbf{X}°] = (x_1 - M[\mathbf{X}°])^2\Pr(\mathbf{X}° = x_1) + \ldots + (x_n - M[\mathbf{X}°])^2\Pr(\mathbf{X}° = x_n)$$

$$= [x_1^2 Pr(X^o = x_1) + \ldots + x_n^2 Pr(X^o = x_n)] - M[X^o]^2$$

$$D[X^o] = \text{SQUARE ROOT of } V[X^o]$$

Theorems

T1. $0 \leq Pr(p) \leq 1$.

T2. If ϕ and θ have logically identical truth conditions,[8] $Pr(\phi) = Pr(\theta)$.

T3. If ϕ is logically true,[8] $Pr(\phi) = 1$.

T4. If ϕ is logically false,[8] $Pr(\phi) = 0$.

T5. $Pr(p \vee q) = Pr(p) + Pr(q) - Pr(p \,\&\, q)$.

T6. If $\phi \,\&\, \theta$ is logically false,[8] $Pr(\phi \vee \theta) = Pr(\phi) + Pr(\theta)$.

T7. $Pr(-p) = 1 - Pr(p)$.

T8. T1–T7 apply to conditional probabilities.

T9. $Pr(p_1 \,\&\, \ldots \,\&\, p_n) = Pr[p_1 / (p_2 \,\&\, \ldots \,\&\, p_n)] \times Pr[p_2 / (p_3 \,\&\, \ldots \,\&\, p_n)] \times \ldots \times Pr[p_{n-1} / p_n] \times Pr[p_n]$.

T10. If p and q are statistically independent, $Pr(p \,\&\, q) = Pr(p) \times Pr(q)$.

T11. $$Pr(p/e) = \frac{Pr(e/p)Pr(p)}{Pr(e/p)Pr(p) + Pr(e/-p)Pr(-p)}.$$

Method for Determining Probabilities of N-Stage Processes

1. Conceptualize the process as a tree diagram.
2. Assign probabilities to each branch B emanating from a branching point P so that:
   (a) The probabilities of the branches emanating from P sum to 1 and
   (b) The probability assigned to branch B is the probability of the process following branch B given that the process has followed the path up to the branching point P.
3. (a) The probability of a complete path is the product of the branch probabilities on it, and
   (b) Each such complete path is a basic event of the entire *n*-stage process.
4. To determine the probability of any statement ‘p’ about the entire process, sum the probabilities of the basic events of the *n*-stage process that realize ‘p’.

8. At least relative to the description of the probability space.

SELECTED ANSWERS

Chapter 2

Selected Answers to Section 2.1

(a) OB claim: There are no practical doubts about whether or not I am presently experiencing pain.

(g) PF claim: Banks, TV, newspapers, etc., are expert sources which make this claim available to me and there are no practical doubts about my memory or the reliability of the sources on this matter. [Some students may legitimately claim that they have no idea whether this is true or false—in that case it is a problematic claim for them.]

Selected Answers to Section 2.2

1. (a) An OB claim about what she is seeing. (One could argue whether one can see that it's a kitchen knife, but it's reasonable to construe it as an OB claim.)

   (d) No. At best this relies on Mr. Crispin's testimony (and even if one did, his having gotten his freedom by killing her can differ from his killing her to get his freedom.)

2. (a) Yes. The claim is limited to what happened at a particular time and place and there is not likely to be any controversy among experts; the claim is made available to me by what I can presume to be an expert source—the *Los Angeles Times.*

   (b) Yes. Much the same reason as (a).

   (c) No. The paper only vouches for Haig *refusing to characterize himself* as optimistic or pessimistic. For all we know, he may be pessimistic (or optimistic).

   (d) No. *Sounding* a note of anxiety is different from being anxious.

   (e) No. The paper only vouches for Haig *saying* that the situation is dangerous. [If we allow the transmission of expert testimony (as we shall do later), and if we count Haig as an expert, this would be a transmitted PF candidate which is transmitted from the expert (Haig) to me by the *Los Angeles Times* (acting as the transmitter).]

5. (f) Not a candidate. It's too complicated for an INT candidate. It's not a SM candidate because it isn't general and it isn't a PF candidate since there isn't any presently available expert testimony on the correctness of the multiplication.

   (j) A difficult example with three possible answers: (i) If one is very smart and can just "see" that the long conditional statement has got to be true, it would be an INT candidate. (ii) Taking the statement to give the relation between *any* small sphere and the Earth, this statement can be taken as a

SM candidate which is a general claim of mathematics and is (in effect) vouched for by the *Britannica* which can be presumed to be an expert source. (iii) One could claim that this isn't a candidate because it isn't an OB, PF, or INT candidate and the actual statement in the *Britannica* is a completely general statement which doesn't involve reference to the Earth; seen this way, (j) is an inference one could make from the perfectly general claim of mathematics made by the *Britannica*—as such, it would be inferential rather than a candidate for unproblematic acceptance.

Selected Answers to Section 2.3

1. (c) This is a PF claim. It is a candidate for unproblematic acceptance because I can presume that it is recently acquired, memorable, and corroborated: (1) Based on its contents I presume it to be recently acquired—for things like presidential elections, the last election is recent. (2) It can be presumed to be memorable due to its content and things like presidential elections being memorable. (3) Based on (i) content, most people knowing the truth of the matter, and the likelihood of their having made the claim to me or my not having been contradicted in making the claim to them, as well as (ii) inferences from (seeming) memories of who the current president is, I can presume that it is a corroborated claim.
[One of these three answers would suffice. Vis-à-vis answer (1), one should remember that "recent" is content dependent—four years is recent for presidential elections but not recent for what one ate for breakfast.]
2. (a) It is an OB candidate for unproblematic acceptance. One can presume that it is appropriately initiated by Square & Frustrated's observation (because he presents himself as having experienced this). Furthermore, we can presume that the event was memorable for Square & Frustrated, and that the remaining links in the transmission (Abby and the *LA Times*) are expert transmitting sources.
3. (b) Transmitted SM candidate. It is a general claim of mathematics such that: (1) it can be presumed to have been appropriately initiated since one can presume that it can be easily checked in expert sources, and (2) it can be presumed to have been corroborated for the persons in the chain of transmission.
   (g) Not a candidate unless it has been transmitted to one and one can presume that it can be easily checked in an expert source OR one has personally confirmed this a number of times so that it becomes a general claim of common sense. I satisfy none of these conditions and it is not a candidate for me. Perhaps your situation differs.

Selected Answers to Section 2.4

Problem 1

1. "B"
6. "C"—Silky's presumed expertise on hats doesn't cross over to shoes; so it's at best an OB candidate. But then there is a significant possibility of error in the surrounding circumstances: seeing a pair of shoes at night from a distance isn't getting a good enough look to determine whether those were Bally shoes made in Switzerland or Bally shoes made in Italy or perhaps even some other shoes.
11. "C"—since he is being suspected, Silky may well be the murderer, and if he is, he has a motive (to deceive) which would cast doubt on the impartiality of his testimony. That is, he may well have the motive to make it appear that his anger was directed toward Mr. Ricardo (or whoever he is) rather than his girlfriend.

Problem 2

2. Presumption of appropriate initiation becomes dubious. While a gossip column isn't entirely reliable, there are some doubts as to whether Jane Fonda was on Rodeo Drive to be seen by Silky. While the gossip column doesn't seem to be a strong enough basis to undermine the presumption of appropriate initiation completely, an acceptable answer would be that claim 2 is no longer a candidate.

Selected Answers to Section 2.5

Problem Set A

1. c. {(3), (5), (2), (6)}
   Given (3) and (5), we are forced to assert that if Jim's father loves Jill, Jim's father doesn't love Jim. But given (2) as well, we are forced to assert that Jim's father doesn't love Jim and thereby forced to deny (6).
2. c. (3), (5), (8)
3. c. (1), (5)

[In Problems Sets B and E, starred comments are optional.]

Problem Set B

Problem 1:

Claim	*Cand?*	*Rel Grade*	*Mem of RCC S?*	*OK or Reason for Elimination*
(1)	T-OB	B	Y	Least preferred member of S.
(2)	no			Inferential.
(3)	D-PF	A	Y	OK
(4)	CS	B	Y	OK
(5)	T-OB	B	Y	Least preferred member of S.
(6)	INT	A	Y	OK

Comments:

(1) Since one's situation is a day after the observation, (1) has to be seen as transmitted by memory.

Problem 2:

Claim	*Cand?*	*Rel Grade*	*Mem of RCC S?*	*OK or Reason for Elimination*
(1)	T-OB	C		Significant chance of error in circumstances
(2)	no			Inferential.
(3)	D-PF	A		OK
(4)	CS	B		OK
(5)	T-OB	B		OK
(6)	INT	A		OK
(7)	T-OB	B		OK
(8)	no			Too much judgment for direct observation.

Comments.

*(1) Given the news about the twin brother, one's circumstance of (allegedly) seeing Tom go into The Liquor Barrel involves a significant possibility of error.

Problem 3:

Claim	*Cand?*	*Rel Grade*	*Mem of RCC S?*	*OK or Reason for Elimination*
(1)	T-OB	C		Significant chance of error in circumstances
(2)	no			Inferential.
(3)	D-PF	A		OK
(4)	CS	B		OK
(5)	T-OB	C		May well have a motive to deceive.
(6)	INT	A		OK
(7)	T-OB	C		May well have a motive to deceive.
(8)	no			Too much judgment for direct observation.
(9)	D-PF	B		OK

Comments:

(1) Since the story of Tom's wife can't be completely discounted, the significant possibility of error remains.

*(5)(7) Since Tom would now seem to be a suspect, his wife may well have a motive to provide him with a (false) alibi. It may be thought that since the alibi won't stand up at all if it is false, given a presumable minimal intelligence on the part of Tom's wife, there are no grounds for giving a "C" grade to (5) and (7); if so, the grade of "B" will stand, but this reason should be clearly stated in an answer.

Problem Set E

Problem 1:

Claim	*Cand?*	*Rel Grade*	*Mem of RCC S?*	*OK or Reason for Elimination*
(1)	D-OB	B		OK
(2)	no			At best a PF claim but controversial.
(3)	D-PF	B	Y	Least preferred member of S
(4)	D-PF	B	Y	Least preferred member of S
(5)	CS	B	Y	OK
(6)	INT	A	Y	OK
(7)	T-OB	B		OK
(8)	no			Appropriate initiation isn't presumable.
(9)	T-OB	C		Dreyfus may well have a motive for lying.
(10)	no			Inferred from flimsy evidence.

Claim	*Cand?*	*Rel Grade*	*Mem of RCC S?*	*OK or Reason for Elimination*
(11)	T-OB	B		OK
(12)	no			Inferential at best.
(13)	T-OB	B		OK

Comments:

(1) The letter itself makes the promise and the letter is directly available to the judges—hence it seems to be a direct observational claim. Some students may consider the letter a transmission of a promise (made in the author's heart)—this seems less satisfactory but perhaps an acceptable answer.

(2) Since no one is claiming to have seen Dreyfus writing the letter, it would be a PF claim at best; but it is controversial since the experts disagree.

(3) This could also be considered a T-OB claim if we take the testifying government officials to have observed the documents to have been absent and unanticipated prior to July.

(4) From the military judges' point of view, French Intelligence can be presumed to be an expert source on this sort of a matter.

(5) Since one was asked to assume this to be an unproblematic claim, it would seem it has to be a CS claim.

(7) Since there is no reason to doubt Major Henry, that he was warned of a spy in the War Office seems to be a transmitted claim of Henry's own observation.

*(8) At best it would be a T-OB or T-PF claim—but the source was not specified (beyond being a "man of honor"), and one cannot presume that an equally good source is readily available (if there was, presumably French Intelligence would have produced the person).

(10) There are other possible answers here: (a) One could treat it as a PF claim by an alleged expert source—The French Intelligence—and yet cast doubt on their expertise in this area since the evidence they produced is extremely flimsy. In that case, it would be a PF claim with the grade C or not a candidate at all. (b) Less plausibly one might claim that it is a PF claim with the grade of B by presuming that they had lots of better evidence that they didn't bother to give. Perhaps the judges took it this way, but one would have to wonder why they didn't "bother" to give the better evidence.

*(13) A link in the transmission from Panizzardi's presumed observation (of his taking precautions and warning the emissary) is the decoding of the telegram by the Foreign Service; the judges may presume that the Foreign Service is an expert transmitting source of this type.

Selected Answers to Section 2.6

2. *Ignorance:* No reasons against 'Mateuse is good' → Mateuse is good.
7. *Hasty Generalization:* The Japanese walk around with cameras when touring in America → The Japanese regularly walk around with cameras; NOT {The behavior of touring Japanese is a fair sample}. What the Japanese do (especially with their cameras) when they are touring is not a fair sample of what they regularly or generally do.
14. *Ad Populum:* 61% of the voters rejected this kind of measure ⇝ This kind of measure deserves to be rejected.
17. *False Cause:* Bottle bills are frequently attended by lower beverage prices → Bottle bills cause (bring about) lower beverage prices.
    [*Hasty generalization* is another possible answer—but neither the size nor the fairness of the sample is clearly questionable. Furthermore, a causal claim is made. Thus, False Cause seems to be a better answer.]

Chapter 3

Selected Answers to Section 3.1

2. (i) The reason is a true reason because both conjuncts comprising the reason are true.
   (ii) The reason is a valid reason: In any possible world, if the given reason is true (in that world),

   The president is the commander-in-chief

   is true (in that world); but then the only way

   If the president is the commander-in-chief, the armed forces are led by a civilian

   can be true (in that world) is that 'The armed forces are led by a civilian' is true (in that world), that is, in any possible world, if the given reason is true, so is the inferred conclusion.
   (iii) The president is the commander-in-chief.
   If the president is the commander-in-chief, the armed forces are led by a civilian.

   The armed forces are led by a civilian.
   (iv) The argument is sound because of (i) and (ii).

Selected Answers to Section 3.2

1. a. It is not the case that [   ].
   e. If [   ] or (   ), then [   ].
2. [a] *Answer:* (2) is false. *Justification:* The argument is valid since it's an instance of [B]. Premise (1) is true by (i). The conclusion (3) is false by (ii) and (iii). Thus, by relation (b), premise (2) must be false.
   [b] *Answer:* (3) is true. *Justification:* The argument is deductively valid since it's an instance of [A]. Premise (1) is true by (iv). Premise (2) is true by (iii). Thus, by relation (a), the conclusion (3) must be true.
   [c] *Answer:* [c] is deductively invalid. *Justification:* It is clear that premises (1) and (2) are both true and that the conclusion (3) is false. Thus, by relation (c), the argument is invalid.
3. (a) (3) If [   ], then (   ).
   (4) If [   ], then (   ).
   (b) (3) If no [   ] is a (   ), then no (   ) is a [   ].
   (4) If all [   ] are (   ), then all (   ) are [   ].
4. [a] The relevant argument form is

   (1) If [   ], then it isn't the case that (   ).
   (2) (   ).

   ---

   (3) It isn't the case that [   ].

   This relevant argument form shows the argument to be valid. Take any possible world and any way to fill the blanks which makes the conclusion (3) false. In that case the rectangle got filled by a true statement; but then if (1) is to come out true, the oval must be filled by a false statement which would force (2) to come out false. Hence, in no possible world can we fill the blanks so that the conclusion comes out false while all the premises come out true.
   [b] The "least course" logical form is:

   (1) If [   ], (   ).

(2) ⬭.

---

(3) ☐.

Fill the rectangle by ‘Reagan won every state in his last election’ and the oval by ‘Reagan won his last election’. The premises clearly come out true while the conclusion comes out false (since Reagan lost Minnesota). Hence the argument is invalid since we considered the “least coarse” form.

5. [a] A logical form of the argument is:

    (1) All ☐ are ⬭.
    (2) Some ☐ are ⬡.

    ---

    (3) Some ⬡ are ⬭.

    Take any possible world and let ‘X’, ‘Y’, and ‘Z’ be any way of filling the three blanks in their order of appearance. If (2) is to come out true, there must be at least one object which belongs to the class of X’s as well as the class of Z’s—let b be any such object. If (1) is also to come out true, all the X’s must be included among the Y’s; therefore, b must also be among the Y’s. Since b was also among the Z’s, b belongs both to the class of Z’s and the class of Y’s, and (3) comes out true. Hence there is no possible world in which the blanks could be so filled that both premises come out true and the conclusion false. Thus, the argument is valid.

6. [b] In each of the following we give the “least coarse” form, and the way of filling the blanks which makes the premises all true and the conclusion false. This suffices to show each of the arguments to be deductively invalid.

    No [trees] are (dogs).
    All (dogs) are [animals].

    Some [trees] are [animals].

7. [a] You might as well say: The time has come to change our research efforts; four years of cancer research is enough!

Selected Answers to Section 3.3.1

1. (c) False $[-T \vee F = F \vee F = F]$
   (f) True $[-T \supset -T = F \supset F = T]$

Selected Answers to Section 3.3.2

1. a. p: F, q: T, and r: F gives:

$(F \supset T) \supset F$,	$F \supset (T \supset F)$	or
$T \supset F$,	$F \supset F$	or
F,	T.	

2. b. $-s \vee -(u \vee t) \vee (s \supset (p \vee r))$.

Selected Answers to Section 3.3.3

4. (The boss is watching if Tom is playing) & (the boss is working)
   (Tom is playing $\supset$ the boss is watching) & b
   $(p \supset w)$ & b
12. [Tom is playing] & [if the boss is watching and some other people are working, the work will get done]

p & [(the boss is watching and some other people are working) ⊃ (the work will get done)]
p & [(w & s) ⊃ d]

16. [The boss's working is a necessary condition for Tom's working] ⊃ [the boss's watching is a sufficient condition for Tom's not playing]
[(Tom is working) ⊃ (the boss is working)] ⊃ [(the boss is watching) ⊃ (Tom is not playing)]
[t ⊃ b] ⊃ [w ⊃ −(Tom is playing)]
[t ⊃ b] ⊃ [w ⊃ −p]

Selected Answers to Section 3.3.4

[c] VALID: The only way the premise can come out true is that 'p' and 'q' are assigned opposite truth values; but then 'p ≡ q' comes out false and the conclusion true.

[d] VALID: The only way the conclusion can come out false is for 'p' to be assigned True and 'r' to be assigned False. But then if 'q' is assigned True, the second premise comes out false and if 'q' is assigned False, the first premise comes out false. Thus, it's impossible to make both premises true and the conclusion false.

[e] INVALID: The following assignment makes the premises true and the conclusion false:

p: T q: T

Selected Answers to Section 3.4

1. (a) The Truth Table Analysis below shows that (a) is a tautology:

p	q	$q \supset (p \supset p)$	
T	T	[T]	T
T	F	[T]	T
F	T	[T]	T
F	F	[T]	T

2. [d] The Truth Table Analysis below shows that [d] is valid:

p	q	r	$[(p \supset q)$	$\& (q \supset r)]$		$\supset$	$(p \supset r)$
T	T	T	T	T	T	[T]	T
T	T	F	T	F	F	[T]	F
T	F	T	F	F	T	[T]	T
T	F	F	F	F	T	[T]	F
F	T	T	T	T	T	[T]	T
F	T	F	T	F	F	[T]	T
F	F	T	T	T	T	[T]	T
F	F	F	T	T	T	[T]	T

3. [a] The Truth Table Analysis below shows (a) is not a pair with logically identical truth conditions:

p	q	$-(p \vee q)$		$\equiv$	$(-p \vee -q)$		
T	T	F	T	[F]	F	F	F
T	F	F	T	[T]	F	T	T
F	T	F	T	[T]	T	T	F
F	F	T	F	[F]	T	T	T

4. (a)

p	q	$p \supset (q \,\&\, -q)$	
T	T	F	F F
T	F	F	F T
F	T	T	F F
F	F	T	F T

Consistent: Comes out true when ‘p’ is false whatever value ‘q’ may have.

5. a. A tautology. *Justification:* If a statement form $\emptyset$ comes out false under an assignment of truth values, its negation comes out true under that assignment. Hence, if $\emptyset$ is inconsistent and comes out false under all assignments, its negation would come out true under all assignments and thus be a tautology.

Selected Answers to Section 3.5.1

1. [c] (i) None.
   [h] (i) CDil. (ii) (p v q) v (r & u) [or: p v q v (r & u)]
2. (a) If the Russians bomb us back, we will suffer damages. [This makes the argument an instance of HS.]

Selected Answers to Section 3.5.2

1. [e]

(1)	$(p \vee q) \supset [(p \vee q) \supset r]$	Pr
(2)	$p \vee q$	Pr
(3)	$(p \vee q) \supset r$	(1) (2) MP
(4)	r	(2) (3) MP

[h]

(1)	$p \supset (r \vee s)$	Pr → Activate the three premises on which SDil can be used in the forward strategy.
(2)	$p \vee q$	Pr
(3)	$q \supset (r \vee s)$	Pr
(4)	$r \vee s$	(1)–(3) SDil
(5)	$r \supset t$	Pr → Again activate premises useful for SDil.
(6)	$s \supset t$	Pr
(7)	t	(4)–(6) SDil

2. [c]

(1)	$p \supset q$	Pr
(2)	$q \supset r$	Pr
(3)	$p \supset r$	(1) (2) HS
(4)	$(p \supset r) \supset (r \supset -t)$	Pr
(5)	$r \supset -t$	(3) (4) MP → Using the backward strategy and asking how to get ‘p ⊃ −t’ may suggest another use of HS on (3) and (5).
(6)	$p \supset -t$	(3) (5) HS

[f]

(1)	$q \supset t$	Pr → Activate the three premises which will allow for a use of CDil.
(2)	$p \vee q$	Pr
(3)	$p \supset (q \vee s)$	Pr
(4)	$q \vee s \vee t$	(1)–(3) CDil → Switch to the backward strategy:

$(n-2)$	t	?
$(n-1)$	$t \supset (p \equiv q)$	Pr
(n)	$p \equiv q$	$(n-1)(n-1)$MP

How can we get 't'? The first two premises have 't' in the consequent position; if we can get the disjunction of the antecedents, we could use SDil—but that's what we have in (4).

(5)	(s v t) ⊃ t	Pr
(6)	t	(1) (4) (5) SDil
(7)	t ⊃ (p ≡ q)	Pr
(8)	p ≡ q	(6) (7) MP

Selected Answers to Section 3.6.1

1. [a] (i) MT (ii) −(u ⊃ s)
   [e] (i) Doesn't match. [To imagine a match applies Rd to part of the line.]

3. [d]

(1) −p ⊃ s — Pr → Since only the first and third premises can be used for anything, we work on them.
(2) s ⊃ p — Pr
(3) −p ⊃ p — (1) (2) HS
(4) p — (3) IA
(5) −(r ⊃ −p) ⊃ −p — Pr
(6) r ⊃ −p — (4) (5) MT
(7) −r — (4) (6) MT

[f]

(1) p ⊃ q — Pr → We activate the premises on which something can be used.
(2) q ⊃ r — Pr
(3) p ⊃ r — (1) (2) HS
(4) −(p v q) ⊃ −(p ⊃ r) — Pr
(5) p v q — (3) (4) MT
(6) q v r — (1) (2) (5) CDil → Switch to backward strategy:

The only plausible way to get '−q' is to get a line 'q ⊃ −q', and something like 'q ⊃ X' and 'X ⊃ −q' seems to be the best bet to get 'q ⊃ −q'. Given (2), we aim for 'r ⊃ −q'; that is,

(*n* − 2)	r ⊃ −q	?
(*n* − 2)	q ⊃ −q	(2)(*n* − 2) HS
(*n*)	−q	(*n* − 2) IA

(6) and the remaining premise bridges the gap.

(7) (q v r) ⊃ (r ⊃ −q) — Pr
(8) r ⊃ −q — (6) (7) MP
(9) q ⊃ −q — (2) (8) HS
(10) −q — (9) IA

4. [b] The missing premise is shown as "*Pr," and the argument shown to be valid is the one given in the problem augmented by the premise indicated in the chain by *Pr. To the side, comment is given on how the answer might have been found.

(1)	p v q	Pr
(2)	q ⊃ (r ⊃ s)	Pr
(3)	p ⊃ (r ⊃ s)	*Pr [Forward strategy and SDil suggests this.]

(4) $r \supset s$ (1) (2) (3) SDil
(5) $-s$ Pr
(6) $-r$ (4) (5) MT

Selected Answers to Section 3.6.2

1. [d] S [f] Not an instance.
2. [d]
(1) $(p \vee q) \supset (r \& s)$ Pr
(2) $(-r \vee u) \& p$ Pr → The forward strategy gives nothing unless (1) and (2) are somehow used. Using S on (2) should suggest using Add to tap (1) by MP.
(3) p (2) S
(4) $p \vee q$ (3) Add
(5) $r \& s$ (1) (4) MP → Use S on (5) to use third premise.
(6) s (5) S
(7) $s \supset (u \supset t)$ Pr
(8) $u \supset t$ (6) (7) MP → Switch to backward strategy:

$(n-1)$ u ?
(n) t (8) $(n-1)$MP

S on (2) and (5) followed by MTP bridges the gap.

(9) $-r \vee u$ (2) S
(10) r (5) S
(11) u (9) (10) MTP
(12) t (8) (11) MP

[i]
(1) $p \vee q \vee r$ Pr → While MTP with '$-r$' is obviously suggested, this seems to get nowhere; another look shows CDil could be used first followed by 2 MTP's with '$-r$'.
(2) $(q \vee r) \supset (r \vee u)$ Pr
(3) $p \supset (w \vee r)$ Pr
(4) $r \vee u \vee w \vee r$ (1)–(3) CDil
(5) $-r$ Pr
(6) $u \vee w \vee r$ (4) (5) MTP
(7) $u \vee w$ (5) (6) MTP

3. [c] Given argument:

$m \vee p$
$\underline{a}$
t

(1) a Pr → Two considerations: (a) The two premises need to be connected and '$a \supset -m$' would help. (b) Ask: what would be the case if he brings out the animal in her? Presumably knowing her mentally isn't enough. So, both considerations suggest (2) as a missing premise.
(2) $a \supset -m$ *Pr
(3) $-m$ (1) (2) MP
(4) $m \vee p$ Pr

(5) p	(3) (4) MTP → Switch to backward strategy: (n − 1) p ⊃ t ? (n) t (5) (n − 1) MP There is no evident way to get 'p ⊃ t' and presumably if she wants to get physical, she wants to hear his body talk. So this is added as a missing premise.
(6) p ⊃ t	*Pr
(7) t	(5) (6) MP

Selected Answers to Section 3.7.1

5. ⊃/v. 8. E/I. 13. Not an instance.

Selected Answers to Section 3.7.2

1. [b]	(1)	−(p & q)	Pr
	(2)	−p v −q	(1) DeM
	(3)	−p ⊃ r	Pr
	(4)	−q ⊃ r	Pr
	(5)	r	(2)–(4) SDil
[e]	(1)	−p ⊃ q	Pr
	(2)	−q ⊃ p	(1) Cont
	(3)	r ⊃ −q	Pr
	(4)	r ⊃ p	(2) (3) HS
[h]	(1)	p ≡ −q	Pr
	(2)	−(p ≡ q)	(1)–(≡)/≡(−)
	(3)	r ⊃ (p ≡ q)	Pr
	(4)	−r	(2) (3) MT
2. [a]	(1)	(q v s) ⊃ −(q v s)	Pr → Activate the premise that can be used right away.
	(2)	−(q v s)	(1) IA
	(3)	−p ⊃ (q v s)	Pr
	(4)	p	(2) (3) MT
	(5)	−[p & −(s ⊃ t)]	Pr → Use DeM or −(&) /⊃ so (4) can be used with it.
	(6)	−p v (s ⊃ t)	(5) DeM
	(7)	s ⊃ t	(4) (6) MTP
	(8)	t ⊃ r	Pr
	(9)	s ⊃ r	(7) (8) HS

3. [a]	(1)	p	Pr	
	(2)	(p & q) ⊃ r	Pr →	Use E/I to use MP with (1)
	(3)	p ⊃ (q ⊃ r)	(2) E/I	
	(4)	q ⊃ r	(1) (3) MP →	To backward strategy:
	(5)	−r v s	Pr	(n − 1) r ⊃ s ?
	(6)	r ⊃ s	(5) ⊃/v	(n)) q ⊃ s (4) (n − 1) HS
	(7)	q ⊃ r	(4) (6) HS	Third premise and ⊃/v bridges the gap.

4. [b]	(1)	−(p ≡ q)	Pr → Drive through '−' since a conjunction is ultimately needed and '≡' becomes a conjunction.

	(2)	p ≡ −q	(1) −(≡)/≡(−)
	(3)	(p ⊃ −q) & (−q ⊃ p)	(2) ≡/⊃ → Use −(&)/⊃ to get conclusion.
	(4)	−(p & q) & −(−q & −p)	(3) −(&)/⊃ [twice]

5. [c]	(1)	(p ⊃ q) ⊃ (r ⊃ s)	Pr	
	(2)	−p v q	Pr →	Create a match by ⊃/v
	(3)	p ⊃ q	(2) ⊃/v	
	(4)	r ⊃ s	(1) (3) MP →	Go to backward strategy:
	(5)	−(r & −s)	(4)–(&)/⊃	(*n* − 2) −(r & −s) ?
	(6)	u v −(r & −s)	Pr	(*n* − 1) u v (r & −s) Pr
	(7)	u	(5) (6) MTP	(*n*) u (*n* − 2) (*n* − 1) MTP

[i]	(1)	(p & r) ⊃ s	Pr → Use the only two premises that can be used.	
	(2)	(s & u) ⊃ q	Pr	
	(3)	s ⊃ (u ⊃ q)	(2) E/I	
	(4)	(p & r) ⊃ (u ⊃ q)	(2) (3) HS →	Use Cont, E/I, and Com to get conclusion as consequent. [This is a kind of hybrid between the forward and backward strategies.]
	(5)	(p & r) ⊃ (−q ⊃ −u)	(4) Cont	
	(6)	(p & r & −q) ⊃ −u	(5) E/I	
	(7)	(p & −q & r) ⊃ −u	(6) Com	
	(8)	(p & −q) ⊃ (r ⊃ −u)	(7) E/I →	First premise should play some role and 'p & −q' would be helpful. Looking at the premise, one may eventually spot that it can be converted into a form for IA. [If this spotted right away, (1)–(8) would have been more obvious.]
	(9)	(−p v q) ⊃ (p & −q)	Pr	
	(10)	−(p & −q) ⊃ (p & −q)	(9) DeM	
	(11)	(p & −q)	(10) IA	
	(12)	r ⊃ −u	(8) (11) MP	

Selected Answers to Section 3.8.1

[d]	(1)	p	As
	(2)	p ⊃ (q v r)	Pr
	(3)	q v r	(1) (2) MP
	(4)	q ⊃ (s ⊃ −p)	Pr
	(5)	r ⊃ (s ⊃ −p)	Pr

(6)	$s \supset -p$	(3)–(5) SDil
(7)	$-s$	(1) (6) MT

[i]

(1)	$(-p \vee -q) \supset (p \,\&\, q)$	As →	This line doesn't match the other lines very well. Can we get anything from (1) alone? Yes, we can convert it to a form where IA can be used.
(2)	$-(p \,\&\, q) \supset (p \,\&\, q)$	(1) DeM	
(3)	$p \,\&\, q$	(2) IA	
(4)	$q \supset (-q \vee s)$	Pr	
(5)	q	(3) S	
(6)	$-q \vee s$	(4) (5) MP	
(7)	s	(5) (6) MTP	
(8)	$(r \,\&\, p) \supset -s$	Pr	
(9)	$-(r \,\&\, p)$	(7) (8) MT →	Use DeM, to use MTP with (3) 's' 'p.'
(10)	$-r \vee -p$	(9) DeM	
(11)	p	(3) S	
(12)	$-r$	(10) (11) MTP	

Selected Answers to Section 3.8.2

[b]

(1)	$-[(q \supset p) \supset p]$	As
(2)	$(q \supset p) \,\&\, -p$	(1)–$(\supset)$/&
(3)	$q \supset p$	(2) S
(4)	$-p$	(2) S
(5)	$-q$	(3) (4) MT
(6)	$(p \supset q) \supset q$	Pr
(7)	$-(p \supset q)$	(5) (6) MT
(8)	$p \,\&\, -q$	(7)–$(\supset)$/&
(9)	p	(8) S
(10)	$p \,\&\, -p$	(4) (9) Adj

Selected Answers to Section 3.8.3

[a] If we could get '$p \supset q$' and '$p \supset r$' by separate chains, we can use that and Adj in the main chain. This suggests two conditional chains:

[D1] $\dfrac{p \supset (q \,\&\, r)}{p \supset q}$

(1)	p	As
(2)	$p \supset (q \,\&\, r)$	Pr
(3)	$q \,\&\, r$	(1) (2) MP
(4)	q	(3) S

[D2] $\dfrac{p \supset (q \,\&\, r)}{p \supset r}$

(1)	p	As
(2)	$p \supset (q \,\&\, r)$	Pr
(3)	$q \,\&\, r$	(1) (2) MP
(4)	r	(3) S

The main chain then becomes:

(1)	$p \supset (q \,\&\, r)$	Pr
(2)	$p \supset q$	(1) [D1]
(3)	$p \supset r$	(1) [D2]
(4)	$(p \supset q) \,\&\, (p \supset r)$	(2) (3) Adj

[c] We start with a conditional chain as the main chain:

(1) $p \supset q$ As

(2) $p \supset (q \supset r)$ Pr →

We would somehow like to get '$p \supset r$' from (1) and (2)—so we try for that by a separate conditional chain:

[D] $p \supset q$
$\underline{p \supset (q \supset r)}$
$p \supset r$

(1)	p	As
(2)	$p \supset q$	Pr
(3)	q	(1) (2) MP
(4)	$p \supset (q \supset r)$	Pr
(5)	$q \supset r$	(1) (4) MP
(6)	r	(3) (5) MP

We can now finish off the main chain.

(3) $p \supset r$ (1) (2) [D]

Chapter 4

Selected Answers to Section 4.1

Answers will vary depending on one's epistemic situation, and the answers given are with the epistemic situation of an ordinary knowledgeable person in mind. Even within that kind of epistemic situation, alternative answers are often possible.

1. a. (i) is a supporting reason for (ii) since it's somewhat more likely that he has chicken pox if he recently played with children having it than if he didn't.
   (ii) is a supporting reason for (i) since it's somewhat more likely that he recently played with children having chicken pox if he now has it than if he doesn't have it now.
   [Both answers assume ignorance as to whether or not he had chicken pox earlier in his life.]
   d. Since we know perfectly well that Carter didn't beat Reagan in 1980, the truth or falsity of (i) has no effect on making (ii) more or less plausible. So, (i) isn't a supporting reason for (ii).
   (ii) is a supporting reason for (i) since it's more likely that Carter would have carried at least two states if he had defeated Reagan than if he hadn't.
2. d. (ii) is a completely legitimate reason for (i).
3. a. Merely acceptable. Even though the probability of a major earthquake in southern California in the next 30 years is quite high, (a) the next ten years is another matter, *and* (b) the chances of it being centered close to Los Angeles (which is needed for decimating L.A.) seems to be not that high. Odds are L.A. won't be decimated in the next 10 years. [One could urge that the claim is highly justified on grounds (b).]
   d. Epistemically neutral. Beyond knowing that neither were of the celibate type, I have no idea who was more active in having lovers.

Selected Answers to Section 4.2

1. [B] The conclusion is completely justified (and hence acceptable) by relation (i) and assumption (b) since the missing premise is completely justified.

[D] The missing premise is not acceptable. Furthermore, if the missing premise is false, the conclusion of the argument is false even if (1) and (2) are true. Thus, by relation (ii), (3) is not acceptable and (1)–(2) constitute a bad reason for (3).

Selected Answers to Section 4.3

Part A

1. *Step 1:* Main point: Democrats are to be trusted in times of economic woe.

   Step 2:

   r: Roosevelt saved the country from the Great Depression.
   d: Roosevelt was a Democrat.
   t: Democrats are to be trusted in times of economic woes.

   Sentence 1: r.
   Sentence 2: Since d, t. ['t' is the main point.]

   Step 3:

   - The inference indicator in sentence 2 shows that 'd' is used as a direct reason for 't'.
   - But 'd' by itself isn't much of a reason for 't' unless it is joined with 'r'.

   Thus the "reason for" tree becomes:

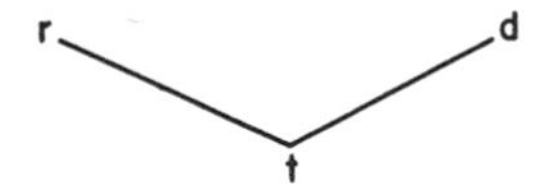

   Step 4: The extracted argument thus becomes:

   r
   d
   ―
   t

5. *Step 1:* Main point: Mary is going to leave him.

   Step 2:

   j: He is in love with Jane.
   s: He is spending much money on Jane.
   m: Mary is going to leave him.

   Sentence 1: j.
   Sentence 2: Otherwise, −s.
   Sentence 3: j ⊃ m.
   Sentence 4: So, m. ['m' is the main point.]

   Step 3:

   - The inference indicator 'otherwise' shows that 's' is being given as a direct reason for 'j' which acts as an intermediate conclusion.
   - The inference indicator 'So' shows 'j ⊃ m' possibly along with something else is being given as a direct reason for 'm', and the something else is clearly the intermediate conclusion 'j' (which will also make the main argument valid).

Thus the "reason for" tree becomes:

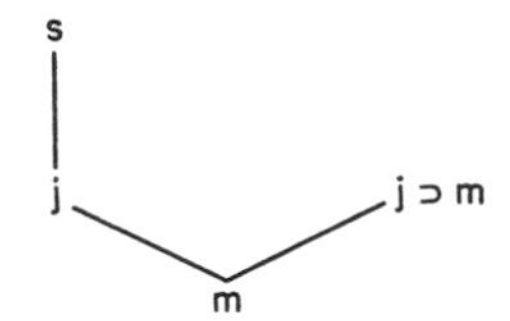

Step 4: The extracted arguments thus are:

[A] j ⊃ m

$\frac{j}{m}$ [a] $\frac{s}{j}$

Part B

1. *Step 1:* Main point: The dairy assistance program must be (immediately) cut.

Step 2:

f: The food assistance programs are being slashed.
p: The food assistance program was cut 14% last year and a cut of 18% more has been proposed for this year.
d: The dairy assistance program is mushrooming.
i: The dairy assistance program has increased from $270 million in 1979 to $1.3 billion in 1980, to more than $2 billion in 1981, and this year's price tag is likely to be at least $2.2 billion.
m: Cuts must be made fairly and across the board.
c: The dairy assistance program must be cut.

Sentences 1, 2, and first half of 3: Background to be edited out.
Sentence 3 (second half): f.
Sentence 4: p.
Sentence 5 (first half): d.
Sentence 5 (second half) and 6: i.
Sentence 6: m.
Sentence 7: c. [main point]

Step 3:

- 'p' is used to support 'f' and 'i' is used to support 'd'.
- 'f', 'd', and 'm' together clearly form the reason for the main point 'c'—if any one of the three were assumed to be false, 'c' would be less plausible.

Thus, the "reason for" tree becomes:

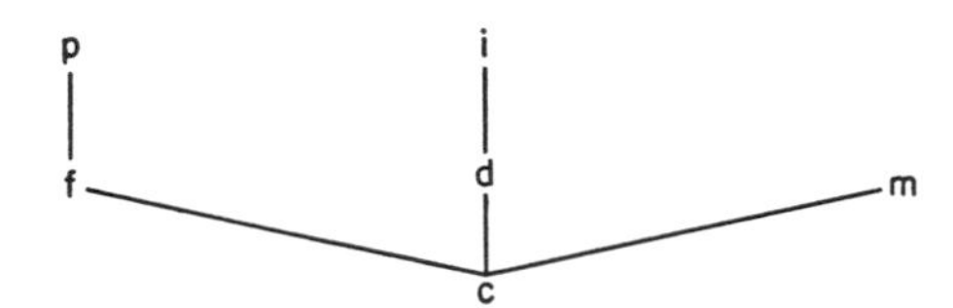

The extracted arguments therefore are:

[A] f
d
m
―
c

[a1] $\frac{p}{f}$ [a2] $\frac{i}{d}$

Selected Answers to Section 4.4

Part A

2.
(1)	$h \supset m$	Pr	
(2)	$o \supset u$	Pr →	A dilemma would be useful, and it seems reasonably plausible in the context of the argument that he is going to eat at home or go out to eat. So, '$h \vee o$' is suggested as a missing premise.
(3)	$h \vee o$	*Pr	
(4)	$m \vee u$	(1) (3) CDil →	Backward strategy suggests that '$(m \vee u) \supset d$' would be useful and this is clearly plausible. [One could also use '$m \supset d$' and '$u \supset d$' and use SDil.]
(5)	$(m \vee u) \supset d$	*Pr	
(6)	d	(4) (5) MP	

Part B

3. Since none of the sentence letters match, we must look for some connection. What would the first two premises naturally suggest? Presumably that parents of private schoolchildren are doing more than their share to support public education. This would connect the first two premises to 'm' and this in turn would allow for the use of MP. Thus, we have:

(1)	p	Pr
(2)	$a \supset b$	Pr
(3)	$p \& (a \supset b)$	(1) (2) Adj
(4)	$[p \& (a \supset b)] \supset m$	*Pr
(5)	m	(3) (4) MP
(6)	$m \supset d$	Pr
(7)	d	(5) (6) MP

Switching to the backward strategy, '$d \supset v$' would carry us home—and it seems reasonably plausible: if they deserve the help provided by the Proposition 9, one presumably should vote for Proposition 9. Thus, the chain is completed as:

(8)	$d \supset v$	*Pr
(9)	v	(7) (8) MP

Part C

1. Clearly, the bare bones of the argument is in effect already given as i / c. Using the hint, the first line is

(1)	$-c$	As

If the Christian belief isn't false, what should we expect? Presumably God's omnipotence and benevolence. So we continue as follows:

(2)	$-c \supset (o \& b)$	*Pr
(3)	$o \& b$	(1) (2) MP

Somehow (3) is supposed to be incompatible with innocent suffering. This suggests the following backward strategy for a *reductio* chain:

$(n-2)$	$-i$	?

$(n-1)$	i	Pr
(n)	i & −i	$(n-2)(n-1)$ Adj

Returning to the forward strategy, how should we arrive at the lack of innocent suffering from (3)?—presumably, a benevolent being would prevent it if he had the power. So we add:

(4)	b ⊃ (p ⊃ −i)	*Pr
(5)	b	(3) S
(6)	p ⊃ −i	(4) (5) MP

We are home once we can get 'p'—but isn't that obviously suggested by his omnipotence. Thus, we finish as follows:

(7)	o ⊃ p	*Pr
(8)	o	(3) S
(9)	p	(7) (8) MP
(10)	−i	(6) (9) MP
(11)	i	Pr
(12)	i & −i	(10) (11) Adj

If we were treating the above chain as a conditional chain for '−c ⊃ (i & −i)', the main chain would list the premises, use what is shown by the conditional chain, and use Rd to get the conclusion 'c'.

Selected Answers to Section 4.5

1\. b. i. '[(f ⊃ a) & m] ⊃ s'—if freedom of religion requires the absolute separation of state and church and freedom of religion must be protected, then the separation of church and state should be pursued—is an unproblematic INT claim.

'm'—that freedom of religion must be protected is an evaluative INT claim for me.

Given our understanding of 'absolute separation' as the government not dictating on religious issues, it would appear that 'f ⊃ a' is an INT claim—the very meaning of 'freedom of religion' seems to require that the government not dictate on religious issues.

ii. The weakest link seems to be 'g ⊃ d'—if there is a genuine possibility of the government dictating on religious issues, the absolute separation of state and church is endangered. Given our understanding of the expressions, though there is a genuine possibility because attempts might be made by some in the government to dictate on religious issues, it seems to me extremely unlikely that such attempts will succeed in the United States with its tradition of separation of state and church. Given our understanding of 'absolute separation', this only requires that the government not dictate; thus, the absolute separation does not seem to be endangered. I would therefore rate this premise to be epistemically neutral or worse. [Compare: there is a genuine *possibility* that I will be murdered in walking to my classroom—instructors have been murdered on campuses; thus, my life is endangered in walking to class.]

The remaining premises—'t ⊃ g' (if there are tuition tax credits, there is a genuine possibility . . .) and '[s & (t ⊃ d)] ⊃ o' (if we should pursue the separation and tuition tax credits endanger the separation, tuition tax credits should be opposed)—seem at least acceptable.

iii. Since 'g ⊃ d' is epistemically neutral or worse for me, the conclusion has not been made evident.

2. a. 'l', '(l & s & f) ⊃ s*', 'e', 't', '(s* & e & t) ⊃ v', 'r', and '(v & r) ⊃ −m'. In the case of 't', it seems to be part of the definition of 'abortion' that the life of the fetus is taken in an abortion. Thus, all these premises seem to be INT or evaluative INT claims. If 'abortion' is understood as a surgical procedure, 't' might be taken as an unproblematic SM claim.

   b. It would seem she would consider 'f' to be at least acceptable given the limitation to reasonably well advanced fetuses. Clearly she questions 's' and it would seem she regards it to be unacceptable, perhaps even that its falsity (in its general form) is highly or completely justified. Thus, she would assess that the argument has not made its conclusion evident since 's' is not acceptable.

Selected Answers to Section 4.6.1

1. a. $1&−N, $1&N, $0&−N, $0&N, G&−N, G&N

   b. The ranking is in the order given in #a. Clearly any outcome with −N is preferable to the same outcome with N. Since getting the dollar is stated to be positive while d($0&−N) = 0, $1&N is preferred over $0&−N. Given the very high negative desirability he attaches to being grounded, a plausible ranking would seem to put $0&N ahead of G&−N.

   c. d($1&−N) = 3, d($1&N) = 1, d($0&−N) = 0, d($0&N) = −2, d(G&−N) = −8, d(G&N) = −10.

   Given the relative importance he assigns to the $1 and avoiding being grounded, some figure like 3 and −10 for the extremes is not implausible. Given that d($0&−N) = 0, d($1&N) must be somewhere between 0 and 3; hence, one such number was used. It's not all that implausible that the cost of nervousness is about the same in all the outcomes and is additive with respect to the other components in an outcome—these assumptions give us the remaining figures.

   d. By assumption (3), we do not have to worry about p_A(O) for O's having −N, and p_{-A}(O) for O's having N—these figures are all 0. Thus the following may not be an implausible assignment of probabilities:

   p_A($1&N) = .2, p_A($0&N) = .6 p_A(G&N) = .2
   p_{-A}($1 & −N) = 0 p_{-A}($0&−N) = .9 p_{-A}(G&−N) = .1

   e. U(A) = (.2)(1) + (.6)(−2) + (.2)(−10) = −3.0
   U(−A) = (.1)(−8) = −.8

Evidently Timmy should not ask for the $1.

Selected Answers for Section 4.6.2

Part A

1. A: All men are [I: Some men are]
   t: Tom is a male chauvinist. M: male chauvinists

   A[M]
   −t ⊃ I[−M]
   ---
   t

(1)	A[M]	Pr	(4)	A[M] ⊃ −I[−M]	(3) S
(2)	A[M] ≡ −I[−M]	Pr[S]	(5)	−I[−M]	(1) (4) MP

(3)	(A[M] ⊃ −I[−M]) & (−I[−M] ⊃ A[M])	(2) ≡/⊃	(6)	−t ⊃ I[−M]	Pr
			(7)	t	(5) (6) MT

Part B

2. Modal Fallacy with ⟨⟩: Taking '⟨⟩' as epistemic possibility, ⟨⟩ (He was at the vault when the money was stolen) & ⟨⟩ (he was at the vault when the money was stolen ⊃ he stole the money) → ⟨⟩ [He was at the vault when the money was stolen & (he was at the vault when the money was stolen ⊃ he stole the money)].

   The conclusion '⟨⟩ (he stole the money)' is derived by using the pattern of inference '⟨⟩ [p & (p ⊃ q)] / ⟨⟩q' (which is in fact valid).

Selected Answers for Section 4.7

Part A

1. *Affirming the Consequent:* (If his wife's car broke down, she is late for hours) & she is late for hours → his wife's car broke down.
2. *Irrelevant Conclusion:* A Brezhnev-type unilateral freeze will not reduce the danger of nuclear war (C*) ⇝ The freeze proposed in Proposition 12 will not reduce the danger of nuclear war (C).
   - By assumption C* is argued—but C isn't.
   - C if C* is implausible if made explicit: A unilateral freeze may not reduce the danger of nuclear war because (a) there is no potential military loss attached to abandoning the freeze and (b) a military loss may be attached to maintaining it if the other side continues to build up the arsenal. In a bilateral mutually verifiable freeze, (a) abandoning the freeze is likely to be met by the other side also abandoning the freeze (thereby incurring the potential military cost that the other side may build better nuclear weapons), and (b) there is no military loss by maintaining the freeze since the other side is also not building up their arsenal. Thus, the inference from C* to C is not plausible.
   - The superficial similarity lies in both C and C* being concerned with freezes and their effects on reducing the dangers of nuclear wars.
3. *Begging the Question:*

   (1) My client did not kill her husband.

   (2) If (1) is true, my client is innocent of the charge of murdering her husband.

   ---

   (3) My client is innocent of the charge of murdering her husband.

   (a) Since the second premise is relatively uncontroversial, we take it as unproblematic. Thus in this context (1) amounts to the denial of

   C*: My client is guilty of the charge of murdering her husband.

   (b) Since we are to assume that no reasons for or against (1) and C* have been given or accepted, in this context there is no more reason to accept (2) than there is reason to accept C*.
4. *Accident:* It is cruel to kill animals → It was cruel for Farmer Jones to kill his lame horse; NOT {the general negative characterization of killing animals applies to the case at hand}.
   - The general negative characterization should be taken as coming with some qualification like 'In the absence of special circumstances'. In the case at hand, there is the special circumstance that it would be crueler for the horse to endure the slow and painful death attending a lame horse which can no longer stand.

7. *Ad Hominem:* The opponents acknowledge that the public pension funds are having troubles ⇝ The public pension funds are having troubles (which should be alleviated by adopting the practices suggested in Proposition 6).

Part B

1. *Begging the Question*

   (1) No foreign country has the right to interfere with the actions of a legitimately constituted government.

   (2) The Republic of South Africa is a legitimately constituted government.

   (3) If (1) and (2) are true, America has no right to interfere with the actions of the South African government.

   ---

   (4) America has no right to interfere with the actions of the South African government.

   (a) Since (2) is likely to be the most controversial premise, we assume that the other premises are unproblematic or at least accepted as such by the parties to the debate. Thus, (2) amounts to the denial of

   C*: America has a right to interfere with the actions of the South African government.

   (b) Since we are to assume that reasons against C* and (2) cancel out, we only need to worry about reasons for (2) and C*. Also by assumption, every reason for (2) is matched by a reason against (2) which in turn is a reason for C*. Thus every reason for (2) is matched by a reason for C* and there is no more reason for accepting (2) than for accepting C*. Thus, the Fallacy of Begging the Question is committed in the assumed context.

Chapter 5

Selected Answers to Section 5.1

1. (c) Let 'm' be 'There is some method of entry to Jane's house which was available to Tom'. As in (a) and (b), clearly 'h, h ⊃ m / m' is deductively valid and 'h ⊃ m' is clearly completely or highly justified. Furthermore, reading (c) in the way indicated in the problem (i.e., having a duplicate key is a method of entry to Jane's house which was available to Tom), 'm' is an indeterminate variant of (c). Thus, 'h' explains (c).
2. (a) (i) Using obvious abbreviations, clearly 's, s ⊃ b / b' is a deductively valid argument with a highly justified second premise. Thus, 's' explains 'b'. (ii) Another explanation (to be abbreviated as 'd') might be 'Since the 1960s Americans have desired to have fewer children and The Pill allows them to realize their desire'. (iii) 'd, d ⊃ b / b' is deductively valid and 'd ⊃ b' appears to be highly justified. Thus, 'd' also explains 'b'.

Selected Answers to Section 5.2

Problem Set A

2. **Problem a:** One is at least highly justified in thinking that Douglas got the time and date right, especially if he made the witticism accredited to him by Cutts. Thus, '(c & t) ⊃ −f' and 'c ⊃ −p' both seem highly justified. Clearly, 'c, t, (c & t) ⊃ −f/−f' and 'c, c ⊃ −p / −p' are valid as MP with and without Adj show. Since 't' and 'p' were given as highly justified and 'f' as completely justified, 'f' and 'p' are negative evidence for 'c'.

Problem b: Consistent with all the assumptions, the only obvious supplemental hypothesis is that Douglas got the time and date wrong. (i) If this hypothesis were sufficiently justified, '(c & t) ⊃ −f' and 'c ⊃ −p' would both be less than highly justified, and 'f' and 'p' both depart from 'c''s data base. (ii) But independent of 'c', this supplemental hypothesis does not have a shred of direct evidence in its favor. Furthermore, it is highly implausible—since Douglas's joke depended on getting the time and date right, it's unlikely that he botched it, and if he did botch it, one might think the papers would have carried it. Thus, the supplemental hypothesis is ad hoc (i.e., has no evidence in its favor beyond saving 'c') and highly implausible as well (i.e., general considerations make it likely to be false). Finally, 'c' can hardly be said to be the only plausible hypothesis surrounding what data there are. Under these circumstances, there is no reason to revise the assessment (in problem a) that one is highly justified in thinking that Douglas got the time and date right. As a result, the supplemental hypothesis is not sufficiently justified to defuse the negative evidence.

Problem Set B

Problem 1: In (A) there is positive evidence for 'h', in (B) there is negative evidence for 'h', and in (C) there is no evidence for or against 'h'. What shows this is the following consideration:

One of the auxiliary premises that would be needed throughout is '(h & a & c & t) ⊃ u'. This seems to be highly justified—if Chubby hamburgers are better, are equally available in equally nice places, cost the same, and have been "taste-tested" by the consumers, then one would expect consumers to choose Chubby over McDonald's with the result that the sale of Chubby hamburgers would be up after the posttrial period (when compared to the pretrial period). The following is a valid argument: h, (h & a & c & t) ⊃ u, a, c, t / u'. Three steps of Adj followed by MP show this. The second premise has just been urged to be highly justified, the third premise 'a' has been given to be highly justified, and for problem 1 we were to take 'c' to be completely justified. In outcomes (A) and (B), because the sales go up significantly during the ad campaign, we are completely justified in taking significant number of people to have tried Chubby hamburgers, and we were also given that it is highly justified that virtually all who try Chubby hamburgers have tried McDonald's burgers—so in (A) and (B), the last premise 't' is also highly justified. Thus, in (A) the completely justified 'u' is positive evidence for 'h', and in (B) the completely justified '−u' is negative evidence for 'h' (since 'h' explains 'u' or '−u'). The situation with (C) is that we cannot take 't' to be highly justified—the ad campaign failed to get consumers even to try Chubby burgers; without their having tried Chubby burgers, there is no evidence available for or against the superiority of Chubby burgers.

Problem 3

(b) Instead of '(h & a & t & c) ⊃ u' being highly justified, we would have 100 such statements for each of the stores; similarly there would be 100 valid arguments instead of the previous one, and each will have 4 auxiliary premises which at least initially are highly or completely justified. The result is: 'u1'–'u3' is positive evidence for 'h' and '−u4'–'−u100' is at least initially negative evidence for 'h'. The parallel thing happens for the McDonald hypothesis 'm' with the principal auxiliary premise being '(m & a1 & t1 & c) ⊃ r1'; as a result, at least initially '−r1'–'−r3' constitute negative evidence for 'm' while each of 'r4'–'r100' is positive evidence for 'm'. As a result 'm' has more positive evidence than 'h'. Since the auxiliary premises are justified to the same degree, there is no difference in the strength of the explanations. To cope with the negative evidence the Chubby people will claim that 'a4'–'a100' are false while the McDonald's people will claim 'a1'–'a3' to be false. By the directions for all problems, this defuses the negative evidence against 'h' and 'm'. None of the supplemental hypotheses appears to be well supported; thus, 'm' needs fewer poorly supplemental hypotheses than 'h'. Just because 'm' has so much positive evidence going for it and 'h' so little, it could be claimed that 'm''s supplemental hypotheses are better supported than 'h''s. Since the simple denial of one of the 'a' statements doesn't explain why the customers went to the other store, neither set of supplemental hypotheses are strong supplemental hypotheses. Thus the situation relative to Preference Rules 1, 2, and 4–6 is this: Rules 1, 4, and perhaps 5 favor 'm', while Rules 2 and 6 favor neither hypotheses.

Problem Set D

Problem 1. From the diagram and the accompanying description, 'T ⊃ d1' appears to be completely justified. Since one use of MP shows 'T ⊃ d1, T / d1' to be valid, 'd1' is positive evidence for 'T'. The second paragraph of the article completely justifies '0 ⊃ d1', and again MP shows '0, 0 ⊃ d1 / d1' to be valid. Thus, 'd1' is positive evidence for '0' as well.

Since '0 ⊃ i' is trivially true, given the assumption, the auxiliary premises of the following argument are at least highly justified: '0, 0 ⊃ i, i ≡ d2 / d2'. The argument can be shown to be valid by MP, ≡/⊃, S, and MP. Thus, d2 is positive evidence for '0'. The article also makes clear that 'T ⊃ −i' is highly justified—two quasars having (virtually) identical properties is a highly unlikely coincidence. But then the auxiliary premises of 'T, T ⊃ −i, i ≡ d2 / −d2' are highly justified. The argument is shown valid by MP, ≡/⊃, S, and MT. Thus, 'd2' is negative evidence for 'T'.

The Rule 1 favors '0' because '0' has both 'd1' and 'd2' as positive evidence while 'T' has only 'd1'. Rule 2 does not seem to come into play, since '0 ⊃ d1' and 'T ⊃ d1' both appear to be completely justified. Rule 3 also favors '0' because '0' has no negative evidence while 'T' does. Thus, the Rules of Fit show '0' to be the better hypotheses relative to the data given.

Problem 3. If 'b v s' were sufficiently justified, '0 ⊃ −d3' would end up being less than highly justified since black holes and relatively small one dimensional "weird creatures" would presumably be difficult to find. In fact 'b v s' would seem to be a strong supplemental hypothesis because '(b v s) ⊃ d3' would seem to be highly justified, and one use of MP shows the validity of 'b v s, (b v s) ⊃ d3 / d3'—i.e., 'b v s' would explain 'd3'.

If 'c' were sufficiently justified, 'T ⊃ −i' would be less than highly justified and the negative evidence 'd2' would be defused. 'c' also seems to be a strong supplemental hypothesis: 'c ⊃ i' is trivially and completely justified, and 'd2 ≡ i' was by previous assumption at least highly justified. Thus, the auxiliary premises of 'c, c ⊃ i, d2 ≡ i / d2' are at least highly justified. A use of MP, ≡/⊃ and S followed by another use of MP shows the argument to be valid. Hence, 'c' would explain 'd2'.

Selected Answers to Section 5.3

2. Type (ii). General claim concerning the bending of light rays around large masses. [If one relied on the highly justified claim that no two quasars have virtually identical characteristics, the argument would not be essentially nondemonstrative.]
4. Type (iv). Given the assumption, the vocabulary of the observations doesn't contain talk about gravitational fields and bending light rays.

Selected Answers to Section 5.4

Problem Set A

Problem 1. We may take all the premises except 'E' in the following argument to be at least highly justified: 'E, E ⊃ e[1], s[1], s[1] ⊃ (e[1] ⊃ d([1]) / d[1]'. Furthermore, three MP's show the argument to be valid. Thus, given that '−d[1]' seems to be completely justified, '−d[1]' is negative evidence experiment 1 provided for 'E'.
Problem 3. A needed auxiliary premise in the argument which shows '−d[1]' to be negative evidence for 'E' is 's[1]'. Thus, if 's[1]' were not highly justified, experiment 1 would no longer yield negative evidence for 'E'. But if 's[E]' were sufficiently justified, 's[1]' would no longer be highly justified—hence 's[E]' is a supplemental hypothesis which would defuse the negative evidence against 'E' if it were sufficiently justified.

Problem Set B

Problem 1. RE 'd1': A *conditional* chain with three MP's aside from various uses of S and Adj shows the following argument to be valid:

P1 & P3 & P4
[P1 & P3 & C(r)] ⊃ [HC(r) ⊃ (mf & pa)]
C(r)
*(P4 & pa) ⊃ i
———————————
HC(r) ⊃ (mf & i) [= d1]

Aside from the hypothesis being tested, the nonstarred premises are completely justified by assumption. But surely if phlogisticated air is incapable of supporting combustion or animal respiration (P4) and the surrounding air is phlogisticated ('pa'), the surrounding air is incapable of supporting combustion or respiration ('i'). Thus, the last premise is also completely justified, and 'd1' is positive evidence for 'P1 & P3 & P4'.
Problem 4. RE P and 'd4': One use of Adj and three uses of MP suffice to show the following to be valid.

P1 & P2
M(m)
H(m)
*[P1 & P2 & M(m)] ⊃ [H(m) ⊃ PG(a)]
*PG(a) ⊃ −L(a)
———————————
−L(a) [= −d4]

Aside from the hypotheses being tested, the nonstarred premises are completely justified by assumption. The starred premises can be seen to be completely justified as follows: if heating a metal ⟨phlogiston + calx⟩ results in the phlogistons escaping into the air, the air gains these phlogistons and the air should weigh more, not less. Thus, 'd4' is negative evidence for P.
Problem 8. RE 'd4': The argument showing 'd4' to be negative evidence for P (in problem 4) needs merely to be altered by adding 'S[P]' as a conjunct in the first premise and replacing the last premise as shown below:

P1 & P2 & S[P]
M(m)
H(m)
[P1 & P2 & M(m)] ⊃ [H(m) ⊃ PG(a)]

[S[P] & PG(a)] ⊃ L(a)
L(a) [= d4]

Being of the same type as earlier valid arguments we have considered, the argument can be taken to be valid. Furthermore, except for the last premise, all the premises that need to be highly or completely justified have already been discussed in Problem 4. The last premise is also completely justified: if phlogistons have negative weight, increasing the phlogistons will reduce the weight. Thus, 'S[P]' along with the other hypotheses of P explain 'd4'; hence, 'S[P]' is a strong supplemental hypothesis in the extended sense.

Problem 12. RE 'd9': Aside from steps of Adj and S, two uses of MP and a use of MTP show the following argument to be valid:

L5
D(m)
C(o, nms, m) ⊃ [aig v −R(ig)]
−(aig)
*[L5 & D(m)] ⊃ C(o, nms, m)
−R(ig) [= −d9]

Aside from the hypotheses being tested, the nonstarred premises are completely or highly justified by assumption. The last premise is also completely justified: if acid is oxygen plus a nonmetallic substance ('L5'), and a metal is dissolved in acid ('D(m)'), clearly oxygen, a nonmetallic substance, and a metal are combined ('C(o, nms, m)'). Thus, 'd9' is negative evidence for L.

Problem 14. The portion of the answer relevant to 'd9': Aside from steps of Adj and S, two uses of MP show the following argument to be valid:

L1 & L6 & S[L]
D(m)
[L6 & S[L] & D(m)] ⊃ [C(ow, m) & (cf ⊃ f(ac) & rw]
*rw ⊃ R(ig)
R(ig)

Aside from the hypotheses being tested, the nonstarred premises are completely justified by assumption. But, if the residue of the water is inflammable gas ('rw'), the release of such a gas ('R(ig)') is clearly indicated and the starred premise is also completely justified. Thus, 'd9' is explained.

Selected Answers to Section 5.5

1. Using the categories "corpuscular absence in days 1–5," "corpuscular absence in days 6–35," and "other considered factors," the initial data of 1867 can then be recast as:

Brood	*Corp. Absent Days 1–5*	*Corp. Absent Days 6–35*	*Other Considered Factors*	*Made Good Cocoons*
A1	−	−	+	−
A2	−	−	−	−
B1	+	−	+	+
B2	+	−	−	+
C1	+	+	+	+
C2	+	+	−	+

Step B produces the following list of sufficient factors:

A[1–5] + A[6–35] + 0, A[1–5] + 0
A[1–5] + A[6–35] A[1–5]

The "crossing out" operation leaves us with A[1–5] and the behavior of brood A2 shows that this factor is causally relevant for the production of good cocoons and cannot be eliminated. Since the data are coherent and only one total cause remains, the best explanation of the data relative to the factors considered is that A[5] is the sole cause of producing good cocoons.

4. (a) The following data would justify the elimination of food and temperature as total causes of the departure date:

Year	*Food/bird/day*	*Mean Temp. of Prior Week*
1922	22 grams	68 degrees
1923	98 grams	54 degrees

(b) Given these data and using 1921 as the base year, we can display the data as follows:

Year	*Food*	*Temperature*	*Departure Date*
1922	<	>	=
1923	>	<	=

Since variation in the food and temperature aren't matched by variations in the departure date, there is negative evidence for the availability of food and temperature being total causes of the departure date.

7. Clearly two uses of MP show 'H, H ⊃ f, f ⊃ e / e' to be valid; furthermore, by assumption (a), the second and third premises as well as 'e' are completely justified. Thus, 'e' is positive evidence for 'H'. By assumption (b), 'e' is therefore also positive evidence for x1 + x2 being a total cause of f1 + f2 which is the sum of all the forces acting on Uranus. Since 'a', i.e., 'x2 is a total cause of forces f2 acting on Uranus', is completely justified by assumption (a), by the Method of Residue, 'e' is positive evidence for 'x1 is a total cause of force f1 acting on Uranus'; i.e., 'e' is positive evidence for the unknown postulated planet of mass m on path p being a total cause of force f1 acting on Uranus.

Chapter 6

Selected Answers to Section 6.1

2. *Use/Mention:* 'Smith' is an ordinary (name). → Smith is an ordinary (person).
6. *Use/Mention:* The decimal representation of π begins with the numeral '3'. → π begins with the numeral '3'.

Selected Answers to Section 6.2.1

1. (a) RE 'raths outgrabe': a predicate expression where
   (A) 'to rath' is a verb referring to some action and 'outgrabe' indicates a place of action or a way in which the act is done, OR
   (B) 'to rath' is a dummy verb like 'to do' and 'outgrabe' is a verb indicating an action or 'to rath outgrabe' is a compound verb like 'take off'.

Selected Answers to Section 6.2.2

1. (b) i. 'Blind sleep' along with 'spying senses' are the source of aberrance and some nondeviant substitutions are:

   And when the book drops on the vase
   And when the brick drops on the ant

   ii. Being a thing with dead weight is a feature of books and bricks, and being a delicate thing that can be broken or a creature that can be killed is a feature of the vase or the ant. Since it is plausible, we may hypothesize that the line conveys: (a) (blind) sleep is like a thing with dead weight which can destroy things, and that (b) the (spying) senses are like delicate things which can be broken or like creatures whose life can be extinguished.

2. (a) i. Some alternatives to 'He isn't without means' are:

   (1) He is rich.
   (2) He has some means.

   ii. The contrast with (1) conveys that he is not wealthy or overly rich. The specific difference with (2) conveys or suggests that the background contains the appearance or the claim that he is without any means. Thus, 'He isn't without means' conveys that though he may not be wealthy, contrary to what may be believed, he does have some means.

3. (a) i. 'Precious', 'beautiful', 'rare', 'without any flaw (or mixture of cheap metals)' are some of the things that are plausibly true of pure gold.

   ii. Since these substitutions are plausible, we hypothesize that part of what is conveyed by 'Is she not pure gold, my mistress?' is: Is she not precious, beautiful, rare, and without flaw, my mistress?

*4. c. [First portion of the answer:] Some nondeviant uses of the interrogative are:

   Will you go to dinner with me tonight?
   Shall we go visit him?
   Will you buy me a present?

   These utterances are requests or proposals, and a feature ϕ of these utterances is:

   ϕ: that they are addressed to people who can refuse the request or proposal, that is, to people whose autonomy has to be respected.

Selected Answers to Section 6.2.3

1. *Complex Question*

Any answer to 'How could you let such a wonderful woman slip away?'

She is a wonderful woman.

One cannot answer the question without committing oneself to the potentially controversial claim that she is a wonderful woman.

2. *Amphibole*

(1) The professor will give no more extensions in the future.
(2) If (1) is true, the professor will give the same extensions in the future as he has up to now.

---

(3) The professor will give the same extensions in the future as he has up to now.

(a) (1) is ambiguous between E1 and E2:

E1: —(The professor will give more extensions than he is giving now).
E2: —(The professor will give any extensions in the future).

(b) For premise (2) to be at all plausible, (1) in (2)'s antecedent has to be taken as E1; thus, to have good reasons for the conclusion one must at the very least disambiguate (1) as E1 throughout the argument.
(c) But (1) is based on the professor's say-so, and s/he may well have meant (1) as E2; thus, premise (1) may well be plausible only when (1) is disambiguated as E2.

Selected Answers to Section 6.3.1

2. 'mammal', 'animal', 'living organism which isn't a plant', 'living organism'.
6. No, they do not have the same meaning. The rule for determining something to be an Indian nickel (i.e., determining it to be a 5¢ coin with a picture of an Indian) and the rule for determining something to be a buffalo nickel (i.e., determining it to be a 5¢ coin with a picture of a buffalo) are not the same. Thus, though they do have the same extension (in our actual world), the two terms do not have the same meaning and may be expected to have different extensions in some possible worlds.
8. (a) The rule for determining the extension of 'ex-husband' requires that the person be a male and the rule for determining the extension of 'housewife' requires that the person be female; since no object can be both male and female, the statement is semantically deviant by being precluded from being true.

   'Cooking', 'doing the laundry', 'taking care of the kids' are some of the things that are plausibly true of housewives. Since the substitutions are plausible, we hypothesize that part of what is conveyed is that Mary's ex-husband has been a person who does such things as cooking, doing the laundry, and taking care of the kids.
9. (a) You don't like her → You dislike her; NOT {'liking her' and 'disliking her' exhaust all the relevant possibilities}.

Selected Answers to Section 6.3.2

1. (a) i. [Partial answer]

   S: We have a free country.
   S[B]: We have as much freedom of speech, movement, etc., as is consistent with the aims of enhancing the public good.

   ii. On the other hand, it is clear that A thinks we would be better off foregoing some of the public services and enhancements of the public good so that we are allowed to do more of what we want to do; B on the other hand thinks that there is no need for reducing the current systems of taxation and control. This is not a verbal dispute, and this disagreement can be expected to persist after the verbal dispute has been cleared away.

   (b) i. [Partial answer]

   S: B is a racist.
   S[A]: B fails to do something which may help prevent a benefit from accruing to an agency which engages in racially discriminatory practices.

2. (a) (1) If Tom is still the jealous type, he will be angry if he knows that you are dating his girl.
(2) Tom isn't angry and he knows that you are dating his girl.

---

(3) Tom is no longer the jealous type.
(a) 'His girl' (E) is ambiguous between his daughter (E1) and his girlfriend (E2).
(b) Validity requires 'his girl' to be used univocally.
(c) The context suggests that (1) is plausible only when E is understood as E2. But since (2) is based on someone's say-so, and since E1 may well have been meant by E, (2) may well be plausible only if E is understood as E1. Thus, the premises may well be plausible only when E is used equivocally.

Selected Answers for Section 6.3.3

2. (a) x is a brother of a parent of y.
3. (a) i. Species: significant portion of speech.
ii. Differentia: some parts have an independent meaning.
iii. Words like 'cat' which are not built up out of several morphemes.

*5. (a) y's parents are ancestors of y.
(b) Any parent of an ancestor of y is an ancestor of y.
(c) Nothing is an ancestor of y unless its being so follows from (a) and (b).

*8. $p \supset q$: $-(p \,\&\, -q)$.

Selected Answers to Section 6.3.4

1. b. The speaker must be determined by the context (to fix the referent of 'I'). The time of the utterance must be determined by the context (to fix the relevant time t for which it is being claimed that at (or by) t I was twice divorced).
3. a. *Accent:*

(1) I say nothing eloquently.
(2) If I say nothing eloquently, even when I say nothing, I do so eloquently.

---

(3) Even when I say nothing, I do so eloquently.
(a) 'I say nothing eloquently' (E) can mean different things when it is accented as E1 and E2:

E1: I say *nothing* eloquently: everything I say fails to be eloquent.
E2: I say nothing *eloquently:* what I say amounts to nothing but I say it eloquently.

(b) The argument is valid only if E means the same thing throughout.
(c) Premise (2) is plausible only when E is accented as E2. But since (1) is accepted on someone else's say-so and s/he accented it as E1, (1) is plausible only when E is accented as E1.

c. *Equivocation:*

(1) The fortune-teller said that I would marry the girl next door.
(2) If the fortune-teller said that I would marry the girl next door and I did marry the girl next door, the fortune teller was right.
(3) I married Jill and Jill was the girl next door.

---

(4) The fortune-teller was right.
(a) 'The girl next door' (E) is ambiguous between E1 and E2:

E1: picking out the girl living next door in the condo I moved into
E2: picking out the girl living next door in some other contextually specified place I lived

(b) The validity of the argument requires that E be used univocally.
(c) Premise (3) is clearly plausible only when E is understood as E1. On the other hand it is extremely implausible that the fortune-teller disambiguated E as E1 when she made her prediction; thus, assuming that the fortune-teller made any statement which actually has a truth value, (1) is plausible only when E is taken as E2. Thus, the premises are plausible only when E is used equivocally.

[The validity of the argument does not actually require that E be used in the same sense in *all* of its occurrences. As a result, a more fully correct analysis would take steps (b) and (c) as:

(b) The validity of the argument requires E being used univocally in (1) and (2)'s first antecedent, and it being used univocally in (3) and (2)'s second antecedent.
(c) For premise (2) to be plausible, E can be taken either as E1 or as E2; however, premise (2) is plausible only if E is used in the same sense in both of its occurrences. Premise (3) is clearly plausible only when E is understood as E1. (1) is plausible only when E is taken as E2 (for the reason given above). Thus, all the premises are plausible only when E is used equivocally either in (1) and (2)'s first antecedent or in (3) and (2)'s second antecedent. In either case, the Fallacy of Equivocation is committed.]

Selected Answers for Section 6.3.5

2. c. *The conveyed content of U is true in W if 'the 16th president' is given a de dicto use.* '___ is believed to be the 17th president' is an extensional context and in W Douglas is believed by Joe to be the 17th president and Douglas is the 16th president. Thus, the 16th president in W is believed by Joe in W to be the 17th president. If 'the 16th president' has a *de dicto* use, the conveyed content of the actual world utterance U is true in W as long as the person who is the 16th president in W is believed by Joe in W to be the 17th president.

3. a. *Ignoring Intensional Contexts:* extension of 'her son' = extension of 'the murder they are talking about in the papers' & −(she is scared that her son will come to her house) → −(she is scared that the murderer they are talking about in the papers will come to her house); NOT {'she is scared that ___ will come to her house' is an extensional context}.

   b. [Likely argument omitted.]

   Ignoring De Re Uses: The conveyed content of the actual world utterance 'The rod in Paris by which the length of 1 meter is defined is less than 1 meter long' is true in W → the object which in W is the rod in Paris by which the length of 1 meter is defined is less than 1 meter long in W; NOT {the use of 'the rod in Paris by which the length of 1 meter is defined' is a *de dicto* use in the actual world utterance}.

Selected Answers to Section 6.4.1

1. An abuse which is an insincerity.
6. A misinvocation due to the person not satisfying the conditions for raising the bet. (Misexecution could be another answer because to raise correctly requires having the money.)

Selected Answers to Section 6.4.2

1. (1) Illocutionary Force: Assessing or grading (the paper as a C, where the Professor's grading it as a C makes it a C).
   Statement to be T-assessed: The grade of C is a legitimate or just grade for the paper—i.e., the paper was not a good one.
   (4) Illocutionary Force: Criticizing (the paper as having various defects); one could also take the illocutionary force to be stating or describing (features of the paper).
   Statements to be T-assessed: Taken as a statement, the truth or falsity of 'Plato was misquoted', 'The paper got Plato's point wrong', etc. As a criticism, this plus the truth of these statements constituting defects a student paper should avoid.
2. a. Re (M1): The first part of the speech act—'Todd isn't there'—has the illocutionary force of stating that Todd isn't there. The second part of the speech act—'I believe that Todd is there'—typically has the illocutionary force of stating (perhaps in a somewhat qualified way) that Todd is there. Thus, the "net" illocutionary force of (M1) is to state an outright contradiction, and it is reasonable to take this to be a misexecution—the procedure of making a statement is not gone through correctly. Hence, the attempt to make a speech act with (M1) insures a misfire and the utterance of (M1) is illocutionarily deviant.
   b. Re (M1): If it is felicitous, the illocutionary force of stating that Todd isn't there must avoid an insincerity—thus, I must believe that Todd isn't there. But since I don't have contradictory beliefs, believing that Todd isn't there results in the second part of (M1) being false, and hence (M1) as a whole is false; that is, (M1) is felicitous only if it is false.
3. b. Conrad's cartoon suggests that Falwell ('s statement that he too is of the cloth should be interpreted to mean that he) is (much like) a KKK member $\rightsquigarrow$ Falwell ('s statement that he too is of the cloth should be interpreted to mean that he) is (much like) a KKK member.

   A political cartoon comes with an "illocutionary force" of "This is a story."

Selected Answers to Section 6.5

1. a. 'You are likely to (or have some chances of) meeting interesting women at Oscar's Nightclub.' The Maxim of Relations to be relevant to A's remark engenders this implicature.
   b. 'Only the smarter students enter college and the intellectual level is higher as a result, more is expected of students in college, etc.' B's remark is pragmatically deviant by flouting the Maxim of Quantity to be informative. Using the Method of Paraphrase on 'high school' (and in effect cancelling the double negation), we get the suggested implicature.
2. b. The Maxim of Quantity to be appropriately informative is violated by just picking out one place he didn't go last night. Since this is plausibly explained as being needed to abide by the more stringent Maxim of Quality to have adequate evidence, it is implicated that the Maxim of Quality can be obeyed only by violating the Maxim of Quantity—i.e., that the speaker does not have adequate evidence to say more about George's whereabouts last night and thus does not know where George was last night.

3.2. (b). 'And I also happen know where he was, but I'm not going to tell you because you may get the wrong idea about George.'

5. a. RE M2: Let 'p' be 'Todd is there'. By the general Maxim of Quality, it is conversationally implicated that in uttering the first half of M2—i.e., 'p'—the speaker is trying to say something that is true. But this is denied by the second half of M2 which states that the speaker doesn't believe 'p'.

Selected Answers for Section 6.6.1

1. [A wide variety of answers is possible. It may be desirable to put some of the items into more clearly observational terms—on the other hand, since observationality seems to be a matter of degree, there is no need to be too finicky about what is to count as specifying the observable content of the claim.]

   a. 0+: He is observed killing Sissy, he was seen coming out of her house or bedroom shortly after the time the coroner determined to be the time of death, the murder weapon is found to have his fingerprints on it, he confesses killing Sissy, etc.

      0−: Sissy is still alive, Sissy is determined to have died of cancer, someone else was observed to be killing Sissy, Jack was observed miles away from the murder scene at the time of the murder, the murder weapon has someone else's fingerprints on it, etc.

2. Clearly a variety of answers is possible. The answers given form just one possible set of answers.

   a. (i) *B:* From part of what you said, it would seem you would regard your statement false if certain things were observed. If a Boy Scout saved the life of a person and didn't know that there was a medal attached to it, would that be an unselfish act? If tax deductions were eliminated and most of the person's friends and acquaintances regard contributions as stupid, would a charitable contribution by such a person be an unselfish, generous act? In short, if we devised a way of detaching the obvious external awards and approbation attached to alleged generous, unselfish acts, and some people still continued to perform such acts, would your claim then be falsified?

      A: Yes. And evidence would favor my claim if we found people in such a situation ceasing to do acts which are alleged to be unselfish.

      (ii) *B:* [Same starting statement as in (i).]

      A: No, because it would still remain that if it was a generous act, it was one the person wanted to do, and if he wanted to do it, it was a selfish act.

      B: Let's grant that if a person wants to do A, the person takes some pleasure in doing A. But why are all such acts selfish? What would falsify 'If one takes some pleasure in doing A, A is a selfish act'?

      A: Clearly nothing could or would falsify it—if one takes some pleasure in doing A, A must be a selfish act.

      B: But now what you are saying seems to true just by definition. Normally, we mean by a selfish act an act where one puts one's personal benefits above that of others. You on the other hand seem to regard any act as selfish as long as one takes some pleasure in doing it. But then given that a generous act requires taking some pleasure in the well being of others, nothing could falsify your claim and it is true by the aberrant definition you have attached to 'selfish' that all generous acts are selfish.

Selected Answers to Section 6.6.2

Part A

A. 1. The party that *perpetrated the Watergate scandals* [i] got a *badly needed shot in the arm* [ii] from the *sleepy resort town of Santa Barbara* [iii].
N: The Republican party received support from Santa Barbara.
E: The Republican party is responsible for the misdeeds of Watergate [i] and is a sick party needing a shot [ii]; the people of Santa Barbara are unaware of what is happening [iii].
O: The Republican party received well-deserved support from the independently minded city of Santa Barbara.

C. 3. When those *little yellow punks* [i] from Taiwan beat us five straight years, we *chickened out* [ii] and limited the Little League Championships to *our own little pond* [iii].
N: After the team from Taiwan beat us five straight years, the Little League Championships were limited to American teams.
E: The teams or people from Taiwan are not worthy of respect [ii], and five straight losses to them led us to take the cowardly course [ii] of avoiding competition with the rest of the world [iii].
O: After suffering the frustrations of losing five straight times to those highly trained and overly competitive teams from Taiwan, we recognized that Little League is after all mainly for fun—so, we decreased the level of competition by limiting the championships to teams from America.

Part B

1. *Illicit Redefinition:*

(1) If gay couples live together, give each other financial support, and are intimate in other ways, gay couples are married couples.
(2) Any married couple may file a joint tax return.
(3) If (1) and (2) are true, gay couples may file a joint tax return.

---

(4) Gay couples may file a joint tax return.

(a) 'Married couple' is ambiguous between the standard sense where it means something like legally married under the eyes of the law and the tacitly introduced new sense where it means living together, giving each other financial support, etc.
(b) The validity of the argument requires 'married couple' being used univocally.
(c) Premise (1) is plausible only in the newly defined sense of 'married couple' while premise (2) is plausible only under the standard sense of 'married couple'. Thus, the premises are plausible only when 'married couple' is used equivocally and the Fallacy of Illicit Redefinition is committed.
[To be more fully correct, steps (b) and (c) should read:
(b) The validity of the argument requires 'married couple' being used univocally in premise (1) and premise (3)'s first antecedent and it being used univocally in premise (2) and premise (3)'s second antecedent.
(c) Premise (3) is plausible only if 'married couple' is used in the same sense throughout. But premise (1) is plausible only in the newly defined sense of 'married couple' while premise (2) is plausible only under the standard sense of 'married couple'. Thus, the premises are all plausible only when 'married couple' is used equivocally either in premise (1) and premise (3)'s first antecedent or in premise (2) and premise (3)'s second antecedent. Hence, the Fallacy of Illicit Redefinition is committed.]

Chapter 7

Selected Answers to Section 7.1.1

[O statements can become I statements, and E statements A statements, by taking 'G' in the negative form.]

1. A. F: philosophers. G: tiresome people (beings).
8. O. F: people. G: people who love him.
10. I. F: people. G: people who admire her.
13. E. F: times (up to now). G: times at which John kissed Mary.

Selected Answers to Section 7.1.2

(1) VALID (9) INVALID

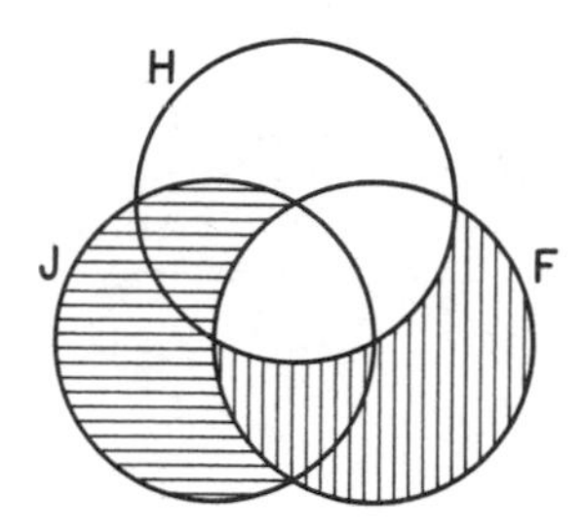

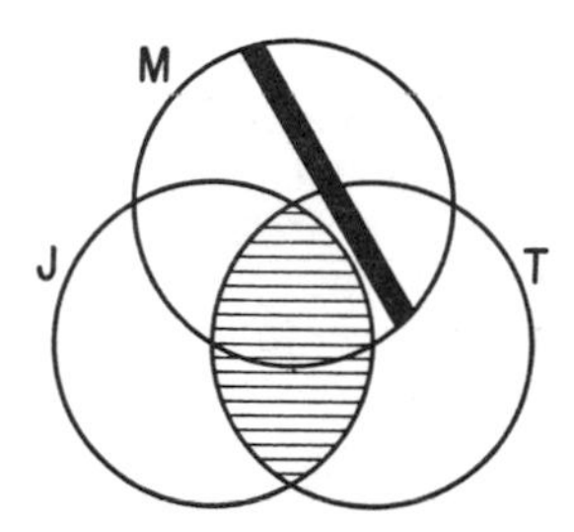

Selected Answers to Section 7.1.3

1. e. (x)[(x is a nun) ⊃ −(x is a daughter of a nun)]
   (x)[Nx ⊃ −(∃y)([x is a daughter of y] & [y is a nun])]
   (x)[Nx ⊃ −(∃y)(Dxy & Ny)]
   g. (Some philosopher is a king) v (no king is admired by a philosopher)
   Some philosopher is a king:
   (∃x)[(x is a philosopher) & (x is a king)]
   No king is admired by a philosopher:
   (x)[(x is a king) ⊃ −(x is admired by a philosopher)]
   x is admired by a philosopher:
   (∃y)[(y admires x) & (y is a philosopher)]
   (∃x)(Px & Kx) v (x)[Kx ⊃ −(∃y)(Ayx & Py)]
2. a. TRUE. If everything in the universe is an F and everything in the universe is also G, then any given thing in the universe must be both an F and a G. Thus, it's impossible for both premises to be true and the conclusion false, and the argument form is valid.
   b. FALSE. Let 'F' be filled by 'is a boy' and 'G' by 'is a girl'; then in our universe both premises are true—there is at least one boy and there is at least one girl. But it is not true of anything that it is both a girl and a boy. Thus, the premises can be true while the conclusion is false, and the argument form is not valid.

Selected Answers to Section 7.2.1

2. (a) The odds are 1:2 in favor of 'p' if and only if the ratio of the amount lost to the amount won is 1/2. Thus, a \$3 bet will result in winning \$6 plus getting back the \$3 one bet if 'p' is true, i.e., getting 1:2 odds is equivalent to putting \$3 into a betting pool which pays back \$9 if 'p' is true. But, Pr(p) = 0.3 for an ideally rational gambler in an epistemic situation if and only

if \$3 is the maximum he or she is willing to put into a betting pool which pays back \$10 if 'p' is true. Since the payoff is worse with 1:2 odds, the ideally rational gambler will not accept 1:2 odds.

Selected Answers to Section 7.2.2

2. a. In throwing 2 dice, the first die can come up in one of 6 ways, and for each of these ways, the second die can come up in 6 ways. So, there are 36 different equiprobable ways the two dice can land. The sums of the spots on the two dice are distributed as follows:

2	1 way	6	5 ways	10	3 ways
3	2 ways	7	6 ways	11	2 ways
4	3 ways	8	5 ways	12	1 way
5	4 ways	9	4 ways		

This chart is derived by the following sort of consideration: the spots can sum to 4 by the first die coming up 1 and the second 3, by the first coming up 3 and the second 1, and by both dice coming up 2, i.e., altogether there are 3 ways the spots on the two dice can sum to 4. Thus: The probability that the player loses on the first play—i.e., gets 2, 3, or 12—is $(1 + 2 + 1)/36$ or $4/36$.

Selected Answers to Section 7.2.3

1. b. Let us use the following abbreviation:
a: A = 4 (i.e., die A resulted in 4) b: B = 4

$$\begin{aligned}\Pr(a \,\&\, b/a \vee b) &= \Pr[a \,\&\, b \,\&\, (a \vee b)] \,/\, \Pr(a \vee b)] \\ &= \Pr[(a \,\&\, b \,\&\, a) \vee (a \,\&\, b \,\&\, b)] \,/\, \Pr(a \vee b) \\ &= [\Pr(a \,\&\, b) + \Pr(a \,\&\, b) - \Pr(a \,\&\, b)] \,/\, [\Pr(a) + \Pr(b) - \Pr(a \,\&\, b)] \\ &= (1/36) \,/\, (1/6 + 1/6 - 1/36) = (1/36) \,/\, (11/36) = 1/11\end{aligned}$$

[Much of this can be simplified by using the passing remark that conditional probabilities which are conditional on 'q' simply amount to the altered probability space where 'q' is taken to be true. Thus, the basic events of the altered probability space are: ⟨4, 1⟩, ⟨4, 2⟩, ⟨4, 3⟩, ⟨4, 4⟩, ⟨4, 5⟩, ⟨4, 6⟩, ⟨1, 4⟩, ⟨2, 4⟩, ⟨3, 4⟩, ⟨5, 4⟩, ⟨6, 4⟩. This space is equiprobable, and since both dice coming up 4's is only realized by ⟨4, 4⟩, the answer is 1/11.]

3. a. By Bayes Theorem (T11),

$$\begin{aligned}\Pr(m/s) &= \Pr(s/m)\Pr(m) \,/\, [\Pr(s/m)\Pr(m) + \Pr(s/-m)\Pr(-m)] \\ &= (.95)\Pr(m) \,/\, [(.95)\Pr(m) + (.10)\Pr(-m)]\end{aligned}$$

Thus, with a 50–50 male/female split, we have:

$$(.95)(.5)/[(.95)(.5) + (.10)(.5)] = 0.905$$

Selected Answers to Section 7.2.4

1. We can conceive this problem as a 10-stage process (10-stage tree diagram) with each stage (branching point) having the possible outcomes S (six) and N (not six). Since it's a fair die, at each stage or branch, $\Pr(S) = 1/6$ and $\Pr(N) = 5/6$. The probability of getting 0 S's in the 10 tosses corresponds to the path with N's at each of the 10 branches, where the branch probability is 5/6 in each case. So,

(a) $\Pr(0 \text{ S's in } 10 \text{ tosses}) = (5/6)^{10}$

As for exactly getting 1 S in the 10 tosses, there are exactly 10 complete paths on the tree or in the probability space which realize this—one corresponding to getting the lone S in the first toss, one corresponding to getting the lone S in the second toss, etc. Each of these paths will have one branch probability of 1/6 and 9 branch probabilities of 5/6. Thus,

(b) Pr(1 S in 10 tosses) = $10 \times (1/6) \times (5/6)^9$

Given (a) and (b), we have:

Pr(getting less than 2 S's in the 10 tosses) = Pr[(0 S's in the 10 tosses) v (1 S in the 10 tosses)]

= Pr(0 S's in the 10 tosses) + Pr(1 S in the 10 tosses) [by T6]

= $(5/6)^{10} + [10 \times (1/6) \times (5/6)^9] = (5/6)^{10} \times [1 + 2] = 3 \times (5/6)^{10}$

4. (b) [Partial solution:] This is a messy problem. The Brute Force method would be the following: The first draw can result in A, 2, 3, J, or some other card C. The portion of the tree diagram when A is drawn is given by:

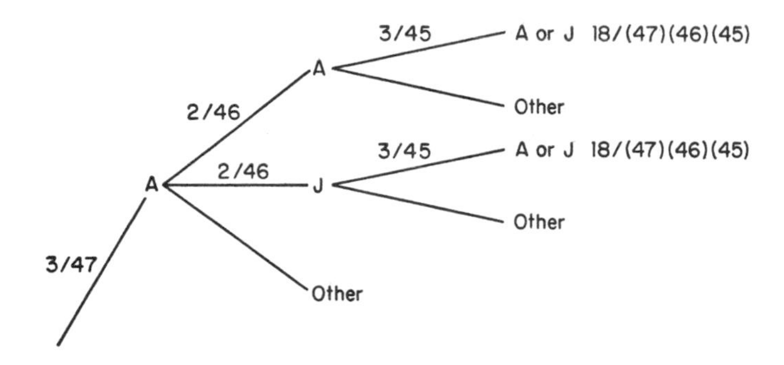

Thus, thc basic events which start with the drawing of an ace give the probability of 36/(47)(46)(45) for getting a full house or four of a kind. The exactly same situation occurs if one draws a 2 or 3 on the first draw. Thus, the basic events that start with A, 2, or 3 give the probability of

(3)(36)/(47)(46)(45) = 108/(47)(46)(45)

for getting a full house or four of a kind.

One would now have to consider the case where one draws a jack first and the case where we first draw a card C other than A, 2, 3, or J.

Alternate Method: A smarter way to deal with this problem is first to conceive the matter as a 3-stage process whose outcomes are M (matches a prior card) or D (different from all prior cards). With only one M you can get at best either three jacks or two pairs. So at least two M's are needed. But three M's are impossible since there are only four jacks. So the complete paths which give rise to a full house or four of a kind are:

[A] —2/27— M(=J) —1/46— M(=J) —45/45— D 90/(47)(46)(45)
[B] —2/47— M(=J) ———— D ———— M
[C] —45/47— D ———— M ———— M

In [B] and [C] we can't directly figure out the M probabilities because it depends on whether the different card was A, 2, or 3 (one of which was discarded) or some other card D. Thus, these cases need to be further analyzed.

Selected Answers to Section 7.2.5

2. The probability distribution of S° is given by

x	Events realizing S° = x	Pr(S° = x)
2	⟨1,1⟩	1/36
3	⟨1,2⟩, ⟨2,1⟩	2/36
4	⟨1,3⟩, ⟨3,1⟩, ⟨2,2⟩	3/36
5	⟨1,4⟩, ⟨4,1⟩, ⟨3,2⟩, ⟨2,3⟩	4/36
6	⟨5,1⟩, ⟨1, 5⟩, ⟨4,2⟩, ⟨2,4⟩, ⟨3,3⟩	5/36
7	⟨6,1⟩, ⟨1,6⟩, ⟨5,2⟩, ⟨2,5⟩, ⟨3,4⟩, ⟨4,3⟩	6/36
8	⟨6,2⟩, ⟨2,6⟩, ⟨5,3⟩, ⟨3,5⟩, ⟨4,4⟩	5/36
9	⟨6,3⟩, ⟨3,6⟩, ⟨5,4⟩, ⟨4,5⟩	4/36
10	⟨6,4⟩, ⟨4,6⟩, ⟨5,5⟩	3/36
11	⟨6,5⟩, ⟨5,6⟩	2/36
12	⟨6,6⟩	1/36

M[S°] = (2 + 6 + 12 + 20 + 30 + 42 + 40 + 36 + 30 + 22 + 12)/36 = 7
D[S°] = SQR ROOT OF
[4 + 9(2) + 16(3) + 25(4) + 36(5) + 49(6) + 64(5) + 81(4) + 100(3)
+ 121(2) + 144(1)]/36 − 49
= 2.4

INDEX